In memory of my mother and father

About the Author

᪥ ᪥ ᪥ ᪥

Janice J. Beaty, professor emerita, Elmira College, Elmira, New York, is a full-time writer of early childhood college textbooks and a consultant in early childhood education from her home in Cape Coral, Florida. Her textbooks include *Skills for Preschool Teachers*, 8th Ed., *50 Early Childhood Literacy Strategies*, 2nd Ed., *Early Literacy in Preschool and Kindergarten*, 2nd Ed. with Linda Pratt, and *50 Early Childhood Guidance Strategies*. She is also engaged in a literacy mentoring program with the Foster Grandparents Program in Columbia, Missouri.

Preface

ᦥ ᦥ ᦥ ᦥ

Observing Development of the Young Child presents a unique system for observing and recording development of children ages 3 to 5 in early childhood classroom settings. It is based on a progression of children's skill development in six major areas. The text is designed for use by college students preparing to be teachers in prekindergarten programs, child-care centers, Head Start classes, and preschools. The book can also be used in such programs by the teachers and assistant teachers who want to learn more about children to make individual learning plans, as well as for making assessments of individual children for program development. Staff members preparing for Child Development Associate (CDA) Assessment will also find this textbook helpful with its suggestions for classroom activities that are developmentally appropriate for young children. The text not only teaches readers how to observe, record, and interpret development of children 3 through 5 years of age, but also discusses what these children are like and how to support them in their development with exciting hands-on activities.

The text focuses on six major aspects of child development: emotional, social, physical, cognitive, language, and creative that are readily observable. It divides each of these aspects further into specific areas: self-esteem and emotional development, social play and prosocial behavior, large and small motor development, cognitive development, spoken language, emergent writing and reading skills, art and music skills, and dramatic play skills. Students can use the observation records they make of children's development in the children's portfolios. Finally, teachers learn to share their observational data with children's families.

THE CHILD DEVELOPMENT CHECKLIST—A PRACTICAL TOOL

The six areas of child development previously identified are outlined in a *Child Development Checklist* that includes specific, observable child behaviors in the sequence in which they occur. Each of 11 chapters discusses one of these areas, using the eight observable items on the checklist as subheads for the chapter and giving ideas for classroom activities for children who have not demonstrated that specified behavior. The most recent child development research in each area is presented as background for the checklist items as they are discussed. Each chapter concludes with a discussion of an actual child observation in the particular area and an interpretation of the data gathered.

The text serves college students as a guide for observing and recording development of young children in their student teaching and coursework. The book is especially well suited as a supplementary text for child development courses. It also can help in-service teachers and assistants who are upgrading their skills in observing children, as well as those who are learning to plan for individuals based on their developmental needs.

Unique aspects of *Observing Development of the Young Child* include discussions of how to *observe* young children, how to *interpret* the data recorded, and how to *plan* for individuals based on the observations. Important topics include children's emotional development, how young children make friends, how to help second-language speakers learn English, how to help children develop empathy toward others as the basis for conflict resolution, how children use exploratory play to learn, how to help young children emerge into reading and writing, and how to develop children's creativity through art, music, and dramatic play.

NEW FEATURES IN THE SEVENTH EDITION

New features in the 7th edition include the following:

- How to become an observer; how to get started; when and how long to observe
- How to accomplish observing and assessing children, which are different but important tasks
- Discussion of alternative approaches to assessment
- How to use visual documentation and documentation panels
- Learning how to "see" properly
- New information on observing the development of a secure child attachment relationship with the teacher
- New information on how to recognize parallel play as a bridge between onlooker and cooperative play
- New information on physical exercise to promote blood flow to the brain for improving permanent memory
- A new discussion of dexterity and handedness
- Observing how using cooking tools increases brain synapses that improve memory
- The importance of listening to the teacher to construct meaning and build concept frameworks
- The value of the child's home language when learning English
- Discussion of oral storytelling as "decontextualized talk"
- Why to treat early drawing as writing
- Observing how dramatic play makes children's thinking visible
- How to develop collaborative child portfolios with parents
- How to use the 134 new books and 85 books with multiethnic characters as lead-ins to children's activities

USE AS A COMPANION TEXT

This seventh edition of *Observing Development of the Young Child* is designed to be used as a companion volume with the author's text, *Skills for Preschool Teachers* (Merrill/Prentice Hall, 2008). Although *Observing Development of the Young Child* is intended as a child development textbook, the companion volume—*Skills for Preschool Teachers*—is a teacher development book focusing on 13 areas of teacher competencies.

Like this textbook, *Skills for Preschool Teachers* is also based on an observational checklist, the *Teacher Skills Checklist,* which documents teacher competencies in the 13 Child Development Associate (CDA) "functional areas": safe, healthy, learning environment, physical, cognitive, communication, creative, self, social, guidance, families, program management, and professional.

Together, the two textbooks form a cohesive, complete training program for preservice teachers, beginning teachers, and in-service teachers preparing for the CDA credential. Preservice teachers can use these complementary texts as especially effective guidance in their student teaching field experiences. Both books focus on positive behaviors in children and teachers. Both the development of children and the training of teachers look at "areas of strength and confidence" and "areas needing strengthening" to set up individualized training plans.

Children's Art on Cover

This art from Head Start children in Missouri is not only creative and colorful, but also gives the informed observer important information about the development of each child. The front cover artist has developed beyond his first sun-face human to a full-body figure. He's showing perspective (difficult even for an adult artist!) as he stands on a blanket at a picnic. He also writes a story about the picnic in scribble-writing at the top.

One back cover artist shows not only high-level thinking but also creativity in solving the problem of getting food to hungry people. His two helpers jump out of a plane with parachutes to bring food to hungry people in the world.

The other back cover artist illustrates his favorite food with a tongue-in-cheek drawing saying, "Strawberries are out of this world!" But his knowledge of Earth, planets and sun, the printing of their names, and his understanding of such humor show special high-level cognitive development.

SUPPLEMENTS TO THE TEXT

The following online supplements are available for downloading by instructors at **www.pearsonhighered.com:**

- **Online Test Bank.** The *Test Bank* features items for evaluating student comprehension, including multiple choice and true-false items, designed to assess student understanding.

- **Online Instructor's Manual.** The *Instructor's Manual* provides materials to support the text by highlighting key chapter points, providing activities, and suggesting additional resources of interest, such as Web Sites, videos, and books.

ACKNOWLEDGMENTS

My special thanks for the new edition of this text goes to the directors, teachers, parents, and children of Williams Family Head Start Center, We Care Child Center, and Almost Home Day Care in Mexico, Missouri, and the Tiger Paws Head Start and Park Street Head Start in Columbia, Missouri. It is always inspiring for me to visit these fine programs and photograph the children as they work and play together, developing their own unique selves. Ann Gilchrist, director of the Central Missouri Foster Grandparents Program, once again deserves my gratitude for setting up my observations in these centers and allowing me to participate with her grandparents who have given so much of themselves to the young children in these programs. My appreciation also goes to Elaine West, Executive Director of the Missouri Association for Community Action, Inc., for allowing me to use some of the exciting children's art created for the annual MACA calendar. Thanks to the young artists and their teachers from Eldon Head Start Center, Lampe Head Start Center, Northwest Missouri Head Start, Lexington Head Start Center, and the Southwest Area Head Start; to my editor Julie Peters, for her guidance and encouragement, and finally to the following reviewers of the text: Alice M. Atkinson, The University of Iowa; Jan Jewett, Washington State University, Vancouver; Carol Dixon Sammis, Tompkins Cortland Community College; and Louise Vlasic, Everett Community College.

Brief Contents

1   Observing and Assessing Children's Development   2

2   Collecting and Recording Observational Data   24

3   Self-Esteem   52

4   Emotional Development   86

5   Social Play   122

6   Prosocial Behavior   154

7   Large Motor Development   182

8   Small Motor Development   212

9   Cognitive Development   242

10   Spoken Language   280

11   Emergent Writing and Reading Skills   314

12   Art and Music Skills   348

13   Dramatic Play Skills   378

14   Sharing Observational Data with Families   410

References   434

Web Sites   443

Index of Children's Books   444

Index   447

Contents

☙ ☙ ☙ ☙

1 Observing and Assessing Children's Development   2

Watching versus Observing 3
   For Curriculum Planning 4
   For Assessment 4
   A Different Point of View 5
   Why Assess Young Children? 6
Assessing Through Observation 7
   The Child Development Checklist 7
   How Do You Become an Observer? 8
   Confidentiality 9
   How Should You Record Your Observations? 9
   How Do You Get Started? 9
   When and How Long Should You Observe? 10
   How Should You Plan for Observing? 10
   Using Systematic Observation 11
   Setting Up Systematic Observation 12
Tests as Tools for Assessing Young Children 12
Alternative Approaches to Assessment of Young Children 14
   Play-Based Assessment 15
   Child Interviews 15
   Visual Documentation 17
   Photographs 18
   Videotapes 19
   Audiotapes 19
   Documentation Panels 20
Learning How to See 20
   Practicing Observation Skills 21
   The Chapters to Follow 22
Learning Activities 22
Suggested Readings 22
Children's Books 23

2 Collecting and Recording Observational Data   24

Recording Observational Data 25
   Narratives 25
   Anecdotal Records 26

Running Records 28
Observer Errors 30
Recording Information 33
Using Your Own Shorthand 33
Learning Center Logs 33
Sampling 34
Rating Scales 36
Rating Scale Observer Errors 37
Checklists 37
Choosing the Method for Observing and Recording 39
Using the Child Development Checklist 41
Using One Checklist Section at a Time 41
Using the Entire Checklist 41
Interpreting the Data 48
Chapters to Follow 49
Proceeding from the General to the Specific 49
Proceeding from the Specific to the General 49
*Use of the Checklist by Preservice Teachers and Student
    Teachers 50*
Observation of Each Child 50
Learning Activities 51
Suggested Readings 51

3   Self-Esteem   52

Developing Self-Esteem 53
Separates from Primary Caregiver Without Difficulty 55
Initial Attachment 55
Initial Separation 56
School Separation 57
Develops a Secure Attachment Relationship with Teacher 60
Children with Insecure Attachments 61
Completes a Task Successfully 62
Makes Activity Choices Without Teacher's Help 64
Seeks Other Children to Play With 66
Plays Roles Confidently in Dramatic Play 68
Stands Up for Own Rights 72
Cultural Differences in Standing Up for Own Rights 73
Displays Enthusiasm About Doing Things for Self 75
Observing, Recording, and Interpreting Self-Esteem 77
*Making a Running Record and Transferring Data to
    the Checklist 77*
Evidence 78
Inferences 80

Conclusions   82
Learning Prescription   82
Learning Activities   84
Suggested Readings   85
Children's Books   85

4   Emotional Development   86

Developing Emotions in Young Children   87
Releases Stressful Feelings in Appropriate Manner   90
Distress   90
The Teacher's Role   91
Expresses Anger in Words Rather than Actions   94
Anger   94
Aggression   97
Can Be Calmed in Difficult or Dangerous Situations   99
Fear   99
Overcomes Sad Feelings in Appropriate Manner   103
Handles Surprising Situations with Control   106
Surprise   106
Shows Fondness, Affection, Love Toward Others   109
Affection   109
Shows Interest, Attention in Classroom Activities   111
Interest (Excitement)   111
Smiles, Seems Happy Much of the Time   114
Joy   114
Humor   115
Observing, Recording, and Interpreting Emotional Development   117
Learning Activities   119
Suggested Readings   119
Children's Books   119

5   Social Play   122

Developing Social Play Skills   123
The Importance of Play   124
Other Early Play Research   125
Social Play Development   126
Access Rituals   126
The Teacher's Role   127
Spends Time Watching Others Play   128
Plays by Self with Own Toys/Materials   130

Plays Parallel to Others with Similar Toys/Materials   133
Plays with Others in Group Play   135
Makes Friends with Other Children   137
Gains Access to Ongoing Play in a Positive Manner   141
Maintains Role in Ongoing Play in a Positive Manner   144
Resolves Play Conflicts in a Positive Manner   146
Observing, Recording, and Interpreting Social Play   150
Learning Activities   152
Suggested Readings   152
Children's Books   152

6   Prosocial Behavior   154

Developing Prosocial Behavior   155
Shows Concern for Someone in Distress   157
    Empathy   157
Can Tell How Another Child Feels During Conflict   160
    Empathy   160
Shares Something with Another   163
    Generosity   163
Gives Something to Another   166
    Generosity   166
Takes Turns Easily   169
    Cooperation   169
Complies with Requests Easily   171
    Cooperation   171
Helps Another Do a Task   173
    Caregiving   173
Helps (Cares For) Another in Need   175
    Caregiving   175
Observing, Recording, and Interpreting Prosocial Behavior   178
Learning Activities   180
Suggested Readings   180
Children's Books   180

7   Large Motor Development   182

Developing Large Motor Skills   183
    Need for More Exercise   184
    Motor Skills in the Preschool Years   185
Walks Down Steps Alternating Feet   186

Runs with Control over Speed and Direction   189
Jumps with Feet Together   191
Hops on One Foot   194
Climbs Up and Down Climbing Equipment   195
Throws, Catches, and Kicks Balls   198
   Throwing   199
   Catching   200
   Kicking   201
Rides Trikes, Bikes, and Scooters   203
   Trikes   203
   Bikes   204
   Scooters   204
Does Creative Movement   205
Observing, Recording, and Interpreting Large Motor
   Development   207
Learning Activities   209
Suggested Readings   209
Children's Books   210

8   Small Motor Development   **212**

Developing Small Motor Skills   213
   Reflexes   214
   Timing   214
   Dexterity and Handedness   215
Turns Knobs, Lids, Eggbeaters   216
   Puzzles   217
   Cooking   218
Pours Liquid Without Spilling   220
Fastens/Unfastens Zippers, Buttons, Tabs   222
Picks Up and Inserts Objects with Dexterity   224
   Manipulative Materials   224
   Children's Skills   225
   Gender Differences   225
Molds Play Dough/Clay with Dexterity   228
Uses Drawing/Writing Tools with Control   231
Uses Scissors with Control   233
Uses Hammer with Control   235
Observing, Recording, and Interpreting Small Motor
   Development   237
Learning Activities   239
Suggested Readings   240
Children's Books   240

9   Cognitive Development   242

Developing Cognitive Concepts   243
Brain Research   246
Using Play   248
Stages of Exploratory Play   248
Classification   249
Assessing Development   251
Sorts Objects by Shape, Color   251
    Shape   251
    Color   255
Classifies Objects by Size   257
    Comparing   257
    Using Opposites   258
    Collections   258
Places Objects in a Sequence or Series   260
Recognizes, Creates Patterns   262
Counts by Rote to 20   264
Displays 1-to-1 Correspondence with Numbers   266
    *Using Marks, Picture Symbols, and Number Symbols
        to Record   267*
Problem-Solves with Concrete Objects   269
    Types of Reasoning   269
Problem-Solves with Computer Programs   273
Observing, Recording, and Interpreting Cognitive
    Development   276
Learning Activities   277
Suggested Readings   278
Children's Books   278

10   Spoken Language   280

Developing Spoken Language   281
Stages of Language Acquisition   282
    Stages of Language Production   283
Listens But Does Not Speak   285
    Preproduction Stage   285
    Provide a Stress-Free Environment   286
    Listening to the Teacher Speak   288
Gives Single-Word Answers   289
    Transition to Production   289
Gives Short-Phrase Responses   291
    Early Production   291

Does Chanting   293
  Early Production   293
  Chanting   295
Takes Part in Conversations   296
  Early Production   296
  The Rules of Conversation   297
  Teacher–Child Conversation   298
  Child–Child Conversations   299
Speaks in Expanded Sentences   301
  Expansion of Production   301
  Second-Language Speakers   303
Asks Questions   305
  Expansion of Production   305
  Linguistic Scaffolding   306
Can Tell a Story   307
  Expansion of Production   307
  Decontextualized Talk   308
  Retelling Stories from Picture Books   309
Observing, Recording, and Interpreting Spoken
  Language   310
Learning Activities   312
Suggested Readings   312
Children's Books   312

11   Emergent Writing and Reading Skills   314

Developing Early Literacy Skills   315
Pretends to Write with Pictures and Scribbles   318
Makes Horizontal Lines of Writing Scribbles   321
Includes Letterlike Forms in Writing   324
Makes Some Letters, Prints Name or Initial   326
  Alphabet Letters   327
  Printing Letters   328
Holds Book Right-Side Up; Turns Pages Right to Left   332
Pretends to Read Using Pictures to Tell Story   335
Retells Stories from Books with Increasing Accuracy   337
  Predictable Books   339
Shows Awareness That Print in Books Tells the Story   341
  Song Storybooks   342
Observing, Recording, and Interpreting Emergent Literacy
  Development   344
Learning Activities   344
Suggested Readings   346
Children's Books   346

12   Art and Music Skills   348

Developing Art Skills   349
  Right Brain versus Left Brain   352
Makes Basic Scribble Shapes   352
Combines Circles/Squares with Crossed Lines   356
Draws Person as Sun-Face with Arms and Legs   357
Combines Objects Together in a Picture   360
Observing, Recording, and Interpreting Art Skills   364
Developing Music Skills   365
Moves Legs and Feet in Rhythm to a Beat   365
  Dance   366
Moves Arms and Hands in Rhythm to a Beat   368
Plays Instruments   369
Sings with Group or by Him-/Herself   371
Learning Activities   375
Suggested Readings   375
Children's Books   375

13   Dramatic Play Skills   378

Developing Dramatic Play Skills   379
  Observing Children in Dramatic Play   381
Does Pretend Play by Him-/Herself   382
Assigns Roles or Takes on Assigned Roles   384
Needs Particular Props to Do Pretend Play   388
Takes on Characteristics and Actions Related to Role   391
Can Pretend with Imaginary Objects   393
Uses Language for Creating and Sustaining the Plot   396
  Spoken Words for Internal Images   397
Enacts Exciting, Danger-Packed Themes   398
  Superhero and War Play   399
  Group Play   401
Uses Elaborate Themes, Ideas, Details   403
Observing, Recording, and Interpreting Dramatic Play Skills   405
Learning Activities   406
Suggested Readings   407
Children's Books   407

14   Sharing Observational Data with Families   410

Involving Families in Their Children's Programs   411
  Focusing on the Child   411
  Using the Child Development Checklist   412

Making Parents Partners   414
Sharing Observation Results   415
   Communication Methods   415
   Interpreting Checklist Results   416
   Sharing Checklist Results with Staff   422
   Sharing Checklist Results with Parents   422
   Planning for the Child Based on Checklist Results   423
   Ongoing Observations by Parents and Staff   425
   Parent Observation in the Classroom   425
Developing Collaborative Portfolios   426
   Why Make Portfolios?   427
   What Form Should a Portfolio Take?   430
   How Can Portfolios Be Used?   431
Learning Activities   432
Suggested Readings   432

References   434

Web Sites   443

Index of Children's Books   444

Index   447

Note: Every effort has been made to provide accurate and current Internet information in this book. However, the Internet and information posted on it are constantly changing, so it is inevitable that some of the Internet addresses listed in this textbook will change.

1

Observing and Assessing Children's Development

WATCHING VERSUS OBSERVING

Most teachers of young children love to watch the children in their classrooms as they work and play together or apart. Which ones are excited about the activities? Who has found a new buddy to play with? Which one stands around and watches? As the days progress, so do the children, growing taller, speaking clearer, showing sparks of creativity they never before revealed. And you are the wonderful witness of it all. Watching children in this spontaneous manner can easily become a most engrossing habit.

Today, however, teachers of young children are being asked to do more than merely *watch* the children. They are being asked to *observe* the children in their classrooms. They are being asked to do *a focused looking* at each child to gain certain particulars about him or her. What are these facts? This textbook is most concerned with evidence involving the *child's development*. Wortham (2008) defined development as: "the process of change in an individual over time" (p. 128).

We realize that all children grow and change. Some do it more rapidly than others. Some do it more slowly. This change is affected by the child's age, the child's rate of maturity, and the child's experiences. Thus children of the same age may not be at the same level of development. Their rate of maturity may be different. Their life experiences may be different. But their development, nevertheless, is continuous. It occurs in certain stages or sequences. All children everywhere go through these same stages and in the same order—but not at the same rate. Most important for us as child observers: *These stages can be observed*. We are able to tell where a child stands in his or her development by observing the stage or sequence the child is in. Then as teachers we are able to provide activities that will help the child progress. Figure 1–1 shows how child development occurs.

Figure 1–1 How Child Development Occurs

- Development is continuous.
- Development occurs in a certain order.
- Development occurs in stages or sequences.
- All children everywhere go through every stage.
- Each child's rate of development may differ.
- Each child's development depends on age, maturity, and experience.

Once you know the stages or sequences of the various domains of child development, you will be able to make sense of the *focused looking* at children that is currently required of us as teachers. What is the purpose for such child observation? Gronlund and James (2005, p. 4) noted two principle ways for using the data obtained:

- For curriculum planning
- For assessment

For Curriculum Planning

To make daily and long-term curriculum plans for the children, you will need to know how the child is progressing in the domains of:

1. Emotional development
2. Social development
3. Physical development
4. Cognitive development
5. Language development
6. Creative development.

Although we treat these domains separately, young children's development occurs in all of them simultaneously. To set up activities in the various curriculum centers of the classroom that will help children progress, you will need to know where a child stands in each of these developmental areas. How will you do it? The most appropriate method we have discovered is by observing each child in a regular, continuous, systematic manner. By observing each child, you will be able to gather the necessary data to help you plan your daily and long-range program. This textbook, *Observing Development of the Young Child,* will provide the methods and the tools to help you accomplish this goal.

For Assessment

Assessment is the process by which teachers collect information about a child's capabilities. Teachers look at children's skill levels, interests, strengths, and weaknesses. Ahola and Kovacik (2007) call assessment: "The ongoing process by which qualified professionals together with families, look at all areas of a child's development through standardized tests and observation. Both areas of strength and those requiring support and intervention are identified" (p. 9).

Assessment of preschool children is a current issue of great importance and concern for early childhood educators. Programs for young children have always attempted to determine children's needs and to evaluate their accomplishments, sometimes successfully, sometimes not. The number of instruments currently available for assessing the learning, progress, and behavior of preschool children is mind-boggling. Literally hundreds of instruments and procedures have come into use in the past 20 years. Behavior rating scales, tests of visual perception, performance inventories, developmental profiles, portfolios, language batteries, self-concept screening devices, social competence scales, sociometric tests, personality inventories, pictorial intelligence tests, case studies, developmental screening tests, performance-based interviews, and video or audio recordings are only a few.

Some of these assessment tools and procedures use the observation of children; some do not. Some need to be administered by professional testers; others don't. Some assessment procedures place children in artificial rather than authentic situations. Many ask children to perform contrived activities. Although such tools and tasks may be helpful to researchers and professionals who are evaluating children for developmental problems, most are not appropriate for the nonspecialist teacher in the early childhood classroom.

A Different Point of View

A great deal of the assessment and evaluation of children today focuses on questions such as, "What's wrong with the child?" and "How can we intervene to help him or her?" This textbook takes a different point of view. It looks for answers to the questions: "What's right with the young child?" and "How can we use his or her strengths to help in the continued development of the child?"

We are then, of course, faced with the problem of how to determine what is "right" with the young child. How can we tell where children stand in their physical, cognitive, socioemotional, language, and creative development? Do we test them, measure them, compare them, put them through a series of tasks—or what?

As early childhood professionals, we have found that in most instances the best method to determine a child's strengths is *for the teacher to observe the young child in the regular classroom based on a particular set of criteria*. Early childhood specialist Seefeldt (1998) agreed when she declared: "Not only can observations reveal much about children's growth and development, their perceptions of self and others, patterns of behavior, and their strengths and weaknesses, but they take place naturally and spontaneously" (p. 316). She and many others have found that observation is one of the best ways to assess an individual young child. It might not work so well with an older child, but it is eminently suited to a preschooler:

As Seefeldt (1998) mentioned:

Young children, who have a limited repertoire of behaviors that can be assessed, may best be studied through observation. In fact, to assess young children, who are unable to express themselves fully with words, with any other than direct observations may not be possible. Further, young children reveal themselves through their behaviors. Unlike older children and adults, the young are incapable of hiding their feelings, ideas, or emotions with socially approved behaviors, so observing them often yields accurate information. (p. 317)

The best method to determine a child's strengths is to observe the child in a regular classroom.

Why Assess Young Children?

The reasons to assess young children are many and varied. Some early childhood programs do assessments of children as a program evaluation tool. Are the children progressing as they should? Should changes be made in the curriculum? Other programs do assessments because they are mandated by the state or federal government to prove their effectiveness to receive ongoing support and funding.

Our professional organization, the National Association for the Education of Young Children (NAEYC), along with the National Association of Early Childhood Specialists in State Departments of Education, has issued a Joint Position Statement on Early Childhood Curriculum, Assessment, and Program Evaluation, adopted in November 2003. It calls for programs to "make ethical, appropriate, valid, and reliable assessment a central part of all early childhood programs." In an earlier publication, the NAEYC defined assessment as "the process of observing, recording and otherwise documenting the work children do and how they do it, as a basis for a variety of education decisions that affect the child" (NAEYC, 1991, p. 32). In a recent statement, they give the specific reasons for assessing young children as:

1. making sound decisions about teaching and learning,
2. identifying significant concerns that may require focused intervention for individual children,
3. helping programs improve their educational and developmental interventions. (NAEYC, 2004, p. 52)

ASSESSING THROUGH OBSERVATION

This textbook concurs with the NAEYC definition and reasons, but takes them a step in a somewhat different direction. The focus in this text is on assessing *children's development* through observation. The purpose for such assessment is to plan curriculum activities for children that will promote their growth and success in the classroom. Teachers need to know where each child stands developmentally to plan activities that will speak to his or her needs. The work of the Russian early childhood theorist Lev Vygotsky supports this focus. He believed that careful observation of children should be considered as valid as their scores on a test (Mooney, 2000).

Observing and recording the actions of young children in the classroom, as previously mentioned, are the primary means for gathering such data on the accomplishments of individuals. Observation can also be used to determine the level of children's development. Once these data are collected and interpreted, teachers can identify the strengths of each child as well as areas that need strengthening. Appropriate activities can then be planned that address both individual and group needs.

The Child Development Checklist

This text gives students of child development and teachers of young children ages 3 through 5 a tool for observing and recording this natural development, the "Child Development Checklist," described in Chapter 2. It is a recording tool that can help observers determine where each child stands in the six areas of emotional, social, physical, cognitive, language, and creative development. The text then incorporates the items from the checklist as an outline for discussing each area of child development in the chapters to follow.

All children go through an observable sequence of development. From large to small motor coordination, from simple ideas to complex thinking, from one-word utterances to lengthy sentences, from scribbles to representational drawings—all children everywhere seem to proceed through a step-by-step sequence of development that can be traced by an observer who knows what to look for. The observer then records these data and later interprets them to make appropriate plans for individual children.

The Child Development Checklist, the basis of this text, helps observers focus on each of the six major areas. These areas are in turn divided into 11 topics of child development (Figure 1–2). Each chapter treats one of these topics of development, and each topic focuses on eight observable items of child behavior based on recognized developmental sequences or progressions. Rather than including every detail of development on the checklist, eight representative items are discussed. This makes observations inclusive enough to be meaningful, but not so detailed to be cumbersome for the observer.

For items the observer does not check as apparent when observing a child, a section of ideas in the chapter following the item called *If You Have Not Checked This Item: Some Helpful Ideas* can be useful in planning for individual needs. Chapters 2 and 3 discuss in detail how the Child Development Checklist can be used for observing and recording child development.

Figure 1–2   Checklist Topics

- *Emotional*
    Chapter 3—Self-Esteem
    Chapter 4—Emotional Development
- *Social*
    Chapter 5—Social Play
    Chapter 6—Prosocial Behavior
- *Physical*
    Chapter 7—Large Motor Development
    Chapter 8—Small Motor Development
- *Cognitive*
    Chapter 9—Cognitive Development
- *Language*
    Chapter 10—Spoken Language
    Chapter 11—Emergent Writing & Reading
- *Creative*
    Chapter 12—Art and Music
    Chapter 13—Dramatic Play

The purposes for assessing children's development in this manner are twofold: (1) It allows students of child development to gain an in-depth understanding of real children and their sequences of growth, and (2) it helps teachers of young children to become aware of each child's growth and to support individual development with appropriate activities and materials.

How Do You Become an Observer?

To become an observer of children, you must first step out of the role you normally hold. If you are a teacher or teaching assistant, you must temporarily give that role to another staff member. This can be planned ahead of time at a staff meeting. Each staff member should take on an observer's role for brief periods every week. Student interns can participate, adding another dimension to this important information-gathering task.

As an observer, you should step back unobtrusively and position yourself close to, but not interfering with, the child you are to observe. You may be seated, standing, or walking around—whatever it takes to get close enough to the child without calling attention to yourself. Try to avoid making eye contact with the child you are observing. If he or she looks your way, you can look around at the other children.

Young children are often much more observant than we give them credit for. Despite your best efforts, the child you are observing will often pick up the fact that you are watching him or her if you keep at it long enough. Most children soon forget about the scrutiny they are undergoing and continue their participation in their activity. If you find, however, that a child seems uncomfortable with your presence, and even may try to get away, you should break off your observation. Try again another day, or let another staff member or student observe that particular child.

Children actually like teachers to observe them in this focused way. They relish such one-on-one attention. Children who are not being observed sometimes complain about it. The problem is that you, the observer, want to see what your child is doing with materials and with other children, without her looking over her shoulder at you. If she realizes she is being watched, her normal behavior may change. Psychologists call this the Hawthorne effect (Ahola & Kovacik, 2007, p. 7). Thus, you must try your best to observe a child without being noticed.

Confidentiality

If you are not the teacher, be sure to have the permission of the proper authority before you begin observing. The information you gain about a child during your observations should not be shared with anyone. It should be completely confidential. Use a fictitious name for the child in your recordings and in any reports you write. Use numbers or letters rather than names for other involved children.

How Should You Record Your Observations?

Many observers prefer to use a clipboard with paper or the Child Development Checklist on it. Several such boards can be left on countertops or the tops of room dividers in each learning center, to be picked up and used by observers whenever the occasion calls for it. If children see you writing on a clipboard for any length of time, some will come over to see what you are doing and want to write with your pencil. Tell them you are busy with your work this morning and that they need to do their own work now. If they persist in wanting to write with your tool, direct them to the classroom writing center, where you can keep a similar clipboard with pencil and paper.

Because children love to imitate you, you could ask those children to observe something like the guinea pig. If they continue to demand your attention, tell them you are busy at the moment but you will attend to them when you are finished. Some observers redirect other children to another staff person or give them a chore to accomplish in one of the learning centers.

Do not announce to the class that you are now doing observations and should be left alone. For youngsters of this age, such an announcement only calls attention to yourself, making everyone stop to look at you. Instead, you should be doing just the opposite: making yourself invisible. Then the child you are observing will continue his or her actions undisturbed. Once you have started observing regularly, most children will soon understand and respect your need for privacy.

How Do You Get Started?

Once you begin observing regularly you will soon find yourself getting hooked and never want to stop. The problem is getting started. If observing is something you have never done before, you may keep putting it off. What will the children think? Won't you look foolish just standing around? Even though you understand that making observations of individuals is just as important as teaching, it may still be hard for you to drop your regular tasks and begin. Getting started demands conscious effort, assert Jablon, Dombro, and Dichtelmiller (2007, p. 143). They suggest several ideas for helping an observer get started:

- No more excuses, just take the plunge.
- Don't let worries get in your way.
- Work with a colleague or a partner at first.
- Observe one child's development area at a time.
- Keep reflecting on what you have learned from this observation.

When and How Long Should You Observe?

When is the best time to observe? Any time! You understand how important it is for you to acquire baseline data about each of the children in your program to plan for them. You must therefore *make* time in your busy schedule to gather the necessary information about each child through observation. The time of day to do your observing depends on what you want to learn about a child.

Do you want to see how she makes the transition from home to school in the morning? Which learning centers attract her attention? How long she stays with an activity? How she interacts with others in the dramatic play center? How she handles tools such as scissors, paintbrushes, or pencils? Whether she knows how a particular book "works"? Plan to observe her, then, in each of the centers where these activities take place any time of day.

It does not take long. Only *5 to 10 minutes a day* of focused observing on the part of each staff member will produce a surprising amount of information on children. Make plans to spend your 5 to 10 minutes observing a child you would like to know better. Every day for a week observe the same child for a different 5 to 10 minute period, and soon you will accumulate enough data for a nearly complete profile of her development.

How Should You Plan for Observing?

Because observing and recording are such important aspects of a teacher's commitment to child development, you should explore ways to make it easier for yourself and other staff members to carry out this responsibility. As noted by one observer: "Making the commitment to observe during the course of a busy day necessarily includes preplanning and organization. Teachers should survey their classrooms to determine how best to approach the task. The focus during this phase should be on identifying ways to use the classroom itself to support your efforts" (Benjamin, 1994, p. 16).

Only 5 to 10 minutes a day of formal observing will produce a surprising amount of information about a child.

Some teachers plan to do their most in-depth recording during free-choice time, when children are busily engaged in all the classroom learning centers. Others preplan by placing an "observation chair" in an unobtrusive spot near children's activities. Having notebooks or clipboards and pencils ready at strategic locations also helps.

Some programs include a small cassette recorder as a tool so teachers can tape-record their observations for transcription later instead of writing them down at the time. You should consider anything that makes your task easier. Share ideas with other staff members and find out what works best for them. Then everyone can get into the act of observing, recording, and planning for children. This entire process is known as *systematic observation*.

Using Systematic Observation

Systematic observation—using a particular system to look at and record children's behavior—has thus become an important part of a classroom staff's daily responsibilities. More educators around the country and the world are finally coming to recognize that:

> Observation is used to chart children's development, to gain insight into children's behavior, and to guide curricular decision making. Observation also plays an important role in assessment, either by replacing or by supplementing standardized evaluation instruments. (Benjamin, 1994, p. 14)

Many teachers using such systematic observation for evaluating child development have concluded that it has a number of advantages as an assessment process (Figure 1–3).

Figure 1–3 Advantages of
Systematic Observation for Child
Assessment

1. Gives observers an otherwise unavailable in-depth look at a
   child

2. Focuses on a child's natural behavior in the classroom
   setting

3. Focuses on what a child can do (not what he cannot do)

4. Helps observer to recognize stages of child development

5. Enables classroom staff to make appropriate plans for individuals ·

6. Helps classroom staff determine how program is working

7. Gives classroom staff appropriate data on which to base
   decisions about children, curriculum, and reports to parents

Setting Up Systematic Observation

Systematic observation of young children requires that you have a plan you will be following to do the observing and recording of a child. Steps in such a plan may include

1. Identifying the information you want to gather

2. Identifying the child you plan to observe

3. Identifying the method you plan to use

4. Setting up a schedule for observation

5. Following the observation schedule

Chapter 2 discusses how such systematic observation can be carried out.

TESTS AS TOOLS FOR ASSESSING YOUNG CHILDREN

Although observation is important, testing—the traditional means for evaluating
children—remains a useful assessment tool if selected carefully and used properly. Many
testing instruments and procedures have been developed and validated by researchers in
the field. When they apply to young children, however, the results are often mixed. What
works with older children does not seem to work as well with preschoolers and kinder-
gartners. Test developers sometimes blame the validation procedures used in developing
the tests. Early childhood educators nod wisely and think to themselves: "It's the kids."

Young children have little interest in tests. Why should they? They don't need to
prove to anyone what they can or cannot do. It's true that they can be talked into coop-

erating with a test-giver. The teacher can administer a test to a child and occasionally get valid results on a particular day. Next week the results may be different with the same child. Honest researchers have had to admit such things as: "The major conclusion of this study is that it is inadvisable to routinely test young children prior to or immediately after their entry into kindergarten" (Wenner, 1988, p. 17). Wenner found that even highly respected and widely used tests predicted little more than a quarter of the actual academic performance of kindergarten children.

Romero (1999) pondered the problem of distinguishing "the young child's inability from his or her refusal to cooperate." Sometimes a child's response of "I don't know" may really mean just that, but often it can mean "I don't want to." Romero concludes that:

> Although there is no unequivocal way of knowing whether a child is not cooperating, is too frightened to respond, or is sincerely trying but still failing, examiners who have experience with preschoolers and thorough knowledge of the testing instruments being administered will be able to discern more clearly the child's intent and motives. (1999, p. 60)

Nevertheless, assessment procedures routinely include tests of many kinds. Although many are reliable and valid instruments, for their results to be used with confidence, teachers and testers alike need to be aware of this "young child factor." Young children do not test well. Thus assessors need to include other more informal but reliable types of assessment—such as observations of children in the regular classroom—to round out the picture when they are evaluating young children.

Dodge, Heroman, Charles, and Maioca (2004) also pointed out that government mandates to test preschoolers, seen more frequently these days, are the wrong reason for administering tests. Ongoing assessment should support children's learning and lead to appropriate curriculum, not gather statistics about children and programs for a political agenda. The tests used for such purposes are often inappropriate as well. As Dodge and others have noted: "Researchers recommend assessing children based on observations of the processes children use rather than on simple, concrete, disconnected indicators or milestones" (p. 21).

If tests are used, it is especially important that the classroom teacher learns to administer the instrument themselves whenever possible. If an outside tester is the administrator, be sure to help such a person establish rapport with individual children. Invite the tester to the classroom ahead of time. Help her or him to become acquainted with individuals by playing with them, reading to them, and talking with them before the testing begins. Otherwise, results for young children are sure to be suspect.

Much testing of young children constitutes misassessment because the testing is not developmentally appropriate. Tests often present young children with a series of demands to answer here and now, although young children may not be inclined to respond immediately. Classroom teachers who need child assessment data to plan activities that will support individual needs must first understand the meaning of "developmentally appropriate assessment" before choosing such a test or other data-gathering procedure.

The National Association for the Education of Young Children (NAEYC) and the National Association of Early Childhood Specialists in State Departments of Education, developed a position statement in 2004 urging programs to "make ethical, appropriate,

Figure 1–4 Indicators of Effectiveness of Assessment Practices

Note: Excerpted from National Association for the Education of Young Children (NAEYC) and National Association of Early Childhood Specialists in State Departments of Education (NAECS/SDE). 2004. *Where We Stand on Curriculum, Assessment, and Program Evaluation.* Online: www.naeyc.org/about/positions/pdf/standlcurrass.pdf

- Ethical principles guide assessment purposes.
- Assessment instruments are used for intended purposes.
- Assessments are appropriate for ages being assessed.
- Assessment instruments follow professional criteria for quality.
- What is assessed is developmentally and educationally significant.
- Assessment evidence is used to improve learning.
- Assessment evidence is gathered from a realistic setting.
- Assessments use multiple sources of evidence.
- Screening is always linked to follow-up.
- Use of individually administered standardized tests is limited.
- Staff and families are knowledgeable about assessment.

valid, and reliable assessment a central part of all early childhood programs. To assess young children's strengths, progress, and needs, use assessment methods that are developmentally appropriate, culturally and linguistically responsive, tied to children's daily activities, supported by professional development, inclusive of families, and connected to specific, beneficial purposes" (p. 4). Figure 1–4 lists an adaptation of their 11 indicators of effectiveness of assessment practices.

It should be stressed again that the classroom teacher, rather than a tester from outside the program, should be the primary assessor. The assessment should be based on activities in which children typically engage within the classroom, and not contrived activities in artificial situations. Assessment should not threaten children, nor should it focus on wrong answers or what children cannot do.

ALTERNATIVE APPROACHES TO ASSESSMENT OF YOUNG CHILDREN

In addition to testing instruments, the assessment of preschool children can be done using alternative techniques. Many of them include child observation, but also the collecting of representative work in play-based assessment, child interviews, and visual documentation. Linder, Holm, and Walsh (1999) observed that:

> Many early childhood specialists appear to be moving away from the exclusive use of standardized or criterion referenced tests and relying more on a combination of traditional techniques with experiential, observational approaches. A survey of school psychologists found that play-based assessment was one of the most frequently cited alternative approaches. (p. 163)

Play-Based Assessment

Because play for young children is their natural means of interacting with the world around them, it makes sense to assess children's development while they are engaged in play activities. Toys and specific artificial play situations have long been used by psychologists to observe and record children's behavior using standardized instruments. Play-based assessments, on the other hand, vary from these traditional assessments in that the child is observed doing whatever the child typically does in the environment. Although standardized assessment instruments may be used for the observations and analysis of children's behavior, the observer records the child interacting naturally with play materials, peers, or even parents or teachers in the classroom environment.

Play-based assessment is defined by an organization called Zero to Three as "a form of developmental assessment that involves observation of how a child plays alone, with peers, or with parents or other familiar caregivers, in free play or in special games. This type of assessment can be helpful because play is a natural way for children to show what they can do, how they feel, how they learn new things, and how they behave with familiar people" (Zero to Three, 2005). Three types of play-based assessment are typically used:

- *Nonstructured:* identifies all behaviors occurring during a play session; assessors often watch a parent playing with the child
- *Structured:* uses a previously designed set of play behaviors using specific play items
- *Transdisciplinary:* uses a team of assessors observing the child simultaneously, each team member looking for specific information

Play-based assessment (Figure 1–5) has also become the method of choice for assessing children with special needs (Ahola and Kovacik, 2007, p. 14).

Child Interviews

Assessment interviews done by a teacher and a child can provide important information about a child not easily obtained by any other means. As Wortham (2008) tells us: "Interviews are especially appropriate for young children who are just beginning to develop literacy skills and cannot yet express themselves with a paper-and-pencil activity"

Figure 1–5 Advantages of Play-Based Assessment

- Provides an opportunity to assess behavior of a child who cannot or will not perform in a formal testing situation
- More can be seen in watching children play than in asking them to perform
- All the developmental domains of a child can be witnessed at the same time

Assessment interviews done by a teacher and a child can provide important information about a child not easily obtained by any other means.

(p. 212). The strategies followed can be similar to those used by Swiss psychologist Jean Piaget to understand children's thinking. He used questioning, then asked more questions based on children's initial responses.

Such interviews are best conducted on an informal basis during a free-play situation. As the teacher interacts or plays with the child, she or he can talk about what is happening. For example, while making an animal puzzle with Nicole, the teacher can make remarks about Nicole's skill in finding and matching the puzzle pieces. This may lead Nicole to tell how she does it. What does she guess the animal will look like when the puzzle is finished? If teachers listen closely to what children have to say, they can use children's responses to lead them to new questions that will elicit further information about their development. Teachers can then record their interviews either on a tape recorder or by writing them down afterward.

According to Wortham, interviews should be short. Ten minutes is an appropriate length of time. Children should also be given plenty of time to think about and respond to the teacher's questions. Reading a picture book to an individual child can serve as an informal interview if the book is carefully chosen and the questions carefully framed to elicit desired information.

For example, one teacher knew that one of the highly active boys, Rinaldo, loved dinosaurs and was always pretending to be one. For her informal interview with Rinaldo, the teacher chose the simple picture book *Ten Terrible Dinosaurs* (Stickland, 1997) because she knew it would hold the boy's short attention to the end. She read the book to herself, thinking about how she would use it with Rinaldo. She guessed that he would enjoy the pictures of the dinosaurs, but would want to interrupt after every page of the simple one-line text to make comments about what was happening. This suited her purpose perfectly because she could then elicit needed information about Rinaldo's thoughts and feelings without interrupting the flow of the story.

Because *Ten Terrible Dinosaurs* is a count-down story, she could also find out what Rinaldo knew about the numbers from 10 to 1, as well as how good he was at hypothesizing what he would find on the next page. "Ten terrible dinosaurs standing in a line," read the first double page. "Soon began to push and then there were . . ." continued the next page. Would Rinaldo know the answer is "9," and would he be able to identify which animal is missing on the following page? Look for picture books that show a fascinating character with a problem to solve that will capture a child's attention for an informal interview. Here are some suggestions:

- *I Will Never Not Ever Eat a Tomato (Child, 2000).* Big brother Charlie tries to convince his little sister Lola to eat various items of food. He is unsuccessful until Lola turns the tables on him.
- *Tabitha's Terrifically Tough Tooth (Middleton, 2001).* Tabitha discovers her tooth is loose and tries all sorts of bizarre but unsuccessful ways to pull it out—until she finally sneezes.
- *Freckleface Strawberry (Moore, 2007).* A girl with red hair and freckles is teased so much about her freckles, she tries to get rid of them, until a baby who laughs instead of teasing changes her mind.

Most teachers find such simple informal interviews to be so valuable that they tailor book readings to particular children and develop forms for recording elicited information. These forms are kept in a child's documentation folder or portfolio along with other observational data. Seefeldt (1998) concurs:

> Interviews possess a number of virtues that make them an ideal tool for assessing young children. They are flexible. The interviewer can go over the same questions, probe others more intently, and direct and adapt the interview until clarity is reached and as much information as possible has been collected. (p. 321)

You can develop your own interview questions on a recording form or use questions like those in Figure 1–6.

Visual Documentation

Visual documentation is something we can look at to gain insight into a child's development, say Ahola and Kovacik (2007, p. 57). With young children, it can take many forms: photographs of children involved in activities, photographs of children's work, video recordings, audio recordings, or samples of children's work.

You can add another dimension to your observation of children by using digital cameras, cell phone cameras, camcorders, and cassette recorders in addition to conducting play-based assessments, interviews, or traditional classroom observations. Such visual

Describing
1.   What's happening on this page?

Predicting
2.   What do you think will happen next?

Problem solving
3.   What else could the character do to solve the problem?

Empathizing
4.   How do you think the character feels about what is happening?

Creating
5.   What would you do if you were the character?

Recalling
6.   Do you remember what the character did at first?

documentation can capture important moments on film or tape to be used to document observational data already gathered about the children. They also can serve as foci for team discussion regarding each child's development or to help make decisions on follow-up activities for the children in question. These observations can then be placed in each child's portfolio or documentation folder.

Photographs

Photos of children are easy to take with digital cameras these days, so be sure to snap a series of the same child or same incident for later recording. These photos are for your use, not the children's. They should be captioned with content descriptions, dated, and placed in the same file as your recorded notes—perhaps in a child's portfolio (see Chapter 14).

Photos have other uses as well (Figure 1–7). You can use the photo of a child interacting with others or engaged in a classroom activity as the focus of an *assessment interview*, just as you would use a picture book. Jot down simple questions you will want to ask the child about the photo to elicit assessment information. Be sure the questions are open ended enough for the child to respond in creative ways you may not expect. You may want to tape-record your conversation or record the results on file cards with the picture attached.

Photographs of individual children taken with a digital camera open other avenues for child assessment. Using appropriate software, these photos can be printed out on regular computer paper, making several copies of each for use in child or parent interviews, or for inclusion in child portfolios. They also can be used as pages in a book children can create with their own stories written under the photos. Digital photos can also be shown *on* computer or television screens for use in staff planning sessions on individual children or for parent conferences.

Figure 1–7 Uses for Photos in Child Observation and Assessment

- Captures image of child at the moment of his/her action
- Serves as memory aid for teachers of what happened
- Promotes child's self-image
- Can be used in assessment interview
- Can be used in parent conferences
- Can be used in a book child creates
- Can be used in turn-taking devices
- Can show child's products
- Can be used in portfolios, documentation panels
- Helps staff interpret child's development
- Helps staff interpret child's behavior
- Helps staff plan for child

Digital photos are especially well suited to on-the-spot recording. In areas where a child needs strengthening, such photos can be especially useful. For example, if Jessica experiences difficulty at arrival time in making the transition from home to school, be sure to take photos of her every morning for several days, whether or not she continues to encounter the difficulties. Keep a running record (Chapter 2) of her actions at the same time and then mount the daily photos together with your written observations on file cards or portfolio pages. Interpreting children's behavior and making plans to help them improve it are more effective when you can see firsthand the visual evidence of their actions long after it occurs (Entz & Galarza, 2000).

Videotapes

Videotapes serve the same purpose as photos. Use a camcorder to tape a child's actions for later observation and discussion with other staff members or parents. After you have previewed the tape and know what areas of development it documents, ask staff members to check off that particular section of the Child Development Checklist (see Chapter 2) when they view the video. Checklists can be used like this with videotapes, treating them like live observations. A group discussion of the tape can be recorded and added to the observational data for making individual plans or for documenting the assessment.

Audiotapes

A cassette tape recorder can also add depth to your written observations by recording a child's spoken language or verbal interactions with other children. Speak the child's name, your name, the date, and the classroom location into the recorder before placing it with a running tape on a table or countertop near the child. After listening to the tape, make notes or check off appropriate items on a checklist to be placed with the tape in the child's portfolio. Audiotapes can also be made of child interviews, as noted previously. Some observers also prefer to speak softly into a cassette recorder instead of taking notes during their observations of children. Later, a transcription of the tape can be made.

Documentation Panels

Another alternative assessment method for observing children's development is the documentation panel. Photographs of children along with their products (e.g., painting, writing, and science collections) are displayed on a board or a panel on the wall of the classroom. The Reggio Emilia schools in Italy promoted this approach, believing that documentation should be a part of the learning process. Teachers and parents alike need to see visually what children have accomplished. As Ahola and Kovacik (2007) tell us: "Documentation serves as an agent for planning, communicating, and reflecting. Children's experiences, including all of the processes of those experiences, are visually recorded and displayed for others to consider" (p. 60).

For instance, the children in Noah's Ark Preschool in Taos, New Mexico, built their own playhouse outside on their playground from adobe bricks over several weeks. Fathers of the Hispanic children helped them plan the dimensions, mix mud and straw, fill square frames, set the bricks out to dry, and then build up the walls and roof. Each step of the process was photographed. Children tape recorded what was happening. Then they wrote stories and made drawings. This material was then assembled on poster board panels as a visual day-by-day diary of the project.

Although the children and parents viewed these panels simply as pictures of their exciting playhouse project, the teachers understood that this was a permanent record of how the children were developing. It displayed their large and small motor accomplishments over time. Their cognitive skills of measuring and counting emerged. Turn-taking and helping one another were captured on film. Their creative skills of making up stories about the playhouse and then reenacting them in real life materialized. These panels could then be shared with other professionals and afterward kept for future planning.

LEARNING HOW TO SEE

Before you become too deeply involved in child observation, you need to ask yourself: "What do I really see when I look at a child?" For most of us, we tend to take a cursory look, make some sort of judgment, and then dismiss it. Bentzen (2005) explained that "our brains enable us to see in ways that far exceed the camera's ability to 'see.' But observation becomes complicated precisely because we do more with sensory information than the camera is able to see. All of us look at and organize the objects and events in our world according to our past experiences, what we know, and what we believe" (p. 6). In other words, we judge what we see.

This means that two people looking at the same child engaged in play will come away with two different views. On the other hand, the more each of us knows about child development, the more similar our observations of the same child will be. As you practice observation according to this book's suggestions, try doing it with a partner so you can compare your notes. You will find the more you observe, the better you become. The more you learn about young children, the more you will see when you observe. The old adage "We see what we look for" holds true with child observations. When we are not looking for specific details, we tend not to see them. Thus it behooves us to become aware of as many details as possible.

Curtis and Carter (2006) quoted Corita Kent, who tells us: "It takes practice for us to recover our ability to see. For many years we have been learning to judge and dismiss. And we've lost the complex realities, laws, and details that surround us. Try looking the way the child looks, as if always for the first time" (p. 1).

Children "see" with all their senses, not just their eyes. They use sight, sound, touch, smell, taste, and movement to "see" the environment that surrounds them. As an observer of young children, you will need to use as many of these senses as possible for every observation you make. You will also need to record as many details as possible for each of these five senses plus movement.

Practicing Observation Skills

It is important to practice your observing skills before you begin observing children. Look at a person near you or a photo of a person and jot down all the descriptive details you can see. Do this exercise with a team member and compare your results. Do it again and try doubling the details. Next zero in on one aspect of a person, for instance, his or her facial expression, and describe it in detail: eyes, eyebrows, lashes, nose, mouth, lips, cheeks, chin, forehead, ears, and movements. Now take the eyes alone, and describe them in detail: eye color, winking, blinking, twinkling, flashing, sparkling, staring, gazing, glancing, opening, closing, squinting, peeking, peering, laughing, scowling. Be careful about being judgmental. Use objective terms only.

Read to a child from a picture book that focuses on careful observation. See if the child can discover hidden objects. See if you can. In *Looking for a Moose* (Root, 2006), four children hike into the woods, a swamp, the bushes, and up a hillside in search of a moose. Only parts of the moose are visible in each location, but no one sees anything at all until the moose finally bugles its call. Zany sound words that accompany the search add to the excitement.

In *The Forest Has Eyes* (Maclay, 1998) the artist, Bev Doolittle, has hidden faces of Indians and animals in the rocks, trees, and streams of each of the illustrations. Readers and listeners are asked to find them. Can they? Can you?

Through Georgia's Eyes (Rodriguez, 2006) is a children's biography of Georgia O' Keefe, the great American painter of the Southwest. She saw things differently from most people: close-ups of giant red poppies, flowers from inside out, bleached white cow skulls on the empty desert, blood red canyons, gray hills as elephants with white sand at their feet. Bring in a book of O'Keefe's paintings (e.g., *Georgia O'Keefe,* Frazier, 2004), or obtain prints from a gallery. How do the children respond to them? How do you?

Observation of young children is critical for a number of reasons, concluded Bentzen (2005). "The most basic reason is that ultimately we learn about reality by observing it, by having contact with it through one or more of our five physical senses. If we are to understand children, we must watch them, listen to them, and touch them. Moreover, we must think about the information we have gotten in these ways and make some sense of it in order to act with and toward children in appropriate and meaningful ways" (p. 17).

The Chapters to Follow

The chapters to follow can serve as guidelines in evaluating children's strengths and needs and for planning activities to help individuals or small groups of children with similar needs. Chapter 2 discusses collecting and recording observational data, including using the Child Development Checklist; how to interpret recorded results; and how to apply your interpretation in making plans for children. Chapters 3 through 13 discuss each of the 11 developmental areas of the Checklist. Chapter 14 concludes with a discussion of sharing observational data with parents.

Ideas for helping children, listed in each chapter under the heading *If You Have Not Checked This Item: Some Helpful Ideas*, should not only assist children in their areas of need but also stimulate your own creativity for developing your own activities. Once you have learned where the child stands developmentally, you will know how to make appropriate activity plans for each of the children in your program.

LEARNING ACTIVITIES

1. If all children everywhere go through the same stages of development, why are some 3-year-olds at different stages than others? How can you tell? What makes the difference?

2. What is the difference between using systematic observations and paper-and-pencil tests to assess young children? Which would you prefer to use, and why?

3. What is the first step for becoming an observer of young children? How would you go about taking it?

4. Look at the Indicators of Effectiveness of Assessment Practices (Figure 1–4) and decide which of the 11 indicators your program has been following and how you can improve your assessment process. If you are not in a program, describe how you would set up a developmentally appropriate method for assessing children in a preschool program.

5. How can photos of children be used in documenting the assessment of preschool children? How would you go about accomplishing this?

SUGGESTED READINGS

Gullo, D. F. (2005). *Understanding assessment and evaluation in early childhood*. New York: Teachers College Press.

Helm, J. H., Beneke, S., & Steinheimer, K. (2007). *Windows on learning: Documenting young children's work* (2nd ed.). New York: Teachers College Press.

Jones, J. (2004). Framing the assessment discussion. *Young Children, 59*(1), 14–18.

Marion, M. (2004). *Using observation in early childhood education.* Upper Saddle River, NJ: Merrill/Prentice Hall.

McAfee, O., Leong, D. J., & Bodrova, E. (2004). *Basics of assessment: A primer for early childhood educators.* Washington, DC: NAEYC.

McLean, M., Wolery, M., & Bailey, D. B., Jr. (2004). *Assessing infants and preschoolers with special needs* (3rd ed.). Upper Saddle River, NJ: Merrill/Prentice Hall.

Mindes, G. (2007). *Assessing young children* (3rd ed.). Upper Saddle River, NJ: Merrill/Prentice Hall.

Mooney, C. B. (2000). *An introduction to Dewey, Montessori, Erikson, Piaget, and Vygotsky.* St. Paul, MN: Redleaf Press.

Puckett, M., & Black, J. (2008). *Authentic assessment for the young child: Celebrating development and learning* (3rd ed.). Upper Saddle River, NJ: Merrill/Prentice Hall.

Seita, H. (2008). The power of documentation in early childhood. *Young Children, 63*(2), 88–93.

CHILDREN'S BOOKS

Child, L. (2000). *I will never not ever eat a tomato.* Cambridge, MA: Candlewick Press.

Maclay, E. (1998). *The forest has eyes.* Shelton, CT: The Greenwich Workshop Press.

Middleton, C. (2001). *Tabitha's terrifically tough tooth.* New York: Phyllis Fogelman Books.

Moore, J. (2007). *Freckleface strawberry.* New York: Bloomsbury USA Children's Books.

Root, P. (2006). *Looking for a moose.* Cambridge, MA: Candlewick Press.

Stickland, P. (1997). *Ten terrible dinosaurs.* New York: Dutton.

Rodriguez, R. (2006). *Through Georgia's eyes.* New York: Henry Holt.

2

Collecting and Recording Observational Data

RECORDING OBSERVATIONAL DATA

As you begin the actual observation of young children, you need to keep in mind that important criteria apply to the details you are discovering and recording. Curtis and Carter (2006, p. 15) refer to them as "components of observation skills." They include

- *Being objective:* You must observe each child without judging.
- *Being specific:* You should look for and record even the smallest details.
- *Using direct quotes:* You should listen closely and record what each child says.
- *Using mood cues:* You should describe the emotional mood of the child.

Systematic observation of young children always implies recording. Not only must observers have a particular reason to observe a child and know what to look for, but they also need a method for recording the information they gather. A number of useful methods have been developed over the years by observers of young children. A sampling of these methods is included for discussion in this chapter. (Figure 2–1).

Narratives

The most popular methods for recording child observations fall under the heading of "narrative recording," that is, written descriptions of children's actions. Two of the

Figure 2–1 Recording Methods

- Narratives
  Anecdotal records
  Running records

- Sampling
  Time sampling
  Event sampling

- Rating scales
  Graphic scales
  Numeric scales

- Checklists
  Developmental

25

several types of informal narratives most widely used are anecdotal and running records.

Anecdotal Records

Anecdotal records are brief narrative accounts describing an incident of child behavior that is important to the observer. Anecdotes describe what happened in a factual, objective manner, telling how it happened, when and where it happened, and what was said and done. Sometimes they include reasons for the child's behavior, but the "why" is better kept in the commentary part of the record. These accounts are most often written *after* the incident has occurred, by someone who witnessed it informally, rather than *during* its occurrence, by someone who was formally observing and recording. Anecdotal records have long been made by teachers, psychologists, social workers, and even parents who record when their babies first walk and talk.

As McFarland (2008) tells us: "Careful documentation about what is happening in the classroom with each child enables a teacher to gain important insight on children's development and needs" (p. 32).

Although anecdotal records are brief, describing only one incident at a time, they are cumulative. A series of them over a period of time can be extremely useful in providing rich details about the child being observed. As McFarland noted: "Children who lack appropriate progression in particular areas over time can be identified by referring to anecdotal records regularly" (p. 33). Teachers can also use anecdotal records with the Child Skills Checklist to describe more fully the evidence they offer when checking an item. When combined with photos, anecdotes written as captions for photos provide very rich visual information about each child's development. Other advantages of using anecdotal records include the following.

Advantages

1. The observer needs no special training to record.

2. The observation is open ended. The recorder writes anything and everything he or she witnesses and is not restricted to one kind of behavior or recording.

3. The observer can catch an unexpected incident no matter when it occurs, for it is usually recorded at a later time.

4. The observer can look for and record the significant behavior and ignore the rest.

As in all observational methods, there are also disadvantages. Observers need to decide why they are observing, what they want to find out, and which method will be most useful. Some of the disadvantages of the anecdotal method include the following.

Disadvantages

1. It does not give a complete picture because it records only incidents of interest to the observer.

2. It depends too much on the memory of the observer because it is recorded after the event. Witnesses to events are notoriously poor on details.

3. Incidents may be taken out of context and thus be interpreted incorrectly or used in a biased manner.

4. It is difficult to code or analyze narrative records; thus, the method may not prove useful in a scientific study.

Such records can be more useful if recorded on a vertically divided page with the anecdote on the left side and a space for comments or interpretation on the right, or the page can be divided horizontally with the anecdote at the top and the commentary at the bottom. Figure 2–2 is an example of the latter format.

This anecdote tells what happened in an objective manner. Especially good are the direct quotes. The anecdote could have included more details about the child's facial expression, tone of voice, and gestures. The reader does not get the feeling of whether the boy was enjoying himself as a helper, trying to ingratiate himself with another child who was not paying much attention, or desperately trying to gain the attention of the other boy. Such details are sometimes missing from anecdotes because they have not been written down until the end of the day or even later. By then, much is forgotten.

The comments contain several inferences and conclusions based on insufficient evidence. Obviously this observer has spent some time watching Stevie, based on her comments, "Stevie is often involved" and "Once engaged in play, he likes to continue, and

---

ANECDOTAL RECORD

Child's Name _____ Stevie _____ **Age** __4__ **Date** __2/23__

Observer _____ Anne _____ **Place** _____ HS _____ **Time** __9:00–10:00__

INCIDENT

Stevie went over to the block corner and asked two boys, Ron and Tanner, if he could help them build. They told him it was okay. As they were building he accidentally knocked some blocks down. "I can put it back up," he said, and handed the blocks to Ron. For awhile he watched Ron build and then said, "I found a smokestack, Ron," and handed him a cylinder block. Ron told him where to put it, and Stevie began getting cylinders off the shelf and handing them to Ron and Tanner to place. Finally he started placing his own cylinders around the perimeter of the building. The teacher asked him if he wanted to finger paint but he replied, "I'm not gonna finger paint unless Ron finger paints."

COMMENT

Stevie is often involved in a lot of dramatic play with several other boys. He especially likes to be near or play with Ron. He seems to look up to him. Whatever rules Ron sets in the play, Stevie follows. Once engaged in play, he likes to continue, and will usually not let another child, or even the teacher, distract him.

Figure 2–2   Anecdotal Record of Observation

The observer infers that Stevie likes to be near or playing with Ron.

will usually not...." She would need an accumulation of such anecdotes to make valid statements like this based on evidence. If this were one page in an accumulation of anecdotes about Stevie, the comments would perhaps be more accurate.

The observer infers that Stevie "likes to be near or playing with Ron," although there is not sufficient evidence here to make that definite an inference. Perhaps she should have said: "Whatever rules Ron sets in the play, Stevie follows," if Stevie actually placed a cylinder block where directed. However, this was only hinted at and not stated. Particular words are very important in objective recording. Her conclusion about Stevie not letting another child or even the teacher distract him is only partially accurate because the observer recorded no evidence about another child.

If you were writing the comments about his particular anecdotal record, what might you infer from the incident? Can you make any conclusions based on this information alone, or is it too limited? Are there things you might want to look for in the future when observing this boy that you would include in the commentary?

It is also helpful to indicate what the purpose is for the particular observation. Most observation forms do not provide a space for this, but the usefulness of the observation is enhanced if it is included. In this case, the observer was looking for evidence of involvement in social play for this child.

Running Records

Another popular informal observing and recording method is the running record. It is a detailed narrative account of behavior recorded in a sequential manner as it happens. The observer sits or stands apart from the children and writes down everything that occurs to a particular child over a specified period, which may be as short as several minutes or may be recorded from time to time during a full day. The running record is different from the anecdotal record because it includes all behavior and not just selected incidents, and it is written as the behavior occurs instead of later. Sentences are often short, and words are abbreviated to keep up with the pace of the action. Ahola and Kovacik (2007) tell us: "The running record is beneficial because it allows us to record minute details, but it is not considered practical when trying to collect a great deal of information about a child" (p. 23).

The information you should record in a running record includes the items shown in Figure 2–3.

As with all factual recording, the observer must be careful not to use descriptive words and phrases that are judgmental. The running record has a number of advantages for persons interested in child development.

Advantages

1. It is a rich, complete, and comprehensive record not limited to particular incidents.

2. It is open ended, allowing the observer to record everything he or she sees, and not restricting the observations to a particular kind of behavior.

3. Because it is written at the time of the incident, it tends to be more accurate than accounts written later.

4. It does not require that the observer have special observational skills and therefore is particularly useful to the classroom teacher.

There are also several disadvantages to using this method, once again depending on the purpose for gathering the information.

Disadvantages

1. It is time consuming, making it difficult for observers to find periods of uninterrupted time.

2. It is difficult to record everything for any length of time without missing important details.

3. It works best when observing an individual, but is inefficient when observing a group.

4. Observers must keep themselves apart from the children for long periods.

Figure 2–3 Information to Record

- Facial expressions
- Interactions with materials
- Interactions with people
- Body movements
- Body language
- Spoken language
- Attention span

Observer Errors

Insufficient Evidence

Look at the running record for Katy (Figure 2–4). Has the observer, Rob, omitted any information that would be important for any conclusion he might make about Katy?

Look at the "information to record" in Figure 2–3. Check off each item as you reread the Katy running record. Was anything overlooked or omitted? What about "facial expressions" and "body language"? Can you comment on the "emotional mood" of the child from this running record? What conclusions can you make about Katy from this record?

In another situation if we see a child come into the room in the morning, refuse to greet the teacher, walk over to a table and sit down, push away another child who tries to join him, and shake his head in refusal when the teacher suggests an activity, how can we record it?

A running record of the situation might read like this:

Jonathan walks into the room this morning as if he is mad at the world. He will not look up at the teacher or respond to her greeting. He sort of slumps as he walks across the room and plunks himself down in a chair at one of the activity tables. Richie tries to join him but is pushed away. The teacher goes over and asks him if he wants to help mix play dough, but he shakes his head no.

This record is rich enough in detail for us to visualize it, but is it factually objective? No. The words *as if he is mad at the world* are a conclusion based on insufficient evidence. The recorder might better have described his entrance objectively like this:

Jonathan walks into the room this morning with a frowning kind of look on his face. He lowers his head when the teacher greets him, and does not respond.

This behavior is unusual for Jonathan, the staff knows. Later the teacher found out that he was not "mad at the world," but sad because his pet cat had been killed by a car the night before. We realize that frowning looks, lowered head, and refusal to speak or participate may be the result of emotions other than anger. If the observer records the child as "acting grumpy this morning," he needs to avoid this judgment and instead record the actual details that explain what happened, such as: *"Jonathan wouldn't respond to the teacher's greeting at first, and when he did, muttered 'good morning' in a low voice with head bent down."* It is up to us to sift out our inferences and judgments and make sure we record only the facts.

The following are judgmental phrases and sentences sometimes found in observation records. Should they ever be used? If not, why not? What could you substitute for them?

He was a good boy today.	*Lost his temper*
Marcie was mad at Elena.	*Got upset*
Shouted angrily	*Made a big mess*
Acted happy	*Couldn't wait to go home*

RUNNING RECORD

Name _____ Katy _____ Age __4__ Date ____2/9____

Observer _____ Rob _____ Place __S. Preschool__ Time __930—10__

Observation	Comments
Katy is playing by herself with plastic blocks, making a gun; she walks into playroom; "Lisa, would you play with me? I'm tired of playing by myself; They walk into other room to slide & climber area.	Clips blocks together to make gun; copies it to make gun for Lisa; clever; shows creativity; does teacher allow guns?
K: "I am Wonder Woman."	
L: "So am I."	
K: "No. There is only 1 Wonder Woman. You are Robin."	Seems to be the leader here as in other activities I have observed.
L: "Robin needs a Batman because Batman and Robin are friends."	Lisa is the friend she most often plays with.
All this takes place under slide & climber; Lisa shoots block gun Katy has given her; Katy falls to floor.	
L: (to teacher) "We're playing super friends and Wonder Woman keeps falling down.	
K: Opens eyes; gets up; says: "Let's get get out our Batmobile & go help the world." She runs to other room & back making noises like a car.	Katy switches roles here. She shows good concentration & spends much time on one play episode.
L: "Wonder Woman is died. She fell out of the car." She falls down.	
K: "It's only a game; wake up, Lisa. You be Wonder Woman. I'll be…….	She can distinguish reality from fantasy.
L: Let's play house now."	
Katy begins sliding down the slide. Says: "Robin is coming after you!" she shouts to Lisa, running from slide to other room.	Shows good large motor coordination. Spends much time every day like this, running around room. Seems to know she is good at this & spends a lot of time doing it.
L. "Katy, here is your doll's dress." John joins girls.	
L. "I'm Wonder Woman."	
K. "I'm Robin."	
J: "I'm Batman. Where is the Batmobile?"	
K. "John, we are not playing Superfriends any more."	Seems to be more comfortable playing with only 1 child at a time.

Figure 2—4 Running Record

Omitting or Adding Facts

Other observer errors include (a) omitting some of the facts, (b) recording things that did not happen, and (c) recording things out of order. Here is the "Jonathan incident" again with some of these errors included. Can you find them?

> Jonathan walks in the classroom this morning. He doesn't look at the teacher but goes straight to a seat at one of the tables. The teacher wants him to help mix play dough, but he refuses. Richie comes over to play with him, but he pushes him away.

Facts *omitted* from the observation:

1. Has a frowning look on his face.
2. Does not respond to teacher's greeting.
3. Walks across the room with shoulders slumped.
4. Drops himself down into seat at activity table.
5. When teacher asks him to help mix play dough, he shakes his head no.

A fact *added* to the observation:

1. Richie comes over "to play with him."

A fact recorded *but of order*:

1. Richie tries to join him before teacher asks him to help mix play dough.

Such errors can creep into an observation almost without the recorder being aware. You need to practice with at least two observers recording the same incident, and then compare results. If you find discrepancies between the records, check carefully that you have followed the guidelines in Figure 2–5.

Figure 2–5   Guidelines for Objective Recording

- Record only the facts
- Record every detail without omitting anything
- Do not interpret as you observe and record
- Use words that describe but do not judge or interpret
- Record the facts in the order that they occur

RECORDING INFORMATION

Using Your Own Shorthand

Children often move from one area to another very rapidly. Even within the same learning center they may not settle down. To catch all the action in your notes, you will want to develop your own shorthand by using abbreviations. Use children's initials for their names and abbreviate words: *child* = ch, *teacher* = tch, *with* = w/, *different* = dif, and so on. Use descriptive verbs whenever you can. Instead of "walks over to sink," can you be more specific? Try to paint a picture with words. Figure 2–6 suggests descriptive verbs to be used for the word *walks*.

Practice makes perfect, and you will soon be developing your own observational shorthand and vocabulary. Complete sentences are not necessary on a running record. Instead, catch the moment on paper as quickly and completely as you can. Afterward, you can draw a line under the recording and write any comments or interpretive remarks that may help explain what you saw happening. Your first 5-minute running record may be rather short, perhaps not more than a half-page of notes. But as you hone your skills, you will soon be filling up more than one page because the more experienced you become, the more you will see.

Be sure to record as much of the spoken language as possible. Also include how the child sounds as she or he speaks. Figure 2–7 lists some of the many verbs describing speaking that you can use instead of the word *said*.

You may want to keep a card with you listing descriptive verbs to substitute for *walks* and *said* and other frequently used but nondescriptive verbs.

Learning Center Logs

Some programs have found that the best way to observe and record on-the-spot actions is to keep a small spiral notebook on the top of the room divider for each learning center. Staff members are asked to record what they see happening in a center whenever they are in the vicinity and to date their observations. The teacher later gathers these logs and transfers the information onto the Child Development Checklists being used for each of the children.

Figure 2–6   Descriptive Words for *Walks*

marches	prances	strolls
stomps	tiptoes	skips
shuffles	toddles	strides

Figure 2–7   Descriptive Words
for *Said*

whispered	stammered	muttered
shouted	grumbled	argued
declared	insisted	announced

This is a way to collect data for several children at once, as well as for child interactions in several learning centers at once. Some programs divide the pages of their logs into the headings of *Child, Actions,* and *Language* to help remind observers of what information to record. If the teacher notes that nothing has been recorded in one of the centers by the end of the day, she or he can discuss this with the staff. Did no children play in that particular center, or did none of the staff happen to observe what was going on there?

Using learning center logs like this helps to alert staff members not only to what is occurring throughout the classroom during the day, but also as a reminder to record what they see happening. As a result, the teacher can piece together a record for more than one child's entire day of activities as seen by several different observers. In addition, no one feels burdened by stepping out of the role as a teacher to observe. Child observation occurs naturally as a part of the staff's normal checking of learning centers to see how children are doing.

All the staff, including the teacher, benefit from this sort of ongoing assessment of children. They learn where each child is developmentally, which centers and which activities seem to attract the most children, and which centers need changing. Learning center log recording like this gives the entire staff a better feel for what is really happening in the program. Martin (1994) also pointed out, "The log system requires a teacher to be diligent in record keeping. It can provide a detailed analysis of what the child is doing. For the child who has a diagnosed special need, this type of record keeping can provide data which can be interpreted and form part of the planning process" (p. 227).

Sampling

A different way of observing children is to look at samples of certain behaviors to discover how often, how long, or when a particular behavior occurs. When using samples, it is important to combine them with other forms of recording—such as developmental checklists—so that a whole picture of the child emerges.

Time Sampling

In time sampling, the observer records the frequency of a behavior's occurrence over time. The behavior must be overt and frequent (at least once every 15 minutes) to be a candidate for sampling. For example, hitting or crying are behaviors that a teacher might want to sample for certain children because they can be seen and counted. Laughing and helping to pick up are other overt behaviors. Problem solving is not a good candidate for time sampling because this behavior is not always clear to the observers, nor can it be counted easily.

Time sampling thus involves observing a specified behavior of an individual or group and recording the presence or absence of this behavior during short time intervals of uniform length. The observer must prepare ahead of time, determining what specific behavior(s) to look for, what the time interval will be, and how to record the presence or absence of the behavior. Such time sampling is often used in *behavior modification* interventions. If the behavior is an inappropriate one, it is also important to use other assessment tools (such as a developmental checklist) to give a complete picture of the child. Time sampling is thus a useful method for observing children for some of the following reasons:

Advantages

1. It takes less time and effort than narrative recording.

2. It is more objective and controlled because the behavior is specified and limited.

3. It allows an observer to collect data on a number of children or a number of behaviors at once.

4. It provides useful information on intervals and frequencies of behavior.

5. It provides quantitative results useful for statistical analysis.

Disadvantages

1. It is not an open method and therefore may miss much important behavior.

2. It does not describe the behavior, its causes, or results because it is more concerned with time (when or how frequently the behavior occurs).

3. It does not keep units of behavior intact because its principal concern is the time interval, not the behavior.

4. It takes the behavior out of its context and therefore may be biased.

5. It is limited to observable behaviors that occur frequently.

6. It usually focuses on one type of behavior (in this case an inappropriate behavior) and thus may give a biased view of the child.

Event Sampling

Event sampling is another method in which the observer waits for and then records a specific preselected behavior. Event sampling is used to study the conditions under which particular behaviors occur or their frequency. It may be important to learn *what triggers* a particular kind of behavior—biting, for instance—to find ways to control it. Or, the observer may want to find out *how many times* a certain behavior occurs. Time sampling could be used if time intervals or time of day were the important factor. If the behavior occurs at odd times or infrequently, event sampling is more appropriate (Martin, 1994).

The observer must first define the event or "unit of behavior." Then, the setting in which it is likely to occur must be determined. The observer takes the most advantageous position to observe the behavior, waits for it to occur, and records it.

Recording can be done in several ways, depending on the purpose for the observation. If the observer is studying causes or results for certain behaviors, then the so-called ABC analysis is especially useful. It is a narrative description of the entire event, breaking it down into three parts: A = antecedent event, B = behavior, and C = consequent event. Each time the event occurs, it is recorded.

If *frequency* of occurrence is the main concern, the observer can record with tally marks rather than narrative description. However, this procedure tends to be more useful for research than for practical classroom applications. The advantages and disadvantages for using event sampling include the following:

Advantages

1. It keeps the event or behavior intact, making analysis easier.

2. It is more objective than some methods because the behavior has been defined ahead of time.

3. It is especially helpful in examining infrequent or rarely occurring behaviors.

Disadvantages

1. It takes the event out of context and thus may minimize other phenomena that are important to the interpretation.

2. It is a closed method that looks only for specified behavior and ignores other important behavior.

3. It misses the richness of detail that anecdotes, specimen records, or running records provide.

Rating Scales

Rating scales are observation tools that indicate the degree to which a person possesses a certain trait or behavior. Each behavior is rated on a continuum from the lowest to the highest level (or vice versa) and is marked off at certain points along the scale. The observer must make a judgment about where on the scale the child's behavior lies. As an observation tool, rating scales work best where particular degrees of behavior are well defined or well understood by the observer and where there is a distinct difference in the behavior at the various points on the scale.

These tools are useful in diagnosing a child on several behaviors at the same time. The observer watches the child and checks off or circles the point on the scale that indicates the child's current position in regard to the behavior or ability. Such scales are simple to make: Simply state the behavior, draw a line, then mark off a number of points or intervals along the line. Five intervals are often used so that there is a middle (neutral) position, with positive and negative intervals on either side of it.

Rating Scale Observer Errors

A different kind of observer error can affect the use of rating scales. Contrary to other types of observation, this tool calls for the observer to make an on-the-spot judgment, rather than an objective description. It is extremely difficult for observers to be totally unbiased and objective. They may be influenced by other things they already know about the child or the child's family, or by outside influences completely unrelated to the situation they are observing. For example, one observer persistently gave lower ratings to an overweight child. When asked about it later, the observer admitted a prejudice against overweight children because he had been one himself.

To guard against these tendencies, the observer should rate all of the different children being observed on the same trait before going on to another trait. To check objectivity, a second rater can observe the same children and compare results.

Rating scales may be used on their own, implemented with other observation methods as a part of the procedure, or filled in after the observation is completed from data gathered from running records. As with the other observation methods, rating scales have certain advantages and disadvantages.

Advantages

1. They are easy to design and less time consuming to use.

2. They provide a convenient method to observe a large number of traits at one time or more than one child at a time.

3. They make it possible to measure difficult-to-quantify traits—shyness, for example.

4. They can be used by nonspecialist observers.

5. They are easier to score and quantify than most other methods.

Disadvantages

1. Rating scales use a closed method. They examine specified traits and may overlook other important behavior.

2. They feature the negative as well as the positive side of each trait.

3. Clearly differentiating between each point on the scale is sometimes difficult, both for the designer and the observer.

4. It is difficult to eliminate observer bias when judgments must be made quickly on so many different traits.

Checklists

Checklists are lists of specific traits or behaviors arranged in a logical order. The observer must indicate the presence or absence of the behaviors either when observing them or when reflecting on the observation. Checklists are especially useful for types of behaviors or traits that can easily and clearly be specified. We tend to see what we look for.

Thus a checklist can prove to be a valuable tool for focusing attention when many different items need to be observed. A survey or inventory of a situation can be done more efficiently with a checklist than with almost any other observation tool. If the observer needs to know whether a child displays the specified behavior, a checklist is the instrument of choice to use.

Both checklists and rating scales often include large numbers of traits or behaviors. The difference between the two is not necessarily in their appearance but in their use. An observer using a checklist merely checks off the presence of the trait (a blank denotes its absence). The observer using a rating scale must make a snap judgment about the degree to which the trait is present.

Checklists can be used in a number of ways, depending on the purpose for the observation. For instance, a different checklist can be used for each child in the class, if the results are to be used for individual planning. On the other hand, all of the children's names can be included on the same checklist along with the checklist items, if it is the observer's purpose to screen children for certain traits.

The items on a checklist can simply be checked off, or the date or time when they first appear can be entered to make a more complete record. A different checklist can be used for each observation, or a single checklist can serve in a cumulative manner for the same child all year if dates are recorded for each item. A single checklist can be used by one observer or by several observers who will add to the cumulative data over a period of time.

Finally, information gained from anecdotal and running records can be transferred to checklists to make interpretation easier. It is much simpler to scan a list of checked behaviors than to read through long paragraphs of wordy description when attempting to interpret observational evidence. However, it is obvious that checklists need to be prepared carefully.

Whether you plan to make your own checklist or use a prepared list, make sure the items listed are specified very clearly in objective, nonjudgmental terms. The user should be able to understand the items easily; thus, it makes sense to put items through a pretest before actual use in an observation tool. All checklist items should be positive, unlike rating scale items, which include a range of behavior from positive to negative.

Checklist items not observed are left blank, indicating absence of the particular behavior. If the observer does not have the opportunity to witness certain behaviors, these items should not be left blank, but denoted by some symbol (e.g., N, meaning no opportunity to observe). Some suggestions for developing checklist items are listed in Figure 2-8.

Overall, the checklist format should allow the observer to scan the items at a glance. The Child Development Checklist is an example of an observation tool that looks at 11 important areas of child development, breaking down each area into eight observable items: Each item is brief, represents an important aspect of development, is parallel in construction (beginning with a verb), and is positive. The eight items are listed in either a sequence or a progression of known child development. Together, they form the profile of a whole child as he or she works and plays in the environment of an early childhood classroom. Advantages for using checklists of this nature include the following:

Figure 2—8   Checklist Items

- Short, descriptive, understandable
- Parallel in construction (word order, verb tense)
- Objective and nonjudgmental
- Positive in nature
- Not repeated elsewhere in checklist
- Representative of behavior, not all-inclusive

Advantages

1. They are easy, quick, and efficient to use.
2. The nonspecialist observer can use them with ease.
3. They can be used in the presence of the child or later from remembered behaviors or recorded narrative observation.
4. Several observers can gather the same information to check for reliability.
5. These checklists help to focus observation on many behaviors at one time.
6. They are especially useful for curriculum planning for individuals.

Checklists have a number of disadvantages as well. Observers must weigh one against the other, always keeping in mind their purpose for observing.

Disadvantages

1. They are "closed" in nature, looking at particular behaviors and not everything that occurs; thus they may miss behaviors of importance.
2. They are limited to "presence" or "absence" of behavior.
3. They lack information about quality and duration of behavior and a description.

CHOOSING THE METHOD FOR OBSERVING AND RECORDING

Table 2–1 compares the various methods for observing and recording young children discussed in this chapter. Each has advantages and disadvantages that an observer needs to consider before choosing a particular method. The final choice often depends on the purpose for the observation.

A checklist was chosen as the basis for this book because of checklists' unique ability to give the observer an overview of child development. It is a teaching tool as well as an observational tool. The Child Development Checklist will thus assist the observer not only in gathering information to help plan for specific children, but also in learning the

Table 2–1 Comparison of methods of observing and recording

Method	Purpose	Advantages	Disadvantages
Anecdotal Record: A narrative of descriptive paragraphs, recorded *after behavior occurs*	To detail specific behavior for child's record; for case conferences; to plan for individuals	Open-ended; rich in details; no special observer training	Depends on observer's memory; behavior taken out of context; difficult to code or analyze for research
Running Record: A narrative written in sequence over a specified time, recorded *while behavior is occurring*	To discover causes and effects of behavior; for case conferences; to plan for individuals	Open-ended; comprehensive; no special observer training	Time-consuming; difficult to use for more than one child at a time; time-consuming to code and analyze for research
Time Sampling: Tallies or symbols showing the presence or absence of specified behavior during short time periods, recorded *while behavior is occurring*	For behavior modification baseline data; for child development research	Objective and controlled; not time-consuming; efficient for observing more than one child at a time; provides quantitative data for research	Closed; limited to observable behaviors that occur frequently; no description of behavior; takes behavior out of context
Event Sampling: A brief narrative of conditions preceding and following specified behavior, recorded *while behavior is occurring*	For behavior modification input; for child development research	Objective; helpful for in-depth diagnosis of infrequent behavior	Closed; takes event out of context; limited to specified behaviors
Rating Scale: A scale of traits or behaviors with checkmarks, recorded *before, during, and after behavior occurs*	To judge degree to which child behaves or possesses certain traits; to diagnose behavior or traits; to plan for individuals	Not time-consuming; easy to design; efficient for observing more than one child at a time for many traits; useful for several observers watching same child	Closed; subjective; limited to specified traits or behaviors
Checklist: A list of behaviors with checkmarks, recorded *before, during, and after behavior occurs*	To determine presence or absence of specified behaviors; to plan for individuals; to give observer an overview of child's development or progress	Efficient for observing more than one child at a time for many behaviors; useful for an individual during a period of time; a good survey or inventory tool; useful for several observers at once; no special training needed	Closed; limited to specified behaviors; no information on quality of behavior

sequences of child growth in the areas of emotional, social, physical, cognitive, language, and creative development. Ahola and Kovacik concurred, saying: "Checklists that are well-designed and appropriately used can be useful in understanding children's development and in developing curriculum" (p. 27).

USING THE CHILD DEVELOPMENT CHECKLIST

The Child Development Checklist in Figure 2–9, around which this book is written, is as much a learning device for the observer as it is a planning tool for helping the child. With sequences of child development as its focus, it presents the areas of emotional, social, physical, cognitive, language, and creative development by dividing each of these areas into two major categories, then subdividing each category into eight representative items of development. (See Figure 1–2.)

Emotional development, for example, is divided into "self-esteem" and "emotional development," with a chapter devoted to each of these topics. These chapters illustrate representative behaviors in the sequence of emotional development that can be seen in the early childhood classroom.

Using One Checklist Section at a Time

As a learning device for the observer, the checklist is best used one section at a time. To understand the sequence of emotional development as it appears in the early childhood classroom, for instance, the observer should first plan to use the Self-Esteem section of the checklist in observing a child *for enough time to see if all eight items are present.* This means coming into the classroom early enough to see how the child enters the room, what she does when her parent/caregiver leaves, and how she interacts with the teacher(s). It also means coming early to the classroom *more than once* to observe how the child behaves on different days, and to record this information. The observer should not only check off the items as they appear, but also record evidence for each item in the space provided.

The observer should then read Chapter 3, "Self-Esteem," paying special attention to the items that were not checked, to gain insight into why the child may not have performed certain items. The Helpful Ideas section after each item in the chapter gives suggestions that may assist the observer/teacher in planning for the child to help her accomplish the items not checked.

Using the Entire Checklist

Once you are familiar with each of the checklist areas and items, you can use the entire checklist for one child to gain a complete overview. How should you begin? You may want to learn something about a particular child in a certain area of development.

CHILD DEVELOPMENT CHECKLIST

Name _____   Observer _____

Program _____   Dates _____

Directions:
Put an **X** for items you see the child perform regularly. Put **N** for items where there is no opportunity to observe. Leave all other items blank.

Item	Evidence	Dates
1. Self-Esteem		
___ Separates from primary caregiver without difficulty		
___ Develops a secure attachment with teacher		
___ Completes a task successfully		
___ Makes activity choices without teacher's help		
___ Seeks other children to play with		
___ Plays roles confidently in dramatic play		
___ Stands up for own rights		
___ Displays enthusiasm about doing things for self		
2. Emotional Development		
___ Releases stressful feelings in appropriate manner		
___ Expresses anger in words rather than negative actions		
___ Can be calmed in difficult or dangerous situations		
___ Overcomes sad feelings in appropriate manner		

Figure 2–9   The Child Development Checklist

Item	Evidence	Dates
___ Handles surprising situations with control		
___ Shows fondness, affection, love toward others		
___ Shows interest, attention in classroom activities		
___ Smiles, seems happy much of the time		

3. Social Play

Item	Evidence	Dates
___ Spends time watching others play		
___ Plays by self with own toys/materials		
___ Plays parallel to others with similar toys/materials		
___ Plays with others in group play		
___ Makes friends with other children		
___ Gains access to ongoing play in positive manner		
___ Maintains role in ongoing play in positive manner		
___ Resolves play conflicts in positive manner		

4. Prosocial Behavior

Item	Evidence	Dates
___ Shows concern for someone in distress		
___ Can tell how another feels during conflict		
___ Shares something with another		
___ Gives something to another		

(*Contd.*)

Item	Evidence	Dates
___ Takes turns without a fuss		
___ Complies with requests without a fuss		
___ Helps another do a task		
___ Helps (cares for) another in need		
5. Large Motor Development		
___ Walks down steps alternating feet		
___ Runs with control over speed & direction		
___ Jumps with feet together		
___ Hops on one foot		
___ Climbs up, down, across climbing equipment		
___ Throws, catches & kicks balls		
___ Rides trikes, bikes & scooters		
___ Does creative movement		
6. Small Motor Development		
___ Turns knobs, lids, eggbeaters		
___ Pours liquids without spilling		
___ Fastens/unfastens zippers, buttons, Velcro		
___ Picks up & inserts objects with dexterity		

Figure 2–9 *Contd.*

44

Item	Evidence	Dates
____ Molds play dough/clay with dexterity		
____ Uses drawing/writing tools with control		
____ Uses scissors with control		
____ Uses hammer with control		
7. Cognitive Development		
____ Sorts objects by shape, color		
____ Classifies objects by size		
____ Places objects in sequence or series		
____ Recognizes, creates patterns		
____ Counts by rote to 20		
____ Displays 1-to-1 correspondence with numbers		
____ Problem-solves with concrete objects		
____ Problem-solves with computer programs		
8. Spoken Language		
____ Listens but does not speak		
____ Gives single-word answers		
____ Gives short phrase responses		
____ Does chanting		

(Contd.)

Item	Evidence	Dates
___ Takes part in conversations		
___ Speaks in expanded sentences		
___ Asks questions		
___ Can tell a story		

9. Emergent Writing and Reading Skills

Item	Evidence	Dates
___ Pretends to write with pictures & scribbles		
___ Makes horizontal lines of writing scribbles		
___ Includes letter-like forms in writing		
___ Makes some letters, prints name or initial		
___ Holds book right-side up; turns pages right to left		
___ Pretends to read using pictures to tell story		
___ Retells stories from books with increasing accuracy		
___ Shows awareness that print in books tells story		

10. Art and Music Skills

Item	Evidence	Dates
___ Makes basic scribble shapes		
___ Combines circles/squares with crossed lines		
___ Draws person as sun-face with arms & legs		
___ Combines objects together in a picture		

Figure 2–9 *Contd.*

46

Item	Evidence	Dates
___ Moves legs & feet in rhythm to a beat		
___ Moves arms & hands in rhythm to a beat		
___ Plays instruments		
___ Sings with group or by him/herself		
11. Dramatic Play Skills		
___ Does pretend play by him/herself		
___ Assigns roles or takes assigned roles		
___ Needs particular props to do pretend play		
___ Takes on characteristics & actions related to role		
___ Can pretend with imaginary objects		
___ Uses language for creating & sustaining plot		
___ Enacts exciting, danger-packed themes		
___ Uses elaborate themes, ideas, details		

Perhaps she has difficulty getting involved with the others in the pretend play during free-choice period. Plan to begin your observation during this period. You will want to look at the items in the Social Play section. Other checklist areas that can often be seen at the same time as Social Play include the items under Self-Esteem, Emotional Development, Prosocial Behavior, Spoken Language, and Imagination. Either check off the items as you see them, writing in the evidence, or do a running record of everything the child does and says and convert it to the checklist afterward.

We need to step back from children and observe them impartially and objectively.

Be sure to make notes after each item, jotting down the evidence that prompted you to check the item (or leave it blank). If you leave the item blank, it is still important to write down your reason—the evidence for leaving the item blank. If you use the same checklist on more than one day in a cumulative manner, be sure to put the date after each item as well.

The time of your next observation may be determined by the areas you have not had the opportunity to observe. For Self-Esteem, for instance, you will want to observe the child when she arrives in the morning, especially at the beginning of the year. Emotional Development items also need to be observed during lunch or snack time, toileting, and naptime.

Interpreting the Data

Once you have observed a child and recorded data about her in a running record, then transferred to the Child Development Checklist, the next step is to interpret the information. Learning to know and understand a child is a fascinating process. Objective observing and recording like this make possible a deeper understanding than a lifetime of merely being around children can do. We need to step back from children and look at them impartially and objectively. Only then do we truly see who they are and what they are. Only then do we begin to understand how we can help them reach their greatest potential.

Interpreting the information your observations have provided takes knowledge and skill. You need to know a great deal about child development both from reading and studying about children and from actual experience with them. Then you can begin to make valid inferences and conclusions about children based on your observations.

This textbook is organized to help you gain such knowledge. Using the Child Development Checklist will focus your attention on important child behaviors in each area of child development. Reading the chapters that feature these areas will help you to acquire knowledge of that particular area. Interpreting the data you acquire will then be more meaningful to you and helpful to the child as you apply it in your individual planning.

CHAPTERS TO FOLLOW

The chapters that follow in this text can serve as guidelines for evaluating children's strengths and needs and planning activities to help individuals or small groups of children with similar needs. The suggestions listed under Some Helpful Ideas should prove useful not only in assisting children in their needs, but also in providing the stimulus for your own ideas for activities.

Proceeding from the General to the Specific

As you study the 11 separate areas of child development included in this observational program, you will note that most of the aspects discussed follow a similar pattern in the growth of the child *from the general to the specific*. Children learn to control large muscles before they master fine motor control. Children recognize overall patterns of cognitive discrimination before the details become clear. They speak single words to include whole categories of things before they learn the names for each thing. They draw a circle to represent a person before they learn to add the details, and they pretend in stereotyped roles as mothers and fathers before they add the personal touches identifying specific family members.

Proceeding from the Specific to the General

This book, on the other hand, proceeds in the opposite direction: Specific categories of development are detailed first. We look in some depth at self-esteem, emotional development, social play, prosocial behavior, large motor development, small motor development, cognitive development, spoken language, emergent literacy, art skills, and imagination.

The child is, of course, a whole being whose development in all these areas is proceeding *simultaneously*. Once you understand the details of this growth, it is possible to make an overall assessment of the developmental skills that each of your children possesses by using the Child Skills Checklist as a whole. Such an assessment then allows you to draw a total picture of the child and formulate individual plans that will promote continued development.

Use of the Checklist by Preservice Teachers and Student Teachers

Preservice teachers and student teachers can use the Child Development Checklist just as a classroom teacher does, making a series of observations of a single child until all the items have been noted. In case the observer has no access to live children in a classroom, it is possible to observe and record using videotapes of children in a classroom.

For student observers who observe and record live children, you need to rewrite your notes as soon as possible after you have finished your observations. As an experienced observer notes:

"Memory is a notoriously poor recorder, so make it a practice to transcribe your notes soon after you visit a classroom. You are more likely to remember accurately if you rewrite your notes the same day that you observe. As a courtesy, you might offer a copy of your observation notes to the classroom teacher in situations in which sharing would be appropriate" (Benjamin, 1994, p. 190).

To interpret the checked items or blanks, the observer should read the particular chapters that discuss these areas. It is especially helpful for such observers to make a written report or case study that includes an interpretation of the child's development in all of the 11 principal checklist areas. Such a report should include not only specific information from the observations, but also whatever inferences and conclusions the observer can draw from the observational data collected, based on his or her knowledge of child development.

OBSERVATION OF EACH CHILD

It is important to observe each of the children in this kind of detail throughout the year. Teachers report they can learn more about each child by stepping back and making a relatively brief, focused observation like this, than by having the child in their program for an entire year. It is an eye-opening experience to look at one child in-depth from an observer's point of view, rather than from the perspective of a busy teacher involved with the activities of many other lively youngsters.

Child-development students report that an in-depth examination of a real child makes textbooks and courses come alive, as well. Parents, too, benefit from the information that objective observations provide. Not only do the parents learn new activities to use with their children at home, but they also often become involved in the fascinating drama of how their own children develop, why their children act the way they do, and how they, as parents, can best help their children realize their full potential. (See Chapter 14.)

LEARNING ACTIVITIES

1. Have a team of observers make a 10-minute observation of a child at play in a preschool classroom. One team member should make a running record of the child at the time of the observation. The other should write up an anecdotal record of the same observation at the end of the day. Compare the results. Which one showed the most details?

2. Have two different observers use the Child Development Checklist to observe the same child at the same time for three days. Compare results. How similar were the observations? In what areas were there differences? How could you improve future observing and recording?

3. Make an anecdotal record for a child after you have observed the child for a half-hour.

What inferences can you make about this child based only on your observation? What specific evidence is each inference based on? Can you draw any conclusions? Why or why not?

4. Make learning center logs and place them around the classroom in each of the learning centers. At the end of the day, collect the recorded data in each of the logs and transfer it to one or more Child Development Checklists. How helpful were these logs? What more needs to be done to complete the checklists?

5. Use the Child Development Checklist to observe a child for 10 minutes on three different days. Be sure to record the evidence for each of your checkmarks. Based on these brief observations, what are several areas of strength the child displays? What are the areas needing strengthening?

SUGGESTED READINGS

Bentzen, W. R. (2005). *Seeing young children: A guide to observing and recording behavior* (5th ed.). Clifton Falls, NY: Delmar.

Curtis, D., & Carter, M. (2006). *The art of awareness: How observation can transform your teaching.* Upper Saddle River, NJ: Merrill/Prentice Hall.

Gronlund, G., & James, M. (2005). *Focused observations: How to observe children for assessment and curriculum planning.* St. Paul, MN: Redleaf Press.

Jablon, J. R., Dombro, A. L., & Dichtelmiller, M. L. (2007). *The power of observation for birth through eight* (2nd ed.). Washington, DC: Teaching Strategies.

3

Self-Esteem

☑ SELF-ESTEEM CHECKLIST

____ Separates from primary caregiver without difficulty

____ Develops a secure attachment relationship with teacher

____ Completes a task successfully

____ Makes activity choices without teacher's help

____ Seeks other children to play with

____ Plays roles confidently in dramatic play

____ Stands up for own rights

____ Displays enthusiasm about doing things for self

DEVELOPING SELF-ESTEEM

From the moment of birth, the young human being is engaged in the dynamic process of becoming himself or herself. The child continually develops into a whole person with a temperament, personality, and value system—with a physical, cognitive, language, social, emotional, and creative makeup that is uniquely his or her own. It is an engrossing process that may take most of a lifetime to complete, but its early stages are perhaps its most crucial, for they set the pattern for all that is to follow. According to Baumeister, Bushman, Campbell, Krueger, and Vohs (2004), "It is widely believed that a strong link exists between children's self-esteem and their success in school."

Among the most important aspects of the child's growing persona is his development of **self-concept**: his sense of self that includes both his **self-image** (his inner picture of himself) and his **self-esteem** (his sense of self-worth). Although these three terms are often used interchangeably, they actually refer to different aspects of the self. A person's self-image is his internal image or picture of himself that includes his looks, his gender, his ethnicity, his standing in the family, and his abilities. A child acquires this image as he grows and sees himself as a separate individual. Self-image is not judgmental, it is descriptive.

On the other hand, **self-esteem** is an emotional evaluation of these aspects: the child's feeling about her looks, her gender, her standing in the family, and her abilities. She needs to feel that she is capable, significant, successful, and worthy. She acquires this sense of self-worth through her interaction with the other people around her as well as her own judgmental view of herself and what she is able to do.

Harter (1998) believes that self-esteem does not fully emerge until middle childhood (p. 21). Self-image and self-esteem then come together to form a child's self-concept. As Kosnik (1993) noted:

> These two areas combine to form our self-concept. Throughout our lives a continuous dialogue exists between these two aspects of self. Our self-concept determines who we are, what we think we are, what we think we can do, and what we think we can become. (p. 32)

Self-esteem formation is a continuous process, but once it has taken some form, it is difficult to change as the child gets older. As the child receives incoming information about the way she is treated by others or by her experiences of success or failure, she uses such data to confirm what she already feels about herself. For example, if the child feels good about herself because of the way she is treated in her family, then she will see a teacher's good treatment of her as confirmation of what she already knows. She then acts out these feelings in the classroom by being happy and cooperative. This, in turn, keeps those around her treating her positively.

If, on the other hand, a child has negative feelings about himself because of the way he is treated in his family, even a teacher's good treatment may not change his self-esteem readily. Instead, he may rationalize it by thinking that the teacher is being nice to him because she feels sorry for him because he is so bad. He may act out his negative feelings about himself by being aggressive toward other children, disruptive of activities, or by withdrawing into himself and not participating. Any scolding or other negative response to such behavior only promotes a feeling that he is no good.

How then can a teacher of preschool children help youngsters become convinced that they are truly worthy people? Teachers must be persistent and consistent in their positive messages to every child *every* day. Sometimes we think we have done our duty by greeting a child whenever we have time as long as some staff member is at the door to do the greeting in the morning. This is not enough. You must personally deliver your positive messages *every* day to *every* child.

As Kosnik (1993) continues with her vital message:

> For children to believe that they are valuable members of the community, they must feel individually noticed and they must feel wanted. By getting to know the children and highlighting their abilities, the teacher validates the children. She is one step closer to increasing the children's self-esteem. (p. 36)

Egertson (2006) added that children with a healthy self-esteem do not have a constant need for adult approval (p. 58).

This chapter will discuss some of the developmental progressions that are observable in children 3 to 5 years of age as they strive to develop a healthy sense of self in the

No matter how good a child feels about himself, initial school separation from a parent is sometimes difficult.

early childhood classroom. Although children carry with them their own unique package of genetic traits and home influences, the teachers they meet and the daily care they receive in the classroom have a strong bearing on their future development.

Each item of the Child Development Checklist will be discussed separately in this and the chapters to follow. Each checklist item is positive in nature and should be checked if the observer sees the child performing in the manner described. If left unchecked, it may indicate help is needed for that particular item. Suggestions for helping and supporting the child's development in the unchecked items will follow the discussion of the item.

The eight items in the Self-Esteem Checklist section show a progression of steps many children take as they separate from their parents or primary caregivers and make the sometimes difficult transition into preschool. It is important for a teacher to determine at the outset where each child stands in this progression to assist the children in developing a strong, positive sense of self.

 # SEPARATES FROM PRIMARY CAREGIVER WITHOUT DIFFICULTY

Initial Attachment

Most studies of young children agree that a key ingredient to their successful development is a strong initial attachment to a primary caregiver, usually the mother. Many psychologists, in fact, regard attachment as the seminal event in a person's emotional development: "the primary source of a child's security, self-esteem, self-control and social skills" (Eliot, 1999, p. 30). It seems a great paradox, then, to suggest that for successful development to continue, the young human must learn at the same time to separate from the parent. But such is the case. This separation should occur first in the home—not only with the child, but also with the parents, who must let go of the child and encourage the child to become independent of them.

Many current attachment/separation studies are based on the initial work of John Bowlby (1969) and Mary Ainsworth (1974), who talk about children's attachment to their parents as a condition of trust in their parents' reliability. Attachment occurs during the first year or two of life as a result of many interactions between infants and parents. The first separation of the child from the mother is, of course, the physical one that occurs at birth. Some psychologists believe that much of life thereafter is the developing person striving to achieve that perfect state of oneness once again with another human (Kaplan, 1978, p. 43).

This is the beginning of the strong initial attachment that both the infant and caregiver need for later separation to occur successfully. Such an attachment leads to a sense of security and trust on the part of the infant. The lack of such an attachment often interferes with the child's ability to build trust in future relationships. In fact, the failure to thrive in infancy is frequently the result of the breakdown of this initial attachment relationship (Seagull & Kallen, 1978, p. 8).

Psychologist Erik Erikson describes young children's psychosocial development in terms of ages and stages. In each stage he noted that a particular task must be accomplished for their personality to develop smoothly. Erikson called the important task during an infant's first year "trust versus mistrust." How infants are treated by those around them helps them to develop feelings either of trust or mistrust of people. These feelings can affect a person's actions or interactions for the rest of his life, Erikson believed (Mooney, 2000, p. 38).

Psychologists like William Damon talk in terms of an initial attachment between an infant and its mother or primary caregiver that needs to develop over a period of time. He agreed that it takes most of the infant's first year to develop the relationship with a caregiver (Damon, 1983, p. 29). But without such an attachment, it is difficult for the infant to develop trust in anyone else, and it becomes doubly difficult for the infant or developing child to separate from the caregiver. After all, if she cannot trust her primary caregiver, how can she risk trusting anyone? The attachment between the infant and primary caregiver, in fact, serves as a model for future human relationships.

Initial Separation

The initial separation of the infant from its mother or primary caregiver begins when he first recognizes he is separate from that person. This develops within the first 6 months of life as the baby recognizes there is a difference between himself and the caregiver—and later, between himself and others. At this time, his first memories—visual in nature—are occurring. Some psychologists call this the "psychological birth" of the baby (Kaplan, 1978, p. 121). It is the first glimmering of self-identity.

Toward the end of the first year, as the infant learns to move about by creeping and by her first unsteady steps, an interesting pattern of interaction with the caregiver often emerges. The youngster uses the caregiver as a base from which to explore her environment. She moves out a bit and comes back, moves farther and returns, moves out again, and this time may only look back, making the eye contact that will give her the reassurance to continue exploring. Teachers may also notice this same pattern of touching or eye contact between child and parent during the initial preschool entrance period (Gottschall, 1989, p. 14).

During the last half of the child's first year (or sometimes before), "separation anxiety" also emerges: The infant sets up a strong protest of crying or clinging if the caregiver attempts to leave. This pattern of distress is also exhibited when a stranger appears, making it obvious that the baby recognizes the difference between the caregiver and others. Thus self-esteem develops as the toddler ventures out and scurries back, clings and pushes away, holds on and lets go. But the stronger the initial attachment, the more secure the developing child should feel each time he or she lets go.

The young human learns who he is by the way other people respond to him (how others seem to be affected by his behavior). Hopefully, this response is mainly positive, so that by the time he enters child care, preschool or Head Start, he already will be feeling good about himself.

School Separation

No matter how good the young child feels about herself, the initial school separation from a parent is often difficult. At 3 years old, the sense of self is still a bit shaky. Although the child has an identity at home, at school the child is in a strange environment. As Balaban (2006) tells us: Separation from parents or primary caregiver frequently makes young children unhappy. They often feel abandoned, cast aside, and uncared for. They may be frightened and just as often angry" (p. 2). To complicate matters, the parent/caregiver may be experiencing the same "separation anxiety" and may not want to let go of the child, which the child often senses.

Each child handles the situation in his or her own way. One child may be accustomed to being taken to the home of a loving babysitter and will take this new "playroom" in stride. Another may cling to her mother and scream whenever the mother attempts to leave. The child who is used to playing with others may quickly join the group in the block building center. A shyer child may need the teacher's urging to join in. One fussing, crying child may stop crying as soon as his mother leaves. Another may withdraw into herself and sit in a corner sucking her thumb.

You—as a teacher, student intern, or assistant—hope that children will become adjusted to this separation within a few days or a week or so. Most of them will. One or two may not. How can you help them develop a strong enough sense of self that they feel free to let go of their primary caregiver?

If You Have Not Checked This Item: Some Helpful Ideas

One or more of the children in your classroom may have self-esteem checklist items that are not checked. Because you are aware that each item represents a step in the developmental progression of young children, you may be able to lend children support at the outset by arranging your schedule or setting up your classroom ahead of time to address their problems. Here are some ideas that may help preschoolers separate from their parents or caregivers with less difficulty.

■ Make Early Initial Contact with Parent/Caregiver and Child

If the child and the parent have met you ahead of time, they may feel less reluctant to separate on the day that school begins. For the child, it is better if this meeting takes place close to the time of school opening rather than the spring before. Memories of a brief visit several months before school begins have little meaning for the young child. An immediate follow-up is more effective. If you visit the child's home, take a camera to make a photo for later use in the classroom to help the child make an easier transition from home to school.

■ Try Staggered Enrollment

Rather than having all the children in your class begin school on the same day at the same time, you might consider having half of them begin on the first day, and half the second—or half in the morning and the rest in the afternoon. This will allow staff members to devote more time to the individual children and their parents. In addition, the first day may not be so overwhelming for the children if only half of the class is present at once.

■ Create a Simple Initial Environment

The more complex the classroom environment, the more overwhelming it is for certain children. You might plan to have the classroom arranged with fewer activity areas for the first weeks, and less material on the shelves. As the children settle in and become more secure, you can add activities and materials as needed.

■ Use Transition Materials

Children can make the transition from home to school and separate more easily from their parents if familiar materials help bridge the gap. Water is one such material. A water table or basin with an egg beater, funnel, and squeeze bottles may take a child's mind off his parent long enough to get him happily involved in the center. Toy trucks and dolls often have the same effect. Have a special set of little toys you can allow children to take home with them at the end of the day and return again in the morning to make the transition less difficult.

■ Utilize Parent/Caregiver Visits

Allow the parents to stay as long as necessary on the first days or come in for visits from time to time. The shy child may use her parent as a base for exploration in the classroom, venturing away from the parent and returning just as she did as a toddler at home. If the separation is a difficult one, have the caregiver return early to pick up the youngster. Little by little the children should be able to stay longer without their parents.

■ Show and Foster Acceptance of the Child

Up until now the child's self-esteem has evolved from the reactions of his family to him. Now that he is in your classroom, you and your coworkers and the other children will be adding details to the child's interior picture of himself. These details need to be positive, happy ones. You need to support this process first by accepting the child and his family unconditionally. Information is relayed to children through words, facial expressions, and actions (Ariza-Evans, 2004, p. 21). Show your acceptance both verbally and nonverbally. Smile at him frequently. Greet him personally *every day,* telling him how glad you are to see him. Say goodbye to him at the end of *every day,* telling him "See you tomorrow, don't forget!" Demonstrate that you enjoy being near him and having him near you. You are the behavior model for the other children as well. If they see that you accept a child no matter what, they will be more likely to do the same.

■ Read a Book

Children like to hear stories about other children that have feelings the same as theirs. Try reading a book about separation to children having difficulty in this area. If the characters of the story are children from a different cultures, all the better. Children learn to accept one another when they see picture books featuring various cultural and ethnic characters. In *See You Later, Mom!* (Northway, 2006), the story of William, an Anglo boy's first week in preschool, shows his teacher to be Asian and his best friend, African. William wants to play with the children, but is too uncomfortable to let go of his mother for long. Every day he asks her to stay and she does. Little by little he lets go of her until on Friday, he quickly joins the others and waves to Mom, "You can go home now, Mom. See you later!"

As Wardle (1995) noted,

> Much of a child's personal identity is determined by the way the environment responds to the characteristics the child has, based on his group belonging (gender, race, family lifestyle, religion). For example, if a program does not support a child's home language, that will impact on self-image. If a child does not see pictures, books, and people in his program that look like him, that too will affect his self-image. (p. 45)

Another fine school separation book is *My First Day at Nursery School* (Edwards, 2002), in which a mother hands over her anxious little girl to the teacher in a room full of toys and activities. But the girl whines, "I want my mommy," and then, "I want my ...," and finally, "I ...," as she gets more deeply involved in the school doings. When mommy finally comes to pick her up at the end of the day, the little girl, of course, wants to stay at school.

*Children with secure attachments
to their parents usually have little
difficulty developing a secure
relationship with their teacher.*

DEVELOPS A SECURE ATTACHMENT
RELATIONSHIP WITH TEACHER

Children who have already formed a secure attachment with their parents or primary caregivers usually have little trouble developing a secure relationship with their teachers as well. As Balaban (2006) says: "When a child trusts, she transfers her loving feelings from parents to teachers" (p. 5). Such securely attached children tend to view teachers as trustworthy and themselves as worthy of care. They are willing to enter into a cooperative relationship with their teachers in which the teacher guides and supports them, and the children comply with the teacher's requests (Watson, 2003, p. 13). They trust that the teacher will help them when they need help and protect them from danger when necessary.

Teachers, on the other hand, need to expect and welcome such an attachment on the part of the children. They need to be there for the children in good times and bad, to provide support and opportunity for children to establish friendships, to know individual likes and dislikes, to provide a stimulating environment where children can become involved in exciting activities, and to give children choices as well as time to complete their projects. They need to show a caring attitude toward each child and display an interest in things the child does or says.

Lucos (2007–08) talks about how emotional togetherness along with a passion for working with children helps a teacher not just to be present, but to be wholly available to children on emotional, cognitive, and physical levels. For appropriate engagement with a child to take place, a teacher needs to know where each child is developmentally. This calls for "purposeful observation." As Lucos continued, "Children desperately need educators who understand how to observe and come to know children for who they are, what they are struggling with, and what they need" (p. 88).

As an observer of the children, how will you know if children have developed this secure relationship with their teacher? Their behavior toward their teacher is the best indication. Some of their behaviors may include

- Asking the teacher to help them solve a problem
- Accepting help or support from the teacher
- Allowing themselves to be comforted by the teacher in times of stress
- Showing affection toward the teacher
- Wanting to be close to the teacher
- Paying attention and listening to the teacher
- Complying with the teacher's requests
- Taking part in conversations and activities with the teacher

Children with Insecure Attachments

Children with insecure attachments to parents or primary caregivers often view themselves as unworthy or incompetent. This feeling frequently follows them into the classroom and affects their relationships with teachers and staff members. They may feel that they cannot rely on any adults to meet their needs, thus their classroom relationships are built on mistrust rather than trust. They may show little interest in becoming involved in classroom activities or with other children. Some may be disruptive, interfering with what other children are doing or calling attention to themselves in other inappropriate ways. They expect to be scolded or punished, and if this does not happen, they may act out in an even more disruptive manner.

If you notice that a disruptive child continues to look over at you once he has interfered with another child, it may be a sign that his behavior is really directed at you rather than the other child. As Watson (2003) noted, "Children with a history of insecure attachment tend to expect adults to be hostile, unresponsive, and unreliable" (p. 14). It is almost as if his behavior is calling out to you: "What are you going to do about me?" or "I want attention, too!" If your attention takes the form of making the child sit in the "time-out chair," this is a punishment response and is not conducive to building a trusting relationship with the child.

What should you do, then, to help this child build a secure attachment relationship with you? Howes and Ritchie (2002) believe that "children who enter classrooms with insecure attachment organizations at home will be helped to move toward secure attachment organizations if the teacher first acts as an organizer rather than as a partner" (p. 70).

If You Have Not Checked This Item: Some Helpful Ideas

■   Stay in Physical Proximity to the Child

When she first enters the classroom, if the insecure child sees you standing or working nearby, she may begin to relax and feel better about being in a new environment. You can look up and smile at her from time to time, or walk over and say a few words of encouragement. Be sure to show the child on a daily basis that you are aware of her. She may eventually come over and stand by you for a few minutes and then return to her activity. Howes and Ritchie agree,

> For young children, using the adult as organizer usually involves keeping the adult in physical proximity. Young children want to know that when they look up from play and exploration, their teacher will be nearby. (p. 70)

■   Provide Positive Individualized Attention

You need to show genuine interest in the child. If this is a child who has made you feel annoyed, find a way to change your feelings. Make a daily list of positive things about the child and tell the child how you appreciate what he is doing or saying. Find out what he likes to eat, do, wear, or play with. Look through a back issue of a magazine or catalogue together. Have him cut out the items that interest him and start a scrapbook of "Things I Like." Bring in a picture of your own to add to it. By giving him positive individualized attention like this, you are helping to break down the child's mistrust and his old patterns of interaction with an adult who has perhaps mistreated or neglected him.

■   Engage in Joint Activities with the Child

Eventually you should be able to play with the child, ask her to help you, share ideas with the child, and ask for her input. You can be her partner for a while, but eventually she will need to partner with another child as she becomes acclimated to the classroom and able to trust that you care about her and will take care of her no matter what. Having more than one adult in the classroom makes it possible to spend such time with children in need—and every child.

 ## COMPLETES A TASK SUCCESSFULLY

You are also helping the child to construct a new and secure relationship by showing him he is a competent human being who can succeed in things. Perhaps he has been overly criticized at home and therefore has little confidence in his ability to succeed at anything. Once you know what things interest him, bring in some books he will enjoy about these topics. Set up a simple art project that he can complete. Have him collect some natural objects and display them in the science center. Help him write his name as

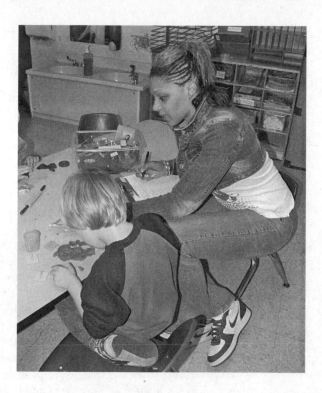

Observe to see which children can successfully complete an activity you have set up.

large as he can and outline each letter with glitter sprinkled on transparent glue. Then he can see who he is: big and strong and beautiful!

Observe to see which children are successful in the activities you have set up in art or science or math. Watch to see which ones can perform self-help skills such as getting dressed. Success is such an important ingredient of self-esteem. Even a child's partial success in a task should be recognized. Ellen and Moratz (2007) believe that giving "descriptive praise" to even the smallest of children's efforts helps them toward mastering a complex skill—and feeling good about themselves. "Look at that! You laced all your shoes by yourself!" (no mention of the skipped eyelet). They claim that recognizing children's accomplishments "is the major and most essential component of a child's self-esteem" (p. 7).

Because "we see what we look for," have you actually looked for such successes? Keep track of successful accomplishments no matter how small for each of the children. Be sure to acknowledge them with descriptive praise, describing exactly what they have done, and not empty praise (phrases such as "good job").

Some children are afraid to start anything, let alone finish it. Also watch for children who enter an activity area, start an activity, but leave before it is finished. Sometimes a first step is all a child needs. Sit next to the child who tells you he can't make the puzzle, and put in a piece yourself. Then ask him to look for the next one. Stay with him until he completes the puzzle. Then ask him to try it again on his own. Give him positive verbal support all the way, but refrain from helping this time. When he has finished, recognize his accomplishment with descriptive praise and/or a photo of him and his puzzle.

If You Have Not Checked This Item: Some Helpful Ideas

■ Create a Sorting Task with Child's Favorite Items

If you know the child has a cat for a pet, bring in set of dog and cat counters and a sorting tray or plastic containers. Ask child to sort out items that are alike.

■ Read a Book

Read a picture book about a character who has a problem to solve and stays with it until it is solved. In *Drum, Chavi, Drum* (Dole, 2003), the Hispanic girl Chavi wants to play the conga drums in Miami's Calle Ocho Festival, but she is not allowed to because she is a girl. Nothing stops Chavi, the best drummer on the street, who finally wins a spot by dressing like a boy and fooling everyone. When they hear how good she drums, they let her ride on a festival float as herself. In *Jingle Dancer* (Smith, 2000), Jenna, a Muscogee Creek Indian girl, dreams of doing a jingle dance at the next powwow just like her grandma did. But her dress has no jingles, and there is no time to make them. Jenna uses her wits to acquire one row of jingles at a time until she has enough for her dress. She and her grandma sew them on in time for Jenna's dance.

Feeney and Moravcik (2005) find, "Picture books for young children play a major role in shaping their emerging images of themselves, others, and the larger society. When the story lines and images are positive in the books that they read, children are likely to develop healthy self-concepts and favorable views of others" (p. 22).

■ Use the Computer

Take special time in helping the child who seldom completes activities successfully to use the computer. Choose a simple program (e.g., *Dr. Seuss's ABC*). Stay with him until he learns how to use it, as you did with the puzzle. Then have him use it on his own. Using the computer successfully is an especially strong booster of a child's self-esteem.

■ Read a Humorous Book

Sometimes humor gets a child going if he can laugh about something. In the humorous story *Magic Thinks Big* (Cooper, 2004), Magic the cat is sort of silly, sleepy, and stuck in one spot. He has all kinds of wonderful ideas of what to do next, but just can't get going. Magic stays with his problem until—he falls asleep! What would your listener do?

MAKES ACTIVITY CHOICES WITHOUT TEACHER'S HELP

One of the next observable indicators of a child's feelings about herself in your classroom is her willingness to choose on her own the activity she wants to engage in. Once she feels confident enough to leave your side, she needs to explore the new environment and try out the various materials and activities on her own. Many children have a strong enough self-esteem to go immediately to the activity areas upon first entering the room. Others use the adult who accompanies them as a base for their explorations, going into an area and coming back to the person, much as they did during their initial separation from their primary caregiver when they were infants. Some also use the teacher as this base.

Numerous studies have found that "children who are securely attached to their primary caregivers will approach peers expecting positive interactions and responses. Conversely, children with insecure attachments to their caregivers will expect and initiate less than optimal interactions" (Mitchell-Copeland, Denham, & DeMulder, 1997, p. 28). In addition, they found that the more secure the child–teacher attachment relationship, the less likely the young child was to be irritable and isolated. Thus, it is important to help a child build this relationship initially. It is also important to observe which children are able to become involved with activities independently—and which are not quite ready, possibly because their teacher attachment or self-esteem is not yet strong enough.

Your goal for children who do not participate independently in activities will be to help them develop a sense of security with you and within the classroom. Once they develop this feeling of security, they may take the next step toward developing their self-esteem by becoming involved in classroom activities on their own. It is so tempting for teachers to help children make decisions, and the children to agree. They will even ask for help. They are used to having adults tell them what to do. You must resist the temptation. Invite them to look for themselves, then support them in their exploration. It is so much simpler for you to make up their minds for them, you may argue. But then they will have lost the opportunity to take the next step in their development of self-esteem. Give them this chance.

If You Have Not Checked This Item: Some Helpful Ideas

■ Provide an Explorable Environment

For younger children, your environment needs to display fewer activity areas and a small number of items within each. This applies especially to 3-year-olds. Some environments are just too complex for many of these children to be comfortable. When too many things are going on, the children may respond by refusing to explore or get involved. For this age group you need to simplify your physical environment—at least at the beginning of the year. Later, the children will be ready for additional activities.

On the other hand, 4- and 5-year-olds need the stimulation of complexity, novelty, and variation. This age group tends to be less fearful of new things and more adventurous. A more complex physical environment may encourage rather than discourage their exploration.

■ Give Children Time

Once children feel secure with you and your classroom, they should be able to make activity choices on their own if you will give them enough time. Let them wander around at first during the free-choice period. Don't force them into an activity before they are ready to go. Some children need more time than others. Others need to try out many things before they settle on one.

■ Act as a Base for Children's Explorations

Sit or stand in an area of the room where children can see you, near but not in any one activity area. Those who still need the security of an adult attachment can make eye contact, receive your smiles of support, and even come over for a moment or so before you encourage them to go off on their own again. The child who is still clinging can explore with her eyes. When she feels secure enough, she will join the others, knowing you are nearby.

■ Read a Book

Hearing a book read about a preschool classroom and all the interesting activities it contains may motivate the insecure child to look around her own classroom and be more willing to make activity choices on her own. Invite an insecure child to hear you read a book such as *D. W.'s Guide to Preschool* (Brown, 2003) from the Arthur's Adventures series. Arthur's sister D. W. tells the listener what goes on in preschool from the moment she says goodbye to her mother ("It's no big deal.") to all the positive things that might help an insecure child feel better. They start the day with "hello's" to everybody, even the classroom pet. Their teacher, Mrs. Morgan, fixes their boo-boos and gives them hugs. They have bathroom breaks whenever they need them. They play with blocks, sand, puzzles, tools, and also learn to share. They eat lunch together, play on the playground, learn numbers and letters, and sometimes go on field trips. After story time, their parents come back for them ("Look! I told you.").

A simpler book is *Mouse's First Day of School* (Thompson, 2003) in which mouse discovers a whole new world by hiding in a child's backpack and being taken to preschool. What excitement! He finds blocks, a toy car (Vrim, vrum, vroom!), a drum he can dance on, tiny plants to climb on, paint tubes to squish, crayons to squiggle, snacks to crunch on, and best of all: friends. What can your child find to do?

SEEKS OTHER CHILDREN TO PLAY WITH

Although this particular item seems to relate more to the child's social rather than emotional development, it actually indicates both. Seeking other children to play with is a part of the progression of developing self-esteem as well as a step on the sequence of socialization.

As the preschool child moves away from the parent in the early childhood classroom, and then as he moves away from the teacher to make activity choices on his own, his next step in the development of his self-esteem should involve joining the other children in play. Yet he often does not join the others, at least not right away. Depending on his previous experience with peers—or lack of it—he may prefer to play on his own at first. In other words, other children do not replace a child's primary or secondary care-givers as objects of attachment. When children finally do seek other children to play with, it is indeed an indication of stronger self-esteem.

Children seem to recognize that other children are like themselves; that is, they, too, depend on the teachers. From their self-centered perspectives, children may see peers as competitors for the attention of the teachers and for their use of materials and activities. Through socialization, they will find ways to get along with other children, as well as to share and take turns with materials—and even people—in your classroom. Through development of a stronger self-esteem, children will eventually feel secure enough to seek contact with others like themselves.

By the time the young child has entered your class, he or she in most instances has had a number of contacts with peers. Their interactions, however, are not the same as with adults. Children look to the adult as their base of attachment. They look to their peers as a reflection of themselves. Those children with a strong self-esteem will have less difficulty interacting with the other children from the outset. They are indicating by this behavior how far along they are in their development.

Those who need help developing this sense of security within themselves may not seek other children to play with at first. You may need to help the children progress. Don't expect success to occur overnight in this particular area. Some children are just not ready for many days or even weeks to make contact with peers. By looking at and treating each child in your class as an individual, you will begin to elicit clues about each that can help you support their development in this crucial area. As before, you will need to use acceptance and patience whenever a child is slow in moving ahead.

If You Have Not Checked This Item: Some Helpful Ideas

■ Help the Child Find a Buddy

For many young children who are used to dealing with a limited number of people at a time, a roomful of lively peers is overwhelming. You may need to help find a partner for the hyperactive child who has been teased by others or the shy child who may be able to relate on a one-to-one basis with one other child before she can cope with a group. Choose someone who gets along with others and ask that child to do an errand for you—perhaps mix paints or play dough, wash the doll clothes, or get out the cots for nap time. Or you might ask the buddy to show the child how to use the saw or how to record her voice on the tape recorder. Make the activities as personal as possible to attract the child's interest and get her to focus on the activity or material instead of on her unsure feelings about herself. Once she successfully relates to one other child, she may begin to seek others to play with on her own.

■ Have Small Groups

Young children are better able to relate to peers when in small groups. You can arrange the physical environment of your classroom so that each of the activity areas accommodates only a certain number of children (say, no more than four). Methods to accomplish this include placing four chairs around a table; using masking tape on the floor to divide the block center into four building areas; or providing only four aprons for water play, two saws or hammers for woodworking, three pillows in the book area, and so forth. When you read, read to two or four children rather than the total group.

■ Use a Material or Activity for Two Children Together

This idea is more often used in European programs to teach children to share, but you might also design or designate a certain material or activity in your classroom as always for use by two children together. You might attach one of your wagons to a trike so that one child must pedal while one rides. Your job chart of daily chores could require that pairs or teams work together to do the jobs. Can you think of other team enterprises?

■ Read a Book

In *Building a Bridge* (Begaye, 1993), two little girls experience their first day of school on the Navajo reservation with excitement but also with butterflies in their stomachs. Anna, an Anglo girl, meets Juanita, a Navajo girl, when their teacher asks Juanita to see if Anna wants to play with a box of purple and green blocks because they're "magical." At first Anna decides to build a bridge with the green blocks and Juanita does the same with the purple ones. But soon the two girls are putting their blocks together to build a huge bridge because it doesn't matter if the blocks are different colors. Differences are magical.

Two children can learn to play together even if they do not speak the same language. In *Margaret and Margarita* (Reiser, 1993), two little girls, one who speaks Spanish and one who speaks English, go to the park with their mothers. At first they are shy when they see one another. Then they begin a dialog in each language on opposite pages. "Hello"… "Hola." Soon they become friends and strike up a conversation in both languages.

 ## PLAYS ROLES CONFIDENTLY IN DRAMATIC PLAY

Once the young child has begun playing with others in your classroom, you need to be cognizant of another indicator of his developing self-esteem. Is he able to take on and play a role in the pretend situations that abound in early childhood programs? Can he pretend to be father or brother or baby in the housekeeping center? Is she a nurse or doctor or famous skater in the dress-up area? Can he be a race car driver, helicopter pilot, or crane operator on the playground? When a child can play a pretend role with confidence in your center, then he is presenting observable proof that his self-esteem has taken on an even more mature aspect.

To play a pretend role, children need to be able to see things from a different point of view than their own. Their perspective, in other words, cannot be egocentric. Some young children cover their eyes and think you cannot see them because they cannot see you. That view is, of course, highly egocentric. At some point in time, however,

3- and 4-year-olds seem to be able to step out of themselves and pretend quite realistically to be someone else.

It is not clear whether this ability is stronger or appears sooner in some children because of opportunity, encouragement, and practice at home, or whether certain children are instinctively or temperamentally more imaginative. No matter what causes the behavior, it indicates to the observer of children that a child has reached a milestone in her development of self-concept. A child's ability to play a role other than her own says a number of things to the observer, including

- The child can distinguish reality from fantasy (i.e., she knows she is pretending).
- The child is able to symbolize things (i.e., represent a real person or event in a make-believe manner).
- The child can see things from another person's perspective.
- The child has strong enough self-esteem to step out of herself and be someone else.

Until all four of these statements are true for the young child, she is really unable to play make-believe roles. Once she can perform this behavior, she is able to explore in a wholly new way. She can try out roles. She can see what it's like to be the mother, the older sister, the baby. She can dominate the situation. She can make her "father" or "brother" do what she wants him to. This ability is a heady discovery. Of course, in a group situation, she herself is often dominated or controlled to some extent by the others and must remain in an assigned or assumed role. If she plays the role "wrong," she will be reprimanded by those often strict conformists, her peers.

Adults in the early childhood classroom may wonder aloud: "Is this what we want our children to do? Isn't it wrong to encourage fantasizing like this?" Not at all, say child development specialists. This is a natural progression in the young child's development. This "fantasizing" is the way young children explore concepts about people and events in the world around them. While adults look askance at the "Walter-Mitty-type" adult who seems to live in a world of make-believe, it is not only natural but imperative that our children have the opportunity to use their imaginations playfully in exploring their own world (see Chapter 13, "Dramatic Play").

Besides, this playful use of the imagination is the next step developmentally for the young child in creating strong self-esteem. He started as a new human being so attached to his mother that he thought she was a part of him. Then he made the separation in which he not only recognized he was separate, but also realized he could move out from her. Next, he developed enough confidence to come to a new environment and allow other adults to be caregivers. From these adults he moved out to explore his new environment and interact with his peers. Now he has developed enough self-esteem that he can try out being someone else.

Child development researchers find strong support for dramatic play of this type in preschool and kindergarten, recording results such as: "Virtually all teachers in this study recognized that sociodramatic play helps children to succeed in school. Most of the benefits they cited were benefits relating to the child's socioemotional development and self-esteem" (Kemple, 1996, p. 27).

A great deal of power surrounds gaining control over people and situations, even imaginary ones. Up until now, the young child has been virtually powerless in a world controlled by adults. But when she plays a role in dramatic play, she is able to take a stand, be what she wants to be, and make things come out the way she wants them. Her self-esteem is thus strengthened as she expands her horizons, gains control over ideas and feelings, and receives immediate feedback from the other players on how her role affects them.

Also, in playing such pretend roles, the player gets to find out more about herself. The other children's reactions to her role and her own reactions to it help her realize their capabilities and understand her limits. She can explore gender roles more fully—what it's like to be male or female. Children in our society are treated differently from the moment of birth, it seems, depending on their gender. Now the young pretender can try out being the mother, father, sister, or brother in the family. Because children often play these familiar family roles in a very stereotyped, exaggerated manner—their own interpretation of the way real family members act—the players soon learn which roles are considered the "best" and how the others feel about mothers and fathers, boys and girls.

For a child who did not participate in dramatic play on first entering your program, now doing so signifies a major step. It means he not only has a strong enough sense of self to try being someone else, but he also now has this unparalleled opportunity to practice his budding interpersonal and communication skills, thus strengthening his self-esteem in a manner that was impossible before. Again a paradox exists: Once he is able to be someone else, he becomes more of himself. As Davidson (1996) noted:

> Although pretend play may look insignificant to the casual observer, there is enormous learning occurring—learning that can be expanded when the adult provides appropriate props, space, time, and guidance. (p. 9)

If You Have Not Checked This Item: Some Helpful Ideas

■ Provide Dramatic Play Materials

Have at least one area of your classroom set up for dramatic play. This section can be a family area with child-size table, chairs, refrigerator, stove, and sink; a bedroom area with doll beds, dresser and mirror, and chest of drawers; a store with shelves of empty food containers and a toy cash register; or any other such setting. If you take your class on a field trip, you should consider setting up a similar pretend area in your room for them to try out the roles they saw enacted on the trip: a doctor's office, a clinic, a laundromat, a beauty shop, gas station, or post office.

In addition to life-size settings and props, you need miniature toys to encourage role-playing as well. Little cars, trucks, people, animals, boats, and planes can be placed strategically in the block corner, at the water table, and with the table blocks. A box full of dramatic play props can be taken out on the playground. Pictures of people in a variety of roles—from family members to community helpers—can be hung at children's eye level around the room to encourage the exploration of roles. Ask the children what kinds of roles they would like to try out and have them help you assemble the props.

■ Allow Time to Pretend

Because the best dramatic play is spontaneous—even though you may have provided the props—you need to set aside a particular time during the day for free-choice activities to occur. Often these activities are scheduled at the beginning of the day, but they can take place any time. Allow enough time for children to become involved in their roles. The length may vary from day to day, depending upon the children's interests and yours, but free-choice activities should be scheduled to occur at the same time every day so that the children can depend on a set period for pretending and playing roles.

■ Play a Role Yourself

Sometimes the only way to help the nonparticipant become involved is to play a role yourself. Obviously, if a child is not ready emotionally, your efforts may be wasted. But some children who are ready to play a role may not know how to get started. In that case, you might pretend to be a mother and invite the child to go on a pretend errand with you, ending up in the dramatic play area where the other children are often delighted to see the teacher playing like they are. If the child accepts your lead and becomes involved with the others, you can gradually withdraw.

■ Be an Observer of Pretend Play

It will help you immensely in your understanding of children if you take time out to observe and record the various children's engagement in pretend play. Station yourself unobtrusively in an area of the room where a particular child is playing and jot down as many details as possible in a running record. Do this for several days, if possible. Some of the things to look for can include

- Theme of the play
- Role the child is playing
- Who else is playing and what their roles are
- Type of interaction with other children
- Who was leader and who the follower
- Length of time the child sustains the role

What can you conclude about the child from your observations? Have you learned anything that can help you plan your program differently so that other children will become more easily involved in dramatic play? Could you add props or suggestions to help the children sustain their play? Chapter 13, "Dramatic Play," has additional suggestions.

■ Read a Book

In *What Shall We Play*? (Heap, 2002), three friends gather and decide to play dress up. Lily May wants to play fairies. But Matt wants to play trees. So they play trees swaying in the wind. Every time Lily May says "fairies," Martha says "cars" or "cats" or Matt says "wibbly-wobbly Jell-O." Finally, Lily May gets her wish, and they dress up with cutout paper wings, a cape, and Lily's magic wand and have a grand time as flying fairies. Does this simple story help your children think of fun roles they can take?

 ## STANDS UP FOR OWN RIGHTS

For preschool children to stand up for their rights within the classroom, they need to have developed strong enough self-esteem to believe in themselves as individuals with a point of view worth other people's consideration. Thus far in their development of self-esteem, they have been able to make the separation from their parents, develop a secure attachment relationship with the teacher, complete various tasks successfully, choose activities on their own, seek other children to play with, and try out pretend roles confidently in a dramatic play situation because they could see things from another person's point of view. Now the children are progressing further by developing their own points of view they feel are worthy of other children's consideration.

What are some of the classroom rights such a self-confident child might insist on? One is *the right of possession*. If a child is playing with a piece of equipment, he should be able to continue using it unless some previous turn-taking rule is in effect. Many childhood squabbles take place over toys or materials, often because of children's egocentric perspectives. A child believes he should have a toy because he wants it. The fact that another child is playing with it does not count in his mind. The development of mutual respect is difficult among 3- and 4-year-olds because many of them lack the ability to understand the other's perspective. The child who feels his right is worth defending will often refuse to give in.

A child's *choice of participation* is another personal right often established in early childhood classrooms. If a child opts to join or not join a particular activity, you and the other children need to honor her choice. Use enticements rather than force if you feel the child should be involved when she chooses not to be.

Completing independent projects in her own way is a right that self-confident children will defend. If a child is doing a painting, modeling clay, constructing a building, or dressing a doll on her own, she should be able to do it as she sees fit as long as she is not interfering with others. Similarly, others should not be allowed to interfere with her. The child with strong self-esteem will continue in her own manner, disregarding or rejecting the attempts of others to impose their will.

Protecting property is another right that self-confident children will insist on. Toys or games they have brought from home are often the focus of conflict. You need to provide a private space like a cubby for each child to store his possessions. Block buildings are also important to the children who have built them. The child who insists on saving his building may want help in making a sign informing others: "Please Leave Dion's Building Standing."

Children may stand up for their own rights in a number of ways. They may physically prevent another child from doing something or make the child do something. They may verbalize their position with the other child. They may tell the teacher. Some of their actions may not be acceptable in a classroom full of children. Use of power or aggression is not appropriate. You need to help such children find more acceptable means for standing up for their rights.

As you observe your children on this particular item, look to see which ones do not allow another child to urge or force unwanted changes on them and which ones do not back down, or give up a toy or a turn. At the same time, take note of children who always give up or give in to the demands of another. They may also need your support in strengthening their self-esteem.

Cultural Differences in Standing Up for Own Rights

Whereas Western cultures consider a child's standing up for his rights as an indication of his self-esteem, Eastern cultures place a greater emphasis on maintaining harmonious relationships (Markus & Kitayama, 1991). Parents from Chinese families teach their children self-restraint and control of their emotions. Their children might very well give in to the demands of another because they have been taught self-restraint. They consider their children competent if they are shy, reticent, and quiet, whereas North American teachers may see such children as lacking self-confidence. Puerto Rican mothers focus on respectfulness of others, and traditional Navajo mothers teach their children to stand back and observe rather than go forward in their play. Many African, Latin-American, and southern European cultures also bring up their children to have respect for others rather than asserting themselves. Marshall (2001) tells us:

> Educators need to expand their views of what is considered important to self-concept beyond the typical notions of autonomy, self-assertion, self-enhancement, and uniqueness, and include characteristics such as empathy, sensitivity to others, modesty, cooperation, and caring as well. (p. 21)

If you find that nonassertive children in your classroom are from another culture, you need to look for other indications of their self-esteem, including respect for others and being sensitive to others' points of view.

If You Have Not Checked This Item: Some Helpful Ideas

■ Model Your Own Behavior

You need to model the behavior you want your children to follow. Stand firm on your decisions. Let your children know why. If you are "wishy-washy" or inconsistent in your treatment of them, they may have trouble standing firm themselves.

■ Allow Children Choices

One way to help a child learn that her rights can count is to give her a chance to make choices that are important to her. Let her choose a favorite activity to participate in or a toy to take home, rather than forcing your choice on her.

■ Stand Up for the Child

When it is clear to you that a child's rights have been infringed upon by another child, you should take a stand supporting the child, and at the same time let the others know "why Shandra can finish her painting now and Tyrell can't," for example.

■ Read a Book

Do animal characters have rights that they want to stand up for? The cows and hens and ducks do in the hilarious book *Click, Clack, MOO Cows That Type* (Cronin, 2000). Farmer Brown can hardly believe it when he begins hearing "click, clack, moo; click, clack, moo!" all day long coming from his barn. His cows have found his old typewriter and now they are making demands by writing notes to him: "Dear Farmer Brown, The barn is very cold at night. We'd like some electric blankets. Sincerely, The Cows." Cows that type? And cows that want electric blankets? "No, way!" says Farmer Brown. But then the cows type, "No milk." At last the cows make a compromise with the farmer and give him the typewriter if he will give them electric blankets

Ella Sarah, in the book *Ella Sarah Gets Dressed* (Chodos-Irvine, 2003), stands up forcefully for her right to wear what she wants, even when her mother, father, and sister try to convince her to wear something else. They lose the arguments, and Ella Sarah dresses to suit herself and her equally fancifully dressed friends.

The children's favorite is often the Charlie and Lola book, *I Will Never Not Ever Eat a Tomato* (Child, 2000), in which Charlie's little sister Lola stands up strongly for her right not to eat certain foods. Charlie accepts her forceful food decisions until he finally finds a creative way to change her mind.

The most successful learners are often those who want to do things for themselves.

DISPLAYS ENTHUSIASM ABOUT DOING THINGS FOR SELF

The lifelong pursuit of a self-concept is, in the final analysis, a struggle for autonomy. If young children are successful in this quest, they will be able and willing to behave independently in many ways. Your observations in the area of self-esteem will help you determine which children in your class are well on the road to developing strong self-concepts and which ones are not. The most successful learners will be those who can and want to do things for themselves. They will have achieved enough self-assurance about their own abilities to be able to try and eventually succeed in doing things on their own. Achieving this competence will then allow them a measure of independence from the adults around them.

What are some of the activities you may observe such children performing independently in your classroom? Here is a partial list:

dressing and undressing	*painting with brush*
tying or fastening shoes	*mixing paints*
using own cubby	*getting out toys*
toileting	*putting toys away*
washing hands and face	*returning blocks to shelves*
brushing teeth	*dressing dolls*
setting table for eating	*handling hammer, saw*
pouring drink	*cutting with scissors*
dishing out food	*cutting with knife*
handling eating implements	*mixing dough*
eating	*using climbing equipment*
cleaning up after eating	*making puzzles*
using computer	*using tape recorder*

The adeptness of 3-, 4-, and 5-year-old children in these various activities depends on their self-esteem, the practice they have had at home or elsewhere, and the encouragement or discouragement the adults around them have offered. This author has noticed that many children from low-income families are often more adept at accomplishing self-help skills than children from middle- and upper-income families. We might infer that children in low-income families have had to do many self-help activities on their own and thus became skilled sooner than their middle- and upper-income counterparts.

Similarly, children who have always had things done for them by the adults around them often give up the struggle for autonomy. You and your coworkers need to beware of the temptation to "help the little children" more than necessary. Children can do many more things for themselves than we realize. You need to allow time for children to learn to zip up jackets and pour their own drinks. Otherwise, you are denying them an unparalleled opportunity to develop their independence.

The way adults behave toward children during these formative years can indeed make a difference in children's feelings about themselves and thus in the way they behave. Research regarding gender stereotyping has found that mothers and fathers often treat their young daughters differently when it comes to independent behavior. Parents often allow and encourage boys to behave independently earlier than girls in such areas as using scissors without adult supervision, crossing the street alone, playing away from home, and riding the bus. When girls ask for help they often get it, but boys more often receive a response telling them to do it themselves. Boys are encouraged to manipulate objects and explore their environments, whereas girls are more often discouraged. Thus it seems that many parents value independence in boys more than in girls.

This type of discriminating behavior may of course result in girls feeling less capable than boys and therefore attempting fewer things on their own. Or this behavior may cause girls—and therefore women—to become dependent on men and less willing to risk using their own capabilities. Is this still the case among your children even with all the focus in the world around them on gender equality?

You and your coworkers need to take special care that stereotyped attitudes about the roles of men and women do not color your behavior toward the boys and girls in your classroom, or that such stereotyped ideas brought in by the children are handled appropriately. As in all areas of development, your goal should be to help each child become all he or she is capable of being. When each shows enthusiasm about doing things independently, you know they are well on their way to developing strong self-esteem.

If You Have Not Checked This Item: Some Helpful Ideas

■ Assess Your Classroom for Independent Possibilities

What can children do in your classroom? It gives them great satisfaction to accomplish difficult tasks on their own. Walk around your physical area and make a list of things that children can do. Items on your daily job chart for individuals or teams to choose can include

feeding the rabbit	*taking own attendance*
cleaning the aquarium	*getting out playground toys*
watering the plants	*sweeping the floor*
scraping carrots for snack	*sponging off the tables*
delivering mail to the office	*getting out cots for naptime*
tape-recording a story	*turning on and using the computer*

■ Encourage Performance of Self-Help Skills

Teach children how to tie their shoes when their small motor coordination allows them this capability. Or have another child help them get started with buttons, zippers, or Velcro tabs. Allow enough time for even the slowest child to perform this task on his own.

■   Be Enthusiastic Yourself

Enthusiasm always scores very high on lists of the competencies of successful teachers. You, as a behavior model in your classroom, need always to be enthusiastic and positive about everything you do. If children see you acting vigorously on your own, they will want to do likewise.

■   Read a Book

One of the most enthusiastic books about preschool is Neubecker's *Wow! School!* (2007). Izzy, a mountain girl goes to school on a little school bus, but when you turn the page, Izzy's excitement suddenly explodes into a double-page spread full to the brim with an entire WOW! CLASSROOM! Children, activities, easel, sand table, art table, book corner, and walls burst forth in stunning colors. The next two pages turned vertically show a foot-and-a-half tall WOW! TEACHER! with multiethnic kids crowding around. And so on through double pages of WOW! ART! BOOKS! LUNCH! PLAYGROUND! MUSIC! ABCs! SCIENCE! NUMBERS! and FRIENDS! Can your listeners contain their excitement?

OBSERVING, RECORDING, AND INTERPRETING SELF-ESTEEM

Self-esteem was chosen as the first topic on the Child Development Checklist because this is the first area of child development a teacher should be concerned with when she meets new children in her classroom for the first time. Here is an example of how one teacher used the checklist.

Making a Running Record and Transferring Data to the Checklist

To use the checklist most effectively, many observers prefer to make a running record of the child they are observing. Afterward they transfer the data they have gathered by checking items on the checklist that they observed the child performing and by recording running-record evidence for their checkmark in the space provided. This combines the best of both methods of observation: the open-ended and rich descriptive advantages of the running record with the focus on a particular sequence of behaviors from a developmental checklist. Here is a running record made for 3-year-old Sheila on October 22:

Sheila's mother brings her into classroom.

Sheila holds tightly to her hand. She begins to cry.

Mother says: "Now, Sheila, you like it here. Be a good girl. See you later."

Mother leaves. S. stands at entrance to room crying.

When teacher comes over S. looks at her & takes her hand.

Tch. takes S. over to girls in doll corner & says something.

S. shakes her head "no."

When tch. lvs. S. begins following tch. around.

Tch. sits S. down at small table with box of crayons in middle & blank sheets of paper in front of 2 chairs.

S. finally takes 2 crayons & starts coloring on paper.

Beth comes over & sits down at table.

Beth takes crayon out of box & starts coloring on her paper.

No talking at first.

Then Beth asks S. "May I borrow your orange?" It is on table.

S. says "No" & covers crayon with hand.

Beth grabs her hand, takes crayon with other hand & pops it into her mouth!

S. says "That's not fair!" and calls tch.

When tch. comes S. says, "She ate my orange crayon so I can't finish my pumpkin!"

Tch. says to Beth, "People shouldn't eat crayons."

Tch. is distracted by other ch. & leaves area.

S. gets up & goes to book corner & takes book.

S. carries book around room, looking carefully at what is going on, but not joining in.

S. whispers to Brian, "Becky painted yesterday & she's going to paint again today. See!" & points to easel.

Brian doesn't respond. S. whines to tch., "I wanna paint!"

Tch. tells her she can paint when Becky is finished.

The observer then takes this running record and fills out the Self-Esteem section of the checklist, as shown in Figure 3–1. As the observer reads the chapter on self-esteem, she should pay special attention to the items that she did not check. She will learn from her reading that a 3-year-old like Sheila may still not be secure enough to let go of her mother easily when she first comes to the preschool. The observer then notes that she does transfers her clinging to the teacher, just as 3-year-olds often do at the beginning of school. But she does not play with the other children. The Helpful Ideas section after each item in Chapter 3 gives suggestions that may assist this child to make the transition from home to school more easily. Because Sheila has been in school for a month and still has difficulty making this transition, she may need this special help.

Evidence

It is important to record evidence as brief, nonjudgmental statements of what you actually saw. If you are observing and recording directly onto the checklist, these statements

CHILD DEVELOPMENT CHECKLIST

Name _____ Sheila age 3 _____   **Observer** _____ Connie R _____

Program _____ Head Start _____   **Dates** _____ 10/22 _____

Directions:

Put an X for items you see the child perform regularly. Put *N* for items where there is no opportunity to observe. Leave all other items blank.

Item	Evidence	Dates
1. Self-Esteem		
_____ Separates from primary caregiver without difficulty	clings to mother & cries	10/22
__X__ Develops a secure attachment with teacher	clings to teacher when mother leaves	10/22
_____ Completes a task successfully	starts coloring but stops when Beth comes	10/22
_____ Makes activity choices without teacher's help	teacher places her at art table	10/22
_____ Seeks other children to play with	no, she does not	10/22
__N__ Plays roles confidently in dramatic play		
__X__ Stands up for own rights	tries to stop Beth from taking crayon	10/22
_____ Displays enthusiasm about doing things for self	watches others but does not play with them	10/22

Figure 3—1   Self-Esteem section of Child Development Checklist (for Sheila)

can be brief descriptions of the child's actions and language that you see and hear. If you are transferring data from a running record, enter that evidence. If you did not have the opportunity to observe the child for a particular item, place *N* instead of a checkmark beside it. If the child has the opportunity to perform a checklist item, but does not do it, leave the item blank, but write an explanation.

For example, in Figure 3–1, the observer leaves the first item blank but includes under Evidence what she saw the child doing. Instead of checking "Separates from primary caregiver without difficulty," the observer notes that "Sheila clings to mother & cries." It is important for the teaching staff to have such information in interpreting the checklist results and making plans for this child.

From the running record previously made about Sheila, the observer can continue to complete the Child Development Checklist under the 10 other areas, checking off items and filling in the Evidence column. Obviously a number of other observations need to be made of Sheila at various times during the day and on different days during arrival, free choice, snack, outdoor play, lunch, nap, and departure to provide a comprehensive picture of the child.

As you can see, the Child Development Checklist *is not a test,* but a listing of developmental items that children may or may not perform. If observers leave certain items blank because the child does not perform them, this may mean one of several things:

1. She cannot because she has not yet reached that level of development.

2. She does not because she is not interested in doing what the item describes.

3. The classroom itself is not set up to encourage the child's performance.

You should not ask children questions about whether they recognize certain colors, for instance. The youngsters' performance on the items should become evident as you observe the children in their natural play activities. Set up activities that will engage the children in the areas you wish to observe. Be sure these activities are spontaneous and not forced. If a child does not get involved in Art Skills, even though art activities are available every day, you should leave the items blank. Do not use N, no opportunity to observe, when in fact the child has the opportunity to participate in art activities, but chooses not to. You may want to make a note, though, after the items that "Easel painting and art activities are available, but B. does not get involved in art."

From the running record previously made, the observer can check off items and fill in evidence for Sheila under Emotional Development for "Shows interest, attention in classroom activities"; under Social Play for "Plays by self with own toys/materials"; under Small Motor Development for "Uses drawing/writing tools with control"; under Spoken Language for "Speaks in expanded sentences"; and under Art Skills for "Makes pictorial drawings." Other observations on Sheila can be made, recorded, and dated on the same checklist until a comprehensive picture of her emerges.

Inferences

The first step in interpreting the data you have gathered is to read it through carefully, both the running record and especially the checklist, to see if you can make any inferences about the child. An inference is a statement of interpretation considered to be true,

Incident	Faulty Inference	Valid Inference
Sheila would not let Beth borrow her orange crayon	Sheila does not know how to share	Sheila was not finished using the crayon
Sheila whispers to Brian Becky painted yesterday & she's going to paint today	Sheila likes to tattle on other children	Sheila is alert to what Becky did with paint yesterday & today

Figure 3—2   Types of Inferences

tentatively at least, because it is founded on objective information believed to be true. In other words, it is a possible explanation derived from the behavior you have witnessed. To make an inference, you must actually have seen and recorded objectively the behavior on which you are basing the inference.

Looking back at the running record made for Sheila, we might consider making the inferences shown in Figure 3–2.

After reading carefully the first incident in the running record involving Sheila (which states that she says "no" when Beth asks to borrow her orange crayon, then covers the crayon with her hand), we need to ask ourselves what we can infer, if anything, from this. Do the words tell us that Sheila does not know how to share? They do not seem to indicate this. Then the inference "Sheila does not know how to share" is probably not a valid one. We just do not have enough information to make this particular inference. We may want to observe Sheila further to see if she is able to share materials with others before we can infer that she does not know how to share. Does the running record tell us that Sheila was not finished using the orange crayon? Yes. The words say, "She ate my orange crayon so I can't finish my pumpkin." Thus we can infer that Sheila was not finished using the crayon.

The second incident, in which Sheila whispers to Brian that Becky painted yesterday and she's going to paint again today, should be approached in the same way. What, if anything, can we infer from this incident? Does it mean Sheila likes to tattle on other children? Because we do not have any indication this is true, such an inference is faulty. We can infer that Sheila is alert to what Becky did with paint yesterday and now today. That is about all. We may want to infer that Sheila is using such an approach to gain access to an activity she likes, or that Sheila whispers about others to get attention, or that Sheila just likes to stir up things in the classroom in this manner—but we truly do not have such information about Sheila, and thus cannot make any of these three last inferences.

Try making your own inferences from an anecdotal or running record you have made after observing a child. One thing you will learn from such an exercise is the importance of recording with rich detail in the first place. You need to learn this skill through practice as you observe children. You can always add something more to a running record: facial expressions, gestures, reactions of other children. They may be the keys to the inferences you are trying to draw about a child.

The principal stumbling block in making valid inferences based on recorded observational data is that *we often try to read more into the data than is actually there.* We are used to making judgments continuously about people and situations in our lives. Often they are faulty judgments based on insufficient or misinterpreted information. Do not allow yourself to be misled like this when you have the written observational data before you. Look at the data and ask yourself the question: Is there evidence to support my inference? If there is not, then you cannot make it.

Conclusions

The final step in your interpretation of recorded data about children is to make whatever conclusions you can. A conclusion in this case is a reasoned judgment based on *valid inferences made from accumulated observational evidence.* As with inferences, you cannot make such a judgment unless you can show sufficient evidence. Read through your observational data. Based on what you have recorded, what can you conclude about the child? In Sheila's case, very little can be concluded from one brief running record. We cannot really conclude that she is always so alert to other children and activities in the classroom unless future observations show this to be the case. It may be that she is only concerned with painting. To make valid conclusions, an observer needs a great deal of recorded information about a child. Observing, recording, and interpreting in this careful, objective manner should help you sort out what children are really like. You may be surprised by what you discover.

Learning Prescription

Creating a *learning prescription* for Sheila is the next step in the process of planning for an individual child based on interpreted observational data. To create such a prescription, you should look over the Child Development Checklist to find at least three *areas of strength.* Although her checklist is far from complete, it is still possible to come up with real strengths for Sheila. For example, she:

1. Stands up for her own rights
2. Speaks in expanded sentences
3. Enjoys art and displays art skills

These three areas of strength can be entered on Sheila's initial learning prescription. *Making a reliable overall assessment of a single child should not be done based on only one observation.* You should have as much information as you can gather from as many different days, activities, and points of view as possible. The best overall records are a compilation from the entire classroom staff. Have each person put a date by the items observed. Individuals may want to indicate their checkmarks and evidence with a symbol, initials, or color coding if everyone is using the same checklist for all the observations.

In Sheila's case, for the purpose of illustrating the checklist planning process, we will make an initial learning prescription based on this one observation. After you have decided on Sheila's strengths, you need to look for her areas that need strengthening. We do not call these *weaknesses*, a negative term, because they are not weaknesses. Words are important, as previously noted, and we should use them carefully. If we talk in terms of negatives, we will think in terms of negatives regarding Sheila and our other children. If we think in terms of areas that need strengthening, we should be able to plan a positive program for Sheila that will help her to continue in her development and improve in areas that need improvement.

Three areas that need strengthening can also be taken from Sheila's checklist from items not checked. For example, Sheila:

1. Needs to separate from her mother more easily

2. Needs to make activity choices on her own

3. Needs to play with other children

Finally, the learning prescription needs to include specific ideas for helping the child to improve by *drawing on her strengths*. Specific ideas for activities can come from your own experience or from the ideas listed in the various chapters after every checklist item, called If You Have Not Checked This Item: Some Helpful Ideas. Because Sheila speaks well and seems to want to do particular things, it might be well to get her involved as a leader with one other child. Presenting such an activity as a transition from home to school when she first arrives might help her separate from her mother more easily. Being the leader in another activity with the same child might help her to make activity choices on her own. Her interest in painting could also keep her involved with the other child and the classroom activities.

With these thoughts in mind, the staff proposed the three Activities to Help as shown on an initial learning prescription for Sheila (Figure 3–3). Future observations would help the staff determine if these activities did help Sheila or if different activities would be more appropriate. The teachers in Sheila's class will want to continue their observing and recording to evaluate how these activities help Sheila and the other children, as well as to determine what other individual plans are needed.

Be sure that observation of such children is an ongoing process in your center. Do a follow-up of children who seem to need special help. Has your learning prescription been helpful? Did the activities you planned really help this child? Share your observations with your classroom team and with the child's parents. Ask them to make similar observations. Include their ideas, as well as your team's, in your individual plans for each child.

```
┌─────────────────────────────────────────────────────────────────┐
│                     LEARNING PRESCRIPTION                         │
│  Name____Sheila_____Age__3__Date____10/22_____             │
│                                                                   │
│  Areas of Strength and Confidence                                 │
│  1. _Stands up for her own rights_____         │
│  2. _Speaks in expanded sentences_____         │
│  3. _Enjoys art & displays art skills_____         │
│                                                                   │
│  Areas Needing Strengthening                                      │
│  1. _To separate from mother more easily_____         │
│  2. _To make activity choices on her own_____         │
│  3. _To play with other children_____         │
│                                                                   │
│  Activities to Help                                               │
│  1. _Transition activity when S. arrives; S. & Becky could clean the rabbit │
│     _cage & feed the rabbit_____         │
│  2. _S. could record her voice & then show Becky how_____         │
│  3. _S. & Becky could paint large cartoon for class "space ship" & others could join in │
└─────────────────────────────────────────────────────────────────┘
```

Figure 3–3   Learning Prescription for Sheila

LEARNING ACTIVITIES

1. Observe all the children in your classroom each morning of the first week of school, using the items in the self-identity checklist as a screening device. Note which children can separate without difficulty from their parents and which children cannot. Make a written Learning Prescription for a particular child to help him or her overcome this initial anxiety. Discuss the plan with your supervisor and then implement it. Discuss the results.

2. Choose a child who seems to have difficulty getting involved with other children or activities. Make a running record of everything the child does or says during three different arrival periods. Transfer this information to the

Child Development Checklist under "Self-Esteem." How do you interpret the evidence you have collected? Can you make any conclusions yet about this child?

3. Meet with one of the parents of children in your classroom. Discuss how children develop their self-esteem, and give the parents ideas that can be used at home to help strengthen their child's self-concept. Ask them for suggestions about how they would like you to work with their child. If you are not in a classroom, make a written report of how you would do this.

4. Observe a child playing a role in dramatic play for 3 days. Keep a running record of everything

the child does or says. Pay special attention to the characteristics of play listed on page 71. What conclusions about the child's self-esteem can you make based on these observations?

5. Choose a child for whom you have checked "Displays enthusiasm about doing things for self." Observe this child during the first half-hour of class for 3 days. Which of the other items can you check for this child based on your observations? What physical evidence can you place in the child's portfolio about her self-esteem?

SUGGESTED READINGS

Balaban, N. (2006). Easing the separation process for infants, toddlers, and families. *Young Children, 63*(6), 14–20.

Gallagher, K. C., & Meyer, K. (2006). Teacher-child relationships at the forefront of effective practices. *Young Children, 61*(6), 44–49.

Hyson, M. (2004). *The emotional development of young children: Building an emotion-centered curriculum* (2nd ed.). New York: Teachers College Press.

Seefeldt, C., & Waskik, B. A. (2006). *Early education: Three-, four-, and five-year-olds go to school* (2nd ed.). Upper Saddle River, NJ: Merrill/Prentice Hall.

Szamreta, J. M. (2003). Peekaboo power: To ease separation and build secure relationships. *Young Children, 58*(1), 88–94.

CHILDREN'S BOOKS

Begaye, L. S. (1993). *Building a bridge.* Flagstaff, AZ: Northland.*

Brown, M. (2003). *D. W. 's guide to preschool.* New York: Little, Brown.

Child, L. (2000). *I will never not ever eat a tomato.* Cambridge, MA: Candlewick Press.

Chodos-Irvine, M. (2003). *Ella Sarah gets dressed.* San Diego: Harcourt, Inc.*

Cooper, E. (2004). *Magic thinks big.* New York: Greenwillow Books.

Cronin, D. (2000). *Click, clack, MOO Cows that type.* New York: Simon & Schuster.

Dole, M. L. (2003). *Drum, Chavi, drum!* San Francisco, CA: Children's Book Press.*

Edwards, B. (2002). *My first day at nursery school.* New York: Bloomsbury Children's Books.

Heap, S. (2002). *What shall we play?* Cambridge, MA: Candlewick Press.*

Neubecker, R. (2007). *Wow! School!* New York: Hyperion Books.*

Northway, J. (2006). *See you later, Mom!* London, England: Frances Lincoln's Children's Books.*

Reiser, L. (1993). *Margaret and Margarita.* New York: Greenwillow.*

Smith, C. L. (2000). *Jingle Dancer.* New York: Morrow Junior Books.*

Thompson, L. (2003). *Mouse's first day of school.* New York: Simon & Schuster.

---

*Multicultural.

4

Emotional Development

EMOTIONAL DEVELOPMENT CHECKLIST

_____ Releases stressful feelings in appropriate manner

_____ Expresses anger in words rather than negative actions

_____ Can be calmed in difficult or dangerous situations

_____ Overcomes sadness feelings in appropriate manner

_____ Handles surprising situations with control

_____ Shows fondness, affection, love toward others

_____ Shows interest, attention in classroom activities

_____ Smiles, seems happy much of the time

DEVELOPING EMOTIONS IN YOUNG CHILDREN

The emotional development of the preschool child is somewhat different from other developmental aspects. Although emotional growth happens simultaneously with physical, social, cognitive, language, and creative development and is interdependent on them, it may seem as if youngsters do not stay developed. They seem to repeat the same sequences of emotional reactions over and over—throughout life. However, it is not the emotion itself that is repeated, but the response to it. As LeDoux (1996) tells us: "An emotion is a subjective experience, a passionate invasion of consciousness, a feeling" (p. 267). It is the _response_ to this feeling that may change in the child over time due to his maturity, environment, the reactions of others around him, or the coaching he receives from you.

Emotional development does have a physical and cognitive basis for its development, but once the basic human abilities are in place, emotions are much more situational. If we agree that emotions are particular reactions to specific stimuli, then we note that these reactions may not change much in a developmental sense over a person's lifetime. Many of us get red in the face when we are angry and cry when we are sad, both as infants and as adults. In other words, it is for the most part the situation—the stimulus—rather than our developmental level that seems to govern our emotional responses.

Actually, emotional development is even more complex. Whereas physical and cognitive development seem to be based on the genetic traits children inherit plus the environment in which they are raised, Izard (1977, 1991) suggests emotions have three internally interacting dimensions:

1. The conscious feeling or emotional experience
2. The process in the brain and nervous system
3. The observable expressive patterns or reactions

Obviously, the brain and nervous system, because they are physical, can exhibit inherited traits. But can emotions themselves be inherited and then develop through maturation and surroundings just like the ability to think? Yes. Brain research makes it clear that "brain maturation influences much of what children are capable of emotionally at different ages" (Hyson, 2004, p. 144). Developmental researchers also recognize that certain emotional responses seem to be universal. Separation anxiety, for instance, occurs at about the same time and for the same reasons in infants and toddlers around the world. Similarly, other types of emotions seem to trigger the fight-or-flight response in humans everywhere.

Developmental psychologists studying universal responses talk in terms of the functions of emotions (i.e., how they help the human species adapt and survive). These scientists note that certain emotions that trigger necessary survival responses in infants have outlived their usefulness when they occur in older children and adults. The acute distress the infant feels and expresses in tears and screams when mother leaves the house, for example, has outlived its usefulness if it is a daily occurrence for a 4-year-old whose mother leaves him at preschool. Although such basic emotions seem to serve in helping to preserve the self or the species, the higher emotions serve social purposes, and their appropriate responses must be learned in a social context.

Thus we need to focus on the response—not the emotion itself—when we speak of emotional development in preschool children. And what most concerns us is not the development, but the child's control of the response—its regulation. In the areas of physical and mental development we want the young child to grow, mature, and extend his abilities to the utmost. With emotional development, we want the child to learn to make appropriate emotional responses, and especially to control negative responses.

Brain research has given us more clues about emotional control. For instance, the right hemisphere of the brain is more responsible for processing negative emotions, intense emotions, and creativity. The left hemisphere is more responsible for positive emotions, language development, and interest in new objects and experiences, Gallagher reports (2005, p. 17). Because the right hemisphere experiences greater growth during the first 3 years of life, it is important that early childhood teachers work closely with young children helping them learn to regulate their negative emotions. Such self-regulation is difficult for many children without adult help. Gallagher tells us: "When young children become distressed and have difficulty regulating their own behavior, caregivers help to minimize the children's stress and provide comfort" (2005, p. 17).

This chapter, then, looks at observable emotional responses of young children in eight different emotional areas: distress, anger, fear, sadness, surprise, interest, affection, and joy. Each discussion is followed by suggestions for helping the child improve his or her behavior if the particular response is not demonstrated. Each of the checklist items refers to a particular emotion. It should be noted, however, that the order in which the items are listed is not a developmental sequence, because sequence as such does not seem to be an important factor in emotional development.

Many psychologists recognize 10 or 12 basic sets of emotions. These are sometimes listed as interest-excitement, enjoyment-joy, affection-love, surprise-startle, distress-anguish, anger-rage, disgust-revulsion, contempt-scorn, fear-terror, shame/shyness-humiliation, sadness-grief, and guilt-remorse (Izard, 1977, 1991). The emotional responses of preschool children seem to be involved principally with the following eight emotions:

1. distress
2. anger
3. fear
4. sadness

5. surprise
6. interest
7. affection
8. joy

To help children develop emotionally, the preschool teacher should be concerned with promoting positive responses and teaching management of inappropriate responses. Although techniques to accomplish this control may vary depending on the emotion and the situation, the following five strategies can be used in helping most children manage their inappropriate reactions:

Helping Children Manage Inappropriate Emotional Reactions

1. Remove or reduce the cause of the emotion.
2. Diffuse the child's negative response by allowing him to "let it out" through crying, talking, or transferring his feelings into nondestructive actions.
3. Offer support, comfort, and ideas for self-control.
4. Model controlled behavior yourself.
5. Give children the opportunity to talk about negative feelings appropriately.

Once a child can verbalize, he or she can begin to take charge of her emotions. She may be able to tell you what happened or how she feels. This is the first step toward self-mastery of emotions. But many children do not possess what Deerwester (2007) calls "emotional literacy," that is, the proper words that express how we feel. She stresses: "We can teach our children how to identify their own feelings by looking at the faces and the body language of others, as well as how to choose the best way to express emotionally charged perspectives" (p. 7). They need to build an "emotional vocabulary" of words like *happy, sad, angry, surprised, disappointed, excited, grumpy, jealous*, and many more. These are new words for many 3-, 4-, and 5-year-olds. They may have heard them, but have little idea what they mean.

Once a child can verbalize, she can begin to take charge of her emotions.

For you as a teacher, you may need to start with emotion word games, word songs, word books, word puppets, and word stuffed animals. At a time when everyone is calm, you or they can act out such feelings one at a time. Specific ideas are discussed under *If You Have Not Checked This Item: Some Helpful Ideas.*

Your goal for the children should be the same as in the other aspects of their development—for them to gain self-control. To help children acquire this control, you first need to find out where they stand in their present responses. Do they cry, whine, or complain much of the time? Do they ever smile? Do they show anger or aggression toward others? The Child Development Checklist lists eight representative items of emotional behavior that can be observed in preschool children; each item represents one of the eight emotions previously listed. Observe the children in your class to determine which youngsters have accomplished the emotional self-control described in the checklist. Children who have not exhibited these checklist behaviors may benefit from the ideas and suggestions discussed in the remainder of the chapter.

 RELEASES STRESSFUL FEELINGS IN APPROPRIATE MANNER

Distress

Children who cannot handle their feelings during stressful times are exhibiting the emotion known as distress. At its lower extreme, distress may result from physical discomfort due to pain, extremes of temperature, or noise; at its upper level, distress may take the form of anguish or depression due to loss. A basic cause of distress throughout life is physical or psychological separation, especially from a loved one. Children who perceive themselves as having been abandoned by an adult, even when this is not the case, experience the same emotions as children who actually have been abandoned. Children also feel distress when negative things happen to them at home, especially abuse and neglect.

Brain research tells us that the body produces chemicals called hormones that help regulate body functions and reactions to the environment. One such hormone is cortisol, which is released in response to stress and helps the body respond to challenging situations. Even daily stressors such as being hungry or hearing a loud noise can cause increases in cortisol levels. But as Gallagher (2005) tells us: "Too much cortisol production over a long period of time is not good and can lead to problems with memory and self-regulation. Frequent and intense stress can harm abilities like remembering and controlling negative emotions or behavior" (p. 15). Thus, it is important for teachers of preschool programs to create a calm environment where children feel cared for and secure, and where children can learn to regulate stress-producing emotions.

Children express distress by crying, whining, or showing a sad face. Sometimes they cling to an adult caregiver. Distressed children may feel uncomfortable, disappointed, or rejected. Because distress is not the most severe negative emotion found in children, adults do not always take it seriously. They should. Distress is an indication that all is not well with a child. Failure to reduce the distress or its causes over time tends to break down children's trust in adults. Furthermore, they may learn to become unsympathetic to others who are distressed because that is the way they have been treated.

What are the principal causes of distress in the preschool classroom? For many youngsters, separation from their mother or primary caregiver is the greatest stressor. Physical discomfort or pain, rejection by peers, bullying by peers, dissatisfaction with a performance, and lack of a skill are other causes of distress. A stressful situation in the family, such as the birth of a new baby, a death, a hospitalization, a move, or a divorce, may also be carried over into classroom behavior by the child who is disturbed by it.

The Teacher's Role

How can you help? Your principal role in the children's emotional development should be to help them master or regulate their feelings. You should not be the controlling device yourself, but instead you should help them find a way to control their feelings from within. Adults are often tempted to take control of an emotional situation. Young children, in fact, look to you to solve the emotional problems that so often overwhelm them. You do children a disservice if you comply. Your role should be that of a facilitator, not a controller. Otherwise, without you, the children will be no better off the next time the emotional situation occurs. As with other aspects of development, your overall goal for children should be to help them develop emotional competence—in other words, emotional self-control.

Although the particular situation may determine your response, distress most often requires that you first give comfort to the child. She is upset and uncomfortable; she may be whining or crying. You can show your concern through comforting words and actions such as holding or hugging. As noted by Raikes (1996):

> Teachers who are close to their children often report child anxiety during such times as a divorce, the birth of a sibling, or family illness. During times of child stress, teachers may give extra hugging, holding, or one-on-one time. (p. 62)

Requiring a child to stop crying right away is not usually the way to help him master his emotions. Venting through tears is, after all, a catharsis. He may think you are not sympathetic to his plight if you insist he stop crying. He may in fact stop on his own when he hears your comforting words or feels your touch. Recent studies have found that crying is of therapeutic value not only psychologically, but also physically. Chemical toxins that build up during stress are released in tears. Even blood pressure, pulse rate, and body temperature seem to be lowered by crying (Frey & Langseth, 1985). As psychologist Solter (1992) pointed out:

> Crying is not the hurt, but the process of becoming unhurt.... A child who has been allowed to cry as long as needed will feel happier and more secure at school, in the long run, than a child who has been repeatedly distracted from her feelings. (p. 66)

Bowling and Rogers (2001) asked, Where do such feelings go when they get stopped? They tell us what every teacher knows: "The feelings erupt as kicking, hitting, screaming, or they are pushed inside and the child retreats and clings to a blanket or thumb" (p. 80). They suggest that the best way to help children release feelings and heal emotionally is to give them complete focused attention, one-on-one. During this special time, the teacher can interact with the child using one or more of the strategies in Figure 4–1.

As for mastering distress so that it will not happen again, this is probably not possible and certainly not appropriate. Distress may be relieved and perhaps controlled to some extent, but not completely mastered. Nor should we want it to be. Distress is a necessary symptom signaling that all is not well with the individual. In your classroom, you should hope to relieve, not prevent, distress in a child. If you are successful, a distraught child will allow herself to be comforted or redirected. But if her sense of self is not strong enough or if the distress is too overwhelming, she may not even allow this. What can you do to help such a child?

Figure 4–1   Relieving Stress

- Give comfort

- Allow child to cry

- Redirect attention

- Help the child to verbalize

If You Have Not Checked This Item: Some Helpful Ideas

■ Hold and Rock

It's a good idea to have an adult-size rocking chair in your center. Sometimes the best help for a distraught child is to hold and rock him.

■ Have the Child Hold a Huggable Toy

A child is often comforted by holding something soft. That is why toddlers carry "security blankets." Your classroom should have cuddly stuffed animals or similar toys available, not only for play but also for stressful situations. The child who does not allow you to comfort her may help herself by holding such a toy. Be sure the toy is washable so it can be cleaned for use by other children.

■ Use a Material with Soothing Properties

Water play and finger painting are activities with soothing qualities. Distressed children can take out their frustrations by moving paint around a surface with their hands or by swishing water and squeezing sponges, thus transferring their negative energy in a harmless fashion.

■ Have the Child Talk to a Puppet

Verbalizing distraught feelings is one of the best ways to defuse and control them. You could designate one of the puppets in your room as a "feelings" puppet and keep it in a special place for the times when children are feeling upset. They can talk to the puppet about how they feel and ask the puppet how it feels. Model the use of this puppet yourself when upsetting occasions arise so that the children can follow your lead when they feel bad.

■ Read a Book

Sometimes distraught children will allow you to read a favorite book to them. You might also keep particular books for them to look at on their own during troubling times. The following books are especially suitable for stressful situations.

The Story of My Feelings (Berkner, 2007) is narrated by a little girl who feels sad, then happy, then angry, and finally peaceful. To make herself feel better, she cries when she is sad, laughs when she is happy, yells when she is angry, and sighs when she is peaceful. This is a song storybook with music that accompanies the words, and even a song CD is included. When any of the children express these feelings, they can sing their troubles away or more privately, listen to the CD on a headset. Music is a good way to calm ruffled feelings.

The Way I Feel (Cain, 2000) includes a cast of multiethnic youngsters, one-by-one feeling silly, being scared, feeling disappointed, feeling happy, feeling sad, being angry, being thankful, being frustrated, feeling shy, being bored, being excited, being jealous,

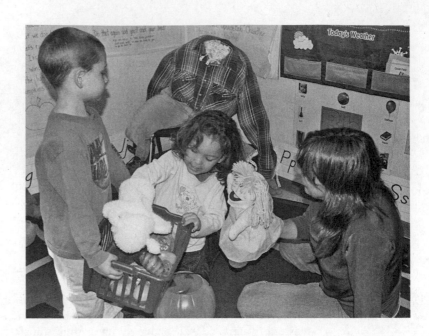

Model the use of a feelings puppet that children can talk to about how they feel.

and being proud. The author wrote and illustrated the book with its expressive, colorful characters to give readers the language for their emotions. She encourages adults to talk to children when someone feels like one of these characters. She encourages listeners to use these emotional words themselves.

Do animals have feelings, too? In *Hurty Feelings* (Lester, 2004), a humorous story about a hippo named Fragility, she never cries when she stubs her toes, but when any of the jungle animals say even nice things about her, she takes it as a criticism and cries because her feelings have been hurt. Then Rudy, a big rude elephant appears and begins insulting Fragility. But everything he says applies to him as well, and soon he is the weeping one, and Fragility the comforter.

☑ EXPRESSES ANGER IN WORDS RATHER THAN ACTIONS

Anger

Anger is the emotion of most concern not only in the classroom, but also in society at large, perhaps because anger has the potential for such harm. We are very much concerned that people learn to control their anger. Therefore we begin teaching what to do—or rather what not to do—very early. We are usually not very successful. There is, however, a positive approach to controlling anger that can diffuse the anger so that children do not turn it against others or themselves.

First, we need to look at the emotion itself to understand what it is, what causes it, and what purpose it serves. Anger is the emotion or feeling that results when we are physically or psychologically restrained from doing something, frustrated in our attempts, interrupted, personally insulted, or forced to do something against our will. We feel hurt, disappointed, and irritated. We frown, our face gets hot, our blood "boils," our muscles tense, our teeth clench, our eyes stare. At anger's highest level, we feel rage that threatens to erupt in an explosive manner. At the other extreme we feel hostility, a cold type of anger.

With anger comes a sense of physical power and greater self-assurance than with any other negative emotion (Izard, 1977, p. 331). The body, in fact, rallies its resources in readiness to strike out against the cause of the anger. In primitive humans, anger mobilized the body's energy quickly and was important for survival. In modern humans, the anger still appears, but its primary purpose has all but vanished.

Here we are, then, ready to turn this rush of physical energy against the "enemy." What should we do with it? This energy needs to be released or somehow diffused, otherwise we will turn it against ourselves. Repressed anger has been implicated as one of the causes of skin diseases, ulcers, migraines, hypertension, and certain psychological disorders (Izard, 1977, p. 351).

Most parents teach their children from the start not to display anger. When they allow angry feelings to begin to show on their faces, children sense their parents' displeasure. Many children soon learn to conceal or disguise anger. Others let anger out in acts of aggression. Neither response is satisfactory, yet many of us carry these responses throughout life.

Instead, we need a positive approach that teaches children from the start what they should do (expression) rather than what they must not do (repression). Anger definitely calls for some sort of release, but children and adults need to "let off steam" harmlessly.

One of the most satisfactory methods used by many preschool teachers coaches children to verbalize their feelings as they did during stressful situations. Verbalizing involves neither yelling nor name-calling, but expressing in words how the child feels about whatever is causing the anger. This approach has at least two advantages: It gives children an acceptable release for their strong feelings, and it puts the children in control. They—not adults—deal with the situation. And solving the problems on their own strengthens the children's self-esteem.

Strong feelings such as anger overwhelm and thus frighten young children. A method for learning control from the inside and not being controlled from the outside will help children in the future when adults are not around. The anger emotion calls for action. But if children learn to speak out rather than strike out, they will not have to suffer the guilt or remorse afterward for an unacceptable act. As child development specialist Furman (1995) recommends:

> The identification and verbalization of feelings can be taught or reinforced in schools, child care centers, and family child care homes as an important part of the early childhood educator's job. (p. 37)

Expressing anger in words is not easy in the beginning. It does not come naturally for young children, whose communication skills are still limited. It is even more difficult for the child caught in the throes of an overwhelming emotion who finds it simpler to strike out physically, shout, or cry. Yet 3-, 4-, and 5-year-olds can learn the response of telling how they feel in words.

How do you teach them? First, you need to model this behavior yourself. When you become angry, tell the individual or the group how you feel and why you feel this way: "I feel very upset to see you dropping the tape recorder on the floor like that! If you break it no one can enjoy the music anymore," or "Luis and Victor, I am so angry to see you ganging up on Juan again! Two against one is not fair!" As Marion (1997) noted,

> Adults who are most effective in helping children manage anger, model responsible anger management by acknowledging, accepting, and taking responsibility for their own angry feelings and by expressing anger in direct and nonaggressive ways. (p. 65)

You must also convey to your children that their actions—not them as individuals—make you angry. You must show you still respect and like the children no matter how angry they get or how upset you feel over their actions. Show the children both verbally and nonverbally that you still accept them as good people.

You also must intervene *every time* the children display temper, and you must help them repeatedly to express their feelings in words: "Sarah, tell Jessica how you feel when she takes your book." "Roberto, don't hit Luther. Tell him how you feel." Make eye contact with the children. Help them to make eye contact with one another to diffuse their anger: "Roberto, look Luther in the eyes and tell him."

How will young, inexperienced children know what words to use when they are angry? As previously noted, you can help them learn the words through activities such as mounting a picture of an angry face and asking the children to help you tell how the person must feel. Write down words that express anger and mount them beside the face. What might they be? What about: *mad, upset, furious, enraged, irritated, irate, incensed?* Obviously, some of these are adult words, but if you use them yourself, as well as going over your list every time someone expresses anger, you may be surprised to hear children using them, too.

Teaching children to express anger in words is a time-consuming process, but so is all learning. If you believe children must gain inner control over their anger, and if you understand they must have some acceptable way to vent their feelings, then you will find it worthwhile to put in the time and effort necessary to divert anger's destructive energy into words. You will know you have been successful when the children begin telling one another, "Don't hit him, Jamar, tell him!"

If You Have Not Checked This Item: Some Helpful Ideas

■ Talk About Feelings

Establish a "feelings" corner in your room with pictures of people looking sad, angry, and glad. Ask the children to tell you what they feel when they look like that. If you have no pictures, make photocopies of feelings pictures from books. Provide a feelings hand puppet that the children can hold and talk to about the feelings they have.

■ Read a Book

Read books about feelings to a child or small group at any time of day, not only when tempers are short. ***When Sophie Gets Angry—Really, Really Angry …*** (Bang, 1999) is a brilliantly illustrated story for both boys and girls showing little Sophie going to extremes with her emotions: "She kicks. She screams. She wants to smash the world to smithereens." After she roars her red volcano roar, she cries. But then she goes outside where there are rocks and trees and birds. She climbs a tree and feels the wind and is comforted. Ask your children what comforts them when they are this angry.

In ***Sometimes I'm Bombaloo*** (Vail, 2002), Katie Honors tells the story about how she is usually a good kid, happy, and gives excellent hugs. But sometimes when her baby brother knocks down the beautiful castle she just made she becomes Bombaloo, scrunching up her face and using her feet and fists instead of her words. Then finally a laugh at something funny makes her Katie again. How would your listeners handle this?

Aggression

Aggression is not an emotion but often the expression of anger. It is the action an individual commonly takes as a result of anger or frustration. Hostile actions or angry words are intended to harm, defeat, or embarrass the person who caused the anger. Aggressive behavior in the classroom most commonly takes the form of hitting, throwing things, name-calling, spitting, biting, kicking, pushing or pulling, physically forcing someone to do something, restraining someone, destroying property, or forcefully taking someone else's possessions or turn.

Young children who have not learned to control their anger often resort to aggressive behavior. Children who have been neglected or treated harshly sometimes use aggression to strike out at the world around them. Children who have had to fend for themselves among older peers without much adult guidance may have learned aggressiveness as a survival strategy. Other children with highly permissive parents may have learned certain aggressive acts to get their own way by hitting or name-calling, for instance.

Research tells us that boys are more aggressive than girls. Since Helen Dawe's early observational study of the quarrels of preschool children in 1934, most findings have shown boys to be more aggressive (Brooks-Gunn & Matthews, 1979). Fabes, Eisenberg, Nyman, and Michealieu (1991) found that preschool boys expressed more anger than girls. Aggression, we realize, is an expression of anger. We can blame boys' aggression on genetics—physical development and hormones—but we also need to look at society's expectations for boys and girls as well as adult interpretations of their behaviors.

Adults tend to read different messages into the nonverbal behavior of girls and boys. In talking about gender differences in her class of 4-year-olds, Ilene described how some parent volunteers attributed angry or aggressive intent to boys' behavior, while interpreting the same kind of behavior quite differently in girls (Hyson, 2004). Society expects boys to be more aggressive than girls; thus boys are *allowed* to be more aggressive.

If aggressiveness were considered a common feminine trait, then no doubt the findings would quickly change.

Some seeming aggressiveness, however, is not done in anger but in play. Some young children, especially boys, engage in rough-and-tumble play using pushing, tackling, and restraining one another in fun. How can you tell the difference? Listening to their voices. Are their tones angry-sounding or more fun-like? Look at their faces and eyes. Do they show anger? Rough-and-tumble play usually has no place inside the classroom but may be allowed outside on the playground if it doesn't get too rough. If you have to stop the roughness, talk to the children involved and have them decide on a calmer mode of interacting.

How else can you help children of both genders control aggressive behavior? Putting negative feelings into words, as previously discussed, helps achieve inner control. But if their actions are physically aggressive against another child, they need to be stopped and firmly reminded that you will not let them hurt their friends. Focus most of your attention on the child who has been hurt, offering comfort and aid, while directing the aggressor into another activity until he or she calms down.

If You Have Not Checked This Item: Some Helpful Ideas

■ Redirect Aggressive Acts

Certain classroom activities lend themselves to the redirection of out-of-control children. Children with explosive tempers or who strike out aggressively can be redirected to pound a ball of clay or play dough with their hands, to throw a beanbag at a target, to punch a pillow, to pound with a hammer, to hit a tetherball, to kick a soccer ball, or use rhythm band percussion instruments. Activities that will calm overwrought children include finger painting, water play, sand play, working with play dough, or listening to music or a story.

■ Hold the Child on Your Lap

Sometimes you must physically restrain a child from hurting others. Because you are bigger, you can hold the child so she cannot hit or kick until she calms down enough to control herself. Hold the child on your lap and restrain her from using her arms. If she also kicks, you may need to remove her shoes. This child is totally out of control and needs your help to restore herself to normalcy. Do not lose control yourself. Children are afraid of their own overwhelming emotions. They need you to remain calm and to prevent them from doing damage. If you are in a rocking chair, rock back and forth, humming a tuneless song over and over. Finally ask the child if she feels calm enough for you to let her get up. If she can't tell you, she is not ready.

■ Read a Book

Little llama in *Llama Llama Mad at Mama* (Dewdney, 2007) sits in the shopping cart as his mama shops at the Shop-O-Rama store, but soon loses his patience and starts to whine. Finally he loses his temper and starts throwing things—all in rhyme. His mama calms him down by lifting him out of the cart and inviting him to help her shop. How would your listeners have handled this tantrum?

Bootsie Barker Bites (Bottner, 1992) tells the tale of the dominating Bootsie, who comes with her mother to visit the little girl narrator's mother and always ends up playing as roughly as a ferocious dinosaur, trying to bite and frighten the little girl. The girl finally resolves the problem next time, scaring Bootsie by pretending to be a dinosaur-hunting paleontologist.

Biting in preschool children sometimes starts as an impulsive act that is mishandled by adults when children are younger. Brazelton and Sparrow (2001) have this to say about it:

> Any impulsive behavior such as biting or hurting is frightening to the child. She doesn't know how to stop. She repeats it over and over as if she were trying to find out why it produces such a powerful response. Biting, scratching, and hitting all start out as normal exploratory behaviors. When adults overreact or disregard the behavior, the child will repeat the behavior as if to say, "I'm out of control. Help me!" (p. 40)

Deerwester (2006) suggests that you discreetly shadow the child who has been biting to prevent him from hurting again. She claims: "This is critical for hitting, pinching, and especially biting. The only way to stop those behaviors is to intercept the child *before* the behavior occurs" (p. 5).

■ Substitute a Biting Toy

One mother gave her biting child a little rubber doggie bone to hang around her neck for use when she had the urge to bite. Teachers need to talk to a biting child and ask what she could do instead of biting someone. Perhaps she would agree to use a biting toy.

CAN BE CALMED IN DIFFICULT OR DANGEROUS SITUATIONS

Fear

Fear first appears as an emotion in the second half of the first year of infancy, according to many psychologists. Somewhere between 5 and 9 months of age, babies begin to notice an unfamiliar face and are afraid of it. Before that point, their physical and cognitive development have not progressed to allow them to distinguish between friend and stranger. After that recognition occurs, infants see unfamiliar faces as a possible threat—until they learn differently.

Thus, the emotion of fear is caused by the presence of something threatening or the absence of safety and security (Izard, 1977, p. 356). Fear may result when the possibility of harm appears, when a strange person, object, or situation is confronted, and when specific fright-producing elements—heights, the dark, thunderstorms, emergencies, violent scenes on TV, and certain animals such as dogs and snakes—are present. When humans are afraid, they feel anxious and alarmed. They may tremble, cower, hide, run away, cling to someone, or cry, depending on their degree of fright. They often seek protection.

Fear is in some ways age-related. Young children are generally not afraid of heights, the dark, or animals before their second year. It is as though they really don't know enough to be frightened before then. As they grow older, children add new fears and drop some of the old ones. Fear, like distress, seems to serve as a warning signal for the human species. Reduce the threat or seek protection. When this warning feeling persists but is no longer useful to the young human, you as a teacher need to intervene.

We know, of course, that extreme fear can be paralyzing, but we need to realize that even lesser fears like anxiety produce tension of some sort: a tightening up of the body and the mind. Anxiety "is the most constricting of all the emotions" (Izard, 1977, p. 365). The anxious person has trouble relaxing and feeling at ease in tense situations.

Tense situations that may cause children to be fearful in a preschool classroom these days can be caused by any number of things: an adult raising her voice at a child, an out-of-control child hurting someone, an emergency such as a building evacuation because of fire or a bomb threat, a storm or natural disaster, or an accident causing personal injury. Even loud noises such as an emergency vehicle siren going by outside or the sudden loud banging of doors inside may cause children to tighten up, huddle together, or cry. When children see, hear, or sense the presence of something threatening, they become afraid.

It is up to you and your staff to help the children remain calm and in control no matter what happens. How can you do it? First of all, you must remain calm and in control yourself. Try to anticipate what emergencies you might face. Practice evacuation drills ahead of time. Show the children by your facial expression, voice, and actions that you are calm and not panicked. As McDevitt and Ormrod (2004) pointed out: "Children learn to guide their actions on the basis of other people's emotional expressions" (p. 376). They will look to you to see how you are handling any tense or threatening situation. Hyson (2004) says that "starting as early as 12 months, children are especially likely to look to adults for emotional information in new, uncertain situations, a process that has been called "social referencing" (p. 67). Be ready to show them your unruffled composure, your quiet voice, your confident actions.

For you to show fear in the face of danger can cause panic among the children. How will you respond to such an emergency event as a shooting, bombing, or explosion? If you fall apart, many of the children may too. As Farish (2001) tells us:

> Helping young children deal with their feelings and thoughts is especially challenging when we adults haven't had time to deal with our own reactions, when we are grieving, afraid, and angry ... we should remember that even very young children notice a great deal and they can quickly tune into any sorrow or anxiety that surrounds them. (p. 6)

You will need to anticipate such emergencies and discuss with the staff how each of you will handle them. Taking roles and acting out emergency situations with the staff ahead of time helps everyone understand their role and gain control of themselves. Walk staff through a practice fire drill without children before you involve the children. Afterward, observe to see which children follow your lead during emergencies or tense situations, and which cry or lose control. Should only one or two children be unable to contain their fear, you or one of the staff members can give support and comfort to them while you involve the others in a calming activity to take their minds off the situation.

If You Have Not Checked This Item: Some Helpful Ideas

■ Remove or Reduce the Cause of Fear

If you know what is causing the fear in a child, it may be possible to remove the cause. If you don't know, ask the child. You may find that she is fearful of an adult who will come to pick her up. Tell her you will contact her parent and work out another solution. Let her know that you will be right there with her no matter what happens. If a child is afraid of a dog on the playground you can take the child inside while another staff member shoos the dog away. If children express fear of lightning or thunder you can reduce the cause by pulling the curtains shut, gathering everyone together in a Happiness Circle on the floor and singing some funny songs (Beaty, 2004, p. 17). When children see violent scenes on television, it is important to talk about them in a class discussion where children can express their fears, and you can help them feel safe at school.

■ Give Support and Comfort to the Child

Fearful children can be comforted by being touched, hugged, held on your lap, rocked in a rocking chair, or sat close to while you talk quietly or read a story to them. Neuroscientists have found that a soothing touch causes the brain to release growth hormones. On the other hand, emotional stress needs to be released or it can cause the release of the steroid cortisol, high levels of which may interfere with connections between brain cells in children (Newberger, 1997, p. 5).

■ Allow Child to Cry

As mentioned previously, chemical toxins that have built up during stress can be released in tears. Do not stop a frightened child from crying. Talk soothingly to her and tell her it's okay to cry. Many young children release their fearful feelings through tears. Venting through crying is a catharsis. Later when it is appropriate, you can try to calm her down by holding her or taking softly to her.

■ Redirect Children's Attention with Calming Activities

Children in the grip of fear may be calmed down by certain art activities. Have them work with play dough. Squishing dough through their fingers or rolling it out on a countertop helps them release pent-up feelings. Finger painting is another activity that allows children to paint out their fears by swishing paint around with their fingers. Or they can get down on the floor and move the paint around on butcher paper with their arms and hands, or stamp their handprints on the paper with slaps that dissipate their fear. Play at the water table is also calming. Children can squirt water into containers with squeeze bottles, whip up bubbles with eggbeaters, blow bubbles in the water through straws, or pour water from one container to another.

■ Help Children to Verbalize Feelings with Puppets

Talk to the children in a small group with a soft, calm voice. When they see you are not afraid of the situation, they may calm down. Then you can offer them a chance to talk about how they feel and what made them feel that way. Children in the group may be surprised to hear that others feel the same as they do. Do not force shy or upset children to talk. Instead, you can go around to each child in a small group at first and ask him to whisper to you. If he allows it, you can then tell the others what he said. Sometimes this action opens up others to talk aloud. Bring in two hand puppets, one for you and one for someone from the group. Your puppet can talk quietly to the child's puppet telling how the situation made it feel and asking how the child's puppet feels. Pass the puppets around for others to participate.

■ Involve Children in Helping Others

Helping another child in a fear-producing situation can take the helpers out of themselves and their own fears. Not all children are able to do this, but those who can often find that their own fears are lessened. They can look at a book together, play with puppets, put a puzzle together, or listen to a music tape with a child who seems upset by the situation. Children are more likely to give help to another when they are with someone. You can ask two children to help a third by playing with materials together. All three children will then be distracted from the fear situation.

■ Read a Book

Fear of the Dark

Francis the Scaredy Cat (Boxall, 2002) tells a simple story in large font words about the cat Francis who loves the boy Ben. But he is secretly afraid of the dark and the hissy monster he hears in a tree on stormy nights. One night Ben doesn't come home as usual, and Francis is afraid the hissy monster might have captured Ben, so he swallows his fears, goes out, and climbs up the tree to rescue him. He finds the monster to be a large but kind black cat, who in turn rescues Francis and helps him climb down. What are your children's fears?

In *The Owl Who Was Afraid of the Dark* (Tomlinson, 2000), Plop the baby barn owl tells his parents he doesn't want to be a night bird because the dark is too scary. His mother sends him out to find out more about the dark from a boy with fireworks, an old lady remembering good times, a Boy Scout at a campfire, and a girl who gives him a sock to hang up for Santa Claus. Now he can't wait till it gets dark.

"I'm Not Scared" (Allen, 2007) tells a simple story of baby owl who decides to take a stroll in the moonlit woods one night with his little owl doll Owly. One by one a badger, a bear, a bat, and finally father owl, pop up saying "Don't be scared, Baby Owl." The little

owl replies fiercely, "I'm not scared!" but the illustrations show him acting scared. As the sun comes up father owl reads him a bedtime story and tucks him in, telling him it's okay to be a little scared of the dark.

Fear of Fire

Stop Drop and Roll (Cuyler, 2001) tells the story of Jessica, a first grader who worries about everything. They are studying about fires, smoke alarms, and fire drills at school and what to do if you should catch on fire: stop, drop, and roll. She is so upset about it all that she can't get the words right: "stop, slop, and troll," or "Mop, pop, and bowl." Finally at Tom's birthday party when he lights the candles on his cake and Jessica sees the fire, she yells: STOP, DROP and ROLL!

Fear of Storms

Aunt Minnie and the Twister (Prigger, 2002) tells the tale of a Kansas woman in the 1930s who inherited nine orphaned nephews and nieces who live with her on her farm. When she wants the kids' attention, she stands on the front porch and rings an old school bell, and the kids come running. One summer when black storm clouds rolled across the sky, Minnie rushes to the porch and clangs the bell. The kids come running, hold onto one another, and follow fearless Minnie into the root cellar. It is a tornado. They are safe, but the old farmhouse is completely turned around. So they put on a new front porch, a new back room, and celebrate with a picnic because they still have each other. What do your children's families do in a storm?

Fear of Being Left Alone

In *Don't Forget to Come Back!* (Harris, 2004), the feisty girl narrator, learns that a babysitter is coming and her parents are going out for the evening. She tries to stop them by telling about all the bad things that will happen when they are gone, especially that a moose will come in and eat her up. But nothing stops them. Sarah, the babysitter, turns out to be cool, letting the girl do silly things. The next morning, the girl wakes up to find her parents didn't forget to come back and she tells them that Sarah didn't let a single moose in the house.

 ## OVERCOMES SADNESS FEELINGS IN APPROPRIATE MANNER

The emotion of sadness may not be as prevalent as emotions such as anger or happiness; nevertheless, some sadness from a variety of causes is sure to be experienced. Fabes et al. (1991) found that girls seem to express more sadness than boys, who express anger more often. How is this emotion expressed? Facial features will alert teachers that something is wrong. Often down-turned corners of the mouth, tearful eyes, or outright crying tell the tale. Hanging of the head, speaking in low tones, or withdrawing in silence are other expressions. Denham (1998) found that the subtlety and complexity of children's emotional expressions increases markedly throughout the preschool years (p. 28).

What causes sadness? Children become sad when they experience a loss, when they want something they can't have or don't get, when a toy gets broken, when friends move away or they themselves move, when they must stay away from home for long periods, when family members become sick and die, or when pets become sick and die. The most severe form of sadness is, of course, the grief felt when someone close dies.

Death is especially difficult for preschool children to understand or accept, just as it is for adults. Young children, however, often expect that the deceased person will wake up or come back to life. As Hopkins (2002) noted: "Preschoolers believe strongly in the power of their wishes, which often leads them to conclude that death is temporary, reversible or partial" (p. 41). But some children are so overcome that they cannot seem to stop crying.

If You Have Not Checked This Item: Some Helpful Ideas

■ Demonstrate Sympathy

Teachers can best help children who are experiencing sadness by leaving them alone when they need to be, talking quietly with them when they are ready, and showing sympathy in words and deeds. Hugging them or holding and rocking can be helpful. Giving the child a stuffed animal to hold may help.

■ Provide a Quiet Space

Just as with the other emotions, children need to express sadness in appropriate ways. Let them cry quietly if they need to. Provide them with a comfortable place to sit away

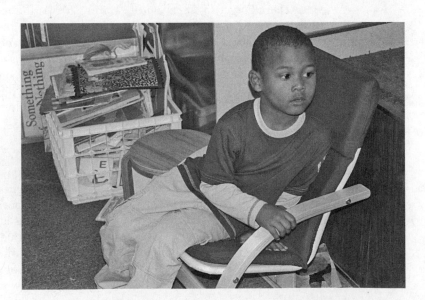

Provide children with a private space where they can be away from the group to relax or calm themselves.

from everyone. A rocking chair, a beanbag chair, or a clump of floor pillows can be moved into a corner. Have the child help if she can. Such a private space is important. As Seefeldt and Wasik (2006) remind us:

> Young children, like all humans, need space to be alone. Wherever or whatever it is, this space is set aside where children can go to be away from the group to think, relax, or calm themselves (pp. 95–96).

■ Give the Child Time

Think of yourself and how you deal with sadness. Sometimes it just takes time. Allow time for the child to come back into herself. Some may take longer than others. But be sure to offer her activity possibilities to join when she is ready or things to do on her own such as making a puzzle, dressing a doll, listening to a music tape, or feeding the classroom animal pet.

■ Talk Privately to the Child

Some Head Start classrooms use a strategy called Pillow Talk when the children have settled down on their cots for their afternoon naps. Teachers go around talking quietly to individuals, making sure to spend enough time with children who may be emotionally upset. As Soundy and Stout (2002) described it:

> Pillow Talk is a ritual that can anchor the day for the children. Regular and predictable one-on-one talks with the teacher give a child a sense of security. They also offer a chance to discuss issues that might never get talked about otherwise and allow children to bring out and express their private "inner songs." (p. 21)

■ Read a Book

Feeling Sad

The book *Yesterday I Had the Blues* (Frame, 2003) tells the tale of an African-American city boy who describes himself, his family, and his friends in terms of the colors of their feelings. When he has the blues (sadness), it is not "the broken skateboard blues," but the "hold a pillow wish it was tomorrow blues." Next day he has the greens, while his dad has the grays, the "don't ask for a new skateboard till tomorrow grays." That's okay because what they all have is a family, and that is golden.

In *I Miss You Every Day* (Taback, 2007), a little girl has such strong longings for her grandparents, who have gone back home after a visit, that she imagines wrapping herself up and mailing herself to them! The illustrations are double-page spreads showing the process of how she would look in a package with a ribbon around it, sending it to the post office, and then air-mailing it on a plane till it arrives in her grandparents' mailbox. One line of rhyming text on top of each page describes what is happening, interspersed with the words, "I miss you every day."

Moving

In *Two Cool Coyotes* (Lund, 1999), a talking-animal story, coyote pup Frank has one best friend, Angelina, who lives in the den next door and plays all day with him. She is one of a kind. But one day Angelina has to leave with her family. They exchange bandanas and promise to be best friends forever. Frank cries for 2 days. Finally a new coyote family moves in with a pup Frank's age named Larry. Soon the two of them are playing together, not exactly like Angelina, but Larry is one of a kind, too.

Lost Pet

In *Patches Lost and Found* (Kroll, 2001), Jenny, a little school girl, is sad because she has to write a story when she would much rather draw pictures. Then she is really sad when she gets home and finds that her pet guinea pig Patches is missing. She draws lost and found pictures and puts them up around the neighborhood. Finally, her neighbor, Mr. Scooter, finds Patches. By then Jenny has so many pictures of the whole episode that her story is laid out for her. She just has to write the words.

Death

Reading a book to a child does not overcome the grief and sadness caused by the death of a loved one. Even the death of a pet can be traumatic for a child. But sometime later, the child might be able to listen to a book about another child whose pet has died. In *Goodbye Mousie* (Harris, 2001), a 3-year-old boy gets up one morning to find that Mousie won't wake up. His father tells him Mousie is dead. The boy won't believe it, but is soon shedding tears. They bury Mousie in a shoe box in the back yard with a sign to mark the spot and two sparklers. The boy tells Mousie he is mad at him for being dead, but sad too. Finally, he says goodbye.

 ## HANDLES SURPRISING SITUATIONS WITH CONTROL

Surprise

Surprise is different from the other emotions in that it lasts only for a moment, although its results may continue for some time with young children. A sudden or unexpected external event causes a reaction of surprise or startle. The event could be a loud noise such as an explosion or clap of thunder at one extreme, or the unexpected appearance of a person at the other extreme. A startled person's mind goes blank for an instant, and his muscles contract quickly. He may even jump or let out a sound if the incident is surprising enough. Depending on the situation, the person may be shocked, bewildered, confused, or embarrassed because of his reaction. Or he could be delighted.

Although a startle reflex appears in babies a few hours after birth, this reflex does not seem to be the same as the emotion of surprise, which occurs in infants between the fifth and seventh month. By that time, enough cognitive development has occurred to enable the infant to form expectations (Izard, 1977, p. 283). Because everything is new for the child, there will be many startling events in her young life. If most of her surprises are pleasant ones, she will come to view surprises positively. If the opposite is true, then surprises may cause the child to cry or exhibit defensive behavior.

Many mothers help prepare their children for surprises, perhaps unintentionally, by playing low-key surprise games such as peekaboo with their children. The surprise is always a pleasant one: the revealing of mother's hidden face. But if children are scolded or ridiculed too severely at home when they cry or make a fuss over unexpected happenings, they may become fearful of anything different whether or not it is sudden.

On the other hand, most adults view surprise as pleasant. Their experience has taught them this. Young children do not necessarily show the same response. Perhaps because their experience is limited or because the occurrence of sudden happenings leaves them overwhelmed, they tend not to greet happily unexpected things as adults do. Most young children, for instance, do not react happily to surprise birthday parties. Many young children, in fact, are more likely to cry or withdraw. It may take some time for the shock to wear off and for them to become their pleasant selves again. Sensitive adults will not impose such startling events on children. Let children enjoy the pleasant anticipation of parties, rather than the startling surprise.

What about the children in your center or classroom? How do they respond to the unexpected? They need to be prepared for it in their lives, and they need to be able to control their responses. Surprise serves the useful function of preparing an individual to deal with an unexpected event. But if a child's reaction is one of such alarm as to immobilize her, then you need to help her deal with it in a better way.

What are some startling events you might anticipate? Most centers have fire alarms that they may or may not be able to control. Ask your building supervisor if your children can have a chance to practice a fire drill with the alarm until they are able to do it with ease. Practicing simulated emergency situations is one of the best ways to learn to deal with real emergencies. In addition to practice, the children can learn to handle sudden changes or surprising events by acting the way you do. You need to be calm and collected yourself, modeling the behavior you would like the youngsters to emulate.

Some children go to pieces when they are startled even by pleasant surprises. They may be the ones who have not developed enough self-esteem or a sense of trust in the people around them. These children may cry, cling, or withdraw long after the event is past. How can you help them?

If You Have Not Checked This Item: Some Helpful Ideas

■ Read a Book

Children may be helped to overcome their negative responses if they hear how others like themselves deal with surprises. Books about startling situations should be read not only to a group of children, but also to individuals who have exhibited a poor emotional response to a surprise.

Granddad bakes a surprise birthday cake for Grandma in *Whopper Cake* (Wilson & Hillenbrand, 2007) that is sure to be a surprise for all your listeners. Although he follows the recipe carefully: 4 fresh eggs (in go 86), 2 cups flour (in go 10—10 bags, that is), 1 cup cocoa (in go 24—24 boxes, that is), it soon appears he will need a bigger mixing bowl (the bed of his pickup, that is). As the hot July sun bakes the cake and it starts raising (10 feet high, that is), a crowd gathers to wait for Grandma to come home. Your listeners will wait breathlessly till you turn the page and everybody yells: "Surprise!" Grandma loves the whopper cake and has only one wish. Have your readers guess what it is.

Stuck in the Mud (Clarke, 2007) seems to be a traditional tale where one of hen's chicks gets stuck in the mud of the barnyard, and everyone who comes to help pull him out one-by-one gets stuck there too: the hen, the cat, the dog, the sheep, the horse, and even the farmer. But then, surprise! Turn the pull-out page and you'll see the chick jumping out of the mud by himself. He was never stuck in the first place! And he thanks them all for playing in the mud with him.

In *What Pet to Get?* (Dodd, 2008), Jack wants a pet, but he doesn't know what kind to get. First he says an elephant, but his mother wonders how they could take it on vacation. (Gigantic pictures of the elephant and all his choices fill the pages.) Then he considers a lion, but his mother thinks it might frighten the mail carrier. What about a polar bear? He wouldn't like central heating. A Tyrannosaurus Rex? No, they are extinct. A giraffe? Too tall. A hippo? Too wide. And on and on. Finally Jack decides on a dog. His mother agrees, so they start out in their car to choose a "lovely little puppy." But where is the surprise? Open the fold-out page and you will see: A huge, wild-looking, wolflike dog in a stud collar called "Fang!"

In *Big Bug Surprise* (Gran, 2007) Prunella, a little girl bug collector, covers the glass case of her favorite bug with a sheet to take for show-and-tell. She knows everything about bugs, which she proceeds to tell everyone she sees and bore them. They all go ho-hum, "not now Prunella." When it is finally her turn to show-and-tell, the surprise is on her. A bee flies in the window, which Prunella identifies it as a queen bee—they never fly alone. In comes a swarm of bees, following their queen. The children scream. But Prunella knows just what to do and soon has the swarm outside. Then she shows the class her surprising, incredible dung beetle—nature's pooper-scooper. The class yells yuck, gross, nasty, and—tell us more, Prunella. And she does.

■ Make a Surprise Bag

Give each child in a small group a paper grocery bag. Have them go to one of the learning centers and put an item in it. You make one, too. Members of the group should keep their eyes closed. When everyone is ready have the children try to guess what is in each bag, one-by-one. If no one guesses, have the bag holder shout "surprise" and pull out the item.

SHOWS FONDNESS, AFFECTION, LOVE TOWARD OTHERS

Affection

Young children learn affection when those around them are affectionate. They learn to love when those around them show them love. They develop fondness when their caregivers give them consistent caring and love. From infancy on, fondness, affection, and love are as necessary for children's growth and development as food and water. Without them, an infant may eventually wither away and even die.

Greenspan (1997) described the important stage of infant development, when "caregiver and child mutually fall in love," that is necessary for the later blossoming of the child's capacity to feel empathy and love (p. 50). He tells how the parent–child duo "create a matched pair of radiant grins, one on an infant face, the other on an adult's; a chorus of purrs or coos or giggles; smiles at rocking or being rocked; whoops of delight at swinging or being swung" (p. 50). In fact, Goleman (1997) admitted that "Making love is perhaps the closest approximation in adult life to the intimate attunement between infant and mother" (p. 101).

If such affection has not been expressed between children and their primary caregivers at birth or soon after, young children may have difficulty showing fondness, affection, or love to others around them. It is not too late for you and your team of teachers or caregivers to help correct this situation. As "significant others" in a child's life, you may be the ones to offer such unconditional affection and love to each child in your class—no matter who they are, what they look or act like, or where they come from. All young children need this warmth from the adults around them if they are to reciprocate and learn to show warmth to others. You need to forge a real connection with them, as discussed in Chapter 3 if they are to fashion one with you and the others in the class.

Do you have trouble with such a notion? Are you, perhaps, not an affectionate person yourself, and thus find it difficult to show affection to others? It is important that you review your role as a teacher or caregiver of young children. Young children need warm and affectionate adults around them. You may want to reconsider your position if you cannot respond in this manner.

Even though the child may not have received such unconditional love from an adult in his family as described earlier, classroom adults can show such affection and love through:

1. Nearness (standing, sitting, holding on lap)

2. Touch (hugs, pats, arm around shoulders)

3. Nonverbal cues (smiles, eye contact, nods, waves, handshakes, handholds)

4. Verbal affirmations ("I'm so glad to see your happy face today!")

Most children will respond to your warm attention with smiles, touches, and hugs in return. But some may hold back and be slower to show affection or make genuine connections with the adults and children in the classroom. These may be the children who have not formed a strong attachment with the primary caregivers in their family. Do not give up on them. If you observe that any of your children do not seem to exhibit some of the four displays of fondness, affection, or love listed, you may want to try the following.

If You Have Not Checked This Item: Some Helpful Ideas

■ Read a Book

Mama, Do You Love Me? (Joosse, 1991) is the classic arctic story of a little Native Alaskan girl, Dear One, asking her mother how much she loves her. When her mother replies in the affirmative, the little girl "ups the ante" on every other page by playing a what-if game. "What if I put salmon in your parka, ermine in your mittens, and lemmings in your mukluks?" The mother would be angry, but still she would love her—to the end.

In *Papa, Do You Love Me?* (Joosse, 2005) the same author moves the story to Africa with a little Maasai boy, Tender Heart, asking his papa the same question. When the boy asks, how much he loves him, the father answers in African terms about warriors, elders, wildebeests, hippos, and resting under a Greenheart tree. The little boy keeps asking what-if questions, but he cannot discover one thing that would keep his father from loving him.

A unique book in the colors and countenances of the Southwest, *Calor* (Pena, 1995) means "warmth" in Spanish. An Indian/Hispanic child offers a sentence in Spanish above the same sentence in English on one page with a brilliant illustration on the next of Navajos and Hopi people, demonstrating the meaning of warmth: of mother's love, of grandmother's warmth, the power of the uncles' warmth, of warmth created when people dance, of baking bread in the *horno*, of giving gifts of baskets and pottery, and finally the love warmth in the heart for everyone who has filled his life with happiness.

An Asian, African-American, and Anglo child feel tenderness and love from their families in *K Is for Kiss Good Night, A Bedtime Alphabet* (Sardegna, 1994) as the children are tucked in and the lights turned down.

In *Love Is a Family* (Downey, 2001) the little Anglo girl, Lily, complains to her mother that their family is too small—no father, no brothers, no babies, no sisters. She thinks their family will look weird at Family Fun Night at her school, with only the two of them. But as it turns out, there are families full of stepdads and stepmoms, half brothers and half sisters, single moms and single dads—all of them laughing and showing their love by being together. That's what makes a family, Lily learns: love!

Full, Full, Full of Love (Cooke & Howard, 2003) shows African-American Jay Jay going to his Grannie's house for Sunday dinner. Jay Jay is so hungry he can't wait, but Granny hugs and cuddles him, has him feed the fishes, get out the dishes, and watch for the others to come: uncles, aunties, cousins, friends, his Mama and Daddy. And then there is food in overflowing rhymes: buttery peas, macaroni and cheese, chicken and yams, potatoes and ham until everyone is full of: hugs and kisses, tasty dishes, all kinds of fishes, and full, full, full of love.

■ Bring Two Together

Start with two children whom you will bring together to hear one of the preceding stories or to tell one to you. One of the children can be openly receptive of affection and love; the other, more reticent. Be sure to show them both your affection and love. Afterward, ask them if they can include one other child in this reading group and show him or her the book just heard read while you remove yourself. Later do the same with two other children and a puzzle or little people figures to act out the story.

 # SHOWS INTEREST, ATTENTION IN CLASSROOM ACTIVITIES

Interest (Excitement)

Hyson (2004) tells us: "Interest—what some may call curiosity—seems to be a fundamental human emotion. Teachers can serve as important models of interest and fascination in finding out more about the world" (p. 69). Interest is the most frequent and pervasive positive emotion that human beings possess. Children show interest by directing their eyes toward an object or person who catches their attention, and then exploring it with their eyes and, if possible, their other senses. Interested people are alert, active, self-confident, and curious. Interest is the motivator for much of children's learning, as well as for their development of creativity and intelligence. Thus it is crucial for growing children to have their interest stimulated by the interesting people, materials, and ideas in their environment.

Psychologists believe that change or novelty is the basis for the interest emotion. The novelty of an object first attracts the person's attention. Once he is aroused and curious, he is motivated to find out more about the object, thus increasing his knowledge, skill, and understanding. Interest, in other words, is the impulse to know, which then sustains our attention in the things we are curious about. Excitement is the most intense form of interest.

For an infant to perceive an object, she must first pay attention to it for a time. It is the emotion of interest that keeps her attention. Without this emotion, she may become passive, dull, and apathetic, with little initiative or movement. The final result may be developmental lags or even retardation.

The interest emotion appears very early in an infant's life. Interest is evident in the attention she shows to the human face: eyes riveted to her mother's face and turning to follow it. Objects such as rattles, bottles, mobiles, her own fingers and toes are fascinating fields for exploration with her eyes and then her mouth. Later she shifts from external exploration to manipulation. What will objects do when you kick them, throw them, drop them?

When he throws his cereal dish on the floor, the child is not being naughty, only normal. He finds out about his world this way. Acts like this against physical objects obviously teach the child many additional things about the feelings of the people around him. If the family is strict or harsh or punitive about his actions, this will inhibit such interest-motivated exploration. If the child is punished too many times, he may cease exploring altogether, which poses dire consequences for his future development. On the other hand, encouragement to explore, play with things, and be curious will stretch his mind, his senses, and his physical skills.

Poverty frequently interferes with the development of strong interests and attention because the variety of objects or activities available in the child's environment is often limited. In cases where the parents must also spend much of their energy struggling to survive, they may have little or no time to interact with their youngsters. The parents may, in fact, actively discourage them from exploratory endeavors. If, in addition, negative emotions dominate the atmosphere, interest quickly fades away.

Thus it is important for you to know which children in your classroom have retained their native curiosity and which have not. The interest and attention individual children pay to classroom activities may give you a clue. But you need to remember that interest is stimulated by novelty and change, so a truer test might be to set up a new activity area and observe which children notice it, who plays in it, and for how long. Because interests by now are very much individualized and personalized, what interests one child will not necessarily cause a flicker of attention in another. For this reason you must provide a wide range of activities and materials for your group. Remember also to add something new once in a while.

The basic interest emotion also affects attention span. Children must first be attracted to an activity through interest that is activated by change or novelty. If they find the activity interesting, they are likely to spend more time doing it and pay more attention to it. Although we know that age and maturity have a great deal to do with how long a child's interest can be held (i.e., the older, the longer), we can also increase the attention span by providing highly attractive materials and activities. Because children must attend (i.e., pay attention) to learn, the length of attention span is crucial in every learning situation. Teachers thus need to know what kinds of things 3-, 4-, and 5-year-olds find attractive.

If You Have Not Checked This Item: Some Helpful Ideas

■ Focus on the Self

Although children's interests are widely varied, all humans—especially egocentric youngsters—have a basic interest in themselves. Think of something new and different about the child who shows little interest in center activities. Make it some kind of question, problem, or challenge that is intriguing and fun. Then turn the child loose with it. For instance, have a Cool Shoe Contest that the child who shows little interest can start. Have her make some kind of paper design that she can tape to the top of her shoes. This makes her Ms. Cool Shoe for the day. Then have her slap out a rhythm with her shoes, which you tape-record. Play the tape. Let other children try to copy it and tape-record their own shoe slaps. Let her choose who will be the next Mr. or Ms. Cool Shoe.

■ Arouse Curiosity

Children love mysteries. Invite a mystery guest (an adult dressed in a costume and mask) to visit the classroom. Let children guess who it is. Or bring a big stuffed animal in a bag and let the children guess what it is. Give them hints about what it eats or the noise it makes. Maybe the slow-to-respond child would like to think of a name for it once it is out of the bag.

■ Read a Book

Saturday Night at the Dinosaur STOMP (Shields, 1997) is a splashy enough book to attract almost any child, especially those with a yen for these prehistoric monsters. Its illustrations seem to leap and stomp, twirl and tromp just like the dinosaurs themselves, to the rhythm of the Ankylosaurus drumming on his hard-shelled back: Boomalacka, boomalacka, whack, whack, whack! Afterward, children can make dinosaur heads from paper bags, have dinosaur races with dinosaur figurines in trucks from the block center, or tape-record their own voices singing like the different dinosaurs in the story. What else might grab their attention?

All of Yolen's *"How Do Dinosaurs ..."* books create enormous interest and arouse instant curiosity of children who can't get enough of these prehistoric monsters. *How Do Dinosaurs Go to School?* (Yolen, 2007), one of the latest, is just as electrifying. A giant yellow and blue-striped ceratosaurus on the cover not only shows off for the teacher but grabs a reader's attention right away. No books look quite like Yolen's with its double-page spread for each of the comical giants rough-housing, stealing a lunch bag, fidgeting, or stirring up the classroom in one way or another. Your children can enjoy making their own outrageously colored dinosaur masks and playing these roles themselves.

I Saw an Ant in a Parking Lot (Prince, 2006), with its comical cartoon ant and big face of Dot, the parking lot attendant on the cover, are sure to arouse the children's curiosity. What's going on here? Dot narrates the story in rhyme about the ant and a red minivan heading toward the same spot. Neither sees the other, but Dot sees both. What to do? She finally saves the day by tossing her chocolate-covered donut at the spot. The van screeches to a stop. The ant hops on the donut and soon is sharing breakfast with Dot back in Dot's station.

☑ SMILES, SEEMS HAPPY MUCH OF THE TIME

Joy

Joy, the most positive of the emotions, is also the most elusive. Seek it and you may not find it. Try to experience it directly, and it may elude you. But live a normal life, and it will appear spontaneously. Joy does not occur so much on its own as it does as a by-product of something else: a pleasant experience, a happy thought, a good friendship. In other words, this emotion is indicative of feeling good about oneself, others, and life in general. Hyson (2004) says: "Feelings of joy are accompanied by confidence, vigor, and self-esteem. Joy opens our minds and hearts to new experiences, making our mental processes more creative and flexible" (p. 113).

The absence of joy tells us that the child is not feeling good about these things. We need to observe children carefully to see where they stand in regard to this important indicator of inner feelings, and we need to take positive actions if this emotion is missing.

Joy is the feeling of happiness that may precede or follow a pleasant experience: sensory pleasure such as a hug, a kiss, or a back rub; psychological pleasure such as the remembrance of good times; and the anticipation of seeing a loved one or of having fun with friends. For young children the most reliable source of joy is play (Hyson, 2004, p. 113). People express joy with smiles, laughter, the lighting up of eyes, increased heartbeat, an inner feeling of confidence, a sense of well-being, or a glow. The emotion itself is fleeting, but the good feeling it creates may color a person's actions and responses for many hours.

As with the other emotions, the capacity for joy is inherited and is different for each individual (Izard, 1977, p. 239). Its development, however, depends greatly on how the mother or primary caregiver responds to joy in the infant. A person cannot teach another person to be happy, but she can influence the occurrence of happiness by creating a pleasant environment in the first place, then responding positively when joy occurs.

Babies may smile during the first days of life. At first they smile in reverie or dreams, then during waking hours when a pleasant, high-pitched voice talks to them, and finally, by the fifth week at the sight of a friendly face coming close (Izard, 1977, p. 239). The elicited smile that comes as a result of a voice occurs within the first week. By the second or third month, infants are smiling spontaneously without seeing or hearing anyone—that is, if they have been responded to pleasantly by their caregivers. But the human face remains the single most effective stimulus to smiling (Izard, 1977, p. 248).

Laughter has its own developmental sequence. It first occurs between 5 and 9 weeks, usually in response to patty-cake-type games or tickling. Scientists believe a child's motor development has some relationship to development of laughter. But both laughter and smiling can be stimulated by the same expressions of joy on the part of another person.

Situations that discourage or prevent the emotion of joy from occurring include poor physical health, fatigue or boredom, harsh treatment or neglect, conditions of poverty that limit a child's possibilities, and lack of joy on the part of caregivers.

Children often experience humor when in a happy, joyful state.

Recognition of a familiar person, object, or situation helps stimulate or encourage the expression of joy. Whereas change and novelty seem to stimulate the emotion of interest, familiarity and being comfortable with things set the stage for joy. Keep this in mind in your classroom. A little change is challenging, no change at all is boring, and too much change is overwhelming for young children. They need a stable schedule of daily events they can depend on and a physical arrangement of equipment that does not change too drastically overnight. Then they can look forward with joy to coming to the center every day.

Humor

McGhee (2005) believes that the relationship between joy and humor is a two-way street. In other words, children are more likely to experience humor when in a happy, joyful state. They sometimes seem to think everything is funny and burst into giggles, silliness, and laughter. But they can also create joy and happiness that wasn't previously there by engaging in humor (p. 17).

Thus, some of the children's books described here are about creating joy by doing or having funny things happen.

If You Have Not Checked This Item: Some Helpful Ideas

■ Talk with Parents

Children who express no joy probably are not very happy. You will need to converse with the joyless child's parents in a sensitive manner, trying to elicit how the child reacts at home, whether any particular problems or pressures are affecting him, and what his basic personality is like. Is the child fundamentally happy? What are his favorite foods, colors, toys, activities? What makes him laugh? Perhaps you can use some of these favorites as a focus for an activity to make him feel joyful.

■ Be a Joyful Person

Children and others feel joy when they meet a person who thinks they are delightful and wants to be around them. Make yourself that kind of person.

■ Read a Book

I Love It When You Smile (McBratney, 2005) is the story of mother and baby kangaroo. Baby Roo feels grumpy and won't smile. Nothing the mother can do makes him smile. He doesn't even want to play with his friends. Tickles, flipping, peek-a-boos—nothing works. So off they go looking for breakfast with Roo in his mother's pouch, and his mother doing silly hops down a hill. At the bottom is a muddy pool, and suddenly she slips, slides, and slops into it. When Roo sees his mother covered with mud from top to bottom he just has to—smile.

In *Ha, Ha, Baby!* (Petty, 2008) Human Baby is not laughing. His face looks like thunder. Nothing anyone can do makes him laugh: not Ma's tickling, Pa's tossing him up, Grandma's peek-a-boos, Grandpa's bubbles, the dog's tricks, the cat's tail-chasing. Nothing. Then the little Brother comes home and informs everyone that maybe Baby doesn't want to laugh today. So he comes up close and starts a staring contest with Baby. Absolutely no laughing. You know who wins: Brother—because Baby can't keep himself from grinning, chuckling, and then chortling: OUR BABY LAUGHED! Huge faces fill the pages, and large font print makes it easy for emergent readers to follow along. Have your children try staring at a partner without smiling or laughing and see how long they can hold it.

Aliens Love Underpants (Freedman & Cort, 2008) bursts with built-in laughter. Just the word "underpants" alone starts children giggling. Then, when they see the pictures of the zany-looking aliens on the cover wearing underpants on heads and bottoms, they can't wait to open up the book. A spaceship of aliens lands in your backyard and begins playing with the underpants on the clothesline. They start diving into long johns, bouncing off an undie trampoline, and holding undie races—all in rhyme. Can your children paint their own pictures of aliens in underpants, making them look even funnier?

■ Childhood Emotions in the Classroom

Table 4-1 helps you see at a glance the causes and results of these common feelings. Such awareness can assist you in helping children develop more positive responses in emotional situations.

Table 4—1   Childhood emotions in the classroom

Emotion	Common Cause	Possible Results
Distress	Separation from loved one, abandonment	Crying, whining, clinging
Anger	Physical or psychological restraint, insult	Red face, loud words, screaming, aggression
Fear	Presence of threat	Tightening of muscles, trembling, clinging, crying
Sadness	Loss, friends leaving, sickness, death	Crying, withdrawing, head hanging down, low tones
Surprise (startle)	Loud noise, unexpected appearance or event	Crying, withdrawing, clinging
Interest	Change, novelty	Looking at something, exploration with senses, wide eyes
Affection	Displays of affection toward child	Standing, sitting near teacher, others; touches, hugs others; smiles, holds hands
Joy	A pleasant experience, happy thoughts, friendship	Smiling, laughing, lighting up of eyes, talking happily

OBSERVING, RECORDING, AND INTERPRETING EMOTIONAL DEVELOPMENT

To understand and interpret the emotional growth of individual children, it is helpful to fill out the emotional development section of the Child Development Checklist for specific children. Using data gathered during observations, her teacher filled out this section of the checklist for Sheila, the child discussed in Chapter 3, as shown in Figure 4–2

Sheila has connected with the teacher. However, she does not seem to be all that comfortable with the other children: She does not play with them yet, and she runs to the teacher whenever anything upsetting happens. The other important indicator is the fact that she does not smile or seem happy. Perhaps Sheila does not display happiness because she is ill at ease with the other children.

This observation was made at the beginning of the school year before all of the children were used to each other and to the center. Some of the activities listed under "If You Have Not Checked This Item: Some Helpful Ideas" may help Sheila feel more comfortable with the others. The fact that Sheila goes around the room trying out everything is a sign that she will eventually want to get involved in everything. Perhaps Sheila can do an art activity with another child. Her teacher may want to pair Sheila with a child who is already at ease and will thus help Sheila feel more at home in the classroom.

CHILD DEVELOPMENT CHECKLIST

Name _Sheila_ **Observer** _Connie_

Program _Head Start_ **Dates** _10/22_

Directions:

Put an **X** for items you see the child perform regularly. Put **N** for items where there is no opportunity to observe. Leave all other items blank.

Item	Evidence	Dates
2. Emotional Development		
__x__ Releases stressful feelings in appropriate manner	Lets teacher calm her down when Beth takes her crayon	10/22
__x__ Expresses anger in words rather than negative actions	When Beth takes her crayon she says to her: "That's not fair!"	10/22
__x__ Can be calmed in difficult or dangerous situations	Yes. Lets teacher calm her	10/22
__x__ Overcomes sad feelings in appropriate manner	Shows sadness when mother leaves but lets teacher redirect her	10/22
_____ Handles surprising situations with control	Cries or runs to teacher when upsetting things happen	10/22
__x__ Shows fondness, affection, love toward others	Touches, stays close to teacher	10/22
__x__ Shows interest, attention in classroom activities	Goes around room trying out everything	10/22
_____ Smiles, seems happy much of the time	Rarely smiles, no evidence of being happy	10/22

Figure 4–2 Emotional Development for Sheila

LEARNING ACTIVITIES

1. Observe the children in your classroom for a week in the eight areas of emotional control. Which children exhibit behavior that seems to show emotional control? Which ones have not yet learned inner control? How can you help them? Write out and discuss a plan with your supervisor.

2. Choose a child who has trouble allowing his or her aggressive behavior to be redirected. Observe the child for three mornings, making a time sampling of the behavior. Use some of the ideas as discussed in Chapter 3 to see if you can reduce the number of times this negative behavior occurs. What are the results of your follow-up observation?

3. Work with one of the children in your classroom who has difficulty expressing his or her anger in words. What actions can you take to help the child? Observe and record the results.

4. Work with a child who seems to exhibit fear and read one of the books described in the chapter. Describe the results.

5. Choose a child for whom you have checked "Smiles, seems happy much of the time." Observe this child on three different days. Which of the other items can you check on the checklist based on your observations? What is your evidence for each checkmark? What conclusions can you make about this child based on these observations? Do you need any additional evidence to make conclusions?

SUGGESTED READINGS

Carlson, F. M., & Nelson, B. G. (2006). Redirecting aggression with touch. *Dimensions of Early Childhood, 34*(3), 9–15.

Fallin, K., Wallinga, C., & Coleman, M. (2001). Helping children cope with stress in the classroom setting. *Childhood Education, 78*(1), 17–24.

Fox, L., & Lentini, R. H. (2006). "You got it!" Teaching social and emotional skills. *Young Children, 61*(6), 36–42.

Novick, R. (2002). Learning to read the heart: Nurturing emotional literacy. *Young Children, 57*(3), 84–89.

Puckett, M. B., & Black, J. K. (2005). *The young child: Development from prebirth through age eight* (4th ed.). Upper Saddle River, NJ: Merrill/Prentice Hall.

Riley, D., San Juan, R. R., Klinkner, J., & Ramminger, A. (2008). *Social and emotional development*. St. Paul, MN: Redleaf Press.

CHILDREN'S BOOKS

Allen, J. (2007). *"I'm not scared!"* New York: Hyperion Books for Children.

Bang, M. (1999). *When Sophie gets angry—really, really angry*. New York: Blue Sky Press.

Berkner, L. (2007). *The story of my feelings*. New York: Orchard Books.

Bottner, B. (1992). *Bootsie Barker bites*. New York: G. P. Putnam's Sons.

Boxall, E. (2002). *Francis the Scaredy Cat*. Cambridge, MA: Candlewick Press.

Cain, J. (2000). *The way I feel*. Seattle, WA: Parenting Press.

Clarke, J. (2008). *Stuck in the mud*. New York: Walker & Co.

Cooke, T., & Howard, P. (2003). *Full, full, full of love*. Cambridge, MA: Candlewick Press.*

Cuyler, M. (2001). *Stop drop, and roll*. New York: Simon & Schuster.

Dewdney, A. (2007). *Llama llama mad at mama*. New York: Viking.

Dodd, E. (2008). *What pet to get*. New York: Arthur A. Levine Books.

Downey, R. (2001). *Love is a family*. New York: HarperCollins.

Frame, J. A. (2003). *Yesterday I had the blues*. Berkeley, CA: Tricycle.*

Freedman, C., & Cort, B. (2007). *Aliens love underpants*. Hauppauge, NY: Barron's.

Gran, J. (2007). *Big bug surprise*. New York: Scholastic Press.

Harris. R. H. (2001). *Goodbye Mousie*. New York: McElderry Books.

Harris, R. H. (2004). *Don't forget to come back!* Cambridge, MA: Candlewick Press.

Joosse, B. M. (1991). *Mama, do you love me?* San Francisco: Chronicle Books.*

Joosse, B. M. (2005). *Papa, do you love me?* San Francisco: Chronicle Books *

Kroll, S. (2001). *Patches lost and found*. New York: Winslow Press.

Lester, H. (2004). *Hurty feelings*. Boston: Houghton Mifflin Co.

Lund, J. (1999). *Two cool coyotes*. New York: Dutton.*

McBratney, S. (2005). *I love it when you smile*. New York: HarperCollins.

Pena, A. (1995). *Calor*. New York: Lectorum.*

Petty, K. (2008). *Ha, ha, baby!* London: Boxer Books (New York: Sterling Pub. Co.)

Prigger, M. S. (2002). *Aunt Minnie and the twister*. New York: Clarion.

Prince, J. (2007). *I saw an ant in a parking lot*. New York: Sterling Publishing Co.*

Sardegna, J. (1994). *K is for kiss good night, a bedtime alphabet*. New York: Doubleday.*

Shields, C. D. (1997). *Saturday night at the dinosaur stomp*. Cambridge, MA: Candlewick Press.

Taback, S. (2007). *I miss you every day*. New York: Viking.

Tomlinson, J. (2000). *The owl who was afraid of the dark*. Cambridge, MA: Candlewick Press.

Vail, R. (2002). *Sometimes I'm Bombaloo*. New York: Scholastic.

Wilson, K., & Hillenbrand, W. (2007). *Whopper cake*. New York: Margaret K. McElderry Books.

Yolen, J. & Teague, M. (2007). *How do dinosaurs go to school?* New York: The Blue Sky Press.*

*multicultural

5

Social Play

SOCIAL PLAY CHECKLIST

_____ Spends time watching others play

_____ Plays by self with own toys/materials

_____ Plays parallel to others with similar toys/materials

_____ Plays with others in group play

_____ Makes friends with other children

_____ Gains access to ongoing play in positive manner

_____ Maintains role in ongoing play in positive manner

_____ Resolves play conflicts in positive manner

DEVELOPING SOCIAL PLAY SKILLS

The social development of the preschool child is revealed in how he or she gets along with peers. Often, we think of social actions as manners and politeness, but in the study of young children, social actions refer to how children learn to get along with their peers. Getting along for this age group rarely involves manners and usually is not very polite. Young children, in fact, frequently struggle to develop social skills. Children start out completely self-centered, which seems to stem from a survival mechanism in infancy. By the time they arrive in your classroom, children have begun to know themselves as individuals but mainly in relation to their adult caregivers. Now they must deal with their peers.

Children who have developed strong self-esteem should do well away from home. They will be able to let go of their primary caregiver more easily and will be more willing to try new things and to experience new people. Reviews of current research support this point of view: "The quality of the child's attachment relationship with his mother in infancy has been found to predict the child's social acceptance in preschool," according to the studies examined by Kemple (1991, p. 51). In addition, if the children have siblings at home, they will have learned to respond and react to other children.

Peers in the early childhood classroom, however, pose a different problem for the young child. Many, if not most, 3- and 4-year-olds simply have not developed the social skills for making friends or getting along with others. The focus of these children is on themselves. For many, everything has been done for them. Even if a new baby has replaced them as the youngest in the family, they still struggle to be first in the eyes of their parents.

This egocentric point of view does not serve them well in the world at large because sooner or later they must learn to deal with others and be treated as part of a group. They may have been enrolled in your program to learn precisely this. The purpose of many preschools is to help young children develop basic social skills.

What do these preschoolers need to learn? If socialization is not concerned with politeness and manners, then what social actions are involved in the early childhood classroom? Some important aspects include the following.

Important Social Learning for the Preschool Child

1. Making contact and playing with other children
2. Interacting with peers, to give and take
3. Getting along with peers, to interact in harmony
4. Seeing things from another child's point of view
5. Taking turns, waiting for a turn
6. Sharing with others
7. Showing respect for others' rights
8. Resolving interpersonal conflicts

Preschoolers' success in developing these skills, either on their own or with your help, may make the difference in how they get along for much of the rest of their lives.

This chapter is particularly concerned with the young child's ability to make contact, interact, and get along with peers. To determine where each of your children stands in the development of these skills, you need to be aware of behaviors that indicate their development level. Because children engage in play—often together—and because play is an observable activity in the preschool classroom, we will focus on observing social play in this chapter. Stone (1995) and other researchers agree that playing with others offers young children the best opportunity to learn social skills:

> Play is the primary mode for children's social development. Play encourages social interaction. Children learn how to negotiate, resolve conflicts, solve problems, get along with each other, take turns, be patient, cooperate, and share. Play also helps children understand concepts of fairness and competition. (p. 49)

THE IMPORTANCE OF PLAY

Vygotsky was one of the first early childhood researchers to be concerned primarily with the social interactions of children. He coined the term *zone of proximal development* (ZPD) to refer to the conditions through which children's comprehension is furthered as a result of social interactions. He looked at children's social play as the essential ingredient. "Play is the source of development and creates the zone of proximal development" (Vygotsky, 1976, p. 16). Although Piaget, too, considered play and social experience to be important, his work focused mainly on individuals rather than their social interactions (Van Hoorn, Nourot, Scales, & Alward, 2003, pp. 29–30).

OTHER EARLY PLAY RESEARCH

Many early childhood specialists have been interested in determining how children develop the skills to get along with one another. Social play has been the focus of such research since Parten first looked at "Social Participation among Pre-School Children" in the late 1920s and published her findings in 1932. She found that social participation among preschoolers could be categorized and that the categories correlated closely with age and maturity.

Parten (1932) identified six behavior categories that have since served as a basis for determining children's social skills level in several fields of study. Her categories include

1. *Unoccupied behavior:* The child does not participate in the play around him. He stays in one spot, follows the teacher, or wanders around.

2. *Onlooker behavior:* The child spends much time watching what other children are doing and may even talk to them, but he does not join or interact with them physically.

3. *Solitary independent play:* The child engages in play activities, but he plays on his own and not with others or with their toys.

4. *Parallel activity:* The child plays independently but he plays next to other children and often uses their toys or materials.

5. *Associative play:* The child plays with other children using the same materials and even talking with them, but he acts on his own and does not subordinate his interests to those of the group.

6. *Cooperative play:* The child plays in a group that has organized itself to do a particular thing, and whose members have taken on different roles (pp. 248–251).

Since 1932, many other researchers have used Parten's categories and find them still observable. Frost, Wortham, and Reifel (2005) noted that the validity of Parten's stages has been confirmed by numerous researchers over the years, and that these stages are also useful in describing any other social event, not just play. Although they see that many of today's children may be progressing through these stages at an earlier pace, their main point is "that for any child, we see a developmental progression in the type of social involvement that child exhibits, and the onset of each type is roughly linked with age" (p. 43).

Researchers like to use Parten's "play categories" when observing children at play because these behaviors really can be seen in the play interactions of young children. Yet since Parten's day, a great deal of new information about the social development of young children has surfaced. Today we acknowledge that these early play categories are indeed a valuable beginning point for gathering observational data about a young child's social development, but we also need to incorporate other up-to-date information. Thus, the Child Development Checklist uses four of Parten's play categories under Social Play, but then uses four categories relating to children's play behavior in making friends, gaining access to ongoing play, maintaining a play role, and resolving play conflicts. Other social competencies such as sharing and turn-taking are discussed in Chapter 6.

SOCIAL PLAY DEVELOPMENT

Because development of social play is very much age-related, the preschool teacher can observe it in a particular sequence as children progress from solitary play through parallel play to cooperative play. "Age-related development" thus signifies that the child's social skill level depends on cognitive, language, and emotional maturity. It also infers that the older the child, the more experience he probably has had with social contacts. Observers have noted that infants first begin to imitate one another in play toward the end of their first year. Howes' (1996) study of early friendships found that:

> By the end of the first year, children form differential relationships with their peers. That is, they seem to be capable of selecting one particular child from among their playmates, initiating and responding more often to this child than to others in the group. (p. 68)

Early in their second year, they are already engaging in peer play whenever they have the opportunity. Two-year-olds often begin peer play by playing alongside another toddler in a parallel manner. If they interact with an age mate, it is with only one. Two-year-olds have difficulty handling more than one playmate at a time. A threesome does not last long for children of this age.

Three-year-olds, as they become more mature and experienced, are able to play with more than one other child at the same time. As they become less egocentric and more able to understand another child's point of view, 3-year-olds have more success with social play. Using more mature language, listening to their play partners, and adjusting their behavior to the situation all support such play.

Access Rituals

The trick for many children in your classroom, you will note, is to gain access to play already in progress. Sociologists call these maneuvers "access rituals." Children new to the group may try different strategies to get involved: (a) The youngest children may use nonverbal appeals such as smiles or gestures of interest as they stand nearby and watch, hoping a player will take note and invite or allow them in; (b) other children may walk around and watch, or stand and watch, waiting for an opportunity to insert themselves; (c) they may engage in similar play parallel to the original players, hoping to join the original players if their own parallel play is accepted; (d) they may intrude in a disruptive manner claiming that the space or the toys are their own; and (e) the oldest preschoolers often use words, asking, "Can I play?" or "What are you doing?" to gain access.

One successful strategy for a child to gain access to ongoing play seems to be en-gaging in parallel play. The least successful strategy is to be disruptive. Researchers have noted that parallel play among preschoolers decreases as group play increases. Still, par-allel play seems to be one of the principal modes of social play for 3- and 4-year-olds in most centers and classrooms.

THE TEACHER'S ROLE

Many teachers today are concerned about the apparent increase of children who exhibit poor emotional regulation, undeveloped social skills, and a fascination with violent play themes, according to Dunn (2003). She reported that:

> A typical early childhood classroom of 18 students contains one or two children with serious and persistent behavioral problems, and up to nine children exhibiting the effects of multi-ple emotional and social stressors in their lives. (p. 18)

How can teachers help children overcome these problems? Many children learn how to interrelate and play with peers in an early childhood program without the teacher's assistance. Others, however, need your help. Newcomers, shy children, imma-ture children, and children from dysfunctional families often have difficulty on their own. Rodrigues et al. (2007) also report that "many preschoolers with developmental delays have been found to have an increased risk for social, language, and cognitive dif-ficulties that negatively influence their social competence. They have lower rates of so-cial interaction and fewer friendships" (p. 317).

If yours is a multiage classroom, it is often the youngest children who have the most difficulty gaining access to group play, sustaining their role in the play, or resolv-ing conflict when it appears. These children definitely need your help. Yours is a spe-cial role in helping children develop the social skills for peer acceptance. It involves several steps:

Helping Children Develop Social Skills for Peer Acceptance

1. Set up the physical arrangement of the classroom to accommodate small-group activities.
2. Observe and record the social skills of the children to determine: (a) who is unoccupied, (b) who watches, (c) who plays alone, (d) who plays parallel to others, (e) who initiates play activities, (f) who gains access to play, (g) who can maintain his play role, and (h) who can resolve conflict.
3. Help children initiate contacts with other children.
4. Help children gain access to ongoing play.
5. Help children maintain their play roles.
6. Help children learn to resolve conflicts with others.

How the teacher carries out this important role in children's social skills development is discussed under each of the checklist items to follow. All four of the checklist items—onlooker, solitary, parallel, and group play—are, of course, descriptive rather than judgmental. We are interested in observing individual children on each item to try to discover the child's level of social skills. We must be careful not to judge a child negatively if we do not check a certain item. The items themselves are neither negative nor positive; they merely describe behavior. What we infer from the checkmarks or lack of them will be more meaningful if we also look at the recorded evidence on which the checkmarks or blanks are based. It is just as important to record descriptive evidence on *items not checked* as on those items you have checked.

 ## SPENDS TIME WATCHING OTHERS PLAY

By using the Child Development Checklist to determine the social play level for the children in your classroom, you can identify children who have not yet become involved in play with others. These may be some of the children described in Chapter 3 who have had difficulty letting go of their mother or primary caregiver, especially at the beginning of the year. The shyness of children and the newness of the environment may also cause some children to hold back at first.

If the youngsters have not had experience with other children their age, a large group of peers can be overwhelming. This lack of experience with other children may deter them from gaining access to group play. Three-year-olds, especially, have usually had more experience with adult caregivers than with other children their age and may not know how to behave in a peer group.

Some children who are new to a program begin by watching. They may walk around the room to see what is going on, but not join in. Parten (1932) described the **onlooker** this way:

> The child spends most of his time watching the other children play. He often talks to the children whom he is observing, asks questions, or gives suggestions, but does not overtly enter into the play himself. This type differs from the unoccupied in that the onlooker is definitely observing particular groups of children rather than anything that happens to be exciting. The child stands or sits within speaking distance of the group so that he can see and hear everything that takes place. (p. 249)

Onlooker behavior is often the first step toward group participation. Some children take longer than others to become involved with group play. They need to know what is going on around them, who is doing what, and how they can enter this play. If the child seems engaged in watching a group at play, it may be best to leave him alone at first. He may join the others once he is at ease in the classroom. On the other hand, some children do not seem to know what to do or say to get others to play with them or to allow them to join in.

More recent observations of preschool children in the various play states have uncovered some interesting new information. Although the progression of children through the stages of play still holds true, the situation is more complex than we thought. Anderson and Robinson (2006) have discovered that onlooker play is more than merely an immature step toward higher levels of social interaction. They say, "Onlooker play apparently serves a very important information-gathering function for children that has never been fully appreciated or considered"(p. 13). For some children, it seems to help them shift into parallel play and then into cooperative (group) play. But they don't necessarily stay shifted. Some shift back again into onlooker play when new play situations occur. It takes careful observation over time to determine what is really going on with active children.

Anderson and Robinson also noted, "Preschool children use the onlooker-to-parallel-to-cooperative interaction shift not only to make the initial transition into cooperative play, but they continue to use this strategy to step back out of cooperative play and back into cooperative play many times during a single play scenario" (2006, p. 13). How is it with your children? Be sure you observe them for an entire play scenario and note on your checklist what is happening. Is it only the more mature children that make the shifts? Do others follow them? Your careful observations may add even more information to this new discovery about children's social play.

If You Have Not Checked This Item: Some Helpful Ideas

■ Arrange Parts of the Room for Two Children

Set up a few small tables, especially at the beginning of the year, for two children to participate in an activity: two puzzles, two table games, two sheets of paper and boxes of crayons, two individual chalkboards and colored chalk, two books to look at, two easels next to one another. This may be all it takes for the unoccupied child to become involved

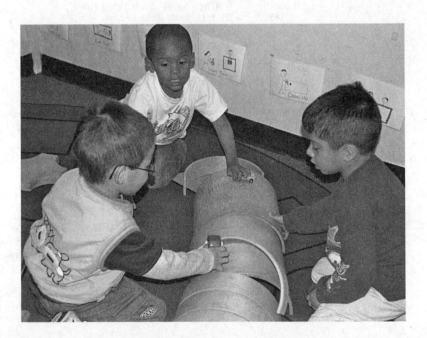

Some children use onlooker behavior to shift into cooperative play.

as soon as she feels comfortable. Playing with one other child is not so overwhelming as a whole group. Furthermore, because children imitate one another, the immature child can actually learn how to play in this new environment by copying her tablemate.

■ Give Children Enough Time

As adults, we sometimes forget that it takes more time for young, inexperienced children to accomplish anything than it does for us. Be sure you give children enough time to try out new activities and associations. Keep your "arrangements for two" set up for as long as necessary at the beginning of the year. Your observations of the children will tell you how long. It may be weeks.

■ Suggest an Initiating Activity

New children need to establish connections with other children in the classroom. They can do this by initiating a conversation with another child. If the onlooker child has not done so, you can suggest that he go to another child and tell him what he would like to do. "Tell Paul you like to play with blocks. Say to him: 'Let's build a house with the blocks.'"

■ Suggest Parallel Play

If, after some onlooking time has elapsed, the child still has not joined in with the others, you may want to suggest that he erect a building next to Paul's, or play with clay at Ricardo's table, or drive his toy car through Sondra's tunnel after he asks her permission. As mentioned previously, parallel play like this is one of the most successful strategies for a child's gaining access to ongoing play.

 ## PLAYS BY SELF WITH OWN TOYS/MATERIALS

Many young children, when they first enter a preschool program, start out playing by themselves. This may occur because of the strangeness of the situation or their lack of self-confidence with unfamiliar children. Solitary play also occurs because children are attracted by the toys and materials and want to try them out by themselves. Some solitary play may occur because certain programs encourage it or because children have an independent project they want to accomplish. You will need to observe and record the child's actual activity during solitary play, as well as the youngster's overall involvement or lack of it with other children. Even after children have advanced to cooperative play, many continue playing by themselves on projects of their own and should not be discouraged from doing so.

Parten (1932) described "solitary independent play" as follows:

> The child plays alone and independently with toys that are different from those used by the children within speaking distance and makes no effort to get close to other children. He pursues his own activity without reference to what others are doing. (p. 250)

For some children, solitary play is truly a beginning level of social play that precedes their becoming involved in playing with others. If your children do not play at all with others or only play parallel to them, you might consider solitary play as a beginning level of play for such youngsters.

Research by Smilansky in the 1960s and Rubin in the 1970s and 1980s has looked at children's play in terms of their cognitive development in addition to their social skills. They maintain that levels of play are determined not only by whether children play by themselves or with others, but also by what children do during play.

To determine whether your solitary players are, indeed, at a beginning level of social play, you should note in your observational data what they are doing. If children are manipulating toys and materials or trying them out to see how they work, they are at a beginning level of play. In block play, for instance, beginners often pick up a block, put it down, pound with it, or put it in a container and then dump it out. More mature players stack blocks into towers, line them up into roads, or build buildings with them.

If you observe a child constructing or creating something by herself, this may indicate something altogether different from the beginner who is manipulating materials alone. If the builder is purposefully using materials toward some end—for instance, making a building, a painting, or a play dough creation—she may be exhibiting higher-level creativity skills. This higher level of skill development may have enabled such children to get satisfaction from making something on their own. Instead of discouraging these children from solitary constructive play, you should provide them with many opportunities for expressing this creativity. Such children will join in group play again when the time is right for them.

If you observe a solitary player constructing something by herself, it may indicate higher-level creativity skills.

Our high-tech society is creating another type of solitary player these days: the young child who spends large amounts of time playing by himself with play stations or interactive video games. Fromberg (1998) noted:

> Among more affluent families, access to personal computers, including CD ROM with voice synthesizers and motion pictures, provides different opportunities for solitary play. . . . As access to refined forms of software increases, along with Virtual Reality simulation technology, the empowerment of players may extend in some ways and contract in others, limited by the imaginations of the software creators. . . . Wholesome opportunities to play, however, need a balanced schedule that also includes sufficient interaction with peers. (p. 200)

Such children may need your program to introduce them to traditional play materials as well as to other players. Does your program include a television or any of these high-tech play materials? Such materials, with the exception of the computer, belong in the home rather than the preschool if you plan to help children develop social skills. Even children's use of the classroom computer should not be a solitary activity, but needs to involve two children together at the keyboard (see Chapter 9).

However, if a child is neither engaged in solitary play nor any other kind of play during the free-choice period, you can help her in several ways.

If You Have Not Checked This Item: Some Helpful Ideas

■ Give Child a Familiar Material

Many children are familiar with dough at home but have not had an opportunity to play with it. Have the nonplaying child help you mix a bowl of play dough. Then give him some implements such as a small rolling pin and cookie cutters—and let him play.

■ Read a Book

Read a book about a child in a preschool, such as *Chatterbox Jamie* (Cooney, 1993). Jamie is a little boy who feels out of place when he first comes to school because he is without his Mom and Dad. At home he is a regular chatterbox, but at nursery school he is silent. On the first day he watches all the different activities, but doesn't join in the play of his multicultural classmates. The second day he starts playing on his own and finally joins in. But it takes several weeks before he finally talks at school.

In *My First Day at Nursery School* (Edwards, 2002), mentioned in Chapter 3, the little girl does not want to be there at first. Then she goes around discovering a playhouse with a blue tea set, painting easels, glue and shiny paper, musical instruments, little trampolines, and friends to play with, and gets involved in all of them.

PLAYS PARALLEL TO OTHERS WITH SIMILAR TOYS/MATERIALS

Parallel play is a fascinating phenomenon. If you are unfamiliar with this type of play, you have to see it to believe it. Parallel play often involves two children who seem to be playing together. As you get close enough to witness what is going on, you find that each child is actually playing a different game from a different point of view but often with similar toys. If language is involved, the two children seem to be talking to themselves rather than each other.

Parten (1932) described parallel play this way:

> The child plays independently, but the activity he chooses naturally brings him among other children. He plays with toys that are like those which the children around him are using, but he plays with the toy as he sees fit, and does not try to influence or modify the activity of the children near him. He plays beside rather than with the other children. There is no attempt to control the coming or going of children in the group. (p. 250)

All kinds of parallel play go on in the preschool setting. More seems to occur with younger children than with older ones. Parallel play, as previously mentioned, seems to enable younger children to learn to play cooperatively with others in an early childhood classroom. This idea makes a great deal of sense when you consider that your room consists of a large group of highly egocentric youngsters who are strangers for the most part. They come together in a physical setting full of toys and activities just for them. How are they to deal with such a setting?

They begin by trying out things on their own. Then they play side by side using the same materials but playing a different game. Finally the children begin to cooperate, to interchange ideas, and to come together to play as a group with self-assigned roles and tasks. It was once thought that children who have learned to play cooperatively, may abandon parallel play altogether. Researchers Anderson and Robinson (2006), as noted earlier, are more inclined to believe that parallel play can also serve as a bridge for children moving from one play state to another.

Observers need to watch parallel players closely. Anderson and Robinson witnessed two boys making subtle shifts from group play back into parallel and onlooker play that could easily go unnoticed. "Parallel play maintained a pivotal position as the boys transitioned into cooperating, watching, or playing alone" (p. 12).

If You Have Not Checked This Item: Some Helpful Ideas

■ Try Finger Painting for Two

Set up a small table where two can sit side by side; put out finger paints to be shared. Invite one of your reluctant participants and one other child to paint. Do not force the reluctant child. Perhaps you could first involve him in a solitary manner and then ask him if another child could work next to him. This time he will be working not only parallel to the other child, but also with the child, because the paints have to be shared.

Set up a computer program for two where one child can help the other.

■ Set Up Tape Recording for Two

It is important to have two cassette tape recorders in your program. They are invaluable because they provide an opportunity for two people to play individually with the same materials in a parallel manner. Tape recording is personal and fun. Even the shy child can talk as softly as she wants as long as she holds the mike up close. She can say anything about herself she wants: her name, the names of her brothers or sisters or pets, her favorite foods, or where she lives. Then comes the fun of listening to what she has spoken. Two children can record at the same table if they each talk into their own microphones. They may eventually want to talk into each other's mikes.

■ Set Up a Computer Program for Two

Place two chairs in front of the computer and bring up a simple program that two children can take turns using. If no one is using the computer, ask a child who knows how to use it to try the program you have set up. Suggest to a child who usually plays by himself that there is an empty computer chair waiting for him—that the other child will help him get started if he wants.

■ Read a Book

The story **Building a Bridge** (Begaye, 1993), mentioned in Chapter 3, can help children understand how two children who are playing separately but parallel to one another can come together. The Navajo girl Juanita and the Anglo girl Anna each build their own bridge with different-colored blocks, but then decide to put them together to build a bigger and better structure.

 # PLAYS WITH OTHERS IN GROUP PLAY

When children play together in a group using the same materials for the same purpose or doing pretend play around a common theme, we say they are engaging in group or "cooperative" play. A great deal of group play occurs in most early childhood programs, although not every child joins in. The observer can often spot children engaged in group play in the block center where they are building structures together or in the dramatic play center where they are playing house or doctor.

Van Hoorn et al. (2003) noted,

> Cooperative play involves sophisticated efforts to negotiate joint play themes and constructions with peers, and is characterized by children stepping in and out of their play to establish roles or events. For example, three children playing restaurant may alternate their roles in the play as customer, cook, and waiter with comments about the plot made from outside the play such as, "And pretend the hamburger got burned." (p. 39)

Group play like this is the principal activity for many children during free-play time, whereas others have not yet learned the social skills necessary to enter the play or sustain their roles. They are the children often engaged in parallel play alongside the group players. Some children are perfectly content to play alongside others without joining in, whereas other youngsters may need your help to join the fun.

Whatever you do, don't force the issue. Some children are not yet enough at ease in the classroom to join in with others in their group play schemes. Give them a chance to get used to the program. Children fare very well on their own, and most will join in their own good time. Because this is the most sophisticated type of play in preschool, many children need time to play on their own or in a parallel situation. They need to become acquainted with the other players and perhaps make friends among them. They also need to have an interest in what the group is doing.

Your role should be to encourage group play by giving children the opportunity for it to occur during the free-choice period, by supporting children in their own play schemes or giving them ideas for new play projects from time to time, by giving them plenty of time to carry on this play, and by inviting anyone interested to join the play.

For children who want to play but do not know how to join in, see the suggestions under Gains Access to Ongoing Play in a Positive Manner later in this chapter. If you do not see much group play of any kind occurring in the classroom, you may need to take stock of your room arrangement or materials. Is your classroom divided into learning centers or curriculum areas with enough space for several children in each area? The block area should have room for at least four to six children to create structures on the floor, but not be so large or open that all the children try to occupy it at once. Block shelves can be pulled away from the walls to partially enclose the area. The shelves themselves should be filled with wooden unit blocks, enough for groups of children to build really large structures. Building accessories can include people, animals, small vehicles, and dollhouse furniture.

Many children first come together in group play in the block center. They may start by playing with blocks by themselves, then build parallel to other builders, and finally join in with a group. Do your space and materials allow for this to happen?

A second area highly conducive to group play is the dramatic play center. Most classrooms have a housekeeping area with child-size kitchen furnishings, a full-length mirror, dolls, and dress-up clothing. In addition, you can add shelves, a desk and toy cash register, and empty containers and bags for creating a pretend store. If there is space for several children and materials for several play themes, you may see more than one play group in operation at once.

If You Have Not Checked This Item: Some Helpful Ideas

■ Follow-Up Field Trips

Whenever you go on a field trip, whether near or far, be sure to set up some trip-related props in one of the learning centers for children to play with cooperatively. Children can then spontaneously re-create the trip or play out some aspect of it that interests them. For example, put out firefighters' gear (hats, raincoats, boots) in the dramatic play center; or put out little fire trucks, plastic tubes for hoses, and figures of people in the block center.

■ Follow-Up Book Readings

Another way to initiate spontaneous group play is to read a favorite story and then put out props for children to reenact or follow up some aspect of the story. *Feast for 10* (Falwell, 1993) is a simple, vividly illustrated story of an African-American family with five children, mother and father, grandparents, and a friend joining together for a wonderful feast. It is a counting story in rhyme, with the mother and children buying the necessary food in the grocery store, loading it in the car, preparing the meal, and finally sitting down to eat. You can follow up by putting out plastic food props in the dramatic play area along with bags and cash register, pans, ladles, hot-pad gloves, and dishes in the house area, just like the book characters used.

In *Tar Beach* (Ringgold, 1991), another African-American family goes to the "beach" on the roof of their apartment building during hot summer nights in New York City. Little Cassie, the narrator, lies on a blanket and looks up at the George Washington Bridge and other lighted buildings. Then she takes off in her imagination and flies over the city. This book also comes with a doll figure of Cassie that can be used as a prop in your block center along with black squares of paper for the "tar beach" roofs of your own block buildings and dollhouse furniture such as tables and chairs. Can your children build tall buildings with black rooftops? Put the book and Cassie doll in the block center after reading this story and watch to see what group play ensues.

Children of every race enjoy pretending to be book character
have African-American children in the class, your youngsters c
characters like Cassie and thus feel good about such children. 7
portant to have picture books showing people of many races an
your children to look at. As noted by Ramsey (1991):

> When children role play situations and characters in a book, they learn how to perceive situations from a variety of perspectives and literally be in another person's shoes. By engaging children in stories, we enable our young readers and listeners to empathize with different experiences and points of view and experience a wide range of social dilemmas. (pp. 168–169)

Ellis, Gallingane, and Kemple (2006) agree. They noted, "Researchers have found that children's stories, fables, and fairy tales have a profound effect on children's social skills when linked with their personal and social experiences" (p. 31). This means you must be sure to talk with the children afterward about whether their own experiences are like those in the book.

■ Start a Play Group Yourself

Children love to have the teacher play with them. If you take on a role and pretend, all the better. Choose an unoccupied learning center and set out a few props to entice children to participate. Perhaps the sand table is free. You can be a paleontologist going on a dig for dinosaur bones for a museum. Put on safety goggles, your explorer's hat, and take a little shovel along. Bury some of the block center toy dinosaurs in the sand. Have extra goggles and some block center trucks on hand to carry the dinosaurs back to the museum. If no children have noticed what you are doing, make an open invitation: "I need four children to go on an expedition with me to the Gobi Desert to search for dinosaur bones." If more than four want to participate, have them sign up for the next turn. Be sure to have a dinosaur picture book on hand for identification purposes, as well as the class camera to take photos of the finds. Once the children are involved, you can withdraw quietly and let the players carry on.

Afterward read to a small group at a time the simple book *Bones, Bones, Dinosaur Bones* (Barton, 1990) about six diggers who look for dinosaur bones, find them, dig them up, wrap them up, transport them to the science museum, and assemble them into the bones of tyrannosaurus rex. Will your children want to create their own museum?

 # MAKES FRIENDS WITH OTHER CHILDREN

Is making friends with peers really important to young children, you may wonder? For instance, are they worried about finding a friend when they first come to school? Whether they express this idea openly, it is often uppermost in the minds of many youngsters when they first come into the unknown environment of the preschool classroom. Will the other children like them? Will there be a friend waiting for them? Just like human beings everywhere, young children also need to feel welcomed and accepted wherever they go.

This is part of being human. All human beings need to be accepted as part of a group outside our families. And within that group, we need at least one other person we can relate to and who relates to us as a friend. The needs of preschool children are no different. But they are different in their ability to make friends. How does one go about making a friend when one is 3 or 4 or 5 years old?

Some children have no difficulty. Others seem to bumble about without much success. A few others don't even try. Not so many years ago, friendship was the main reason that parents enrolled their children in preschools. They called it "socialization." They wanted their children to learn socialization skills before they went to elementary school. In other words, they wanted their children to learn to get along with other children.

Somehow, in the intervening years, many people have changed their goals for preschool children. When parents, teachers, and society at large talk about preparing children for elementary school, they seem to mean children's learning of academic skills such as reading, writing, and numbers. What happened to the social skills of making friends and learning to get along with peers? Don't children still have to learn that? Kemple (2004) emphasized, "Until a child's essential needs, including positive association with others, have been met, they are limited in their ability to move beyond those realms into academic areas of learning" (p. 6).

This textbook takes the point of view that all development occurs simultaneously. Social skills are just as important as cognitive skills, and support for their development should not be neglected. For preschoolers who do not develop competence in interpersonal social skills, the results can be disastrous in later years. As Riley, San Juan, Klinker, and Ramminger (2008) pointed out, "In the extreme case, children who are rejected or ignored by others may develop problems in personal adjustment, social skills, and learning"(p. 36). Other studies have correlated poor peer relationships in early childhood classrooms with later delinquency, as well as emotional and mental health problems (Parker & Asher, 1987).

As children move away from their families by coming to preschool, they necessarily form new relationships with the people around them, especially their peers. Although such relationships are usually thought of as friendships, they are quite different from the friendships of older children or adults. Being preoccupied with their own interests and needs makes it difficult for preschool children to form friendships based on personality. They are more likely to look on a friend as a momentary playmate who is doing something interesting or is fun to play with. As Ramsey (1991) noted,

> During preschool, children form "playmateships" in which children think of their most frequent companions as their friends. Friendships are defined by the current situation. Children sometimes say "I can't be your friend today" when they really mean "I'm playing with somebody else right now." Because frequency of association is often determined by availability and proximity, some friendship choices may reflect convenience more than personal preference. (p. 21)

Until children can truly see things from another person's perspective, their relationship with that person will always be somewhat one sided. For the egocentric child

Friendship often starts with two children coming together to play.

of 3 to about 6 years, friendship is more of a one-way street than a two-way relationship with each partner contributing. Young children are preoccupied with their own needs. They believe that others want what they want. That is the reason that play among preschoolers may suddenly break down into conflict, because the players cannot see things from the other person's point of view.

How does friendship come about, then, among young children? When toddlers and the youngest preschoolers talk about a friend, they usually apply the word to any special person who has been called a friend for them. They do have favorite peers and can form strong attachments, but the concept of friendship itself does not have much meaning for them at first.

With older preschoolers, friendship often starts with two children coming together. Each needs to be recognized as a person by the other, and then accepted. These children may indeed be true friends, but often the reason for their friendship in preschool is based on playing together rather than liking one another's personality. The most important aspect of this type of friendship in an early childhood program is whether the child is *included* in the play with a partner or a group.

It is important for teachers to help children make friends for a number of reasons. Riley et al. (2008) say: "Preschool-aged friends appear happier during their interactions and are better at dealing with conflict than nonfriends. Young children are also more skilled and competent when interacting with a friend than a nonfriend" (p. 40).

Teachers can best help young children make friends with others first by observing and then recording the children to determine who has been included or excluded from group activities. Keep your eye on disruptive children who often engage in verbal and physical aggression; they may be children who have not found friends. They may wander around the room, hovering close to others but not really included. Other onlookers may be shy or withdrawn children who have not been rebuffed but ignored by their peers. And still others may be children who are new to the class and have not yet found a way to be included by others. Children who are perceived by others to be different because of looks, language, age, or a physical disability are also sometimes excluded.

Once you have determined which children do not seem to have a friendly attachment to anyone in the group, you can decide whether such youngsters need to resolve their own friendship problems or if you should intervene to help them. If children come to you or cling to you, it may be a sign for you to bring them together with one other child. On the other hand, if an onlooker seems content to play parallel to the others, she may need more time to become comfortable with the activities and children before finding a friend on her own. Children with disabilities may also need your help to find a friend. As Rodriguez et al. (2007) pointed out, "approximately 50% of inclusive preschool students with disabilities are at risk for social rejection by peers and require 'evidence-based' intervention to promote their social competence" (p. 317).

If You Have Not Checked This Item: Some Helpful Ideas

■ Help Children Find Partners (Playmates)

Play singing games or circle games where children have a partner to participate with. Do not ask children to go around choosing a partner, because some children, such as shy children, will be left out. Instead, the teaching staff can help children pair up quickly and quietly without a fuss. Playing partner games like this every day may help outsiders feel included enough to begin playing with their partner in an unstructured activity afterward.

■ Do Not Make a Fuss About Friends

Teachers who talk a great deal about which children are friends with which other children may unknowingly be putting pressure on children who do not have identifiable "friends." Finding a personal friend is not the point in preschool. Most children have not yet developed to this level. Having a playmate is more important, but talking about it is not.

■ Create Size-Restricted Play Spaces

Have a number of spaces or tables set up for two children. For example, two to tape record their names; two to listen to a book tape; two to build with LEGO blocks; two to paint with finger paint; two to count with tiny dinosaur counters. Children, especially those with visual or hearing impairments, can be directed to these activities to play with one other child. Be sure to call their partners by name so they will get to know the other child better.

■ Model the Contact Behavior

If the child seems unable to make any contact with someone to play with, you can model the behavior yourself. "C'mon, Terrell, you take that car, and I'll take this car. We're going to build a garage for our cars. Let's see if we can get someone to help us. Let's ask Lavon. Hi, Lavon. We're going to build a garage for our cars with the blocks. Want to help us?"

You should be successful because children enjoy playing with the teacher and like to be chosen by the teacher to do things. However, if Lavon refuses, then approach another child with the same request. This helps Terrell learn what to do should he be refused. You can extract yourself unobtrusively from this play once the children are engaged.

■ Read a Book

Some preschool children may have an imaginary friend at home, but seldom does this "friend" come to preschool. In *Jessica* (Henkes, 1989), little Ruthie has an imaginary friend named Jessica who goes wherever she goes and does whatever she does. Her parents tell her in no uncertain terms, "There is no Jessica!" But for Ruthie, there is. When Ruthie turns 5 and goes to kindergarten, Jessica goes along reluctantly—just like Ruthie. But when the children in school line up with partners, another girl comes and stands by Ruthie. Her name is Jessica, and they end up being good friends.

In *I Am Too Absolutely Small for School* (Child, 2004), another humorous Charlie and Lola book, Lola tells Charlie all the reasons she can't go to school, one being Loren Sorenson her invisible friend who is feeling slightly not very well. Charlie replies to all her reasons, so off she goes with Loren. When she returns she is with a real visible friend and they sit down together at home to have pink milk. But there is a space between the two girls. Can your listeners see what might be in that space?

In *Hunter's Best Friend in School* (2002), Hunter and Stripe are two little raccoon boys who like the same things and do everything together in preschool. But when Stripe starts making mischief, Hunter feels bad about copying his teasing and making a mess. He finally finds a way to turn Hunter's tricks into something they all enjoy.

 ## GAINS ACCESS TO ONGOING PLAY IN A POSITIVE MANNER

During free play periods in most preschool classrooms, you see groups of children busily engaged in building in the block corner, dressing up for pretend roles in the dramatic play area, racing little cars, playing with table blocks, painting, molding play dough, playing with puppets in the reading area, or playing in the water or sand tables. Not every child is engaged. Onlookers, shy children, new children, and others may want to get involved, but don't know how. Some have tried but been rejected. Others may need your help to get started.

But why should child players keep out other children in the first place? Corsaro's research has shown: "The children's desire to protect interactive space is not selfish. In fact, they are not refusing to share, rather they want to keep sharing what they are already sharing" (2003, p. 40). He also noted that "in their experiences in the preschool settings the kids came to realize that interaction is fragile and acceptance into ongoing activities is often difficult. Therefore the kids concentrate on creating, sharing, and protecting their play" (p. 69).

In her survey of research on preschool children's peer acceptance, Kemple (1991) found, "Researchers have recognized for a long time that generally positive behaviors, such as cooperation, are associate with being accepted by peers, and generally antisocial behaviors such as aggression, are associated with being rejected" (p. 49). Children who successfully enter ongoing play have learned to adopt such positive strategies such as those in Figure 5–1.

Communication skills also seem to play an important role in children's gaining acceptance in group play. Outsiders need to talk with the players, understand what their replies are, then respond again, replying to their concerns. If the group is pretending to take their babies to the doctor, for example, a successful strategy Charlene might use for gaining entrance is to get a doll from the housekeeping area and bring it along with the others, saying, "My baby needs to be examined, too." In this case, she has adopted the group's frame of reference (doctor play) as well as contributing something relevant to the play (bringing her baby to be examined). But just as important, she uses words and does not crash unannounced into the play. Instead, she gets a doll, brings it along with the others, and then communicates clearly.

Had she merely asked, "Can I play?" it would be easy for the group to reject her. Had she taken one of the other children's dolls or tried to take over the role of the doctor, she would probably have been rejected. Children who have difficulty seeing things from another person's point of view may not understand what is required of them to join ongoing play. Then it is up to you to help.

Rosa, a shy little girl in Head Start, had trouble gaining access to much of the group play because she tended to be so unassertive. She would watch the others play, but whenever she shyly asked, "Can I play?" she was usually refused. Then she went off by herself. She should not have given up so easily. Over half of the requests made to join preschool play groups are denied, Corsaro (2003) discovered. But because group play in preschool is so fluid and brief, outside children have many opportunities to join in during a typical day. Just because a child is denied access once does not mean she will be denied if she tries again.

Figure 5–1 Positive Strategies to Gain Access to Ongoing Play

- Observing the group to see what is going on
- Adopting the group's frame of reference as in parallel play
- Contributing something relevant to the play
- Acting interested; walking round and round the play
- Asking again if she can play

Many children like Rosa do not try again. Then it is up to the teacher to coach them on their next step or to model a more successful strategy that they might try. If nothing seems to work for Rosa and the group itself will just not accept her, then the teacher may want to spend some time coaching the group later on how to admit an outsider.

The teacher, however, should not herself force the child on the group. Being the adult in charge, the teacher has the power to make the group accept Rosa, but she will not be solving Rosa's problem by doing so. Instead, the group may become resentful toward Rosa, who was forced on them by the teacher. The social dilemmas that preschool children face are actually important learning situations for them. If the teacher solves the problem, the child has missed the opportunity to try to work it out for herself. Whenever a teacher intervenes, it should be as a last resort after a child has had more than one chance to attempt the resolution herself.

If You Have Not Checked This Item: Some Helpful Ideas

■ Use Puppets with the Child and/or the Group

When it seems appropriate, bring out two hand puppets and introduce them to Rosa with names such as Ollie Outsider and Purely Personal. Tell her that Ollie wants to play with Purely, but Purely won't let her. Ask Rosa what she thinks Ollie can do to get Purely to let her play. Whatever Rosa suggests, you can try out with the puppets. Let the Ollie puppet succeed if Rosa's suggestions seem appropriate. Give your own suggestions if nothing of Rosa's seems to work.

Use this same sort of puppet play to coach a group that will not let an outsider join. First ask the children how they think Ollie feels when Purely won't let her play. Then ask the group why they think Purely won't let Ollie join in. Finally ask the group what Ollie can do and what Purely can do so that everyone can play together. Then act out with a puppet on each hand the suggestions given by the group. Finally, let a child be one of the puppets while you play the role of the other one in a repeat of this social role play.

■ Provide a Time for Everyone to Join a Group

It is much easier for children to join a play group at the outset. Once the group has started, the outsider usually encounters resistance entering an established group. Therefore, it is important for the preschool teacher to provide a time and opportunity for everyone to become involved in playing with someone else. This can be at the beginning of the free-choice period. Perhaps a brief circle time can acquaint the children with the activities available. Then each child can join the activity group of his choice.

Be careful that you do not choose the activity for the child and force him into it. The child must learn on his own how to gain access to a group. If a certain child holds back and does not join with any others, you can make a suggestion. You can urge the child to choose an activity or a partner. But do not pressure. He may not be ready yet.

☑ MAINTAINS ROLE IN ONGOING PLAY IN A POSITIVE MANNER

Developing the skill to enter ongoing play is not the end of social skill development for the preschool child, but rather the beginning. He must also be able to continue playing with the others. If the play situation is a pretend one, then the child needs to get along with others in the role he has chosen or been assigned. If he is building a block structure with another child, then the child needs to be able to cooperate with his play partner and complete the building. This give-and-take among preschool youngsters is not always smooth. To maintain his role in ongoing play, a child needs to be able to do the tasks in Figure 5–2.

In a spontaneous dramatic play situation, the child must also be able to pretend, take a role, take turns, and show respect for others' roles—all within a playful framework. Quite a complex agenda for 3-, 4-, and 5-year-olds. No wonder not all children are successful at it. Yet being successful at group dramatic play helps young children to practice and learn the social skills necessary to be *successful in life*. That is why group dramatic play in the preschool classroom is one of the most important activities. Some of the social skills children can learn through group dramatic play include those in Figure 5–3.

Most classrooms provide a place for group dramatic play, that is, the taking of spontaneous roles in an imaginary situation made up by the children during free play. A clear sequence of pretend play in young children has emerged over the past 20 years of research. By age 2, children can pretend and often play with imaginary objects. The more complex group dramatic play mentioned here cannot happen until children can articulate verbally, which occurs between 2 and 4 years of age. Such play gradually becomes more complex with 5-year-olds in kindergarten until about age 6, when the frequency of group dramatic play begins to decline. By age 7, games with rules are more prominent, and group dramatic play seems to disappear altogether (Smilansky, 1968, pp. 10–11).

Thus, the early childhood classroom needs to take advantage of this recognized sequence of children's activities and provide the materials, equipment, space, and time to allow and encourage children to engage in group pretend play—the practice field for the social skills of life itself. Chapter 13 discusses the development of the child's dramatic play skills and themes he or she choose when making up the roles and situations for group dramatic play. In this chapter, we are concerned with the young child's personal interactions with peers that will allow him to continue his play with them. Engaging in group pretend play like this helps to transform a preschool child from an egocentric being who is the center of all attention into a socialized human being who recognizes the existence of others' points of view and can respond appropriately.

Figure 5–2 Maintaining a Role in Ongoing Play

- Carry on a conversation
- Maintain eye contact when speaking
- Listen to and watch other speakers
- Adjust own conversation content in order to be understood

Figure 5–3 Social Skills Learned
Through Group Dramatic Play

- Adjusting their actions to the requirements of their role
- Being tolerant of others and their needs
- Not always expecting to have their own way
- Making appropriate responses to others
- Helping others and receiving help from them

If You Have Not Checked This Item: Some Helpful Ideas

■ Make Prop Boxes for Field Trip Pretend Play

You will be taking your children on field trips to stores, farms, fire stations, hospitals, laundromats, fast-food restaurants, parks, zoos, pet shops, and construction sites. Upon your return, you will want to provide a variety of ways for children to represent and talk about their experiences. An excellent activity involves providing props for them to play the roles seen at the field trip site. Many teachers make up a prop box after every field trip, filled with paraphernalia to be used in pretending the different roles.

A trip to the post office, for instance, could produce a prop box with stamps (cancelled postage stamps or stickers of some sort), a stamp pad and stamper, envelopes, a mail bag (tote bag), a mail carrier's hat, and a picture book about a mail carrier. Label each box with a picture and words the children will soon recognize. Allow the children to take such boxes from the shelf and play with the equipment during free-choice period. If children have shown interest in the field trip, they are more likely to become involved with pretend play afterward.

■ Change Your Dramatic Play Area from Time to Time

Everyone is stimulated by change. If you have had housekeeping equipment in your dramatic play period for a number of weeks, try converting the area to something else: perhaps a store or a hair salon. Talk with the children and have them help stock it with empty or discarded items from home.

■ Put New Accessory Items in the Block Area

Group pretend play takes place in areas other than the dramatic play center. Children can do their follow-up pretending after a field trip in the block center, as well. Mount pictures of the field trip site at eye level on the wall to give children seated on the floor ideas for creating new kinds of buildings. Add appropriate accessories to the shelves within the block area as well. If you have been to a construction site, put out little trucks, figures of people, string (for ropes and wires), plastic tubing, even stones if you want to be very realistic. Accessories can also be put at the sand or water table, although pretending in these areas is more often solitary or parallel than group play.

■ Read a Book

In *Saturday at The New You* (Barber, 1994) African-American Shauna goes every Saturday to help her mother in her beauty shop, The New You. A delightfully realistic story, some of your girls may want to pretend to be Shauna in their own pretend beauty shop. Read the book to find what props they will need.

In *Haircuts at Sleepy Sam*'s (Strickland, 1998), three African-American brothers hurry down to Sleepy Sam's barber shop on Saturday morning to get their hair cut—the way they want it. Your boys may want to join the barber shop fun, pretending to be one of the three fun-filled barbers at Sleepy Sam's.

Two books that can serve as motivators for creating a pretend eating establishment in the classroom are *Mel's Diner* (Moss, 1994) about an African-American family that runs a diner, as told by their little girl who helps; and *In the Diner* (Loomis, 1993), another day-in-the-diner book with a similar story line, told in rhyming words such as "bacon sizzles; syrup drizzles."

RESOLVES PLAY CONFLICTS IN A POSITIVE MANNER

Not only does group play teach children the social skills of gaining access and maintaining a role in the playing, but more important, it also gives young children the opportunity to learn to get along together. This is not always easy to learn. Conflicts of all kinds occur with high frequency in an early childhood classroom. Children need to learn how to resolve such disagreements in a positive manner. Unfortunately, many children have learned from television that it is acceptable to resolve conflicts with violence (Johnston, 2003, p. 28). Your job is to help them learn a different type of resolution. During group play, major conflicts often focus on (1) roles, (2) direction of play, (3) turns, or (4) toys.

Pretend roles are important to the children who take them. In spontaneous dramatic play, certain children often insist on being mother, or father, or doctor. If several children want the same role, a conflict often results. This does not necessarily mean a physical fight, but usually an argument and sometimes tears. If the children involved cannot resolve the conflict quickly, play is disrupted and sometimes disbanded.

Conflict also occurs over play themes in dramatic play (e.g., "Let's play doctor." "No, let's play superheroes"), as well as the direction of the action, which is generally made up on the spot. Egocentric young players often want their own way and frequently disagree over who will do what, what they are going to do, and what's going to happen next.

"It's my turn!" or "It's my toy!" are other comments frequently heard during group play in early childhood classrooms or playgrounds. Youngsters 3, 4, and 5 years old are still for the most part focused on themselves and their desires. It is most annoying for them to find that someone else got there first, or has what they want, or won't listen to them.

Often children turn to the teacher to resolve these conflicts. You need to be aware, however, that the youngsters themselves have the capability to resolve social play conflicts on their own. That, in fact, should be your goal for the children: to help them resolve play conflicts by themselves in a positive manner. How do you do it? To begin with, your observation of individual children will tell you which youngsters are able to resolve conflicts on their own and which ones are not.

Rather than focusing on the negative behaviors during such conflicts, spend some time observing how certain children are able to settle their disputes positively. We can learn a great deal from children if we are willing to try. Consider the following running record that looks at 4-year-old Alex:

> *Alex, Calvin, and Dominic are on top of the indoor climber pretending to be astronauts in outer space. Alex is the captain of the space shuttle. All three boys make zooming noises and motions. Alex pretends to steer. Two other boys climb up the ladder to try to join the group but are ignored and finally leave.*

Alex:	*"Duck! There's a meteor!"*
Calvin:	*"It's my turn to be captain, Alex."*
Alex ignores Calvin and continues steering.	
Dominic:	*"No, it's my turn. I never get a turn."*
Alex:	*"We're being bombarded by meteors! You need to duck!" (He ducks his head.)*
Calvin:	*"I'm captain now."*
Alex ignores Calvin and continues steering.	
Dominic (to Calvin):	*"You can't be captain. Alex is still captain."*
Alex:	*"You can be copilot. They always have copilots."*
Calvin begins pretending to steer.	
Alex:	*"Bang! We've been hit by a meteor! Abandon ship!" (He slides down to floor and runs across room; other boys follow.)*

This exciting adventure in outer space is typical of the vigorous dramatic play preferred by 4-year-olds. It should also be exciting for an observer to see a 4-year-old like Alex handle a role conflict with such composure and success. Alex is often the leader in such play, and from the way he uses ideas and words, it seems obvious that he is an experienced player. Children who play together a great deal learn by trial and error what works in resolving conflicts and what doesn't. They also find out what works with particular children and what doesn't work.

The first strategy Alex uses is *ignoring*. Alex ignores the boys who try to join his shuttle play. They finally go away, so he certainly notes that this kind of ignoring is a successful way to keep out unwanted players. Then another potential conflict emerges: Calvin wants a turn to be captain. At first Alex ignores this request as well. Then Dominic joins in and also wants to be captain. Now Alex tries another strategy: *distracting*. He tells them that they are being bombarded by meteors and wants them all to duck. A strategy like this may sometimes work. In fact, here it seems to work with Dominic, who gives up his own demand to be captain and cooperates with Alex. But it does not work with Calvin because he has not given up his demand. So Alex tries another strategy: *negotiating*. He offers Calvin another role: copilot. Calvin accepts and the play continues. This does not mean that either boy knows exactly what a copilot is. But it must sound satisfactory to Calvin because he *compromises* his demand to be captain, accepts the new role as copilot, and plays the role the same as Alex plays the captain's role.

Alex may very well have known that he had to do something to satisfy Calvin, or perhaps Calvin would have: (a) gotten up and left or (b) continued his complaints and disrupted the play. Obviously Alex wanted the play to continue and wanted to keep his own role as captain and leader. He was successful in *negotiating a compromise*.

Did all of this actually happen in so short a dramatic play incident, you may wonder? Yes, it did. Observe a child involved in group play for yourself and record everything that happens. Then step back and interpret what you have seen. Obviously the children do not talk or think in terms of strategies. These are adult interpretations. Young children do not conceptualize in this manner. They just do it. Trial and error has taught certain alert youngsters what works for them and what doesn't when conflict arises. Children who are successful in resolving play conflicts in a positive manner often use such strategies as those in Figure 5–4.

If your observations turn up children who do not seem to know how to resolve play conflicts like this, then you may want to consider some of the following solutions.

If You Have Not Checked This Item: Some Helpful Ideas

■   Have Child Observe and Discuss Play with You

For a child who often tries to resolve play conflicts by hitting or shouting, you can have him observe a group play situation with you and then discuss it. If the child had sat next to you as you observed and recorded the Alex-Calvin-Dominic play incident, you might say to him:

Alex is captain of the space shuttle, isn't he? But Calvin wants to be captain, and so does Dominic. What does Calvin do? Yes, he tells Alex that he wants to be captain. Does Alex let him? No, he doesn't pay attention to him. So then what does Calvin do? Does he yell at Alex? No. Does he hit Alex? No. He tells him again that he wants to be captain. Does Alex let him? He lets him be a copilot. Is that like being captain? What would you do if you were on the space shuttle with Alex, Calvin, and Dominic? Do you think your ideas would work?

Figure 5—4   Strategies to Avoid Conflict

- Ignoring
- Distracting
- Reasoning
- Negotiating
- Cooperating
- Compromising

If the play situation you observe with the child contains some aggressive behavior, ask the child what the result of the behavior was. Most children will not continue to play with peers when they act aggressively. Often they won't allow such peers in their play groups in the first place.

■ Use Puppets

For a child who gets into arguments frequently with his playmates, try using two puppets to enact a similar situation. Name your puppets something like Tong-Talk-Back and Fronz-Friendly. Put one on each hand and enact a play situation where Tong argues with Fronz over something, with the result that the playing is discontinued. Ask the child what Tong could have said to keep the play going. Ask what the child would have done.

■ Coach the Child on How to Act

Sometimes you need to go to a child and coach him or her on how to act or what to say in a conflict situation. You must make it clear to children that you will not let them hit anyone or hurt anyone or call them names. When they are upset about something, children must learn to express their feelings in words. You may need to coach those who do not know how:

> Tell Jenny how you feel, Teresa, because she took your egg beater. Don't call her names. Tell her why you are upset. Say it in words. Say: "Jenny, you took my egg beater. That makes me feel bad. I wasn't finished using it. Please give it back."

■ Do a Group Role Play

Sometimes the play group itself doesn't know how to resolve conflicts peacefully. In that case, you can consider having a group role play sometime after the children have settled down. The players should be other children, so that the children having conflicts can watch. Take a role yourself if it seems appropriate. Then you can help direct the play. Give a few other children names and roles to play. Describe a brief conflict situation. Then have the children act it out. Stop the play at any time to discuss what has happened and whether there is a better way to resolve the conflict. Try each of these techniques to see which ones work best with your particular children.

■ Read a Book

There are other ways to get what you want besides aggressive actions. Read to one or two children at a time. In *What Shall We Play?* by Sue Heap (2002), as discussed in Chapter 3, Lily May wants to play fairies and Matt wants to play trees. So they played trees. Again Lily May wants to play fairies, but Martha wants to play cars. So they play cars. Still again Lily May wants to play fairies, but Martha wants to play cats. So they play cats. Of course Lily May still says fairies, but Matt wants to play wobbly Jell-O. So that's what they play. Finally Lily May says, "Now let's play fairies and I have a magic wand."

So they play fairies and all of them fly. Ask the children how Lily May finally got them to play fairies.

For children who want to pretend about astronauts there are several good books. *Hedgie Blasts Off* (Brett, 2006) is an exciting adventure of a hedgehog astronaut who flies to the planet Mikkop to save Big Sparkler, the volcano that shoots out sparkles. *If You Decide to Go to the Moon* (McNulty, 2005) is a more scientific but imaginary journey of a boy blasting off and traveling to the moon and back, with a foldout of the beauty of Earth and all its creatures. *Zoom! Zoom! Zoom! I'm Off to the Moon* (Yaccarino, 1997), for younger preschoolers, has a little boy astronaut blasting off for the moon and returning to a big celebration with simple rhyming words at the top of every page.

OBSERVING, RECORDING, AND INTERPRETING SOCIAL PLAY

How should you use the Social Play Checklist section with your children? The following description shows how one classroom team put the checklist to use:

When 3-year-old Lionel entered the classroom as a new child in January, he seemed to have a great deal of trouble interacting peacefully with the other children. By the end of the third week he still had not joined any of the group activities. The staff members decided to make a running record of Lionel during the free-play period for several days and then transfer the results to the Child Development Checklist. Here is a typical example of a running record made on Lionel:

> Lionel gets two little cars from box in block corner & sits on floor moving cars around, one in each hand. Makes car noises with voice. Plays by himself with cars for five minutes. Moves closer to block building that two other boys are constructing. Plays by himself with his cars. Then L. tries to drive his cars up wall of building. Boys push him away. L. waits for a minute, then tries to drive car up wall of building again. Boys push him away. L. crashes one car into building & knocks down wall. One of boys grabs L's car & throws it. Other boy pushes L. away. L. cries. Teacher comes over & talks with all three. L. lowers head & does not respond. Boys say: "He was trying to knock down our building with his cars." and "We don't want him to play with us."

When the staff members reviewed the running records and checklist information recorded for Lionel (see Figure 5–5), they concluded that he knew where to find materials and toys in the classroom and how to use them. They also interpreted his Social Development Checklist results to mean that Lionel was beyond onlooker behavior, and that he played by himself and in parallel play as closely as possible to other children because he wanted to join them. His methods for gaining access to a group (e.g., driving his car up the block building wall and crashing his car into the wall) were neither successful nor acceptable.

Staff members also determined from the Language Skills checklist that his language development was not as advanced as that of many of the children in the classroom. That may have been the reason he did not express his wants verbally. Perhaps because he was a new outsider, he had not made friends with the other children, and his aggressive actions had prompted some of the boys to keep him out of their play.

CHILD DEVELOPMENT CHECKLIST

Name___Lionel_____   Observer_____Barb_____
Program _Preschool-K2_____   Dates___1/20_____

Directions:

Put an **X** for items you see the child perform regularly. Put **N** for items where there is no opportunity to observe. Leave all other items blank.

Item	Evidence	Dates
3. Social Play		
_N_ Spends time watching others play	L. is beyond this level of play	1/20
_x_ Plays by self with own toys/materials	Plays with little cars	1/20
_x_ Plays parallel to others with similar toys/materials	Moves close to block building with his cars	1/20
____ Plays with others in group play		1/20
____ Makes friends with other children		1/20
____ Gains access to ongoing play in positive manner	Tries to gain access by driving cars up bldg—then crashes car	1/20
____ Maintains role in ongoing play in positive manner	Does not gain access	1/20
____ Resolves play conflicts in positive manner	Crashes car into bldg when boys won't let him play	1/20

Figure 5-5   Social Play Development Observation for Lionel

The staff decided to try pairing up Lionel with Adrian, a more mature player, who might help Lionel get acquainted with the others and gain access to their play. They asked Lionel and Adrian (who also liked cars) to build a block garage for the little cars, and said they would take a photo of it. Eventually two other boys joined them in this activity.

This type of observing and recording can assist individual children in their development of social play skills and help them grow and learn in your program.

LEARNING ACTIVITIES

1. Use the Child Development Checklist, Social Play Development, as a screening tool to observe all of the children in your classroom. Which ones engage mainly in solitary play? In parallel play? In group play? Are any unoccupied or onlookers?

2. Choose a child whom you have observed engaging in solitary play. Do a running record of the child on three different days to determine what kind of solitary play was performed. How could you involve the child in the next level of play? Should you do it? Why or why not?

3. Choose a child whom you have observed engaging mainly in parallel play. What kind of play does the child do? How can you help the child get involved in the next level of play? Use one of the suggested activities and record the results.

4. Choose a child who is not able to gain access to ongoing group play, and use one of the activities described to help the child enter and play with a group.

5. Make a running record of a child observed in group pretend play. Afterward, determine which of the discussed strategies the child used to resolve conflicts. If the child is not successful, describe why and how you would propose to assist him.

SUGGESTED READINGS

Fox, L., & Lentini, R. H. (2006). "You got it!" Teaching social and emotional skills. *Young Children, 61*(6), 36–42.

Gallagher, K. C., & Mayer, K. (2006). Teacher–child relationships at the forefront of effective practice. *Young Children, 61*(6), 44–49.

Lamm, S., Grioux, J. G., Hansen, C., Patton, M. M., & Slaton, A. J. (2006), Creating environments for peaceful problem solving. *Young Children, 61*(6), 22–28.

Ma, I. (2006). Temperament and peer relationships. *Childhood Education, 83*(1), 38–43.

Riley, J. G., & Jones, R. B. (2007). When girls and boys play: What research tells us. *Childhood Education, 84*(1), 38–43.

Wohlwend, K. E. (2004/05). Chasing friendship: Acceptance, rejection, and recess play. *Childhood Education, 81*(2), 77–82.

CHILDREN'S BOOKS

Barber, B. E. (1994). *Saturday at The New You.* New York: Lee & Low.*

Barton, B. (1990). *Bones, bones, dinosaur bones.* New York: HarperCollins.*

Begaye, L. S. (1993). *Building a bridge.* Flagstaff, AZ: Northland.*

Brett, J. (2006). *Hedgie blasts off.* New York: G. P. Putnam's Sons.

Child, L. (2004). *I am too absolutely small for school*. Cambridge, MA: Candlewick.*

Cooney, N. E. (1993). *Chatterbox Jamie*. New York: Putnam's.

Edwards, B. (2002). *My first day at nursery school*. New York: Bloomsbury.*

Elliott, L. M. (2002). *Hunter's best friend at school*. New York: HarperCollins.

Falwell, C. (1993). *Feast for 10*. New York: Clarion Books.*

Heap, S. (2002). *What shall we play?* Cambridge, MA: Candlewick Press.*

Henkes, K. (1989). *Jessica*. New York: Puffin.

Loomis, C. (1993). *In the diner*. New York: Scholastic.*

McNulty, F. (2005). *If you decide to go to the moon*. New York: Scholastic.

Moss, M. (1994). *Mel's Diner*. Mahwah, NJ: Troll Communications.*

Ringgold, F. (1991). *Tar Beach*. New York: Crown.*

Strickland, M. R. (1998). *Haircuts at Sleepy Sam's*. Honsdale, PA: Boyds Mills Press.*

Yaccarino, D. (1997). *Zoom! Zoom! Zoom! I'm off to the moon*. New York: Scholastic.

*Multicultural

6 Prosocial Behavior

PROSOCIAL BEHAVIOR CHECKLIST

___ Shows concern for someone in distress

___ Can tell how another feels during conflict

___ Shares something with another

___ Gives something to another

___ Takes turns without a fuss

___ Complies with requests without a fuss

___ Helps another do a task

___ Helps (cares for) another in need

DEVELOPING PROSOCIAL BEHAVIOR

A second area of young children's social development that is of great concern to early childhood caregivers is the positive aspect of moral development, better known today as *prosocial behavior.* It includes behaviors such as *empathy*, in which children express compassion by consoling or comforting someone in distress or by expressing how another child feels during interpersonal conflict; *generosity*, in which children share or give a possession to someone; *cooperation*, in which children take turns willingly or cooperate with requests cheerfully; and *caregiving*, in which children help someone complete a task or help someone in need.

These are some of the characteristics that help people get along in society, motivate people to interact with one another, and help make us human. Young children are not in the world alone. They are part of a family, a clan of relatives, a neighborhood, a community, a country, and a world of similar beings. To be an integrated member of the "human tribe," the young child needs to learn the tribe's rules of behavior from the beginning.

This learning, you may argue, should happen in the home, and it certainly does happen in an informal manner, whether or not parents realize they are teaching their children pro- or antisocial behavior. Children absorb everything that happens around them: what mom does when the baby cries, what dad does when someone upsets him, and what family members do when they disagree. Every emotional situation presents the young human with forceful patterns of behavior he can model. We know only too tragically that adult child abusers often come from families where they were abused as children. Riley, San Juan, Klinker, and Ramminger (2008) tell us research has shown that "children are more accepted by peers when their parents are warm, responsive, and in tune with their children" (p. 54). The opposite is also true. Children have more difficulty getting along with peers when parental interactions are hostile and overcontrolling.

Prosocial behavior can be modeled as well. Both the home and the school should be aware of the powerful lessons taught by behavior modeling, which the child absorbs so readily at this early age, especially in emotional situations. What does the teacher do when out-of-control children upset her? It is so important for the other young children around her that she does not let her negative feelings burst out.

Children also learn behavior by methods other than examples in both the home and the preschool. Formal—often restrictive—rules for "proper behavior" have been drummed into children from time immemorial. Children are scolded or punished when they behave in an unacceptable manner. They may cry, sulk, or slink away, or they may try to behave correctly next time. But just as often, they stick out a tongue in defiance and grumble, "Try and make me!"

There is a better, easier way. Many early childhood specialists these days are turning to focus on the so-called **prosocial behaviors** in a search for ways to raise more humane members of the race. Not only does the learning of prosocial behaviors promise positive results, but it also offers more satisfying responses for both the child and the caregiver. Mitchell-Copeland, Denham, and DeMulder (1997) found, in fact, that it is the quality of the relationship between a teacher and a child that predicts how prosocial a child will behave toward the other children:

> Prosocial behavior is behavior that reflects care or concern on the part of one child toward another; for example, by helping, comforting, or simply smiling at another child. The present study found that such caring behavior in response to others' emotional overtures is predicted by the quality of the relationship between a teacher and a child. Simply, the more secure the child-teacher relationship, the more prosocial a child is toward his or her peers. (p. 35)

Empathy, generosity, cooperation, caregiving: How do you teach such behaviors, anyway? They sound so elusive. Aren't some children just "good" naturally? If children seem to be good, they probably are mature and have a good "home start." You can reinforce that maturity and home influence by the way you treat children in the early childhood classroom and by the way you model behavior yourself. But first, as with other areas of development, you should know where each child already stands concerning his or her development of prosocial behaviors. You will need to observe every child on the eight checklist items and then make plans to provide individual support or activities.

Each of the checklist items in this chapter is an observable behavior that shows if the child possesses a particular prosocial capacity.

 # SHOWS CONCERN FOR SOMEONE IN DISTRESS

Empathy

Empathy is the capacity to feel as someone else feels. A person with empathy is able to understand another person's emotional response to a situation and to respond in the same way—in other words, "to feel for him." Empathy is a step beyond mere sympathy in which one person can respond emotionally to another but from his own perspective. With empathy, you respond from the other person's perspective and participate in his feelings.

For the child to separate his or her viewpoint from another's is a necessary step toward acting prosocially. Riley et al. (2008) describe two kinds of perspective-taking skills: social and emotional. Social perspective-taking means the child has to sense what another person wants. Emotional perspective-taking means the child has to sense how another person feels (p. 50). This is not an easy task for most egocentric young children, although some seem to sense it intuitively. But most learn perspective-taking, and thus empathy, through their interactions with peers and through modeling and direct teaching on your part.

Some psychologists believe empathy is the basis for all prosocial behavior. Without this capacity, a child will be unable to behave naturally in a helping, sharing, compassionate manner. Obviously, the child can be forced to perform prosocially whether or not she understands what she is doing. But this forced performance is not empathy. Forced behavior has little to do with the prosocial skills of our concern. Behavior must be natural and spontaneous to show that children possess empathy. Are children born with empathy, or do they learn it? Probably a little of both. Eliot (1999) tells us:

> Emotional learning begins immediately, in the form of imitation. Infants just a few hours old are capable of mimicking certain facial expressions or hand gestures.... Imitation is important because it serves as the basis for the development of empathy, the ability to experience what another person is feeling. (p. 300)

Although newborns appear to have the rudiments of this emotion, true empathy requires the conscious recognition of another person, which doesn't emerge until months or years later. Until this cognitive development has occurred, the child may have difficulty expressing empathic concern for others because he is still too egocentric and therefore unable to see things from another person's point of view. Because they lack this empathy, infants and toddlers often mishandle their animal pets. The youngsters have no idea that pulling a puppy's ear or squeezing a kitten might hurt the animal. If these actions do not hurt the children, they think, why should the pulling or squeezing hurt their pet? This egocentric point of view eventually changes with cognitive maturity and experience, but until a child can view things from another's perspective, as mentioned, he may have difficulty showing empathic compassion for another's distress.

When does this change take place? It happens gradually, of course, as does all development. Yet, some part of the human capacity to respond to distress is genetic, for even infants 1 day old will become upset and cry when a nearby baby starts crying. Then, somewhere between 1 and 2 years of age, the cognitive change takes place. Toddlers, although they may not act appropriately, begin to show genuine concern for others. These youngsters have been observed giving up their favorite stuffed animal to an older sibling who is crying. They feel comforted by the animal, so why not give it to another in distress? The act of giving demonstrates their developing capacity for empathy.

From 2 to around 6 years of age, children begin to react more appropriately to the distress of others around them. The ages of the children in your class fall within this range. You will be observing them to determine which ones show concern for another child in distress. Distress may be displayed by someone who is hurt, sad, or sick. She may be crying or even screaming. It also could be less dramatically disclosed by a child who puts her head down on a table, goes into a corner, or leaves the room after an upsetting incident.

You will note that some children immediately come to the side of the upset child. Others do not. The children who display this empathic concern, of course, may be special friends of the upset child. On the other hand, highly sensitive children who have no particular friendship with the child also will come close. Some youngsters just stand by the side of the distressed child and look at him or her, or look for the teacher. Others actively console the child, touching or speaking to him or her.

If a teacher causes the distress, a similar thing may happen. A child being reprimanded or scolded often will attract a circle of observers. In this case, you will have more difficulty determining empathic behavior because some of the observers are more concerned for themselves and how the teacher feels about them. Others are simply curious. Before you check this item about them, watch and see who comforts the child after the teacher leaves. The children who comfort the child are not necessarily taking the distressed child's side against the teacher. If they stay with the child after the teacher leaves, they more than likely have true compassion for the child.

The classroom worker should also know that family life and cultural background have a definite influence on empathic response in children. If families stress prosocial behavior, their children will exhibit it more than children from families that do not teach or demonstrate it.

Some cultures stress consideration of group members more than others. Communal-type cultures, such as the American Indian, Pacific Island, and Asian cultures, often stress concern for group members more than the mainstream U.S. culture does. Our culture seems to stress competition among individuals more often than cooperation. The individual is glorified in our society, sometimes at the expense of the group. As a teacher in the multiethnic, multicultural society that makes up the United States, you need to be aware of such differences.

Research has shown that community size and the role of women also influence a child's prosocial inclinations. Children from a rural rather than urban setting, from a small rather than large city, or from a society where women have an important economic function outside the home are more inclined to show concern for others (Damon, 1983, p. 132). If the mother works outside the home, the children often learn to take on responsibilities at an early age. Learning helping and caretaking tasks so early obviously inclines children toward prosocial behavior. Thus, the teacher needs to know something about the individual child's background to assess the child's behavior accurately.

Individual differences in children also influence behavior, as Damon (1988) noted:

> Like the capacity for empathy itself, such individual differences in empathic responding show up very early in life. Children as young as one and two respond differently to others' distress. Moreover, these differences between individual children endure, at least through the early childhood years. (p. 18)

If you have not checked this item for many of your children, do not be alarmed. Showing concern for someone in distress is one of the more difficult prosocial behaviors for preschoolers to learn. Distressful situations that happen to others upset onlookers, too. Before the onlookers can respond, they often need to overcome their own anxieties. They thus are more apt to step back and let the adult show the concern. Your own prosocial response, however, can involve your children in this humane act.

If You Have Not Checked This Item: Some Helpful Ideas

■ Model Empathic Behavior in the Classroom

You must serve as a model for the children. When something distressful happens to someone, you should show your own concern by going to the person; touching, hugging, or holding the person if this is appropriate; talking to the child; and giving the youngster time and space to feel better again. You can also convey your own empathy for distressed children by listening carefully to what they are saying and responding appropriately, so that they feel you understand their fears, worry, or anger. Marion (2003) tells us: "Research shows that a child is highly likely to imitate models when it comes to prosocial behavior. Modeling is an extremely powerful way to encourage children to act prosocially" (p. 310). But then you must be consistent and practice what you preach.

A second way to model this behavior is through your actions in distressful situations that happen outside the classroom. If someone is hurt or dies, if a tragic event is shown on television, or if something upsetting happens within their families, you must let the children know you are concerned, too.

■ Help the Children Show Their Own Concern

Talk to the children both privately and in a group about distressful happenings that have occurred. Encourage the children to ask questions about things they do not understand. Show them that it is all right to cry and express emotions openly. When a class member is in the hospital, have the class make and send a card.

When children are pretending in dramatic play about people or pets being hurt, listen to see if the youngsters express compassionate feelings even in pretend. You can model a concerned role in pretending, too, by expressing your own sympathy when one of the players is pretending to be hurt or a baby is getting a shot from the doctor.

■ Read a Book

Sometimes when something is wrong a person or animal feels *grumpy,* like bulldog Gloria does in *Grumpy Gloria* (Dewdney, 2006). The children in the family do everything they can think of to help her feel better. Nothing works. The large exciting illustrations show why. Gloria feels left out because the littlest girl with a new doll ignores her. When Gloria's bike crashes into her doll buggy, Gloria falls into it and finds that there's room for two. Wonderful rhyming words express emotions (sullen, scowly, sulky, slumpy), along with expressive faces, helping children understand distress. Can they reenact this story with their own scrunched up faces?

In *Ha Ha, Baby* (Petty, 2008) the family is distressed because baby is not laughing or smiling. What's wrong? One by one they try to make baby laugh. Ma tickles him. He scowls. Pa picks him up and tosses him. Baby glares. Grandma plays peek-a-boo. Baby turns away. Grandpa blows bubbles. Baby harrumphs. When they all gather round and coo at baby, he cries. Then the little boy comes in and sees baby glaring. So he comes up close and stares at baby with no laughing until . . . first a dimple, then a smile, and out comes a laugh. Baby is okay. How would your children resolve the distress?

 # CAN TELL HOW ANOTHER CHILD FEELS DURING CONFLICT

Empathy

Empathy for another child is sometimes difficult to feel when one youngster is in conflict with another. But you can actually *teach* children to become aware of what another child feels to convert the conflict to positive feelings. This new approach to conflict resolution is called "other-esteem conflict conversion" and often works when no other behavior management strategy succeeds.

Feel what the other child feels. Can a young child actually do this? Researchers have found that with the beginning of a role-taking capability, at about 2 or 3 years, children become aware that other people's feelings may sometimes differ from theirs. More important, because children now know that the real world and their perceptions of it are not the same thing, and that the feelings of others are independent of their own, they become more responsive to cues about what the other is feeling.

Most conflicts in preschool revolve around possession disputes. Someone wants something that another child is playing with, or someone takes something away from another child. Most such conflicts are brief interruptions in play, resolved by the children themselves, as they should be. Occasionally the conflict becomes so overpowering an adult must intervene. When hitting, fighting, throwing things, or crying breaks out, it is time for an adult to take action.

Suppose Samantha has been playing with the baby buggy and Kimberly takes it away from her; Samantha then hits Kimberly, making her cry. What will you do? You might try "other-esteem conflict conversion." Take the two girls aside, and when they are calm enough to talk, ask each to tell you what happened. Accept whatever they say. Samantha will talk about her buggy being taken, and Kimberly will complain that Samantha hit her. Accept both of these two points of view.

The conflict can now be converted to a feelings solution by asking each girl in turn to tell you how she thinks the other girl feels. "Look at her face, Kimberly. What does that tell you about how she feels?" Kimberly may insist that it is Samantha's fault because Samantha hit her. You can say, "Yes, you already told us about that. But now we are talking about feelings. How do you think Samantha feels?"

You can ask Samantha the same question about Kimberly. "She's been crying, Samantha. How do you think she feels?" But Samantha may still be talking about Kimberly taking her buggy. The conversion will occur when you can get her to consider the other girl's feelings, not her own. "Yes, you told us about Kimberly taking your buggy, but now we are talking about feelings. Look at her face. How do you think she feels?"

Many children are surprised to find another side to the conflict. Most have never been asked to consider the other child's feelings. But when they realize this is what you want them to do, they are relieved to find that you do not blame them and are not going to punish them. Instead, you are asking them to consider the other girl's feelings.

Each child has attention focused on her in a positive way. You have listened to her side of the conflict. You are asking the other child to look at her and tell how she feels. Finally, you will be asking the other child to think of something that will make the first child feel better. Just taking this action makes her feel better already. The same focus then switches to the other child, and she also begins to feel better.

Finding out about another child's feelings is often a great revelation to young children. Nobody has asked them to do such a thing before. Preschool children are extremely sensitive to feelings because they are so open with their own feelings and have not yet learned to conceal them as older children and adults do. When you point out to them that other children have feelings that can be hurt, most youngsters are willing to try to make amends. Nobody is being blamed for the conflict. They are only being asked to consider the other child's feelings, then to do something that will make the other child feel better. Many "other-esteem converted conflicts" like this end up with a hug. As Marion (2003) pointed out: "Children are more likely to be cooperative, helpful or compassionate if they understand another's perspective" (p. 314).

Teachers can help children become more responsive to cues of what the other child is feeling by directing the attention of the children in conflict to each other's faces as noted earlier. "How do you think Samantha feels, Kimberly? Look at her face." She should have no trouble identifying a basic emotion. Research has found that even infants as young as 6 weeks of age can distinguish between one facial expression and another, whereas children 2 and 3 years old have no trouble associating basic emotions with facial expressions (Hyson, 2004, p. 52). Still it may be hard for many teachers to believe that a complete conflict turnaround can happen when children become aware of one another's feelings.

Wittmer & Honig (1994) described one such incident:

> A preschool teacher kneeled to be at eye level with a child who had just socked another child during a struggle for a bike. The teacher pointed out the feelings of the other child: "He's very sad and hurt. What can you do to make him feel better?" The aggressor paused, observed the other child's face, and offered the bike to the crying child. (p. 7).

Children may, however, have difficulty with the words for expressing emotions because of their limited verbal skills. Here is where you come in. Be sure to spend time talking to individuals and small groups about their feelings. Read books about feelings as suggested in Chapter 4, and mount pictures around the room of children's faces expressing particular feelings. Can children name the feelings they see? With your support they can develop this ability to verbalize feelings. As Ramsey (1991) noted,

> Because even very young children resonate to others' emotions, children can empathize and communicate on an emotional plane before they are consciously aware of others' perspectives. (p. 18)

If You Have Not Checked This Item: Some Helpful Ideas

■ Use Mirrors

Bring in several small hand mirrors and place them on a table set for four to six children. Let children look in each mirror and make faces of their own. Have them make a happy face, a sad face, an angry face, a surprised face. Then have them make a face for their tablemates and let the others guess what kind of face they are making.

■ Use Puppets

Put a hand puppet on each of your hands and let them engage in a conflict over a toy. You can be the voice for each puppet. Then you can stop the conflict as the teacher and ask each puppet:

What happened? How do you think the other puppet feels? What would make the other puppet feel better? Ask the children in your small group to join in, too. Ask them how they think each of the puppets feels and what would make them feel better.

■ Read a Book

How Are You Peeling? Foods with Moods (Freymann & Elffers, 1999) is a goofy food book with one or two scrunched up fruit or vegetable faces on each page asking such questions as: Happy? Sad? Feeling blue? Feeling bad? Oranges and lemons discuss being jumpy, worried, or grumpy. Onions wonder about feeling secure or not so sure. Children are sure to identify with the whimsical facial expressions of potatoes and tomatoes that in turn can help them learn the words to express their own feelings during conflict.

Figure 6–1 Nicole has Drawn a Picture of Herself and How all the Vegetables Feel Good with Smiley Faces Except the Strawberry.

The Way I Feel (Cain, 2000) is a feelings word book with a different child expressing a different emotion every two pages. Colorful cartoon-like characters bounce, scrunch, or erupt across the pages. Even the words themselves (silly, scared, disappointed, happy, sad, angry, thankful, frustrated, shy, bored, excited, jealous, and proud) display the characteristics of that emotion. Have your listeners find a page that describes them if they can. If not, what would one look like?

■ Draw a Picture

Children can also draw their own pictures of what they would look like. The silly food faces from the former book may interest some of them. In fact, they may want to combine their face pictures into their own book. See Figure 6–1.

SHARES SOMETHING WITH ANOTHER

Generosity

Sharing and helping may be the easiest prosocial behaviors for young children to learn because these behaviors occur most frequently in the early childhood classroom. This is understandable considering the many opportunities children in a group have to learn to share materials with one another. Sharing also is easier to do than some of the other prosocial acts because the child suffers only a temporary loss. The youngster must give up something, but only temporarily.

Genuine sharing must be a spontaneous act of generosity with play materials or play space, claim Hearron and Hildebrand (2005). "Forcing children to share only makes a child feel that adults are on the other child's side. Children who have difficulty sharing should be helped to have long, sustained experiences with equipment and supplies that no one forces them to relinquish, so they can finally feel that they have 'enough'" (p. 234).

Again, the child's ability to perform such an action depends on her cognitive maturity as well as the lessons she has learned from those around her. The younger the child, the more inclined she is to consider the toy she is playing with as her personal possession, whether it is or not. Children still retaining this egocentric view also will try to take the toys they want away from others, and they will be upset if the others do not comply. The fact that these egocentric children want the toy makes it theirs, according to their reasoning.

To prevent squabbles, early childhood teachers need to establish rules governing "property rights" at the outset. When children first enter the classroom, they are confronted with a treasure trove of materials to enjoy. The youngsters need to understand that these materials belong to the center, not to specific children. Individuals can use the materials, but the items must be shared, which means letting other children use the items either at the same time (as with paints), or one after another.

Nevertheless, some squabbles over equipment can be expected. The primary way young children learn rules is to test them. Who gets the favorite toy first? Favorites are often trikes and eggbeaters. Some teachers consider it best to have several favorites to avoid problems. Other teachers believe that such problems afford good opportunities for children to learn how to share and take turns.

Researchers find that older children are more likely to share than younger ones. Sharing with peers, in fact, increases dramatically between the ages of 4 and 12. If a toy belongs to the center, young children are more likely to share the item than if it belongs to them personally. Most teachers ask children to keep toys from home in their cubbies. The youngsters can show the toys to the class at circle time, but afterward, the toys must be put away until it is time to go home.

Because sharing is such an important prosocial skill in the preschool center, everyone must spend time helping individuals learn the skill. You may want to start by observing the prosocial behavior of every child in your class to see which children already know how to share and which ones may need help in learning this skill. Some children will share toys, food, and turns when asked by another child, but many still need the teacher to make the request.

More children will share if the teacher makes sharing important for everyone. As noted by Honig and Wittmer (1996):

> Sharing increases among preschool children whose teachers give them explanations as to why sharing is important and how to share. (p. 64)

Some children will share materials when asked by another child.

If You Have Not Checked This Item: Some Helpful Ideas

■ Model Sharing

Sharing is one of children's behaviors that definitely reflects adult modeling behavior. Adults often ask children to share with their peers, but how often do adults ask a child to share with them? Try it. Set up a situation where a child who has had difficulty in sharing must share a seat, a piece of equipment, or an activity with you. For example, invite him to paint at your table. Then, set out one jar of paint that the two of you must share. Verbalize as you work on your painting. Let the child know he is doing well in sharing the paint.

■ Use Group Toys

Encourage a small group of two, three, or four children to construct a building using one set of Lego blocks. Have several children work on a large puzzle together. Have one child hold the wood while another pounds at the woodworking table. Tie a wagon to the trike and let one child pedal while another rides in the wagon.

■ Set Up a Food-Sharing Experience

Bring in one apple, one orange, or one melon for each small group at your snack tables. Discuss with the children how they can share the piece of fruit. Let them help you divide it equally.

■   Take a Photo

Use a digital camera to capture an incident of children's sharing. Show it to one small group at a time and talk about it with them. Children remember visual images like this almost better than words.

■   Read a Book

In *Mine! Mine! Mine!* (Becker, 2006) Gail tells the story of her "greedy" cousin Claire, who comes to visit her, touching all her stuff and trying to play with her toys. Gail throws a fit, telling Claire not to touch or play with anything. Soon Claire is in tears. Gail's mother demonstrates sharing, but Gail will still only share her discarded toys and food she doesn't like. Sharing of favorite toys is still beyond her ability. Her mother talks more about sharing, saying she will get better and it will get easier as she grows. How would your children handle Gail's problem?

 GIVES SOMETHING TO ANOTHER

Generosity

A great deal of research has been done on this aspect of prosocial behavior, perhaps because researchers find it easy to measure whether children are willing to give one of their possessions to someone else. Most studies show that as children increase in age, their generosity also increases. What is not so clear is why.

We assume that as children become cognitively more mature, they will be less concerned with themselves as the center of everything and more aware of others and their needs. We also expect that as children grow older they will have more experiences with social customs through the teachings of their family, friends, school, and church. In other words, children will have learned how society expects them to behave.

Other things also affect young children's giving. Length of ownership is one. Children seem more willing to give up a possession they have had awhile than something they have just obtained. Perhaps the novelty eventually wears off. The item they are giving also makes a difference. It may be a toy, an item of food, a piece of candy, or money. Whether they have more of the same also makes a difference. Reasons for the giving have a bearing, too. Is the item given out of friendship, because someone asks, because someone has a need, or because an adult suggests that it might be a nice thing to do? Older children are more apt to respond to adult suggestions or pressure.

Children are more likely to share a favorite toy rather than give it up totally. Formal occasions for giving, such as birthdays or religious holidays, teach children about giving. The child's egocentric nature often shows itself when he or she wants to give mom a toy truck or doll for her birthday.

Teaching generosity, however, is tricky in our society. We send children mixed messages. We tell them it is a good idea to give to people in need, but then the youngsters see us turn away charity solicitors at our front doors. Children hear us refuse to lend a lawn mower or power tool to a neighbor who has a need. "Let him buy his own," we say. "Let him work as hard as we did to buy this one."

Ours is a very material possession–oriented culture. Children learn this from television and our responses to the messages TV sends. Children also witness how strongly we feel about our cars, flat-screen TVs, and computers. It is an interesting commentary on our values to see families with fewer material possessions being much more generous with them.

Not all cultures value personal material possessions so highly. American Indians and Pacific Islanders, for instance, teach their children that giving is more important than possessing. Many of these people practice what they preach by simply giving a possession to a neighbor or relative who admires or has need of it. These people believe they are enhanced by the person accepting something from them.

Nevertheless, as preschool teachers, we need to be aware of how this prosocial behavior works with children in our classroom, regardless of our society's confusion over the issue. Use the Child Development Checklist to determine which children will give a possession to someone else. Are these the same children you have checked on the other prosocial behaviors? What other characteristics do these children share? Do they come from families where they have been given a great deal of responsibility? Prosocial behavior such as generosity is often more evident in such children. Do these children seem more mature in all areas of development? We know that generosity increases with age and maturity.

Use the Child Development Checklist to see which children will give or permit another child to take one of their toys.

If You Have Not Checked This Item: Some Helpful Ideas

■   Be a Model of Generosity

Let children see you give up something to someone in need: an item of clothing, a book, food, or money. How do you feel about this? As adults, we are often reluctant to begin this kind of giving ourselves. Will it get out of hand? Will people take advantage of us? How genuine is your own generosity? We have been conditioned to acquire material possessions and guard against losing them.

■   Articulate Generosity

When situations arise where giving is appropriate, talk to your children about it. Maybe they could donate some money or services to help someone in need. Perhaps you could put up a box for pennies, clothing, or canned goods to be given to fire, storm, or flood victims. Or perhaps you could take a small group at a time to the collection center with their donations.

■   Read a Book

A Birthday Basket for Tia (Mora, 1992) is the story of Cecilia's gathering of gifts for her Great-Aunt Tia's surprise birthday party. She goes through her house choosing items that she and Tia have enjoyed together, putting them in a birthday basket. When Tia comes to the surprise party, Tia shows her appreciation for each item.

   Coconut Mon (Milstein, 1995) is a lovely, lilting Caribbean counting story with a coconut vendor calling out and selling his wares one by one until only one coconut remains. This he whacks apart with his machete and gives to a little boy, who in turn invites everyone to come and share his DE-LIC-I-OUS coconut.

   In *Flower Garden* (Bunting, 1994), a little African-American girl and her daddy purchase a tray full of potted flowers at the supermarket and carry it page-by-rhyming-page on a bus, up the stairs, and into their apartment where they transplant pansies, daisies, daffodils, geraniums, and tulips into a rainbow jamboree of flowers in a window box just in time for Mom's birthday. What do your children give as birthday gifts?

   In *Rabbit's Gift* (Shannon, 2007), Rabbit sees that snow is coming and it's time to find more food. After he finds two turnips, he wonders if Donkey has enough to eat, so he rolls his extra turnip over to Donkey's house. When Donkey finds the turnip she wonders if Goat has enough to eat, so he carries the turnip over to Goat's house. When Goat finds the turnip she wonders if Deer has enough to eat, so she rolls it over to Deer's house. Deer has plenty but he wonders about Rabbit, so he carries the turnip back to Rabbit's house. Rabbit is surprised to find the turnip and decides to share it with all of them together. Can generosity spread like this in your classroom?

TAKES TURNS EASILY

Cooperation

Cooperation includes a wide range of prosocial behaviors, including turn-taking; alternating the use of toys, equipment, or activities; complying with requests; coordinating actions to accomplish goals; accepting other children's ideas; and negotiating and compromising in play. Certain of these behaviors were discussed in Chapter 5 under Social Play. In this item we are specifically looking at alternating behaviors: that is, going in a certain order, first one and then another; waiting for another child to have a turn; or alternating the use of toys and equipment with other children.

Taking turns is another type of behavior that must be learned. To maintain a smoothly running program, you must help children learn at the outset how to take and wait their turns in a group situation. Those with brothers and sisters at home may have learned this already, although it is sometimes the inappropriate behavior they learn, such as the biggest or strongest gets the first turn.

To evolve from an egocentric being whose only concern is satisfying his own wants and become someone who understands the wants of others, the young child must learn to see things from another person's perspective, as previously mentioned. To do this, the child needs the freedom to be able to function on his own in an open environment. His parents can support this development best by helping him understand others' views and by encouraging him to participate in decision making about his own behavior. Following the dictates of authoritarian parents gives the child little opportunity to develop these skills. Warm, supportive mothering also makes a difference in the development of prosocial behaviors in young children. As children move into elementary school, the best support they can have at home is a nonauthoritarian mother who allows and encourages her children to act on their own.

In preschool, however, children must learn to take and wait for turns. You can help them by setting up the environment so that it speaks to these needs. Arrange activity areas for three, four, or five children at the most, and put signs or symbols for these numbers in every area. Then children can regulate their own numbers during free play. Let children take tags to hang on hooks or pegboards, tickets to put in pockets mounted on the wall, or their pictures covered with clear contact paper to hang in the area where they want to work. Or have activity center necklaces hanging in each center for children to wear when they play in the particular center.

Many programs start the day with a circle time. The teacher lets the class know what activities are available, and the children choose activities by taking tags or necklaces. If a child finishes playing in her chosen area before free-choice time is over, another child can pick up the tag and take his own turn. This is how children learn about taking turns and waiting their turn.

Nevertheless, the teacher must let them do it on their own. Directing individuals into particular areas is the same as the authoritarian parent telling his or her children what to do. If we want children to develop prosocial behaviors, we must not short-circuit the process by trying to do it for them. To learn the necessary social interactions, they must be allowed to experiment with turn-taking on their own.

Giving children this freedom takes forbearance on the part of the preschool staff. It is so much easier for adults to make choices for children. After all, children take *so long* to make up their minds. But we must remember the purpose of the free-choice period in the first place: to allow children to learn how to make their own decisions based on their own interests and needs, and how to deal with the consequences of their choices. Through freedom of choice, children also learn that another child may have the same choice as theirs, and that they may have to wait their turn before their choice is available.

Children also learn by using timing tools such as a kitchen timer or 3-minute hourglass when several children want turns using favorite toys or equipment. One child can hold the timer while another uses the toy for 3 minutes. When it is the next child's turn, the child after her gets to hold the timer. Some children enjoy controlling the timer as much as playing with the toy!

Children can also learn to take turns by "signing up" for a turn. Put a list on a clipboard with a pencil near the activity, and have children sign up (print or scribble their names) one after the other. When their turn is finished, they can cross out their names. Some children whose names are far down the list may need to wait until another day. But then they find they are near the top of the list.

If You Have Not Checked This Item: Some Helpful Ideas

■ Have Children Practice Turn-Taking in Dramatic Play

Set up a particular play area, such as a beauty or barber shop, and put out two or three chairs for the customers. Then the children will have to wait their turn, just as in real life. Or set up a bakery or other facility where people must take numbered tickets to be waited on. Have tickets available for the children to take. One child can be the ticket taker.

Set up a traffic light in the classroom for the children to use in their big truck play. The light can be a cardboard milk carton with holes cut out and covered with clear food wrapping paper colored red, yellow, and green. Not only will children learn safety rules, but they also will realize that cars and people must wait their turns before using the road at a street crossing.

■ Bring in a Special Plaything or Activity to Teach Turn-Taking

Introduce a new toy at circle time and have the children help set up the rules for playing with it, such as the number of people who can use the toy at one time and for how long. The children may want to use the kitchen timer you have provided to keep track of the time. One child will surely want to keep the time. The teacher can also help children sign up for turns on a chart.

■ Read a Book

Me First (Lester, 1992) is the humorous tale of Pinkerton, a pig who always has to be first in everything he does with the other little pigs in his scout troop. Then one day on a picnic to the beach, he hears a voice asking, "Who would care for a sandwich?" He rushes ahead of the others shouting "Me first!" Suddenly he finds himself in the clutches of a "sand witch" who demands all kinds of care from him, finally teaching Pinkerton that it does not pay to be selfish.

In *Haircuts at Sleepy Sam's* (Strickland, 1998), as discussed in Chapter 5, three African-American brothers go to the barbershop and must wait their turns for a haircut.

COMPLIES WITH REQUESTS EASILY

Cooperation

A second aspect of cooperation involves complying with requests. This includes following directions, but more especially, it looks at how children cooperate with one another by complying with something another child or the teacher requests of them. For example, a child or the teacher may request another child to help, to wait, to give up something, to take a different role, to give information, or to do something in a certain way.

Complying with requests in a cooperative way is not blind obedience; for example, "Josh, move your truck," may not result in Josh doing anything. Children should know the reason they are being asked to do something. They should be expected to behave in a reasonable way if the request is reasonable: "Josh, Anna Maria needs you to move your truck so she can get her coat out of her cubby."

Nor is cooperative compliance a submission to a demand. Before you decide on checking this item for a child or leaving it blank, be sure it is compliance to a request and not to a demand that you are witnessing: not "Get out of the way, Josh," but "Anna Maria needs you to move your truck" or "It's pickup time, Andy. Please help Jerome pick up the blocks."

Children are more likely to comply with a teacher's request if they are given choices. As Wittmer and Honig (1994) noted,

> Toddlers and preschoolers struggling to assert newly emergent autonomy cooperate more easily with caregiver requests if they feel empowered to make choices. Adults can decide on the choices to be offered. (p. 11)

For example, a child who resists helping with block pickup can be given an interesting choice of pushing the blocks over to the shelf with a big "bulldozer" block or loading blocks in the truck and driving them over to the shelf.

Once a child has complied with a request, he can expect to be thanked for doing it. If you are the one who made the request, don't forget to thank the child. When you notice a child complying with another child's request, be sure the requesting child thanks him or her. Cooperative behavior like this implies reciprocal behavior on another's part. You may need to point this out in a pleasant, not correcting manner: "Anna Maria, Josh really moved his truck for you in a hurry. Don't forget to thank him."

If You Have Not Checked This Item: Some Helpful Ideas

■ Model This Behavior

Make a point of complying with reasonable requests a child makes of you. When you do this, be sure to articulate what you are doing so that other children understand it. For example, you might say aloud as you help pick up blocks, "Andy and Jerome asked me to help them pick up the blocks because they have to leave early today." This should help children understand that you comply with their requests just as you expect them to comply with yours. In addition, it gives them the reason for your response so they will know you may not always help everyone pick up blocks on a daily basis. Do the children thank you for helping?

If children are demanding things of one another and not getting the desired results, you can also model the behavior that they should use: "Rhonda, why don't you say to Anne, 'Please give me my doll. It's time for me to go home. I'll bring it back tomorrow.'"

■ Read a Book

Carlos and the Squash Plant (Stevens, 1993) tells the story of the Hispanic boy Carlos who helps his father grow vegetables in their garden but hates to take a bath afterward. His mother says if he doesn't wash his ears a squash plant will grow in them—and one day it does! Carlos is so embarrassed that he covers his head with his big straw sombrero and even wears it in the house. Large colorful illustrations show Carlos working, eating, and finally washing—making the squash plant disappear. This book is written in English and Spanish.

In *Pedrito's Day* (Garay, 1997), little Pedrito's father has gone north to work, so Pedrito is expected to help his mother and grandmother. He shines shoes in the market of his Nicaraguan home. On the day of this story, Tia Paula asks Pedrito to run an errand for her and get change for a bill she gives him. Although he complies with this request without a fuss, on the way he stops to play soccer with some older boys and loses the money. Now he must face up to the moral dilemma of accounting for the loss. What would your children do?

In *Some Dog* (2007), George, an old basset hound, leads a comfortable but lazy life with a man and woman until a new little lively dog called Zippity joins the family. He dashes around, bringing in the newspaper, even catching fish when they go fishing. "Some dog," they say. George is jealous. But one day a terrific thunderstorm roars in and scares Zippity so badly that he zips around knocking over things until they put him out. When the man and woman realize Zippity is lost, they beg George to "go find Zippity." He doesn't really want to in the middle of the storm, but when they give him

Zippity's blanket to sniff, he knows he can track a scent anywhere, so he does. Through rain and wind, over a seesaw and slippery trail he goes, until he finds the little dog sinking into thick, oozy muck. He rescues him and returns home, to be called "some dog," once again.

HELPS ANOTHER DO A TASK

Caregiving

Along with sharing, this is by far the most common prosocial behavior exhibited in the preschool classroom, possibly because it is much less of a cognitive act. Children simply assist someone in doing a task. They may be asked or they may volunteer to help when they see that a peer or the teacher needs help with something. The children do not need to understand or intellectualize about what is happening. They do not need to take another person's perspective. They just need to lend a hand. Most children have already learned this activity at home, and they soon realize that the early childhood classroom also expects children to help out.

Research shows that this behavior may occur three times more than any other prosocial act. Even so, helping others do a task is not all that frequent in proportion to other behaviors. Seeking help occurs about six times more frequently than giving help among 3-year-olds (Moore, 1982, p. 77). But as children grow and develop through the early childhood years, helping behavior increases. Whereas slightly more than half of the youngest children (3-year-olds) assessed in one study gave some form of help, 100 percent of children 9 and 10 years old gave help (Smith, 1982, p. 216).

The youngest preschoolers, nevertheless, may have some problems with helping. They may not know when to help or how much help to give. Sometimes children overdo their help, becoming bossy and not knowing when to stop. Other times children don't do enough and simply stand around watching before the task is finished. The best way for them to learn the cues for appropriateness in such social behavior is to plunge in and try it. Other children are not shy about telling peers what they are doing wrong.

You, on the other hand, need to set up activities that require children to give assistance. Setting tables for snacks and lunch is one; getting out cots or mats for naptime, getting out paints and mixing them, filling the water table, feeding the pets, and helping with cleanup are a few of the others. These tasks are multiple learning situations for cognitive concepts as well as learning when and how to help.

Children may have favorite chores as well as chores they try to avoid. Making up a "helpers chart" gives every child a chance at every chore. Let the children help design the chart. It can contain pictures as well as titles for every job. Children can hang their name tags on it daily at circle time or once a week if they decide to keep the same job for a week. New jobs can be added from time to time as needed. Use your creativity to invent the jobs. Here are a few you may want to include:

mail carrier delivers notes to office

zookeeper: takes care of pets

aquarium attendant: feeds fish

door attendant: opens and closes door

chef: helps prepare snacks

server: sets tables, passes food

nap attendant: gets out and puts away cots

gardener: waters plants

You cannot expect young children to do all the work in the classroom. Picking up the block corner is a case in point. One or two children can easily empty the shelves while building a complicated construction. Putting all the blocks back in proper order during cleanup time may be an overwhelming chore for two. A teacher should get down on the floor with them and lend her assistance, just as the children help her from time to time.

If certain children are not helping at all, you need to engage them in chores. Chores do not need to be drudgery. Children enjoy doing grownup things. Youngsters have no idea that pickup is any less interesting than getting toys out, unless adults make pickup seem less glamorous. In fact, you should make cleanup in your room a fun thing to do by treating it as a game and not a chore.

If You Have Not Checked This Item: Some Helpful Ideas

■ Invite a Helper to Your Class on a Weekly Basis

Anyone engaged in an occupation is a helper. Perhaps a different parent could visit the classroom on a weekly basis to talk to the children about how he or she helps. One class created a new job on the helpers' chart each week after the helper had visited. Sometimes the children had to stretch their imaginations to create the new job. After a telephone installer had visited the room, they finally decided to add the job "telephone attendant" in which one child would be allowed to answer the classroom phone each day.

■ Use Games for Pickup and Cleanup

Block shelves fill up much easier when they are hungry monsters waiting to be fed by the children, or when children do pickup to music, trying to finish before the song is over. Long blocks can be bulldozers pushing the blocks or toys over to the shelves. Have your children help you think up other pretend games at cleanup time.

■ Read a Book

In *Too Many Tamales* (Soto, 1993) Maria helps her mother make tamales for the Christmas party they are having. Maria's mother takes off her diamond ring to knead the dough. Maria puts it on her own thumb and continues to help. Later during the party she remembers the ring, and thinks it must have fallen into the dough. She enlists her cousins to eat all the tamales, carefully looking for the ring before her mother finds out. But the ring ends up on her mother's finger and everyone has to help to make more tamales.

In *Dumpling Soup* (Rattigan, 1993), set in Hawaii, Marisa gets to help wrap dumplings for the first time for Grandma's midnight soup at the family's annual New Year's gathering. Hawaiian, Japanese, Korean, and English words are scattered throughout the story, reflecting Marisa's "chop suey" family. She loves to help, but worries that no one will want to eat her lumpy dumplings. They do—even though they call them "elephant ears"!

HELPS (CARES FOR) ANOTHER IN NEED

Caregiving

This particular behavior is perhaps the most difficult of the prosocial skills for young children to attain. Helping another in need is an extension of the first checklist item, Shows Concern for Someone in Distress. Whereas showing concern involves "compassion," a psychological support, helping another in need involves "caretaking" or "giving nurturance," a physical act of giving help. The help may consist of giving affection (e.g., a hug, a touch), positive attention (getting help, giving help), reassurance (verbalizing support), or protection (standing by, physical protection).

For young children, giving these things is difficult because the youngsters must first overcome their own anxiety caused by the stressful situation. They must also have an understanding of how to act. In emergency situations, even adults are often confused and have difficulty knowing what to do.

Very young children have been observed taking action when another child or person is in distress, but the instances are rare compared to other prosocial acts. Toddlers have been seen giving their bottles or cuddly toys to siblings who cry in distress. Giving something to the victim seems to be the main response of young children. They more often seek help than give it, however. In addition, those who seek help in the preschool approach adults more than peers, although older preschoolers are beginning to turn to their companions for help.

Crying or uttering distressful sounds is supposed to trigger an empathic response in others, according to psychologists. Scientists look to the animal world and note the intricacies of response in many species. Have we humans lost much of this seemingly instinctive concern? We read in the news or see on television the instances of adults ignoring victims who call for help. Much of this inattention seems to be a defensive reaction on the part of people who either do not want to get involved in the trouble or fear they might be victimized themselves.

Can children learn helping? Studies show that children can learn helping behaviors in pretend or symbolic situations, but when the real thing occurs, they still may not

Older children can help younger children on the playground.

respond. Children with nurturing caregivers do give more help and express more sympathy. It seems, then, that modeling behavior does promote prosocial helping (Yarrow, Scott, & Waxler, 1973, p. 254). As Robinson and Curry (2005–06) point out: "Educators must create opportunities for natural caring in the classroom if children are to develop their own instinctive caring" (p. 70).

What kinds of situations calling for help might occur in the classroom? Injury is one. Children may fall and hurt themselves, cut themselves, or burn themselves. Losing something is another situation that requires help. Children may lose mittens, money, or a toy. Accidental damage also necessitates assistance. Children may spill paint on themselves, fall in the mud, or spill milk or other food. They may drop and break a piece of equipment.

How can children help? Depending on the situation, they could go for help if an adult is not in the immediate vicinity. They could comfort the victim by talking or touching. They could help pick up spilled substances, look for lost items, or give information to help the adult solve the problem.

Children are more likely to give help to others when with someone. Teachers should take advantage of this by involving the children in helping situations whenever possible, rather than doing all the helping themselves. When children are involved on their own, teachers should step back and allow the youngsters to do what they can.

You can also check off this care-giving item if you observe children giving care in pretend situations to their dolls or classroom pets. Does someone put a blanket around her doll saying that she is cold and might catch the flu? Does someone notice that the guinea pig is out of water? If elderly people or babies visit your classroom, watch which children show signs of caring. Does someone get a chair for the guest without being asked?

If You Have Not Checked This Item: Some Helpful Ideas

■ Discuss Helping with the Children

When helping behavior occurs, spend time in small and large groups talking to children about it. Sometimes television events such as natural or man-made disasters seen by children are good discussion items. How do people help the victims?

■ When You Model Helping Behavior, Talk About It

You will be helping children all year long. Talk aloud to the children about what you are doing, and help them find ways to assist you.

■ Draw a Picture About Helping

Children in one classroom had been talking about how people in America can help people in other parts of the world. They decided to draw pictures about helping people around the world.

Figure 6—2 One Child Drew People Jumping Out of a Plane with Parachutes to Take Food to People in the World.

■ Read a Book

Love Can Build a Bridge (Judd, 1999) illustrates a number of incidents of multiethnic children's caregiving of one another. One boy helps another who has been hurt on a slide; a boy helps a girl who has fallen while rollerblading; another boy helps a girl who has injured her arm while jump-roping. What would your listeners do in the same situations? It is always important to discuss books after reading to see what children understand about them.

In the humorous story *Clink, Clank, Clunk* (Aroner, 2006), a gentleman rabbit drives his open-top car on his way to town, when various mechanical problems start popping up with loud clunking noises. Meanwhile, various animal friends along the way beg for a ride. Rabbit helps them all: mole, squirrel, porcupine, possum, beaver, crow, skunk, fox, and cow. When the car finally runs out of gas everyone has to get out and help rabbit push till they get there. Then he junks his clunker, buys a big new car, and they all ride home together. Vroom! What would your children do in such circumstances?

Another humorous talking-animal story is *Stuck in the Mud* (Clarke, 2008), in which mama hen is frantic because one of her chicks is stuck in a deep, thick, mud hole. She tries to pull it out, but instead becomes stuck herself. Cat hears hen calling and rushes to help. But she becomes stuck too. Dog hears cat, comes, and gets stuck as well. Sheep comes and gets stuck. Horse comes and sinks in, and even the farmer gets stuck. The reader should then open the folded-over page to see little chick hopping out of the mud by himself and telling them he was never stuck—but thanks for playing with him. What do your children think about this helping scenario?

OBSERVING, RECORDING, AND INTERPRETING PROSOCIAL BEHAVIOR

Sandra is a 4-year-old who rarely performs any of the prosocial behaviors on the checklist unless forced to by the teachers—for example, sharing a toy or waiting for her turn (see Figure 6–3). The teachers have noted that she also seems immature in the area of social skills and plays only by herself, not parallel to the others or with a group. The teachers have concluded that Sandra may not have developed the ability to see things from a perspective other than her own. Therefore, she has little or no empathy for others who need help or who are in distress.

A suggestion to help Sandra develop empathy is to give her two hand puppets, one with a bandage on its arm and the other a helper. You can put the bandaged puppet on your hand. Ask her to find out what happened to the injured puppet. If she likes this kind of play, she may be willing to "branch out" and play "helping puppets" with a second child.

Observe the other children in the classroom for these same prosocial skills. If you find other children who have not performed many of the items on the checklist, try pairing them with a child who does display these skills and give the pair a social task to perform together, such as helping you help anyone who needs assistance putting on boots or jackets.

Child Development Checklist

Name___Sandra_____   Observer___Angie_____

Program___Pre-K_____   Dates___11/5_____

Directions:

Put an **X** for items you see the child perform regularly. Put **N** for items where there is no opportunity to observe. Leave all other items blank.

Item	Evidence	Dates
4. Prosocial Behavior		
_____ Shows concern for someone in distress	Moved away from Mark when he got hurt	11/5
_____ Can tell how another feels during conflict	Does not answer when asked how another child feels	11/5
_____ Shares something with another	Would not give up her doll to Betty	11/5
_____ Gives something to another	Has not done this	11/5
_____ Takes turns without a fuss	Cried when she could not be first on the swing	11/5
_____ Complies with requests without a fuss	Always says "I can't" or "I don't know how" when asked to do something	11/5
_____ Helps another do a task	Same as above	11/5
_____ Helps (cares for) another in need	Would not help when Mark got hurt	11/5

Figure 6–3   Child Development Checklist Observation for Sandra

LEARNING ACTIVITIES

1. Use the Child Development Checklist for prosocial behavior as a screening tool to observe all the children in your classroom. Which ones demonstrate the most prosocial behavior? Do they also have friends in the class? Which children show few prosocial skills? How do these children get along with the other children in general?

2. Choose a child who exhibits few of the prosocial skills. Do a running record of the child on three different days to determine how he or she works and plays with the others. Do an activity with the child to help him or her share, take turns, or help. Record the results.

3. Choose a child who is a good helper and try to involve him or her in getting another child to participate in helping. Discuss the results.

4. Try two of the ideas under If You Have Not Checked This Item with a child who shows few prosocial skills. Discuss the results.

5. Read one of the children's books from this chapter with a group of children or do an activity with the group to promote prosocial skills. Discuss the results.

SUGGESTED READINGS

Beaty, J. J. (1999). *Prosocial guidance for the young child.* Upper Saddle River, NJ: Merrill/Prentice Hall.

Eisenberg, N. (1992). *The caring child.* Cambridge, MA: Harvard.

Fox, L., & Lentini, R. H. (2006). "You got it." Teaching social and emotional skills. *Young Children, 61*(6), 36–42.

Kemple, K. M. (2004). *Let's be friends: Peer competence and social inclusion in early childhood programs.* New York: Teachers College Press.

Lillard, A., & Curenton, S. (1999). Do young children understand what others feel, want, know? *Young Children, 54*(5), 52–57.

Puckett, M. B., & Black, J. K. (2005). *The young child: Development from prebirth through age eight* (4th ed.). Upper Saddle River, NJ: Merrill/Prentice Hall.

Stockdale, D. F., Hegland, S. M., & Chiaromonte, T. (1989). Helping behaviors: An observational study of preschool children. *Early Childhood Research Quarterly, 4*(4), 533–543.

CHILDREN'S BOOKS

Aroner, M (2006). *Clink clank clunk!* Honesdale, PA: Boyds Mills Press.

Becker, S. (2006). *Mine! Mine! Mine!* New York: Sterling Publishing Co.

Bunting, E. (1994). *Flower garden.* San Diego: Harcourt Brace.*

Cain, J. (2000). *The way I feel.* Seattle, WA: Parenting Press.

Clark, J. (2008). *Stuck in the mud.* New York: Walker & Co.

Casanova, M. (2007). *Some dog!* New York: Farrar, Straus, & Giroux.

Dewdney, A. (2006). *Grumpy Gloria.* New York: Viking.

Freymann, S., & Elffers, J. (1999). *How are you peeling? Foods with moods.* New York: Scholastic.

Garay, L. (1997). *Pedrito's day.* New York: Orchard Books.*

Judd, N. (1999). *Love can build a bridge.* New York: HarperCollins.*

Lester, H. (1992). *Me first*. Boston: Houghton Mifflin.

Milstein, L. (1995). *Coconut Mon*. New York: Tambourine Books.*

Mora, P. (1992). *A birthday basket for Tia*. New York: Simon & Schuster.*

Petty, K. (2008). *Ha ha, Baby!* London: Boxer Books (Sterling Publishing Co.)

Rattigan, J. K. (1993). *Dumpling soup*. Boston: Little, Brown.*

Shannon, G. (2007). *Rabbit's gift*. Orlando, FL: Harcourt.

Soto, G. (1993). *Too many tamales*. New York: Putnam's.*

Stevens, J. R. (1993). *Carlos and the squash plant*. Flagstaff, AZ: Northland Press.*

Strickland, M. R. (1998). *Haircuts at Sleepy Sam's*. Honesdale, PA: Boyds Mills Press.*

---

[1]Multicultural

7

Large Motor
Development

☑ LARGE MOTOR CHECKLIST

____ Walks down steps alternating feet

____ Runs with control over speed and direction

____ Jumps with feet together

____ Hops on one foot

____ Climbs up, down, across climbing equipment

____ Throws, catches, and kicks balls

____ Rides trikes, bikes, and scooters

____ Does creative movement

DEVELOPING LARGE MOTOR SKILLS

Physical development for young children involves two important areas of motor coordination: movements controlled by the large or gross muscles and those controlled by the small or fine muscles. This chapter will focus on large motor development, involving movements of the whole body, legs, and arms.

We understand that a child's physical development depends upon his biology, but we need also to consider Vygotsky's contention that environmental conditions are just as important (Sanders, 2002, p. 18). In the classroom it is the teacher who provides assistance (*scaffolding*) according to the child's *zone of proximal development*—the level of difficulty at which he can accomplish a task with the help of an adult or skilled peer. Thus, teacher-designed activities for individuals and small groups play an important role in this chapter.

Because motor development is so obvious and visible an aspect of children's growth, we sometimes take it for granted. Of course children will grow bigger, stronger, and able to perform more complicated motor tasks as they increase in age. Of course they will learn to run and jump on their own. Why should we be concerned with motor development in preschool? Sanders (2006) tells us:

Most children naturally develop at least a minimal level of physical skills simply by moving through their home and school environment on a daily basis. But too many children never get the opportunity to refine these physical skills to a level where they feel competent to participate in popular games and physical activities. Children who do not participate and are not physically active are the ones who are more likely to become overweight or obese. (pp. 4–5)

Need for More Exercise

The fact that many youngsters today are leading much more sedentary lives than children did formerly causes great concern among health professionals. The increase in television watching along with the decrease in safe outdoor play areas has cut down tremendously on the motivation and opportunity for young children to run, jump, and move their bodies. Up to half of U.S. children may not be getting enough exercise. We know that exercise and physical activity are necessary to build healthy bones and muscles, to control weight, to decrease blood pressure, and even to reduce the risk of later heart disease and diabetes (Staley & Portman, 2000, p. 68).

Current brain research adds impetus to the need for physical exercising in preschool children. As Leppo, Davis, and Crim (2000) pointed out:

The early years of life are ideal opportunities for children to learn to develop control of their muscles and movement. During this critical period, neural pathways develop [in the brain] through the process of myelinization. Myelin, a fatty insulating substance, covers axons and expedites the transmission of neural impulses in a predetermined pattern. The process is most rapid from birth to 4, then continues at a slower pace until around 20. The process of myelinization permits children to develop control over their motor functions and sensory abilities, and also facilitates their cognitive functioning. (p. 142)

Even more important, these motor pathways in the brain of the developing child are refined through use. The more a particular pathway is activated through consistent use, the likelier it is to be stabilized. Hunter (2000) concurred when he told us: "Sitting still makes us dumber. The brain doesn't grow. Without movement, the body doesn't grow either. Muscles are weaker and bones are too. Certain injuries among teenagers now have never been seen in such numbers, probably because in early childhood so many bodies sat around, often in front of screens, both television and computer" (p. 50).

Lack of exercise in the early years has other serious consequences. When children sit watching television, they often snack on junk food. Soon they are putting on excess body weight that may lead to obesity. Sanders (2002) reported that: "Physical inactivity has contributed to the 100% increase in the prevalence of childhood obesity in the United States since 1980" (p. xiii). Obesity, in turn, may lead to childhood diabetes and other serious ailments.

Preschool teachers often feel that their programs already serve the physical needs of their children by providing first-rate playgrounds for daily use with swings and slides, climbing and balancing equipment, and trike paths with trikes, scooters, and wagons. Isn't this enough, they ask? Not according to many specialists. They quote studies that show:

For four- and five-year-olds on the playground for one-half hour of free play, only 11% of the children participated in vigorous activity such as riding tricycles, playing tag, or dribbling balls, while 60% of the children participated in sedentary activities such as sitting, standing, and talking (Staley & Portman, 2000).

How is it on your playground? Are your children getting enough exercise? Using the checklist items, observe each of them on your outside playground to see who is running, jumping, climbing up ladders and sliding down slides, pumping swings, and negotiating monkey bars. Record the names of children engaged in vigorous play and those who are not. Do you agree or disagree with the specialists about the percentage of children involved? They also say that "a total of 30 to 60 minutes of daily vigorous exercise, with the heartbeat above 140 BPM, is necessary for optimal health of children under 18 years of age" (Werner, Timms, & Almond, 1996).

For most programs this means that teachers must do more than merely provide children with equipment and time to use it. It means *you will need to lead all the children in exercising every day.* Young children can complete such a 30-minute regimen in several short time segments of 10 or 15 minutes either inside or outside the classroom. Make it fun. This chapter includes a number of creative exercises for everyone—including you.

In addition, some preschool children may need special help with large motor skills. To determine who they are, you should observe and record how each child accomplishes the eight skills on the large motor portion of the checklist. Although all children develop physically in a predictable sequence of skills that can be observed, there are definitely individual differences. These can be determined through observation.

You also need to become familiar with the sequence of normal large motor development. You can then apply this knowledge to particular children to determine whether they are developing predictably within the normal range, or whether they may need some special help. Finally, you can assemble a repertoire of activities to motivate all the children in your program, including those who may be lagging behind in this development.

Motor Skills in the Preschool Years

The eight items under large motor development on the Child Development Checklist are neither a complete list of large motor skills, nor a sequence of skills, although one skill may precede the other. Instead, these eight items represent a sample of important basic motor behaviors that children should have acquired by age 5.

It is important to screen all the children in your class at the outset using this or a similar list of skills to identify children needing special help. You and your coworkers can play physical games with the children doing running and jumping while another staff member observes and records on a single sheet. At another time, walk up and down stairs with children and give them opportunities to move their legs and feet and arms and hands in rhythm as someone observes. Still another time, toss various types of balls to the children for catching, throwing, and kicking practice.

List the children's names on the left side of the sheet. At the top put the eight skills in abbreviated order: Walks/Runs/Jumps/Hops/Climbs/Throws & catches/Rides/Creative movement. Observers can check off when they see the children completing each of the skills. Remember, this should not be a test, but an observation of natural accomplishments from activities set up in the classroom and on the playground. Take as many days as necessary to complete these observations. You will then have an idea of the nature of the large motor skills each child possesses. Setting up developmentally appropriate activities is possible once you have this important information about the children. Observe and record individual accomplishments whenever children become involved in these activities.

 ## WALKS DOWN STEPS ALTERNATING FEET

Most 3-year-olds walk in adult fashion. Their trunk is no longer top-heavy as it was at age 2, and they have mastered walking to the extent that they no longer need to watch their feet or balance with their arms. They swing their arms as they walk just like adults. They still may fall occasionally on uneven ground, but they are not so far from the ground that falling hurts too much. Now they can walk up stairs alternating feet unaided, although many 3-year-olds put two feet on a step coming down. This is what you will be looking for. The balance of some children this age is good enough to allow them to walk straight, one foot in front of the other, on a line or a balance beam.

Although growth occurs in a predictable chronological sequence, it seems to happen in spurts. It seems as though the body has to stop and assimilate all the development that has occurred before going forward again. This "assimilation stop" often happens at the half-year age. Children who walked and ran smoothly at 3 may seem to have a "relapse" at 3½. They suddenly act uncertain with their large motor skills and may even seek the hand of an adult as they walk along. This happens especially going up or down stairs. They may have good days when everything about their bodies seems to work well, and bad days when they stumble and fall.

Four-year-olds have control of their bodies and take great pleasure in using them. Children age 4 walk confidently in many ways: forward, backward, sideways, tiptoeing, or striding along. They are able to walk a circular line for the first time without losing their balance. Most can walk both up and down stairs, alternating their feet. Although their skipping is not at all perfected (most can do it only with one foot), some start to roller skate.

Four is an age of great exuberance and expansiveness. If you do not provide enough walking, running, and climbing activities in your center, 4-year-olds may make their own. They definitely need an opportunity to practice their large motor skills both inside and outside the classroom.

Five-year-olds are at the adult stage in walking. This is another period of great growth when children spurt up as much as 2 or 3 inches in a year. Much of this growth occurs in the legs, which lengthen more quickly than the other body parts. Boys may be a bit taller and heavier than girls, but they are about a year behind them in physiological development (Caplan & Caplan, 1983, p. 237).

Children of this age can walk a straight line for about 10 feet without stepping off it. Many can skip with alternating feet now. Even the less-active 5-year-olds now can walk down stairs alternating feet. Five-year-olds are less expansive and more controlled than 4-year-olds in all their actions, but children age 5 still love to use their large motor abilities in play.

If You Have Not Checked This Item: Some Helpful Ideas

■ Practice Walking

Studies show that children between the ages of 2 and 6 demonstrate observable improvement in basic motor patterns after repeated performance with adult encouragement. Instruction in the movement doesn't seem to help, but practice does. Play follow-the-leader in the classroom and outside with yourself as the leader who sets the pace. Do all kinds of walking motions and be sure everyone has a chance to copy you before you change to the next movement: march, shuffle, stride, giant-step, tiptoe, bunny hop, skate. Do trotting and high-stepping around the trike path. Bring out a cassette player and put on peppy marching music. Have half the group stand and clap while the other half marches to the beat.

Clappers are exercising too. Gellens (2005) pointed out: "Physical activity helps the blood flow to the brain and helps move information from temporary memory to permanent memory. Clapping out a telephone number or address helps young children memorize this important information" (p. 14). Think of all the clapping games your children can do.

Also set up a walking-hopping-sliding trail in your classroom or large motor room with contact footprints stuck to the floor in various patterns of movement with one foot or two. Use the trail with one small group at a time to see if they can change their steps when the footprints change. Two prints together mean "stamp, stamp" in place.

■ Practice Step Climbing

If your room is in a building with a second story, make it a practice to take children up and down the stairs every day. If you have no stairs, go for a field trip to a building that has stairs, or get a rocking-boat-steps piece of equipment to practice on. Some playground equipment also has stairs, but ladders are not the same.

■ Play Animal Charades

Have two or three children demonstrate how an animal walks and let the others guess what animal it is. Try elephant, horse, rabbit, kangaroo, snake, and turtle walks.

■ Have a Dinosaur/Mammoth Stomp

Children love to imitate animals. Let them walk like dinosaurs to heavy-sounding music with a slow beat. Read them *Saturday Night at the Dinosaur Stomp* (Shields 1997), to get them going. Stop when you come to the dinosaur movements and have a few children at a time demonstrate how they "trampled and tromped," "made tracks," "plodded

Children can practice step climbing on a playground slide.

on big fat legs," and "capered and twirled." Read **Mammoths on the Move** (Wheeler, 2006) where dazzling pictures of gigantic wooly mammoths migrate during winter months with "stepping, stomping, marching, tromping" in rhyme. Can your children tromp through the classroom as you read?

■ Walk Through the Woods

Your trees can be empty 2-liter soda bottles that you set up like a maze in one section of the classroom. Children can make the trees by wrapping the bottles in colored peel-off paper. Children can tramp their way around and through the woods to drum beats or more clapping. Play follow-the-leader or make up a story about being lost in the woods (Sanders, 2002, p. 22).

■ Read a Book

Some preschool teachers involve their children in various kinds of classroom walking when they take them on a "bear hunt," walking in place. This imaginative experience is available in two lively picture books. One is the traditional *We're Going on a Bear Hunt* (Rosen & Oxenbury, 1989). The other is *Oh, Look!* (Polacco, 2004), in which three little goats escape from their pen "can't go over it; can't go under it; can't go around it" so they go through the open gate for a series of great adventures that your children can repeat—always standing in place and moving their feet while you read the story.

Funny Walks (Hindley, 1994) shows people and animals walking in all sorts of ways: hopping, skipping, bounding, slinking, shuffling, scurrying, and marching. Then it invites the listeners to do their own funny walks. *Rap-a-Tap-Tap: Here's Bojangles, Think of That!* (Dillon & Dillon, 2002) has this famous African-American dancer high-stepping in rhyme through city streets.

RUNS WITH CONTROL OVER SPEED AND DIRECTION

Running may be the large motor skill you think of when you consider young children. They seem to be perpetual motion machines. This is the principal method of movement for some children. Others run awkwardly and spend much less time doing it than the rest of your children. What should you expect of the 3-, 4-, and 5-year-old children in your program? As with walking, you will need to know about the range of development for this skill before you can decide where each of your children stands and how you best can help.

Running is smoother for 3-year-olds than it was when they were younger. Their body proportions have grown and changed from a top-heavy appearance. Their legs are now longer and more coordinated in their movements. They have more control over starting and stopping than 2-year-olds, but they still have not mastered this skill completely. Because their large motor skills are so much more automatic, they can abandon themselves to the pure enjoyment of running.

Then at about 3½, many children go through an awkward stage where some of the smoothness of their large motor movements seems to disappear. Teachers need to be aware of these "disequilibrium" times so they can support the child during his "difficult days," knowing he will reacquire his smoothness of motion sometime soon.

The sensitive teacher needs to work with each child, encouraging and supporting him to accomplish all he is capable of. Pressure and ridicule simply have no place in the early childhood classroom. The teacher needs to find interesting motor activities in which children showing awkwardness can succeed and to avoid activities that pit one child against another. A wide range of individual differences exists in physical development as in every other aspect of development. Some children simply will never be highly coordinated. Others may grow up to be professional athletes.

Providing a wide range of interesting motor activities that are fun to participate in seems the best answer. Three-year-olds are at an ideal age to begin such a program. And because some so-called awkward children are simply beginners in skill development, they should not be labeled as such or treated differently. Children are children; they are all different in looks, likes, and abilities. Each of them needs your special affection and support as he or she progresses through the sometimes rocky road of physical development.

You need to be aware of these ages and stages as they apply to your children, nevertheless. Take time to visit this year's class next year and you may see some surprises. This year's awkward boy may be the best runner in another year. The sedentary girl who would never join in may be the leader of the physical activities. A year makes such a difference in the development of young children.

Expansive 4-year-olds are good runners. Their movements are strong, efficient, and speedy. They can start and stop without difficulty, and they like to zoom around corners. They seem to know what their bodies can do and enjoy putting them through their paces. Give them space and time to run. Play running games in and out of the classroom to get them started.

Five-year-olds seem to spurt up in height, mostly in their legs. They are more mature runners than 4-year-olds, and many love to join in games that test their abilities. Their speed and control have increased, and they seldom fall when running across uneven surfaces as 4-year-olds sometimes do. Their running games, like the rest of their actions, are usually not as noisy and out-of-bounds as those of 4-year-olds.

If You Have Not Checked This Item: Some Helpful Ideas

■   Offer Simple Running Games

Preschool running games should not be competitive. The "awkward" child may give up trying if he or she is always last. Instead, simple circle games may serve the same purpose. Old classics like "duck, duck, goose" are still favorites of 3- and 4-year-olds as they walk around the outside of the circle and tap someone who then chases them around to the empty space. No one wins or loses. Games with rules are often too complicated for preschoolers, but they can learn to make the right responses in simple games like this and enjoy the running portion. You can join in too and let some of the less-skilled runners catch you.

■   Employ Directed Running

You can make up all kinds of inside and outside running activities. For instance, one child at a time can run to the tree and back until all have had a turn. Make the activity more complicated by having them follow a second direction: run to the tree, run around it once, and then run back.

■   Have the Children Run to Music

Have children run to music in the large motor area. Have them run fast or slow, loudly or quietly, according to the music. Then have them run like animals to music. How would a deer run through the woods?

■   Involve the Children in Running in Place to Chants

Young children need to run. If you do not have the inside space, or the weather outside is bad, have them run and hop in place to a simple chant you have made up:

I'm a kangaroo-roo-roo;

See me run-run-run;

Have some fun-fun-fun;

In the sun-sun-sun.

Watch me hop-hop-hop;

Never stop-stop-stop;

Then I run-run-run;

In the sun-sun-sun.

■ Try Imaginative Running

Let children pretend to be cowboys or cowgirls riding stick horses or be jet planes zooming down the runway. Have them pretend to be animals that run, such as deer or dogs. Put up pictures of animals that run and have the children imitate them. Have an imaginative "Running Romp" in the classroom for 10 minutes at a time. If you have no room, they can run in place. Clements and Schneider (2006) remind us that preschool children should not be sedentary more than 60 minutes at a time except when sleeping (p. 4). How is it in your classroom?

■ Read a Book

The simple book *Clip-Clop* (Smee, 2006) can be made into a game for children's running. The horse invites each of the barnyard animals for a ride on his back. "Up you get" he says to each as he moves along. So cat, dog, pig, and duck hop up for a ride. As you read the book, have the all the children stand in a circle with one child being the horse, who walks around on the outside of the circle. Choose four of the circle children to be the four animals each time you read the story. Each time an animal wants a ride, the horse says, "Up you get" and that child can leave the circle and follow closely behind the horse who continues clopping along. When all four animals are on board, they ask the horse to go faster, so he does. Have your horse and children speed up around the circle until you shout, "Whoa!" The horse should stop and everyone falls down. Read the story again with new children for the animals if the children like it.

JUMPS WITH FEET TOGETHER

Jumping is a skill that involves taking off with one or two feet and landing on both feet. Jumping is sometimes confused with leaping, which involves taking off on one foot and landing on the other, or hopping, which is done all on the same foot. The checklist item mentions "two feet together," so observers will not confuse jumping with leaping or hopping.

The jumping skill has three parts: takeoff, flight, and landing. Teachers can demonstrate each phase so children needing help can practice it correctly. For takeoff, you should bend your knees slightly, crouch your body, and swing your arms forward and upward. For flight, you should continue raising your arms into the air as your body leaves the ground. Land with your two feet slightly apart and your body over your feet. Children can practice bending their knees, crouching, and swinging their arms forward. When they feel ready, have them spring up into a real jump.

Jumping as a large motor skill for preschoolers should be done in place with the child springing up and landing in the same spot. Once they are competent jumpers, they can jump forward, jump from the floor over an obstacle, or jump from a height such as a hollow block and land on the floor.

Jumping is not only going up and down but also discovering the properties of the material being jumped on. Will the surface withstand your impact? Will it throw you back, absorb you, rebound, or stretch? Is it different to jump on something hard or soft, or into water, sand, leaves, or snow? You can jump on something (such as a board), over something (such as a rope or a crack in the sidewalk), to different heights, or across things (a puddle or a stream of water) (Olds, 1994, p. 34).

Some children become quite proficient jumpers by age 3, but many do not, and we should not expect them to. They must have developed the strength first, and then must be encouraged to practice the skill (most parents do not encourage their children to jump off steps or from furniture). Three-year-olds, though, are becoming more long-legged and coordinated. If they are not too heavy, most may be able to do some jumping with encouragement and practice. In jumping over an obstacle, most children start by leading with one foot. This is leaping. Springing up with both feet simultaneously in a jump is more difficult, but possible for some children.

Four-year-olds are much more proficient jumpers, and by age 4½, most can accomplish any type of jumping: up, down, forward, or over. They may not be able to do a sequence of different actions, though, such as hopping, leaping, and jumping, although they perform some or all these actions separately. Four-year-olds can jump higher in the air and farther down from higher elevations. The second step from the bottom of the stairs is now their big challenge, one you may want to discourage.

Five-year-olds, as you might expect, are long, high, far jumpers if they have had practice. Maturity is important, as previously noted, but practice of the skill is just as necessary, along with encouragement and compliments from adult observers. If children have been ridiculed because of their awkwardness or lack of physical accomplishment in the past, you may have to spend more time helping them to improve their self-image before you start jumping improvement.

Most 5-year-olds soon will feel secure enough to jump anywhere. This is the age when rope jumping first appears. Girls may try to make it their exclusive sport, but teachers can be the rope turners so that every class member who wants to participate can have a turn. Again, do not force the awkward child. Before you introduce a jump rope to 5-year-olds, be sure to check out the jumping skills of all your children individually, so that no one will be embarrassed in front of peers if he or she tries to jump rope and fails. This failure sometimes happens, and it may prevent a child, especially a boy, from ever putting himself in such an embarrassing situation again, which means he may not participate in group sports in school.

Competition has no place in the early childhood large motor program, as mentioned previously, but neither do total group activities that play up the weaknesses or inabilities of individual children. Total group games such as jump rope seem like such innocent fun, but they are not for an awkward child. However, if you and another staff member are the turners, everyone can try to run through the rope as it turns without stopping to jump. Observing and recording the large motor abilities of individual children will help you decide what new activities to introduce.

A jumping activity everyone can try is shooting hoops. Bring in a free-standing, preschool-size basketball hoop and have children try jumping with two feet together while throwing a ball through the hoop. A sponge ball or soft basketball is best for indoors.

If You Have Not Checked This Item: Some Helpful Ideas

■ Work with Individual Children Who Show Poor Skills

If children are age 4 and 5 and still cannot jump, you should try an activity such as jumping over a line. If children are 3 or younger, you do not need to be so concerned because their jumping ability may not yet be well developed. If a child has a physical impairment, she may want to jump but not be able to. Her legs may be in braces, but if her arms are strong, you may be able to place her between two stationary objects like tables or room dividers where she can support herself with her arms and bring her feet up off the ground in a sort of jump, if this is appropriate. As Olds (1994) noted:

> In working with differently abled children, the challenge always should be to identify opportunities for action—find every means possible to maximize the use of capabilities that are strong, and exercise to the fullest extent faculties that are weak. (p. 33)

■ Try Concept Jumping

When children are learning the concepts "up," "down," "over," "forward," and "in place," you might try having them act out the motions by jumping. Ask the others to guess what kind of jump a child made. Or let one child call out a concept and another child try to demonstrate by jumping it. Jumping up can also be jumping in place. Jumping down needs to be from a large hollow block, a step, a stool, or another high item. This jump can also represent jumping forward.

■ Utilize Jumping Animals

Place pictures of jumping (leaping or hopping) animals on the walls at children's eye level and have them try to imitate the animals (e.g., kangaroo, kangaroo rat, frog, toad, rabbit, deer, horse).

■ Read a Book

Hoops with Swoopes (Kuklin, 2001) shows the full figure of WNBA basketball star Sheryl Swoopes against a white background making all her famous basketball moves: jump, catch, step, shoot, and jump again. As you read the single words for every move, have children demonstrate their own moves one-by-one.

One, Two, Three, Jump! (Lively, 1998) shows a little green frog that wants to be somewhere else, but always seems to jump right into the path of danger. A dragonfly who can see everything in the garden all at once keeps warning him of the danger and getting him to jump just in time. Have a few of your children imitate the frog every time he needs to jump. Set up your own lily pads with a series of mats and have children jump from one to the other as you read the story.

The Magic Moonberry Jump Ropes (Hru, 1996) shows older African-American girls trying to get some other children to jump rope with them, but with no luck—until Uncle Zambezi comes along with magic moonberry ropes brought back from East Africa. Then their wish for new friends comes true.

Five Little Monkeys Jumping on the Bed (Christelow, 1989) shows a mother monkey trying to put her five lively monkey children to bed. But as soon as her back is turned they start jumping and, of course, one falls off and bumps his head. This is a rhyming cumulative chant that your children can have fun reenacting as you read it. When all five monkeys are finally asleep, the worn-out mother turns to her own bed—and jumps on it!

 ## HOPS ON ONE FOOT

Hopping is the large motor "bounding" skill in which the child springs off the floor on one foot and lands on the same foot. Jumping uses both feet together, while leaping uses alternating feet to take off and land. A child can hop in place or hop forward for one or more steps. This checklist items asks you to identify the children in your class who can hop.

Children need balancing skills before they can hop. They also need the leg length and strength to jump first. This means that not that many will be truly hopping before 3 years of age, and maybe not until 3½. In fact, hopping for most children is not well developed before the age of 4.

You will see large individual differences in this skill as you do in other areas of development, but the largest difference is in gender. Girls 4 and 5 years old almost always hop more and better than boys. Hopping is a girl's skill in our society. Games such as hopscotch and jump rope, which appear among 5- and 6-year-olds are examples. These games are generally played by girls, not boys. Challenge a boy to play hopscotch, and he soon finds that girls his age are much more skilled hoppers, just as girls are better rope jumpers. However, preschool children who play few or no hopping games may have difficulty doing any hopping, whether they are boys or girls.

To help nonhoppers get started, ask them if they can hold one leg off the floor and hop up and down on the other. Have them lean forward slightly in the direction of the hopping leg as they spring up. If they lose their balance, have them try hopping next to a wall. Have them put out one arm to balance themselves against the wall, lift up one foot and try hopping on the other foot. Can they do it? They may need to practice balancing first. How long can they balance on one foot? Because hopping is more difficult than jumping, children need to practice it frequently but briefly. Their large muscles should be strengthened but not strained.

If You Have Not Checked This Item: Some Helpful Ideas

■ Create a Hopping Trail

Make a hoping-tiptoeing-walking trail in your classroom or large motor room with cutout contact footprints that show hopping steps on one foot; then walking steps with both feet; then hopping on the other foot; tiptoeing and jumping. Place a hopping trail next to a wall for inexperienced hoppers to balance against with one arms as they hop.

■ Hop to Music

Find a bouncy but slow tape or CD and let children try to hop and jump to it. Most 4-year-olds will not be able to do more than three or four hops at a time, but the children can switch to jumping if they want.

■ Hop to Drumbeats

Let children make different movement to different drumbeats you play. A one-thump beat can mean to walk, a two-thump beat can signify to hop, and a quick-time beat can indicate to run. See if they can follow your rhythm. Don't change your beat too quickly, because most children are beginners when it comes to moving to rhythm.

■ Read a Book

In *Bounce* (Cronin, 2007) a dog invites readers to bounce like different animals, including himself, a bunny, a frog, a ballerina, a volleyball or soccer player. The bouncing shown can be hopping or jumping. Have your children try it as you reread this book.

Ready, Set, Skip! (O'Connor, 2007) is the story of a little girl who wishes she could skip like the other kids. She can leap. She can creep. She can twirl. She can skate. Her mom asks her if she can hop. Yes. She can hop and never stop. Then hop on one foot, then quickly on the other: that is skipping says her mother. She tries it, slowly at first and then faster. She is skipping! Your younger children may not have the strength or co-ordination to skip, and shouldn't be expected to. But some of the more mature children may be able to skip. If not, tell them to wait another year.

CLIMBS UP AND DOWN CLIMBING EQUIPMENT

Climbing involves use of the arms as well as the legs. It is, in fact, an outgrowth of creeping. Most children begin climbing as soon as they can creep over to an item of furniture and pull themselves up. If they are allowed, they will creep up the stairs. They will try to creep down, too, and soon find out that a backward descent is the only kind that works.

Many 3- and 4-year-olds enjoy climbing on all sorts of things: jungle gyms, ladders, ladder climbers, dome climbers, slides, rope climbers, trees, rocks, poles, and drainpipes.

By the time they are in your program, children this age should be able to climb down and up with ease.

Although it takes bravery as well as muscle strength and coordination to be a successful climber, many of your children will be able to accomplish this skill if they have the opportunity. You should consider providing climbing equipment and climbing possibilities both inside and outside your classroom. First of all, safety factors need to be considered. Because falling is the main concern with climbing, be sure that floor or ground surfaces are cushioned. Padding can be used inside. Sand or wood chips are preferable to grass or hard surfaces outside.

Not all children will attempt to climb. Do not force the reluctant ones. You can encourage them and help children if they try to climb, but if they refuse, they should not be forced to try. Not all children will want to accomplish climbing skills, which is perfectly acceptable. Children have as much right to personal choices and interests as adults. Were you a climber when you were 4?

On the other hand, the excitement of accomplishing such a physical feat as climbing to the top of a climber is wonderful to behold. As noted by Cherry (1976):

> If I had room for only one piece of play equipment, my unhesitating choice would be something to climb on. Climbing strengthens muscles, develops postural control, and orients children to varying views of the world. For small children who spend so much time having to look "up" it must be an exhilarating experience to be in places where the view is "down." Few experiences can make a child feel so important as sitting on top of a jungle gym. (p. 53)

For children who indicate they would like to attempt this sort of climbing, you can help them best by standing close enough to catch them if they should falter, to encourage them if they turn to you for help, and to congratulate them when they succeed. They may climb only halfway to start. Then, little by little, they gain courage and expertise enough to complete their climb. You should accept any attempt they make, but not prod them to go all the way if they are not ready.

Some children may need to strengthen their leg muscles before they can succeed in climbing very high. One fun method is to have them practice using leg muscles with the traditional song *The Grand Old Duke of York*. Have the children sing it as they sit in a line or a circle and stand all the way up on the word "up," sit down on the word "down," and "stand half-way-up" on those words. You try it with them. You may be the only singer at first as they try to do the movements.

(Tune: "The Farmer in the Dell")

The Grand Old Duke of York	*And when you're **up**, you're **up**,*
He had ten thousand men,	*And when you're **down**, you're **down**,*
*He led them **up** the hill*	*And when you're only **half-way up**,*
*And then he led them **down** again*	*You're neither **up** nor **down**.*

Go very slowly at first until the children get used to what they are supposed to do. Some may just not be able to follow it. But those who can will enjoy it even more as you speed up the song. Soon they will be all mixed up trying to go up or down. It all ends in laughter—and stronger leg muscles! Do it again, teacher!

If You Have Not Checked This Item: Some Helpful Ideas

■ Provide a New Piece of Climbing Equipment

A packing crate (with splintery edges sanded down) is often a tempting piece of home-made climbing equipment that can be used either inside or outside. Ladder steps can be fastened to the outside of the crate if necessary, or children may use a step stool to climb up the crate. Cargo netting is also a fine piece of climbing equipment. Fasten it to a classroom wall with padding underneath or to a horizontal bar outside on the playground.

■ Build a Loft

Lofts not only give preschool children extra space for various new activities, they also provide a new perspective on the activities below. Some lofts use ladders to reach their tops, others use steps or stairs. Some have several means of entrance and exit. Even nonclimbers often learn to manage all the methods of access because being up in the loft is such fun.

■ Have a Multiple-Access Slide

A multiple-access slide is one of the most valuable pieces of large motor equipment you can purchase if your center can afford only one piece of equipment. Children are motivated to learn to climb to get to the platform at the top of the slide. There are usually steps, bars, a climbing wall or ladders to help children reach the top, and the youngsters soon know how to use them all. If you have space inside, an indoor multiple-access slide can serve as a loft as well as a large motor device.

■ Make an Obstacle Course

Use planks, sawhorses, barrels, ladders, and boxes to create an obstacle course for climbing. Rearrange them frequently. Children can climb up, over, and under.

■ Read a Book

The title *Chicken Chickens* (Gorbachev, 2001) means "Scared Chickens" and so they are, your listeners will soon find out. Mother Hen takes her two little chickens to the playground for the first time. When they see all the little animal-children swinging, sliding, playing ball, riding the teeter/totter and merry-go-round, they're scared. Finally Mice persuade them to go up the steps of the slide. They're still afraid to go down until Beaver carries them down on his tail. Then they do it again all by themselves. Can your children handle your playground equipment, or do they need your help?

Read *From Head to Toe* (Carle, 1997), in which every other page challenges children to make a particular movement like a different animal. A full-page penguin asks if

Table 7–1   Large motor skills

Age	Walking	Running	Jumping	Climbing
8 months–1 year	Walks in a wide stance like a waddle			Climbs onto furniture and up stairs as an outgrowth of creeping
1–2 years	Walks in a toddle and uses arms for balance (arms are not swung)	Moves rapidly in a hurried walk, in contact with surface	Uses bouncing step off bottom step of stairs with one foot	Tries climbing up anything climbable
2–3 years	Walks upstairs two feet on a step	Runs stiffly, has difficulty turning corners and stopping quickly	Jumps off bottom step with both feet	Tries climbing to top of equipment, although cannot climb down
3–4 years	Walks with arms swinging; walks upstairs alternating feet; walks downstairs two feet on step	Runs more smoothly, has more control over starting and stopping	Springs up off floor with both feet in some cases; jumps over object leading with one foot	Climbs up and down ladders, jungle gyms, slides, and trees
4–5 years	Walks up and down stairs alternating feet; walks circular line; skips with one foot	Displays strong, speedy running; turns corners, starts and stops easily	Jumps up, down, and forward	Climbs up and down ladders, jungle gyms, slides, and trees
5–6 years	Walks as an adult; skips alternating feet	Shows mature running, falls seldom, displays increased speed and control	Jumps long, high, and far; jumps rope	Displays mature climbing in adult manner

they can turn their heads and a child replies, "I can do it," and does. Can your children?

Table 7–1 lists the progression of movement skills in children from infancy to age 6.

THROWS, CATCHES, AND KICKS BALLS

Many preschool children do not get the opportunity to play with balls until they are older, perhaps when they enter primary school. Although their arm, hand, and leg muscles are not so well developed and coordinated during the preschool years, your program can encourage this coordination. Children enjoy playing with balls when it involves balls they can handle at their level of accomplishment. Using the smaller, softer balls available for indoor play makes this possible.

Throwing

Throwing and catching are two important upper body large motor skills. Throwing appears first. There are several ways to throw, such as overhand, underhand, and sidearm, and with two hands or one. Young children seem to go through a general progression, starting with infants who throw small objects overhand but downward, to the two-hand underhand throw, the one-hand underhand throw, and finally the one-hand overhand throw. The size and heaviness of the thrown object also made a difference as to the type of throw (Pica, 1995, p. 116).

Two-year-olds frequently try to throw things such as food or clothing, sometimes in frustration. Their throwing action is more of a jerky, sidearm movement. If they should try to throw a ball, they often stand facing the target, using both forearms together to push a ball forward. The ball often dribbles away, almost accidentally. Some youngsters who have the smaller, softer indoor balls at home may develop one-hand overhand throws even before preschool. How accurate they eventually become depends on maturity and practice. Photographic studies made of children throwing reveal four distinct patterns in the development of throwing:

- Two- and 3-year-olds throw mainly with their forearms, using little or no footwork or body rotation.
- Three-and-a-half-year-olds throw with more body rotation and arm range.
- Five- and 6-year-olds start to throw with a forward step on the same side as their throwing arm.
- Six-and-a-half-year-olds throw maturely, stepping forward with the opposite foot (Zaichkowsky, Zaichkowsky, & Martineck, 1980, p. 40).

The children in your classroom should be able to develop throwing skills. Throwing takes practice—not so much instruction as opportunity. Children have to work out how to throw by themselves as their muscles and coordination mature. Give the youngsters many throwing opportunities, and they will do the rest.

What can they throw? Let them try inflated beach balls, yarn balls, sponge balls, Nerf balls, foam balls, squeezable balls, squish balls, beanbag balls, grip balls, tactile balls, and punching balloons. Balls come not only in dozens of materials these days, but also in a huge variety of sizes and shapes, from golf-ball size to giant balls as big as the children. Some are made from soft materials to resemble soccer balls, footballs, basketballs, and baseballs.

Where can children throw? Because accuracy is not the point at first, they will need to become familiar with the throwing action itself. Have them throw foam or yarn balls against a wall. When they are ready, have them throw at a large target like a hula hoop hung on the wall or a box standing upright against a wall. A freestanding basketball

Children can throw all kinds of balls on the playground.

backboard at preschoolers' height can be used even in the classroom if a foam ball is thrown. Girls and boys alike enjoy throwing balls. But neither will develop this skill to a mature degree without practice.

Evidence shows that practice counts with this large motor skill. Earlier, our society considered boys to be better throwers than girls. "To throw like a girl" was a derogatory comment often made about boys who threw poorly. It describes the throwing stance of stepping forward on the same foot as the throwing arm and throwing from the elbow: the stance of an immature thrower.

In order to develop their arm muscles children need to be involved in many of the activities your classroom provides. Block building is one that offers special strengthening of arm muscles. It also activities the brain. As Gellens (2005) tells us: "When children play with blocks, the entire brain is activated. Brain connections are made in many parts of the brain simultaneously. Both hemispheres of the brain are aroused. Repetition of both large- and small-motor movements brings permanence in brain connections. Large plastic bricks, big cardboard blocks, or hollow blocks require the use of large muscles" (p. 20). Once again we are reminded that all development is simultaneous.

Catching

Because catching a ball is more difficult than throwing, it develops later. In addition to having upper body maturity, children also need eye–hand coordination to track the thrown ball and catch it with their hands. Many of your children may not develop this skill as easily as they did throwing. Most 3½-year-olds are still at the stage of trying to catch by holding their arms straight out in front of their bodies. They will be successful only if the ball is large and thrown directly into their arms with little force. Even 5-year-olds catch a chest-high ball only 60 to 80 percent of the time (Cratty, 1982, p. 126).

In addition to the necessary practice, this particular skill also requires nervous system maturity. The child is being asked to respond to moving objects of varying speeds. His response time is much slower than that of an older child or adult. Even when he seems to be ready for the ball to arrive in his hands, he may not be able to bring them together in time.

Preschool girls seem to be more successful than boys in ball catching, perhaps because they have more mature eye-hand coordination. All children need as much practice in catching as in throwing. You, however, need to be aware that they may not succeed as well in catching because they are not developmentally ready.

Some children show fear as the ball approaches them. You may want to start catching practice by throwing soft, colorful objects such as beanbags, yarn balls, beach balls, and foam balls. Better yet, have children begin by catching their own bounced ball. Once they are used to this activity, you can stand close to them and toss a large, soft ball to them. Catching success does not happen in one day or even one week. Let children take their time, but be sure to provide frequent opportunities. Once children have achieved some success, challenge them to catch an object they themselves have tossed up in the air—the hardest challenge of all.

Kicking

Kicking a ball with the leg and foot is not as easy as it looks for preschoolers. Besides having leg muscle development, children need balancing skills and eye–foot coordination to kick a ball. Kicking for distance and not accuracy is more important for preschoolers (Gallahue, 1993).

Have children start by placing their nonkicking foot next to the ball. Tell them to look at the ball, then kick with their other leg. They can begin by kicking a beach ball any way they want. Once they get the hang of it, have them kick smaller foam balls at a wall. If you have little space for kicking balls, have children kick punchball balloons. If children want to kick harder rubber balls, find a space outside where they will not kick the ball into another child (Sanders, 1992, p. 79).

If You Have Not Checked This Item: Some Helpful Ideas

■   Try Some Kicking Games

Have children take several steps backward from a ball on the ground, then run up and kick the ball. How far can they kick? Another day, put two traffic cones about 6 feet apart. Have children stay behind a line at about 6 feet and try kicking a ball between the cones (Sanders, 1992, p. 81).

■   Use Targets for Throwing

Make targets out of cardboard boxes. Paint a simple animal face or clown face on the box. Cut a large hole for the mouth, much larger than the ball or beanbag. Have children stand behind a line not too far away and try to throw into the hole.

■ Throw Newspapers

Sanders (2002, p. 38) suggests another fun throwing activity: throwing rolled up newspapers into a box placed in front of a drawing of a house. Children can pretend to be newspaper boys and girls delivering the morning paper. Can they throw it in the box while moving in front of the house? How close do they need to be for accuracy?

■ Use Pillows

For children who are having difficulty catching a ball, try throwing a small soft pillow to each one. Stand close enough at first for them to succeed without difficulty. Then step back a little at a time until you are farther away when you throw and they must track the pillow with their eyes.

■ Read a Baseball Book

You are not going to be teaching or playing baseball in preschool programs, but such a game promotes the skills of throwing and catching that young children need to practice. Thus, several baseball books are appropriate for young children. *Luke Goes to Bat* (Isadora, 2005) tells a long ago story of Luke, a little African-American boy in Brooklyn when Jackie Robinson played for the Brooklyn Dodgers. The big boys won't let Luke play in their street stickball games street at first. When he finally plays, he strikes out. But his grandma tells him never to give up. She takes him to a game at Ebbetts Field where Jackie hits a home run over the fence. Later when Luke finds a ball on his roof he knows it is the one Jackie hit and he promises never to give up.

In *Just Like Josh Gibson* (Johnson, 2004) an African-American girl hears the story her Grandmama tells about how her father teaches her to play baseball just like Josh Gibson, the best Negro League player. How she is as good as any boy, but is never allowed to play on the boy's teams until the day her cousin Donny hurts his arm during a game, and there is no one to take his place but Grandmama. She puts on his shoes and hits the ball a mile that day, catches everything that is thrown, and does everything else just like Josh Gibson.

In *Hit the Ball Duck* (Alborough, 2006), Duck and his animal friends drive out to the park for a hilarious game of baseball in rhyme. Duck grabs the bat and hits the ball up high—into a tree where it is stuck. He throws up his bat to knock it down, but it gets stuck too. So he throws up his glove to knock them both down, but of course it gets stuck as well. Then they climb up one on top of the other until Frog can almost reach the ball, but Duck sways and they all come tumbling down. Then down come the bat, glove, and finally the ball—right into Frog's hands. Duck, you're out!

Harry and Willy and Carrothead (Caseley, 1991) tells the story of Harry, who was born with no left hand and so wears a prosthesis, and his friends Willy and Carrothead. The story takes place at school when the boys are 5 and shows all three engaged in physical activities, especially baseball, where Harry is a great player.

Be sure all your children have practice in throwing, catching, and kicking—even the differently abled children. Bring in a wheelchair and let everyone take turns throwing and catching a ball while seated in the chair. Make it possible for children in leg braces to practice kicking while standing between two chair backs.

 # RIDES TRIKES, BIKES, AND SCOOTERS

Trikes

Riding a trike on the preschool playground is one of the great joys for most children in your program. Most children are so anxious to be on the trike that there may be fights unless you have more than one or unless you set up a turn-taking arrangement. Do you know who the trike riders are and who never rides the trikes? If not, you need to observe and keep track. Those who do not know how usually stay far away from the trikes. You will want to have a game where each child, one at a time, can pretend to be a race car driver and ride the trike a short distance to the starting line, a mark you make on the sidewalk.

Remember, this is not a test, but a game. Do not force reluctant children to ride. Make note of who they are and take some time during another day to work with them on a one-to-one basis. You can do the same with children who try to ride but can't seem to make the wheels go around. Make the lessons private. Don't embarrass them by trying to teach them in front of other riders.

Making the wheels on the trike go around has to do with leg and foot coordination. Have the child try to push a pedal down with one foot at a time and then the other foot. Push down with the right foot, which raises the left pedal. Then push that pedal forward and down with the left foot. Have them take the other foot off the pedal for a moment while they are learning how each foot works. Finally, have them try both feet at once, pushing easy, not hard. Down-up-down.

Children who cannot make a trike go are usually trying to push too hard with both feet at once, instead of pushing down with one foot while allowing the other foot to raise up. It is a matter of coordination that most children can learn with practice. Have them sit on a chair inside and make their legs go down and up until they get the idea. You can sit down and model the movement. Or have all the children sit in a circle and pretend to be trike riders going slowly at first and then faster. Afterward, set one of your trikes aside for use in practicing for those who need more help.

Once the beginners get their feet to work in the down-up-down motion, they next need to concentrate on steering with their arms and hands. They should be able to teach themselves once their feet are working properly and the trike is moving. If not, you can walk alongside them and, with your own arms and hands, demonstrate in the air the motions they should be making. Children who learn to ride a trike in your program are receiving a tremendous boost in their self-esteem, as well as a new leg muscle exercising tool.

All your drivers and passengers should also be wearing bike helmets for safety. Preschool-size helmets can be ordered from Childcraft (1-800-631-5652) or Lakeshore. Children love the grownup idea of wearing a helmet, and reluctant riders may soon be asking to learn to ride so they can wear one, too.

Some children may need private lessons to help them learn how to make a trike go.

Bikes

Can preschool children learn to ride two-wheel bikes? Some can if they learn on the small easy-ride bikes from Lakeshore with extra-wide wheels and a low design that resists tipping while children are getting used to balancing on two wheels. Their feet will reach the ground when they sit on the 13½-inch seat.

Scooters

Scooters are popular again and being made for young children. Lakeshore has a three-wheel scooter for 3- to 6-year olds, as well as a larger two-wheel scooter for children 3 to 7. It can stand upright alone because its wide wheels resist tipping. Children learn to stand on the wheeled platform while holding and turning handlebars to steer and pushing backward with one foot on the ground. They may have already learned this pushing maneuver while sitting on your wheeled vehicles and pushing them around inside the classroom. Scooters can be a special challenge for the trike riders, as they require balancing, steering, and foot-pushing to make them go.

If You Have Not Checked This Item: Some Helpful Ideas

■ Have a Parade

Line up your riding vehicles on the trike path and have a parade. Some of the children can bring out the rhythm instruments and march behind the riders. The riders will have to learn to keep together—no racing ahead. As for racing itself, children can go fast when they are on their own, but try to discourage racing one against another where someone wins and the other loses.

■ Have a Safety Demonstration

Put up street traffic signs on your trike path indicating *Stop, One Way, Yield, No U Turn, People Walking* (Childcraft, 1-800-448-4115). Talk about what drivers should do to obey the signs, and why. Then have one or two riders at a time take their vehicles around the traffic course to see if they can obey the rules. Make it fun.

■ Read a Book

Mike and the Bike (Ward, 2005) is a fabulous book for bike lovers. Its author is a cyclist, guitarist, and song writer whose CD "Mike and the Bike" accompanies the book. The story of Mike's bike and its fantastic rides is written in rhyme with cartoon-like illustrations. Take the CD and a player outside and play it as your trike riders zoom along.

Sally Jean, the Bicycle Queen (Best, 2006) is Sally Jean's biking story from the time she turned two and got her first trike, to her yard-sale bike with two small balance wheels in back at age 4. Then at age 5 the training wheels came off, and age 6 the seat was raised and she called her bike "Flash." When she got too big for her bike, she began fixing other kid's bikes to earn money for parts. Finally she began to recycle junk and was able to put together a brand new recycled bike that she called "Lightning." She was once again Sally Jean the Bicycle Queen.

Duck on a Bike (Shannon, 2002) is the story of a barnyard duck who spies a farm boy's bike and decides to go for a ride. As he passes each of the farm animals (cow, sheep, dog, cat, horse, chicken, goat, pigs, mouse), they make a snide comment. Suddenly a bunch of kids on bikes comes riding up to the farmhouse. They park their bikes and go inside. Bikes for the animals! They all hop on and go for a wonderful spin around the barnyard. If you have a small two-wheeler, your children can also reenact this story as you read it by the trike path.

 ## DOES CREATIVE MOVEMENT

An entire class of preschool children can gain tremendously from creative movement activities if the activities are led by a sensitive teacher and held in a creative environment. The teacher can use a drum, tom-tom, tambourine, or simply hand-clapping for the beat, but she must be sensitive enough to pick up the pulse or rhythm of the group instead of imposing her own rhythm on them. Tapes or CDs can be used, as well, but again, the teacher needs to rely on the group rhythm, which is usually different—often slower—than that of a tape. The environment should be attractive, orderly, and comfortable. If a gymnasium is used, it should be uncluttered. If the preschool classroom is large enough, clear a space for expansive movements. Preschoolers need to be able to run, leap, and gallop.

The teacher should be the leader—a sensitive and creative leader. If a child does not want to participate, don't make her. You can take her hand and swing it gently to the music. The teacher should be prepared, as well, with a series of simple movement activities for the children to try. Children do not like to be told: "Do whatever you want to do," or "Move any way you want to the music." This only leads to confusion.

Instead, you should lead the children into creative movement activities through the stimulus of a steady, rhythmic beat. They need to master the basic locomotor movements of walking, running, crawling, leaping, and galloping to music or to a beat. Start by beating the tom-tom slowly and having children walk across the floor to the beat. Then increase the tempo of the beat and have them come back across the floor a bit faster. Try other movements, at first slowly and then faster.

They also should master some of the nonlocomotor movements such as swinging, swaying, rocking, bending, and stretching. Not all at once. Try one movement at a time. Continue using a drum or tap on a tambourine to set the beat for movement. Have seated children tap their feet to the beat. Then have them sway or rock or bend while still seated. Change the beat, making it faster or slower, louder or softer. Then have them stand up and make the same movements as you change the beat. Whatever you do with rhythm, make it fun and do not expect perfection from these developing children.

The short attention span of preschoolers makes it necessary to keep the sessions short (15 to 20 minutes) and include a variety of movements and dance activities. Young children like activities that take place on the floor, so be sure to include "snake" and "worm" dances where children can wriggle and crawl. Four-year-olds especially love to run. You will want to include a "jet plane zoom" or a "race car rally" in which children can run to music or a beat.

Because children love making animal movements, some teachers focus on those for their creative movement activities. The book *Move* (Jenkins, 2006) shows all kinds of animals making two of their typical moves on every other page with a gigantic word giving the names of the movements: swing, walk, dive, swim, leap, slither, climb, fly, run, dance, float, slide, and waddle. Children can look at the pages, then get up and try to make the movement.

You can also do a follow-the-leader activity in a line where you as leader set the pace. You can march, tramp, slide along, trip along on tiptoes, or walk in cadence, calling out a beat (e.g., "one-two buckle your shoe, three-four shut the door"). Put on a record with a strong beat, and have the children move around the room keeping time. You may want to wind down your session with a slower record. Choose an appropriate tune for a "monster shuffle" or a "dinosaur clump." Children are usually happily exhausted after such a creative movement session.

Creative movement like this calls on children to use more than their large muscles. They must also use their imaginations. As Pica (1997) pointed out:

> Creative movement activities give children many opportunities to imagine. They must imagine the slowness of a turtle to replicate its movement. They must recall a time when they were not happy to move as though sad. They must envision a partner balance or group shape in order to achieve it. (p. 9)

If You Have Not Checked This Item: Some Helpful Ideas

■   Walk to Music

Play different records or pieces of music with different rhythms, and have your children try to walk around the room keeping time with the beat. Then have them walk to the rhythm of your drum beats or to a clicker. If you do not have a percussion instrument, tap on a glass. Speed up the tempo. Slow it down. Make it syncopated.

■   Use Rock Music

Rock music is characterized by its strong beat. Bring in several CDs or tapes with a beat and let children move/dance to them in the classroom.

■   Move to Chants or Poems

Books with chants and body action rhymes, such as *Mother Goose, Numbers on the Loose* (Dillon & Dillon, 2007), are wonderful sources of verses with a beat that children can move to. So is a book like *Arroz con Leche: Popular Songs and Rhymes from Latin America* (Delacre, 1989).

■   Read a Book

In *Down by the Cool of the Pool* (Mitton, 2001) frog cries Whee! Can you dance like me? This starts a wild melee of flapping by duck, wiggling by pig, stamping by sheep, bounding by cat, and frisking by dog. Your children can choose to be one of the animals and do their own movements to the peppy music you play.

In *Hilda Must Be Dancing* (Wilson, 2004), Hilda Hippo loves to dance so much she never stops. But she doesn't know what it sounds like to the other jungle animals: crash, smash, thumpity bump, boom, bang, bash! Children are convulsed by the hilarious rhymes as Hilda's thumping in her favorite pair of heels "knocks bananas in gooey heaps, shaken from their peels." The animals try to get her to take up knitting or try some singing or take up swimming. She finally does, and soon her water ballet absorbs the thumping sounds and delights them all, even Hilda.

Twist with a Burger, Jitter with a Bug (Lowery, 1995) has colorful cartoonlike characters dancing mambos, snapping to raps, swaying to the tune, and polkaing after supper with a fork and spoon. The rhythm and rhyming of the book's exuberant words will soon have children on their feet to act out the movement.

OBSERVING, RECORDING, AND INTERPRETING LARGE MOTOR DEVELOPMENT

It is important at the beginning of the year to screen all your children using the Large Motor Development section of the Child Development Checklist. List the name of each child along the left side of a lined sheet of paper. At the top, indicate the eight items of the checklist. Draw vertical lines separating the eight items. Check off the large motor skills you observe for each child. For children who have few checkmarks, you may want to do an in-depth observation on each of the items.

Lionel, whose social play observations appeared in Figure 5–1, was observed for large motor development. Figure 7–1 shows that information. These observational data

---

Child Development Checklist

Name _Lionel_   **Observer** _Barb_

Program _Preschool-K2_   **Dates** _1/20_

Directions:

Put an **X** for items you see the child perform regularly. Put **N** for items where there is no opportunity to observe. Leave all other items blank.

Item	Evidence	Dates
5. Large Motor Development		
_____Walks down steps alternating feet	Holds onto rail & puts 2 feet on each step when going down	1/20
_____Runs with control over speed & direction	Does not run often	1/20
__N__Jumps with feet together		
__N__Hops on one foot		
_____Climbs up, down, across climbing equipment	Does not attempt to climb	1/20
__N__Throws, catches & kicks balls		
__N__Rides trikes, bikes, & scooters	No equipment	1/20
__X__Does creative movement	Taps feet to drum beats; claps in time to CD	1/20

Figure 7–1   Large Motor Development Observations for Lionel

gathered for Lionel were helpful to the classroom staff. They could see that Lionel spent more time in sedentary activities. He seemed more at ease sitting and playing than running around engaged in large motor activities.

During a parent conference, the teachers learned that Lionel lived in a large apartment building and had little opportunity to run outside and play. However, the staff was also concerned that the program itself offered few large motor experiences for the children. The "N" designation, meaning "no opportunity to observe," was listed for most of the children because the program has neither a playground, gymnasium, nor indoor climbing equipment. Children are taken for walks, weather permitting, and are allowed to run around on the lawn outside the building. But it is obvious that additional large motor activities need to be provided.

Because Lionel and many of the other children showed skills and interest in rhythm activities, the classroom team decided to incorporate creative movement and dance activities at one end of the large classroom on a daily basis. As children become accustomed to moving to music and drumbeats, the teachers plan to take the children outside on the lawn for more expansive creative movement exercises. They are also negotiating for indoor climbing equipment.

LEARNING ACTIVITIES

1. Use the Child Development Checklist for large motor development as a screening tool to observe all the children in your classroom. Which ones are the most physically accomplished? Which need the most help? What are their ages?

2. Choose a child who seems to need a great deal of help in large motor development. Do a running record on three different days to determine what the child can do physically. Do an activity with the child to promote a skill for which he or she needs help. Record the results.

3. How do the girls and boys of the same age in your program compare with one another in each of the large motor checklist items? How do you explain any differences or similarities? Can you make any inferences or conclusions about gender differences based on your observations?

4. Choose a child who needs help with creative movement. Involve the child using one or more of the ideas from the text. Discuss the results.

5. Have a staff member involve children in a new large motor game while you observe and record. Discuss your results as compared with the original screening you did. What conclusions can you draw?

SUGGESTED READINGS

Armistead, M. E. (2007). Kaleidoscope: How a creative arts enrichment program prepares children for kindergarten. *Young Children, 62*(6), 86–83.

Beaty, J. J. (2008). *Skills for preschool teachers.* Upper Saddle River, NJ: Merrill/Prentice Hall.

Bernath, C., & Masi, W. (2005). Movin' and grovin': Integrating movement throughout the curriculum. *Dimensions of Early Education, 33*(3), 22–26.

Chenfeld, M. B. (2004). Education is a moving experience: Get movin'! *Young Children, 59*(4), 56–57.

Council on Physical Education for Children. (2000). *Appropriate practices in movement programs for young children ages 3–5.* A position statement of the National Association for Sport and Physical Education. Reston, VA: NASPE.

Miller, S. E. (1999). Balloons, blankets, and balls. Gross-motor activities to use indoors. *Young Children, 54*(5), 58–63.

Pica, R. (2006). Physical fitness and the early childhood curriculum. *Young Children, 61*(3), 12–18.

Pica, R. (2007). *Moving and learning across the curriculum.* Clifton Parks, NY: Cengage.

Sutterby, J. A., & Frost, J. L. (2002). Making playgrounds fit for children and children fit on playgrounds. *Young Children, 57*(3), 36–41.

Weikart, P. S. (2003). *Movement in a steady beat.* Ypsalanti, MI: High/Scope Press.

CHILDREN'S BOOKS

Alborough, J. (2006). *Hit the ball duck.* La Jolla, CA: Kane/Miller.

Best, C. (2006). *Sally Jean, the bicycle queen.* New York: Farrar, Straus, & Giroux.

Carle, E. (1997). *From head to toe.* New York: HarperCollins.

Caseley, J. (1991). *Harry and Willy and Carrothead.* New York: Greenwillow.

Christelow, E. (1989). *Five little monkeys jumping on the bed.* New York: Clarion Books.

Cronin, D. (2007). *Bounce.* New York: Atheneum.

Delacre, L. (1989). *Arroz con Leche: Popular Songs and Rhymes from Latin America.* New York: Scholastic.[*]

Dillon, L., & Dillon, D. (2007). *Mother Goose: Numbers on the loose.* Orlando, FL: Harcourt.

Dillion, L., & Dillion, D. (2002). *Rap-a-tap-tap: Here's Bojangles, think of that!* New York: Blue Sky Press.[*]

Gorbachev, V. (2001). *Chicken chickens.* New York: North-South Books.

Hindley, J. (1994). *Funny walks.* Cambridge, MA: Bridgewater.[*]

Hru, D. (1996). *Magic moonberry jump ropes.* New York: Dial.[*]

Isadora, R. (2005). *Luke goes to bat.* New York: G. P. Putnam's Sons.[*]

Jenkins, S. (2006). *Move.* Boston: Houghton Mifflin.

Johnson, A. (2004). *Just like Josh Gibson.* New York: Simon & Schuster.[*]

Kuklin, S. (2001). *Hoops with Swoopes.* New York: Hyperion.[*]

Lively, P. (1998). *One, two, three, JUMP!* New York: Simon & Schuster.

Lowery, L. (1995). *Twist with a burger, jitter with a bug.* Boston: Houghton Mifflin.[*]

O'Connor, J. (2007). *Ready, set, skip!* New York: Viking.

Polacco, P. (2004). *Oh, look!* New York: Philomel Books.

Rosen, M., & Oxenbury, H. (1989). *We're going on a bear hunt.* New York: McElderry Books.

Shannon, D. (2002). *Duck on a bike.* New York: Blue Sky Press.

Shields, C. (1997). *Saturday night at the dinosaur stomp.* Cambridge, MA: Candlewick Press.

Smee, N. (2006). *Clip-clop.* London: Boxer Books (New York: Sterling).

Ward, M. (2005). *Mike and the bike.* Salt Lake City, UT: Cookie Jar Publishing.

Wheeler, L. (2006). *Mammoths on the move.* Orlando, FL: Harcourt.

Wilson, K. (2004). *Hilda must be dancing.* New York: McElderry Books.

*Multicultural.

8

Small Motor Development

SMALL MOTOR CHECKLIST

___ Turns knobs, lids, eggbeaters

___ Pours liquids without spilling

___ Fastens/unfastens zippers, buttons, tabs

___ Picks up/inserts objects with dexterity

___ Molds play dough/clay with dexterity

___ Uses drawing/writing tools with control

___ Uses scissors with control

___ Uses a hammer with control

DEVELOPING SMALL MOTOR SKILLS

Small motor development involves the fine muscles that control the extremities. In the case of young children, you should be especially concerned with control, coordination, and dexterity in using the hands and fingers. Although this development occurs simultaneously in children along with large motor development, the muscles near the trunk mature before the muscles of the extremities, which control the wrists and hands.

Thus it is important for young children to practice use of the large muscles as they become involved in small motor activities. Delays in developing large motor coordination may very well have a negative effect on the development of small motor skills. But once children can accomplish small motor movements, preschool teachers should encourage them to engage in all types of manipulative activities so they can learn and then practice the skills needed to use their hands and fingers with control and dexterity.

Reflexes

Surely infants and toddlers use their hands and fingers without much previous experience, you may counter. Why, then, do 3-, 4-, and 5-year-olds have a different situation? The difference is important. It involves voluntary versus involuntary movements. Infants move their arms, hands, and fingers through reflexes, not voluntary movements. The nervous system assimilates these involuntary movements as it matures, allowing children to control their movements voluntarily. As these initial reflexes disappear, children must purposefully learn to replace them by using and controlling their hands and fingers.

A very large number of reflexes are present in the infant. They include the Moro, or startle reflex, in which the infant throws out its arms with a jerk and lets out a cry; the rooting reflex, in which the infant turns its head and opens its mouth when touched on the side of the cheek; the sucking reflex, in which the infant sucks if its lips or mouth are touched; the walking reflex, in which the infant makes stepping movements when held in an upright position on a surface; the swimming reflex, in which the infant makes swimming movements when held in the water with its head supported. Many more reflexes exist (Eliot, 1999).

The reflex most connected with small motor hand skills is the grasping reflex or palmar grasp in which the baby clamps its fingers around anything put in its palm. This grasp is so strong in the beginning that it will support the infant's weight and can be used to lift the baby entirely off the surface on which it is lying. It is difficult, in fact, for the infant to let go. You may have to pry its fingers apart.

Involuntary responses such as this have their origin in the lower brain stem and spinal cord and eventually come under the control of the higher brain centers of the nervous system as the child matures. This higher part of the brain inhibits these initial reflexes after they have finished their task of aiding the survival of the helpless newborn; the higher brain center then allows voluntary movements to replace them.

The grasping reflex lasts until about 9 months. Infants cannot start to control hand and finger actions voluntarily before this. Infants may reach for things—but not very accurately—before the age of 6 months; letting go is the infants' main problem. Even year-old children may struggle to release an object voluntarily, and some do not gain control of "letting go" before 1½ years of age. This is called "prehension," the ability to grasp an object and let go. Children in your program will be using prehension to handle painting and writing tools as well as small manipulative objects.

Timing

We understand that, like the large motor skills, voluntary small motor skills do not just happen; they must be learned naturally and then practiced by young children. Is there a certain time period when particular skills can be learned best? When is the child's neuromuscular system mature enough for him to control his movements and perform certain actions? Should we wait until he is ready? Not really. As with large motor skills, we should encourage children to use their small muscles as soon as they can. Because each child's development is different, this time period may differ with various children.

All of us carry within us an inherited biological clock. For some of us, small motor development occurs in textbook fashion, just as the charts for average physical growth indicate. For others, this development happens just a bit behind or ahead of the charts. This staggered individual development will exist in all the children in your program. Each child has his or her own built-in biological clock. Neither you nor the child knows what time it is for the child, except in general terms. Because everyone's development occurs in a particular sequence, the best we can do is to assess the child's development through observation and provide him or her with appropriate activities, materials, and encouragement.

Is there a "critical moment" when small motor skills must be learned or it will be too late? Again, not really, except in broad general terms. The best time to learn a small motor skill seems to be when the skill is changing most rapidly. But because this is not easy to determine, it is best to offer many types of activities for all your children and to help them get involved with activities that offer both success and challenge.

In other words, all your children are "ready" to begin developing their small motor skills when they enter your program. You do not need to wait. The question is not whether they are "ready," because they are, but whether *you* are ready to assist them in this important area of development. To do this successfully, you will first need to know where each child stands in small motor development, so that you can help them continue in their growth and learning.

You may want to screen them using the eight Small Motor Checklist items. These items are observable behaviors that demonstrate acknowledged small motor skills of young children in the areas of rotation, manipulation, and dexterity, as well as handedness.

Dexterity and Handedness

Dexterity calls for quick, precise movements of the hands and fingers. Four- and 5-year-old children must be dexterous to manage small buttons and zippers and write legible letters and numerals. Young 3-year-olds may not have matured to this level. It all depends on a neurological process, with certain abilities becoming localized in the left and right hemispheres of the brain. Handedness is an outgrowth of this process but may not be fully dominant until 6, 7, or 8 years of age (Puckett & Black, 2005).

Puckett and Black further tell us that both right- and left-handedness facilitate the use of small motor activities, leading to refined coordination and therefore dexterity. They say that "some children ages 4 and 5 whose handedness is not clearly established use both hands with facility; some use one hand for eating, and the other for another activity, such as throwing or reaching. There is no reason to encourage the use of one hand over the other, as this process is governed by intricate neurological connections in the brain" (p. 319).

The best advice at the moment, it seems, advocates helping young children develop small motor dexterity, no matter what their hand preference. Children need to succeed. A strong hand preference may help them perform small motor tasks with dexterity. If you know what that preference is for any of your children, you can help them develop it further with practice and positive feedback.

TURNS KNOBS, LIDS, EGGBEATERS

Twisting or turning movements—done with the wrist, hand, and fingers by rotating the wrist and/or forearm—take several forms. The child may enclose a doorknob with her hand and try to twist and then pull it to open the door. Depending on the size and stiffness of the knob and door, she may or may not succeed at first. Or she may not be tall enough to make her small motor skills work effectively. Turning a key in a lock involves this same type of motion.

Another form of small motor rotating involves vertical turning at the wrist or rotating the forearm while the fingers are gripping an implement: a cranking type of movement. Manual eggbeaters, food mills, and can openers use this motion. Still another type of small motor rotating involves using the fingers to twist a nut onto a bolt, turn a screw into a hole, or twist a lid onto or off a jar or bottle.

Children at an early age can accomplish this motor skill. Two-and-a-half and 3-year-olds, for instance, can turn a doorknob if they can reach it. They love to screw and unscrew lids or tops on jars and bottles. Have parents collect empty plastic bottles and containers of all sizes along with their screw-top lids, and keep the items in a box in the manipulative area of the classroom for the children to practice on.

Small motor control is far from perfect, especially with the younger children; things have a way of slipping out of their fingers from time to time. Thus it is important to use only unbreakable containers such as plastic—never glass—in the classroom.

Turning the knobs on an Etch A Sketch to draw a picture gives a child practice in this small motor skill.

In wooden puzzles children need to rotate the piece to match the shape of the hole.

Puzzles

This same hand-rotating skill is used by 3-year-olds and older children as they try to put together a puzzle. Whereas 2-year-olds will often try to jam a puzzle piece into place and will give up if it doesn't fit, older children will rotate the piece to try to match the shape of the hole. Watch and see how your children make puzzles. Obviously perceptual awareness (i.e., what the piece looks like) is also at work in this instance, but children first need the small motor rotating skill to use their shape recognition ability.

Wooden puzzles of differing complexities should be an item on your shelves of manipulative materials. These puzzles offer excellent practice for finger dexterity and eye-hand coordination, as well as the cognitive concepts of matching shapes, and part-to-whole relationships. Puzzles can help teachers, too. As Maldonado (1996) noted,

> Puzzles provide teachers with a fine observation and assessment tool, allowing teachers to easily observe children. Their concentration, body movement, language, thinking in the form of problem solving, and making choices are accessible to the observer. It is important for teachers to program enough time to sit with each child at a puzzle at least once a month. (pp. 9–10)

Young children can also teach their teachers a thing or two about puzzles—strange as it may seem. Two preschool teachers at a faculty meeting happen to make the comment that one child had brought to school a 100-piece puzzle and another had brought a 150-piece puzzle and was making it with his classmates. Could 3- and 4-year-old children actually make puzzles of such size and difficulty? No one had ever given them the opportunity. But when they had the chance, yes, they were able to work on such complex multipiece puzzles successfully and, over time, complete them.

As Barron (1999) noted,

The child who selects the puzzle works on it throughout the day—interspersed with other activities—and typically over a few days. Classmates spontaneously come by and assist from time to time. Doing puzzles is a social literacy activity rich with conversations about the process, about the story represented by the picture, about the children's personal experiences connected to the picture. (p. 11)

Cooking

Three-year-olds can also use this hand-turning skill to operate an eggbeater, and they love to do it. Be sure to have more than one eggbeater at your water table because the eggbeater is usually a favorite implement and the focus of many squabbles if only one is available. Children like to try turning food mills and can openers as well, but do not always have the strength to succeed if the items to be ground or opened are too difficult.

Research has found that objects of differing shapes and those that can be modified are more interesting to children than rigid and unchangeable objects. Novelty is also an important quality in encouraging children to handle and manipulate objects. When the novelty wears off, children are less interested in playing with the items. Teachers should respond to such findings by including a variety of items in the manipulative area and by changing them from time to time (Cratty, 1986, p. 214).

In addition, teachers should include cooking experiences in the classroom on a daily or weekly basis. Children can help with "cool cooking," that is, food preparation without heat, such as daily snacks. They can scrape carrots and cut celery for dipping; mix cream cheese with flavorings for dips; whip cream into butter and grind peanuts into peanut butter (check first for peanut allergies). They can also help with "hot cooking" by whipping eggs with eggbeaters for scrambled eggs or grinding cooked apples or pumpkin through a food mill.

Gellens (2005) pointed out:

Children not only enjoy preparing food, but in doing so, every sense is engaged, so multiple areas of the brain are stimulated simultaneously. Measuring, cutting, stirring, and pouring are good for eye–hand coordination and small and large muscular development. The more the senses are associated with a given activity, the stronger the synapses and the stronger the memory. (p. 18)

More and more teachers are making food preparation a part of their curriculum with the advent of convenient appliances such as electric fry pans, hot pots, microwaves, and toaster ovens. It is an activity with special significance for children's development of small motor skills. Or as Cosgrove (1991) pointed out:

Many kinds of learning are involved in cooking: motor, sensory, conceptual, and social skills all play an important part in food preparation. All five senses are involved. Stirring, beating, and rolling improve muscle control. Measuring, boiling, and freezing illustrate change. Following directions requires listening. Sharing, cooperation, and good manners encourage social skills. And waiting for someone to say "OK, it's done—let's eat" develops patience. (p. 44)

But before you begin hot cooking be sure to check on safety codes followed in your building or community.

If You Have Not Checked This Item: Some Helpful Ideas

■ Provide a Collection of Food Utensils for Cooking and Play

Visit a hardware store having a large assortment of food preparation utensils and stock up on all kinds of grinding, squeezing, and cranking types of implements. Better still, visit a flea market and buy the same sorts of things secondhand. Some of the old-fashioned hand tools of great-grandma's kitchen will make a big hit in your classroom. Keep some of the items in your housekeeping area for pretending, and some near the water table or on your manipulative shelves for small motor practice. But be sure to let children use these utensils when you do real cooking.

■ Use a Food Mill

Gellens (2005) suggests: "Have children use a food mill to strain cooked apples to make applesauce. This requires arm strength and stamina. Children see sequencing first hand when they follow recipes and see foods change from one state to another" (p. 18).

■ Make a Nuts-and-Bolts Board

Fasten bolts of differing sizes to a sanded-down board, and give children a box of nuts to screw onto the bolts. The children will need to use their size-sorting as well as small motor skills. Such boards are also available nowadays from educational supply houses, but creating your own makes the activity more natural and personal.

■ Collect Old Locks and Keys

Have a box of old locks and keys for children to experiment with. The youngsters will need persistence as well as motor skills to match up and make the locks and keys work. But it is an exciting challenge for them.

■ Get a Toy Hopper with a Hand Crank for the Sand Table

Children love to play with sand. Toy stores, toy catalogs, and stores selling beach toys offer sand implements for sifting and grinding that certain children will use for hours. With a hopper, they can grind sand enough to fill every container available. Don't forget to have children wear safety goggles at the sand table.

■ Try a Citrus Reamer

Bring in a citrus reamer that works by hand and let your children take turns twisting half an orange on it to make their own juice for snack. You may need to help them get started.

■ Read a Book

Duck Soup (Urbanovic, 2008) is a whacky animal tale with Maxwell Duck deciding to make a soup that will be his masterpiece. Ooo-la-la! So he does. But it needs just a little something more, so out he goes to the garden for some chives. In come his friends who smell the soup. But where is Max? They see a feather floating on top of the soup and are horrified to think he has fallen in. Out they pour the soup through a strainer into the kitchen sink, thinking a potato is his head, onions his eyeballs, and carrot slices his feet. Then in comes Max. Oh, no! So they have pizza for lunch and are all happy Max is not duck soup.

Dumpling Soup (Rattigan, 1993) tells the story of the little Asian-American girl, Marisa, who helps her Korean grandmother and her aunts to make dumplings for their annual New Year's celebration in Hawaii. They chop and talk and mix and pound and scrape, scrape, scrape. Be sure to have some real food for your children to prepare after reading this book.

Cook-A-Doodle-Do (Stevens & Crummel, 1999) tells the hilarious tale of Big Brown, Rooster who grows so bored with eating chicken feed that he decides to cook up Little Red Hen's Magnificent Strawberry Shortcake. With the "help" of Turtle, Iguana, and Pot-bellied Pig, they go into the farmhouse kitchen, sift flour, cut in butter, beat an egg, add milk, put it in the oven, and actually end up with a great shortcake with strawberries and whipped cream on top. But Iguana lets the cake slide to the floor on his way to the table, and Potbellied Pig, the taster, eats the whole thing. Before things get out of hand, Rooster says that was just for practice. Who will help me make it again? And they all do.

 # POURS LIQUIDS WITHOUT SPILLING

Two-year-olds are able to hold a glass of milk, at first with two hands, and then with one. Most parents are not really concerned that their children do more than this sort of holding. Pouring tends to be an adult activity that mothers do even for their preschool children. Many nursery school teachers and child-care personnel feel the same way. Why should children learn to pour? Won't they just make a mess if they spill? Isn't it much quicker and more efficient if the adults in the classroom do the pouring?

Children should learn to pour not only as a helping activity, but also to practice small motor coordination. Pouring is an excellent authentic activity that children can participate in, and that is both helpful to others and, more important, helpful for their own small muscle development. Long ago Maria Montessori, the renowned Italian early childhood educator, recognized the value of pouring by including all sorts of pouring activities in her "daily living exercises," which taught children small motor skills such as eye–hand coordination. Today Montessori children still learn by pouring rice before they finally pour liquids successfully from small pitchers.

The size of the pitcher is the key to successful pouring. Put a small pitcher on each of your children's snack or lunch tables, and let the youngsters help themselves to juice or milk. If they should spill, they can help clean up with a soft sponge, another good small motor exercise.

Allowing children to pour may not be as efficient as having an adult pour the drinks, but you need to think about the purpose of your program. Is it to take care of a group of children, or is it to *help young children develop their own skills* and learn to take care of themselves? Young children take a great deal of pride in being able to do adult-type tasks. Performing these tasks not only makes them feel grown-up but also gives them a real sense of self-worth and accomplishment.

There will be accidents. Spills are part of the price our children pay for the complicated task of growing up. Remember the problem of releasing the grip, in which children actually have to learn how to let go because some traces of the grasp reflex may still remain? And if they do not have their minds on what they are doing, they may release their grip without meaning to. Again, make spilling a learning experience, not an embarrassment. They will enjoy squeezing out the cleanup sponge. Three-year-olds may need to use both hands for pouring. But if the pitcher is small enough, 4- and 5-year-olds can often handle it with one hand.

If You Have Not Checked This Item: Some Helpful Ideas

■ Have Pouring Implements in Your Water Table

Have several sizes and types of plastic pitchers in your water table. Some can be large with lids on the top; some can be small and open at the top. All should have handles. Children can do much of their initial pouring practice here without worrying about spilling. Later, have children sign up to water classroom plants with a small watering can.

■ Use Pouring Implements on Your Food Table

Have small plastic or ceramic pitchers that the children can use to serve themselves. You can fill these small-sized containers as they empty. Again, the flea market is a good source for interesting pouring implements such as vinegar cruets and small metal pitchers.

■ Read a Book

Oliver's Milk Shake (French, 2000) has plenty of pouring, starting with Oliver pouring orange soda for breakfast to the yummy scrummy fruity frothy icy nicy tip-top tasty dreamy creamy milk shake his Aunt Jen helps him make from scratch. What "scratch" means is going out to the farm for fresh milk from a cow—in a carton at the farm stand—and a basket of blueberries. Your children can follow Aunt Jen's recipe for their own yummy, etc. shake.

Warthogs in the Kitchen: A Sloppy Counting Book (Edwards, 1998) shows what happens when one warthog and then another and another get together in the kitchen to make cupcakes. As the hilarious mess progresses, they pour mountains of sugar (instead of four scoops) and a whole bag of flour (instead of seven scoops) into their mixing bowl. The story concludes with two recipes: Cupcakes for Humans and Cupcakes for Warthogs.

Cool Kids Cook (Hay, 2000) is a wonderfully illustrated cookbook for children with recipes for everything from Gringo's Nachos to Frog in a Pond (lime Jell-O). Plenty of pouring of liquids and dry ingredients gives junior chefs great small motor practice.

FASTENS AND UNFASTENS ZIPPERS, BUTTONS, TABS

Fastening and unfastening zippers, buttons, and Velcro tabs are other self-help skills we want children to accomplish not only so they can take care of themselves, but also to help them develop their small motor dexterity. Young children want to do things for themselves. Often they have trouble accomplishing fastening tasks because their motor coordination has not developed sufficiently. But just as often their difficulty has to do with lack of practice because the adults around them do everything for them.

It is interesting to note that economically disadvantaged children frequently develop small motor dexterity before middle-income children do. They have had more practice. In fact, preschoolers in many large one-parent families are expected to help dress themselves when the working mother has her hands full getting herself ready for work every morning, the baby ready for the sitter, and breakfast ready for everybody before she has to leave.

If mothers and fathers do all the buttoning and fastening of clothing for their preschoolers, the children miss an excellent opportunity for learning how to do it on their own. They may even resist when the preschool teacher encourages them to try, wanting the teacher to perform the same function as their mothers.

Three-year-olds are able to unbutton first—always an easier task—but many can also button large buttons on clothing if given the chance to practice. Most 3-year-olds also can fasten regular snaps but may have trouble with the heavy-duty jeans-type snap. Even 4-year-olds seldom have the finger strength necessary to make these heavy-duty snaps work. Four-year-olds should be able to button and unbutton clothing with little difficulty. They can unzip zippers, but often need help getting started with jacket zippers that come apart completely.

Many shoes and articles of clothing are fastened with Velcro-type fasteners. This seems to be the easiest fastener for children to handle. A Velcro fastener is pulled apart by gripping the end between the thumb and forefinger and pulling; it is fastened merely by pushing one Velcro-covered tab against the Velcro backing. Preschoolers have the strength and coordination to do this with ease.

Give children a great deal of the practice putting on and taking off clothing and shoes. Sometimes you need to help a child get started with a zipper, but be sure to show him how and let him try again. Encourage children to dress and undress the dolls they play with. Have them dress them again when they are finished.

If You Have Not Checked This Item: Some Helpful Ideas

■ Use Buttoning/Zipping Boards

Make or purchase several boards that will help your children acquire and practice these skills. If you make your own boards, have only one skill on each board: buttoning on

Encourage children to dress and undress the dolls they play with.

one, zipping on another, snaps on another. Then children can practice one of these skills at a time. Have these boards available in the manipulative area of your classroom.

■ Dress and Undress Dolls

Constructive Playthings (1-800-448-4115) features ten different 16″ tall multiethnic dolls with removable, washable clothes. Extra sets of clothing for sleep time, school days, and outer wear are also available. Eight 18″tall rag dolls representing four different ethnic groups are not only dressable, but also fit into a wheelchair, sold separately.

■ Talk with Parents

Talk with parents about the importance of their child's developing small motor coordination. Let them know the kinds of activities their children will be doing in your class. Suggest some of the activities the children could be doing at home, such as self-help skills like dressing themselves—including buttoning, zipping, and snapping clothing—or helping dress younger members of the family.

■ Read a Book

Ella Sarah Gets Dressed (Chodos-Irvine, 2003) shows a determined little Ella Sarah getting dressed in what she wants to wear and not what her mother, father, and sister have in mind. So she puts on her pink polka-dot pants, her dress with orange-and-green flowers, her purple-and-blue striped socks, her yellow shoes, and her red hat. Ella thinks her outfit is just right, and so do the friends that come to her door—in equally spectacular outfits. Have children reenact this story with dress-up clothes from the dramatic play center.

I Can Do It Too! (Baicker, 2003) is a simple book with a 3-year-old African-American girl imitating each member of her family as her father pours juice into his cup; her sister puts on all her clothes, snaps, zips, and ties the bows; her Grandma bakes a chocolate cake; her Grandpa reads her a book; her uncle plays a guitar; and her best friends play sipping tea in a castle. "I can do it too!" she says on every other page, and she does.

 ## PICKS UP AND INSERTS OBJECTS WITH DEXTERITY

Manipulative Materials

Picking up and inserting objects is the small motor skill most frequently promoted in the early childhood classroom. This skill involves manipulation of items by gripping them between thumb and fingers and inserting or placing them somewhere else. Using puzzles, pegboards, and stacking toys; lacing, sewing, weaving, and stringing beads; and counting, sorting, and matching small items call for this skill. Playing with Lego bricks, geoboards, formboards, bristleboards, and many plastic table games also calls for the picking up and inserting skills.

All classrooms should have a permanent space for manipulative activity of this sort, with shelves at the children's level equipped with many such materials for easy selection and return. There should be a table in the area next to the shelves, as well as floor space for playing with the larger toys. Some classrooms call this area the "manipulative/math center" because preschool math concepts are learned through the manipulation of small objects. Kyoung-Hye Seo (2003) noted,

> A variety of math manipulatives are on the market today—pattern blocks, counters, number towers, base-10 blocks, and Cuisenaire rods, to name a few. The idea behind math manipulatives is that young children learn best through active interactions with concrete objects. (p. 30)

Manipulative objects like this also help children develop small motor coordination and dexterity.

The selection of materials should cover a wide range of children's abilities, as well. Wooden puzzles, for example, should include simple single pictures with pieces showing an entire part of the picture for beginners, as well as more complicated pictures with many pieces for older or experienced children. Table block sets should include large blocks as well as Lego bricks. As Seefeldt and Wasik (2006) point out: "Three-year-olds play better with large blocks than with small Lego pieces. Their fingers do not have the dexterity to manipulate small objects" (p. 44).

Teachers should plan to check all the manipulative materials at least once a week to be sure all the parts and pieces are there. If some pieces are missing, either replace the piece or remove the material. It does not help beginners to try making puzzles or playing games with pieces missing. Many beginners soon give up.

It is not necessary to put out all the manipulative materials that the program owns at once. Add a few new ones to the area every month and remove some of the old ones. Remember that novelty motivates children to use the materials. Save some of the more complicated table toys for challenging the experienced children later in the year. If you have a limited supply of materials, consider trading with other programs.

Children's Skills

You will want to know which children visit the manipulative area during your free-play period. Use the small motor checklist as a screening device to help you find out. Are children avoiding the area because they are not comfortable with small motor skills? Are boys the ones who avoid the manipulative materials?

Once you identify which individuals avoid manipulative activities, you will be able to sit down at a table with a single child and challenge him or her to make a puzzle with you, stack blocks, or sort shapes into a formboard. If you are keeping file card records of each child, you can add this information to these cards. You or your coworkers may need to spend time every day with children who need extra practice with small motor skills. You may need to encourage these children to complete some of the small motor activities on their own. It is important for children to succeed in something on their own.

Preschool puzzles are well suited to helping children accomplish such a task. As Maldonado (1996) says:

> Through puzzle making, young children experience satisfaction by putting things together where they belong. The child is the problem solver by moving through the dissection of the puzzle, finding strategies to complete it, and evaluating the results. Upon puzzle completion, self-gratification is reached. (p. 4)

Sometimes your presence at the puzzle table helps a child to stick to her task until it is completed. Let her do it on her own, but lend your support through positive comments when she tries several pieces and finally finds the right one.

Gender Differences

Our society still seems to encourage girls to engage in small motor activities more than boys. Boys are encouraged to run outside and climb trees or play ball. Girls are given manipulative-type toys for their play. As a result, many girls are more dexterous with their fingers, whereas many boys are more skillful in large motor activities such as running and throwing.

In the end, all children need to be skillful and at ease with both large and small motor activities. Once involved with formal education, both genders will need to handle writing tools and reading activities. Girls who are more skillful with finger dexterity and eye–hand coordination have an edge over boys in writing and reading at present. Is this small motor skill imbalance perhaps the reason more boys than girls have problems in learning to read?

If You Have Not Checked This Item: Some Helpful Ideas

■ Use Bead-Stringing

Put out all kinds of materials for both boys and girls to use in making necklaces. Have macaroni and all sorts of pasta shapes available. The children can color them first by painting. Bring in little seashells with holes drilled in them (hobby shops do this), as well as acorns and horse chestnuts in the fall, plastic or wooden beads, and any other small items you can find. Save tops from plastic bottles and tops of marking pens; punch holes in them and use them for stringing necklaces and bracelets.

An excellent picture book to use as a stimulus to bead-making and stringing is *A String of Beads* (1997) by Margarette S. Reid, showing a girl and her grandmother collecting, naming, and stringing brilliant beads together against a black background. They talk about where beads come from, who uses them, and what they are made of. Colorful pictures give directions for making and baking clay beads. If bead-stringing catches on, your children may want to go on a field trip to a bead store or hobby shop.

■ Make a Geoboard

Make a 1-foot-square wooden board about ½-inch thick and pound in headless nails over the surface of the board in rows 1 inch apart. Allow the nails to protrude above the surface about an inch. Let the children string colored rubber bands over the tops of the nails, making all kinds of designs. Older children can try to copy design cards you have made, as well.

Design cards are foot-square cardboard cards with dots representing the nails in the exact arrangement as the geoboard. On each card draw the outline of a red square or a blue triangle or a yellow rectangle, and let the children try to copy each shape with similar colored rubber bands on the geoboard. These designs must be simple for 3- and 4-year-olds because their copying skills are still at an early level. Kindergarten children have an easier time copying geoboard designs. If this play becomes a favorite activity, you will want more than one geoboard. Such boards can also be purchased from educational supply companies.

■ Make Pegboards

Ask a building supply company for scraps of pegboard it normally would throw away. You can cut the scraps to child-size shapes and sand down the edges. The pegboards do not have to be squares. Triangular pegboards are just as useful and appealing. Get boxes of colored golf tees for pegs, and let the children use the tees the same way colored rubber bands are used on the geoboards. You may want to make simple designs on paper or cardboard for the children to copy on their pegboards, as well. Graph paper is helpful if you do not want to spend time measuring spaces.

■ Ask Parents to Help

Have a parent "Board-Making Bee" to help stock your classroom as well as make enough extra boards to take home for their children to play with. You can almost always attract parents or other family members to help your program if they know they will be making educational games they can also take home. Besides helping their children both at home and at school, the parents themselves can be learning the importance of small motor activities for their children. Too often adults tend to look on all children's activities as play, an unimportant entertainment. Parents need to be aware that play is essential to their children's physical, mental, creative, and social development as human beings. Such parent group activities may change parents' outlook.

■ Hide Objects in Sand Table

No need to purchase manipulatives if you use your imagination. For instance, use your sand table as a beach that the children pretend to visit to look for shells. Collect little shells from a real beach (or a bead store) and bury them in the sand table. Have several children at a time dig for them with their fingers. If you first read *Famous Seaweed Soup* (Martin, 1993), your children may want to prepare their own famous seaweed soup just like Sara. Afterward, have them insert the shells through a hole in the top of a margarine tub cover for safekeeping.

   The sand table can also be a forest floor, where children hunt for acorns you have buried. Or perhaps it can be a dinosaur dig, where the children need to dig up the little plastic dinosaurs you have buried. All these are wonderful for finger exercising. If your program has no funds for purchasing such items, call a company for one of their toy catalogues, cut out and duplicate pictures of the items, laminate them, and bury them in the sand table.

■ Insert Snap Pieces to Build Things

Snap block sets of all types intrigue children. All have colored pieces, some of which are transparent. Children especially like to build things such as bugs (Build-a-Bug set) or dinosaurs (Build-a-Saurus) from Constructive Playthings (1-800-448-4115).

■ Read a Book

In *Grandmother's Dreamcatcher* (McCain, 1998), Kimmy must stay with her Chippewa grandmother in her cabin in the woods while her parents hunt for a house. Seeing that she is worried, her grandmother tells Kimmy they will make her a dreamcatcher to ease her mind at night, and so they do. First, they gather the ingredients: a twig that bends, some feathers, some silver beads, leather string, and thin leather strips. As they make the dreamcatcher, the grandmother tells Kimmy the story of how it works to permit only sweet dreams to come through. It works so well, in fact, they decide to make some for Kimmy's parents and their new house. Instructions for making a dreamcatcher appear on the last page.

In *Cleversticks* (Ashley, 1991), little Ling Sung doesn't want to go to his new preschool any more because he is unable to do most of the things the other children can do with ease: tie his shoes, write his name, button his jacket, and fasten his paint apron. Then one day when his snack cookies break, he picks up a pair of paintbrushes upside down and uses them as chopsticks to pick up each cookie piece and insert it into his mouth. The teacher is delighted and the other children clap. When Ling Sung's dad hears about it, he calls him "Cleversticks." Provide chopsticks for your children to use in pretend and real eating activities.

Busy Toes (Bowie, 1998) illustrates a concept some early childhood people may have overlooked: that toes can do many of the same things fingers can. It is a wonderfully illustrated book of mainly African-American children and infants using their toes to draw with a pencil, dig in sand, splash, squish, fish, dance, count, pick up little toys, push little cars, and cuddle.

 ## MOLDS PLAY DOUGH/CLAY WITH DEXTERITY

Other materials for strengthening young children's small muscles of hands and fingers are play dough and clay. Although they may seem similar, they are quite different. Playdough is the traditional molding material homemade in most preschool programs. It is soft, squishable, and easily molded into many shapes or rolled out flat. Clay, on the other hand, is denser and harder to work with the hands. It takes time and patience to mold, but is even better exercise for young hands and fingers.

Most teachers start with playdough. It is easy to make and allows children to get involved with it immediately. They can measure its ingredients, mix them together, stir it, add a color, divide it into portions, squish it between their fingers, roll it into a ball, flatten it into a pancake, and use all kinds of tools to cut, stamp, pound, and mold it into shapes. As Swartz (2005) says,

> Playdough allows children to practice fine motor skills. Children use hands and tools to pound, push, poke, shape, flatten, roll, cut, and scrape the dough. Through these experiences, children develop eye–hand coordination and control, dexterity, and strength, critical skills they will need later for writing, drawing, and other purposes. (p. 108)

Several different recipes are used to make playdough. Here is one:

2½ cups flour

½ cup salt

2 teaspoons alum

2 tablespoons cooking oil

2 cups water

Boil the water and pour it over the dry ingredients. Stir together and add cooking oil. Set aside to cool. When cool to the touch knead it with the hands until smooth. Store in an air-tight container but do not refrigerate. Many teachers prepare the dough ahead of time at first. Later they involve the children in helping to make it.

Commercial playdough comes in several varieties. Constructive Playthings (1-800-448-4115) features Play-Doh in 6-ounce cans of red, yellow, blue, white, lime, purple, orange, and pink. Also available is Crayola Dough that air dries in two days if children want permanent sculptures, but stays soft in closed buckets. Comes in 3-pound tubs of red, blue, yellow, purple, orange, and green. Lakeshore (1-800-778-4456) has regular dough or wheat and gluten-free dough in 3-pound tubs of red, blue, yellow, purple, orange, green, lilac, lime, pink, turquoise, black, and white. They also carry air-dry lightweight clay in 4-ounce bags of six colors or all white. Tools to work with play dough and clay include rolling pins, cookie cutters, mallets, stampers, and rollers.

Give the children a chance to work the playdough with their hands at first, squishing, squeezing, and molding it. See how many shapes they can make. Another day bring out rolling pins and cookie cutters. Finally use plastic knives, mallets, stampers, and rollers.

After working with playdough or clay with their hands, children like to roll it with a rolling pin.

Also give children the experience of working with pottery clay. Give each child a lump of clay and encourage them to work it with their hands: to squeeze it, twist it, punch and poke it, roll it into a rope or flatten it into a pancake. It is much denser and harder to manipulate than playdough, but children come to like the feel of it. If they are worried about getting dirty, show them how easily it brushes off when dry. Keep the clay in an air-tight container or plastic bag with a damp sponge to keep it moist. Koster (1999), an advocate for children using real clay, has this to say: "Playdough is fine, but clay is real! Clay speaks to a basic need in all of us to touch the earth and play in its life-giving soil. Clay and children belong together!" (p. 22).

If You Have Not Checked This Item: Some Helpful Ideas

■ Visit a Museum or Art Gallery

Take a field trip to an art gallery or museum that displays pottery or other clay objects.

■ Visit a Potter's Studio

Take a field trip to a potter's studio so you can see how potters use clay to make bowls and other objects. Or invite a potter to the class and to show the children what he/she does.

■ Visit a Bakery or Market Where Bread is Baked

Take a field trip to a bakery to watch how bread is made.

■ Make Real Dough with the Children

Make real dough together and bake cookies. Or bring in a bread machine and bake bread.

■ Read a Book

The Empanadas That Abuela Made (Bertrand, 2003) is a wonderful cumulative bilingual tale of how Grandma made her famous pumpkin tarts. The comical illustrations show the gigantic dough "that folds over the pumpkin for the empanadas that Abuela made" is first folding over three laughing children. Next comes the gigantic rolling pin with the children dancing on it. Then Grandpa appears and joins the dancers on the pin rolling out the dough. But somehow Grandma gets to bake her tarts and feed everyone. Can any of your Hispanic children bring in a Spanish speaker to read the story in Spanish, too—and perhaps make pumpkin tarts?

Iggy Peck, Architect (Beaty, 2007) is the outrageous story of a natural building wonder, Iggy Peck, who builds his first tower at age two—out of diapers and glue! Then he builds the Sphinx from mud in his front yard, a temple from modeling clay, and the

St. Louis Arch from pancakes and coconut pie—all in rhyme. But his second-grade teacher prevents him from building anything until the day he saves the class at a picnic on an island when the footbridge collapses, and he builds a new bridge out of boots, tree roots, and string.

The Mud Family (James, 1994) takes the reader far back into the dry canyons of the Southwest where Sosi lives with her family in an ancient cliff dwelling. No rain falls, and her family grows quarrelsome, so Sosi goes down to the dry river bed, where there is one remaining pool of water, and molds her own little family out of mud. When the adults dance for rain, they tell Sosi she is too little to dance. So she does her own rain dance for her mud girl. Then the raindrops splash. Suddenly a flash flood roars down the canyon sweeping away her mud family and almost taking Sosi. Her father snatches her up just in time, saying, "We are your family. You are my mud girl," and carries her back home. Dramatic illustrations bring the story to life.

USES DRAWING/WRITING TOOLS WITH CONTROL

Preschool programs for 3-, 4-, and 5-year-olds should not be concerned with "teaching" children how to draw pictures or write words. Set up your learning centers and let them emerge on their own. Some of your older children may—and probably will—progress to this stage of development and may be able to do some pictorial drawing and word writing naturally. Provide children with opportunities to use writing and drawing implements of all kinds to encourage natural development of their small motor finger strength and dexterity and their eye–hand coordination (see Chapters 11 and 12).

The first time preschoolers use crayons, pencils, or marking pens, they usually hold them in the so-called power grip: all the fingers are clamped fistlike around the implement. This does not give them much control over the marks they will make because the entire hand, wrist, and arm are involved in the movements, rather than the fingers.

As their motor skills develop and they have the chance to practice, they will eventually switch to the *precision grip*: holding the implement between the thumb and fingers. Young children go through predictable stages in their development of writing skills. Cratty has noted that the earliest stage is a grasp in which only the pencil touches the page with the arm and hand unsupported in the air. In the next stage, the little finger and elbow side of the hand are rested on the page of paper, but the hand and fingers are moved as one unit. Finally, children learn to use their hand and fingers separately, with the hand as an anchor on the paper and the fingers moving the pencil. The final stage, however, may not be reached until between 5 and 7 years of age (Cratty, 1986, p. 224).

Watch and see which of the children are using a mature grip on their writing implement and which still seem to prefer the fist clench. Ask their parents what writing or coloring tools they have at home. Some children may not have had the same amount of practice as others, because they have no materials. You may want to send home a few crayons and paper for those who want more drawing and writing practice. Meanwhile, give the children all kinds of practice using writing tools to trace inside and outside objects.

The stubby fingers of preschoolers sometimes have more success gripping a thick tool, although some youngsters prefer regular pencils and crayons. Felt-tip markers are already thick and easy for them to use. Many preschoolers prefer markers to any other writing/coloring implement. The problem for teachers is reminding the children to keep the markers capped so they don't dry out. Most preschoolers just can't remember. Clemens (1991) offers a clever solution:

> You can make a mound of plaster of Paris, take the caps off your markers, and sink the caps upside-down into the wet plaster, so their open ends are flush with the surface. After the plaster dries, the markers, inserted in their caps, stick out like porcupine quills. Children easily return the markers to the mound when they are not using them. (p. 7)

Programs sometimes forget about crayons when so many other drawing tools are available, many children preferring to use felt-tip markers. Nevertheless, crayons are important for their ability to help children strengthen the finger muscles necessary for later holding a writing tool. Cherry (1972) reminds us:

> The child can practice moving his arm, wrist, and lower palm rhythmically on a table top or floor, as he pushes a crayon back and forth and round and round. This prepares him for writing where similar, but more controlled motions are necessary. (p. 46)

Crayons, like most drawing tools, come in different sizes and shapes. Preschool children can have helpful small motor activities with fat crayons, the common slim crayons, and even flat crayons. Althouse, Johnson, and Mitchell (2003) suggest peeling the paper from a few crayons to encourage the children to peel off the paper from the rest themselves. Then using the tips, sides, and bottoms of the crayons can be explored (p. 26).

Chalk is another drawing implement sometimes neglected. Fat, sidewalk chalk is especially helpful in strengthening the small muscles of the hands and fingers. Children can draw on chalkboards, grocery bags, or brown wrapping paper unrolled across the floor. They can use wet paper or wet chalk to brighten the colors and make moving the chalk smoother. Drawing on a sidewalk is yet another exercise for wrists and fingers.

Table painting can be done with small, fine brushes, whereas easel painting takes short fat brushes for preschoolers' stubby fingers to hold. They can be ordered from educational supply companies. Art and writing skills for preschoolers are discussed more fully in Chapters 11 and 12.

If You Have Not Checked This Item: Some Helpful Ideas

■ Have a Writing Center

Place a small table in a quiet area. Have primary pencils, regular pencils, felt-tip markers, ballpoint pens, crayons, and notebooks and tablets of various sizes to scribble on. Make the center into a pretend newspaper office where children scribble or write newspaper reports; a post office where children write and mail letters; a business office where "secretaries" take notes in a notebook.

■ Make Posters

Bring in some posters showing a picture and a brief message and talk about them with the children. Would they like to make a poster for the "parents' potluck picnic" they are planning? Read them the book *Patches Lost and Found* (Kroll, 2001), about Jenny who lost her pet guinea pig Patches, and found him by crayoning dozens of posters that she put up around the neighborhood. They can look at the simple pictures of the guinea pig with a word or two saying LOST PATCHES and listing the phone number to call.

■ Read a Book

My Crayons Talk (Hubbard, 1996) is a wonderful crayoning experience with a little girl and her talkative crayons. Purple shouts, "Yum! Bubble gum," and shows the girl holding a giant purple crayon while blowing a huge purple crayon-colored bubble. Have your children choose their favorite color crayon and make their own drawing (or scribble) for that color. The girl's blue calls, "Sky, Swing so high," as she goes up in a swing with a giant blue crayon blasting off as a spaceship.

USES SCISSORS WITH CONTROL

Learning to cut with scissors takes a great deal of coordination and practice. Children who have had practice with this activity at home may be ahead of those who have not, regardless of age. Sometimes the scissors themselves make it difficult for youngsters to learn how to use them. The blunt scissors found in many preschools are often dull and difficult to manipulate, even by adults. Really good scissors are expensive, but a worthwhile investment when you consider what fine practice they give children in developing strength and coordination in hands and fingers.

A variety of scissors is now available from educational supply companies. Most preschoolers can learn on conventional scissors, but spring-action scissors are also available for beginners and children with limited muscular control. Because you want your children to develop small muscle control, try conventional scissors first. Be sure they are child-size with stainless steel blades and with large enough plastic hand grips for both righties and lefties. Cherry (1972) noted,

> Cutting looks easy, but tiny immature finger muscles are not so easily directed to move in the manner necessary to guide and control their opening and closing. (p. 126)

You can help children who have not learned to cut in several ways. Show them how to hold the scissors with their favored hand. As with crayons, children sometimes pick up scissors with either hand, but will not have much success if they are trying to use the nondominant hand. You may also have to model the use of scissors. As Bodrova and Leong (1996) observed,

> Teachers may have to model how to hold the instrument because children, although they may have seen adults holding it correctly, often do not focus on the most important attributes of the grip. Describe what you do with your hands in words so that the child can use private speech to guide him. For example, say, "To move the scissors, squeeze, squeeze." (p. 154)

To help children hold the paper they are cutting with the opposite hand, you might put a dot on that side of the paper to remind children to hold it with the dot under their thumb. You can then tell them to cut with their thumbs up. Some teachers start by holding a narrow strip of paper stretched taut between two hands for the child to cut in two. Once a child can do this cutting without difficulty, get another child to hold the paper and let each take a turn holding and cutting. Give them a task of cutting all the yellow strips into small pieces.

On another day, show the child how to hold the strip of paper in her own hand and cut with the other hand. She needs to keep her scissors in her dominant hand. Let her practice on different kinds of paper, including construction paper, typing paper, and pages from magazines. Finally, draw a line on a sheet of paper and let the child practice cutting along a line. Be sure to have at least one pair of left-handed scissors.

Most 4-year-olds can cut along a straight line without difficulty, but many have trouble turning corners and following a curved line. Children need practice of all kinds in cutting. Whenever you are preparing art materials for the children to use, especially cutouts that need to be pasted, try to involve the children in helping to do the cutting.

If You Have Not Checked This Item: Some Helpful Ideas

■ Use Wrapping Paper Ribbons

Let children practice cutting wrapping paper ribbons into confetti. Ribbons have more body than ordinary paper and cut easier. Someone may need to hold the ribbon while the other cuts. Save the confetti for a celebration.

■ Use Squeeze Bottles and Sponges

If children have difficulty making scissors work, it may be they need help strengthening finger muscles. Put several squeeze bottles in the water table and let them squirt water into containers, or take them outside and squirt designs on the sidewalk. Make rules ahead of time about not squirting each other or they will lose their bottle. Also cut up sponges into sizes small enough for children to hold and squeeze. They can use them to sponge off art tables or lunch tables—another small-muscle strengthening activity.

■ Set Up a Cutting Table

Put out several pairs of scissors and different kinds of paper scraps to be cut into small pieces: letter paper, wallpaper, old greeting cards, drinking straws, coupons, wrapping paper, and so on. Save the cuttings for later use in making collages.

■ Read a Book

In *Pablo's Tree* (Mora, 1994) Pablo's grandfather Lito plants a tree when Pablo is adopted as a baby, and every year thereafter he decorates the tree with a surprise decoration that he makes: paper streamers, paper lanterns, tiny birdcages, bells, and chimes. Pablo can't wait to visit Lito to see what the next birthday will bring. Have a birthday tree for your class and let children fold and cut paper decorations on their birthday. Be sure to count birthdays of children born during the summer when school is out.

USES A HAMMER WITH CONTROL

Holding a nail and pounding it with a hammer held in the opposite hand is the most complicated small motor skill thus far discussed. Many children will not be able to do it well until they are older and more coordinated. Even adults often have difficulty. Try it yourself and find out.

Arm and wrist strength make a difference. The small toy hammers in play sets should not be used. They are not heavy or strong enough to have much effect other than frustrating the pounder. A small adult hammer is better for pounding in real nails.

Both boys and girls should be encouraged to pound. It is an excellent activity to develop small motor strength and coordination. If you do not have a carpenter's bench in your room, you can set up a woodworking area by hanging tools on the wall from a pegboard and using a tree stump as a pounding surface. Slices can also be cut from a stump and placed on a table for pounding. Nails go into tree stumps easier than into boards. Place a towel or rug sample under each stump to absorb the sound. Leithead (1996) suggests that when the top of the stump is completely covered with nails, it can be sliced off, making a clean surface for new pounding (p. 12).

Leithead has observed that children's first hammering of nails into stumps is random. As they master the skill, they begin to make designs, sometimes their own initials. She noted other uses for pounding:

> The hammering center usually has two stumps and two hammers of different weights. Children can experiment scientifically, predicting which hammer will be the most efficient and then testing their predictions by counting the number of blows each hammer takes to sink a nail. (p. 12)

To get children interested in this or any activity area in your classroom, simply go into the area yourself and begin pounding something. Pounding always attracts attention, and soon children will want to do the same thing the teacher is doing. Again you should check to make sure they are holding the hammer in their favored hand. You can control for safety by limiting the number of hammers or tree stumps available for pounding. Also be sure the pounders wear safety goggles and that an adult is present when tools are being used.

Safety seems to be the primary concern for teachers. But with basic safety limits established before the children use the center or its tools, the possibility for injuries is reduced. If a teacher is uncomfortable using the tools, she or he should ask a carpenter or a parent to demonstrate their use. Why should young children be involved in woodwork in the first place, you may wonder? Huber (1999) tells us:

> As children explore with tools and wood they use large and small muscles. Sawing requires large movement, while holding a screw in place requires small-muscle coordination. Hammering nails helps build eye-to-hand coordination. As children make decisions about design, shape, and types of wood to use, they participate in problem-solving skills. (p. 33)

Andrews (1997) suggests that the following rules or limits should be followed:

- Only two children at a time in the woodworking center
- Wear goggles at all times
- Use only one tool at a time; replace it before taking another
- Hold tools and materials in hands (not mouth)
- Before leaving the center, return tools and materials to proper places. (p. 31)

Other possibilities for hammering include using commercial plastic hammers as shown in the chapter opening photo along with foam boards for pounding in plastic nails or pegs.

If You Have Not Checked This Item: Some Helpful Ideas

■ Use Soft Pounding Materials

Do not start your pounding activities with wood. Most children need to acquire the skill before they can drive a nail through wood easily. Start with a softer material such as fiberboard, ceiling tiles, or Styrofoam.

■ Use Large-Headed Nails

Children should use large-headed nails at first. Most tacks are too short for the pounder to hold, but roofing nails or upholstering tacks are large enough and long enough to work well.

■ Have an Alphabet Hammering Activity

Most early pounding by children is just for manipulating purposes and not to build anything. After children become experienced they may want to pound tongue depressors or other flat sticks together to make letters. Read *Alphabet Under Construction* (Fleming, 2002), in which a mouse creates a huge letter on every other page by airbrushing A, buttoning B, carving C, and so forth. A horizontal poster of the mouse's alphabet is included. For children who would rather pound nails than sticks, can they make the first letter of their name in nails on a stump head?

■   Read a Book

I Love Tools (Sturges, 2006) shows a boy and girl watching their father use hammer, saw, square, ruler, drill, and screwdriver to build a bird box for a bluebird. Outlines of the tools appear on the inside front and back covers. Which of these tools can your children handle?

Thump, Quack, Moo: A Whacky Adventure (Cronin & Lewin, 2008) shows Farmer Brown's animals helping him prepare for the annual Corn Maze Festival. Of course, they make a mess of it with Duck pounding together a ticket booth with no opening. The farmer cuts a wonderful Statue of Liberty maze in the corn while Duck cuts his own secret. When they both go aloft in a hot air balloon to check on the maze, readers must open a flap to see the Statue of Liberty with Duck's head on it! Have your children draw their own maze on a huge sheet of paper.

OBSERVING, RECORDING, AND INTERPRETING SMALL MOTOR DEVELOPMENT

As you did with the large motor checklist items, you should also screen your entire class on the eight small motor checklist items. Make a similar chart with the children's names on one side, and the eight items across the top. Check off the accomplishments for all your children based on your observations. At a glance, you can see by the blanks which of the children may need special help to accomplish small motor skills.

Observe each of these children who need special help separately during the free-choice period, recording their actions in a running record. Later you can transfer this information for an individual onto the entire checklist by checking off items and writing in evidence.

Finally, you should make an individualized Learning Prescription for each child needing special help. The activities you choose to help the child in "Areas Needing Strengthening" should be based on his or her "Areas of Strength and Confidence." For example, Figure 8–1 shows the small motor checklist for Lionel, the new boy discussed at the ends of Chapters 5 and 7. Using the information gained on the social play checklist and the large motor checklist, the staff put together the learning prescription for Lionel shown in Figure 8–2.

Because Lionel shows the ability to make puzzles and to fasten and unfasten zippers and buttons, the staff thought he could use his small motor skills to work with another child in a class project. He likes art activities such as using play dough and finger painting, but does not use paintbrushes, writing tools, or scissors. He is left-handed and seems to have trouble with scissors.

The staff says that they will provide him with left-handed scissors and give him support in the activity of cutting out pictures of cars for the class scrapbook. They do not have a woodworking bench, but Lionel says he has helped his grandfather pound nails. Perhaps

Child Development Checklist

Name ___Lionel_____ Observer ___Barb_____

Program ___Preschool – K2_____ Dates ___1 / 20_____

Directions:

Put an **X** for items you see the child perform regularly. Put **N** for items where there is no opportunity to observe. Leave all other items blank.

Item	Evidence	Date
6. Small Motor Development		
___X___ Turns knobs, lids, eggbeaters	Plays with eggbeater at water table	1/20
___X___ Pours liquids without spilling	Pours own milk at lunch	1/20
___X___ Fastens/unfastens zippers, buttons, Velcro	Dresses & undresses self	1/20
___X___ Picks up and inserts objects with dexterity	Makes puzzles easily	1/20
___X___ Molds playdough/clay with dexterity	Likes to roll out playdough	1/20
_____ Uses drawing/writing tools with control	Does not use markers or writing tools	1/20
_____ Uses scissors with control	Does not use scissors	1/20
___N___ Uses hammer with control	Woodworking not available	1/20

Figure 8—1 Small Motor Checklist Observation for Lionel

he and other children could pound together simple rhythm instruments from wood, paint them, and use them in a rhythm activity (Lionel excels in rhythm). Using things Lionel likes to do and is good at doing may help him get involved with the other children.

Learning Prescription

Name _Lionel_   **Age** _3_   **Date** _1/20_

Areas of Strength and Confidence

1. _Does manipulative activities well by self_
2. _Performs or participates in music and rhythm activities_
3. _Has good small motor coordination_

Areas Needing Strengthening

1. _Needs to develop large motor skills_
2. _Needs to learn to play with others_
3. _Needs to develop small motor skills of writing, drawing, cutting_

Activities to Help

1. _Bring in pair of left-handed scissors & have Lionel cut out car pictures to make a scrapbook with one of the other boys._
2. _Bring in hammer, nails & tree stump; ask Lionel to help another child make rhythm instrument shaker_
3. _Have Lionel & other children paint rhythm instruments they make_

Figure 8–2 Learning Prescription for Lionel

LEARNING ACTIVITIES

1. Use the Child Skills Checklist section on small motor development as a screening tool to observe all the children in your classroom. Note which ones spend time in small motor activities and which do not.

2. Compare the checklist results for the children in your classroom in both large and small motor development. Do you see any relationships?

3. Choose a child who seems to need a great deal of help with small motor skills. Do a running record of him or her on three different days concentrating on small motor skills. Do a learning activity with him based on the results.

4. How do the girls and boys of the same age compare with one another in small motor skills? What conclusions can you make based on your observations?

5. Put out a new small motor activity for the children to use. Observe and record the results.

Why did you choose it? What conclusions can you draw?

SUGGESTED READINGS

American Cancer Society. (2000). *Kids' first cookbook*. Atlanta, GA: Health Content Products Publishing.

Armistead, M. E. (2007). Kaleidoscope: How a creative arts enrichment program prepares children for kindergarten. *Young Children, 62*(6), 86–93.

Beaty, J. J. (2008). *Skills for preschool teachers* (7th ed.). Upper Saddle River, NJ: Merrill/Prentice Hall.

Bisgaier, C. S., & Samaras, S. (2004). Using wood, glue, and words to enhance learning. *Young Children, 59*(4), 22–29.

Edwards, L. C. (2002). *The creative arts: A process approach for teachers and children*. Upper Saddle River, NJ: Merrill/Prentice Hall.

Isbell, R.T., & Raines, S.C. (2007). *Creativity and the arts with young children*. Clifton Parks, NY: Cengage Learning.

Sosna, D. (2000). More about woodworking with young children. *Young Children, 54*(6), 32–34.

CHILDREN'S BOOKS

Ashley, B. (1991). *Cleversticks*. New York: Crown.*

Baicker, K. (2003). *I can do it too!* New York: Handprint Books.*

Beaty, A. (2007). *Iggy Peck, Architect*. New York: Abrams Books.

Bertrañd, D.G. (2003). *The empanadas that Abuela made*. Houston, TX: Pinata Books.

Bowie, C. W. (1998). *Busy toes*. Dallas: Whispering Coyote Press.*

Chodos-Irvine, M. (2003). *Ella Sarah gets dressed*. San Diego: Harcourt.*

Cronin, D., & Lewin, B. (2008). *Thump, Quack, Moo: A Whacky Adventure*. New York: Atheneum.

Edwards, P. D. (1998). *Warthogs in the kitchen: A sloppy counting book*. New York: Hyperion.

Fleming, D. (2002). *Alphabet under construction*. New York: Henry Holt.

French, V. (2000). *Oliver's milk shake*. New York: Orchard.

Hay, D. (2000). *Cool kids cook*. New York: William Morrow.

Hubbard, P. (1996). *My crayons talk*. New York: Henry Holt.

James, B. (1994). *The mud family*. New York: G.P. Putnam's Sons.*

Kroll, S. (2001). *Patches lost and found*. New York: Winslow Press.

Martin, A. (1993). *Famous seaweed soup*. Morton Grove, IL: Whitman.

McCain, B. (1998). *Grandmother's dreamcatcher*. Morton Grove, IL: Whitman.*

Mora, P. (1994). *Pablo's tree*. New York: Macmillan.*

Rattigan, J. K. (1993). *Dumpling soup*. Boston: Little, Brown.*

Reid, M. S. (1997). *A string of beads*. New York: Dutton.*

Stevens, J., & Crummel, S. (1999). *Cook-a-doodle-doo!* San Diego: Harcourt.

Sturges, P. (2006). *I love tools!* New York: HarperCollins.

Urbanovic, J. (2008). *Duck soup*. New York: HarperCollins.

---

*Multicultural.

9

Cognitive Development

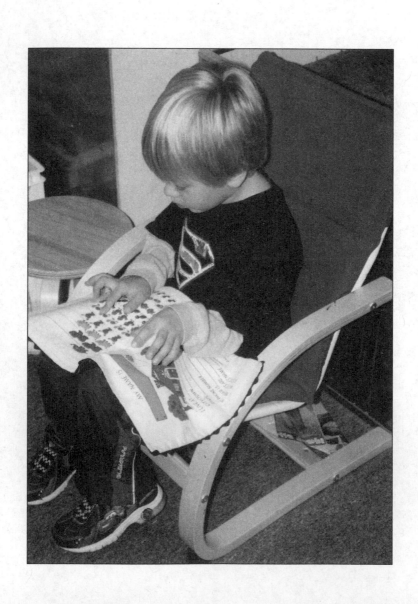

☑ **COGNITIVE DEVELOPMENT CHECKLIST**

___ Sorts objects by shape, color

___ Classifies objects by size

___ Places objects in a sequence or series

___ Recognizes, creates patterns

___ Counts by rote to 20

___ Displays 1-to-1 correspondence with numbers

___ Problem-solves with concrete objects

___ Problem-solves with computer programs

DEVELOPING COGNITIVE CONCEPTS

Cognitive development of preschool children is concerned with how their thinking abilities evolve. We are only beginning to understand how this takes place. The work of pioneer researchers like Swiss psychologist Jean Piaget in his investigation of how knowledge is created (see Table 9–1) has given us new insights into how children think as well as how their thinking evolves. The research of Russian psychologist Lev Vygotsky has added his own theories on cognitive development and helped to apply this information to the classroom. Studies by more recent psychologists have refined those earlier premises and developed theories of their own. The research of neuroscientists continues to provide more insights into how the brain develops and how this affects young children's thinking processes and behavior.

One of the surprising findings resulting from all this research is the fact that young children's thinking is not the same as that of adults. Piaget's Stages of Cognitive Development in Table 9–1 show how children below the age of 7 think mostly in concrete terms and have not yet developed the abstract thinking of older children and adults. Not all modern researchers agree with Piaget's stage theory. As McDevitt and Ormrod (2004)

Table 9–1   Piaget's stages of cognitive development

Sensorimotor Stage (Birth to Age 2)

Child thinks in visual patterns (schemata).

Child uses senses to explore objects (i.e., looks, listens, smells, tastes, and manipulates).

Child learns to recall physical features of an object.

Child associates objects with actions and events but does not use objects to symbolize actions and events (e.g., rolls a ball but does not use ball as a pretend car).

Child develops object permanence (comes to realize an object is still there even when out of sight).

Preoperational Stage (Age 2–7)

Child acquires symbolic thought (uses mental images and words to represent actions and events not present).

Child uses objects to symbolize actions and events (e.g., pretends a block is a car).

Child learns to anticipate effect of one action on another (e.g., realizes pouring milk from pitcher to glass will make level of milk decrease in pitcher as it rises in glass).

Child is deceived by appearances (e.g., believes a tall, thin container holding a cup of water contains more than a short, wide container holding a cup of water).

Child is concerned with final products (focuses on the way things look at a particular moment, "figurative knowledge," and not on changes of things or how things got that way, "operational knowledge"), and he cannot seem to reverse his thinking.

Concrete-Operational Stage (Age 7–11)

Child's thoughts can deal with changes of things and how they got that way.

Child is able to reverse her thinking (has ability to see in her mind how things looked before and after a change took place).

Child has gone beyond how things look at a particular moment and begins to understand how things relate to one another (e.g., knows that the number 2 can be larger than 1, yet, at the same time, smaller than 3).

Formal-Operational Stage (Age 11+)

Child begins to think about thinking.

Child thinks in abstract terms without needing concrete objects.

Child can hypothesize about things.

noted, "Piaget's stages provide a rough idea of when new abilities are likely to emerge" (p. 158). But perhaps the most startling finding to those unfamiliar with this research is that children actively construct their own knowledge.

Using the physical and mental tools they are born with, children interact with their environment to make sense of it, and in so doing, they construct their own mental concepts of their world. The brain seems to be conditioned to take in information about objects and their relationship to one another. What do things look, feel, taste, sound, and smell like? What can they do? How are they like one another? How are they different? What happens if you touch, push, or throw them?

As children manipulate the objects in their environment, they learn to make different responses to different objects. The new knowledge that they gain is assimilated into their previous knowledge, thus helping their thinking patterns evolve. To Piaget, children's cognitive development comes from biological maturation, their interactions with their environment, and their spontaneous discoveries about it. Piaget puts the knowledge that children are constructing into three categories:

- *Physical knowledge* Children learn about objects in their environment by physically manipulating them. They begin constructing the mental concepts of shape, size, and color about these objects.

- *Logico-mathematical knowledge* Children construct relationships about the objects such as alike and different, more and less, which ones go together, how many, how much.

- *Social knowledge* Children learn rules for behavior and knowledge about people's actions through their involvement with people.

As they interact with the objects and people in their environment, young children acquire physical knowledge and logico-mathematical knowledge simultaneously. According to Charlesworth, "As the physical characteristics of objects are learned, logico-mathematical categories are constructed to organize information" (1996, p. 6). Thus cognitive concepts are formed.

Charlesworth continues:

> Early childhood is a period when children actively engage in acquiring basic concepts. Concepts are the building blocks of knowledge: they allow people to organize and catgorize information. (p. 1)

This chapter will look at children's development of particular logico-mathematical concepts as observable examples of where they stand in cognitive maturity.

Although Vygotsky's theories support many of Piaget's findings, Vygotsky believed that after age 2, culture and cultural signs are necessary to expand children's thinking (Charlesworth, 1996, p. 7). In other words, cognitive development does not come from the child alone but also from the adults and mature peers around him, as well as from mental tools (Vygotsky called them "signs") that the child develops such as speech and, later, writing and numbering.

Whereas Piaget emphasized children as explorers and discoverers, constructing their knowledge independently, Vygotsky developed the concept of the *zone of proximal development,* or ZPD, defined as the area between where the child is now in mental development and where she might go with assistance from an adult or a more mature child (Charlesworth, 1996, p. 7).

To gain cultural knowledge, the child needs assistance or scaffolding, which is provided by more mature learners. To Vygotsky, good teaching involves presenting material

Good teaching involves using material that is a little ahead of the child's development.

that is a little ahead of the child's development. Teachers know they have identified a child's ZPD when the child responds with enthusiasm to the activities the teacher provides.

Both Piaget's and Vygotsky's points of view are incorporated into quality early childhood programs today by giving children opportunities to explore and discover on their own, as well as to interact with adults who support their efforts and challenge them in making new discoveries. However, neither Piaget nor Vygotsky had access to the brain research technology currently being used to discover how the brain develops and functions. Although many of these findings support the theories of those pioneer researchers, we are still at the beginning of our knowledge about this amazing organ we all possess: the human brain.

BRAIN RESEARCH

New findings about infants' and young children's brain development are opening our eyes to the importance of early adult–child interactions and a stimulating environment. As recently as 30 years ago, many psychologists believed that the genes children were born with determined the structure of their brains, which could not be changed. Brain research, however, has disproved such a theory. Heredity determines only the basic number of neurons (brain cells) children are born with, but this is just the framework (Newberger, 1997). New brain-imaging technologies such as the positron emission tomography (PET) that allow neuroscientists to study how the brain develops over the first 6 years of life have reported surprising findings.

The brain is in a mostly undeveloped state at birth: "Fully three-quarters of the human brain develops outside the womb, in direct relationship with an external environment" (Shore, 1997, p. 24). The weight of the brain increases from about 1 pound at birth to 2 pounds by age 1 (Bergen & Coscia, 2001, p. 27). It is the electrical activity of the neurons that is most important. Even before birth, these cells fire electrical charges that carve mental circuits into patterns in the brain, actually changing the structure of the brain. You could say that the brain is wiring itself for use.

Immediately after birth, an explosion of learning occurs caused by these same electrical processes. What happens next is up to the people and the environment surrounding the infant. The brain changes dramatically as trillions more synapses (connections) than it can possibly use are produced, laying out circuits for vision, movement, language, thinking, and the functions necessary for life itself. By age 2 the number of synapses reaches the adult level, and incredibly, by age 3 the brain's synapse density is twice that of the adult brain (Shore, 1997). This time the neural activity is no longer spontaneous as it was before birth, but is driven by the sensory experiences the child encounters in his environment.

In other words, for neurons to make connections in the brain, they must be activated through experiences. The importance of these experiences are described by Newberger (1997):

> Positive interactions with caring adults stimulate a child's brain profoundly, causing synapses to grow and existing connections to be strengthened. Those synapses in a child's brain that are used tend to become permanent fixtures; those that are not used tend to be eliminated. Neural plasticity, the brain's ability to adapt with experience, confirms that early stimulation sets the stage for how children will continue to learn and interact with others throughout life. (p. 5)

Chiron and colleagues (1997) used the single photon emission tomography (SPECT) technique to study cerebral blood flow and how it affects young children's brains and thus their behavior. Bergen and Coscia (2001) report that Chiron's group observed greater blood flow in the right hemisphere of the brains in 1-year-old children. Other changes they noted that were related to brain growth included handedness (established between ages 1 and 4), sensory and motor control (established by ages 3 to 4), and perceptual and language growth (between ages 1 and 3). By age 3, children use memory consciously and are learning to use memory strategies such as repetition (Bergen and Coscia, 2001, pp. 29–30).

Not all experiences are the same for every infant and young child, according to Greenspan (1997). Strange as it may seem, it is the emotional interactions with those around young children that have the most crucial role in shaping the intellect. Greenspan further claims:

> Babies' emotional exchanges with their caregivers, rather than their ability to fit pegs into holes or find beads under cups, should become the primary measuring rod of developmental and intellectual competence. (p. 9)

This new understanding of how the mind develops makes it clear that positive emotional experiences are crucial in a young child's growth of intellectual capacities. Thus, as we look at the cognitive development of preschool children in this chapter, we must keep in mind that for intellectual competence to occur, the activities and experiences we provide must be accompanied by positive interactions with caring adults.

USING PLAY

Both Piaget and Vygotsky agreed that children create their own knowledge through exploratory play. They do it by playing with things, people, and ideas. Most people think of play as something recreational, something we do for enjoyment, and something rather inconsequential. For adults, this definition of play may be true, but for infants and young children, play is a way of trying out and finding out about the world around them. Children fool around with toys, their clothing, their hands and feet, sounds, words, and other people. Youngsters use their senses of taste, touch, sound, sight, and smell in a playful manner with anything and everything they can get their hands on, to find out what an object is, what it feels like, what it sounds like, and what you can do with it. The fact is that child's play is sensory practice in learning to think.

From the time he is born, the human infant pursues such information with a single-minded determination. At first, everything goes into the mouth. Then the infant bangs objects against the side of the crib to see what they sound like, to see what they will do, or to find out what will happen. The toddler has an extra advantage. He has expanded his field of exploration by learning to walk. Suddenly the world's objects are his to touch, pick up, shake, throw, taste, and take apart. He uses his senses to "play" with his world and to find out what it is about. And as soon as he can talk, he plays with words and word sounds as well.

All the information extracted through this playful exploration of the environment is filed away in predetermined patterns in the brain, to be used to direct or adjust the child's behavior as he continues to respond to the stimuli around him. We now know that this knowledge is organized by the brain in predictable patterns from a very early age.

STAGES OF EXPLORATORY PLAY

Exploratory play itself occurs in predictable, observable patterns as young children grow and develop. All children seem to go through three definite stages of play every time they explore the possibilities of a new object or activity on their own. To make such stages easy to recognize and remember, we call them "the 3 Ms": manipulation, mastery, and meaning. Children progress through these developmental stages by being allowed to explore new objects and activities on their own. If we make children do things our way, we are short-circuiting their learning process. Our guidance should come after children have a chance to try out things on their own (Beaty, 2008, pp. 92–93).

When children of any age first begin to explore a new object, they play around with it, turning it upside down or inside out, or using it in ways it was never meant to be used.

For example, when children first use unit blocks, they often fill containers or trucks with them and then dump them out. Building with the blocks comes later, after children have become acquainted with the possibilities of blocks through manipulation. With paints, children start by messing around with the brushes and paints, perhaps filling a page with color and then covering it with another color. They are manipulating the medium. With a computer or typewriter, children often start by "piano-playing" the keys; that is, pressing all the keys instead of pressing one at a time and watching what happens. Children need this manipulation experience to discover how things work.

Once they are familiar with the medium, they quickly go on to the next stage of exploratory play: mastery. To master the use of a material or activity, young children need to try it out over and over, much to the distraction of many adults. Repetition is the hallmark of the mastery stage, almost as if children were setting up a natural practice session for themselves. With blocks, they build endless roads or walls or towers. With paints, they often repeat a scribble or line on page after page. With the computer, they call up their favorite screen again and again. You are probably witness to the story-reading mastery phase when children want the same story repeated endlessly. They are wiring their brains to remember; in other words, they are developing memory.

After they have satisfied this urge to master the material, many children go on to a new exploratory stage in which they put their own meaning into the activity. With blocks, they construct buildings. With paints, they create pictures. With computer programs, they may add their own twist such as playing an invented "I stopped you!" game with a partner. With familiar stories they often rename characters, change the plot, or make up their own story. Not all preschoolers reach this meaning stage, but many do if they have been encouraged to develop naturally through exploratory play.

CLASSIFICATION

As Shaw and Blake (1998) tell us: "Sorting and classifying are two important types of activities that encourage deductive reasoning. These activities foster the language of logic and build the base for more mature thinking" (pp. 120–121). Classification, one of the basic processes children use to develop reasoning abilities, is the method of placing objects that are alike in the same class or category. For the brain to classify, children first need to be able to tell what things look like: their shape, color, size, and other attributes. Then they must be able to tell which objects are alike according to particular attributes and which ones are different. Complex mental and physical abilities come into play as children develop classification skills: language and vocabulary; identification of shapes, colors, and sizes; and visual perception in identifying likeness and difference.

How do children learn these complex skills? Micklo (1995) says:

Children learn classification and other mathematical structures the same way that they learn about the rest of the world—by manipulating actual objects and constructing new knowledge after reflecting on their physical and mental actions. (pp. 24–28)

Once they have begun to notice the similar properties of objects, children can begin to separate or classify them, a necessary ability in cognitive development for the brain to sort out and process the wealth of incoming data obtained through sensory activities. Sorting objects and materials gives children practice in this skill and involves identifying the similarities of objects as well as understanding their relationships. The more we learn about young children's development of thinking abilities, the more we realize that thinking is concerned primarily with information processing and retrieval.

Piaget and other researchers have noted that children progress through a sequence of sorting skills, and that each skill is more complex than the previous one. The earliest sorting skill to appear is simple classification, which many 2- and most 3-year-olds can do. Children doing simple classification can sort or group objects that actually belong together in the real world. For example, they can group together all the toy animals that live on the farm in one set and all the fish and creatures that live in the ocean in another set, if the youngsters have had the appropriate experiences concerning such animals. This activity is not quite true classification, because it is based on associations between the animals and their homes, rather than the animals' likenesses or differences.

Another type of simple classification in which young children place things that "belong together" into a group involves putting all of the toy trucks, cars, and motorcycles together in a group because "you can drive them," or putting the proper hats on all the dolls, or putting all the blocks together because they make a house.

A more mature type of classification that many 3-year-olds and most 4- and 5-year-olds can do involves classifying objects into separate sets based on a common characteristic like color, for instance. You can ask the children to place all the red blocks in one set and all the blue blocks in another.

The problem most young children have in doing this kind of sorting involves consistency. They have difficulty keeping in mind the rule on which the sorting is based. Often, they will start sorting objects on the basis of color but will switch in the middle of the task to some other property, like shape, and may even switch back again before they are finished.

Children need to practice with all kinds of sorting games, activities, and collections—and the youngsters love this practice. Give a child a box of mixed buttons and let him sort it any way he chooses. Talk with the child afterward, and ask how he decided on which buttons to put in each pile. Look around your classroom for other objects to sort, such as dress-up clothing, blocks, and eating utensils. By age 5, children with experience can sort objects into intersecting sets based on more than one characteristic: color as well as size, for instance.

Why is it important for children to be able to classify like this, that is, to sort objects into certain categories? Child development researchers believe:

Children make use of categories to expand their knowledge. By simply naming objects we can encourage children to notice how different items are similar and help children gain new information about the world. Furthermore, because children expect items in a category to be alike in nonobvious ways, they are able to learn about "scientific" properties (such as the insides of animals) well before kindergarten age. Both of these implications illustrate that categories are the foundation for later learning in school. (Gelman, 1998, p. 25)

Willis (2007) tells us that the more ways something is learned, the more memory pathways are built in the brain. She calls teachers "memory enhancers"—not just "information dispensers" (pp. 311–312). What other ways can children classify in your classroom? What about organizing collage materials in art; gathering role props in dramatic play; choosing picture books on a certain subject; sorting objects collected on a field trip through the park; choosing musical percussion instruments (Charlesworth & Lind, 2007, p. 142)? Children need to use more than their sight in classifying. They should also use touch, taste, smell, and sound when appropriate.

ASSESSING DEVELOPMENT

How have your children fared in constructing their own knowledge? They need to have built up mental representations of objects: ways to differentiate things by their appearance or by their sound or feeling, ways of telling how things are alike or different, and ways to decide how things fit together as a part of a sequence or a series. These are the patterns or concepts the brain forms in organizing the data it takes in.

You will need to assess each of your children by observing their ability to accomplish the eight checklist items at the head of this chapter. The first two items refer to classification concepts the child needs to know; next is a concept involving sequences; next comes the ability to recognize patterns and create their own; the following two counting items involve children's number sense, including one-to-one correspondence; and finally comes their problem-solving ability, in which they draw on the previous skills to solve problems. Once you have made your assessment, you should plan activities or playful exploration periods for children to continue developing their thinking skills.

SORTS OBJECTS BY SHAPE, COLOR

Shape

Children identify and classify objects by their shapes. Charlesworth and Lind (2007) mention: "Basic two-dimensional geometric shapes include the circle, triangle, square, and rectangle. Each of these shapes is constructed from a straight line" (p. 218).

Development of thinking begins with the infant's seeing, hearing, and feeling things in her environment: her mother's face, or her bottle or mother's breast. Her brain takes in these important visual perceptions and stores them in particular schemes or patterns that are mental representations for the objects and events she experiences. Her brain seems to be conditioned to pay attention to certain things in her environment and ignore the rest.

Research has shown, for instance, that an infant looks longer at the human face than at anything else around her. She seems to have an innate preference for faces or facelike objects. The infant seems, in fact, to prefer visual stimuli that have a contour configuration. She is beginning her construction of knowledge.

The first checklist item on shape is concerned with refinement of the child's perceptual recognition. To think, reason, and problem-solve, the child needs to know and discriminate among basic shapes of things. We start with geometric shapes because the concept of shape is one of the first concepts to emerge in the child's cognitive development. He needs to distinguish among a circle, a square, a rectangle, and a triangle—not to do math problems, but to be able to categorize and distinguish mentally among the objects in his environment.

Young children need to begin sorting and classification activities as soon as they enter your program. Put out a set of plastic shape blocks. They may be red, blue, green, and yellow squares, circles, rectangles, and triangles. Observe to see how the children play with them. Does anyone group all of the circles together? That child is demonstrating discrimination abilities: that one shape is different from the other shapes. Can anyone tell the names of the different shapes? Those children are demonstrating labeling abilities. What about matching? Can anyone find other blocks to match a shape you put out? Can they do sorting; that is, separating the mixed group of shapes into sets of similar shapes Remind the children they need to be looking at the shapes of the blocks, not the colors.

After children have played with all kinds of concrete materials like this, they may be ready to find shapes in the classroom environment. Play shape-finding treasure hunts with them. At an even higher and more abstract level, they can try to find the shapes they know in pictures. Finally, some should be ready to reproduce certain shapes in their

Observe to see how children play with plastic shape blocks. For example, what is this child doing?

art, on geoboards, or in block building. As you can see, this learning takes place not just by a teacher telling the child, "This is a square," "This is a circle," but more effectively by children's hands-on playing or exploring with all their senses about what makes a particular object a circle or what makes another shape a square.

Children in this preoperational stage of development (see Table 9–1) learn best from three-dimensional objects first, before recognizing more abstract symbols such as pictures. Seeing pictures of the various shapes is helpful, but it is too abstract as the only method from which young children can learn. Youngsters first need hands-on activities with concrete materials.

Your program should provide the children with many such experiences. Because the children learn these classification skills through the senses, you should give the youngsters all kinds of sensory play opportunities. Playing with dough, for instance, allows children to make dough balls, which the youngsters flatten into circles with their hands or roll flat with a rolling pin and cut into circular cookies. Sensory learning involves taste, touch, smell, and sight in this instance.

Block building is an excellent medium for creating circles, squares, rectangles, and triangles. In the beginning, you may need to name the shapes the children are making. They probably already know "circle" and perhaps "square," but "rectangle" and "triangle" are interesting new grown-up words. Can the children build a triangle, one of the most difficult shapes for youngsters? Their triangles may be rather rounded in the beginning, because corners are hard for the children to deal with. The diagonal line is the last to appear in children's cognitive learning. This is why triangles and diamonds are very difficult for children to make. Put masking tape on the floor in the shapes of circles, squares, rectangles, and triangles and let children try to build these shapes with their blocks.

If You Have Not Checked This Item: Some Helpful Ideas

■ Start with One Shape at a Time

Children need to focus their attention on one concept before expanding it to include other aspects. The circle is good to begin with because children are used to the roundness or ovalness of the human face. They need to experience examples of all kinds of circles. Let the youngsters find out how many circles they can discover in the classroom. Did they find the wheels on toy vehicles, the casters on the doll bed or office chair, the clock, or the mark on the table made by a wet glass?

■ Give Children Enough Time to Explore

How long should they concentrate on this shape before including a second shape in their explorations? It depends on your children and their interest. Be sure every child has a chance to have enough sensory involvement with circles so that he or she can internalize it. The internalization may take several weeks, depending on the age and experience of your children. If one child needs more time to work with circles before she truly understands the concept, be sure that you provide this time for her.

Time is an important aspect of young children's learning. Most early childhood programs in the United States are not geared to this crucial element. In Europe it is different. For example, the acclaimed preschools of Reggio Amelia in northern Italy give individual children as much time as they need to complete their activities, sometimes days, weeks, or months. In addition, children have the opportunity to use the same materials over and over again until they have gained some control over them and have internalized the concepts involved. We remember this stage of learning as mastery, one of the 3 Ms. As a result, the children get deeply involved in their work/play and produce "astounding" (in the eyes of visitors) arts and crafts products.

As Seefeldt (1995) tells us:

> Time is used differently in Reggio preschools than in preschools in the United States. Experiences and themes last months, as opposed to the one- or two-week units typical in the United States. And children are never expected to move on to something new until they have exhausted their own ideas fully. Often, in Reggio, children were observed painting at easels for an entire morning or working with clay for hours. (p. 42)

Whether U.S. teachers will change their point of view about time is questionable because time is treated differently in this country. Many Europeans tend to be more relaxed about time than their U.S. counterparts. Perhaps what U.S. preschools need to stress instead is that children's experiences need to be repeated over and over for them to learn from the process.

■ Have Children Make Their Own Circles

Use circle-making activities that involve molding clay, shaping dough, finger painting, cutting out circles, cutting out jack-o'-lantern tops, stamping circular shapes on paper, and tracing around circular objects. When the children finally have a strong sense of what a circle is, introduce the square as the next shape, and afterward one shape after another using the same type of activities.

■ Read a Book

In *Mouse Shapes* (Walsh, 2007) Violet Mouse and her friends hide from the cat in a pile of different colored shapes. Soon they begin building things with the shapes. A square with a triangle on top makes a perfect mouse house. After reading this book, put out a collection of cutout shapes of different colors and see what your listeners can make with them.

In *Look! Look! Look!* (Wallace, 2006), three mouse family children discover a normal-size postcard of a beautiful Medieval woman. They look at it by cutting out mouse-size squares of colored paper for viewing frames and looking through them. They see shapes, patterns, and colors. They decide to cut out their own shapes and put them together for their own mouse postcard. Have your children use viewing frames to look at pictures you have on the walls of your classroom. What will they see?

Some foods are flat circles. *The Runaway Tortilla* (Kimmel, 2000) is one. Like the story of the gingerbread boy, nobody in Texas can catch the pesky tortilla that runs away from everyone, except the wily coyote. Afterward, play a "catch the tortilla" game in a follow-the-leader tramp around the classroom. Have one child be the runaway tortilla and the others gather up any circles they may find as they go. Be sure to serve tortillas for lunch after this romp. Children can make their own tacos.

Color

Another way the brain classifies things is by color. Research shows that infants as young as 4- to 6-months old begin discriminating colors. Most children recognize red, green, yellow, and blue along with black and white first before they recognize secondary colors such as violet, pink, and brown (Richardson, Goodman, Hartman, & LePique, 1980, p. 123). Children develop color perception shortly after shape recognition, although they seem to talk about colors first. Adults make more reference to color than shape, and children quickly pick up this fact.

Your children may, in fact, be able to name many colors just as they name numbers, without truly knowing what the name means. Naming colors is a function of language development in which children must link a visual image with a recalled name. Just because a child says "red" does not mean that she can identify the color. Ask the child the color of her shirt. Ask the youngster to find something red in the classroom.

Color, like shape, is an aspect of visual perception that the child's brain uses to help her classify objects and discriminate their differences. Although the child sees colors from the beginning, she now needs to put names to the different ones.

Again, concentrating on a single color at first and then adding other colors is best. Although basic colors are usually easier for children to recognize, you must take advantage of seasonal and holiday colors as well. Orange should certainly be a part of your classroom during the fall pumpkin, Halloween, and Thanksgiving seasons, and pink as well as red for Valentine's Day.

Allow children to play with colors as they do with blocks. Give them things like poker chips or golf tees and let the children see if they can find all the reds. Some children will be able to sort all of the items by color, but don't expect everyone to be so accurate at first. Let the children experiment with the look and texture of "redness" in all of its shades as they mix it with white paint. Give the children plenty of time to experience one color before you focus on another.

As your group begins its investigation of other colors, you can add paint colors one by one to the easel. Have colored lotto cards, colored plastic blocks, and many other table games featuring colors. Be sure to bring in many different items of the color you are exploring. If you have bilingual children, be sure everyone learns color names in both languages.

Differently abled children can learn color concepts along with all of the other youngsters. Set up your activities to allow children with physical and mental impairments to participate. If you keep concept games in the manipulative area, be sure the shelves are low enough for everyone to reach.

If You Have Not Checked This Item: Some Helpful Ideas

■   Let Children Mix Colors

Let children have the fun of mixing colors. Put out squeeze bottles of food coloring, spoons for stirring, and plastic cups or muffin tins full of water. You may want to use only one or two colors at first, or you may want to let children discover how mixing blue and yellow together makes green because this is such a dramatic change. At another time, use cups of predissolved colors, medicine droppers, and muffin tin cups full of clear water.

Children can play with mixing colors in many ways. The youngsters can finger paint with the color you are focusing on. When the children add a new color to their repertoire, add the same one to the finger painting table. Have them mix the old and new colors together to see what happens.

■   Cut or Tear Colored Paper

Colored construction paper can be used in many ways. When children have learned two or three colors, let them cut up or tear pieces of construction paper in these colors for a sorting activity or for making collages. Do not confuse children by combining shape and color activities when they are first learning color or shape concepts.

■   Play Concept Games

Children love to play any game that focuses on them. A game that asks them to identify the color of their clothing makes an excellent transition between activities: "The boy with the blue and white sneakers may go to lunch; the girl with the red and white shirt may go next; all the children with brown pants may go."

■   Read a Book

Butterfly, Butterfly (Horacek, 2007) shows little Lucy playing with a beautiful butterfly out in her garden. The next day it is gone, but she finds a pink worm, a brown spider, a red ladybug, an orange snail, purple caterpillars, a blue dragonfly, and a yellow bee. On the last page the beautiful butterfly suddenly pops up. Take a small group at a time outside to see what colorful insects they can spot.

Maisy's Rainbow Dream (Cousins, 2003) is a simple oversize book about the little mouse Maisy, who dreams in large full-page colors about a red ladybug, an orange fish, a yellow bee, a green leaf, a blue clock, a violet butterfly, and indigo spots. The vivid illustrations should inspire some of your own painters to try their hand at the easels. Put out some of the colors mentioned.

Planting a Rainbow (Ehlert, 1988) illustrates in brilliant colors how a garden full of red, orange, yellow, blue, and purple flowers and green ferns is planted in the spring and grows into a rainbow garden.

CLASSIFIES OBJECTS BY SIZE

As the young child constructs his own knowledge by interacting with the objects and people in his environment, his brain seems to pay special attention to the relationships between things. Size is one of those relationships. Is it big? Is it small? Is it bigger or smaller than something else? The property of size, like the properties of shape and color, is an essential understanding the child needs to make sense of his world.

Early in life the infant develops size constancy, the ability to see the size of an object as constant no matter if it is close or far away. By the time they are in preschool, children need to be able to compare objects that look the same but are of different sizes. These various orders of size are often thought of in terms of opposites: big-little, large-small, tall-short, long-short, wide-narrow, thick-thin, and deep-shallow. Once again, language plays a part because the child has to link a visual image with a recalled descriptive word. Direct comparison of objects based on one of the opposites just listed seems to be the best way for young children to learn size.

Comparing

Comparing one object with another is one of the best ways to investigate the properties of something new or different. This is, in fact, how the brain works. It focuses on, takes in, and evaluates data about the new object on the basis of what the brain has previously processed about a similar object. Charlesworth and Lind (2007) say: "As children develop skills in observation, they will naturally begin to compare and contrast and identify similarities and differences. The comparing process which sharpens their observation skills, is the first step toward classifying" (p. 73).

Information-processing researchers mention three functions that the brain must complete to process new perceptions:

- *Attending*
- *Identifying*
- *Locating*

Attending involves determining what in a situation is worthy of detailed processing. Identifying involves establishing what a perceptual pattern is by relating the pattern to entries already in memory. Locating involves determining how far away an object is, and in what direction (Siegler, 1986, p. 135).

When you are first using comparisons with your children that focus on the concept of size, be sure to use objects that are alike in all their properties except size. This is not the time to use different color or shape items. Instead, try using two similar items, one large and one small. Then talk to the children about how the objects are alike and how they are different.

Using Opposites

Making a direct comparison of two objects that are similar in every aspect except size is one of the best methods for helping children learn the concept of size. Use things such as two apples (a big and little one), two cups, two blocks, two books, or two dolls. Be sure to talk in positive terms ("This one is big. This one is little."), rather than in negative terms ("This one is not big."), which may only confuse the child.

Also be sure the children are comparing the two objects themselves, and not their position in space. Some children look at two similar objects and say that the closer one is bigger because it looks bigger than a more distant object. This tends to happen when children's size constancy is poorly developed or when you are asking them to compare pictures of objects rather than the real three-dimensional objects themselves. Charlesworth and Lind (2007) list the following basic comparisons p. 157.

Use the size opposites big and little in all sorts of comparisons in your classroom before you move on to another aspect of size, such as tall and short. Be sure that you use the words for size opposites whenever you can in the classroom: "Look, Kenya has built a tall building and Rhonda has made a short one." "Can someone bring me a large block from the shelf? Can you find a little one, too?" "Who can find a thick pencil? Who can find a thin one?" A pretend shoe store in the dramatic play area is a fine opportunity to feature size concepts. (See Figure 9–1).

Collections

Once children are familiar with various size, shape, and color categories through their own explorations and the games you have played with them in identifying and naming objects, let them try to apply their skill to collections with more than one attribute besides size. Children enjoy playing with collections of natural objects just to discover what they feel like, see what they look like, and explore how they can play with them. A collection of shells, acorns, or rocks can be kept in plastic containers on the shelves of the manipulative/math area for children to bring to a table in the area and play with.

Figure 9–1   Basic Comparisons

large	small	thick	thin
big	little	wide	narrow
long	short	near	far
tall	short	later	sooner
fat	skinny	older	younger
heavy	light	higher	lower
fast	slow	loud	soft

They need to find out how the items are alike. Once the items are sorted, can they find the biggest one? The littlest? Keys and buttons also make fine collections for sorting.

In case you wonder if such play is actually important, here is what Moomaw and Hieronymus (1995) have to say:

> Collections encourage children to become more flexible in their thinking. There is no pre-determined, correct way to sort the objects. The goal is for children to find a variety of ways to group the materials. Collections can help children take another person's perspective. As they discuss or argue about how to group the items in a collection, they may find that different people view the same objects in different ways. (p. 56)

If You Have Not Checked This Item: Some Helpful Ideas

■ Play Size Transition Games

When you are waiting with the children for lunch to be served, for the bus to come, or for something special to happen, it is a good idea to have a repertoire of brief transition games, finger plays, or stories to tell. This time provides an excellent opportunity for concept games, such as: "The girl wearing the shirt with wide stripes may stand up." "The boy wearing the T-shirt with narrow stripes may stand up." Or play a guessing game with your fingers. Hold your hands behind your back and ask the children to guess which hand has a big finger held up and which has a little finger held up. Then show them. Can one of your children then be the leader of this game?

■ Sort Blocks During Cleanup

Have children help sort out the largest unit blocks during cleanup before putting them back on the shelves. This activity will give you an indication of who can and cannot sort objects based on size. Make the activity a game, though, and not a task.

■ Use a Computer Program

In *Millie and Bailey Preschool* (Edmark) several of the games feature math concepts: "Matching" asks players to match shoe sizes; "Build a Mouse House" has players build a house from shapes; in "Cookie Factory" counting, shapes, and patterns are featured.

■ Read a Book

How Big Were the Dinosaurs? (Most, 1994) shows a large picture of a different dinosaur on every page, along with comparisons or measurements the children can relate to. Triceratops, for instance, has a head bigger than a front door. It takes two horizontal pages to show how Supersaurus is longer than a supermarket aisle.

Just Enough Carrots (Murphy, 1997) takes place in Star Supermarket, where Mother Rabbit and her two children compare amounts of food they are buying with what the other talking animals have in their carts. Horse has more carrots, Bird has the same, but Elephant has fewer. Children learn the meaning of comparison words through the book illustrations and the Rabbits' conversation.

 ## PLACES OBJECTS IN A SEQUENCE OR SERIES

In observing children to determine their cognitive development, we have been concentrating thus far on the classification aspects of what is known as "logico-mathematical knowledge." Children display three aspects of this knowledge:

- *Classification abilities:* The ability to understand particular characteristics or attributes of objects and the ability to group things into classes with common properties
- *Seriation abilities:* The ability to understand "more than" or "less than," and the ability to arrange things systematically in a sequence or a series based on a particular rule or order
- *Number abilities:* The ability to understand the meaning and use of numbers, and the ability to apply them in counting and ordering (Saunders & Bingham-Newman, 1984, p. 120)

This next checklist item involves seriation abilities in children. To arrange objects in a sequence, the child first has to recognize their properties and relationships. How are they alike? How different? What is the common thread that connects them? Then the child must understand order: that one comes first (perhaps the biggest), one comes next, and next, and finally last. His practice in sorting items by likenesses should help him note both properties and relationships among objects as well.

Just as the young child often changes the rule he is using as he sorts a number of things, he also displays inconsistency in arranging objects in a sequence. It is as if his immature mind cannot hold for long the rule on which the sequencing is based. Simple seriation asks us to observe children to see if they can arrange objects in a series from the largest to the smallest or vice versa. Children's previous activities with opposites should prepare them for identifying extreme differences among objects. Because young children can think of only two things at one time, they can usually identify the first and last objects in seriation, but may mix up those in between.

However, young children can usually arrange items in a series if they are provided with cues. Montessori size-cylinders, for instance, can be arranged in a board containing a series of graduated holes. Children try to fit the cylinders from large to small in the increasingly smaller holes. They match the size of each cylinder with the size of each hole by trial and error to see which cylinders do fit or do not fit. Once they have learned the concept, many children can line up the cylinders in the proper order without cues from the board.

Stacking blocks, boxes, and rings work on the same principle of arranging items in a series, usually from the largest to the smallest. Even toddlers soon learn that the smallest ring will not go down all the way on the stacking column. Instead, they have to put the largest ring on first. Then, if one ring is left over, they will need to start over again to find their mistake. Russian matreshka dolls, a classic folk art, are a series of hollow wooden dolls, each smaller than the next, that fit inside one another. The point is that children play these learning games on their own, and thus come to discover the concept of sequencing through their own play.

Most preschoolers understand the concept of bigger and smaller, but when this concept is applied to a series, the complexity of the many comparisons seems to confuse some youngsters. How can an object that is bigger than one item also be smaller than the item that precedes it?

You may find that you have not checked this particular checklist item for any but the most mature children. This finding is to be expected with 3- and 4-year-olds. Five-year-olds, on the other hand, usually are more successful. You may decide to add a number of new series games and activities to your manipulative or science/math areas to promote this skill. Be sure the new materials provide enough cues for your children to succeed. Most of all, be sure these activities are fun to do.

If You Have Not Checked This Item: Some Helpful Ideas

■ Arrange Children

Have groups of three children at a time arrange themselves from shortest to tallest on three boxes of graduated sizes. Let them tell who is tallest. Then let them shift around on the boxes. Now who is tallest? Give everyone a chance to be tallest. To arrange children without the graduated boxes may make the truly shortest child feel bad because children have gotten the idea from us that tallest is best.

■ Read a Book

The traditional classic stories of *Goldilocks and the Three Bears, The Three Little Pigs,* and *The Three Billy Goats Gruff* all feature a graduated series of characters from the littlest to the biggest along with their graduated series of furniture, cereal bowls, houses, and even noises. Children love these stories and will want to join in on the repetitious dialog or sounds as you read or tell the stories. The youngsters may also want to act out the stories as well.

You can cut out the characters from scanned pictures from of each of these books. Then you can mount the cutouts with sandpaper or Velcro tabs and use them with your flannel board activities. Can your children arrange the characters in proper order from littlest to biggest? Children need this hands-on activity to develop the abstract concept of seriation.

Hit the Ball Duck (Alborough, 2006) is a wonderful book full of comical sequences all shown on pages divided in two lengthwise. Listeners need to sit close to see the ball being thrown by goat, being hit by duck, going up, up, up, and landing in a tree; the bat being thrown, going up, up, up, and landing in the tree; the glove being thrown, etc., etc.; the animals climbing one on top of the other, and all falling down; the bat coming down, down, and being caught by duck; the ball coming down, hitting sheep on the head, and being caught by frog. So duck, you're out! As you read the next time through, stop after each action and ask the listeners what comes next. Or you can point to each picture and ask what words describe it.

 RECOGNIZES, CREATES PATTERNS

The concept of patterning involves recognizing or creating a series of objects, words, sounds, or colors that occur in a certain order and are repeated. Why involve preschool children in learning about patterns? Copley (2000) tells us that research has shown "focusing on the concept of patterns effectively facilitates children's ability to make generalizations about number combinations, counting strategies, and problem solving" (p. 89). Learning about patterns also helps preschoolers to predict what will happen next, especially in a story. Many children's lives are governed by patterns (rituals) that must be followed to the letter or loud protests will ensue, even though the term "pattern" is seldom used.

Patterns surround children. The daily schedule occurs in a pattern. The chorus of a song or the words of a jump rope rhyme are patterns. Children enjoy being involved in hand-clapping patterns. Some patterns follow repeated sequences of a preset rule such as designs in wallpaper or tiles. Most children intuitively recognize patterns once the concept is pointed out. Have them look around to find patterns inside and outside the classroom. Rainbows are patterns of color. Dances are patterns of steps. Gardens may be planted in patterns of flowers. Floor tiles may be arranged in patterns. Children's pants and shirts often contain fascinating patterns.

Once children understand what makes something a pattern, they will be happy to search for patterns in their everyday life if you make it a game. They can be "pattern detectives" seeking patterns everywhere. Put a sticker on the shirt of each one who discovers a pattern. Use different stickers so that a row of them on a shirt also forms a pattern. Perhaps they will note that letters can be arranged in patterns; so can numbers.

You can soon tell who understands this concept by the number of stickers they wear. If some children have not received a sticker, play a game with them, perhaps in the book center, so they can find a book with a pattern in it; or in the dramatic play center where the plastic dishes and tablecloth may contain patterns.

Now it is time for them to create some patterns of their own. Bring out sets of manipulative objects such as tubs of little jungle animals or sea creatures, and sets of giant beads, colored blocks, or tiles. First have them sort them into piles according to one attribute (e.g., color, size, or species). Then have children line up or arrange several of them in patterns. One child can start. Try not to use more than three different attributes at first (e.g., red, blue, and yellow; or tigers, elephants, and monkeys). Ask those who are watching: "What is the rule for this pattern?" "Yes, it is first red, then blue, and then yellow." Or "Yes, it is first tigers, then elephants, and then monkeys." What comes next? Do children understand that each pattern starts all over like the first one?

Find out which children can keep the pattern going. Inconsistency is also a problem here with many young children. They start out with the pattern in mind, but soon forget which color comes next and don't understand they can look back at the first pattern to find out. The more they practice, the more accurate they will become. Activities like this give them practice in keeping track of what comes next. Shaw and Blake (1998) noted that "the thought process behind patterning applies to all disciplines and could be called a core curriculum concept" (p. 82).

If You Have Not Checked This Item: Some Helpful Ideas

■ Have Children Become a Pattern

If you recall that young children learn best when they are involved as persons, invite those who are interested to make a pattern of themselves. Have six children tie different single-color scarves around their necks. Use only three colors (e.g., red, blue, and yellow). Can they stand in a line so the six are in a pattern? It could be: red-red, blue-blue, and yellow-yellow; or red-blue-yellow, red-blue-yellow; or something similar that is repeated in the same manner. Challenge three more children to wear the same colored scarves and keep the same pattern going.

■ Build a Block Construction In a Pattern

As children learn to build with unit blocks, they often intuitively arrange them in a pattern. Once they learn about patterns, have them build a wall, a road, or a tower using several sizes of blocks in a pattern. Can they keep it going? It is obvious how creating patterns also helps children with memory development.

■ Paint a Pattern at the Easel

Put out three different jars holding three different colors of tempera paint at an easel with a brush in each. Ask the painters to paint something in a pattern. Afterward, ask who can find their patterns. Not all the children use all three colors. One painter used all one color but painted a line of x's and o's in a pattern.

■ Find Hair Patterns

Hairstyles are patterns, too. Have the children look for different patterns among children's hair in their class. Do they have names? Then read them *Hats off to Hair!* (Kroll, 1995), with impressive pictures of children's faces and hair illustrating 36 different hair patterns! Does anyone understand that the rhyming words of the story are also in patterns?

■ Read a Book

Although books are more abstract than blocks or paints or people's hair, certain books contain fantastic patterns that even the youngest children can recognize. *Kente Colors* (Chocolate, 1996) is a glorious ode to the colors of Africa: "Kente colors bright and bold; red, yellow, blue; black and gold." Different colors of Kente cloth have different meanings. The end papers and page borders show the cloth in brilliant geometric patterns.

Maya Angelou's *Kofi and His Magic* (1996) is a first-person narration by a boy from Ghana, West Africa, with color photos telling how Kofi makes his magic with his imagination. Dozens of people in the book are clothed in Kente cloth with more patterns than anyone could envision. Have your listeners sit close to see what other patterns besides cloth are found in Ghana.

Luka's Quilt (Guback, 1994) tells the colorful story of the Hawaiian girl Luka, who loves colors, and her grandmother Tutu, who preserves the traditional ways. When her grandmother makes Luka a traditional Hawaiian quilt, Luka expects it to be as full of brilliant tropical flowers as the ones surrounding her house. But it is white on a green background. It is the pattern that is most important, not the colors. Luka and Tutu have a falling out until Lei Day when everyone gathers to make the traditional flower necklaces. Luka insists on putting every flower available into her lei instead of just the traditional one flower. Tutu finally realizes a person's own sense of beauty can be acceptable, too. Have your children find dozens of other brilliant patterns in this book: in the yard, in the kitchen, at the store, and at the market.

 ## COUNTS BY ROTE TO 20

No need to emphasize how important the learning of the concept of numbers is for the children. They will be dealing most of their lives with numbers involving size, distance, amount, time, temperature, cost, money, and measurement. In their mind's quest to create its own knowledge, the children will be going through a predetermined sequence of development, internalizing the information gained from their sensory interactions with the world around them.

Rote counting involves reciting the names of the numerals in order from memory. It seems such a simple thing to do, but it involves memory skills (remembering the names of the numbers), seriation skills (remembering the order of the numbers), and even patterning skills (understanding that numbers from 1 to 10 are repeated in a pattern as the counting proceeds to higher numbers).

Even 2-year-olds display a rudimentary knowledge of numbers when they hold up two fingers to show you their age and count aloud "one-two." For most, this counting is more of a parroting response than a true understanding of "two years." However, some 2-year-olds can count by rote to 10, and many 3- and 4-year-olds are able to count by rote to 20 (Siegler, 1986, p. 279).

Again, this rote counting does not mean the children understand the concept of numbers at first. Often, in fact, children do not get the sequence correct in their counting or may even leave out a number or two. These mix-ups and omissions are understandable because the children are performing a memory task, not a concept task. Their counting is really chanting, as in a nursery rhyme. You will find that many children do not know the meaning of each number word. In fact, their chanting of numbers seems more like one long word instead of 10 separate ones: "onetwothreefourfivesixseveneightnineten."

Nevertheless, chanting numbers like this is important in the cognitive development of the child. Cognitive development, like physical development, proceeds from the general to the specific. Children first chant a line of numbers and then begin to understand specific number names from the line. Listen to the children as they chant. Are they getting the number names right and in the right order? Chant along with them to help them hear the correct pronunciation.

This type of counting is due in part to the children's limited language experience. To understand the meaning of each number word, the child must form a mental image of it. You cannot expect this mental image formation in many 2-year-olds. By age 3, some children will have formed mental images of certain numbers because of their sensory experience with these numbers in their environment. It is therefore important for parents and other adults to use numbers frequently in the children's everyday living, and to involve children in the use of numbers with activities such as chanting, measuring, weighing, counting out items, counting out money, and playing games involving the counting of moves.

Children need to be able to place objects in a series and understand that the objects are more than or less than one another. The youngsters need to know the answers to questions such as, "Which group has the most?" And, of course, they need to know the names of the numbers. Some of these skills are just developing in the preschool classroom, but many children will not fully grasp the concepts of seriation and number much before the age of 7 or second grade.

For children who can count to 10 or 20, but have no real understanding of numbers or of what counting really means, try having them count to 7 or to 13. The children will have to slow down and think about what they are doing. They may not be able to stop at a number other than 10 or 20 at first. Play games with individuals or small groups, asking each to count to a number other than 10 that you will call out. Make such games exciting. Children who have not learned to count will soon be picking up this skill to play the game.

Children love to count. As Charlesworth and Lind (2007) say, "They need repeated and frequent practice to develop counting skills, but this practice should be of short duration" (p. 127).

Rote counting needs to evolve into *rational counting* in which children match each numeral name in order to an object in a group. This is a complex task involving a child's coordination of eyes, hands, speech, and memory. A teacher should not push children to do rational counting with more things than they can count easily and with success (p. 128).

Be sure bilingual children learn to count along with you. They can also count in their native language for the others to hear and learn. Make counting by rote fun for all, but be sure to do it often for short durations. Familiarity with numbers can only happen for preschoolers if the numbers and number games are repeated frequently.

If You Have Not Checked This Item: Some Useful Ideas

■ Chant or Play a Jump Rope Rhyme

Have children learn a jump rope rhyme that includes numbers. There may be as many "how many?" rhymes as there are children in the school. Some involve Cinderella:

Cinderella dressed in white,
Went upstairs to say goodnight.
How many seconds did it take?
One, two, three, four, five....

Cinderella dressed in yellow,
Went inside to eat marshmallows.
How many marshmallows did she eat?
One, two, three, four, five....

Use chants from the wonderful new *Mother Goose: Numbers on the Loose* (Dillon & Dillon, 2007), which includes familiar and not so familiar Mother Goose rhymes containing numbers. Beginning with rhymes containing 1, the verses take readers through all the numbers up to 30.

Some are counting-out jump rope rhymes. All are illustrated by comical talking animals in Medieval garb or light- or dark-skinned people wearing animal-head masks.

Make up some of your own chants using children's names. Have two adults turn a large jump rope outside on the playground while children clap and chant the numbers each time the rope hits the ground. One child at a time can run through the turning rope or stop and jump.

■ Sing Songs Involving Numbers

Sing "Hickory, Dickory, Dock." Have the clock strike a different number and the mouse do something different for each verse: The clock struck two, the mouse said "boo." The clock struck three, the mouse had tea, etc. Sing the "One little, two little . . ." song using different objects (fire trucks, baseballs, rubber bands, etc., but not Indians).

■ Read a Book

Construction Countdown (Olson, 2004) shows a countdown from 10 to 1 showing earth-movers, payloaders, and other construction vehicles.

Astronaut Piggy Wiggy (Fox & Fox, 2002) tells the tale of his journey into space, including a countdown before he blasts off.

DISPLAYS 1-TO-1 CORRESPONDENCE WITH NUMBERS

Next, children must master simple one-to-one correspondence for them to develop number sense. This is what we are asking them to do when they count objects. Learning that a number stands for an object is their next step in the sequence of learning number concepts. At first, many youngsters try to rush through their counting without actually including all the objects. The children seem more concerned with saying all the numbers than with making sure each number represents an object. They eventually come to learn that the key principles governing counting are

- *The number names must be matched one-to-one with the objects being counted.*
- *The order of the number names matters, but the order in which the objects being counted are touched does not matter.* (Resnick, 1989, p. 163)

This is part of rational counting. It will assist children in their awareness of quantity. They come to understand that the last number they name tells how many there are. Preschool children learn these principles not by being taught, but by being involved playfully in hands-on counting. As with learning shapes and colors, concrete objects should be used first, pictures later, and finally numerals.

Children become familiar with the names and the task by repeating them many times in many forms. Through repetition and trial and error, they finally get it right. Most adults are not aware of the importance of learning to count. Cognitive scientists, on the other hand, have a different view. In the words of Unglaub (1997):

> Why is the ability to count rationally so important? If unable to count rationally, the child is not ready to start more formal activities that lead to mathematical concepts. (p. 48)

Thus, it is important that children count or hear you counting every day in the classroom and that you provide youngsters with many opportunities for doing so on their own. Start with fewer items than 20 in the beginning, just as you did with number chanting. Then the children will need to stop before they get to 20. Also have the children touch each item as they count. If they skip one, have them try again. Or have them hand you an item as they count it. But be sure it is fun or interesting for them, and not a task involving right or wrong.

Learning to sort also is good preparation for counting things. Putting a cup with a saucer or a hat on a doll helps them understand one-to-one correspondence. Now they must apply their learning to numbers. They learn by their sensory actions that the number "one" represents the first object, that "two" represents the second, and so on. This learning is a first step. But counting in a progression still is not the same as understanding one-to-one correspondence.

Children may be able to count a row of 10 or even 20 children, and still may not be able to choose four of them. Give them practice. Once they are able to count up to 10 objects in a progression, the youngsters can practice picking out a particular number of items, such as three dolls, five blocks, or seven dominoes. Phrase your questions or directions to give the children practice with both activities. "How many red markers are there?" asks them to count in a progression. "Bring me four napkins," takes them one step further in their development of number concepts.

Put out small collections of items in margarine tubs on the tables of your manipulative area and have children count them. They can do it on their own and record their number on the tape recorder if you have it set up for them. Have "Count Me" signs hanging around the room on objects like your fish aquarium, your painting easel paints, and the hats in your dramatic play area. What other things would the children like to count on their own? Ask them. If they want you to check on their accuracy, you will have to count these things, too—a good modeling behavior.

Using Marks, Picture Symbols, and Number Symbols to Record

To support children's number activities, you or your children can record their counting. You should not use number symbols at first, but simple marks to represent the numbers. For example, keep an attendance chart with all the children's names and mark a symbol for each child present. Then the children can count the marks. Have children keep track with marks on a pad or punches on a card with a paper punch of how many times they feed the guinea pig or water the plants, or of how many cars pass by the building. Then have them count the number of marks or punch holes to get the total.

Use shape symbols, stick figures, or picture symbols for numbers, too. Put signs in each activity area with a particular number of stick figures or peel-off picture symbols to represent the number of children allowed in the area at once. Have a certain number of hooks on the wall with tags on them for use in each area. Have children take the tags while in the areas. Check from time to time with the children in the area, having them count how many participants are in there and whether this is the proper number.

Use charts and bar graphs at appropriate times to record numbers. Hang a calendar chart near the guinea pig's cage and record the number of carrots he eats every day by drawing carrot symbols. Record how tall each child's seeds grow every week by posting a chart with the child's name and having him or her measure the height with a ruler. Help children record the height after their names. Or use a bar graph that can be colored to the height the plant has grown.

Later in the year when the children have shown that they understand one-to-one correspondence, you may want to use the actual numerals along with the picture symbols. Numerals alone are often too abstract for many of the children at the beginning of the year.

If You Have Not Checked This Item: Some Helpful Ideas

■ Have Children Count One Another

Any activity is more meaningful to a young child if it involves her and her peers directly. Have children help you take attendance in the morning by going around and counting how many children are present. Have the counting child touch each child. Give the counters help if they need it with numbers above 10.

■ Have Many Counting Materials

Fill your manipulative or math area with counting materials or games. Use egg cartons for children to fill the sections with items and count how many there are. Use buttons, shells, dominoes, spools, paper clips, and macaroni as items to fill the sections.

■ Do a Follow-the-Leader Counting Walk

Walk around the room with three or four children doing a follow-the-leader, touch-and-count walk. Do it aloud the first time and then silently once children know how. For example, after touching three items silently yourself, stop and ask, "How many did we touch?" Congratulate the ones who get it right, and continue your walk. When all the children have caught on, let one of them be the leader.

■ Have Children Set the Table

Let the children set the table for meals and snacks. They may need eight spoons and eight forks for each table, along with eight plates, cups, and napkins. Can they do it? This real task is an especially powerful activity for teaching one-to-one correspondence.

■ Read a Book

Counting books are as popular as ABC books these days. Here are a few:

We All Went on Safari: A Counting Journey Through Tanzania (Krebs, 2003) shows an extended family of African people walking through various animal habitats. Each day a different child tells the number of the particular species they see from 1 to 10. Can your listeners hear or see any patterns? The rhyme on each page starts with "We all went on safari. . . ." Can they tell how many children went along? Take your children on a counting safari around your classroom to look for toy animals.

In *Max Counts His Chickens* (Wells, 2007), the Easter Bunny has hidden 10 hot-pink marshmallow chicks all over Grandma's house. Little bunny Max and his older sister Ruby pop out of bed on Easter morning, baskets in hand, to look for them. Ruby finds one under her pillow, another in her dollhouse. That makes two she says. Max finds none. She finds another on the tub faucets while Max dumps out the bath-bead bottle; another in the soap dish, while Max squeezes out the toothpaste tube. Numbers and hot-pink chicks appear at the top of each page. Finally Ruby finds all of them and Max, none.

Grandma quickly calls the Easter Bunny, and soon yellow marshmallow chicks come popping through the door mail slot. How many of them? Your children will have to count. Max says: "one, three, ten, two, six, four, seven, eight, nine, five!" Does he understand one-to-one correspondence? How can you tell?

In *Click, Clack, Splish, Splash* (Cronin, 2006), the animals on Farmer Brown's farm, led by Duck, sneak into his house one by one and take all the goldfish out of his aquarium. Then they dump them into the farm pond in a countdown from 10 to 1, while Farmer Brown wakes up from his nap to find an empty aquarium.

PROBLEM-SOLVES WITH CONCRETE OBJECTS

Problem solving involves young children in using higher levels of thinking. They must use creative thinking in which they create new ideas or use materials in new ways. They also use critical thinking to mentally break down a problem into its parts (Segatti, Brown-DuPaul, & Keyes, 2003, p. 12); in other words, to do reasoning. Jensen (1998) believes that "the single best way to grow a better brain is through challenging problem solving" (p. 35).

Types of Reasoning

Several types of reasoning are often employed by young children in their problem-solving efforts. *Intuitive reasoning* is based on appearances of things. They may think one object is bigger than another because it looks that way: for example, the tall thin glass holds more water than the short wide glass. With more information available through measuring, they may find that both glasses hold the same amount. When youngsters do intuitive reasoning like this, you need to ask them "why" they think something is so and "how else" they can tell.

Inductive reasoning is based on perceptions of regularity. Children use it when they are looking for a pattern or for something several things may have in common. Their conclusions may be accurate when applied to specific examples, but may not fit all situations. *Deductive reasoning,* on the other hand, is based on conclusions drawn from information gathered over a period of time (Shaw & Blake, 1998, pp. 117–119).

As children do reasoning, they will be using many of the concepts they have developed previously, especially classification and numbers. The best way for preschool children to apply their newly acquired cognitive concepts is through problem solving with concrete materials. They will be manipulating materials in a trial-and-error exploration of what works and what doesn't work.

Teachers can start with a small group of children at a time in a particular classroom learning center, posing a simple problem. For example, in the block center she might ask: How can you build a road wide enough for two little toy cars to travel side by side? Some children may solve the problem by building a road with two parallel lanes. Others may make one wide lane. If it works for both little cars, then it is a good solution.

Another time, she may put down a wide piece of blue construction paper to represent a river and ask the builders what they can build so their cars can get across the river without getting wet. This more complex problem calls for bridging the river by placing a block on either side for a support and then finding blocks or a board long enough to span the river between the two supports. You may want to talk with them about how they will go about finding a solution. Listen to what they have to say and jot it down. They will need to break down the problem into parts: finding a block or blocks long enough to span the river and finding a way to raise the blocks above the river.

No fair laying the blocks lengthwise in the river, some builders will say. Ask them what would happen in a real river if they did this. Do they know how the water in a real river flows? Finding a block or board long enough to reach the supports is one solution. Often children have trouble finding the right length block and continue trying out blocks that are too short to reach the supports. The concept of length is still a bit fuzzy for many. Can they find another way besides guessing to choose the correct length of a block needed to bridge the space between the two supports? Trial and error is one way. Someone else may suggest measuring it. Yes. Then they will need to apply this measurement to the blocks on the shelf until they find the right length.

If some of the children are unfamiliar with using measuring devices such as a ruler, here is another problem for them to solve. What can they use to measure the space? Does anyone hold her hands apart to show the size of the space between the block supports? Will she be able to keep her hands spread the right distance apart by the time she gets over to the block shelves? Someone else may suggest stretching a strip of paper or length of string from one support to the other. Yes, that would work.

What if none of the blocks on the shelf is long enough? Someone may suggest moving the supports into the river and closer together until they find a block long enough to reach them. Yes, that is another possibility. Let them try it and see. Another child's idea may be to put a third support in the middle of the river to hold a bridging block on either side of it to reach the supports on the river bank. That, too, will work. Then there is the creative child who solves the problem of crossing the river by having a toy helicopter air-lift the cars … or the child who floats the cars over on a boat. Let each small group experiment to discover its own solution.

Another interesting block problem involves running toy cars down a block ramp and seeing how far each one can travel. Can anyone make the cars travel farther without giving them a shove? Through trial and error someone will discover that raising the ramp at one end increases the speed of the cars, which in turn makes them travel a longer distance. Someone else may discover that the size of the cars also matters. Do bigger, heavier cars go farther than little, lighter cars? Have them try it and see. You can jot down all their solutions to these problems on newsprint, even the ones that don't work, to be talked about afterward. How many budding engineers have you discovered?

Keep your eyes peeled for problems with concrete materials that children may run into on their own both inside and outside the classroom in their normal day of work and play. What about the girl who tries to force her doll buggy through the concrete tunnel on the playground that is obviously (to you) too small? Or the boys who are having trouble moving a truck tire from one side of the playground to the other by dragging it? It is not up to you to suggest a better solution, but to observe and record how the children themselves solve these problems, and then talk about how they did it afterward.

Shaw and Blake (1998) pointed out: "While young children may not think logically in an adult sense, they can still develop a trial-and-error thought process that lays the foundation for later problem solving and logical thinking" (p. 112). It is important to talk to the children about how they solved their problems. The questions you will want to find answers to can be outlined as a "scientific method for problem-solving" (see Figure 9–2).

Intuitive problem solving can be talked about either before or after it happens. Then the teacher and children can record the results together by writing, photographing, drawing, or tape recording. One teacher had the children draw their conjectures about how to find out which foods were good for them. Figure 9–3 shows one child's idea: Her hand holds a magnifying glass over each of the foods!

Figure 9–2   Scientific Problem Solving

1.   What was the problem?

2.   How did you decide to solve it? (make a conjecture)

3.   What did you do?

4.   What happened?

5.   What is your conclusion about it?

6.   How can we record this?

Figure 9—3   *"I'm discovering good foods!"*

If You Have Not Checked This Item: Some Helpful Ideas

■   Play Simple Guessing Games in Small Groups

Have your group guess (make a conjecture) about how many unit blocks it will take to line up across the table they are sitting around. Write down the number each child mentions. Then have that child count out the blocks and line them up across the table. Don't make a fuss if they are wrong, only if they are correct.

Have another small group guess how many toy cars it would take to fill the shoebox you place on the table. Have each child who guesses try it and see. Make up several similar guessing games and play them with the children several times a week. Do they improve with experience?

■   Play Simple Problem-Solving Games in Small Groups

Put out a number of hair curlers of different sizes and a purse or plastic container of a certain size. Can anyone find a way to carry all the curlers in this one purse? (Make sure the only way all of the curlers will fit inside this purse is if the children put the little curlers inside the big ones.) Does anyone solve this problem?

Put out cardboard or plastic tubes of different sizes. Put out several tiny cars and trucks of different sizes and a shoebox. Tell the children the only way the cars can get into their garage (the shoebox) is by driving through one of these tunnels (tubes). Have the children take turns guessing which ones will work, and then trying them.

■ Read a Book

In *Magic Thinks Big* (Cooper, 2004), a very large cat sits in front of an open door in his home on a lake in Maine. He contemplates his next move: Should he go in or go out or stay where he is? In his mind, he uses intuitive reasoning to make conjectures about what will happen in each case. The pages illustrate his thoughts: If he goes out, he could catch a salmon and share it with the bears on their island—if a moose would swim him across. Have your children guess (make a conjecture) about what will happen next in each case.

If You Give a Pig a Pancake (Numeroff, 1998) is another favorite book in the author's series about what will happen "If You Give . . ." an animal something. In this case, if you give a pig a pancake she'll want syrup to go with it. If you give her syrup, she'll probably get all sticky and. . . . Have your children guess what will happen next as the little girl character makes conjectures about what hilarious requests the pig will make one after the other. Children will need to use their classification skills (e.g., What goes with pancakes? Syrup. What goes with "sticky"?) to guess what comes next. Here is more practice in intuitive reasoning.

In the book *If I Had a Dragon* (Ellery & Ellery, 2006), Morton tells the story about his little brother who is no fun to play with, but if he'd only turn into a dragon, then maybe they could: Go for walks? Play basketball? Go for a swim? Play hide and seek? Go to a movie? Whistle? None of these conjectures work, especially the dragon's whistling that nearly fries Morton to a crisp! Ask your listeners what they think will happen after each of Morton's conjectures, before you turn the page to see what really happens.

If Mom Had Three Arms (Orloff, 2006) is a little boy's imagination turned loose in a "what-if" counting story. The boy imagines in rhyme what his mother would do with 3 through 20 arms on every other page in this book. Afterward have your listeners make up a new story about what their own mother might do with extra arms.

PROBLEM-SOLVES WITH COMPUTER PROGRAMS

Computers in preschool programs are sometimes seen as controversial. But for teachers who know how to use them, how to select appropriate software, how to help children learn to use them on their own, and how to integrate the software into the curriculum, computers can be powerful learning tools for young children.

Some educators believe that children cannot control computers before they reach Piaget's concrete operational stage (see Table 9–1). The computer screen shows only an abstract two-dimensional image. Others argue that "many children in this stage may show characteristics of the later concrete stage. The strength of the computer is its ability to bridge concrete and abstract thinking and learning" (Fischer & Gillespie, 2003, p. 88). Children seem to learn in the same way computers teach: by trial and error.

The key to successful computer use with preschool children is in the software you select. In this instance, you will be looking for CD-ROM programs that feature activities to help children strengthen cognitive skills such as sorting, classifying, sequencing, and

Figure 9–4 Criteria for Children's Computer Programs

- Tried out by teacher ahead of time
- Attractive to young children
- Based on children's book being used
- Easily used and understood by children
- Teaching appropriate skills
- Tied to learning center activities

patterning, as well as programs that feature counting, numbers, and one-to-one correspondence. The activities in most of these programs use these skills for problem solving.

Because computer programs are more abstract than the concrete materials in the classroom, it is important for you to try them out ahead of time to determine how they can lead to concrete activities in the learning centers. Choosing programs based on one of your picture books is one way of tying them into your classroom activities. As you look for appropriate programs, keep the following criteria in mind (Beaty, 2008, 152). See Figure 9–4.

Preschool children can learn to use a computer with ease and love to do it. Some have used computers at home or watched parents or older siblings use them. Others can't wait to try out this adult-type instrument to see how it works. You can introduce a new program to two children at a time who are seated at the computer. Others can watch and take their turns later. Cooperative learning like this is the best way for them to make use of the computer. They learn to take turns, to talk together, and to teach each other how the program works.

You will already have installed the program they are to use on the hard drive. Children will then be able to access the program themselves. Use only one program at a time until all the children are thoroughly familiar with it. Most software contains multiple games and activities at increasing levels of difficulty, so you will need to know which game is the one your children should start with. What your children need know about operating a computer is shown in Figure 9–5.

Repetition is the key element here. Turn off the program and let them start it up over and over. With two children at the computer, one can remind the other of the next step.

Figure 9–5 What Children Need to Know about Operating a Computer

- How to turn on the computer
- How to wait until the main menu appears
- How to double click the mouse on the proper icon
- How to wait until the program menu appears
- How to click on the activity they want to pursue

At first everyone will want a turn, but after the novelty wears off two children at a time can choose to use the computer during the free-choice period by wearing the two computer necklaces you have provided. After the children have demonstrated their ability to access the program, you can put out extension activities involving blocks, books, and manipulative materials. Here are some computer CD-ROMs appropriate for cognitive learning:

Adventure Workshop: Preschool—1st Grade: Dr. Seuss (The Learning Company)

By choosing the math section, the Cat-in-the-Hat invites the children to proceed. Horton the elephant then leads them into a problem-solving situation to find Sweet Alma Sue's mother. To start the adventure, an outdoor scene appears as a nonverbal picture menu with four activities embedded in it: *Fox in Socks Sorting, Yertle's Counting Turtles, Fish Follies,* and *Sneezlebee's 1, 2, 3s.* Children need to run their mouse around on the scene to find these games. When the right area lights up, they should click on it and wait for the activity to appear.

In *Fox in Socks Sorting*, children are directed by voice to help fox sort out his two different color socks hanging on a clothes line into two different-color boxes. They must click on each sock of the right color and drag it down to the box of that color. Two higher levels of this game are included.

In *Yertle's Counting Turtles*, the scene is a pond with turtles in it. Yertle asks children to choose turtles with a particular number on them and to stack them on top of one another for Yertle to climb on. *Fish Follies* has an octopus asking children to choose one of six colors and color in the white fish displaying a circle, a triangle, or a square. When all the fish are colored in they sing and dance.

Some of these may seem rather sophisticated games for 3- and 4-year-olds, but as soon as they catch on, they will be completing the activities with glee. You may want to go through each game at first with the children, always asking them what to do when each direction is given orally. Then let them try it. Or simply let them figure out how the games work by trial-and-error.

Children can figure out how computer programs work by trial and error.

Be sure to acquire the Seuss books *Fox in Socks, Yertle the Turtle*, and *One Fish Two Fish Red Fish Blue Fish* for reading to the children before they play the computer games. Then make up your own sorting and coloring games. Bring in colored socks and shoe boxes. Have children draw fish with two simple curved lines, color them in, and cut them out. They can be used in a sorting, numbering game you invent. Make turtles out of colored play dough to predict and count how many turtles the children can stack up before they all fall over.

Dr. Seuss character dolls can be found in children's book sections of book stores or ordered from Demco Reading Enrichment (1-800-356-1200). The computer programs can be purchased in computer stores and office supply stores or ordered from Library Video Company (1-800-843-3620). Other computer programs appropriate for cognitive development of preschool children:

Blue's 123 Time Activities (The Learning Company):
  Counting game; weighing game;
  Shape and number game; cash register

Disney's Mickey Mouse Preschool
  Opposites; cause and effect

Disney's Winnie the Pooh Preschool
  Classification; discrimination

Millie & Bailey Preschool (Edmark)
  Matching shoes; cash register; numbers game
  Build a mouse house; Cookie Factory

OBSERVING, RECORDING, AND INTERPRETING COGNITIVE DEVELOPMENT

Sheila, the girl who was observed in Chapter 2, was found to have most items marked on this section of the checklist, as shown in Figure 9–6. When the classroom staff reviewed Sheila's entire checklist, they were not surprised to see her results in cognitive development. Sheila had already seemed to them to be a bright child with exceptional language and art skills, but she seemed to have difficulty gaining access to group play. She preferred to play by herself, although often parallel to others. In fact, one of the staff members predicted that every one of the items for Sheila under cognitive development would be checked. The prediction was almost correct. Sheila had not yet become involved with the computer, perhaps because it also involved having a computer partner.

It is important for staff members to look at the total picture when they observe and record a child's development and to confer with the others about the results. Not every child will accomplish every item in a section, although a girl like Sheila probably will once she accepts working with a partner.

Child Development Checklist

Name _____Sheila_____ Observer _____Connie_____

Program _____Head Start_____ Dates _____10-23_____

<u>Directions:</u>
Put an **X** for items you see the child perform regularly. Put **N** for items where there is no opportunity to observe. Leave all other items blank.

Item	Evidence	Dates
7. Cognitive Development _X_ Sorts objects by shape, color	Know colors; draws & names circles, squares, triangles	10/23
_X_ Classifies objects by size	Plays size matching games	10/23
_X_ Places objects in a sequence or series	Lines up dolls from littlest to biggest	10/23
_X_ Recognizes, creates patterns	Draws color patterns; rainbows	10/23
_X_ Counts by rote to 20	Counts to 20 & beyond	10/23
_X_ Displays 1-to-1 correspondence with numbers	Counts children with accuracy	10/23
_X_ Problem-solves with concrete objects	When no hats were available made paper hat	10/23
___ Problem-solves with computer programs	Does not use computer	10/23

Figure 9–6 Cognitive Development Observations for Sheila

LEARNING ACTIVITIES

1. Use the Child Development Checklist "cognitive development" section as a screening tool to observe all the children in your classroom. For which of your children did you check most of the items? How did these children do on other areas of the Checklist, for example, in small motor development?

2. Choose a child for whom there are few checks under cognitive development. Observe him or her on three different days, making a running record to help you get a more detailed picture of his or her cognitive skills. Plan an activity to help this child and record the results afterward.

3. What are the ages of the children who had the most checks on the checklist? What are the ages of the children with the least checks? What are the children's backgrounds? Can you make any inferences about cognitive development based on this information?

4. Choose a child who needs practice showing 1-to-1 correspondence with numbers and set up activities to help the child practice this skill. Record the results.

5. Read one of the children's books or use a computer program from this chapter with a child you have identified as needing help in a particular area. Plan an activity together based on the book or program. Discuss the results.

SUGGESTED READINGS

Baroody, A. J. (2000). Does mathematics instruction for three-to-five-year-olds really make sense? *Young Children, 55*(4), 61–67.

Berk, L. E. (2001). *Awakening children's minds: How parents and teachers can make a difference.* New York: Oxford University Press.

Epstein, A. S. (2003). How planning and reflection develop young children's thinking skills. *Young Children, 58*(5), 28–36.

Geist, E. (2001). Children are born mathematicians: Promoting the construction of early mathematics concepts in children under five. *Young Children, 56*(4), 12–19.

Jung, M, Kloosterman, P., & McMullen, M. B. (2007). Young children's intuition for solving problems in mathematics. *Young Children, 62*(5), 50–57.

McDonald, J. (2007). Selecting counting books. *Young Children, 62*(3), 38–42.

Moomaw, S. (2005). Math & science go outside. *Dimensions of Early Childhood, 33*(3), 27–32

Wallace, A. H., Abbott, D., & Blary, R. M. (2007). The classroom that math built: Encouraging young mathematicians to pose problems. *Young Children, 62*(5), 42–48.

CHILDREN'S BOOKS

Alborough, J. (2005). *Hit the ball, Duck.* La Jolla, CA: Kane/Miller.

Angelou, M. (1996). *Kofi and his magic.* New York: Clarkson Potter/Publishers.*

Chocolate, D. (1996). *Kente colors.* New York: Walker.*

Cooper, E. (2004). *Magic thinks big.* New York: Greenwillow.

Cronin, D. (2006). *Click, clack, splish, splash.* New York: Atheneum.

Cousins, L. (2003). *Maisy's rainbow dream.* Cambridge, MA: Candlewick Press.

Dillon, L., & Dillon, D. (2007). *Mother Goose: Numbers on the loose.* Orlando, FL: Harcourt

Ehlert, L. (1988). *Planting a rainbow.* San Diego: Harcourt Brace.

Ellery, T., & Ellery, A. (2006). *If I had a dragon.* New York: Simon & Schuster.

Fox, C., & Fox, D. (2002). *Astronaut Piggy Wiggy.* Brooklyn, NY: Handprint Books.

Guback, G. (1994). *Luka's quilt.* New York: Greenwillow.*

Horacek, P. (2007). *Butterfly, butterfly.* Cambridge, MA: Candlewick Press.

Kimmel, E. A. (2000). *The runaway tortilla.* Delray Beach, FL: Winslow Press.*

Krebs, L. (2003). *We all went on safari.* Cambridge, MA: Barefoot Books.*

Kroll, V. (1995). *Hats off to hair!* Cambridge, MA: Charlesbridge.[*]

Most, B. (1994). *How big were the dinosaurs?* San Diego: Harcourt Brace.

Murphy, S. J. (1997). *Just enough carrots.* New York: HarperCollins.

Numeroff, L. (1998). *If you give a pig a pancake.* New York: HarperCollins.

Olson, K. C. (2004). *Construction countdown.* New York: Henry Holt.

Orloff, K. (2006). *If Mom had three arms.* New York: Sterling Publishing.

Wallace, N. E. (2006). *Look! Look! Look!* Tarrytown, NY: Marshall Cavendish.

Walsh, E.S. (2007). *Mouse shapes.* Orlando, FL: Harcourt.

Wells, R. (2007). *Max counts his chickens.* New York: Viking.

[*]Multicultural.

10 Spoken Language

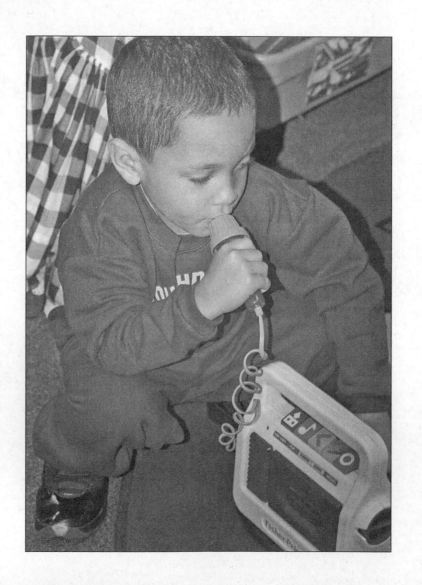

☑ SPOKEN LANGUAGE CHECKLIST

____ Listens but does not speak

____ Gives single-word answers

____ Gives short-phrase responses

____ Does chanting

____ Takes part in conversations

____ Speaks in expanded sentences

____ Asks questions

____ Tells a story

DEVELOPING SPOKEN LANGUAGE

Spoken language is one of the important skills that makes us human beings. We assume, without much thought, that our children will learn to speak the native tongue before they enter public school. Language acquisition cannot be all that difficult, we decide, otherwise how could a little child do it? After all, the child does not have to be taught; language acquisition just seems to happen. It is nothing to get excited about, we think, unless it does not happen on schedule.

As a matter of fact, the acquisition of a native language is one of the greatest developmental accomplishments and mysteries we may ever encounter involving the young child. It is a great accomplishment because the child starts from scratch with no spoken language at birth and acquires an entire native tongue by age 6; sometimes the child acquires more than one language if he is in a bilingual family.

Most linguists agree that human language is an innate behavior. As Eliot (1999) noted,

The reason language is instinctive is because it is, to a large extent, hard-wired in the brain. Just as we evolved neural circuits for eating and seeing, so has our brain, together with a

Figure 10–1   Early Language
Development

- Crying, cooing

- Sound-making

- One-word stage

- Short phrases

- Telegraphic speech

- Expanded sentences

sophisticated vocal apparatus, evolved a complex neural circuit for rapidly perceiving, analyzing, composing, and producing language. (p. 352)

We may not show concern while all goes well, but we should learn all we can about
the kinds of things that help or hinder the acquisition process to smooth the way. The
years from age 3 to 5 are especially crucial in this process. Three-year-olds may acquire
900 to 1,000 words, but by age four their language development explodes to about 4,000
to 6,000 words, as they teach themselves the rules for putting words together to speak
in complex sentences. At age five their vocabularies may expand to 5,000 to 8,000 words
(Seefeldt & Wasik, 2006, pp. 49–50). (See Figure 10–1.) During these years, children are
often in an early childhood program; thus, the language environment you provide can
have a significant effect on their progress.

Kalmar (2008) calls it a "talk-rich environment—an accepting place where teachers
encourage young children to talk, and they model the use of stress, pitch, and dialect to
help children develop and refine their language skills" (p. 89). To support your children's
language development, you should know at the outset how accomplished they already
are as speakers. A good way to start is to use an observation screening device such as the
eight Child Development Checklist items under spoken language to assess all your children at the beginning of the year. Then follow up with written or tape-recorded language
samples of each child's speech.

STAGES OF LANGUAGE ACQUISITION

Language acquisition begins at birth. A child's first language is crying and cooing, an infant's first communication sounds. Mothers, fathers, and caregivers soon learn what
such sounds mean and can respond properly. Crying in its many forms may mean "I'm
hungry," "I'm wet," "I'm sleepy," "I'm uncomfortable," or "Don't leave me." Cooing may
mean "I'm content," "I'm happy," or "So good to see you."

Adults' responses to these first communication sounds are important because infants see that their vocalizations have had an effect on those around them. They will then
make the same sound when they want that same effect. Adults should talk to youngsters

each time they respond to their sounds. "I hear you crying, Lori, and it sounds to me like you're hungry." As adults use the same words over and over, infants continue their own similar communication sounds. By the time they are toddlers, youngsters will be saying "hungie" when they want something to eat, because they have heard that word used by adults in association with feeding.

Infants and toddlers continue their sound-making because it is fun for them. Certain sounds give them great pleasure, especially when adults respond with a similar sound of their own. This playing around with sounds is the *manipulation* stage of exploratory learning discussed in Chapter 9. Children apply the same 3 Ms in learning to speak as they do in learning to play with blocks, paint, use the computer, and every new learning situation they experience. Just as they did with cognitive concepts, they are constructing their own language.

Next comes a "one-word" stage, where toddlers use only one word to express several things. Often the first word is "mama," and the youngster will use it to mean: "Where are you, Mama?" or "Mama, pick me up," or "Mama, I'm glad to see you!" or "Don't leave me, Mama!" The happy or anxious sound of the word conveys as much meaning as the word itself. Davidson (1996) tells us:

> The specific words that children learn and the meanings that they construct for these words will depend on their experiences, interests, and the language that surrounds them. Some children begin by labeling things (learning many nouns); others use words that prompt social interactions (greetings, or words that influence the behavior of others). (p. 84)

As toddlers acquire more names of objects and action words, they say these single words over and over, not necessarily because they are demanding something, but because they are in the *mastery stage* of language acquisition. Repetition is the name of the game. Next, they begin putting words together into short phrases that stand for sentences: "Mommy, hungie." ("Mommy, I'm hungry.) "Go car." ("I want to go in the car.") "All done now." ("I'm all finished eating.") They often put their own meaning into such phrases: "Jeremy TV," which the adult has to figure out. ("Jeremy turned on the TV when he wasn't supposed to!") This compressed form of speech is often called "telegraphic speech" because only important words are used, as in a telegram.

All children everywhere acquire the language they hear spoken in their homes in this manner during their early childhood years. If they hear a second language spoken consistently in the home, they will acquire this language, as well.

An explosion occurs in a child's speaking vocabulary around the end of the second year or the beginning of the third year; 30 to 50 new words a month may be added if the child hears talking around her. (Even the TV counts.) By age 3, she may know almost 500 words (McDevitt & Ormrod, 2004, p. 287).

Stages of Preschool Language Production

By the time children enter preschool around the age of 3, most have progressed beyond telegraphic speech to expanded sentences. However, you may not discover exactly

Preproduction

When children first enter a strange, new language environment they often respond by being silent. Children who are learning English as a second language often concentrate on what is being said rather than trying to say anything.

Transition to Production

When children have become more comfortable, they often begin speaking by giving single-word answers to questions.

Early Production

Children may respond to questions and activities in short phrases. They may be able to engage in simple conversations and even do chants and singing.

Expansion of Production

Children speak in expanded sentences, ask questions, tell stories, do role playing, and carry on extensive conversations.

Figure 10–2   Stages of Preschool Language Production

Note: From *Teaching and Learning in a Diverse World: Multicultural Education for Young Children* (pp. 157–158), by P. G. Ramsey, 1987, New York: Teachers College Press. Copyright 1987 by Teachers College Press. Adapted by permission.

where each youngster stands at the outset because another set of circumstances has come into play. When young children who are still at the beginning stages of language learning leave the comfortable home environment where they are used to the people around them and come into the strange, new environment of the preschool, they may stop speaking altogether at first.

Preschool teachers and assistants must understand that young speakers, no matter what their language and how fluent they are at home, may progress through several stages of language production before they become fluent speakers in the classroom. Although these stages are often applied to second-language acquisition, they can be used by teachers to help all children aged 3 to 5 adjust to the new situation and progress in their language development (see Figure 10–2).

Some children are fluent speakers from the start and have no need to progress through these stages. Others are fluent at home but silent at preschool until they become acclimated to the new situation. How long this takes depends on each child's development. Non-English-speaking children may take longer to progress through the stages as they acquire a new language.

This chapter goes on to describe the four stages of language production with the following eight checklist items. (See Figure 10–3.)

Figure 10—3 Checklist Items of Preschool Language Production

Preproduction

_____   Listens but does not speak

Transition to production

_____   Gives single-word answers

Early production

_____   Gives short-phrase responses

_____   Does chanting

_____   Takes part in conversations

Expansion of production

_____   Speaks in expanded sentences

_____   Asks questions

_____   Tells a story

 LISTENS BUT DOES NOT SPEAK

Preproduction Stage

For many English-speaking children, this first checklist item refers more to the child's emotional adjustment to the classroom than to his or her speaking abilities. As previously noted, a child must feel at ease in the strangeness of the classroom environment and among her peers to speak at all. The so-called nonverbal child is frequently one who lacks confidence to speak outside the confines of the home. The child may have a shy nature or may come from a family that uses little verbal communication; or the child may have a physical disability, such as a hearing impairment, that has interfered with language development.

Spend time assessing a nonverbal child using the entire Child Development Checklist. The areas of self-esteem, emotional development, and social play are especially important. Does the child have trouble separating from her parents when she comes to the center? Can she do things for herself with any confidence? Does she seem happy? Does she play by herself or with others?

Set up a meeting with her parents and discuss the checklist results with them. If the results point toward some type of impairment, the parents will want to have the child tested further by a specialist. If the parents indicate that the child talks fluently at home, then the nonverbal child may be demonstrating her feelings of insecurity in a strange new environment rather than a language or hearing problem.

This classroom is a talk-rich, stress-free environment where teachers encourage children to talk.

Your principal task with the shy or uncommunicative child will be to help her feel comfortable in the classroom. Using pressure to get her to talk before she is at ease may well produce the opposite results. You and your coworkers will need to take special pains to accept the child as she is and to try to make her welcome in the classroom. You can invite her to join appropriate activities, but if she refuses, you need to honor her reluctance. It often takes a great deal of patience and forbearance on the part of an early childhood classroom staff to allow the shy child to become at ease in her own good time.

If the nonverbal child seems to feel comfortable with one other child, you may be able to have that child involve her with the others. On the other hand, sometimes the only solution is to leave the nonverbal child alone. If your environment is a warm and happy one, she eventually should want to participate.

Help the non-English-speaking child feel comfortable, too. Can someone on the staff speak his language? If a number of children in the classroom speak this same language, say Spanish, be sure to provide this language during the day. Bring in a Spanish speaker if none of the staff speaks Spanish. Perhaps a family member or a high school or college student who wishes to practice the language can visit. Language tapes and songs are available and should be used to help all the children learn new words through games and fun. You as a teacher must also learn and use a few words from this second language: hello, goodbye, my name is, what is your name, how are you, do you want to.

Provide a Stress-Free Environment

The environment must be stress free. For many children, speaking among a group of peers is a new and untried experience. To help them feel at ease about speaking, you need to help them feel at ease about themselves by accepting them as they are. Show you accept them with smiles, hugs, and words of welcome and encouragement. Show you are happy to see them every day and want them to participate. Take time when they leave to say you were happy to have them in the class and look forward to seeing them tomorrow.

Ongoing brain research places great emphasis on the importance of caring adults in an emotionally supportive environment during the early childhood years. In addition, as a language facilitator, you need to accept everyone's language, no matter how poorly pronounced or how ungrammatical it is, and whether it is English, a dialect of English, or another language altogether. Language is a very personal thing. It reflects not only the different children's stages of development, but also their families' language.

You must be especially careful not to correct a child's language. Telling him he is saying a word wrong or using the wrong word is a personal put-down for himself and his family. He will learn the correct form himself when the time is right by hearing you say the word and by practicing it with his peers. Nonverbal children watch closely and listen carefully to how you deal with other speakers in the classroom.

You and your coworkers can serve as good language models for everyone, helping and supporting them in classroom activities, but taking care not to correct their speech. Modern linguists now realize that it is pointless for adults to try to correct a preschooler's speech by making him repeat words according to an adult standard that he is not ready to use. Correcting, in fact, is a negative response that tends to reinforce the unwanted behavior and make the child think there is something wrong with him personally. Instead of improving a child's language, correcting often makes the child avoid speaking at all in the presence of the corrector.

Occasionally a child who has been pronouncing words normally will slip back into baby talk or stop talking altogether. She may also display other behaviors such as thumb sucking and wetting. Because this tends to be an indication of stress or an emotional upset, you will want to talk with the parents about the pressures in her life that may be affecting her adversely, causing the temporary language regression. Is there a new baby in the family? A new father or mother? A death or a divorce? Someone in the hospital? Someone out of work? A move? Young children feel these emotional upheavals in their families as severely as adults. Sometimes the first indication of such stress for a child is her slipping back to earlier speech patterns.

But because they are in a group of other child speakers, most young children will quickly revert to the speech patterns and word pronunciations they hear around them once the stress is relieved. Their brains are programmed to do such copying at this stage of their lives. Even non-English-speaking children will soon join the mainstream of language with continued exposure to mainstream speakers. The common mispronunciations of preschoolers should be overlooked rather than corrected. As soon as the development of their vocal apparatus allows them to, they will be pronouncing English words just like everyone else.

You can keep your classroom as free as possible from stressful situations for the young child if you are sensitive to her needs. She should not be put on the spot and forced to perform verbally, creatively, or in any other way. Offer her opportunities and encouragement, but do not force the shy, unsure, or bilingual child to speak.

Listening to the Teacher Speak

Listening is also an important function for all the children in the classroom. Jalongo (2008) defined it as: "Listening is the process of taking in information through the sense of hearing and making meaning from what was heard" (p. 12). As Kalmar (2008) tells us: "From frequent interactions with their teacher, children begin to notice and understand complex sentence structure and multiple meanings of some words. By listening to teachers talk for a variety of purposes, children construct meaning and build conceptual frameworks" (p. 89).

In order to hear what is being said, children need to *attend,* that is to pay attention to the words. In order to understand what the words are saying, children need to *interpret,* that is, to assign meaning to them. It is up to you, then, to make your words clear, to make them interesting, and to repeat them—on the spot, and again later. Repetition in words and in actions is an important key to young children's learning. *Keep it brief, make it clear, and say it often*, should be your motto.

If You Have Not Checked This Item: Some Helpful Ideas

■   Use a Prop for Security

Many young children feel more secure when they have something in their hands, especially something soft and cuddly with the quality of a security blanket. You might want to keep several stuffed animals for children to choose from and hold when feeling out of sorts, or when first coming to the classroom and not yet feeling comfortable. Your "nonverbal child" may even end up talking to her animal. It may be the beginning of her verbal integration into the classroom.

■   Use a Puppet

Almost every child likes the idea of putting a puppet on his hand. Have a box or hat-tree of various kinds of puppets and let the nonverbal child choose a different one every day if he wants. Preschool children tend to play with puppets as if the puppets were a part of themselves rather than a separate toy like a doll. Because puppets have mouths, children often first experiment by trying to bite someone with the puppet—in fun, of course. Later the youngsters get the idea of having the puppet speak with their mouth, perhaps in a whisper or in a different tone from their own voice. Shy children are often more willing to have a puppet speak for them than they are to speak for themselves. You might find yourself able to talk with a shy child's puppet through a puppet you put on your own hand.

Puppets can be played with alone, but they often lead naturally to involvement with other children. Thus, puppets are an excellent transition material to help the shy child integrate himself painlessly into the activities of the classroom.

■   Read a Book

Oliver Has Something to Say (Edwards, 2007) is the story of Oliver, who doesn't talk because everybody in his family talks for him. When his mom asks him a question his big sister answers. When his friend's mother asks how old he is, his father answers. When he enters

You may be able to talk with a shy child through a puppet.

preschool and the teacher asks him what he wants to play with, nobody is there to answer for him, so he finally speaks up—and keeps on speaking up at school, at home, and everywhere.

Chatterbox Jamie (Cooney, 1993) tells the story of Jamie, who talks up a storm at home but when he first goes to nursery school, can't bring himself to say a word. Days pass before he finally gets up the courage to tell about his own baby sister when Kristen's mother brings her baby to school. Ask your listeners about their own baby sisters or brothers. Sometimes when the focus is not on them, they will talk about someone at home.

I Can Do It Too! (Baicker, 2003) shows an African-American girl at home on brightly colored pages imitating all the actions her family members make, saying "I can do it too" (Dad pouring juice; sister putting on clothes; Grandma baking a cake; uncle playing a guitar). Ask your listeners what they can do.

GIVES SINGLE-WORD ANSWERS

Transition to Production

As you observe nonverbal children in the class, you may decide when the time is right to go around the class at circle time to find out who will respond to a simple question that can be answered with one word. (Have you ever seen a live cow? Tell me "yes" or "no.") If the nonverbal child does respond, then you can try asking other one-word questions to a small group that includes the nonverbal child.

Playing question-and-answer games with several children may help the nonverbal or bilingual child feel confident enough to try her own skill at answering. "What is Alex wearing on his feet today?" or "What kind of juice are we having for snack?" These games should be fun and not a test of right or wrong answers. Accept any answers the children give without a fuss. Follow up by repeating what the child said, for instance: "Sneakers. Yes, Alex is wearing sneakers on his feet today."

Play follow-the-leader language games with a few children at a time, including the nonverbal child, having them march around the room behind you and name out loud any item you touch. The nonverbal or bilingual child will hear what the others say and may eventually join in. If children like this game, do it every day, touching more than one item at a time. Children love challenges, so think of other variants of this game you can play with them. How about a "Guess-What-I-Touched" game? Have the children cover their eyes while you go over to a shelf and touch something.

Have a Spanish speaker (or other language speaker) play the same simple games with the children, a small group at a time. Everyone can learn to name the items in Spanish as well as English. Once the nonverbal children join in the answering, you know they will soon be on their way to speaking more fully.

If You Have Not Checked This Item: Some Helpful Ideas

■ Help the Child Succeed at Something

All children need to experience success at this stage of their development. If they are having trouble speaking, help them be successful at something else. Perhaps they can finger paint or model with clay or play dough. Such art activities are also therapeutic for children under stress.

■ Make Name Cards for Items Children Name

Children who can give only single-word answers may be able to name items in the room from your follow-the-leader games. Have anyone who is interested go around the room with you one at a time while you write down each object they can name. Tape this name card to the object.

■ Have a Feelie Bag

Put several familiar objects from the classroom in a bag and ask each child from one of the small groups to put his hand inside, feel the object without taking it out, and try to guess what it is. Encourage everyone to try to name an object. Afterward, have children collect three or four objects themselves from the classroom shelves and make their own feelie bags to use with other children. Make sure nonverbal children and second-language speakers are in the group and have the opportunity to try their skill in guessing and saying the names of the objects.

■   Read a Book

Can You Say Peace? (Katz, 2006). Here is a wonderful introduction to other languages. First ask children what "peace" means. Can they say the word? Read to a small group at a time so each listener can see the large picture of a child from another country saying "peace" in his or her language. (Pronunciation is given.) Go through it again. Have children shout out the word in each language. Talk about the country. Put up a picture of a different country every day, and use its word for peace throughout the day.

Do Donkeys Dance? (Walsh, 2000) asks a series of wacky questions one page at a time and then answers them with the correct answer. See if your children can answer first before you turn the page. Does the nonverbal child join in the answering?

Does a Kangaroo Have a Mother, Too? (Carle, 2000) asks a number of similar animal questions, all of which can be answered "yes," but a whole sentence answer is given along with one of Carle's brilliant animal pictures. Again, have your listeners answer the question before you turn the page.

 # GIVES SHORT-PHRASE RESPONSES

Early Production

As young children become more used to the classroom, they will begin to respond to your questions and comments in short phrases. When second-language speakers pick up enough English from the other children around them they, too, will respond in short phrases and incomplete sentences. When your English speakers learn enough of the second language you have introduced into the classroom, they should be able to repeat short phrases in that language, as well.

Some of the children mentioned earlier may already be fluent in English, but hesitant in speaking in the classroom because they are away from the comfort of their homes. When their comfort level in preschool is high enough, they will join in talking with the others, first with short phrases, then sentences.

Second-language speakers will pick up English quickly if this is the language spoken around them. They learn it not by being drilled with new words, but by hearing the language spoken around them and trying it out as they join the other children in games and activities. They, too, may be hesitant at first in using these new words. You must accept any responses they give to your questions and comments, whether in English, their home language, or in gestures.

They may not pronounce the English words the same as the other children do at first, but they should see by your actions that you accept whatever they say. You can repeat their response to see if you understood them, if this seems appropriate. This gives them yet another chance to hear English responses without being corrected by the

- *Expansion:* Repeat what child has said but add words to it

- *Extension:* Respond to child's statement but add more information

- *Repetition:* Repeat what child says or your response

- *Parallel talk:* As you observe child's actions describe them aloud

- *Self-talk:* As you perform an action, describe it in words

- *Vertical structuring:* After child speaks ask questions to encourage child to continue talking

- *Fill-In:* Make a pause as you speak, so child must fill in the word(s)

Figure 10—4 Strategies to Foster Language Production

Note: From A. M. Kratcoski & K. B. Katz, "Conversing with young language learners in the classroom," *Young Children* 53 (May 1998): 30—33. Excerpted and adapted with permission from the National Association for the Education of Young Children.

teacher. Be sure language is spoken throughout the classroom throughout the day, not in children's shouting or noisy roughhousing, but in busy voices engaged in stimulating activities. You, as a language facilitator, can help children develop their early production of language by using some of the strategies shown in Figure 10—4.

These strategies are natural responses to children's speech that you may already be using. Obviously, you will be listening closely to what a beginning speaker is saying. You may add to it or repeat what was said, validating what the child has told you and encouraging her to continue. If you don't understand the child's speech in the first place, it is better for you to keep listening and try to pick up a word here and there than to keep asking the child: "What did you say?" Repeat the word you heard as an encouragement for the child to continue speaking.

As you serve as a linguistic model for the children, be sure you use simple sentences and speak slowly and clearly enough for children to understand what you are saying. You may also need to vary your tone of voice to emphasize key words. As you get used to the various children's speech and they get used to yours, their early productions should expand naturally. But whatever you do, have fun doing it. Children need to know that your conversations with them are for pleasure, not perfection.

If You Have Not Checked This Item: Some Helpful Ideas

■ Help the Child to Feel Accepted

Children want to talk like the others around them. Their mispronunciation of words may make them feel out of place, whether they are second-language speakers, dialect speakers, or nonfluent English speakers with articulation problems. You need to show by your actions and words that you accept the child as she is, that you are happy to have her in the class, and that you will support and encourage all her endeavors. Preschool-age children have the ability to pick up mainstream English pronunciation quickly when they are surrounded by English speakers. Your acceptance of the way they speak their home language and the way they pronounce English words is an important first step toward their success in language production.

■ Read a Book

Bear Snores On (Wilson, 2002) tells the story of the great brown bear who is hibernating in a cave in the woods when a mouse, a rabbit, a badger, a gopher, and a mole come in to get warm by making a fire, popping corn, and chattering in rhyme. "But the bear snores on," is the phrase repeated each time a new animal joins the group. Have each of your listeners say this phrase in turn as the story continues.

In *Is Your Mama a Llama?* (Guarino, 1989), a little llama goes around asking each of his animal friends (young bat, swan, calf, seal, kangaroo, and llama) if their mama is a llama. All but the last one answer with the phrase "No, she is not," and then give descriptions of their mamas. For the second reading, have your small group of listeners choose to be one of these animals and respond to the question you ask when it is their turn.

Mice Squeak, We Speak (dePaola, 1997) is a simple colorful story with a two-word sentence at the bottom of each page telling how the animal pictured communicates (e.g., lions roar, owls hoot). The three multiethnic child characters (Anglo, Asian, and African American) come forward one at a time as the story progresses to tell what they do: "But I speak." "But I say." "But I talk." Children in your small listening group can reenact this story pretending to be the children as you reread the story.

 ## DOES CHANTING

Early Production

Just as they play with blocks, toys, and each other, children also play with words. Youngsters make up nonsense words, repeat word sounds, mix up words, say things backwards, make up chants, and repeat rhyming words. Most people pay little attention to this activity, as it seems so inconsequential. What we have not seemed to realize is that through this playful activity, children are once more at work creating their own knowledge. This time the content is language rather than cognitive concepts, and this time the child is manipulating the medium (words) with his voice. Once again, he is structuring his experiences by finding out what words do and what he can do with them. Play is once more the vehicle because of the pleasure it gives him.

All children play with words, especially in the early stages of language development, but of course there are great individual differences in the amount of language play you will witness among your children. We do know that children who are involved in rhyming activities at an early age carry over this interest in poetry into adult life, and that children who have had early experience with nursery rhymes are more successful later in reading than children who have not. It behooves us, then, to observe children's language play and provide encouragement and support for all youngsters to become more involved with chanting and finger play rhymes.

Opitz (2002) declared that:

> The only conclusion that can be drawn from research literature is something that experienced teachers have known for quite some time: children appear to hear rhyming words and words that begin the same first. Then they show the ability to hear, blend, and isolate individual sounds in words. (p. 11)

Although mothers often promote language play with their infants by playing word and action games with them such as pattycake and peekaboo, much language play is solitary. Children carry on monologues in which they manipulate sounds, patterns, and meanings of words. These three areas have, in fact, been identified by specialists as common types of word play (Schwartz, 1981, pp. 16–26).

Infants from 6 to 18 months often "talk" to themselves before going to sleep, repeating rhythmic and rhyming sounds. The infants sound almost as if they are really talking, only with nonsense words. With older children, **sound play** contains more meaningful words, consonants, and blends. The children often repeat these words in nonsensical fashion: "Ham, bam, lamb, sam, wham, wham, wham."

Pattern play is a common form of play that involves manipulating the structure of the language. The child begins with a pattern and then substitutes a new word each time he says it: "Bobby go out; Mommy go out; Daddy go out; doggie go out" or "Bite it; write it; light it; sight it; night it; fight it."

Meaning play is not as common among younger children, but it is really more interesting. Here the child interchanges real with nonsensical meanings or makes up words or meanings. An interesting example Schwartz (1981) found was children doing water play with floating and sinking objects and telling the objects to "sink-up," meaning "float" or "sink-down" (pp. 19–20).

Piaget (1976) described much of the talk of 3- to 5-year-olds as egocentric. It is as if much of their speaking is not directed to anyone in particular, but rather produced for their own pleasure. Some children go around muttering to themselves most of the day, especially when they are involved in an interesting activity. The muttering seems to disappear by the time they enter kindergarten, but it may become inner speech instead. Vygotsky (1962), on the other hand, believed that egocentric speech was an "ingrowth stage" linking external social speech and internal thought. As egocentric speech turns inward, it becomes a child's most important tool for structuring thought.

Are any of the children in your class engaged in word play? They will be if you sponsor or promote it. Do finger plays and body action chants with the children during circle time or for transitions between activities.

Chanting

A chant, according to Buchoff (1994), is "any group of words that is recited with a lively beat. Through chanting all children speak together in unison. They learn the importance of clear and expressive pronunciation as their voices combine to make the message of the chant come alive" (p. 26). Everyone can be successful in chanting, even children who speak nonstandard English or no English at all. They can listen and join in with the rest, and soon will be saying the words themselves.

Many chants, especially jump rope rhymes, are just like children's early sound, pattern, and meaning play. Perhaps that's why children enjoy them. Children enjoy the sounds and rhythms of chanting as much as they do singing. As Buchoff (1994) noted,

> Chanting promotes successful language experiences for all children regardless of background or talent. It is useful for children who speak nonstandard English, as well as children who are learning English as a second language. (p. 26)

Like singing, you can chant verses from books or make up your own. Peppy, rhyming verses are best like those from jump rope rhymes and nonsense poetry. Pick out a verse from *Anna Banana, 101 Jump-Rope Rhymes* (Cole, 1989) or *Mother Goose—Numbers on the Loose* (Dillon & Dillon, 2008) and try it out with the children. Have them repeat it with you over and over, making motions if they want, or clapping their hands. Do this on a daily basis, and soon they will have memorized all the chants you share with them. Whether children understand the words makes no difference. Anyone who can speak can chant:

California oranges,	One potato, two potatoes,
Fifty cents a pack,	Three potatoes, four.
Come on, Lashandra,	Five potatoes, six potatoes,
Tap me on the back.	Seven potatoes, more (or make that "pizza").

Have the children themselves create their own chants. Soon everyone will want to join in.

If You Have Not Checked This Item: Some Helpful Ideas

■ Make Up Your Own Chants

Have the children make up new words to a singing/chanting game they already know, and then act it out. For instance, instead of "The Farmer in the Dell," they could chant "The Keeper in the Zoo," and act out the zoo animals that the keeper takes in descending size.

■ Read a Book

The Lady with the Alligator Purse (Westcott, 1988) is another traditional jump rope rhyme acted out in nonsensical verses by Miss Lucy, Tiny Tim, and The Lady with the Alligator Purse, who saves the day by ordering pizza. Children love to chant its verses.

Miss Mary Mack (Hoberman, 1998) is a classic children's chant about Miss Mary Mack, all dressed in black, who watched the elephant jump the fence, and he flew so high he didn't come back till the Fourth of July. A simple hand-clapping/chanting game goes along with it and is illustrated on the inside front cover.

The Seals on the Bus (Hort, 2000) is a silly takeoff on the traditional wheels-on-the-bus song with the seals going errp, errp, errp, the lion bus driver roaring, and the geese honking. After you have read it once, have the children choose the parts of the animal passengers and make their noises when the time comes.

There Was a Cold Lady Who Swallowed Some Snow! (Colandro, 2003) is one of many takeoff books from the old lady who swallowed the fly. In this one, each verse ends with, "I don't know why she swallowed some snow. Perhaps you know." As you read each verse, have your listeners chant the last two lines. In the end when she hiccups out all the things she swallowed, they turn into a snowman!

There Was a Coyote Who Swallowed a Flea (Ward, 2007), another similar book, has a wonderful cartoony coyote swallowing a whole pack of Western items one by one. Listeners can chant the last line of every verse: Yippee-o-ki-yee!

TAKES PART IN CONVERSATIONS

Early Production

Some children still in the early stage of classroom language production may be able to engage in simple conversations with other children or with you. As soon as they are able to converse with ease, their speaking ability will show even greater improvement from practice with their peers, some of whom may speak at a bit higher level. Children improve in speaking most rapidly when in the presence of speakers whose abilities are a bit higher than their own.

For this reason, it is important to have mixed-age groups in preschool programs. The younger children learn language skills from the older ones. The older children have an excellent opportunity to practice their skills with someone a bit younger. Older children seem to be able to adapt their language level intuitively to less-mature speakers, thus enabling younger children to improve their speech.

Just as the infant is predisposed to acquire his own language in a particular manner, he also seems to bring with him in life a preprogrammed way to extract and learn the rules of conversation naturally. Researchers have noted that infants as young as 10 weeks are beginning to learn behaviors necessary for later conversation (Holzman, 1983, p. 3). For instance, to converse, speakers must listen to what someone says, speak one at a time, and then pause for the other speaker to have a turn.

Another interesting finding is that mothers seem to treat their baby's gestures, cries, coos, smiles, and babbling as meaningful contributions to a real conversation. An infant's arm may reach out toward her rattle. The mother responds by picking up and giving the rattle to the child, at the same time conducting the following conservation: "Oh, you want your rattle. Here it is. Here's your rattle." Baby takes the rattle and shakes it. Mother replies. "Yes, your rattle. Your nice rattle." Baby pauses to hear mother say this, shakes the rattle, and smiles. Then the baby pauses to hear the mother again respond. "Oh, you like your rattle. Shake your rattle." The baby shakes the rattle, and pauses once more for the mother's response. The mother smiles and nods her head in approval. "Shake, shake, shake," and so forth. Thus the rules for conversation are learned long before the child can speak.

We may wonder: Who is reinforcing whom? The mother starts the conversation, but the baby listens and replies with her physical response, which makes the mother say the next thing, and the baby responds again. It takes two to have a conversation. Children learn this from infancy, unless there is no one to talk to or no one who will listen. Parents who do not take time to talk to their infants during this preverbal period of development make a great mistake. We need to address children in their native language from the moment they are born if we want to motivate them to become fluent speakers themselves.

The Rules of Conversation

Conversation seems like such a natural activity you may not realize it has its own unwritten "rules." As Weitzman and Greenberg (2002) tell us:

> Learning to take part in conversation is a complex process. Conversations are like a game for two or more players—a game made more complicated because of its many rules. The only way inexperienced players (infants and young children) can learn these rules is by playing the game with a more experienced player (like you). Once they learn the basic rules, their ability to participate in conversations improves, dramatically increasing their opportunities for language. (p. 108)

Some of the rules can include those in Figure 10–5.

Sounds simple, doesn't it? But participating in an adult conversation of any length may not be as simple as it sounds, you often find. Too many adults dominate conversations without giving others a chance to respond. They may not look at you when they are

Figure 10–5   Rules of Conversation

- Look at the speaker while she is talking.
- Listen to what the speaker is saying.
- Respond to the speaker at the appropriate time.
- Send a clear message.
- Stick to the topic.
- Pause and give the speaker a turn while you listen.

talking. Or they may not stick to the topic. But once you are aware of these unwritten rules, you should be able to hone your own conversational skills to help children develop theirs.

Teacher–Child Conversation

You have undoubtedly heard that one of the best things teachers of preschoolers can do is read to their children. This is true. But an even greater contribution to their language development is to converse with children, to listen and respond to them in conversational speech. Because many mothers intuitively treat preverbal youngsters as real contributors to conversations, the youngsters eventually become such. You can do the same with children in your classroom. Remember, however, the conversations you initiate with the children should be natural and not contrived.

As Machado (1995) noted,

> Daily teacher-child conversations become amazingly easy when teachers focus on "children's agenda." Teachers defeat their purpose when the objective is always to teach, or add a new word to the children's vocabulary. The key is to identify the child's interests; words then become meaningful. (p. 269)

Take time to have a personal conversation with each child in the class at least once during the day. Do not "talk down" to children, but instead treat them as equal partners in the conversation. Talk about things that are personally meaningful to the child, such as some activity he is engaged in at the moment. Keep track of who you talk to. If you miss any of the children, start with them the next day. If they do not respond to your

Take time to have a personal conversation with each child.

conversation, fill in for them as best you can. But always leave room for the child to do his part when he is ready. And remember to take turns. If children forget, remind them that speakers take turns with one another when they are conversing.

Research with preschool children at home and in school recognizes the fact that oral language is the foundation of early literacy. The skills needed to carry on informal conversations with friends and relatives become important in children's early reading and writing. Dickinson and Tabors (2002) reported, "Opportunities to hear and use a variety of new and interesting words in conversations with adults were especially important to children in our study" (pp. 10–15).

These researchers also found that *extended discourse* was an important contributor to children's language development. Teachers and parents both extended conversations with their children by adding information to what the children said and waiting for them to respond. Explanations and narratives during mealtime were another source of extended discourse. Children themselves also engaged in their own extended conversations in fantasy talk during toy play. Some ways for you to model and extend your conversation can include the ideas in Figure 10–6.

At the same time, you need to be careful not to dominate the conversation, something easy to do when the child stops speaking. Children did better on the researchers' language assessment used in the earlier study when teachers talked *less* during free play. This may reflect the fact that children need a time to put their ideas into words without adult engagement, and that *teachers may need time to listen more.*

Child–Child Conversations

The classroom environment itself largely determines the nature of children's oral language experience, noted Rojas-Cortez (2001, p. 13). Teachers set the stage for child–child conversations by the way they arrange the learning centers. How many children should each center serve? The number of chairs or activities available helps to determine the number of children who will choose that learning center during free play.

Figure 10–6 Strategies for Extending Teacher–Child Conversations

- Repeating the child's last words and adding your own comment
- Giving information about a past experience
- Giving reasons for what you have said
- Comparing two things you are talking about
- Talking about how you feel
- Wondering about how the child feels
- Giving the topic an imaginary twist (What would happen if ...)
- Asking a question (which gives the child another turn)

The block center and dramatic play center will be the largest with props and materials enough for six or eight. Their role-playing activities often encourage several groups of children to engage in talking with one another. More intimate conversations can occur in the art area if you place two easels next to each other or one basket of crayons on a table set up for four; in the computer center, with two chairs at the keyboard; in the manipulative center, with one puzzle and two chairs at a small table; in the book center, with two beanbag chairs next to one another or a couch with two pillows; in the science/discovery center, with two baskets of seashells to sort and count; or at a small water table, with two eggbeaters.

If You Have Not Checked This Item: Some Helpful Ideas

■ Converse in Small Groups

Spend time every day in conversations with small groups of children. One of the best times is at snack or lunch. Be sure an adult sits at each of the children's tables and helps carry on a conversation. Talk normally about anything that interests you or the children. You do not have to be the "teacher" who is teaching them the names of the fruits on the juice can. Instead, relax and enjoy your snack or meal with the children. Say the kinds of things you would at your own meal table at home. "Whew, isn't it hot today? I think summer is coming early." "What's that you say, Jamal, you like summertime best of all?" "Me too. I love to swim and picnic." "You like to do that too, Marisa?" "Yes, you are lucky to live next to the park." Children who do not take part in this group conversation nevertheless listen to and learn from it.

■ Encourage Dramatic Play

Children's own conversations often take place in dramatic play situations. Puppets and dolls stimulate conversations, even imaginary ones. Bring in props to encourage imaginative play in the housekeeping area, the block center, and the water or sand table. Take props outside to encourage dramatic play there, too.

■ Have Telephone Conversations

Keep toy telephones or cell phones available for pretend phone conversations between children. You should also plan to "call" a child on the toy phones every day if possible, just to get a conversation going. Read children the story *I'm Calling Molly* (Kurtz, 1990), about the African-American boy Christopher and his Anglo neighbor Molly, who frequently call each other on the phone to talk about what they are doing—until one day when Rebekah comes to visit Molly and cuts Christopher out of the loop. Afterward, have the two listeners pretend to be the two children using the toy phones as you read the story again.

Having a toy phone in the dramatic play area promotes child–child conversations.

■ Read a Book

All of Child's popular Charlie and Lola books are written in conversations between the older brother and younger sister and sometimes include Lola's friend, Lotta. Here are some:

I Will Never Not Ever Eat a Tomato (2000)

I Am Not Sleepy and I Will Not Go to Bed (2001)

I Am Too Absolutely Small for School (2006)

 ## SPEAKS IN EXPANDED SENTENCES

Expansion of Production

Young children ages 3, 4, and 5 are just at the age when their speaking develops most rapidly. From the simple phrases they spoke earlier, now they are suddenly able to expand the subjects and predicates of their sentences into longer, more complex thoughts. How did this expanded language come about? Linguists are searching for answers by starting with infants and audiotaping their utterances, videotaping their interactions with their caregivers, and comparing infants' development with deaf children, children from other cultures, and children from a variety of backgrounds.

We know that soon after an infant walks, he talks. We also know that all human infants are predisposed to acquire their native language. Their brains are wired to sort and store the information that will later be used in producing speech. Human infants give their attention to human voices, listening and then responding, at first in babbles, but as soon as possible in word sounds. Then sometime between 1½ and 2 years of age, the infants realize that everything has a name. Immediately their vocabulary starts expanding as they begin to absorb the words for everything they see and touch.

This is the crucial time for meaningful adult intervention. The parent or caregiver can name objects and actions. The children listen and try to imitate. The caregivers will listen to the children and respond; all this interaction takes place in the natural give-and-take manner of parents playing with their children.

This is also the crucial time for an enriched physical environment and the child's freedom to explore it. To learn names for things, the youngsters need to see them, feel them, hear them, and try them out. They learn words by interacting with the things that are represented by words in their environment. The more things the child interacts with, the more words the child will have the occasion to learn, as long as support, encouragement, and good language models are also at hand. Young children induce the meanings on the basis of hearing the words used in life experiences.

Not only are young children predisposed to learn language this way, but adults and older children also seem predisposed to "teach" children language this way. Observers watching mother–infant interactions soon picked up this behavior. The language behavior of the infant seemed to elicit the particular language behavior from the mother that was most appropriate to the infant's level of development. As the infant's ability improved, the mother's level of response expanded (Holzman, 1983, p. 87). Even more surprising is the fact that anyone playing with an infant seems able to adapt intuitively to the infant's language level, even other children.

Studies with 4-year-old boys who had no younger brothers or sisters showed that the boys were able to adjust their language to a 2-year-old with good language ability and another 2-year-old with poorer skills, in explaining how a toy worked. The boys listened to the toddlers' responses to their own instructions and made adjustments intuitively (Holzman, 1983, pp. 107–108). This result may very well indicate that not only are infants born with the method for acquiring their native language, but also that the speakers around them are endowed with a similar skill for helping them acquire it.

By around age 2, children are able to use the proper word order consistently in their primitive sentences. As they suddenly blossom into pretend play at this time, a parallel expansion seems to occur in their language. Their sentences grow longer and more complex, and their vocabularies increase. Once they have absorbed the basic rules for forming sentences, they are on their way, for they will no longer need to rely exclusively on imitating the language around them. Instead, they will be able to produce sentences they have never heard. For most children, this mastery has occurred by age 4. Obviously, it is important for children to be involved with competent speakers of the native language. If youngsters do not hear the language used or do not engage with someone in speaking it during these crucial years, they may have difficulty acquiring it.

You need to know which children in your class are speaking in the expanded sentences that most 3-, 4-, and 5-year-old children should be able to use. Some who are not speaking in sentences may be shy or ill-at-ease children who have the ability but not the confidence to speak in the classroom, as mentioned previously. Others may come from homes where language is not used so extensively. Still others may come from homes where English is not spoken. For these and all of your children, you will want to provide rich language opportunities that allow the youngsters to hear sentences spoken and to respond.

How will you do it? Give them fascinating things to talk about. Look around you: the classroom, the neighborhood, the community. Make a list of possible topics to explore with the children. Ask the children to add their own ideas to the list. What would they like to find out about these topics? Write down questions, too. Your list might start out something like this:

Bridges: the bridge across the river; how it was built

Dolphins: dolphins in the downtown aquarium being mammals and not fish

Guinea pigs: no guinea pigs running around outside like squirrels

Second-Language Speakers

For children learning English as a second language, it was once believed that their parents should learn English and use it with them at home, rather than their native language. That is no longer true. As Ramsey (1987) noted,

> Current research suggests that it is better for parents to continue to speak to their children in their home language. The more skilled children are in their home languages, the more able they are to learn a second language. (p. 159)

In fact, children are quite capable of learning more than one language, "whether simultaneously or sequentially," says Paneque (2006).

Today we are coming to recognize the value of home languages that are different from English and are finally beginning to promote rather than discourage their use by children and their parents. The National Association for the Education of Young Children (1996) position statement that responds to linguistic and cultural differences in early childhood education includes some of the following recommendations:

- Recognize that all children are cognitively, linguistically and emotionally connected to the language and culture of their home.
- Acknowledge that children can demonstrate their knowledge and capabilities in many ways.
- Understand that without comprehensible input, second-language learning can be difficult.
- Actively involve parents and families in the early learning program and setting.
- Recognize that children can and will acquire the use of English even when their home language is used and respected.
- Support and preserve home language usage. (pp. 4–12)

If Spanish is the first or second language for many of the children in your program, be sure to provide opportunities for all the children to be exposed to the language in a natural manner. Have a Spanish hour when nothing but Spanish is spoken. Read books and sing songs in Spanish. Do number games and dramatic play in Spanish. Children love to hear and say new words. Have their favorite chants and songs translated into Spanish, or get new ones from the book *Arroz con Leche: Popular Songs and Rhymes from Latin America* (Delacre, 1989). If you do not speak Spanish, invite a speaker from a nearby high school, college, or the children's families.

But what if your program includes numbers of children who speak many different languages? Inner-city early childhood programs are becoming more language-diverse than ever these days. How can you accommodate such diversity? Ramsey (1987) described a program attended by children of foreign students representing 15 different languages. The program rose to the occasion by requesting the parents to help them make a book with simple sentences in all 15 languages that the teachers often needed, such as "Your mother will be here soon" or "Do you need to go to the bathroom?" The parents and their children then enjoyed coaching the teachers. This activity also gave the foreign families, who were daily experiencing their lack of expertise in English, the opportunity to be the experts (p. 160).

If You Have Not Checked This Item: Some Helpful Ideas

■ Provide Dramatic Play Opportunities

Children's imaginative play is one of the best preschool activities to motivate and promote language growth in young children. Youngsters take on roles in which they must produce dialog. Even the shy, nonverbal, or bilingual child will learn by listening to the others. Be sure to schedule enough time for children to become involved in this pretending type of play. Take a role yourself to help the shy child join the others. Once he is involved, you should withdraw.

■ Assign Buddies

Burton and Edwards (2006) suggested assigning buddies who are good English speakers to bilingual children who need to hear English spoken to become involved in the many activities and experiences in the classroom.

■ Go on Field Trips

Children need many real experiences with their world to process and use information in thinking and speaking. Give the youngsters many new things to think and talk about by going on field trips. These out-of-class experiences do not have to be elaborate or to distant locations. Have one adult take three children down to the corner store to buy something. Take a small group on a walk around the block to see how many different sounds they can hear. Be sure to take a tape recorder along to play back and discuss later. Go on a field trip to a tree every week in the spring or fall to see how it changes. You may want to take along a camera to record the experience and to motivate talk about it back in the classroom. Be sure to use new vocabulary words to label the new things and ideas the children have experienced. Also label them in a second language if this is appropriate. Then use them over and over with the children.

■ Read a Book

Abuela (Dorros, 1991) tells the story of a little Hispanic girl from New York City, Rosalba, and her grandma, "Abuela," who came from Puerto Rico. Your children may be excited to learn another word for "grandma." This grandma takes care of Rosalba while her parents are at work. Because Abuela speaks mostly Spanish, the pages are interlaced with single words and simple sentences in Spanish that Rosalba explains to the readers. They take off (in their imaginations) to soar above the city, out to the airport, and even above the Statue of Liberty. Have your children soar above their classroom and report what they see in Spanish and English.

In *I Love Saturdays y domingos* (Ada, 2003), the little girl who narrates this story loves to visit her Anglo grandparents on Saturdays and her Hispanic grandparents on Sundays, eating foods from each of their cultures and enjoying similar activities together. Spanish words are interspersed with English on Sunday, but easily translated. Choose a day or time to use Spanish words in your classroom.

In *Bebe Goes Shopping* (2006, Elya), Mama rolls Bebe in a shopping cart through the supermarket. While Mama shops, Bebe helps himself to items that interest him, much to Mama's dismay. Then she spies a box of animal crackers, and Bebe is finally satisfied to eat them. Spanish words are interspersed in every sentence Mama speaks. A glossary at the end translates them. Set up a store in your dramatic play area and mark items in both English and Spanish.

In *We All Go Traveling By* (Roberts, 2003), not only do the sentences expand as the children in the school bus go traveling by, but they also accumulate as other vehicles come into view. Can your children remember which ones come next and add them to the long string of words they are producing? Included with the book is a CD with music for a song they can sing, adding their own words if they like.

 ## ASKS QUESTIONS

Expansion of Production

This language skill is another good indication that your children's command of language is developing normally. Most children are able to ask questions as adults do by about age 4. Before that, they go through a predictable sequence in learning to ask questions, just as they do in other areas of development.

Children usually do not learn to ask questions until they have learned to answer them when you ask them something. Between 1½ and 2 years of age, when they are putting a few words together to form primitive sentences, they also ask their first questions, if caregivers have been asking them questions first. The word order of these first questions is the same as a statement but with a rising intonation at the end: "Jamie drink milk?" meaning "May Jamie have a drink of milk?" or "Should Jamie drink his milk?"

Next, they begin to learn the use of the "wh" words at the beginning of questions, words like *what*, *where*, and *who*: "Where Mama going?" or "Where going?" meaning "Where is Mama going?" This type of question becomes quite popular because the adult generally responds, and suddenly the child realizes he has stumbled onto another way of controlling an adult: asking a question that the adult will answer. This is not always true with mere statements. Because he delights in adults' attention and their responses to the things that he originates, he will often burst into a period of questioning. It is not only that he wants to know the answer, but also that he wants an adult's attention.

The next stage in learning to ask questions comes as he expands his sentences to include auxiliary verbs such as *can* and *will*. These questions, though, are often expressed in inverted order; for example, "Where Daddy will go?" instead of "Where will Daddy go?"

The final stage is the expanded question in proper word order, which most children are able to ask at around 4 years: "Can I go with you?" "What are you doing?" "Why doesn't the light go on?"

If you discover through your observation that certain children have not yet attained this level, what will you do? Will you sit down with them and teach them how to ask a question correctly? If you have been reading this text carefully, you know the answer is "no." Young children do not develop language skills by being taught formally. How do they learn? They learn language just as they learn to develop their perceptual skills: They teach themselves word order by hearing the language forms spoken around them and by practicing language themselves when their physical and mental development has progressed to the point at which they can do so.

Linguistic Scaffolding

As teachers of preschool children, you realize your support of their speaking efforts is most important, especially because young children learn language mainly through imitation. *Linguistic scaffolding* is the direct support teachers give to help children build conversations. It may include the use of questioning, expansion, and repetition. (See Figure 10–4.) Otto (2002) tells us:

> The questioning used during linguistic scaffolding serves to lead the children ahead in the dialogue or discourse and maintains the verbal interaction. (p. 40)

In other words, to keep a conversation going, teachers often insert a question. Questions are often used to clarify something the child has said, to check on the child's knowledge, or to gain information. Even young children understand when the teacher is asking a question: by the rising intonation of her words at the end of a sentence, along with her facial expression encouraging the child to respond. As preschool children develop more complex language, they also imitate this kind of questioning to gain information.

If You Have Not Checked This Item: Some Helpful Ideas

■ Ask Questions Yourself

When you understand that children do not ask questions until they have learned to answer them, you will include your own asking of questions in your activities with the children. Circle time is a good time for everyone to hear the English word order of questions and to answer the inquiries if so inclined. Even the children who are not at the point of answering questions in front of a group will learn by listening.

■ Ask Children to Help You Gather Answers to Questions

You can ask a child to ask three or four other children for some information you need. For example, if you are planning a field trip, you might ask several children to go around asking others if their mothers would like to come along. This may not be the most accurate way to gather this information, but it is excellent practice in questioning skills, and you can always check the accuracy of the information with the parents later.

■ Read a Book

Little Raccoon's Big Question (Schlein, 2004) has the little raccoon asking his mother: When do you love me most of all? He asks one question after another about the times, but she answers "no." In the end he finds out: his mother loves him *all* the time. Have your small listening group ask questions about the mother's answer.

Mama, Do You Love Me? (Joose, 1991) is the highly acclaimed story of the little Inuit (Native Alaskan) girl, Dear One, who asks her mother this question over and over, upping the ante each time. Her mother replies in a kind of folk poetry that captivates young children listeners. "How long?" "Till the stars turn to fish in the sky, and the puffin howls at the moon." Vivid illustrations show a puffin howling, ptarmigan eggs breaking, lemmings in mukluks, and Dear One turning into a musk ox, walrus, and polar bear. But still the mother's love holds firm, and the two dance together at last in bright dresses against the white Arctic background.

Papa Do You Love Me? (Joose, 2005) is the follow-up book with a little Maasai boy, Tender Heart, asking his African father this question. What if the boy became hot, or thirsty, or fell asleep while watching the cattle, or was challenged by a lion? Can the boys in your group think of what their fathers or grandfathers or uncles might answer in these situations?

CAN TELL A STORY

Expansion of Production

Children whose speaking has become fluent in all the other checklist items are often competent and confident enough to tell full-blown stories about themselves or those around them to individuals, to small groups, and sometimes to the total group. Not every child will be able or willing to perform such a linguistic feat, but some are. Before children can tell such stories, though, they must first have experienced hearing many stories told and read to them. If the reading and telling of stories holds a prominent place in your program, and if your book center shelves are stocked with some of the fine books mentioned in this text, you should be able to help develop some child storytellers.

Are you a storyteller? If you want your children to participate in storytelling, they need an adult model to imitate. Don't believe you are too shy to tell stories. Anyone can do it. After all, what is a story? An anecdote, an experience, an adventure, a fable, a tale. Not every story comes from a book. Did you tell the children what happened to you on the way home from school yesterday? That's a story. Did you tell them what your pet cat did when the neighbor's dog got into the yard? That's another story. All of life that is happening around you and the children can be woven into story after story.

What happened when the children went on a field trip to the pet store, or museum, or zoo? What about the little kitten in the cow barn at the farm you all visited? How did that pesky squirrel finally reach the birdseed you put up so high in your bird feeder? All these incidents make fine oral stories. Keep your senses alert for such daily storytelling possibilities, and you will soon have a long list.

Decontextualized Talk

Curenton (2006) noted how important oral storytelling is for young children: "Storytelling prepares children for school because it allows them to use a sophisticated form of communication—*decontextualized talk*—that is not bound by the immediate context" (p. 81). This talk is about objects, feelings, and ideas experienced in the past or expected in the future. Contextualized talk is only about the present. Decontextualized talk promotes higher-level thinking such as planning and reminiscing. It sets the foundation for children's school achievement.

You might begin by telling the children some interesting anecdotes at circle time, and they should quickly respond with stories of their own. Maybe something about the new baby, or their pet iguana, or the trick their brother played on them last night, or the trip they are going to take during the summer. When other children see how interested you are about such stories, they will want to contribute, too.

You may want to write down the stories children tell about the field trip they went on or an incident from their lives. Use a big pad of newsprint so everyone can see what you write as the child dictates. Be sure to reread this story aloud over and over in the days to follow. Remember how important repetition is for children's early learning. Children can dictate stories into a cassette recorder, too, and play them back whenever they want. Storytelling in preschool used to be exclusively up to the teacher. No longer. As Soundy and Genisio (1994) pointed out:

> The responsibility for storytelling was once restricted to the teacher's domain. Renewed attention on developmentally appropriate practices, however, has shifted the responsibility to include the child. Children are now being asked to tell their own stories, including original make-believe versions and retelling of old favorites. Teachers are exploring ways to incorporate children's experiential background when guiding children to verbalize stories. (p. 20)

Retelling Stories from Picture Books

Some teachers base children's storytelling on favorite picture books they have read to the children over and over. These need to be stories that are memorable to the children. Choose books with some of the following characteristics:

- Plot incidents that happen in an easily remembered order
- One, two, or three interesting characters who speak
- Attention-getting words, phrases, or incidents that are repeated

Stories with folktale-like plots, where a number of incidents happen in a certain order, are especially good choices. As you read these books to the children, be sure to pause after each incident and ask, "What happens next?" When you come to the repeated words or phrases, have the children join in saying them aloud. At some point you can ask who would like to tell the story out loud—perhaps to a small group at first.

A good book to begin with might be *The Three Billy Goats Gruff* as retold in a new version by Mary Finch (2001). Children will remember the three characters: the little, middle-size, and big billy goats Gruff, that go trip-trap, trip-trap across the rickety bridge to eat the grass on the other side of the stream. They will want to repeat the words of the big hairy troll, who stops each of the goats, saying, "I'll have you for my dinner." Finally, they will remember how the big billy goat kicks the troll into the middle of next week. You may have to begin the storytelling yourself by telling the tale without looking at the book. Every day have a different child retell the story. Accept whatever they say, even if they leave out important parts.

Eventually some of the tellers will want to tell their story to the whole class. Not only will they be demonstrating their skill of using spoken language, but also, as Isbell (2002) tells us:

> A story told by the teacher and retold by children is a powerful literacy tool for the early childhood classroom. Storytelling provides a pleasurable literacy connection that has the power to positively impact children's attitudes toward stories throughout their lives. (p. 30)

If You Have Not Checked This Item: Some Helpful Ideas

■ Tell Group Stories

Keep your senses alert for a good story theme about something that happens in the classroom or on the playground. Afterward, gather the group together and talk about it: what happened when the storm came and the electricity went off; where they think the ambulance was going so quickly with its siren blaring; how Ross felt when he finally had the courage to swing hand over hand across the monkey bar.

Different children can tell their versions of these incidents. Be sure you accept every version. Can anyone make up an imaginary version of the incident? Bring in one of the storybook dolls you may have, such as Dear One from *Mama, Do You Love Me?* or Rosalba from *Abuela*.

How do the children think they would relate the episode? Can anyone do it? What about one of the animals from the block center telling a story? Or how about one of the plastic dinosaurs? What would he have to say?

■ Do Tape-Recorded Stories

You could start a story on the tape and ask interested children to finish it. You might start something like: "As I was coming to school today, I heard a very strange noise. It sounded a little like a train. It sounded like it was coming around the corner. I felt like running away, but I didn't. Instead, I. . . ." You can pass the tape recorder around a small group and have each child in the group add to the story. Afterward, play it for all to hear. Later, children may want to start their own stories and pass the recorder around.

■ Pretend to Be a TV Star Telling a Story

Childcraft Education Corporation (1-800-631-5652) offers an inexpensive sing-along cassette recorder and a sing-along machine, both with microphones for broadcasting stories to a group—just like a TV star.

■ Read a Book

Native Americans consider storytellers to be important members of their communities. The boy narrator of the story **Knots on a Counting Rope** (Martin & Archambault, 1987) is blind, but loves to hear his grandfather tell him the story of his birth and of how he got his proud name "Boy-Strength-of-Blue-Horses." When the boy finally rides his horse across the finish line in the exciting tribal day horse race, his grandfather is able to paint a vivid word picture for the boy about his perilous ride. Then he can tie a wonderful new knot in his storytelling counting rope.

Can your children tell any stories they have heard from their grandparents or others? You might invite a family member to come in and tell such a story to the group. If the relative speaks a language different from English, ask someone to come along who will translate. Encourage the telling of stories in languages other than English.

OBSERVING, RECORDING, AND INTERPRETING SPOKEN LANGUAGE

The language checklist results for Sheila were much like the teachers in her classroom had predicted (see Figure 10–7). Every item was checked except "Takes part in conversations." Although Sheila spoke to other children, it was rarely in the form of

Child Development Checklist

Name ___Sheila___ Observer ___Connie___

Program ___HeadStart___ Dates ___10-22___

<u>Directions:</u>
Put an **X** for items you see the child perform regularly. Put **N** for items where there is no opportunity to observe. Leave all other items blank.

Item	Evidence	Dates
8. Spoken Language		
_N_ Listens but does not speak	She is beyond this level	10/22
_N_ Gives single-word answers	She is beyond this level	10/22
_N_ Gives short-phrase responses	She is beyond this level	10/22
_X_ Does chanting	Yes; likes to repeat rhyming verses:"See ya later, alligator"	10/22
___ Takes part in conversations	Speaks to others but does not converse	10/22
_X_ Speaks in expanded sentences	"She ate my orange crayon so I can't finish my pumpkin"	10/22
_X_ Asks questions	yes	10/22
_X_ Can tell a story	Yes; she tells long anecdotes to teachers, not children	10/22

Figure 10—7 Observation Checklist on Spoken Language for Sheila

conversation, but more often a command or a complaint. Because Sheila showed evidence of "Speaks in expanded sentences," the staff members believed Sheila eventually would join in with other children in classroom activities, including conversation. In fact, Sheila's language skill could be used to help her become involved with the others. The teachers made plans for Sheila to tell several other children, one at a time, how to use one of the computer programs the class had recently acquired that she had finally learned to use on her own.

LEARNING ACTIVITIES

1. Use the Child Skills Checklist spoken language section as a screening tool to observe all the children in your classroom. Which children seem to need help in more than one of the items? How do these children fare in the various areas of cognitive development?

2. Choose a child who seems to be having difficulty with spoken language and observe him or her on three different days doing a running record of language activities. Compare the results with the checklist results. How do you interpret the evidence you have collected? Are any pieces of evidence still missing about this child's language performance?

3. Choose a child whom you have screened as needing help in several of the checklist items, and carry out one or more of the activities listed. Record the results.

4. Teach the children a chant. How did the children perform whom you noted as needing help in this area? What can you do to help if necessary?

5. Do a tape-recorder activity with a small group of children. Have them tape-record their own words and then play them back. They may want to tell about themselves, tell a story, or say a verse.

SUGGESTED READINGS

Hall, N. (1998). Young children as storytellers. In R. E. Campbell (Ed.), *Facilitating preschool literacy*. Newark, DE: International Reading Association.

Kirmani, M. H. (2007). Empowering culturally and linguistically diverse children and families. *Young Children, 62*(6), 94–98.

Novick, R. (1999–2000). Supporting early literacy development: Doing things with words in the real world. *Childhood Education, 76*(2), 70–75.

Selman, R. (2001). Talk time: Programming communicative interaction into the toddler day. *Young Children, 56*(93), 15–18.

Wasik, B. A. (2006). Building vocabulary one word a time. *Young Children, 61*(6), 70–78

Whaley, C. (2002). Meeting the diverse needs of children through storytelling. *Young Children, 57*(2), 31–34.

Woodard, C., Haskins, G., Schaefer, G., & Smolen, L. (2004). Let's talk: A different approach to oral language development. *Young Children, 59*(4), 92–95.

CHILDREN'S BOOKS

Ada, A. F. (2002). *I love Saturdays y domingos.* New York: Atheneum.*

Baicker, K. (2003). *I can do it too!* Brooklyn, NY: Handprint Books.*

Carle, E. (2000). *Does a kangaroo have a mother, too?* New York: HarperCollins.

Child, L. (2001). *I am not sleepy and I will not go to bed.* Cambridge, MA: Candlewick.

Child, L. (2003). *I am too absolutely small for school.* Cambridge, MA: Candlewick.*

Child, L. (2000). *I will never not ever eat a tomato.* Cambridge, MA: Candlewick.

Child, L. (2006). *Snow is my favorite and my best.* New York: Dial.*

Colandro, L. (2003). *There was a cold lady who swallowed some snow!* New York: Scholastic.

Cole, J. (1989). *Anna Banana, 101 jump rope rhymes*. New York: William Morrow.

Cooney, N. E. (1993). *Chatterbox Jamie*. New York: Putnam's.

Delacre, L. (1989). *Arroz con leche: Popular songs and rhymes from Latin America*. New York: Scholastic.*

dePaola, T. (1997). *Mice squeak, we speak*. New York: Putnam's.*

Dillon, L., & Dillon, D. (2007). *Mother Goose: Numbers on the loose*. Orlando, FL: Harcourt.*

Dorros, A. (1991). *Abuela*. New York: Dutton.*

Edwards, P. (2007). *Oliver has something to say!* Montreal, Quebec: Lobster Press.

Elya, S. M. (2006). *Bebe goes shopping*. Orlando, FL: Harcourt.*

Finch, M. (2001). *The three billy goats Gruff*. Cambridge, MA: Barefoot Books.

Guarino, D. (1989). *Is your mama a llama?* New York: Scholastic.

Hoberman, M. A. (1998). *Miss Mary Mack*. Boston: Little, Brown.*

Hort, L. (2000). *The seals on the bus*. New York: Henry Holt.*

Joose, B. M. (1991). *Mama, do you love me?* San Francisco: Chronicle Books.*

Joose, B. M. (2005). *Papa, do you love me?* San Francisco: Chronicle Books.*

Katz, K. (2006). *Can you say Peace?* New York: Henry Holt.

Kurtz, J. (1990). *I'm calling Molly*. Morton Grove, IL: Whitman.*

Martin, B., & Archambault, J. (1987). *Knots on a counting rope*. New York: Henry Holt.*

Roberts, S. (2003). *We all go traveling by*. Cambridge, MA: Barefoot Books.*

Schlein, M. (2004). *Little raccoon's big question*. New York: Greenwillow Books.

Walsh, M. (2000). *Do donkeys dance?* Boston: Houghton Mifflin.

Ward, J. (2007). *There was a coyote who swallowed a flea*. Flagstaff, AZ: Rising Moon.*

Westcott, N. B. (1988). *The lady with the alligator purse*. Boston: Little, Brown.

Wilson, K. (2002). *Bear snores on*. New York: McElderry Books.

*Multicultural.

11

Emergent Writing and Reading Skills

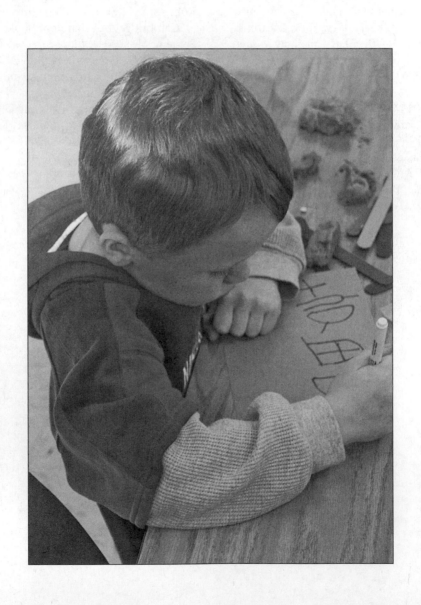

✓ EMERGENT WRITING & READING CHECKLIST

____ Pretends to write with pictures and scribbles

____ Makes horizontal lines of writing scribbles

____ Includes letterlike forms in writing

____ Makes some letters, prints name or initial

____ Holds book right-side up; turns pages right to left

____ Pretends to read using pictures to tell story

____ Retells stories from books with increasing accuracy

____ Shows awareness that print in books tells the story

DEVELOPING EARLY LITERACY SKILLS

Why should a chapter on children's writing and reading skills be included in a book on observing the development of preschool children? Surely learning to write and to read has little to do with child development, does it? Teaching children to write and read should come later when children are in kindergarten and first grade, shouldn't it? The answers to these questions are quite different today than they would have been as recently as 20 years ago.

Today research shows more clearly how writing and reading can be developed naturally by children, how children make sense of their world through playful exploration, and how children's brains take in this information and extract rules from it to help the children use it. Such research has changed our minds forever about the way children develop and how we can best support their growth (Roskos, Christie, & Richgels, 2003, pp. 52–58).

We now know that writing and reading are outgrowths of the same communication urge that drives children to express themselves orally and even pictorially. We also know that given the proper tools and support, all children everywhere go through the same sequence of stages in teaching themselves to write and to read. It is true that learning to write and to read are as much a natural part of a child's development as learning to talk. Child development specialists are finally coming to realize that "learning to write is largely an act of discovery," as one specialist puts it (Temple, Nathan, & Burris, 1993, p. 2).

The term used currently to describe children's early natural development of writing and reading skills is *emergent literacy*. Scholars studying child development have this to say about it:

> As researchers began to observe and report the literacy activities of preschool children, they found that young children engage in a wide range of emergent literacy behaviors, such as listening to stories, discussing stories, making up stories, scribbling "letters" to family and friends, writing their names, and creating invented printlike signs. Today there is a general consensus in the research community that literacy is a process that begins at birth, when babies begin to experiment with oral language. (Gambrell & Mazzoni, 1999, p. 81)

Thus, writing and reading join speaking, thinking, emotions, social, and motor skills as other aspects of development that children can arrive at by playfully experimenting with the materials in their environment. This does not mean, however, that writing and reading development occurs naturally without adult support. Children need regular and active interactions with print and oral and written language. Many youngsters come from families with few toys, let alone books for reading or the tools for writing. Furthermore, most parents are unaware that their children can develop these skills naturally. Children need their parents' support to progress in this natural development. They need the tools to write with, the print materials in their environment, and encouragement to try them out on their own. In addition, children need to practice emergent writing and emergent reading skills over time, just as they do running or speaking.

Without tools to write with at home, preschoolers can do little more than make marks on steamy windows or scratches in the dirt. Without books to look at, preschoolers have little interest in reading. Without parents' modeling their own reading and writing, children have no reason to think this is something they should do. Without parental expectations that they should experiment with writing and reading on their own, children may never try it.

On the other hand, this does not mean teachers should sit down with preschool children and formally teach them how to write and read, any more than they should formally teach them how to walk and talk. Cognitive psychologists worry that preschool teachers, who are in a critical position for nurturing the "roots of literacy" in young children, may not know how to do it. According to Schrader and Hoffman (1987),

> When teachers are unfamiliar with current knowledge about the natural development of literacy in young children, they impose skill-oriented expectations and tasks on these youngsters—copying and tracing standard adult print, for example. Such activities not only are stressful for three-, four-, and five-year-old children, but they do not afford children the opportunity to use their self-constructed knowledge in meaningful ways. (p. 13)

Instead, we should be filling the children's environment with examples of written language and books; we should serve as models by doing a great deal of writing and reading ourselves in the presence of the children; and we should provide them with the tools and encouragement to attempt writing and reading on their own.

All early childhood professionals need to become aware of this research and its implications for supporting young children's emergent literacy. The International Reading Association (IRA) and the National Association for the Education of Young Children (NAEYC) have thus adopted a joint position statement describing developmentally appropriate practices for young children learning to read and write in preschool through third grade (NAEYC, 1998, pp. 30–46). The goals for preschool include the following.

Awareness and Exploration

Children explore their environment and build the foundations for learning to read and write.

Children can:

- enjoy listening to and discussing storybooks

- understand that print carries a message

- engage in reading and writing attempts

- identify labels and signs in their environment

- participate in rhyming games

- identify some letters and make some letter-sound matches

- use known letters to represent written language

Teachers can help them with their explorations (adapted from NAEYC, 1998, p. 40).

Teachers can:

- share books with children, including Big Books, and model reading behaviors

- talk about letters by name and sounds

- establish a literacy-rich environment

- reread favorite stories

- engage children in language games

- promote literacy-related play activities

- encourage children to experiment with writing

Although the natural development of writing and reading occur simultaneously in children, this chapter discusses writing first and then reading. Do any of your children pretend to write, perhaps at the easel, by scribbling letterlike symbols? Do any of them insist on writing their own name on their art products? Assess all the children in your classroom by using the first four items of the Emergent Writing and Reading Checklist. Then set up a writing table or a writing area complete with a variety of writing tools, and watch what happens.

PRETENDS TO WRITE WITH PICTURES AND SCRIBBLES

Young children's first natural attempts to write are usually scribbles. Isn't this drawing, you may wonder? Initial scribbling is also done at the outset in art, you may point out. True, children do not at first distinguish between drawing and writing. At an easel, they may be scribbling a picture or scribbling their own idea of writing, or both together. But if easel painting is new to them, they are probably doing neither painting nor writing. Instead, they may be just trying out the brush and paint; in other words, manipulating the medium, the first stage of the "3 Ms" playful exploration process.

You can ask them what they are doing, but often they are just playing around with the painting tools without any particular product in mind. Both drawing and writing are a fascinating process for young children when they start. They are not planning to produce a picture or a written message. This tends to be an adult's objective. Preschool children may be just learning to control the brush and paint—quite a lengthy process for some children who have had no practice at home with painting or writing tools. Remember that self-directed exploratory learning takes time for preschool children. Give them plenty of time and encouragement to experiment.

At the flat surface of a writing table, the same process is at work, but the tools seem to make a difference. Children recognize that pens and pencils are used for writing. Crayons and felt markers may be used for drawing or for writing. Children often combine the two in their initial attempts. Once again, they may be manipulating the medium, but some will be experimenting with early writing that includes pictures.

Mayer (2007) tells us that at first children do not distinguish between drawing and writing because both convey meaning (p. 35). Baghban (2007) pointed out that it is important for preschool children to continue drawing their stories or drawing daily happenings in their journals because "drawing promotes the first writing, and this writing becomes the first reading that children themselves author" (p. 22). She also tells us that young children may perceive the difference between drawing and writing, but until about age seven they still draw when asked to write. She noted, "It is important that the teacher treat the drawings as writings until the children tell the teacher they are not" (p. 24).

Kevin's drawing of a picnic (Figure 11–1), for example, includes words in scribble writing at the top to tell what it is about.

Children's early attempts at writing vary greatly according to what discoveries they have made about the writing they see done around them at home, in school, on television, in stores, and in restaurants. In dramatic play, they may make a scribble on a pad while "taking an order" at the pretend restaurant. In the classroom writing center, they may cover a page with swirls, lines, and circles that start in the middle and go around the outside. The lines may include a head with arms and legs protruding or an oval with "rabbit ears" as they write a letter to a friend about their pet. On the signup sheet for a turn at the computer, they may print one wiggly letterlike symbol that represents their name, or they may make another head with arms and legs to represent themselves.

Figure 11–1   Kevin Did Scribble
Writing at the Top of the
Drawing to Tell What it is About.

Ferreiro and Teberosky (1982), in their now-classic book *Literacy Before Schooling,*
noted,

> In children's own first spontaneously produced graphic representations, drawing and writing
> are undifferentiated. Gradually some lines acquire forms like drawings, while others evolve
> towards imitations of the most salient characteristics of written language. (p. 52)

Although drawing and writing both represent things symbolically, the two are quite
different. Drawing maintains a similarity to the object it represents, whereas writing does
not. Writing is an entirely different system having its own rules, whereas drawing does
not. Young children are unaware of the difference initially and thus use both pictures
and scribbles interchangeably to convey their thoughts.

As children make new discoveries about print through their own explorations and
their involvement with picture books, they construct their own ideas about writing. At
some point, children seem to recognize that writing is different from drawing, and their
scribbles take a somewhat different form. Children as young as 3 years may recognize
the difference between writing scribbles and drawing scribbles. In fact, some children
do drawing scribbles on one part of an easel paper and writing scribbles that "tell about
the picture" on another part (Vukelich & Golden, 1984, p. 4).

The two kinds of scribbles often look completely different. Writing scribbles may be
smaller and done in a horizontal linear manner across the top or bottom of the page,
something like a line of writing. But not always. Individual differences in writing scribbles vary greatly, with some squeezed together at one side of the drawing and others just

a circle or line in a corner. The children who make such writing scribbles seem to understand that writing is something that can be read, and they sometimes pretend to read their scribbled writing, or they may ask you to read it. This is one of the first steps in the natural acquisition of writing.

If You Have Not Checked This Item: Some Helpful Ideas

■   Set Up a Writing Center

If your goal is to encourage children to explore writing on their own, then you must provide a setting for this to occur. A writing center can be just as exciting for children as a block center. Most programs put a table in their writing center with writing supplies on a nearby shelf. Some centers report that a more enticing piece of equipment is a real child-size writing desk, perhaps the roll-top variety or the type used in children's bedrooms. Drawers can be filled with the tools of writing: pads, tablets, paper, envelopes, cards, stickers, tape, rulers, rubber stamps and stamp pads, paper clips, paper punches, erasers, pencils, pens, and markers. Or keep these items in plastic containers on nearby shelves. Another desk or table can hold a typewriter or computer (or both). A stand-up chalkboard or small individual boards encourage scribbling and writing with chalk, as well. On the wall should be a bulletin board for displaying children's scribbled messages.

■   Fill Room with Environmental Print

What written symbols and signs do you notice in your home environment or on the way to the classroom? You will likely see books, magazines, newspapers, catalogs, phone books, ads on TV, posters, cereal boxes, food containers, T-shirts, letters, computer keys, computer programs, street signs, traffic signs, gas station signs, fast-food restaurant logos, store signs, billboards, all kinds of advertising, and on and on. This is what we mean by *environmental print*. All these symbols and signs can be featured in the classroom as well. Each of the learning centers can have its own signs and labels. Put out old magazines and catalogs and have children cut out pictures of favorite signs to be pasted in a sign scrapbook.

■   Read a Book

In *Bunny Cakes* (Wells, 1997), little bunny Max makes a wonderful earthworm birthday cake for his grandma and wants to put Red-Hot Marshmallow Squirters on it. So when his sister sends him to the store with a list of ingredients she needs for the angel surprise cake she is making, Max scribbles with a red crayon. Of course the grocer cannot read Max's scribbles, so he gives him only what the list says: "eggs." Again and again Ruby sends Max to the store to replace the ingredient Max has broken or spilled, and every time Max makes his red scribbles, but to no avail. In the end Max draws a picture of Red-Hot Marshmallow Squirters, and of course the grocer includes them. What kind of grocery list can your children make?

Carlo Likes Reading (Spanyol, 2001) is a simple story with a line of text such as "Carlo reads his bedroom" or "Carlo reads his breakfast" on every other page. Each page, however, is full of printed labels for every object in sight: window, curtain, clock, pillow, slippers, etc. Carlos is reading the one-word labels for the objects in each room—his own environmental print. Can your children guess what any of the labels say?

In *Patches Lost and Found* (Kroll, 2001), Jenny has lost her pet guinea pig Patches and decides to put up posters about him around her neighborhood. She draws mostly pictures of Patches with a word or two under them: "Patches lost" with her phone number to call. In fact, she draws a whole story using pictures of what might have happened to him before he is finally returned. Can your children draw a picture of their pet, or a pet they would like to have? How will they label it?

MAKES HORIZONTAL LINES OF WRITING SCRIBBLES

Once children's scribbles have become horizontal lines instead of circular or aimless meanderings, they are indicating they understand writing is something different from drawing. Still, their first scribbled lines do not resemble letters or words at all. Temple et al. (1993) noted how different learning to write actually is from what logic tells us it ought to be:

> Learning to write, it would seem, is nothing other than learning to make letters and to combine them into words. But studies of writing development have suggested that young children learn to write through a process that is quite the opposite. Rather than learning to write by mastering first the parts (letters) and then building up to the whole (written lines), it appears that children attend first to the whole and only much later to the parts. (p. 19)

Young children, in fact, seem to have extracted through their own observations only the broad general features of the writing system: that it is arranged in rows across a page and that it consists of a series of loops, tall sticks, and connected lines that are repeated. Only later will children differentiate the finer features of the system: separate words and finally, letters.

Where have they acquired even this much knowledge of written language so early in life? Look around you. They, like all of us, are surrounded by written material in newspapers and magazines, in television advertising, on the labels on food products, on softdrink bottles, in letters in the mail, in the stories read to them, on store signs, on greeting cards, on car bumper stickers, and on T-shirts. The printed word is everywhere. This is the writing referred to previously as *environmental print*.

Some families, of course, encourage their children to print their names at an early age, and may even take time to write out the creative stories that their young children tell them. Some children have older brothers or sisters who bring written material home from school. Some children come from homes with computers. These children see family members engaged in writing or reading and try to become involved themselves. Observe to discover which of your children do pretend writing—this first step in the writing process, which ones have progressed beyond this beginning, and which have not yet started.

As young children create their own knowledge about writing, they will be extracting certain information from the writing around them that Marie Clay, the New Zealand literacy specialist, calls principles and concepts:

Principles and Concepts of Writing Extracted by Young Children

1. *Recurring principle:*   Writing uses the same shapes again and again

2. *Generative principle:*   Writing consists of a limited number of letters from which you can generate a limitless amount of writing.

3. *Sign concept:*   Print stands for something besides itself, but does not look like the object it stands for.

4. *Flexibility principle:*   The same letter form may be written in different ways, but the direction the letter faces is the same.

5. *Page-arrangement principle:*   English is usually written in lines of print from left to right and top to bottom on a page.

(Adapted from Clay, 1991; Davidson, 1996; Temple et al., 1993)

Can you tell which of these principles the children who scribble in horizontal lines have extracted? Probably 1 and 2, and possibly 4. As they repeat lines of loops, sticks, crosses, or circles across the page in their imitation of writing, children are exhibiting the recurring principle of writing: that writing consists of the same moves repeated over and over. Horizontal lines of scribbles like this are not always produced from left to right or top to bottom. Children sometimes start at the bottom or the middle of the page, and they may even write one line from the left and one from the right.

This girl is exhibiting the Page-Arrangement Principle: that English is written in lines of print from left to right and top to bottom of a page.

At the same time, youngsters are also displaying the *mastery* stage of "3 Ms" exploratory play. They will fill pages with lines of scribbled "writing" like this, and it gives them great satisfaction. After playing around with this new skill during the manipulation stage, children now repeat this scribbled writing over and over to master it. At the easel or at the writing table or desk, you will see certain children hard at work filling their papers with these horizontal writing lines, just as if they were writing a letter or a story.

Be sure it is the children who are in charge of this natural emergence of literacy. You should not be the one to set goals for their writing. Instead, observe where each child stands in her own developmental sequence, put out new materials to keep her interested, and comment favorably about what she is doing. "Latoya, you have certainly worked hard this morning filling so many pages with writing. Would you like to put it up on the writing center bulletin board?"

If some children show no interest in becoming involved with emergent writing activities like this, do not pressure them to try. You can invite them to experiment with using markers or chalk or whatever materials you put out daily. If they want to draw pictures like Jenny did in *Patches Lost and Found,* you can accept that. But don't push them into representational drawing before they have explored the medium (Oken-Wright, 1998).

Voluntary and not enforced participation in writing activities should be the rule in your program. Some children need to develop better eye–hand coordination before they engage in flat surface writing. They might learn more from painting at the easel or playing with the utensils you have put out at the water or sand tables instead. If the youngsters can build a tall block tower without its toppling over, can drive a nail straight into a piece of wood, or can use a pair of scissors with ease, their eye–hand coordination is probably developed enough for them to use a writing implement. But they may use it for drawing instead of writing.

If You Have Not Checked This Item: Some Helpful Ideas

■ Put Out a Variety of Writing Materials

Most children will not try to become involved in writing if there is no sign of writing in their environment. If you do not have a special writing center, set up a writing table or desk with different implements, and you may soon have a group of budding writers.

For paper, it is best to use unlined sheets. Children will be placing their scribbles all over the page at first, and lined paper may inhibit this free-form exploration of how writing works. For them to progress to horizontal scribbles, they need blank sheets of paper. Use typing paper or stationery, as well as tablets and pads of different sizes and colors.

For writing tools, you will want to include a variety and change them every week or so. We sometimes think of pencils first, but research with beginning writers shows that pencils are the most difficult of all writing implements for young children to manipulate effectively. Children themselves often choose colored felt-tip markers as their favorites. You should also include colored chalk and a small chalkboard, crayons, and a few pencils, in addition to the markers. It is not necessary to have only the large primary-size pencils. Some preschoolers have great difficulty handling these thick pencils and prefer to use regular pencils. Put out a variety of writing tools, and children will find out on their own what works best for them.

■ Use Sand or Salt Trays or Finger Painting

Put out small trays of sand or salt in your writing area so children can practice "writing" with their fingers. It is easy to "erase" this writing simply by shaking the tray. Finger painting on tabletops or paper also gives the children practice doing "mock writing" with their fingers.

■ Be a Writing Model Yourself

Do a lot of writing in the presence of the children. If they see writing is important to you, they will want to do it, too. If you are doing checklist recording or running records in their presence, children will often want to use your pen and paper to do some pretend writing themselves, as mentioned earlier. Don't give up your writing tools; instead, be sure you have a well-equipped writing center from which they can get their own recording notebook. Or tie a pencil to a clipboard like you use, so the children can "observe and record," too. Serving as a writing model like this will almost always stimulate certain of your children to try their own hand at writing.

INCLUDES LETTERLIKE FORMS IN WRITING

Just as an infant's babbling finally begins to take the sound of real talking, so a child's first linear scribblings eventually begin to look like real writing. For many children, the lines of their scribbles become somewhat jagged and then finally take on features of real letters such as straight, curved, or intersecting lines, although no real letters are formed. Children may paint such letters on easel paper or scribble them on flat paper at writing tables. When this scribbling takes the form of horizontal lines containing letterlike forms, some linguists call it *mock writing* (Temple et. al., 1993, p. 29). This advanced scribbling happens as a natural developmental sequence when children have the freedom and opportunity to experiment with writing on their own. Teaching, in fact, has little or no effect at this point.

We recognize that children extract the elements of writing from their environment and play with these elements using writing tools and paper. Once again, youngsters are manipulating and then mastering the medium (writing) until they have learned how to handle it, what it can do, and what they are able do with it. As Schickedanz and Casbergue (2004) pointed out: "Mock letters, which display many characteristics of alphabet letters, contain the segments that are the building blocks of actual letters" (p. 18). The boy in the photo at the opening of the chapter is making mock letters.

Children practice lines of mock writing over and over just as they did their first horizontal scribbling. But as it begins to look more like conventional writing, some children believe that it must have meaning. If this is writing, they reason, someone who knows how to read should be able to read it. Often they will take a piece of mock writing to an adult and ask her to read it. How should you respond? Be honest about it. "Oh, Sharon, your writing is beginning to look almost real. Can you tell me what it says?" Some children really have a story in mind when they do their mock writing, and they will be able to tell it to you. Others think that their "words" must speak only to someone who can read.

Researchers, however, see something very important when they analyze children's mock writing: Though mock letters clearly are not alphabet letters, they do reveal progress in children's development from scribbling to writing. When mock letters are carefully analyzed they reveal the following concepts of letter form: symmetry, uniformity of size and shape, inner complexity, left-to-right directionality, linearity, and appropriate placement (Hayes, 1990, p. 62).

Observe to see which of your children are at this stage in this experimental writing. What can you do to help them progress further?

If You Have Not Checked This Item: Some Helpful Ideas

■ Encourage Children to Write Messages

Children who are at the meaning stage in their exploratory writing can write messages in mock writing to other children, to their parents, or to you. Have youngsters write notes to their parents inviting them to visit the classroom, or write a block corner sign asking other children to leave their buildings standing. If you want (or if the children ask), you can write the real words under the scribble writing. This is not necessary, though. Many children know what their scribbled messages say, and they can convey the meaning to the message recipients. Specialists who are studying young children's emergent literacy call these early writing attempts *personal script,* whereas mature writing is known as *conventional script.* By using these terms, you can avoid telling children their writing is "not real" or is "nothing but scribbles."

■ Put Up Personal Mailboxes

If there is a reason to produce writing, many children will show an interest. Have children help make personal mailboxes by painting empty cereal or shoe boxes you have collected and opening them at one end. Have them put their name (scribbled or printed) on each box, and stack the boxes on a shelf in the writing center. Don't forget to put up your own box and those of your coworkers. Then you can begin by writing brief messages to the children. Encourage them to answer your notes and to write scribbled messages to one another, to be placed in their mailboxes.

■ Take a Field Trip to the Post Office

Taking a field trip to the post office makes a great deal more sense when children are engaged in emergent writing activities such as those previously mentioned. When they return to the classroom, they can set up their own pretend post office in the dramatic play area with paper, envelopes, stamps, stampers, and stamp pads, along with the personal mailboxes the children have made. Ask the post office for the mail kit it has available for classrooms.

■ Have a Class Mailbox

Put your written communications to children or their parents in a class mailbox. You can have a child take the mail out every day and (with your help) distribute it. You should plan on writing one note to each child on a weekly basis. It should be simple and nice: "Roberto, I love your new sneakers!" or "Sandy, thanks for helping Cheryl today." When the note is delivered to the child or to her mailbox, one of the adults in the class can help him or her read it. This modeling behavior on your part should stimulate children to want to write notes to classmates or answer your notes on their own.

■ Read a Book

In *Nice Try, Tooth Fairy* (Olson, 2000), Emma writes a note to the tooth fairy asking her to return her first tooth so she can show it to her grandfather who is visiting. The tooth fairy returns tooth after hilarious tooth, all belonging to different animals, before she finally gets it right. What would your children write to the tooth fairy?

A Letter to Amy (Keats, 1968), newly reissued, tells the story of Peter, an African-American character in many of Keats' books, who writes a birthday invitation to his friend Amy and takes it outside in the rain to mail. The wind blows the letter out of his hands, and he ends up knocking down Amy in his struggle to retrieve it.

In *Giggle, Giggle, Quack* (Cronin, 2002), Farmer Brown goes on vacation and leaves his brother Bob in charge of his fractious animals with a list of instructions he has written. Duck finds his pencil and substitutes his own outrageous rules such as Tuesday night is pizza night, and Thursday night is movie night. Can the children pretend to be duck and write their own rules?

Duck for President (Cronin, 2004) is full of printed signs showing a list of chores for Farmer Brown's animals, also the farm election, voter registration, and then tallies for duck and his rivals. At the end of this comical tale, duck gives up the presidency, goes back to the farm, and writes his autobiography on a new computer after tossing out the old barn typewriter from the book *Click, Clack, Moo, Cows that Type* (Cronin, 2000). Help your children make their own signs.

MAKES SOME LETTERS, PRINTS NAME OR INITIAL

Just as the 1-year-old begins to say wordlike sounds that parents recognize as words, the preschooler begins to write wordlike forms by making letterlike scribbles. When adults see this, they often point it out: "Oh, Hilary, you made an *l* in your writing, see!" "Yes, you did it again. Do you know that you have an *l* in your name?" Many children have been taught to print the letters of their names. This is different. Scribbles evolve more as cursive writing. But as the child realizes that her scribbles are being recognized by adults as real letters, she tries to make real letters by printing them.

Although adults often intervene at this point, children still learn alphabet letters on their own by being surrounded by letters and hearing them used. This is the way it should be. The youngsters' own names are often the first source. Children may learn to say the letters in their names soon after they recognize their name sign on their cubby. Many children are then able to identify those particular letters wherever they see them. In fact, they tend to include the first and last letters of their names to a significant degree when writing, says McNair (2007, p. 84).

Alphabet Letters

Reciting or chanting the ABCs is not the same. Just as children can chant the numbers from 1 to 10, but not understand what any of the numbers mean, preschoolers often chant the alphabet without the slightest idea of what they are saying. Children's television programs can help children learn the letter names, and some youngsters may have learned letters from this technique, although watching television is a passive method.

Other children may have learned alphabet letters from a computer at home or in the classroom. A number of software programs feature alphabet games for children 2 to 6 years of age. Using the computer keyboard also helps children learn alphabet letters. In many ways, computer programs are superior to television as a learning tool because they actively and playfully involve children in their own learning. Computers should be used playfully with young children, rather than in formal lessons. Children should be free to use a classroom computer during free-choice time the same way they use blocks or dolls or the water table.

Also be sure to have alphabet games on the shelves of your manipulative area; alphabet letters mounted on the wall at children's eye level; alphabet books in the book area; and wooden, plastic, sandpaper, or magnetic alphabet letters available for the children to play with. Play alphabet games with the youngsters, but do not teach the alphabet formally. You will find that if you have filled the children's environment with letters, children will teach themselves the alphabet letters they need to know. Formal teaching, even of the alphabet, is not appropriate during the preschool years because this is not how young children learn.

In recognizing letters, children progress through a particular sequence just as they do in learning to make speech sounds naturally. The first distinctive feature children seem to recognize is whether the line that makes the letter is straight or curved. Letters that are round such as *O* and *C* are recognized first. Then letters with curved lines such as *P* and *S* are noted. Next, curved letters with intersections such as *B* and *R* are distinguished from curved letters without intersections like *S* and *J*. Letters with diagonal lines such as *K* and *X* are among the last to be recognized (Schickedanz, 1986). This pattern follows the one noted in Chapter 9: that young children have difficulty distinguishing shapes with diagonal lines.

Printing Letters

As children begin to print letters, their first attempts are usually flawed. Youngsters make the same mistakes in writing letters that they do in recognizing letters; that is, they often overlook the letter's distinguishing features. Development of children's written language, just as their other aspects of development, progresses from the general to the specific. Until they are able to perceive the finer distinctions in letters, they will have difficulty making letters that are accurate in all the details.

Let the children practice on their own. Pointing out errors is not really productive, just as it was not in their development of spoken language. In time, their errors will become less frequent as the children refine their perception of individual letters and gain control over their writing tools.

One of the children's problems in printing letters correctly has to do with the letters' orientation in space. Children are often able to get the features of the letters accurate, but not the orientation. Children reverse some letters, and some they even write upside down. Occasionally their letters are facing the right direction, but just as often their printing may be a complete mirror image of the real thing.

Part of the answer may lie in the fact that children have already learned that an object's orientation—that is, the direction it faces—makes no difference in identifying the object. For instance, a cup is a cup no matter whether the handle is pointing toward a person or away from her. A flashlight may be lying horizontally or standing on end, but it is still a flashlight. Objects, in other words, do not change their identity because they face a different direction.

But letters do. Letters made with the same features are completely different, depending on the direction they face and whether their vertical lines are at the top or bottom. If children's brains have not extracted these orientation rules for distinguishing letters, they are sure to have trouble identifying and printing such letters as *d, b, p,* and *q*. All four of these letters are made with the same curved and straight lines. Yet it may take some years for children to get their orientation straight. Children often reverse letters even into the elementary grades. As Schickedanz (1986) noted,

> In much of children's early writing, vertical and horizontal placement are mixed. . . . Sometimes letters are reversed; sometimes they are placed upside-down. These characteristics, plus a tendency to write in any direction—left to right, right to left, top to bottom, bottom to top—are all related. Until children understand that space can be organized in terms of coordinates, they do not select any consistent direction in which to place their writing. (p. 84)

One of the problems in children's playing with three-dimensional alphabet letters is the fact that they can be reversed or turned upside down. If you have such letters in your writing area, be sure to have real alphabet letters mounted on the nearby wall *at children's eye level* so that the youngsters can easily see the letter's proper orientation. Magnetic letters are better than letter blocks or plastic letters in this respect. At least the magnetic letters cannot be turned over when placed on a metal backing.

With practice and maturity, children resolve these problems themselves unless they have a learning impairment. It is not up to you to correct them. They are progressing as they should through the fascinating task of creating their own knowledge about letters and words. Your best strategy as a teacher is to fill the environment with words, letters, and occasions to write, as well as to encourage and accept the children's own attempts at writing.

If You Have Not Checked This Item: Some Helpful Ideas

■ Have Children Sign Up for Turns

Children can use their mock writing to sign up for turns to use the computer, to play with blocks, to paint at the easel, or to ride a wheeled vehicle. Put small clipboards or sign-up sheets at the entrances to your activity areas, next to the computer or easels, or wherever children need to take turns in the classroom. Tie a pencil to the clipboards and tell the children to put their names under each other's. Have them cross off their names after they have finished their turns, so that the next person can have a turn. Some children can already print their name or initials. If other children say they cannot write their names, tell them to try. Tell them to use their personal script just as they do at the writing table. They will remember which personal scribble is theirs when it is time for their turn. It is important that children understand that you consider their scribbles as real writing; they will continue in their developmental sequence on their own.

■ Make Alphabet Letters Personal

Children always learn in a more meaningful way if the subject is somehow connected to them. Help children recognize the first letter in their own first name by playing games with it. You can have letter cards on yarn necklaces that the youngsters can wear. Let the children find their own letters. Then let the youngsters see if they can find any other child with a letter like theirs. Be sure to have enough similar letters, and make them big enough so everyone can see them easily.

■ Have Alphabet Cards

Let children play with alphabet cards having a picture of an object on them. That will allow youngsters to see the letter in the proper orientation. The object on the card will also give them a clue to the name of the letter. Some educators feel that it is best to have cards showing both upper- and lowercase letters. Then children will see that each letter can be written in two different ways. They feel it is not helpful for children to use only capital letters because they will need to write in lowercase in the elementary grades. Others believe that using upper- and lowercase letters together will only confuse preschool youngsters at first. Try it and see how it works for your children.

■ Have a Typewriter

Bring in a manual typewriter for the children to experiment with. Children love to play with letters and words that they can type. Let the youngsters teach themselves how to use it. They will need to investigate the keyboard to find each letter they want, and then learn to press one key at a time to print their letters. If they enjoy typing, read them the humorous book *Click, Clack, Moo: Cows That Type* (Cronin, 2000). Farmer Brown's cows have found an old typewriter in the barn and are now writing him messages: "The barn is very cold at night. We'd like some electric blankets." What do your children think the farmer will do?

■ Use Computer Alphabet Games

Computer alphabet programs are good introductory programs for young children. However, most of today's programs are operated with a mouse, which does not give the child an opportunity to use the keyboard to bring up an alphabet graphic on the screen like some of the older programs. Of the many alphabet programs on the market, here are some popular CD-ROMs that can be ordered online from Amazon.com.

Alphabet Express Preschool (School Zone)   Curious George Pre-K ABC's

Arthur's Preschool   Disney Learning Preschool

Blue's ABC Activities   Dr. Seuss's ABC

Chicka Chicka Boom Boom   Reader Rabbit: Great Alphabet Race

Children's books about Arthur, Curious George, and Dr. Seuss's characters should also be available. Character dolls for Arthur, Curious George, and the Cat in the Hat, along with their books, are available from Demco Reading Enrichment (1-800-356-1200) for reenacting the stories.

Computer alphabet programs are good introductory programs for young children.

■ Read an Appropriate Alphabet Book

There are many good alphabet books on the market, but you need to review any you plan to use with your children to see if they are age appropriate. Some alphabet books are for very young children. Looking at the simplicity of the words and pictures may help you determine the age level. If there are pictures of children in the book, are the children in the book the age of yours?

Some alphabet books are too sophisticated for young children. These books often display the talent of the artist rather than help children recognize letters. Other alphabet books are confusing to young children because of the unfamiliar objects used as illustrations. On the other hand, a few of the new books may make your children laugh as they search for the object being illustrated by the letter. You may want to consider the following criteria when choosing alphabet books: see Figure 11–2.

A favorite of every preschooler who hears it, is *Chicka Chicka Boom Boom* (Martin & Archambault, 1989). The letters themselves tell the tale as they scramble up a coconut tree, and then all come tumbling down in various states of disrepair when it gets too crowded at the top. Children really learn their letter names as they repeat them in the rollicking rhyme: A told B, and B told C, "I'll meet you at the top of the coconut tree." The CD *Chicka Chicka Boom Boom* is available from Constructive Playthings (1-800-448-4115), as is a 20-inch free-standing coconut tree and felt letters. Or you can make your own tree and letters for children to use as they follow the story in the book or CD.

Alphabet Under Construction (Fleming, 2002) shows a mouse airbrushing, carving, or gluing every large letter of the alphabet on page after page. What fun! A free poster inside the book shows the entire alphabet just as the mouse has constructed it. Have your children join in by choosing their own letter from the white letters you supply (Constructive Playthings has 9-inch card stock letters) and decorating them with all kinds of tiny collage materials.

In *B Is for Bulldozer: A Construction ABC* (Sobel, 2003), the letters appear in color as the first letter of a word—such as Asphalt, Bulldozer, and other construction items. Children need to work their way through the book to find out what all this equipment is building. Can they recognize the first letter of their own construction toys in the block center?

In *Click, Clack, Quackity-Quack* (Cronin, 2005), Farmer Brown's wily duck leads the other animals one letter at a time to a picnic in the meadow under a tree. If the children already enjoy Cronin's other books of the farm animals who write and read, they'll love

Figure 11–2 Alphabet Book
Criteria

- One large letter to a page
- Colorful objects that children recognize
- A fast-paced story or theme that rhymes
- A lead-in to hands-on activities

this one. Can they take their block animals on a ride around the classroom to a pretend picnic?

In *Max's ABC* (Wells, 2006), another Max and Ruby book, the ants in Max's ant farm escape and climb up Max's pants to get a bite of his birthday cake, letter by letter. Nothing Ruby does gets rid of the pesky bugs until she uses the vacuum cleaner. Then Max empties the bag so they are all free to go home.

These books are more effective if read to one or two children at a time rather than a group. The children need to sit close to the teacher to identify the objects being named and see the shapes of the letters. Have the books on your bookshelves so children can look at them on their own or in the writing center where children are teaching themselves to make letters.

■ Serve Alphabet Soup

Serve alphabet soup for lunch and see if the children can find and identify any of the letters.

■ Have Fun with Pretzels

Have pretzels for snack and see what letters your children can make by breaking off pieces before eating the pretzels. This idea comes from watching what children invent on their own.

■ Have Children Keep Journals

Even if children are still scribble-writing, they enjoy keeping journals because it is such an adult thing to do. Read them *Diary of a Worm* (Cronin, 2003) to give them the idea. Provide them with blank booklets and give them a particular time during the day to write about something that happened that day. Talk about it first. Some will want to draw a picture instead, which is fine. Others will scribble, but may eventually do some mock writing and later, real writing.

HOLDS BOOK RIGHT-SIDE UP; TURNS PAGES RIGHT TO LEFT

Children need many early experiences with books before they finally learn to read independently. It is especially important for you to make sure they have all kinds of book experiences both in the classroom and in the home. Many programs purchase paperback duplicates of books in the classroom for a home lending library. Children sign out for a book each day and return it in the morning. This also gives families the chance to read to their children the same books the youngsters are using in the classroom. Young children need to have their favorites read again and again for them to develop a strong affinity for books and reading. As McVicker (2007) noted, "Reading aloud to children and extending books through interactions and activities hold huge educational benefits for young children, not to mention intensifying their joy" (p. 21).

In the classroom, it is essential for an adult to read to a small group *on a daily basis*. As every major research study on reading has found: "the single most important activity for building these understandings and skills essential for reading success appears to be **reading aloud to children**" (NAEYC, 1998, p. 33).

In addition to group reading, staff members should look for opportunities to read books to individuals during the day. After each reading, talk to the children about the story. Ask questions, have children talk about the pictures, and discuss their favorite actions. As the NAEYC research also found: "It is the talk that surrounds the storybook reading that gives it power, helping children to bridge what is in the story and their own lives" (p. 33).

Finally, books need to be available in an enticing book center—full of book posters, puppets, book character dolls, and stuffed animals—where children can look at the books on their own and play with book extension activities.

But surely, you may exclaim, a preschool child will know how to hold a book, which side is up, and which way to turn the pages. Not necessarily. The youngest children or those with no previous book handling experience may not know how to hold the books or turn the pages. Do not show them how. Let them find out for themselves just as you do with their painting or scribbling.

Observe how each of the children handles books. If you see a child who does not hold the book right-side up, you don't need to correct him. Instead, ask him to pick out a book he would like you to read for him. You might then ask him how you should hold the book. If he still does not have a clue, then say you'd like to look at the pictures together with him. Can he help you hold the book so that both of you can see the pictures? If he gives you the book upside down, ask him: Can you see the pictures if I hold it this way? Be sure to follow up with this child and books in the days to come.

Even though a child may have seen you reading books many times, he still may not know how to hold a book if he has not had the experience. Take special care to observe which children play in the book center and which ones do not. Invite children who do not show an interest in books to choose a book for you to read to them alone. Most children enjoy having the teacher pay special attention to them. Remember that one of your important tasks is to bring together children and books in happy and satisfying ways.

This means that you and your coworkers must serve as good book-reading models. Note in your daily plans who will be the book readers for a particular day. Ask the readers to choose books they especially like, and to tell the children why they like them. Have them plan a book extension activity to use after they have read the books they like. For instance, for some of the books discussed in this text they might do the following:

- *Abuela* (**Dorros, 1991**): Have a child fly a Rosalba doll around the classroom and come back and tell you what she saw.
- *If You Decide to Go to the Moon* (**McNulty, 2005**): Have a child go around the room and choose an item he or she would take to the moon, and then tell why.
- *Duck for President* (**Cronin, 2004**): Have child make a sign for himself as president.
- *My Crayons Talk* (**Hubbard, 1996**): Have the child choose a crayon from a basketful, tell what it says, and then draw with it.

Children need such hands-on experience with books—the more the better. We need to find all sorts of ways to get books off the shelves and into children's hands. As Gottschall (1995) noted,

> When children can easily see the pictures and print, they also gradually gain the prereading skills that they will need for primary school: they learn how to hold a book; that you read from left to right and from top to bottom; that stories have a beginning, a middle, and an end; and that printed words stay the same and can be read again and again. (pp. 30–31)

If You Have Not Checked This Item: Some Helpful Ideas

■ Use Big Books

Although they are more often used in elementary school to teach reading, a few big books fill a useful role in preschool programs. They can help young children understand how a book works, for instance. Use big books when reading to the total group. Put the big book on an easel so children can see the pictures and text, and you can turn the pages easily. At the same time, have one or two small copies of the same book that the younger listeners can hold. Have them turn the page when you do. Big books available from Constructive Playthings (1-800-448-4115) include

Silly Sally

Caps for Sale

Three Billy Goats Gruff

Mean Soup

Stellaluna

■ Put Books in Every Learning Center of the Classroom

Sometimes we categorize things so distinctly that we overlook other possibilities. That seems to be especially true with our use of picture books in the classroom. We usually keep them on the shelves of the book center, and they seldom find their way into other areas of the classroom. If we want children to become involved with books in a hands-on way, we need to consider keeping some books in the other curriculum areas. Perhaps a large plastic baggie hanging from a shelf in each area can contain a picture book suitable for that area. Or a book can be clipped to a large kitchen clip hanging from a string attached to the wall. An adult can read the book to children playing in the area, and children can look at it on their own.

For instance, put *Mike and the Bike* in the large motor center, *Max Counts his Chickens* in the manipulative/math center, *Tar Beach* in the block center, *Diary of a Worm* in the writing center, *My Crayons Talk* in the art center, *Planting a Rainbow* in the science center, *My Family Plays Music* in the music center, and *Violet the Pilot* in the dramatic play center. Don't forget to change them often.

PRETENDS TO READ USING PICTURES TO TELL STORY

As children become more familiar with picture books, they begin looking through them on their own, at first flipping through and missing some of the pages, but later turning each page separately and looking at it intently. As certain books become their favorites, they go through them again and again. They will also ask an adult to read them over and over.

Now it's their turn to read. Children who have handled books and enjoyed hearing them read aloud take just as much pleasure in pretending to read these books themselves, especially to an adult reader. Because young children do not at first understand it is the words that tell the story, they re-create their stories aloud mainly from the pictures or sometimes from memory if they have heard the story repeated many times. Their story may not even include all the pictures in the book at first, but rather the ones that make the biggest impression on them.

Children may also include some real words from the story if they remember them from hearing the story repeated. Other extraneous information may also find its way into their story, especially if the adult reader has discussed the illustrations with them. Thus the story they are pretending to read often comes out quite different from the book version. But children read it along in their own way, turning the pages and saying words just as if they appear that way in the book.

If it is the children's first attempt to retell what is in a book, they may do what is called "picture-naming"; they merely point to a picture on a page and tell what it is, rather than telling the story in a narrative sequence. They still believe it is the pictures and not the words that tell the story. They have not yet developed what is called "a sense of story" (Schickedanz, 1999).

Children take pleasure in pretending to read a familiar book to the teacher.

It is not up to you as a teacher to correct the child's pretend reading of a story. Instead, you should accept it just as you do his pretend writing with pictures and scribbles. This emergent reading is an early stage of a child's learning to read, a wonderful display of his interest and attention to the way a book works and how a story goes. Whether it is accurate is beside the point. Your role is to thank the child for his reading and invite him to do more of it.

You will find that the more reading you do for individual children and small groups, the more you can expect the children to do "pretend reading" for you. If none of the children in your program has offered to do such pretend reading, it may mean that you have never asked them to do it. Or it may mean they are not that familiar with the books because the stories have not been repeated enough. Remember the "3 Ms"—manipulation, mastery, and meaning—and be sure to reread favorite books over and over to help children master the stories.

Using book audiotapes or CD-ROMs is not the same. Children need to see and hear real books read by a live person sitting close to them and talking about the story afterward. They need to do follow-up extension activities of their favorite books by using puppets or doll characters or reenacting the story as a character themselves (Beaty & Pratt, 2007). How will you know which books are their favorites? Listen to the children when you have finished reading. Does anyone say "Read it again, teacher"? That will give you a clue.

If You Have Not Checked This Item: Some Helpful Ideas

■ Read a Favorite Book

Often a favorite book is one that

- Is written about an experience children can relate to
- Has an interesting-looking character with a funny name
- Has simple illustrations in bright primary colors
- Has a brief text with a line or two on a page
- Uses repetition, rhyming words, or distinctive expressions
- Has an exciting or funny story line or cumulative incidents

Here are three books that have become children's favorites. Once you read them to children, they will want to hear them again and again:

1. *Clarabella's Teeth* (Vrombaut, 2003) tells the story of poor crocodile Clarabella who can't come out and play because she has to spend so much time brushing her dozens of teeth. Children love the zany pictures of the animals: Ruby brushing her rabbit teeth, Liam brushing his leopard teeth, Max (hanging upside down) brushing his monkey teeth, and Zoe brushing her zebra teeth. And Clarabella? She is brushing and brushing and brushing. Next comes lunchtime and then tumble time, and you know what Clarabella is doing. When her teeth are finally

brushed clean it is bedtime for her friends. But they have a surprise for her. A gigantic crocodile toothbrush for Clarabella.

Bring in four regular toothbrushes for four animal puppets and a gigantic tooth-brush (a hairbush will do) for Clarabella, for children to reenact this story as you read it over and over. They love to put the animal puppets on their hands and brush their teeth—especially Clarabella's. No rhymes in this book but lots of repetition. Soon you will have several children who volunteer to "read" the story.

2. *How Do Dinosaurs Get Well Soon?* (Yolen, 2003) has an array of funny, ferocious dinosaurs demonstrating outrageous behavior in rhyme, in answer to the title question. What if a dinosaur catches the flu? Does he whimper and whine in between each atchoo? The scenes show one after another of the dinos dropping dirty tissues all over the floor, flinging medicine out the door, dumping out juice, and getting sick in a pail (children love it). But no, that's not really what they do, as they rhymingly obey each of the health rules till they're better.

Here is a book for children to reenact, taking the role of each dinosaur pictured as you read the story to the total group. Make signs for child characters to wear around their necks for each of the ten dinosaurs whose names are on the inside covers.

3. In *I Will Never Not Ever Eat a Tomato* (Child, 2000), big brother Charlie tells the story about his little sister Lola, who is a fussy eater. Lola names off all the vegetables, fruit, and food she will NOT eat as she waits for Charlie to get her dinner. He tells her that is lucky because they are not having any of those things. When he puts down a carrot in front of her, he tells her it is not a carrot but an orange twiglet from Jupiter. So she tries it: Mmm, not bad. The mashed potato is a cloud fluff from Mt. Fuji. Then she wants something from that big bowl on the table. What? Yes, tomatoes! No, she informs Charlie, not tomatoes. They are moonsquirters, her favorite.

How can your listeners reenact this story? Bring out real food or plastic substitutes from the dramatic play center and have your children choose their roles, two at a time to play Lola and Charlie. Any or all of these books can easily become favorites if you read them often enough and have the children get involved in re-creating the humorous in-cidents. Their bright, funny illustrations mark them as books children will remember and be able to retell in pretend reading.

 # RETELLS STORIES FROM BOOKS WITH INCREASING ACCURACY

At the same time young children are pretending to write and beginning to identify let-ters, they are also involved in the natural emergence of reading skills. They are asking parents and teachers to read them stories and scribbling their own stories in mock writing. They are drawing their own illustrations, scribbling mock stories about them, and "reading" them back to the teacher. To children, reading and writing are all the same thing. You write something and you read it back; you read something and you write about it. And it is very exciting to "read" your own "writing"!

Nevertheless, until recently many educators somehow never made the connection that writing and reading can emerge naturally and develop simultaneously in preschool children. Even teachers who note that many more "early readers" are entering kindergarten these days still believe that writing is different. Maybe some children can develop reading on their own, but surely children have to be taught to write, don't they?

Perhaps it is because writing and reading have always been taught as separate subjects in elementary school that educators in the past never looked closely at what was actually happening with younger children. Now, however, the evidence is in. Studies over two decades by child development specialists in the United States, Argentina, New Zealand, and elsewhere agree that:

> The young child's reading and writing abilities mutually reinforce each other, developing concurrently and interrelatedly rather than sequentially. Furthermore, reading and writing have intimate connections with oral language. Truly, the child develops as a speaker/reader/writer with each role supporting the other. (Teale, 1986, pp. 3–5)

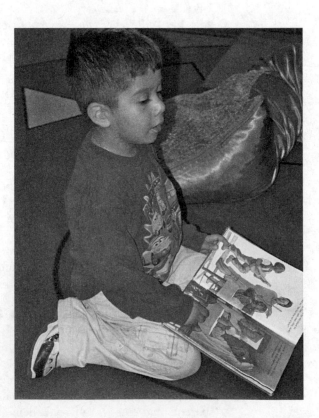

This boy is retelling the story of Abiyoyo.

Figure 11–3 Stages in
Children's Natural Development
of Reading

1. Retells stories from books with increasing accuracy

2. Shows awareness that print in books tells a story

3. Attempts to match telling of story with print in books

4. Wants to know what particular print says

Child development specialist Judith A. Schickedanz (1986) suggests several sequential stages in young children's natural development of reading based on her research with preschool children. The first two of these stages are converted here into checklist items: see Figure 11–3.

Next time a child asks you to read a story, have him choose a favorite tale, one he has heard before. After you have finished, tell him it is now his turn, that he should tell the story to you. He can turn the pages if he wants and "read" the story to you. Make it fun, so that he will want to repeat the activity again and again. This means, of course, that you will need to spend much of your reading time on a one-to-one basis with individuals rather than reading to a whole group. Most teachers find this very rewarding, and so do children.

At first the child may read along with you as you "scaffold" the child's reading. In other words, you do much of the reading of a familiar book but encourage the child to join in whenever he can. In time the child will take over more and more of the reading. After a child has participated a number of times in a scaffolded reading experience with a particular book, he will often attempt to retell the story independently (Strickland & Schickedanze, 2004, p. 30).

The story may not be verbatim, but most children use some words from the book. They tend to tell the story in their own language, at their own developmental level, with the same articulation they use when they speak. If they speak a dialect, they will retell the story in this dialect. If they are learning English as a second language, they will retell the story the way they speak English rather than the way the story is written in the book. The more times the child hears the story, the more accurate her retelling will become.

Predictable Books

The book's structure also influences the accuracy of the child's story retelling. Research has found that the best beginning books for helping children learn to read are *predictable books,* those that "contain selections with repetitive structures that enable children to anticipate the next word, line, or episode" (Bridge, 1986, p. 82). If children are familiar with a story and can anticipate what comes next, they will have a much easier time retelling the story themselves.

If the child is familiar with the book you are reading and is familiar with books in general, she can follow the story more easily if she knows what's coming. If the book is written in a predictable pattern, it is also easier for the child to remember the story line and to recall what comes next. The following books contain *patterns* that make them excellent predictable books to use with preschoolers.

Silly Sally (Wood, 1992)

Snip Snap! What's That? (Bergman, 2005)

Stuck in the Mud (Clarke, 2008)

Twist with a Burger, Jitter with a Bug (Lowery, 1995)

Rhyming and *repetition* are also important qualities of predictable books. Even very young children remember rhymes and love the books that contain them. As Opitz (2000) tells us:

> Is it any wonder that most children develop a sense of rhyme with relative ease? After all, they are surrounded by rhyme in their everyday lives through the songs they are sung by their parents or those they hear while viewing television and movies. Children develop an ear for rhyme if they are provided with opportunities to hear it. And for those children who haven't had such opportunities, immerse them in the delightful books filled with rhyme. (p. 21)

Predictable books can provide that opportunity. Several recent books are favorites because of their rhyming and repetition:

Aliens Love Underpants (Freedman & Cort, 2007)

Drat That Fat Cat! (Thomson, 2003)

Grumpy Gloria (Dewdney, 2006)

Llama Llama Red Pajama (Dewdney, 2005)

In the second book, you will be reading the question, "But was that cat fat enough? **No, he was not!**" six different times. Let your listeners join in as soon as they can. Then, as the outrageous cat gobbles up different creatures, each one's sound is also repeated: "squeak, squeak" for the rat; "quack, quack" for the duck, "woof, woof" for the dog, "drat that fat cat," for the old lady; and "hic, hic, hic, hic, hic" as he coughs them all up. Children quickly remember the words and shout them out with glee. This is one story they will soon be able to retell almost word for word. Morrow and Gambrell (2004) concurred, saying, "Repeated readings promote independent reading; children can confidently revisit a familiar book without adult assistance" (p. 45).

Through listening to stories like these read over and over, young children begin to develop a *story schema,* or sense of story: a mental model of the basic elements of a story. From this mental model, children develop expectations for the setting, the characters, the order of incidents, and how the story will end (Neuman & Roskos, 1993). Neuman and Roskos noted,

> This sense of story comes about by hearing stories, and by being read to on a regular basis. Perhaps no other finding in research is as well documented as the simple fact that reading regularly to young children significantly influences their understanding of what reading is all about as well as their later proficiency in reading. (p. 37)

Do you read daily to individuals in your class? It will be evident by the number of children who are able to retell the stories from your books.

If You Have Not Checked This Item: Some Helpful Ideas

■ Read Predictable Books

In *The Three Billy Goats Gruff* (Galdone, 1973), children who know this traditional story remember the size of the goats, where they were going, how they went across the bridge ("trip, trap, trip, trap"), what the troll said to each goat ("Who's that tripping across my bridge?"), and many more details. They can tell it almost by heart. If they want to tell you the story by pretending to read as they turn the pages, let them. Also ask them to tell the story afterward without looking at the book. You try it first and let them correct you if you leave out anything.

Children who are not as familiar with books and reading may still agree to tell you the story, but theirs may be a story created by them as they look at the pictures. Your acceptance of any story they tell is important. As they progress in their experience with stories and books, their retelling will become more accurate. Eventually with a highly predictable book, some children will memorize the words, and then their retelling may be perfect.

SHOWS AWARENESS THAT PRINT IN BOOKS TELLS THE STORY

The next developmental step in emergent reading skills involves print awareness. If you are reading to children on a one-to-one basis, they already may have indicated something about their print awareness or lack of it. At first children believe that the pictures in the book tell the story as previously mentioned. They may not pay any attention to the text. Even when they do, they may not understand that it is the print and not the pictures that the reader is reading.

Some children are so unaware of the purpose of print that they may cover it unintentionally with their hands if they are holding the book. Others may understand that the reader needs to read the print, but they may also think the reader still needs the pictures to know what the words say.

Researchers have discovered a sequence most children go through in sorting out print from pictures in a picture book:

1. At first the text and the picture are not differentiated.

2. Then the children expect the text to be a label for the picture.

3. At the third stage the text is expected to provide cues with which to confirm predictions based on the picture. (Clay, 1991, p. 32)

As children pretend to read you their favorite stories, some of them use the same narrative style and almost the exact words as the book itself. Are they really reading? If you cover the print as they read, you will discover that most have memorized the words after hearing the book read many times. But eventually these same children, without being taught, will come to notice the print and realize that the print, not the pictures, tells the story in the book. Certain kinds of books help children to make this cognitive leap recognizing that print tells the story. One is the "song storybook."

Song Storybooks

Song storybooks are picture books whose stories are written in the words of a familiar children's song with a line of text on each page. Because children already know the song by heart, they may be able to follow the words along if you run your finger under them as you read. They will be delighted to see the pictures in the book illustrating the familiar song. In addition to following along or chiming in as you read the words, have them sing the words with you from time to time.

Constructive Playthings (1-800-448-4115) has the following song storybooks in big book format along with a CD with songs on it:

Down by the Station

Old MacDonald Had a Farm

There Was an Old Lady Who Swallowed a Fly

This Old Man

The Wheels on the Bus

Other regular-size song storybooks with songs children love to sing (and read, and act out) include

I Love You a Bushel & a Peck (Wells & Loesser, 2005)

If You're Happy and You Know It (Warhola, 2007)

On Top of Spaghetti (Johnson, 2006)

She'll Be Coming 'Round the Mountain (Emmett & Allwright, 2006)

These books are also predictable because the children already know the words and what comes next. When they see the words in a line of print, they will be able to "read" it, that is, recite it from memory. Little by little they may realize that it is the print that tells the story, not the pictures.

You can determine who these children are by asking them where you should look in the book when you read it to them. By now, some of these youngsters may try to match the telling of the story with the print in the books, and some may even want to know what particular print says. In the final stage prior to reading, they will actually begin to read the words. This is how literacy finally emerges naturally—when interested adults bring experimenting children together with appropriate books.

Not all children in preschool will arrive at this stage. Individual development, personal interests, and home background have a great deal to do with children's accomplishments. Your role is to fill your program with exciting books, extension activities, opportunities for reading, and time for children to explore to their heart's content. Then reading to individual children and listening to them read to you may be one of the most satisfying activities any of you engage in.

If You Have Not Checked This Item: Some Helpful Ideas

■ Make Newsprint Stories

Bring a newsprint pad into the book area and have children dictate stories to you that you write on the pad. Can they read them back? Another day paste an interesting picture on the newsprint and have children dictate a story about the people or animals in the picture. Mount these stories around the room and read them with individuals from time to time.

■ Fill the Environment with Print

As mentioned earlier in the chapter, you need to fill the classroom with print: charts, place cards, books, magazines, newspapers, telephone directory, labeled food containers, and signs of all kinds. Have the children help you make the signs. Ask them what should be labeled in the classroom and then spell the words aloud as you print them on the signs: aquarium, door, table, chair, telephone, dramatic play area, and so forth. Have them help mount the signs on the appropriate objects.

■ Read a Book with Large Font Print

Other types of picture books that help children understand that the print tells the story are books with large font type. More and more recent books have some or all the words in large font. For example:

Homemade Love (Hooks, 2002) has a little African-American girl narrating this simple story all in large font red print. It starts with "My mama calls me **girlpie**," with the last word even larger in gigantic letters. As you read it to one or two children at a time, run your finger under the words. On every page there are one or two words printed in huge type. After the children are familiar with the story, they may be able to say the words on the pages in huge type.

In *I Know a Rhino* (Fuge, 2002), the words are in large font black print with one or two words on each page being in gigantic print. The first page shows the little girl having tea with a **Rhino** who takes **three** sugars. This book is also predictable because it rhymes.

My Truck Is Stuck! (Lewis, 2002) is also a rhyming story with the truck going **into a hole** in large black font; going **beep! beep!** to stop a car for help in large green font; **beep! beep!** to stop a van in large blue font; **beep! beep!** to stop a jeep in large red font, and so on.

In *Please, Baby, Please* (Lee & Lee, 2002), the parents talk to their toddler in large font two-line rhymes, with the last line reading, "please, baby, please," or "baby baby baby, please." Can your listeners pick out the words "please" and "baby"?

OBSERVING, RECORDING, AND INTERPRETING EMERGENT LITERACY DEVELOPMENT

Although young children develop emergent writing and reading skills at the same time and in much the same manner that they develop spoken language, we realize that the same emphasis has not been placed on the natural development of preschool writing and reading by many adults around them. Therefore, there may be children who can produce mock writing and letters, but who have not practiced it. There may be some children who are aware of print and try to read it, but have not been noticed. If you screen your entire class using the Child Development Checklist items on writing and reading skills, you may find certain children who exhibit some of these skills. After observing the 4-year-old boy Jeremey previously referred to, the teacher was able to complete the checklist section shown in Figure 11–4.

Jeremey's accomplishments as recorded on the checklist helped the teacher understand that Jeremey was showing real progress in his writing and reading skills. She had not realized how far along he had progressed. She decided to work on a one-to-one basis with him using predictable books. After Jeremey heard the story repeated, perhaps he could retell it. If he really liked the story, she would ask him if he knew what particular print said certain words. She also decided to encourage him to "write a story" about what he was building in the block area.

The teacher also decided that now was the time to expand her writing table to an entirely new and separate classroom writing area with an old rolltop desk, many writing tools and paper, a small table with a manual typewriter, and magnetic alphabet letters. Who knows which other children would emerge with self-taught knowledge of letters and words!

LEARNING ACTIVITIES

1. Use the Child Development Checklist section on emergent literacy skills as a screening tool to observe all the children in your classroom. Compare the children who have checks at the higher levels of the writing skills with their results in spoken language. Can you draw any conclusions?

Child Development Checklist

Name _____ Jeremey _____   Observer _____ Betsy _____

Program _____ Pre—K _____   Dates _____ 5/5 _____

Directions:

Put a **X** for items you see the child perform regularly. Put **N** for items where there is no opportunity to observe. Leave all other items blank.

Item	Evidence	Dates
9. Emergent Writing and Reading Skills		
_N_ Pretends to write with pictures & scribbles	He no longer scribbles but tries to write real words	5/5
_N_ Makes horizontal lines of writing scribbles	Same as above	5/5
_N_ Includes letterlike forms in writing	Same as above	5/5
_X_ Makes some letters, prints name or initial	Prints his name, copies other words	5/5
_X_ Holds book right-side up; turns pages right to left	Yes, likes to look at books	5/5
_X_ Pretends to read using pictures to tell story	Likes to repeat stories in books	5/5
_X_ Retells stories from books with increasing accuracy	Can tell story without book	5/5
_X_ Shows awareness that print in books tells story	Points to word and asks if it says "_____"	5/5

Figure 11—4   Emergent Writing and Reading Checklist for Jeremey

2. Set up a writing area with paper and writing tools and make a running record of how children use it on three different days.

3. Observe and make a running record of children using a typewriter or computer on three different days. How do they go about teaching themselves how to use the instrument or programs? Are they using trial and error to teach themselves? Do they learn from their errors? How?

4. Have a child select a favorite book for you to read; afterward, ask the child to tell you the story page by page. What do you learn about his reading skills?

5. Read a predictable book to an individual child. Does he show any awareness of the print? Can he retell the story?

SUGGESTED READINGS

Beaty, J. J. (2009). *Fifty early childhood literacy strategies.* Upper Saddle River, NJ: Merrill/Prentice Hall.

Fox, M. (2001). *Reading magic: Why reading aloud to children will change their lives forever.* Portsmouth, NH: Heinemann.

Isbell, R. T. (2002). Telling and retelling stories: Learning language and literacy. *Young Children, 57*(2), 26–30.

Hall, K. W. (2008). Reflecting on our read-aloud practices: The importance of including culturally authentic literature. *Young Children, 63*(1), 80–86.

Jalongo, M. R., & Ribblett, D. M. (1997). Using song picture books to support emergent literacy. *Young Children, 74*(1), 15–28.

Johnson, M. H. (2008). Developing verbal and visual literacy through experiences in the visual arts: 25 tips for teachers. *Young Children, 63*(1), 74–79.

Love, A., Burns, M. S., & Buell, M. J. (2007). Writing empowering literacy. *Young Children, 62*(1), 12–19.

CHILDREN'S BOOKS

Bergman, M. (2005). *Snip snap! What's that?* New York: Greenwillow.

Child, L. (2000). *I will never not ever eat a tomato.* Cambridge, MA: Candlewick Press.

Clarke, J. (2007). *Stuck in the mud.* New York: Walker.

Cronin, D. (2000). *Click, clack, moo: Cows that type.* New York: Simon & Schuster.

Cronin, D. (2005). *Click, clack, quackity-quack.* New York: Atheneum.

Cronin, D. (2002). *Giggle, giggle, quack.* New York: Simon & Schuster.

Cronin, D. (2003). *Diary of a worm.* New York: Joanna Cotler Books.

Cronin, D. (2004). *Duck for president.* New York: Simon & Schuster.

Dewdney, A. (2006). *Grumpy Gloria.* New York: Viking.

Dewdney, A. (2005). *Llama llama red pajama.* New York: Viking.

Dorros, A. (1991). *Abuela.* New York: Dutton.*

Emmett, J., & Allwright, D. (2006). *She'll Be Coming 'Round the Mountain.* New York: Atheneum.

Fleming, D. (2002). *Alphabet under construction.* New York: Hyperion.

Freedman, C., & Cort, B. (2006). *Aliens love underpants.* Hauppauge, NY: Barron's.

Fuge, C. (2002). *I know a rhino.* New York: Sterling Publishing.

Galdone, P. (1973). *The three billy goats Gruff.* New York: Scholastic.

Hooks, B. (2002). *Homemade love.* New York: Hyperion.*

Hubbard, P. (1996). *My crayons talk.* New York: Henry Holt.

Johnson, P. B. (2006). *On top of spaghetti.* New York: Scholastic.

Keats, E. J. (1968). *A letter to Amy.* New York: Harper.*

Kroll, S. (2001). *Patches lost and found.* Delray Beach, FL: Winslow Press.

Lee, S., & Lee, T. L. (2002). *Please, baby, please.* New York: Simon & Schuster.*

Lewis, K. (2002). *My truck is stuck!* New York: Hyperion.

Lowery, L. (1995). *Twist with a burger, jitter with a bug.* Boston: Houghton Mifflin.*

Martin, B., & Archambault, J. (1989). *Chicka chicka boom boom.* New York: Simon & Schuster.

McNulty, F. (2005). *If you decide to go to the moon.* New York: Scholastic.

Olson, M. W. (2000). *Nice try, Tooth Fairy.* New York: Simon & Schuster.

Seeger, P. (1994). *Abiyoyo.* New York: Aladdin Paperbacks.*

Sobel, J. (2003). *B is for bulldozer: A construction ABC.* San Diego: Harcourt.

Spanyol, J. (2001). *Carlo likes reading.* Cambridge, MA: Candlewick.*

Thomson, P. (2003). *Drat that fat cat!* New York: Arthur A. Levine Books.

Vrombaut, A. (2003). *Clarabella's teeth.* New York: Clarion.

Warhola, J. (2007). *If you're happy and you know it.* New York: Orchard.

Wells, R., & Loesser, F. (2005). *I love you! A bushel and a peck.* New York: HarperCollins.

Wells, R. (1997). *Bunny cakes.* New York: Dial.

Wood, A. (1992). *Silly Sally.* New York: HarperCollins.

Yolen, J. (2003). *How do dinosaurs get well soon?* New York: Blue Sky Press.*

*Multicultural.

12 Art and Music Skills

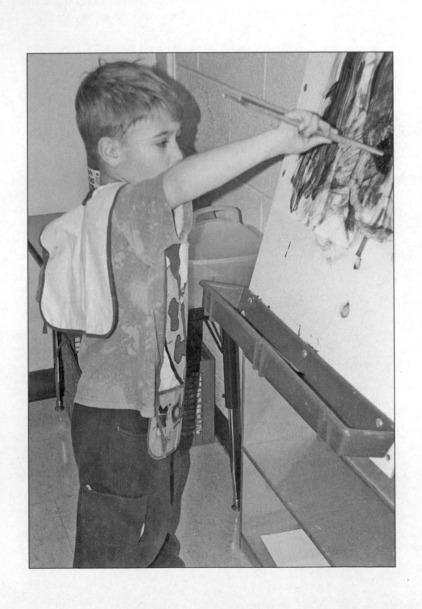

✓ ART AND MUSIC SKILLS CHECKLIST

____ Makes basic scribble shapes

____ Combines circles/squares with crossed lines

____ Draws person as sun-face with arms and legs

____ Combines objects together in a picture

____ Moves legs and feet in rhythm to a beat

____ Moves arms and hands in rhythm to a beat

____ Plays instruments

____ Sings with group or by him/herself

DEVELOPING ART SKILLS

This chapter on the development of children's art and music skills and the following chapter on dramatic play focus on the growth of creativity in young children. Too often creativity is not included in discussions of the major aspects of children's development— emotional, social, physical, cognitive, and language. Yet it is as notable a drive in the development of the young human being as thinking or speaking.

The unfolding of a young child's creative urge is a joy to behold for most sensitive early childhood teachers. To help foster and not suppress such development is just as important as it is for speaking, writing, and thinking skills. Yet somehow we equate creativity with special talent that not everyone displays; therefore we downplay or ignore the development of creativity as more of a frill than a necessity for getting along in life.

In downplaying or ignoring creativity, we deprive the developing human of a basic aspect of his or her expressional capacities. Every child has the potential to become an artist, a musician, a writer, or an inventor, if his interests carry him in that direction and if her teachers support rather than control her urge. The fact that few people become artists is evidence of society's low priority for creativity and high priority for conformity. As Hale and Roy (1996) pointed out:

> When we teach children the visual arts, we really do not teach but rather we provide rich, manipulative, concrete experiences for young children. When a teacher gives children the opportunity to be creative, it requires allowing children to find and solve problems and communicate ideas in novel and appropriate ways. (p. 4)

Creativity connotes originality and novelty. To create, one brings into existence a new form. Creative people have original ideas, do things in new and different ways, and see things from unique and novel perspectives. Creative people do not imitate; they do not follow the crowd. In a word, they are nonconformists.

Who are they? Artists, inventors, poets, writers, actors, musicians, interior decorators, chefs, architects, clothing designers, to name a few—and young children. They are all people who follow their own bent and use their ingenuity to design something new. Young children are naturally creative because everything they do, make, or say is completely new to them. They explore, experiment, put things together, take things apart, and manipulate things in ways no adult would ever think of, because the youngsters don't know the difference.

Children come into the world uninhibited and with an entirely fresh point of view: their own. They continue to follow its bent until they learn how society expects them to behave. Only youngsters with strong enough psyches or strong enough outside support to resist society's inhibitions become the artists or creators whom we value as adults.

Could the children in your classroom become such creative adults? If their natural-born creativity is supported and valued by the adults around them, and if it has an opportunity to blossom and grow, children have the chance to escape the smothering pressure to conform and can enrich their own lives and those of others with the products of their talent.

This chapter on creative development deals in art with representational drawing, not only because such art is an important part of most early childhood programs, but also because many early childhood teachers need help in restructuring their art programs. Too many activities in such programs suppress rather than support creativity. As De la Roche (1996) noted,

> Must all snowflakes and shamrocks and turkeys be the same shape? Do they have to be prepackaged and regular to be lovely enough to be hung up in the window? Is regularity and sameness what we want from preschool, kindergarten and first-grade children? Snowflakes are not regular. (p. 82)

The chapter could just as well deal with the development of science skills, which also depend on children's natural exploratory bent. Yet science at the preschool level has somehow escaped the controlled approach that many teachers take with art. It seems good for children to explore plants and animals in all sorts of ways. But somehow many teachers seem to feel that drawings should be done only in the manner prescribed by adults, because "adults know better." As Wachtel (2008) tells us:

Children's natural creativity may overcome the conformity of coloring-book-like pictures.

Teachers who employ processed art are encouraging children to copy the work of the teacher, without experiencing any creativity. The final art products are duplicates of each other. (p. 18).

When teachers give all the children the same coloring-book-like picture to color in, children's natural creativity may overcome this conformity, but why not let them make their own designs?

The traditional point of view needs to be challenged. We need to step back and take a good look at the development of creativity. When does creativity appear in human beings? What are its characteristics? What can we do to help it grow? How can we keep from suppressing it?

This chapter looks at a developmental sequence in drawing skills that appears in all children in the same order. Even visually impaired children exhibit the beginning steps of the sequence until the youngsters' lack of visual feedback discourages them from continuing. You will note this sequence is similar to the steps children take in developing physical skills, cognitive skills, and especially writing skills with early scribbling.

It is obvious that the brain is programmed to accomplish all kinds of development in this order—from the general to the specific—as youngsters have the opportunity and materials to interact with their environment in a playful manner (manipulating, mastering, and creating meaning), thus discovering what it and they are able to do. The same creativity emerges naturally in all aspects of art, from making collages to modeling clay, but this chapter will focus on the emergence of representational drawing skills as an example. (See Chapter 8, Small Motor Development, for three-dimensional art, and Chapter 9, Cognitive Development, for using colors.)

Right Brain versus Left Brain

The two hemispheres of the brain control different functions in human beings. The right hemisphere or right brain plays a dominant role in holistic thinking, visual-spatial skills, intuition, emotions, art, and creativity. The left hemisphere or left brain predominates in rational, linear, analytical, and sequential thinking, language, reading, writing, and math skills (Eliot, 1999, p. 406). As Eliot tells us: "Babies appear to be born with a slight right-hemisphere advantage." As language skills develop, the left hemisphere catches up; by age 4, communication between the two hemispheres has greatly improved.

Nevertheless, in most people the left hemisphere eventually tends to dominate the right, perhaps because of its focus on literacy and math skills during the school years. In early childhood, the right brain is dominant. Thus it is the preschool years that offer young children the opportunity to develop creative skills that can last for a lifetime during this early right-brain dominance. It is just as important for you (who may be left-brain–dominant) to be aware of this right-brain dominance in young children and become more creative yourself. Young children can teach all of us a great deal about creativity if we will open our minds to them and encourage this originality.

MAKES BASIC SCRIBBLE SHAPES

During their first year of life, children really do not draw. If they have access to a crayon, they are more apt to put it in their mouths than to put a mark on paper. Around the age of 13 months children's first scribbling begins. The first marks they make are usually random. These marks have more to do with movement, in fact, than with art. The toddler is often surprised to find that a crayon, a pencil, or a paintbrush will make marks. Youngsters are often captivated by watching the lines that their movements can make on a surface. The surface is not always paper, much to their caregiver's dismay. Children will mark on walls, tabletops, or anything else that will take a mark.

This first stage of art skill development is purely mechanical and manipulative. The child is gaining control over the art tool, whether it is a crayon, paintbrush, pencil, felt-tip marker, or chalk. The child makes random marks without using eye control. Visually impaired children make the same kind of random marks in the dirt. Writing scribbles also begin like this but eventually veer off in a different direction.

Older children in your program who have had no access to art materials (or those who have been suppressed in their attempts at home) still go through these same stages (Figure 12–1). However, their progression through the stages occurs more rapidly. It takes older children far less time to learn how to handle art materials through spontaneous exploratory play.

You will note that in all these early art experiences, young children are once again teaching themselves through playful exploration of the medium with the "3 Ms" of manipulation, mastery, and meaning. The end results that appear on their papers are not art products, not paintings as such, but the footprints of the process of emerging art skills.

1. *SCRIBBLE*
    UNCONTROLLED
   Marks made on paper for enjoyment. Child has little control of eye and hand movement. No pattern.
    CONTROLLED
   Control of eye and hand. Repeated design.
    NAMED SCRIBBLE
   Child tells you what s/he has drawn. May not be recognizable to adult.

2. *SHAPE AND DESIGN*
   Child makes shapes such as circles, squares, ovals, triangles.

   Child's muscle control is increasing and s/he is able to place shapes and designs wherever s/he wants.

3. *MANDALA*
   Child usually divides circle or square with lines.

4. *RADIALS*
   Lines that radiate from a single point. Can be part of a mandala.

5. *SUNS*
   Formed from oval, square, or circle with short lines extending from the shape. The extending lines take many variations.

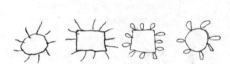

6. *HUMANS*
   Child uses SUN design and develops a face by adding human features. . . a "sun face."

   Child elongates several lines of the SUN design to create arms and legs.

7. *PICTORIALS*
   Child combines ALL stages to make recognizable design or objects.

Figure 12–1   Stages of Art Development

Note: Reprinted with permission of B. Helm.

From about 2 years of age on through 3 and 4, and sometimes later depending on the child, an individual will mark on paper in a scribbling manner. At first the scribbles may be endless lines done in a rhythmic, manipulative manner. Eventually the child will use eye control as well as hand/arm movement to make her scribbles and direct their placement on the paper. One scribble often is placed on top of another until the paper is a hodgepodge of lines and circles. Painters may cover their painted scribbles with layers and layers of paint before they are finished.

The result of this effort has little meaning to the child at first, for she is not trying to create something, but merely experimenting by moving colors around on a paper. The process, not the product, is important to her. Adults, however, think of art mainly in terms of creating a product. Their response to scribbling is often either to dismiss it as unimportant and worthless, or to ask children to tell them what they have drawn. Once children learn that adults expect this sort of information, the youngsters often begin naming their scribbles. This behavior does not mean that they really had something in mind when they began moving the brush or crayon around on the paper. Our comments, instead, should focus on their efforts in the process of drawing, not on the "imperfect" products they first create. "I see that you used three different colors in your painting today, Rosa."

Children work hard at scribbling. Only they know when a scribbled "drawing" is finished—actually, the *process* is finished. Some youngsters go over and over the lines they have made, almost as if they are practicing the way to make a straight or curved line. We understand these children have progressed to the "mastery" stage of exploratory art. Their early products seem to show a greater proportion of vertical lines, especially in easel paintings. But many children are able to make multiple horizontal, diagonal, and curved lines as well. Back and forth the youngsters work, sometimes changing their hand direction when they get tired and sometimes even changing hands. Whereas 2-year-olds place one scribble on top of another, 3- and 4-year-olds frequently put a single scribble on one paper (Kellogg, 1970, p. 18).

Rhoda Kellogg, the art specialist who collected and analyzed thousands of children's drawings from around the world, identified 20 scribbles that children make. Not all children make all 20 scribbles that they are capable of producing. Individuals tend to concentrate on a few favorites and repeat them in many variations. The fact that all children everywhere produce some of the same 20 scribbles spontaneously—and no others— seems to indicate that this early form of art must be genetic in the human species.

Kellogg (1970) considers these scribbles to be "the building blocks of art" (p. 15). The individual's scribble "vocabulary" most easily can be read in his finger painting. He will draw his "designs" with one or more fingers, and then "erase" them before starting over. Because they do not pile up one on top of the other as with opaque paint, it is easier to see which of the 20 basic scribbles he favors.

As children's physical and mental development progresses and they are able to control the brush and paint more easily, their scribbles begin to take on the configuration of shapes. Kellogg (1970, p. 45) has identified six basic shapes in children's early art: rectangle (including square), oval (including circle), triangle, Greek cross (+), diagonal cross (×), and odd shape (a catchall). These shapes do not necessarily appear separately, but rather are mixed up with other scribbles or with one another.

If children have had the freedom to experiment with art as toddlers, they usually begin to make basic shapes spontaneously by age 3. Children's perceptual and memory skills help them to form, store, and retrieve concepts about shapes quite early if they have had appropriate experiences. The particular shapes a child favors seem to evolve from his own scribbles. Attempts at making ovals and circles usually appear early. This form seems innately appealing to young humans everywhere, perhaps because of their preferred attention to the oval human face.

Circular movements in their scribbling eventually lead them to form an oval. The youngsters often repeat it, going around and around over the same shape. Visual discrimination of the shape and muscle control of the brush or crayon finally allow them to form the shape by itself instead of intertwined within a mass of scribbles. Memory comes into play as well, allowing the children to retrieve the oval from their repertoire of marks and to repeat it another day.

In this manner, the child's capacity to draw shapes seems to emerge from his capacity to control the lines he makes in his scribbling. In other words, he makes one of the basic shapes because he remembers it from creating it spontaneously in his scribbling, not because he is copying the shape from his environment. As he experiments, he stumbles onto new ways to make new shapes. But certain ones seem more appealing, and individual children return to them again and again.

Three- and 4-year-olds first create rectangles by drawing a set of parallel vertical lines, later adding horizontal lines at the top and bottom rather than drawing a continuous line for a perimeter. Thus we see why it is important to give them many opportunities and much time to practice. The children are teaching themselves to draw, just as they taught themselves to build with blocks, walk, talk, think, speak, write, and read.

If You Have Not Checked This Item: Some Helpful Ideas

■   Provide Controllable Materials

Beginners will not be able to progress much beyond scribbling unless they can control the materials. Be sure to provide fat, kindergarten-size crayons for children to grip well. Children can use thin crayons, too, but sometimes beginners bear down so hard they break them. Mix your tempera paints with just enough water to make them creamy but not drippy. Add cornstarch or flour to thicken them if they are too thin. Buy short stubby easel paintbrushes that young children can manipulate easily. Wrap ends of colored chalk with masking tape to help gripping and to control smearing.

■   Be Nondirective

Allow children to explore and experiment with paint and chalk, finger paint and crayons, and felt-tip markers and pencils completely on their own. Put the materials out for their use during free play, or have materials invitingly placed on low shelves near art tables for the youngsters' own selection.

■ Provide Materials Children Can Use on Their Own

Easels always should be available. They are one of the best motivators for spontaneous drawing that you can have available. Children soon find out that all they need for painting is to put on a painting smock and go to the easel. There is no need to get out paints, for they are already mixed and waiting. There is no need to ask for help or direction from the teacher. If an easel is free during free-choice time, they can go over to it and paint.

For children who are experienced easel painters, it is always good to challenge them with a new activity. Perhaps they would like to try flat-table painting with paints in a muffin tin. Or you might make a table easel with two sections of cardboard taped together to form an inverted "V" over a table. Paper can be fastened to it with masking tape. Paint can be mixed and waiting in muffin tins or jars taped to the table so they will not spill.

Remember that children are still in the exploratory stage and should not be expected to paint a picture. If they want your comments, you can talk to them about the colors, lines, and shapes they have created. They may want the paper displayed on the wall. If not, label it with their names and dates and add it to their portfolios (see Chapter 14).

 ## COMBINES CIRCLES/SQUARES WITH CROSSED LINES

The next step in the sequence of children's self-taught art skills involves combining two of the shapes they have made. Kellogg has observed and written a great deal about this behavior. The Greek cross (+) and the diagonal cross (×) are favorite shapes. These are often combined with an oval or rectangle to make what is sometimes called a "mandala." Mandalas don't necessarily stand alone on a sheet of paper but are embedded in groups of scribbles. These shapes or others form the bulk of art for many 3- and 4-year-old children.

Pictorial drawing eventually evolves out of particular combinations of shapes. One of the first representations to occur in children's art is the human form. This representation seems to evolve naturally from the child's first experiments with an oval shape combined with a cross inside it (the mandala), which then leads to an oval with lines radiating from its rim (the sun), which finally evolves into an oval with two lines for arms, two for legs, and small circles inside the large head/body oval for eyes (the sun-face human).

From mandalas to suns to humans is the natural sequence that much of children's spontaneous art follows. Watch for this development in the children in your program. Talk to parents about the spontaneous way art skills develop in children if youngsters have freedom to explore on their own. Both you and the parents may want to save children's scribbling and early shape drawings to see if you can identify the sequence of their development. Be sure to date the art.

Not all children make mandalas, but most do. These basic shape combinations are never lost once they have become a part of a person's art vocabulary. Take a look at the doodles adults make in a nonthinking, spontaneous fashion. You yourself still may draw the mandalas you first discovered as a child.

If You Have Not Checked This Item: Some Helpful Ideas

■ Provide Variety in Your Art Materials

Not all children may enjoy painting at an easel. You should include other possibilities as often as possible. Finger painting is one. It can be done on a smooth paper, a tabletop, or a cookie sheet. Paper finger paintings can be hung to dry and are thus preserved if the child wants to save them. Tabletop finger paintings can also be preserved before cleaning the table by pressing a paper onto them and rubbing the back of the paper.

Finger paint itself can be made from liquid starch that is poured onto paper with powder paint shaken into it, from wallpaper paste mixed with water and poster paint to the proper consistency, or with soap powder mixed with a little water and paint powder. Soap powder can also be whipped until stiff and used as white paint against colored construction paper. Shaving cream can also be used for finger painting.

Don't forget to allow plenty of time for your children to manipulate this new medium. Just because they have mastered easel painting does not mean they will be at the same stage in finger painting.

DRAWS PERSON AS SUN-FACE WITH ARMS AND LEGS

A combination of an oval with lines radiating from its rim is often the next step in the child's natural sequence of drawing a pictorial representation. We call this shape combination "sun" because it looks like the symbol adults use to represent the sun. Children do not call their sun-shape a sun unless adults or more experienced peers first give it the name. The youngster is not drawing a sun, but merely experimenting with shapes. If this combination appeals to them, they will repeat it many times. When they finally do begin to draw pictorially, they sometimes call this figure a "spider."

Although this figure seems quite simple to draw, the sun does not appear spontaneously in children's drawings at first. Two-year-olds can make curved and straight lines, but they rarely produce suns before age 3 (Kellogg, 1970, p. 74). The sun figure may well emerge from the children's experiments with the mandala figure. Most of children's early attempts at sun figures include some kind of marks in the center of the figures—either lines, dots, or ovals. Once the children have begun to make a sun with a clear center, they have progressed beyond the mandala to something new. Their early suns with center marks are not forgotten, however. When children begin to draw "sun-faces," their first humans, they include the center marks for eyes, nose, and mouth. We see sun figures in primitive rock art as well. Early civilizations must have followed the same sequence in their progression of artistic representation.

One of the first pictorial figures that the young child draws naturally is a person. He draws it as one large head/body oval with two lines coming out of the bottom for legs, a line from either side for arms (sometimes these are omitted), circles or dots inside the head circle for eyes, and sometimes a nose and mouth. It looks like the sun he has been drawing, only with two side "rays" for arms, two longer bottom "rays" for legs, and sometimes short top "rays" for hair. All children everywhere seem to draw their first humans in this spontaneous manner. They are known in the art world as "tadpole" people because of the resemblance. Here we are calling them "sun-face humans." (See Figure 6–2.)

To adults unfamiliar with the child's sequence of development, these are strange humans indeed: all head and no body, with arms and legs attached to the head. Surely children age 3 and 4 can see that a person's arms and legs are attached to the body and not the head, you may say. Adult concepts about art, however, have little in common with what is happening with the beginning child artist.

All along adults have looked at the products of children's art (the drawings or paintings) as the most important thing, when to the young child, the process is more important. Children are not drawing a picture at first, but developing a skill. Their efforts progress through an observable sequence of development from general to specific, from holistic to detailed drawings in a spontaneous progression.

Production of a human is the transition to pictorial drawing for most young children. The method they apply is the same one they used for making shapes and symbols. They draw *what they know how to make,* and *not what they see.* Out of their practice with mandalas and suns comes this sun-face human with a few of the "sun's rays" for arms and legs. They do not draw stick figures until later, and then only by copying what adults or older children are drawing.

It is not surprising, in fact, that children's first humans are all face. We remember that even infants attend to this image most frequently. The human brain seems programmed to take in details about faces. This, after all, is the most important part of the human being.

As children first create their circle humans, they do not always repeat their drawings exactly. All children make armless humans at one time or another, even though the youngsters may have drawn arm lines earlier. This behavior does not indicate the children are regressing or are cognitively immature. It may appear only because the proportion of two parallel legs to a head is more appealing alone than with arms sticking out at the sides. Children rarely draw legless humans (Kellogg, 1970, p. 101). The behavior may result from the brain's tendency to overgeneralize in early categories. Later details will be more discriminating.

As children have more practice drawing their early people, they often add hair or hats, hands or fingers, feet or toes. The additions may be lines, circles, or scribbles. Children may identify their persons as being themselves or someone else. The actual size of the person named in the drawing is usually not considered by young children. Instead, they often draw the most important person in the picture as the biggest.

Eventually children will add a body to their head drawings. They often do this by drawing two extremely long legs and putting a horizontal line part way up between them. You may remember that this is the common method they used earlier to draw rectangles. Youngsters often will draw a belly button in the middle of the body. By this time they frequently are drawing other pictorial representations, as well. These representations, as you will note, are also based on the children's previous experience, showing once again how development proceeds in a continuous sequence from the general to the specific, as long as children have the freedom to learn naturally.

If You Have Not Checked This Item: Some Helpful Ideas

■ Draw with Chalk

Colored chalk is very appealing to children if they can grip it and control its tendency to smear. Wrap the upper end with foil or masking tape to make gripping easier. Soft, thick chalk is best. The regular size breaks too easily with the pressure some children apply. Chalk should be used dry at first for children to become used to its properties. Then you can wet either the paper or the chalk for a richer effect. Use either a water-sugar solution (four parts warm water to one part sugar) or use liquid starch, and apply it to the paper for children to draw on with dry chalk. Or use the liquid as a dip for children to wet the chalk but draw on a dry surface. Many children like the rhythm of dipping and drawing. Dry chalk marks on wet paper can also be smeared around to create different effects. Draw on brown paper grocery bags for still a different effect.

■ Draw with Felt-Tip Pens

Water-soluble felt-tip pens are always favorites with children. They seem able to control them more easily than paintbrushes or crayons. The pens' thick size and smooth marking ability make them especially well suited to preschool art. Some marking pens have brush-tip rather than felt-tip points. These have the spreading capacity of watercolor paint. It is not necessary or even desirable to give each child an entire set of pens of all colors. Give the youngsters only a few colors at a time until they express the need for more.

■ Keep Art Activities Spontaneous

Do not use pictures, figure drawings, or models for your children to copy. This is not how spontaneous art develops. Even children who have reached the pictorial stage do not need to copy. You will find that they draw what they know rather than what they see.

■ Read a Book

My Crayons Talk (Hubbard, 1996) tells the sprightly story of a little girl with people-size crayons that say things to her. For example, her purple shouts "Yum, bubble gum." Brown, blue, yellow, gold, silver, red, green, orange, black, white, and pink crayons all have other exciting or funny things to say on every double-page spread. Can your children draw a talking crayon? Accept anything they draw no matter what it looks like.

In *Red Red Red* (Gorbachev, 2007), turtle is hurrying through the town to see something red. Each of the animals follows along asking him one by one is it red roses? No. Watermelon? No. Red socks? No. Red paint? No. Red fire truck? No. When they finally get to the top of the hill turtle tells them to look over there . . . red is coming. It's the beautiful red sunset. Before you turn to that page have the children guess what they think it will be. Preschool children are very much attuned to the sun. You will see a sun in almost every picture they draw. Or maybe more than one! (See Figure 12–2.)

Figure 12–2   The Child Who Drew this Picture Says it is: "My Friends with a Garden and the Sun."

■   Talk with Children about Their Art Through Your Observations

Engel (1996) believes that instead of trying to elicit stories about children's artwork or making evaluative comments, teachers should first observe several aspects of the work and then, when it seems appropriate, talk with the child about these aspects. Such aspects could include its medium, shapes, colors, design, scenes, or purpose. The teacher could mention to the child artist what she sees in the drawing/painting and hope that the child might respond.

For example, she might say: "Ricardo, it looks to me as if you started your painting with a lot of red paint and then covered part of it with yellow. Then you have a row of figures down at the bottom in still a different color. Did you paint them first or last? They really give your picture a balanced look." It is then up to the child to respond or not in any way he chooses.

 COMBINES OBJECTS TOGETHER IN A PICTURE

Once children have discovered the way to draw a person, they will often begin drawing animals as well. Youngsters' first animals are hard to distinguish from humans. It is obvious the animals are based on the same practiced form: a head with eyes, nose, and mouth; a body with arms sticking out from the sides and legs coming out the bottom.

Often the animal is facing front like a person and seems to be standing on two legs. We know the drawing is an animal instead of a person because of the two ears sticking up straight from the top of the head. Sometimes these are pointed like cat ears or circular like mouse ears. These are transition animals.

Eventually the young artist will find a way to make his animal horizontal with an elongated body parallel to the bottom of the paper, four legs in a row from the bottom of the body, a head at one end, and often a tail at the other end. The features of the face are still positioned in a frontal pose and not a profile, even though the animal is positioned with its side showing. Most animal head profiles do not appear in children's drawings until around age 5 or later.

In fact, many children do not draw animals until they go to kindergarten. This behavior—or lack of it—may be due to their progress in their own developmental sequence, but drawing animals also reflects the kindergarten curriculum. Often kindergarten teachers give children outline animals to copy that may, in fact, short-circuit the youngsters' spontaneous development.

Kellogg (1970) argues that many teachers believe a child's self-taught system differs too widely from adult drawing, and therefore the child needs to be taken by the hand and taught how to draw "correctly" (p. 114). Children sometimes abandon art in elementary school because of insufficient teacher approval for their natural art.

The first trees are also transitional drawings based on the human figures children have taught themselves to draw. They look like armless humans with two long legs for the trunk and a circular head for the treetop, which often contains small circles or dots that may be leaves, but look more like fruit. The trees are not drawn to size. They may be similar in height to the humans in the picture or even smaller. A few 4-year-olds may draw trees, but most children are age 5 before they begin these drawings.

As children have practice and freedom to draw, more details evolve on trees. The tops of some trees resemble the sun with the rays as branches and balls at the ends of the branches as leaves. Other children make branches coming out from the trunk like arms on a human. The first flowers are also based on a familiar model: a sun with a stem.

Children who are able to draw representational objects with crayons or felt-tip markers may not be able to do this same level of drawing with a paintbrush and paint if they have not used paint before. It is important to realize children must go through the same developmental stages of manipulation, mastery, and meaning with each new medium they encounter.

As Smith (1993) noted,

> Experimentation with paint usually begins when children enter preschool or kindergarten. Often they have already been drawing with crayons and pencils for some time and can produce lines and shapes in these media readily. Nevertheless, consistent with the laws of development, they must begin at the beginning in paint, with rhythmic, motoric actions. . . . They are not lagging behind, but simply building up the necessary knowledge in the paint itself. (p. 18)

A few of the children in your classroom may begin doing pictorial drawings at age 3 and a few more at age 4. Do not expect all youngsters to do so. Let them progress through their own sequences of development at their own individual rates. Those who do draw pictorially will be using the previously discussed repertoire of figures they have developed. Their drawings will be representations, not reproductions, for the young child draws what he knows, not what he sees.

This principle is especially apparent in children's spontaneous drawings at age 6, when many youngsters go through a stage of so-called X-ray drawings that show both the inside and outside of objects at the same time. The children's drawings depict things as the youngsters know them, rather than just what they can see. People are shown inside houses without walls as in a cutaway drawing, for example.

The children in your classroom probably will not have reached this stage, nor will they have developed a baseline in their drawings much before age 5. Objects are still free-floating on their art papers just as their first spontaneous letters are. This different perspective used by young children is sometimes used by adult artists as well.

Children also interpret their pictorial drawings differently from adults. Youngsters often do not start out to draw a particular thing. Instead they describe their art more by the way it turns out than by what they had in mind. The way it turns out may have more to do with the materials they are using than anything else. Runny paint in easel drawings may remind the youngsters of smoke, rain, or fire, for instance, so they draw a picture of rain or a fire.

On the other hand, some children purposefully draw a picture of the post office that the class visited on a field trip. The picture will look, of course, just like the building shape they have learned to do spontaneously, and not at all like the post office itself. Children first draw buildings by combining mostly rectangular shapes in various ways and not by looking at buildings. The drawing often has a door in the middle and at least two square windows above it. Roofs may be flat or pointed and often have a chimney with smoke coming out. The drawing catches the essence of the building, not the reality. Some 4-year-olds also draw cars and trucks, as well as boats and planes. Often it is hard to tell the difference between early cars and trucks.

Once children have a repertoire of figures that the adults around them seem to accept, they will begin to put the figures together into scenes. The size and color of their objects will not be realistic. The more important the object or person, the larger the child will make it. Colors will have little relation to the object being depicted. They depend more on the particular brush the child happens to pick up, or a color the child happens to favor at the moment. Objects will be free-floating, as mentioned, and not anchored to a baseline. But the effect will be balanced and pleasing, nevertheless.

Children who verbalize about their art may tell you things about their drawings that have little to do with what your eyes seem to show you. The youngsters must be speaking about an inner vision of their world, you decide. You are right, of course. And from inner visions come creative ideas. Let's support this beginning urge toward creativity in all children by giving it the freedom to grow spontaneously.

If You Have Not Checked This Item: Some Helpful Ideas

■   Add New Art Activities

Your children may want to try drawing with liquid glue from a plastic squeeze bottle. They may want to draw with a pencil or other marker first and then follow the lines with

Figure 12–3   After a Science Project on Planets and a Field Trip to a Strawberry Patch, this 5-Year-Old Child Drew "Strawberries are Out of this World."

glue. Or they can try the glue without guidelines. Because glue is transparent when it dries, you may want to add food coloring to the bottles. This liquid glue is a much more free-flowing medium; children will need to play with it for a while to see how it works and how to control it just as they did the first time they used paint. They will need to squeeze and move the bottle at the same time, a trick of coordination that may be difficult for some. Don't expect pictorial designs from glue drawing.

■ Encourage Children to Draw About Field Trips

Not all your children can or want to draw pictorially. But for those who do, you can suggest they draw a picture about a trip you have taken together. Children find it satisfying to be able to represent things they know about. They can tell about the things in words, have you write down their words, or record their words on tape. But it is also good to make a drawing or build a block structure about new things they have encountered. Their products help you as a teacher to find out what is important to them and how they conceptualize the new ideas they have gained. Figure 12–3.

■ Encourage Children to "Document" Their Science Projects by Drawing Pictures

In addition to use in their journals, children's drawings can also be used to document their science projects. They can draw whatever it is they are doing for their projects in either single pictures or a series of pictures or panels. For example, children who are planting seeds can draw pictures of the soil, the seeds, and the plants in their stages of growth. Have them explain what the pictures show while you print the words they say at the bottom of the picture. They may even want to create their own picture books of their projects. In the Reggio Emilia schools in Italy and the United States, art is used as a language to reinforce the art concepts children are learning.

As Althouse, Johnson, and Mitchell (2003) explained,

Documentation panels display the child's work with great care and attention to both the content and aesthetic aspects of the display. The documentation describes in the child's own words—and sometimes the teacher's as well—the images, ideas, and processes represented by the child's art work. This form of documentation makes visible the child's learning, since it often shows the processes of the art experience from beginning to end. (p. 10)

■ Read a Book

Peter's Picture (Gorbachev, 2000) is the story of little Peter Bear who draws a big orange flower for his parents, but on the way home he shows it to a series of animal friends who have their own silly ideas of what he should do with it. When he finally gets home his mother admires it, and his father rushes right down to the basement and makes a wonderful frame for it.

Planting a Rainbow (Ehlert, 1988) tells a simple story in large, bold type of a little girl and her mother who plant bulbs and seeds for flowers that grow in rainbow colors. Brilliant flower cutouts against a white background, with color-coded pages of flowers in the center of the book, clearly display the shapes and color categories of the blooms. Be sure you use this book for reading only, and not as a model from which children would be expected to draw their flowers. Young children's art does not evolve from copying models.

OBSERVING, RECORDING, AND INTERPRETING ART SKILLS

If you find that most of your 3- and 4-year-olds have not progressed beyond the random marks or scribbles stages, ask yourself if your program has allowed the children the opportunity, the freedom, and the time to pursue art on their own. Is the children's art truly their own, or have teachers intervened to help them draw a house or animal "correctly"?

As Gellens (1996) noted,

Children's art must reflect the child. Art must be the child's own work from beginning to end. A teacher's hands should never touch the artwork. The art activity must meet the child's developmental level and offer a risk-free environment where the child can create. It must help the child move from one level to the next in a pressure free atmosphere that is fun and exciting. It must be totally child produced. (p. 7)

Do you have at least one easel in the classroom set up and ready to use? Do you have an art area where children can get their own supplies and do their own work without teacher directions? Give children this opportunity and freedom to explore and experiment with art on their own. Then have them apply their skills to illustrating their journal writing and to documenting their science projects.

DEVELOPING MUSIC SKILLS

Most young children love music and respond readily to its sounds and rhythms. Music in the preschool classroom makes them feel happy. Whether it comes from tapes, CDs, instruments, or singing voices, its sounds and rhythms give the whole atmosphere a feeling of release, excitement, and something different happening. It is the essence of creativity. Shore (2005) tells us:

> A wide variety of research and anecdotal evidence suggests that music can do more than change our moods; it can actually change our brains. (p. 4)

Snyder (1997) goes on to say that music is the most direct route to thinking, because it requires neither words nor symbols to be perceived (p. 165). She describes how Frank Wilson, a neuroscientist who registered brain scans of children performing certain tasks, reports that: "When they read words, the language center of the brain lights up. But when they read music, the brain lights up like a Christmas tree!" (p. 168).

Music can help young children synthesize experiences, transition into new activities, calm down during naptime, build self-esteem, and improve performance in language and math (Shore & Strasser, 2006, p. 62). When children sing, they develop the rhythmic patterns of language and recognize the sounds of rhyming words. It taps into the right hemisphere of the brain, which operates both music and memory functions. It connects the right hemisphere with the left hemisphere, which operates speaking and reading. The steady beat of singing develops pathways in the brain that seem to be essential for learning, especially related to reading (Snyder, 1997). Hap Palmer (2001) has even used singing to teach young children to read (pp. 13–17).

With all of these advantages to its credit, music surely should be considered an important part of the early childhood curriculum. Unfortunately, this often is not the case. Too many teachers do not realize the importance of music in child development. Too many teachers may feel awkward and inadequate engaging in musical activities with children. Society seems to support them when it considers music and art education to be frills rather than necessities. Now that you know its importance, it is up to you as a teacher of young children to include music as an important curriculum component. It is also up to you to overcome any reluctance you may feel about using music with your children. Let's start with rhythm first, in which you and all the children can become easily and happily involved.

 ## MOVES LEGS AND FEET IN RHYTHM TO A BEAT

Preschool children's acquisition of musical skills crosses several areas of development, including physical, cognitive, language, and creative. But because music itself involves both rhythm and sound (tempo and tone), we will look first a young children's development of rhythm.

All humans are rhythmical beings, whether or not we recognize the fact. Rhythm, in fact, is the essence of our life: witness the beating of our heart and the breathing of our lungs. It is not so surprising to find, therefore, that even infants can make rhythmical responses with their arms, hands, legs, and feet. These claps, kicks, or wavings seem to be triggered by internal stimuli and not by external sounds or motions, although Cratty (1986) has mentioned that in cultures where dance is important, infants too young to stand have been observed picking up the beat of nearby adult dancers with their own bodies and limbs (p. 257).

Nevertheless, the first voluntary rhythmical movements of young children are stimulated by sounds rather than visual cues. As with other physical development, the young child's rhythmical development proceeds in an observable sequence. First to appear are movement of arms/hands and then legs/feet that can follow a regular and rather slow rhythmic beat. Next, the young child's movements are able to replicate an irregular beat. Finally, children can learn to follow sound cues of different intensities. Horizontal movements are acquired before up-and-down movements of the arms. Rhythmic movements of one leg or one arm appear before the ability to move both limbs rhythmically.

Regardless of development, most young children love to dance and sing. They will make attempts to imitate any rhythmic activity around them. Young children also will follow their own internal rhythms with moving and singing on their own. If we want children to continue these movements, the next move is ours. Adults who notice young children moving rhythmically must compliment them, encourage them to continue their movements, and call others' attention to the children's accomplishments.

Children very quickly pick up on the values of adults around them. If the adults show interest in children's dancing, the youngsters will continue to dance. On the other hand, if adults disregard the action or reprimand children for moving around so much, the children will stop. You need to provide the stimulus in your program for young children to move rhythmically. That means you must schedule such activities early in the life of your classroom. Be creative yourself and think of the curriculum areas that might include dance.

Dance

After reading several of the dance books listed next to small groups, find out who would like to try one of the dances. For ballet, play one of the numbers from the *Nutcracker Suite.* Tell or read children the story. Then have a few children at a time stand and sway to the music. Can anyone raise up on his toes? Gellens (2005) says that children love to move to music, and that dancing stimulates all regions of the brain. She suggests that pairs of children face each other and mirror the other's movement (p. 19). They can swing arms or hold hands and move to the music.

If You Have Not Checked This Item: Some Helpful Ideas

■ Read a Book

In *Ballerina Dreams* (Thomson, 2007), a true story, five little girls have always wanted to do ballet dancing just like other little girls (one is 3, one 4, two 5, and one 7). They come together in a physical therapy class because each of them has a muscle disorder from cerebral palsy that makes movements difficult for them. But their therapist decides to help their dream come true if they will work hard with her and five young helpers. The girls wear leg braces, use a cane or a walker, but all are finally able to perform ballet pieces from the *Nutcracker Suite* and *Swan Lake* at a recital. Their story is illustrated with wonderful real photos of each of them in their tutus and tiaras against the pink pages of the book. After reading this book take special pains to see that each of your children takes part in creative movement and dance in any way they can.

In *The Jellybeans and the Big Dance* (Numeroff, 2008), Emily and three other little animal characters attend a dance class, but only Emily really wants to learn the dance the teacher is teaching them: "Oh, Little Bugs." Finally Emily calls them "the dancing jellybeans" and persuades them to choose a bug they like. This they perform in style, dressed as their favorite bugs. If you are looking at insects in science, what a great way to make them come alive.

In *Josephine Wants to Dance* (French, 2007), Josephine is a kangaroo in Australia who wants more than anything to dance a ballet. Her little brother Joey tells her that kangaroos don't dance, they hop. But when the prima ballerina twists her ankle, Josephine is ready. She leaps through the open theater window and onto the stage. She has learned the role and can jump higher than any dancer the director has ever seen. So they make her a tutu and ballet shoes and she dances the ballet to claps and cheers from everyone.

For children who may have trouble dancing, read them *Giraffes Can't Dance* (Andreae, 1999) about Gerald the tall giraffe who wants to join the other animals in the annual Jungle Dance. When he enters the ring to dance they all make fun of him for his clumsy movements. But a little cricket tells the depressed giraffe that sometimes when you're different you need a different song. So Gerald tries swaying to the grass and bending to the trees, and soon he is dancing.

For children who are not ready or interested in dancing, have them sway in their seats to the background music you play while reading this book. Playing music to reading like this also helps children's memories.

In *Hilda Must Be Dancing* (Wilson, 2004), Hilda Hippo loves to dance so much she never stops. But she doesn't know what it sounds like to the other jungle animals: crash, smash, thumpity bump, boom, bang, bash! Children are convulsed by the hilarious rhymes as Hilda's thumping in her favorite pair of heels "knocks bananas in gooey heaps, shaken from their peels." The animals try to get her to take up knitting or try some singing or take up swimming. She finally does, and soon her water ballet absorbs the thumping sounds and delights them all, even Hilda. Children love to imitate the thumping, bumping moves that Hilda makes.

Twist with a Burger, Jitter with a Bug (Lowery, 1995) has colorful cartoonlike characters dancing mambos, snapping to raps, swaying to the tune, and polkaing after supper with a fork and spoon. The rhythm and rhyming of the book's exuberant words will soon have children on their feet to act out the dancing. Play different kinds of music every time you read this book. Can the children move their legs or sway to the beat as you read?

MOVES ARMS AND HANDS IN RHYTHM TO A BEAT

Here is another way for preschool children to develop rhythm. Most have participated in hand-clapping activities from infancy. They have imitated their mother doing pat-a-cake and imitated others around them who applaud a performance by clapping. Now, in this item, they are asked to perform a musical activity with their hands: moving their arms and hands to a beat. This can mean clapping with their hands or beating out a rhythm with sticks, blocks, or percussion instruments held in the hands. Simple. You can do this too.

As discussed in the previous item, rhythm is a natural part of all of us. Our heart goes on beating whether or not we think about it. Our fingers may tap out a rhythm automatically, but can preschool children clap their hands in rhythm to a beat created outside their body? They can if their physical skills have developed normally and they have had practice clapping in rhythm.

As they develop physically, arm control occurs before hand control, and hand control occurs before finger control. A second sequence of development begins with control of one arm/hand independent of the other (as in waving). Next comes the simultaneous use of both arms/hands (as in clapping), and finally comes alternate movements of two arms/hands (as in drumming).

Although clapping ability appears early in a child's development, the ability to clap with control comes later. Two-year-olds, for instance, enjoy clapping, but usually cannot clap in a pattern without a great deal of help and practice. The concept of clapping in rhythm or clapping out the syllables of a name is beyond most of them. Three-, 4-, and 5-year-old children also may have some difficulty following a clapping pattern. Yet most of them can learn to clap the syllables of their names and enjoy repeating the activity because it is personal.

Once they have reached this maturity, children need to have practice to follow external rhythms. The creative movement activities discussed in Chapter 7 and here under "dance" gave the children practice in moving their feet and bodies to the rhythm that you, the teacher, provide with your hands. Now it is their turn. When you sing songs or play tapes or CDs in your classroom, give children practice clapping to the rhythm. Or use familiar folk songs to practice clapping to different beats.

If You Have Not Checked This Item: Some Helpful Ideas

■ Try Name Clapping

Focusing on a child's name is the surest way to interest a young egocentric child in almost any activity. At circle time or small-group time you can introduce "name clapping," clapping out the syllables in each child's name as the children say the name aloud. Make the activity more interesting by adding other words, such as "hello" or "my name is." Now the children can chant and clap: "Hel-lo-Chris-to-pher," "My name is Sar-ah." As the children become more adept, add their last names to this clapping activity. "My name is Mel-is-sa-Brad-ley."

■ Use a Tape Recorder

Children may want their own clapped rhythms recorded on the tape recorder and then played back for others in the group to try to imitate. Have each child say his or her name and then clap it out in rhythm.

■ Have a Music Play Center

Set up your music area as a play center where children can engage in music as play. Change the materials from time to time. Have all kinds of sound makers and shakers that can be played with the hands. Another time add sound blocks, clackers, maracas, and rain sticks.

■ Read a Book

Summer Beat (Franco, 2007) features a little girl, Em, skateboarding to meet a little boy, Joe, along with her dog Rusty. It is the Fourth of July, and the two of them play together as summer noises make beats in the background: the lawn sprinkler, the hammock, the picnic, chomping corn-on-the-cob, spitting out watermelon seeds, joining a three-legged race, throwing water balloons, lighting sparklers, and watching fireworks. What other summer sounds do your children know?

PLAYS INSTRUMENTS

Moving the two arms/hands alternately in a vertical motion, such as beating on a drum, indicates a more mature development of a child's arm/hand control than does clapping. Young children enjoy beating on drums, pans, wooden blocks, and almost anything that will make a noise. For beaters they can use their hands (fingers, palms, knuckles, fists), drumsticks, mallets, ladles, or anything else they can pound with. Fill your classroom music center with drums and beaters.

The developmental sequence of drumming with the hands follows that of clapping. But children will have more success in beating a drum in a particular rhythm if they first have had many clapping experiences. When your children demonstrate that they can clap in rhythm, it is time to introduce the drum.

Instruments used in preschool programs fall into the same categories of those used by professionals: sound makers, rhythm, melody, and harmony instruments. Sound-makers for young children include pots, pans, glasses, seed pods, stones, and cans with seeds. Rhythm instruments include rhythm sticks, tone blocks, coconut shells, bells, triangles, gongs, cymbals, tambourines, sand blocks, rattles, maracas, and drums, to name a few. Melody instruments include xylophone, marimba, tone bells, tonette, flutophone, and ocarina. Harmony instruments include autoharp, harmonica, guitar, ukulele, banjo, mandolin, accordion, piano, and electric keyboard.

Rhythm instruments such as the drum need to be taken seriously in the preschool: that is, a drum is not a toy, but a real instrument, and should be treated as such. Perhaps because teachers do not understand that rhythm instruments are serious instruments used in real bands, they allow children to treat these instruments as toys. Instead, each instrument should be introduced to children separately, showing them how to use it properly and limits on using it improperly. In this way the children get the most from the experience; they learn how to use the instruments, to appreciate the sound it makes, and to practice the physical skills the instrument affords them.

Unfortunately, rhythm instruments are often used in "rhythm bands" with all the instruments played at once as the children march around to music. The youngsters, of course, may have fun with such an activity, but it adds little to their enjoyment of music, their skill development, or their appreciation for the instruments they hold (whose name they often don't know). Instead, children tend to bang as loud as they can all at once creating a cacophony of sound—noise—which drowns out the sounds of the individual instruments, the music, and the rhythm they are supposed to be following.

Drums come in all sizes and shapes. Some are intended to be played with the hands; some are played with two drumsticks, and some are played with one. Constructive Playthings (1-800-448-4115) features cultural drums and shakers, such as double-headed frame drum from Peru, single-headed frame drum from Java, talking drum from Africa, Chinese tom tom, Caribbean bongo, Chinese gong, seed pod shaker from Zimbabwe, shekere from Ghana, juju nut arm shaker from Ghana, rain dance rattle from Guatemala, and wooden frog guiro from Thailand.

Commercial drums are usually wooden or plastic with a skin or plastic head over one or both ends. Have several drums and drumsticks available in the music center. Take time to introduce their use to a few children at a time rather than merely putting them on a shelf. Talk to them about each drum and how to use it. Let them try each one. Put on music and let them try to keep a beat with their drum. They can use drumsticks or their hands. Pass the drums around until everyone has a chance. Keep this activity going for several days with different music.

If You Have Not Checked This Item: Some Helpful Ideas

■ Send Drum Messages

Children enjoy sending drumbeat messages. If they have learned to clap out names by syllables, they will be able to send drum messages the same way. Let them try sending their names ("My-name-is-Ri-car-do") with drumbeats. Can the other children guess what they are saying on the drum?

■ Make Drums

Various types of drum can be made, depending on the material. Use large cans, ice cream containers, oatmeal boxes, round plastic containers, coffee cans, margarine tubs, or wooden or metal buckets for the body of the drum. Children can decorate the container and drum on its head. But for a realistic drumhead, you can use animal parchments (from music stores), goatskin, heavy plastic, or canvas. Remove one or both ends of the can or container. Cut one or two circular head pieces larger than the container opening. Punch holes around the edge of the drumhead material about 2 inches apart. Soak the parchment or goatskin in water for half an hour. Place the drum head material on either end of the drum body and lace tightly together with cord or rawhide laces.

To make drumsticks, glue small rubber balls on the ends of sticks such as pencils or wooden dowels. Wrap cloth around the ends of wooden ladles, or inset sticks into spools and wrap cloth around the spools.

■ Read a Book

Drum, Chavi, Drum (Dole, 2003) tells the story of the girl Chavi, in a Spanish-American neighborhood in Miami, who is determined to play the conga drum in the Calle Ocho festival. But girls don't play drums everyone tells her. That doesn't stop Chavi. She practices hand-tapping on windows and car hoods in this bilingual book, and finally does drum on a float in the parade dressed as Zorro in black hat, mask, and cape. Her drumming is extraordinary and when the crowd discovers "he" is a "she," they clap even louder and dance to her drumming.

Jazz on a Saturday Night (Dillon & Dillon, 2007). The great jazz musicians of a bygone era play again on the pages of this book (and in the CD that accompanies it): Miles Davis on the trumpet, Max Roach on the drums, Charlie Parker on the sax, John Coltrane on his sax, Thelonious Monk on the piano, Stanley Clarke on the bass, and Ella Fitzgerald singing on each of the double-page spreads. The CD introduces the instruments and features an original jazz number your children will want to move to.

Rock-a-Baby Band (McMullan, 2004) has ten little babies shake, rattle, and roll through the pages of this book (also accompanied by a CD). The babies play drums, rattles a tambourine, maracas, bells, spoons, pan lids, and toy guitar. Then they form a conga line and parade outside on the playground. Play the CD and have your children sing and march along.

 ## SINGS WITH GROUP OR BY HIM-/HERSELF

Children who are not speaking in the classroom or who are speaking only one or two words can sing. Strangely enough, singing, which is controlled by the right hemisphere of the brain, can occur even when speaking, which is controlled by the left hemisphere, is limited. In addition, children who do not speak English can sing songs in English. They may not understand the words, but they can sing or chant them along with the other children. Even shy, nonverbal children often join in singing before they have the courage to speak in the classroom.

With this information in mind, you should be filling your program with songs and chants. (See Chapter 10.) Children who get caught up in the joy of music will

*Even children who do not speak
English can sing English words,
here with a karaoke machine.*

join in. Other children may hesitate at first, but may soon find the musical activities
you provide to be so contagious they cannot resist. Do not force any child to participate. Invite everyone, and have such a good time yourself, no one will want to be left
out.

To teach children songs, you need to repeat them over and over on a daily basis with
everyone joining in. Sing morning greeting songs, transition songs, finger plays at circle
time, singing games in the large motor area; songs for seasonal holidays, songs for rainy
days, sunny days, snowy days; songs about animals, and especially, songs about the children themselves. Use nursery rhyme favorites of your own and make up words to familiar
tunes, using the children's names whenever possible, and you will soon create an interested
group of young singers.

Tapes and CDs are fine for occasional use, but give your children a language
boost by helping them sing their own words to songs and chants. You need not be a
good singer yourself. The children will never know the difference. If you cannot sing,
then chant with the children in unison or in a monotone, and clap your hands. For
example:

(Tune: "Are You Sleeping?")

Where is Carmela?	*Very nice to see you,*
Where is Carmela?	*Very nice to see you,*
Here she is!	*Come and play,*
Here she is!	*Come and play.*

Other tunes you can use with your own words include:

"Row, Row, Row Your Boat"
"This Old Man"
"Here We Go Round the Mulberry Bush"
"On Top of Spaghetti"

Learn folk songs from different cultures through CDs, songbooks, the children themselves, and their family members. Invite family members to visit the class and sing songs in their home language. English-speaking children can sing along, too, just as second-language children can sing songs with English words. All it takes is repetition. Sing the songs over and over. Children are geared to enjoy such repetition. Remember the mastery stage of exploratory play?

Still another opportunity for singing is singing games. They ask for children to listen to the words of the song and then follow the actions called for. You may need to play tape or CD at first so they children can hear the directions. After repeating the singing game many times, children will be able to sing and act out the song without the tape. Traditional singing games can be sung and acted out without tapes or CDs.

Some children may enjoy the song storybooks described in Chapter 11 so much, they will even sing them for you by themselves after the group has finished a song.

This child is singing the song from a song storybook.

If You Have Not Checked This Item: Some Helpful Ideas

■ Have a TV Show

Have a few volunteers put on a pretend TV show for the others in the class. They can sing, drum, or play another instrument. Use your camcorder or tape recorder. Then ask for volunteers in the audience to perform. If you have a karaoke machine, you should have plenty of volunteers. Play back your tape and ask others to join in.

■ Sing Questions and Answers

Sing questions to a group of children and have them sing back an answer. For example, sing: "How are you feeling today?" They can sing the answer: "We're feeling fine"

■ Sing Directions

Sing short direction songs and have others join in. For example, sing:

(Tune: "Farmer in the Dell")

It's time to pick up blocks,	*It's time to pick up trucks . . . etc.*
It's time to pick up blocks	*It's time to go to lunch . . . etc.*
Come on everyone,	*It's time to go outside . . . etc.*
It's time to pick up blocks.	*It's time to say goodbye . . . etc.*

(Tune: "Are you Sleeping?")

Are you hungry?	*Are you sleepy? etc.*
Are you hungry?	*Are you ready? etc*
Time to eat,	*Put your coat on . . . etc.*
Time to eat,	
Come and take a seat now,	
Come and take a seat now,	
Sit right down,	
Sit right down.	

■ Read a Book

Dooby Dooby Moo (Cronin, 2006) has Farmer Brown's animals acting up again. This time they decide to enter the talent show at the county fair, where the first prize is a trampoline. Farmer Brown spies on them. The cows sing "Dooby, dooby, moo." ("Twinkle Twinkle Little Star.") The sheep sing "Fa, la, la, la, baa." ("Home on the Range.") The pigs were going to dance, but they fall asleep. Duck sings "Quack, quack, quaaaak" ("Born to Be Wild.") Next time Farmer Brown spies on them he hears: Dooby, dooby, BOING! You know what they won! Can you have an animal talent show with your children pretending to be animals singing?

In *Take Me Out of the Bathtub and Other Silly Dilly Songs* (Katz, 2001), fourteen wonderful wacky songs appear on every other page to familiar tunes such as "Take Me Out to the Ballgame," "I've Been Working on the Railroad," and "Row, Row, Row Your Boat." With illustrations as wild as the words, your children will love singing them.

LEARNING ACTIVITIES

1. Use the Child Development Checklist for art skills as a screening tool to observe all the children in your classroom. For children with checks at the higher levels in the sequence of art skill development, compare their scores in cognitive development, especially in "Sorts objects by shape/color." Can you draw any conclusions from this comparison?

2. Based on your screening survey, choose one or two children who have not shown much interest or development in art, and try to involve them in an art activity. Use one of the other checklist areas in which they have shown interest and skills as the basis for the art activity. Record the results.

3 Set up your art area so children can use it without adult help or direction. Make a running record of what happened in this area before you changed the setup and afterward.

4. Choose a child who needs help in moving to rhythm. Involve the child using one or more of the rhythm ideas from this chapter. Discuss the results.

5. Observe and record which ones of the children join in the singing activities. For children who are reluctant to join in, read them song storybooks with a small group, and have the group sing along. Or have a "puppet singalong." Does this help them get involved?

SUGGESTED READINGS

Beaty, J. J. (2008). *Skills for preschool teachers* (8th ed.). Upper Saddle River, NJ: Merrill/Prentice Hall.

Cherry, C. (1972). *Creative art for the developing child*. Belmont, CA: Fearon.

Drew, W. F., & Rankin, B. (2004). Promoting creativity for life using open-ended materials. *Young Children, 59*(4), 38–45.

Edwards, L. C. (2006). *The creative arts: A process approach for teachers and children* (4th ed.). Upper Saddle River, NJ: Merrill/Prentice Hall.

Greata, J. (2006). *An introduction to music in early childhood education*. Clifton Park, NY: Cengage.

Kemple, K. M., Batey, J. J., & Hartle, L. C. (2004). Music play: Creating centers for musical play and exploration. *Young Children, 59*(4), 30–37.

Loomis, K. Lewis, C., & Blumenthal, R. (2007). Children learn to think and create through art. *Young Children, 62*(5), 79–98.

Moore, T. (2002). If you teach young children, you can sing. *Young Children, 57*(4), 84–85.

CHILDREN'S BOOKS

Andreae, G. (1999). *Giraffes can't dance*. New York: Orchard.

Cronin, D. (2006). *Dooby dooby moo*. New York: Atheneum.

Dillon, L., & Dillon, D. (2007). *Jazz on a Saturday night*. New York: The Blue Sky Press.*

Dole, M. L. (2003). *Drum, Chavi, drum*. San Francisco, CA: Children's Book Press.*

Franco, B. (2007). *Summer beat*. New York: Margaret K. McElderry Books.

French, J. (2007). *Josephine wants to dance*. New York: Abrams.

Ehlert, L. (1988). *Planting a rainbow*. San Diego: Harcourt Brace.

Gorbachev, V. (2000). *Peter's picture*. New York: North-South Books.

Gorbachev, V. (2007). *Red red red.* New York: Philomel Books.

Hubbard, P. (1996). *My crayons talk.* New York: Henry Holt.

Katz, A. (2001). *Take me out of the bathtub and other silly dilly songs.* New York: McElderry.

Lowery, L. (1995). *Twist with a burger, jitter with a bug.* Boston: Houghton Mifflin.*

McMullen, K. (2004). *Rock-a-baby band.* Boston: Little, Brown & Co.*

Numeroff, L., & Evans, N. (2007). *The Jellybeans and the big dance.* New York: Abrams.

Thompson, L. (2007). *Ballerina dreams.* New York: Feiwel and Friends.*

Wilson, K. (2004). *Hilda must be dancing.* New York: Margaret K. McElderry Books.

---

*Multicultural.

13 Dramatic Play Skills

____ Does pretend play by him/herself

____ Assigns roles or takes assigned roles

____ Needs particular props to do pretend play

____ Takes on characteristics and actions related to role

____ Can pretend with imaginary objects

____ Uses language for creating and sustaining the plot

____ Enacts Exciting, danger-packed themes

____ Uses elaborate themes, ideas, details

DEVELOPING DRAMATIC PLAY SKILLS

A second important aspect of creativity in young children is their development of imagination. For young children, imagination is the ability to pretend or make-believe, to take a role other than their own, to create fanciful situations, or to act out a fantasy of their making. Imagining is a function of the right hemisphere of the brain, and as we know, young children are right-brain dominated. Thus, most young children seem to engage in a great deal of imagining before the age of 7. It is a type of activity that many adults fail to see as significant in the development of the child, because they do not do it themselves. But early childhood professionals have come to recognize children's imagining as one of the most effective means for promoting development of intellectual skills, social skills, language, and most especially, creativity.

One of the basic tools for creating is imagining, the ability to see a picture in your mind's eye. This ability allows you to tap into memories of the past and reform them as possibilities for the present or future. Children's make-believe relies heavily on this capacity to draw on such internal images and to create new ones. The Singers, who have done extensive research and writing on children's imaginative play, believe that imagining is essential to the development of intellectual and language skills as well. Children remember ideas and words they have actually experienced because the youngsters can associate the ideas with pictures in their minds (Singer & Singer, 1977, p. 6). This association reveals why children need to have many real experiences. Otherwise, they have few images stored in their brains to draw on.

A child must utilize previous experiences in new and different ways. She extracts the essence of a familiar experience such as getting ready for bed, and applies it creatively to a pretend activity such as putting to bed her doll, who doesn't want to go. Or she may take the role of the doll herself as well as that of the frustrated mother, who is losing her patience with the stubborn doll.

The child experiments with the situation, playing it this way one time and that way another. If a peer joins in, there is another point of view to reckon with. If the original player strays too far from her role, she may lose it to a player with more definite ideas on how a mother should act. Or she may switch to a different role herself and try on yet another set of characteristics. She learns to recall fragments of past experiences and combine them in novel ways, adding original dialog, fresh nuances to her characterizations, and new directions to her plots. No playwright ever had better practice.

In addition to being her own creative playwright, she is also the actor, the director, the audience for other actors, and an interacter with others, whether she plays her role or steps out of it to make "aside" comments on progress of the spontaneous play. Just as with every other aspect of her development, she is developing her own creativity when she has the freedom and time to participate in imaginative play.

Imaginative play like this in early childhood programs is called dramatic play or sociodramatic play by psychologists. It is described by Edwards (2006) as:

> play that involves social role-playing with others and refers to children's pretend play when two or more children assume related roles and interact with each other. (p. 192)

> She goes on to say that sociodramatic play and creativity enjoy a common thread because both processes are dependent on a child's ability to use symbols and "must be honored as a rich and complex process that facilitates the development of a child's creative potential" (p. 193).

This time the knowledge children create is about real life and the other actors in it: how they behave, how they respond to stressful situations, how they carry out their work roles, how they speak, and how they interact with one another. Adult observers of dramatic play find that most of the make-believe play of children centers around the social problems of the adults with whom children have close contacts. Common themes include the family and home; doctors and hospitals; work and professions; school; and dramatizations of escape, rescue, and superheroes.

Playing at life is not the inconsequential activity many adults seem to think it is. Children who have had extensive practice with dramatic play are often those who are most successful in life as adults. Children who have not been allowed or encouraged to engage in such play may be at a disadvantage as adults, for they have missed an important grounding in social, intellectual, and creative skills.

Chapter 5 discussed dramatic play as it applied to the development of children's social skills in solitary, parallel, and group play. This chapter will look at the same phenomenon

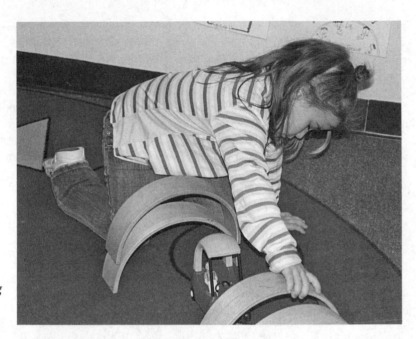

Children pretend about everything they do, both alone and with others.

in relation to the development of creativity in young children. For you to discover where the children in your classroom are in the sequence of their development, assess each child using the eight items of the Child Development Checklist as you observe children pretending in the dramatic play area, at the water table, in the block area, at the wood bench, with science materials, at the painting easels, or on the playground.

You will find young children pretend about everything they do, both alone and with others. Tap into this rich vein of creativity in young children, and you may see life and the world from a completely new and fresh perspective: the *what-if* point of view. This *what-if* perspective is the true magic of childhood, the belief that children can make life anything they want it to be.

Adults know from the hard facts of reality that life cannot be changed so easily—or can it? What if we also believed we could really make life anything we wanted it to be? Does believing make it so? Children act as if this idea were true. Is there a way we can help them develop into adults who will actually be able to make their adult lives come out the way they want them to? Is there a way we can preserve the child in ourselves so we can do the same? Take a hard look at the developmental sequence in imaginative play that follows to see what you need to do to keep this spark alive in children and to rekindle its essence in your own life.

Observing Children in Dramatic Play

The importance of dramatic play for children's development of thinking, speaking, forming relationships, seeing things from another's perspective, and learning social and prosocial skills puts it at the top of the list of daily curriculum activities. But there is another aspect of dramatic play that is sometimes overlooked. For teachers to observe children in dramatic play is one of the best methods for learning about the development of their children. Roskos and Christie (2001) pointed out that it provides a lens through which adults can witness children's knowledge, feelings, and abilities and also "makes visible children's thinking" (p. 66).

If teachers view dramatic play not just as an activity, but as an expression of children's thinking, they can begin to see how children understand their world. Hatcher and Petty (2004) ask you to put on your "x-ray vision" to examine what dramatic play reveals about children's concept development (p. 79). As you observe children's development of dramatic play skills, look for the links between play and concept development.

 ## DOES PRETEND PLAY BY HIM/HERSELF

This checklist item describes one of the earliest of the imaginative play behaviors in young children. Incredibly enough, it appears as early as 1 year (Smilansky, 1968 p. 10). By 18 months, infants may go through the imaginary routine of feeding themselves with an empty spoon and cup, and even saying "Yummy!" The Singers (1977) believe this tendency to play or to replay past events through imagery is one of the basic capacities of the human brain (p. 3). At first the pretend actions involve only the child himself; later they may involve toys, dolls, and eventually people.

The youngsters do not take a role in this play. They are themselves. As Davidson (1996) noted,

> When children first begin pretending, they will engage in single acts of symbolic play, as in the case of a child pretending to drink from a toy glass. Often very young children will pretend with regard to action, without necessarily taking on another role. The child may care for the baby by rocking it, without pretending to be a mother or a father. (p. 32)

This young child is showing an observer she has developed the concept of "you take care of a baby by rocking it."

By 2 years of age, most children spend a great deal of time at home or in a toddler program replaying fragments of everyday experience, if given the chance. Pieces of familiar routines are repeated with little change or little effort to expand them into a longer sequence. The toddler will put the baby to bed by putting the doll in the cradle, covering it, and saying, "Night-night." Then the toddler will pick up the doll and begin the routine all over again. Once a particular routine is established with a 2-year-old, it seems to become quite rigid, almost like a ritual.

Words are not all that important in the pretending of 2-year-olds, however. The youngsters use them sparingly, mainly to accompany actions or for sound effects. Once these youngsters get an idea for pretend play, they try to put it into action immediately. They do not set the stage with words, or search for appropriate props. Props may be used, though, if they are available. Two-year-olds use props realistically, for the most part. Dishes are used realistically for eating, and not as a pretend steering wheel or a flying saucer. Because these youngsters are also impulsive in their behavior, props can influence the type of pretend play they engage in. A toy broom can inspire them to sweep, for instance, even though they had no previous plans for cleaning.

The first imaginative play of youngsters mainly concerns chores and routines, such as eating, going to bed, caring for the baby, talking on the phone, turning on television, shopping, visiting grandma, driving the car, and getting gas for the car. Two-year-olds are very serious about it and take offense if adults make fun of their sometimes comical modes of pretending. Keep track of these play routines for each of your children from time to time and note what new concepts they have learned over time.

Doll play is also a frequent activity for both boys and girls of this age. Dolls are usually undressed, laid in a box or bed, and covered completely over with a piece of cloth in a very ritualized routine. These children are not pretending to be mother or anyone other than themselves because they have not yet developed a perspective-taking concept, that is, the ability to see something from another point of view.

The play of 2-year-olds is frequently solitary and rarely involves more than one other player. They and their age-mates have not yet developed the social skills for coming together in a common endeavor. When two children this age play together, one usually imitates the other. However, others will join in if they see one child doing something, and sometimes a wild melee ensues. The pretend play of children this young is brief at best, and it may disintegrate suddenly into running and squealing if other children are around.

Young 3-year-olds who have not done much imaginative play may start in this manner in your classroom: pretending by playing a familiar home-centered routine, but not taking on a role. They may eventually expand their early single actions into a string of actions composing an episode. For example, they may put the baby doll to bed, get out the dishes, set the table, pick up the baby, and sit down to eat.

On the other hand, some more mature 3- and even 4-year-olds may perform solitary pretend play with little cars, people, or miniature animals. They seem perfectly happy playing out an imaginary scenario by themselves. You can sometimes tap into this play by talking to them about what you see them doing with their props.

As they become more experienced players by interacting with others around them, they are often assigned a role by a more mature player. Whether they can actually play this role depends on their perspective-taking ability: whether they can see things from a different perspective than their own. Some children merely watch what the others are doing. Some continue with their own pretend actions, but with little recognition of a role as such. Others imitate their play partners and little by little learn how to play a pretend role. Observe and record what new concepts the children have learned.

As with stages of social play, children seem to progress from watching others to solitary imaginative play, to parallel play, and eventually to group play. As an observer, you may see this progression more easily with children who play with pretend objects such as dolls, figures of people and animals, or cars and trucks. They may be playing in the block area, house area, manipulative area, or sand table. In the dramatic play area itself, where children are playing roles in a spontaneous drama, it is sometimes difficult to recognize who has a role or who is playing the same theme in the same space but in a parallel manner.

If You Have Not Checked This Item: Some Helpful Ideas

■ Have Appropriate Props Available

Knowing that the youngest children pretend mainly about familiar household routines, you should have eating, cleaning, and sleeping props available in your dramatic play center. Put out all kinds of baby dolls and their beds as well. For older children, be sure your block center contains little cars and figures of people and animals.

■ Read a Book

If I Were a Lion (Weeks, 2004) tells the rhyming story of a girl whose mother has sent her to a time-out chair because she has been acting wild. The child is not repentant but angry because her mother has called her "wild." If she were really wild she would be a roaring lion, or clawing bear, or howling wolf, or snapping alligator. The spirited illustrations show the girl imagining all of these animals acting wild in her house—while she sits meekly in her chair thinking: "Mother doesn't realize that lions don't apologize." Then her mother will finally see that the opposite of wild is—"me." Read this to some of your solitary pretenders. Do they remember what they have pretended in similar circumstances?

Oliver Who Would Not Sleep (Bergman, 2007) does his pretending at night in this rhyming story of how he blasts off in his toy rocketship and flies all the way to Mars and back. Talk with your listening group about how each of them pretends at night in their bedrooms.

ASSIGNS ROLES OR TAKES ON ASSIGNED ROLES

Three-year-olds usually find it is more fun when several children play together. You will have checked on this previously in your observations concerning social play. This item signals the beginning of peer play for most children. Pretend episodes usually do not last long in the beginning because most children of this age are not yet flexible when it comes to differences of opinion. This inflexibility sometimes shows up when it comes to who will play what role.

Many 3-year-olds try to control dramatic play by assigning the roles. The dominant child takes the role he or she wants and assigns the others, who may or may not agree. Most children of this age want their own role. As their creativity blossoms through this type of play, their solutions to role assignment problems are often highly creative and something an adult would not have thought of. Listen to your children to see how they resolve such problems.

The role of mother is a favorite one for girls of this age. What would you do when all four girls playing together want to be the mother and no one will give in? After a few minutes of discussion—or rather argument—when it became clear that Janie (who spoke up first about being the mother) would not change, nor would the other three, a different solution needed to be found. The girls accepted the fact that the household could have only one mother, but they could not accept that they would have to be sisters or babies or grandmothers. Suddenly one of the girls said, "We'll all be other mothers who are visiting Janie this morning," and they were.

Three-year-olds who are playing pretend roles at home often will act the same way in assigning roles, even to adults. "I'll be the mother and you be the baby," is a role reversal commonly proposed by a child to her mother. Go along with the role reversal if you are the adult, and you will enjoy observing how your child plays your role as mother. Here is a typical role assignment situation played by 3-year-olds Sherry and Ann in a preschool and recorded in a running record:

> *Sherry is in the play grocery store holding a box of cereal. She hands box to child playing role of cashier. Walks back to grocery shelves. Picks up box and puts it in grocery cart. "Here's our groceries, Mother," she says to Ann, standing nearby. Picks up bag of groceries and carries it to play house. Walks back to grocery store. "I'm gonna be mother," she says loudly to herself. "Mother, it's time to go home," she says to Ann. Ann gives no response but pays for the groceries. "There are no more groceries. We have to leave now," says Sherry. Still gets no response from Ann. "I'm the mother and you're the grandmother. I'm not a little kid," she says to Ann. No response. They walk to house together. She puts her bag down and helps Ann with hers. "We have to unload everything now." They start to unpack all the groceries. "Oh, no, daughter," she says to Ann, "When it's cleanup time we have to pick all this up." Both girls laugh.*

Because Ann was originally the director of this play episode and Sherry had evidently agreed to the role of daughter by taking it, it is interesting to see what strategies Sherry now uses to get out of an unwanted role. First she states loudly but to herself that she is going to be the mother. Because she receives no response, she retains her daughter role at first, but then states outright to Ann that she is the mother and Ann can be the grandmother. Sherry still gets no response. Silence does not signify consent among young children. Silence may only mean that the challenged child does not want to engage in an argument, not that she agrees to give up her role. Sherry tries calling Ann "daughter," but Ann refuses to get involved verbally, so the role problem is still unresolved before cleanup time ends the play.

Another imaginative play episode previously recorded in Figure 2–4 shows older 3- and 4-year-olds engaged in the type of role assignment problem being discussed here:

> *Katy is playing by herself with plastic blocks, making guns; she walks into other room.*
>
> K: *"Lisa, would you play with me? I'm tired of playing by myself."*
>
> *They walk into other room to slide and climbing area.*
>
> K: *"I am Wonder Woman."*
>
> L: *"So am I."*
>
> K: *"No, there is only one Wonder Woman. You are Robin."*

L: "Robin needs a Batman because Batman and Robin are friends."

All this takes place under slides and climber. Lisa shoots block gun that Katy has given her. Katy falls on floor.

L (to teacher):   "We're playing Superfriends and Wonder Woman keeps falling down."
                   Katy opens eyes, gets up and says:

K: "Let's get out our Batmobile and go help the world." *She runs to other room and back making noises like a car.*

L: "Wonder Woman is died. She fell out of the car." *She falls down.*

K: "It's only a game. Wake up, Lisa. You be Wonder Woman. I'll be. . . ."

L: "Let's play house now."

Katy begins sliding down slide.

K: "We have a lot of Superfriends to do." *(She says this while sliding.)* "Robin is coming after you!" *(She shouts to Lisa, running from slide and into other room.) Lisa has gone into housekeeping area and says to Katy:*

L: "Katy, here is your doll's dress." *(Lost yesterday.) John joins the girls.*

L: "I'm Wonder Woman."

K: "I'm Robin."

J: "I'm Batman. Where is the Batmobile?"

K: "It's in here."

They run into the other room and Katy points under the slide platform, telling John what the Batmobile can do. Then they all run into the other room and back again.

K: "John, we are not playing Superfriends any more."

This typical pretending episode illustrates perfectly the kind of role assignment and switching so characteristic of children this age. It is obvious from the children's easy agreements that they have played together before and therefore accept certain conditions. Katy is the director here and assigns the roles. She takes the role of Wonder Woman and assigns Lisa the role of Robin. Lisa really does not agree (we soon see), but she accepts her assignment. She probably has gone through this with Katy before and knows that if she plays along without making a fuss, her turn will come. It comes quite soon, in fact, when she notes that Katy seems to have abandoned the Wonder Woman role by suddenly getting out the Batmobile and "going to help the world."

Here Lisa announces that she is Wonder Woman and has fallen out of the car and died. Katy agrees to Lisa's new role by saying: "It's only a game. Wake up, Lisa. You be Wonder Woman." When John joins the game and takes the role of Batman, the girls do not object at first. But obviously they know how to get rid of unwanted players by announcing: "John, we are not playing Superfriends any more."

(The teacher later told the observer that she allows superhero play as long as it does not get out of bounds. She does not allow gun play and did not realize that was happening or she would have intervened.)

Observe to discover what other creative ploys your children use to get peers to take role assignments or to get out of assigned roles they don't want and into ones they really want. Other strategies used to resolve play conflicts in a positive manner are discussed in Chapter 5.

If your children are engaged in this kind of dramatic play, you will probably be checking this item. If you leave it blank, it means either that the child is not playing because he has not reached this level of group imaginative play, or that he does not assign roles or accept assignments. If this is the case, he has probably not reached the group play level, because children who play together like this soon come to an understanding about role assignments.

If You Have Not Checked This Item: Some Helpful Ideas

■ Be a Model for Pretend Play

It is not up to you to force a child into group play. Such play should be totally spontaneous. But you can certainly help a shy child become involved with a group by taking a role yourself and inviting the child to take a role and come along with you into the play group. Davidson (1996) suggests other ways the teacher can help support pretending:

> If a child is pretending to cook, the adult can ask about what is cooking, showing that this act of pretending is valued. If a child needs help taking on or expanding a role, adults can model pretending. If an adult picks up a play phone and talks, often a child will then imitate by picking up the other phone and answering. (p. 33)

On the other hand, teachers need to restrain themselves from entering pretend play too vigorously. After all, this is the children's spontaneous creation and should remain so. Teachers can help in many ways to get onlookers involved or to keep the play going on an even keel, but then they should extract themselves unobtrusively as players. Van Hoorn, Hourot, Scales, and Alward (2003) emphasize that timing is everything when entering and exiting children's play: "When teachers enter and exit children's play or shift from one strategy to another, timing is crucial. Teachers need to observe play long enough to see if any intervention is called for or if the children are best served by the teacher in a less directive role" (p. 103).

■ Read a Book

What Shall We Play? (Heap, 2002) involves three children: Lilly May who wants to play fairies, Matt who has other ideas, and Martha, their friend. They are obviously experienced players who go along with one another rather than arguing. When Lilly May says "fairies," Matt says, "No, let's play trees," so they do, each taking a tree role. For their second theme they still do not accept fairies, but "cars" as Martha suggests, all becoming different cars. Next comes "cats" again from Martha and then "wibbly-wobbly Jell-O" from Matt. Finally they take up Lilly May's idea and have a grand time playing fairies with wings and wands. Ask your listeners how they would have responded to these ideas.

NEEDS PARTICULAR PROPS TO DO PRETEND PLAY

Play researcher Sara Smilansky (1968) discusses three types of pretending that occur in dramatic play: pretending with regard to a role, pretending with regard to an object, and pretending with regard to an action. Teachers can support children's pretend play by providing representational props, toys, and dress-up clothes. The youngest children doing pretend play may need more realistic props.

If you have bilingual children, be sure to label the props in both languages. As Burton and Edwards (2006) described,

> For example, Luis, Jose, and Sophie are pretending to go to the subway station. The props are labeled with text and pictures of a train, ticket, money, a caution sign in both languages, so each child knows each object in his or her language. Even though they speak different languages, they are able to recreate what happens at the subway station. (p. 6)

If 3-year-olds have had a chance to pretend when they were 2, they gradually develop new skills and interests in their imaginative play. The fragments of familiar routines that occupied the children earlier become more extended and less rigid as the youngsters mature. Three-year-olds begin to think a bit about the pretending they are about to do, rather than acting on a sudden impulse. This forethought often leads them to preplan the play by finding or gathering certain realistic props. In fact, some 3-year-olds cannot proceed with play until they find the right prop.

The rigidity many 3-year-olds express in their ritualistic manner of pretending thus often carries over in their insistence on particular props to play. Three-year-olds may believe they need a particular hat, costume, doll, or steering wheel to carry out a role. Many times the object is the basis for the play, but not so much on impulse as with 2-year-olds. Three-year-olds very much enjoy dressing up and playing a role, and they have a much broader concept of how to do it.

Props may very well serve the children as an instrument for getting out of themselves. Because 3-year-olds are still strongly self-centered, they may need a prop to break away from their own point of view. Just as shy children can lose themselves in speaking through a hand puppet or from behind a mask, 3-year-olds may need the impetus of an object outside themselves to get them started in pretending to be someone else.

Family activities are a large part of 3-year-olds' pretend play in preschool programs. Play researcher Hughes (1991) noted,

> There are clear indications that threes, unlike twos, begin to identify strongly with adults—to become increasingly interested in what adults do and to imagine themselves doing the same things. Perhaps as a result, threes become interested in dramatic play, in which they have an opportunity to act out adult roles for themselves. (p. 74)

Doll play, hospital play, and pretending to be a community helper are common themes. Three-year-olds also enjoy driving cars and trains, flying jet planes, and being firefighters. They can carry these themes out in dramatic play, block building, table

Rani needs to put on a dress to play the role of mother.

block games, clay creations, the water table, and the woodworking bench, as well as with puppets and toy telephones—anywhere and everywhere children gather.

It is up to you and your coworkers to provide the props that support pretend play in these areas. Bring in a set of jet planes and figures of people, place them in the sand table with posters of planes mounted on the wall nearby, and see what happens. Be sure to provide safety goggles to keep sand out of eyes. Some astute child is sure to point out that pilots of some kinds of planes wear goggles, and soon you may have several goggled "pilots" zooming around the classroom with their planes!

After a trip to the zoo or animal farm, bring in toy animals to the block center along with figures of people, toy trees, cars, and perhaps a little train to carry people around the block center zoo that the children may build. It is important to provide appropriate props for children to pretend with in various learning centers of the classroom after such a trip. Playing with such props is not just a matter of fun, but it helps young children to symbolize in a concrete way the more abstract ideas gained from the trip. Classroom staff can encourage children to remember what they saw on the field trip and build their own miniature trip site, or pretend to be one of the people they met at the site.

Young children learn best through concrete, hands-on activities. The props you provide for imaginative play can help them create spontaneous dramas about any topic of current interest. As Gowen (1995) noted,

> Props relevant to the children's culture and community can enrich the children's efforts to construct and express their understanding of significant events and roles in their lives. (p. 78)

For example, one morning Ricardo's grandmother visited his preschool and helped the children prepare tamales for lunch. Afterward, the teacher put out a plastic set of Mexican food in the housekeeping area for the children to pretend with. She also read them the book *Too Many Tamales* (Soto, 1993).

For days thereafter, a number of the children spontaneously acted out the tamale preparation, but with their own unique twist. Because the Mexican food set included only plastic tacos, the children invented their own tamales by using plastic egg rolls from a Chinese food set and wrapping them with paper for corn husks! Then they hid a toy ring in the wrapping for someone to try and find, just as in the storybook (Beaty & Pratt, 2007, p. 169).

Not every child will be interested in pretending in this manner, just as not every child will like a particular book. Do not force or even urge youngsters to participate who show no interest. Read the story, put out the materials, and let those who want to engage in playing with them. As Gowen reminds us: "As always, the rule in promoting development through play is to follow the child's lead" (1995, p. 78).

If You Have Not Checked This Item: Some Helpful Ideas

■ Have a Variety of Props Available

In the large motor area, have large wooden riding trucks, wagons, and a wheelbarrow, as well as large hollow blocks and floorboards for building child-size structures. Put out a full-length mirror in the dress-up area. Include costume jewelry, scarves, handbags, wallets, belts, vests, shoes, aprons, all kinds of hats, doctor's equipment, goggles, binoculars, badges, umbrellas, and canes. An assortment of men's and women's clothes in teenage size is often easier for young children to handle than adult-size clothing.

Think of the learning centers in your classroom as areas for children's imaginative play to take place. What props can you put in the block area after a field trip to a construction site, for instance? What about construction vehicles and workers, string for wires, straws for pipes, and popsicle sticks for lumber? Think about filling other centers with such accessories: sand table, water table, woodworking area, clay table, writing center, and of course, the dramatic play area.

■ Take Many Field Trips

For children to become involved in spontaneous dramatic play activities, they must have firsthand knowledge about them. Ask children where they have gone with their parents.

If many have gone on picnics, put out picnic props in the dramatic play area. If many children have not experienced a picnic, plan a picnic field trip to a nearby park . . . or even to the playground outside. Afterward, put out the props.

Take field trips to nearby sites of interest to the children such as barber/beauty shop, farm, fast-food restaurant, laundromat, farmer's market, flower shop, pet store, repair shop, gas station, shoe store, fire station, or doctor's clinic. Then put out dress-up props in the dramatic play center and miniature figures in the block area for children to pretend with.

■ Read a Book with Character Cutouts

Amazing Grace (Hoffman, 1991) is a classic book about an African-American girl who loves to pretend. She is Joan of Arc, Anansi the Spider, Pegleg Pete, Hiawatha, Mowgli, Aladdin, Doctor Grace, and finally Peter Pan in her school play. Your girls can dress up and pretend like Grace does; or you can scan the wonderful illustrations of Grace in her costumes, print them off, and cut them out as paper dolls for the children to pretend with on a smaller scale.

My Shoes Take Me Where I Want to Go (Richmond, 2006) takes the reader through a child's fascinating imagination of using shoes to pretend to be a boy basketball player, a girl soccer star, a boy hockey player, a boy pirate, a girl scuba diver, a cowgirl, a boy mountain climber, a girl dancer, and a boy president. Can your children pretend to take on particular roles as they wear the shoes from your dress-up area?

■ Read a Book with a Costume

Ladybug Girl (Soman & Davis, 2008) shows little Lulu all dressed up in her ladybug costume ready to take off for another day's adventures. She helps ants by clearing a rock out of their way; looks for a shark in the pond; picks up rocks that have fallen off a stone wall; and flies down the hill with her wings bubbling behind her. Sixteen other costumes she sometimes wears are illustrated on the end pages. This book should give your girls some good dramatic play ideas.

Violet the Pilot (Breer, 2008) is somewhat older than Lulu, but nonetheless creative. While other girls were playing with dolls, Violet played with monkey wrenches and needle-nose pliers in her father's junkyard. She is a mechanical genius and can build almost anything out of the junk. After building a plane that really flies, Violet rescues some Boy Scouts whose canoe had tipped over. And of course she wears her pilot helmet, goggles, and scarf. Both boys and girls should enjoy this one, and get more ideas for dress-up dramatic play.

TAKES ON CHARACTERISTICS AND ACTIONS RELATED TO ROLE

Four-year-olds have more experience than 3-year-olds when it comes to creating a role in their pretend play. Because they desperately want to participate in the adult world, 4-year-olds try out all sorts of adult roles: mother at work, father at work, doctor, nurse, bus driver, astronaut, waiter, fast-food cook, gas station attendant, mail carrier, firefighter, truck driver, train conductor, or crane operator. In addition, 4-year-olds play their roles with many more realistic details. They select props more carefully, dress up more elaborately, and carry out the role with more appropriate dialog and actions.

If you listen carefully to 4-year-olds when you are observing them doing imaginative play, you will be able to learn a great deal about their understanding of the people and situations in their world. In addition, you may gain quite a respect for their use of creativity in developing their roles. Even the mundane roles of mother, father, brother, and baby are played with new twists and novel solutions to problems. Dialogue is expanded, and the players even express emotions quite eloquently where appropriate.

Language is used more than ever before to set the scene and create the mood. Because the players are beginning to make greater distinctions between real and pretend, they often make aside-like comments about things that are not real, just pretend, so that you, their peers, and even they themselves understand what is real and what is pretend. Four-year-olds are also more flexible about taking different roles. Children who would not take a bad guy's role at age 3 may play it to the hilt with great gusto at age 4.

Your planning, suggestions, and support may be necessary to get the play going, but the children should be on their own. As Edwards (2002) reminds us:

> As you think of ways to provide opportunities for sociodramatic play, remember that play involving role-taking and themes will occur in your classroom with or without your planning. However, you can provide the seed ideas to get children started and suggest roles or themes to initiate play activities. You must be willing to be flexible in your planning, to observe and listen to your children, and to take your cues from them, rather than being in a hurry to move into more teacher-directed and structured activities. (p. 173)

Then you can observe your children carefully as they pretend in the dramatic play area, in the block corner, at the water table, and on the playground. Are they playing roles with greater realism than before, using expanded dialog, showing more emotion, and almost becoming the character? If so, you should mark this item on the checklist.

If You Have Not Checked This Item: Some Helpful Ideas

■ Read a Book

What Eddie Can Do (Gebhard, 2004) shows imaginative Eddie having great adventures diving to a sunken ship, discovering rock writing in a cave, traveling through outer space, exploring the rain forest, taming tigers, and flying with birds, but he doesn't know how to tie his shoes. When he hears his friend Clara next door is being attacked by a double-tailed monster, he rushes home so his mother can show him how to tie his shoes. Then he can tie the monster to a tree with the garden hose, just like tying his shoes.

■ Have Many Sets of Flannel Board or Cutout Characters

Children can use cutout characters from scanned copies of their favorite storybook characters to play with on a flannel board or as paper dolls. Make photocopies of the characters from a favorite book and mount them on cardboard with sandpaper or Velcro backing, or laminate them. Keep the characters in a manila envelope with a copy of the book inside. Then children can look at pictures from the story when they play. The youngsters can act out scenes from the book if they want, or they can have the characters participate in brand-new adventures.

This activity is good practice in role playing with characters the children already know. A child can play by herself or with another child. Keep more than one flannel board in the book area if you want this to be a popular activity. Personal flannel boards can be made by mounting flannel or felt to a piece of cardboard folded in two and hinged at the top so that it stands easily on a table. Some favorite storybooks from which you may want to cut out characters are the following.

Freckleface Strawberry (Moore, 2007)

If You Decide to Go to the Moon (McNulty, 2005)

Iggy Peck, Architect (Beaty, 2007)

Hoops with Swoopes (Kuklin, 2001)

Mike and the Bike (Ward, 2005)

Sally Jean, the Bicycle Queen (Best, 2006)

 # CAN PRETEND WITH IMAGINARY OBJECTS

Children go through a succession of levels in pretending with objects just as they do with roles. Beginners seem to need highly realistic objects for their pretend play: a toy telephone for a real telephone; a plastic apple for a real apple; a toy car for a real car. As they mature and become more experienced pretenders, children are able to use less representational props: a cylinder block for a telephone; a ball for an apple; a unit block for a car. This is called object substitution.

The most highly imaginative children are able to make an even greater leap in substitution of objects. They can pretend without any concrete object at all. They can call on an imaginary telephone grasped symbolically in their hand. An imaginary apple is held somewhat differently with their fingers curled around empty space. An imaginary car can speed along the floor with their hand directing its movements and their voice making sound effects.

Observe your children in the dramatic play area to see how they use objects in their pretending. Often children pay for their groceries with imaginary money, although they may carry a real purse. They may ride around the room on an imaginary motorcycle, but wear a real cycle helmet, or eat pretend food in the housekeeping area, but use real toy forks and spoons. As Gowen (1995) noted,

> The inclusion of imaginary elements in play indicates that the child can entertain these ideas without them being tied to concrete objects and real beings. As the child's representational abilities develop, she can imagine objects and beings and more readily symbolize them with words alone. (pp. 79–80)

Not all children arrive at this stage of using imaginary objects rather than real ones. It is often children with more experience or better use of language who use less representational toys or imaginary ones. Does this mean a teacher should not include so many realistic props in the dramatic play or block centers? Davidson (1996) says:

> There is some research that shows that less realistic props are preferable for older children, since the props do not put a limit on the direction of the play. Although more open-ended props can be provided for older children, it is important to remember that more realistic props may be needed by less skilled older players. (pp. 33–34)

However, many toy companies carry the realism too far, making toys that move by themselves, make their own sounds, and have lights that go on and off. You will not find such toys in most preschools, and with good reason. Children's own imaginations are not challenged if the toy does everything and all a youngster can do is to turn it on and watch it perform. Such toys tend not to hold children's interest for more than a few days, while toys that children must interact with never lose their appeal. Martha B. Bronson (1995), in her book, *The Right Stuff for Children,* also favors giving children materials to construct their own play scenes rather than purchasing prefabricated scenes such as a house, school, garage, airport, or farm. Unit blocks and building bricks "require more flexibility and creativity on the part of the child and support more variety in play" (p. 88).

Nevertheless, children will often choose a representational toy rather than a substitute object. Although it is important to have representational toys, having too many can discourage the development of imagination. Learning centers where imaginative play takes place should also include open-ended materials that children can use to create their own imaginary objects and settings: Styrofoam, tissue tubes, empty boxes of all sizes, pipe cleaners, feathers, plastic bottles of all sizes, cardboard cartons, and other throw-away items that seem appropriate.

There is one other interesting form of object substitution you should look for in your observations of children's pretending with objects. When children play with toy people, animals, and dolls—pretending they can move and talk—they are doing what is called *active agent* object substitution. At first, children play with toy figures as passive recipients of the play. They may feed them or dress them or ride them around in a vehicle. When the toy becomes an active agent, the child walks it around as if it were alive and also talks for it. Gowen (1995) noted,

> An especially sophisticated form of active-agent play occurs when children have two or more toy beings interact with one another. For example, the child hops one toy person into the toy

This girl does "active agent" object substitution when she talks for each of the people and moves the horses around.

car and says in a low voice, "I'm going to work now," then turns another toy person around and says in a high voice, "Okay, I'll see you later." (p. 80)

If you want your children to become involved in this highly imaginative play, be sure to provide appropriate materials: figures of people and animals, especially ones that can stand by themselves, as well as vehicles that can carry the figures.

If You Have Not Checked This Item: Some Helpful Ideas

■ Model the Desired Behavior

Some children need to see an adult pretending to get the idea of what to do themselves. One study showed that the most highly skilled preschool pretenders had mothers who pretended with their children at age 1 (Berk, 1994, p. 36). Be sure you occasionally join the children in their pretending. You need to remember that it is their play, and you should only be a visitor. Better than taking a role may be to make an appropriate comment when you see them doing imaginative play. "Oh, Reggie, I bet those animals really like those pens you are building for them." Or, "Here's a cracker for your doll, Samantha. Do you think she's hungry?"

■ Read a Book

Even Fire Fighters Hug Their Moms (Maclean, 2002) shows a 4-year-old boy playing exciting roles at home while his mom watches and tries to get in a hug. Some of his props are realistic but others are imaginary. He uses a real red helmet and boots as a fire fighter, but also a tank vacuum cleaner hose for water. As an EMT, he drives an inverted wash basket ambulance with a pot cover steering wheel. The front loader he drives as a construction worker is a living room chair with golf clubs stuck between cushions for shifting gears. His rocket to the moon is a cardboard box with an inverted waste basket as a helmet. But his best role is garbage truck driver where he throws all his toys down his playroom slide into the trash-crusher box, and this time gives his mom a big hug. What props can your listeners invent for similar roles in the classroom?

In *My Chair* (James, 2004), a group of children demonstrate what astounding things chairs can do when they pretend. "My chair is a fort." "Mine is a roller skate." "Mine is an intergalactic zoo."

 ## USES LANGUAGE FOR CREATING AND SUSTAINING THE PLOT

Although 2-year-olds do most of their pretending without much language, 3-, 4-, and 5-year-olds depend on language to set the scene and sustain the action. If they are playing by themselves, they often will talk to themselves about what is happening. They also will speak for the characters—all of them. If the youngsters are playing with other children, they often use a great deal of dialogue to carry out their ideas. This behavior promotes their improved use of language and dialogue with others. In addition, it provides yet another opportunity for them to express creativity in the fresh and novel way they use words.

Words direct what the children do, the way they act, who the characters are, the unfolding of the plot, and the way they resolve conflict. Children involved in pretending who do not have the language skills of the more advanced players are able to listen and eventually imitate the advanced players' use of language. Everyone involved gets excellent practice in improving speaking skills, trying out new words, and using familiar language in new ways.

For some children, a new experience is the use of language to express feelings. The characters in these spontaneous make-believe situations need to express how they feel about what is happening to them. Many children have trouble putting their feelings into words. Younger children prefer to "act out" rather than speak out. This type of imaginative play gives them the opportunity to learn how to express feelings.

The youngsters, in fact, are projecting their feelings by expressing what a character feels. Even if the character is a doll, a puppet, or an inanimate figure of a person or an animal, the children have yet another opportunity to speak. Children 3 and 4 years old are often more comfortable expressing the feelings of toy people than their own. The youngsters like to take their dolls or stuffed animals to the doctor's office, to listen to these pretend people express their fears, and to comfort them. In doing so, the children sort out their own impressions about the situation and try out their own sometimes novel ideas for resolving problems. Smilansky (1968, p. 27) has found three main functions of language in this sort of dramatic play:

- Imitating adult speech
- Imagining a make-believe situation (mainly dialog)
- Directing the action

If you listen carefully to the actors in imaginative play, you will note they carry out all three of these functions. They definitely imitate adult speech. You can practically hear yourself speaking if you are the parent or the teacher of any of these children. Children also bring imagery to life in the characterizations they express through dialogue. Finally, someone in the group, usually the self-assigned director, is forever stepping outside her role to explain or reaffirm what is going on.

Spoken Words for Internal Images

If inner imagery allows the child to pretend in the first place, then talking aloud allows her to expand the meaning of what she visualizes. She not only hears himself speaking, but she also receives feedback from others' reactions. This feedback helps her revise and refine ideas and word use. Until she arrives at the point where she can create and sustain the action of pretend situations through language, she will miss the value of using her imagination in this manner. Eventually she must use mainly language and not just imagining in thinking. Thus imaginative play serves as a sort of transitional activity for the preschool child to learn spoken words for her internal images.

Alexander (2005) describes a realist role-play between two girls who are making plans for a shopping expedition. Emily picks up a telephone book and tells Madison her hair looks like a mop and she needs to call the beauty shop to get her hair done before she goes shopping. She actually finds the page in the phone book with a picture of a beautician. She says the phone numbers aloud as she presses their buttons on the toy phone. Then she holds a one-sided conversation with the pretend beautician discussing the best time for an appointment. When Madison also wants an appointment, Emily holds another one-sided conversation. Madison adds: "Tell her I'll pay with a credit card and we can get there right away" (p. 30).

Alexander tells us that pretending like this helps children fit into society and function as responsible citizens. It also helps children build vocabularies and reinforce concepts (p. 31). An observer analyzing the girls' conversations realizes that this scenario does indeed make their thinking visible, as previously mentioned. Concepts the girls' conversations illustrate include

If your hair looks bad you need to get it done in a beauty shop.

You need to make an appointment to get your hair done.

To get an appointment you call the beauty shop.

You use the phone book to get the number.

You can pay for the service with a credit card.

It's important to be on time.

One player can learn from another how you go about making appointments. Obviously Emily learned what to do from others, but in reenacting this scenario out loud she reinforces these concepts. Had she made a mistake or omitted something, another child player, listening to the conversations, would soon correct her. Conversations like this in dramatic play also serve the important function of helping second-language learners use English.

If You Have Not Checked This Item: Some Helpful Ideas

■ Use Hand Puppets

Have a variety of hand puppets available for the children: animals, characters from books, community helpers, adults, and children figures. A puppet theater made from a cardboard carton can help motivate the children's use of puppets as play actors. You may need to put on a puppet show yourself to set the stage, so to speak, for your children's dramas. Younger children tend to use puppets as an extension of their arms, using the puppet's mouth for pretend biting rather than for speaking, as mentioned previously. Your modeling behavior can show the children a better way to use puppets.

It is not necessary to have a puppet theater in the beginning, but your more advanced pretenders may expand their repertoire of imaginative play if a puppet theater is available. Make puppets or purchase them from toy stores, children's book stores, science museum shops, nature stores, store kitchen departments where they are sold as pot holders, or educational supply catalogues such as Demco Reading Enrichment (1-800-356-1200).

■ Encourage Improvisation

As Edwards (2002) tells us: "In improvisation children make up their own dialogue, movements, actions, and expressions" (p. 212). The dialogue is, of course, dependent on the language skills of the children. You can encourage it by proposing a scenario for anyone who wants to take part. For example, you may suggest they can pretend to be on the playground where they hear a strange noise, look up, and see a spaceship coming down and landing, with strange beings coming out of it. What will your children say to them? Then what will happen? Other scenarios for improvisation might include

- How to ride on a whale
- How to talk to a dinosaur
- How to explore Mars
- How to find treasure at the bottom of the sea

 ## ENACTS EXCITING, DANGER-PACKED THEMES

Most 4-year-olds do everything in a more exuberant, out-of-bounds manner than 3-year-olds, including pretending. Four-year-olds are more noisy, active, and aware of things outside themselves. They are fascinated with matters of life and death, and they begin to use such themes more often in their imaginative play. Superheroes and other television characters show up in their pretending. Bad guys are captured. Good guys are rewarded. People get shot and killed.

Adults look askance and blame television. They think that TV-watching surely must be bad for young children. By the age of 4, young children are viewing an average of 4 hours of television a day. Surely this viewing must affect their pretending and imaginations. Research by children's play specialists, the Singers, however, resulted in findings contrary to what they had expected. They found no relationship of statistical significance between watching television and imaginary play. Pretending neither increased nor decreased as a result of watching television.

The strongest correlation the Singers found was between the amount of television watched and overt aggression in the classroom. How true, preschool teachers agree, without perhaps realizing that 4-year-olds have always exhibited aggression in their play. The real reason for the increased aggression could well be that sitting and watching television for long periods does not allow young children to discharge their pent-up energy and aggressive feelings as does normal active play; or that the aggression children see and experience in their families needs an outlet.

Superhero and War Play

Four-year-olds are extremely active and must have daily opportunities to discharge this pent-up energy. It is only natural for this energy to take the form of powerful superhero character roles from the television programs the children watch. Ask adults who were raised before the days of television what form their wildest pretending took, and you will hear tales of cowboys and Indians, cops and robbers, or war play. Such play helps children release fears and build up confidence.

The argument against allowing superhero play in the classroom talks about the television cartoons children see that show superheroes controlling others through threat, force, and violence. Many teachers describe superhero play in their classrooms as being characterized by too-rough, too-loud play that they are forced to intervene in or stop completely. What should a teacher do who has a strong belief in the value of fantasy play, but does not believe the amount of adult intervention required to keep superhero play from bursting out-of-bounds is worth the effort? Should superhero play be banned from the classroom entirely?

No, say many teachers. There are ways to extract important learnings from this powerful play activity that seems to have so many youngsters in its grip. When there is war and violence in our own lives, children pick up on the feelings expressed around them. They may try to act out the scenes of violence they see on television. As Levin (2003) tells us:

> Play with violence tends to end up with children out of control, scared, and hurt. Managing aggressive play and keeping everyone safe can feel like a never-ending struggle and a major diversion from the positive lessons we want children to learn. (p. 61)

What can we do? Banning war play from the classroom does not work as it once did. Children's intense desire to engage in this kind of play leads them to find ways to circumvent the ban. They somehow need to express these strong feelings of fear, rage, and helplessness in nondestructive ways. Some children can be redirected to paint out their emotions with bright and dark contrasting poster paints (red-black, yellow-brown, orange-purple) on paper, poster board, cardboard cartons, or brown grocery sacks. Unroll large sheets of newsprint on the floor or on the wall for a mural and invite children to paint out large scenes of things that have been bothering them. Finger painting also allows children to paint emotionally with whole arm strokes. If they show bombs exploding and people being killed, accept what they do, and have them tell you the story about it if they can.

Some children may want to make "spider webs" with string around the tacks you place on cork boards on the wall. They can cut out figures of people from magazines or picture books to be laminated and played with on the webs, reenacting Spider Man adventures. Others may prefer to draw their spider webs on chalkboards with white chalk, and play out superhero adventures on their webs with red-and-blue chalk figures they move around. Throwing beanbags at targets is another method for redirecting strong energy with the beanbags as superheroes and the targets as buildings.

One of the more creative suggestions is to scale down the most violent play; that is, to turn it into a tabletop activity. Most of the television characters are available commercially in a variety of sizes from dolls to matchbox-scale figures, just right for tabletop play. When children are sitting at a table, running and crashing bodies cease to be a problem. Pretending, after all, can take place anywhere. Again, teachers must control the types of characters and their props brought into the classroom. Use of guns, swords, and other weapons should be discouraged and substitutes found. Figure 13–1.

Children need to talk about the superheroes they like, what powers they have, and how they use these powers. Help them create new superheroes who have powers that solve problems without using violence. Hoffman's (2004) book for teachers, *Magic Capes, Amazing Powers: Transforming Superhero Play in the Classroom,* gives other suggestions for

Figure 13–1 Controlling
Superhero Play

Controlling Superhero Play

- Paint out strong emotions with bright and dark colors on large sheets of newsprint

- Make spider webs with string strung around tacks on corkboards; play scenario with cutout Spiderman figures

- Throw beanbags at cardboard carton targets

- Scale down superhero play with tabletop figures

- Create new superheroes with powers that help people and animals

- Use props such as power bracelets, capes, magic wands, old cell phones painted gold

helping children create good superheroes. Reading the book *Ladybug Girl*, discussed earlier, gives children other ideas about creating a superhero based on an insect and its powers. What other bugs or animals might children choose for their superheroes?

Group Play

Group play comes into its own when children reach age 4. When they first get together, however, it often degenerates, like superhero play, into a wild sort of activity without plot or dialog, almost a regression from children's previous role-playing. This wildness seems to be a natural progression in their learning to get along with one another. The establishment and recognition of dominance is often dealt with in such "rough-and-tumble play." Children also develop coping skills as they focus on the sometimes aggressive actions and reactions of peers. Out of these interactions comes a sense of common group purpose that sets the stage for the more organized play to follow.

Teachers can help by redirecting the energy of wild play into the exciting, danger-packed themes that 4-year-olds favor. Doctor play, always a favorite, can involve taking sick or injured patients to the hospital in an ambulance with a loud siren. One teacher found her children needed help organizing and elaborating on their ambulance plot. Some of the children were running around the room making loud siren noises. The teacher suggested they build an ambulance out of large hollow blocks. Now what could they do? This time, the teacher decided to play a role herself. A running record of an observation of the very active 4-year-old Jessica includes the following:

> *Jessica runs to climber, climbs up & sits on top. Teacher tries to involve children in dramatic play; suggests they use climber as their hospital. They are building an ambulance out of large blocks. Jessica climbs down & begins stacking blocks one on top of the other. Then sits & watches others taping paper plates colored yellow on front to use as headlights. She picks up plate & tapes it to rear of ambulance. Runs to table to get felt-tip marker. "I want the yellow marker. Lots of yellow." She gets marker. "What am I gonna write on? I want to color something. I'll color the wheels black." Jessica drops yellow marker and picks up black one. She colors in back paper plate wheel with marker. "I want to color something yellow." Teacher suggests steering wheel. She does it. She runs & climbs into block ambulance. "I'm the driver." She uses her plate as steering wheel. "I wanna be the patient." Jessica gets up and lies down in middle of ambulance. She gets carried to "hospital" by teacher & other children. She lies by the climber & pretends to be sick, moaning & groaning. Other children leave, but she stays. Then she gets up & runs to table where teacher is helping children to make doctor bags. Teacher asks her what name she wants on her bag. She answers, "I want to be a nurse, not a doctor." Teacher asks what tools a nurse uses. She answers, "Nurses help, they don't use tools. Doctors use tools." Teacher asks, "What does your mother use when you are sick?" She answers, "I don't know." Jessica takes bag & runs back to ambulance with bag on arm, smiling. She yells, "Lisa, lay down, you're the patient." Jessica sits in front seat & drives ambulance using paper plate steering wheel. She hops up again & runs to teacher, asking her to be the doctor. She jumps up & down, urging the teacher to hurry. "Hurry, we're ready," she repeats. Teacher comes & helps carry Lisa to hospital.*

The teacher noted that more children participated in this particular role play than any others she had witnessed. An ambulance had gone by on the street outside earlier in the morning, siren blaring, and the children who saw it were excited but alarmed. This event prompted their building of the block ambulance, but the teacher's own participation in the play certainly stimulated the extra number of children to become involved. The teacher's idea for extending the play by helping the children make doctor bags added immensely to the drama. The running record, however, caught 4-year-old Jessica just as she normally acted, always on the run.

Jessica's stereotyped answers about doctors is also typical of this age. Gender roles seem to become more rigid, with girls insisting on playing the mother, waitress, or teacher, while boys often want to play father, driver, policeman, or superhero. Same-gender groups form about this time, with girls' play becoming more relaxed and verbal, and boys' play faster paced and more aggressive.

Block play, for instance, may get out of hand with 4-year-olds. It sometimes disintegrates into throwing when adults are not around, or even when they are. Try to change the violent direction of the block play by giving players a new task involving excitement or mystery: "Where is the mysterious tunnel I saw on the floor this morning, boys? What, you didn't see it? I'm surprised. I thought you had X-ray vision. I could see it right through the rug. You don't believe me? Well, maybe if you make your own tunnel, you'll be able to see the mystery tunnel, too. Jeff, you and Lorenzo know how to build tunnels. Maybe you could make a mystery tunnel at one end of the rug, and Jesse and Tyrone could make a tunnel at the other end. What will happen if the tunnels come together, I wonder?"

If you observe that individual children who are 4 years old have not started playing with exciting, danger-packed themes, it may be that they are less mature than the others. How do they compare with other 4-year-olds in motor skills, for instance? Obviously, it is not appropriate to push such children into something they are not interested in. Provide them with many opportunities to engage in play themes of their own interests. You will know what some of these are from your observations and conversations with such youngsters.

If You Have Not Checked This Item: Some Helpful Ideas

■ Read a Book

Superhero ABC (McLeod, 2006) shows a cartoonlike superhero for every letter of the alphabet. A is Astro-Man always alert for an alien attack; B is Bubble-Man who blows big bubbles at bullies. Yes, there are some girl superheroes such as G, Goo-Girl who shoots gobs of goo at gangsters and I, Ms Incredible, who becomes invisible in an instant. Children love it, but teachers may not appreciate the violence.

Abiyoyo (Seeger, 1986) is a South African folktale about a boy who annoys everyone by playing his ukulele, which makes people dance, and his magician father, who angers everyone by making things disappear with his magic wand ZOOP! The two of them are put out of town where they live until the people-eating monster Abiyoyo makes his appearance. The boy's playing makes the monster dance till he falls down, and his father's magic wand zoops the monster out of existence. They return as heroes. Children can make their own magic wands from sticks and their ukuleles from shoeboxes if they want to reenact this story.

Way Far Away on a Wild Safari (Peck, 2006) shows a little boy going on a safari to Africa, where in his imagination he meets each animal in a rhyming verse. Back home his grandma is waiting for him with baked animal crackers and milk. This is for your youngest children.

 # USES ELABORATE THEMES, IDEAS, DETAILS

The themes that 4-year-olds use in their pretending are many of the same ones they used at age 3, only much expanded. The youngsters still enjoy playing house. Both boys and girls play with dolls and take roles in the housekeeping corner. Doll play now includes dressing as well as undressing, but the central action usually involves putting the doll to bed. Many girls of this age prefer playing with little girl dolls rather than baby dolls. Play with dollhouses, however, is still too detailed to hold the interest of most 4-year-olds. They like the dolls more than the houses. Even block structures are not played with as much as they will be played with at age 5. At age 4, the pretending takes place during the process of building, rather than with the finished product afterward.

Doctor play is at its peak at age 4, and it will seldom be as popular again. All kinds of themes involving community helpers are used, especially after a visit by a community helper or a field trip to a work site. Superheroes are popular, as you have noted, especially television characters. Monsters sometimes appear, but they are still a bit too scary for most 4-year-olds to handle.

The pretend play of older 4- and 5-year-olds is characterized by the elaborate nature of the drama, no matter whether the theme is a common one or an invented adventure. Five-year-olds add all kinds of details through their dialog, dress-up, props, and imaginations. Their play gets so involved, in fact, that it even carries over from one day to the next. The players remember where they left off the day before and can start right in again.

There is much more talk during pretend play, as well, because 5-year-olds have a better command of the language. With their improved language skills, they clarify ideas and talk out problems. Concerns about sickness, accidents, and death are dealt with more realistically in the imaginative play of 5-year-olds. Although the youngsters like to use props, those with a high level of fantasy can pretend without props.

Boys and girls begin playing more in groups of the same gender by this time. The nature of the play changes somewhat, with girls' play becoming more calm and boys' play becoming more active. Girls still prefer to play house, but boys more often play superhero or monster. Groups are often larger than before, as friendships expand and children learn how to get along with more than one or two peers.

Five-year-olds like to build big buildings and then play inside the structures. Imaginative play is at its height just before and during this period. After children enter first grade and games-with-rules become the norm, make-believe play begins to wane. It is not at all prevalent among children much after age 7.

By about age 7, a cognitive change that allows more abstract thinking has taken place within the child. What happens to pretending? We speculate that it does not disappear at all but becomes a part of the inner self to be tapped by adults in daydreaming as well as in generating creative ideas. Adults who experienced a rich fantasy life as children may be the fortunate possessors of the skill to play around with ideas in their heads, just as they did with props and toys as children in preschool.

As you observe the children in your classroom on the last of the checklist items, you may want to make a list of the themes the children are using in their play. What can you do to help them add more themes to this list? Put out more props? Read more stories? Help the children make more costumes? Take children on more field trips so they will have additional real experiences to draw from? All of these activities are good ideas. Try them, and see how your children respond.

If You Have Not Checked This Item: Some Helpful Ideas

■ Have Big Building Supplies

Four- and 5-year-olds like to build big structures to play in. Have the youngsters use hollow wooden blocks if possible. Or bring in wooden packing crates you get from a wholesaler. Cardboard cartons, plastic milk carton carriers, scrap boards, and lumber can be used for building pretend huts, forts, houses, boats, race cars, and fire engines. Play houses also can be purchased commercially, made out of pup tents, made by covering a card table with a blanket, or by hanging sheets over lines strung in a corner of the room.

■ Read a Book

Foley and Jem (Golding, 2004). If your children are interested in space exploration, bring in several of these fine picture books to give them ideas. In this one, the boy Foley gets the idea of building a rocket ship for his dog Jem, to be the first dog to go to Mars. When he gets to Mars Jem sends back pictures of the barren landscape. Then he walks to the other side of the planet and discovers a whole new world of weird buildings and busy beings: dogs. Now Jem's too busy to send any more pictures, and the book ends with him having a great time on Mars.

Hedgie Blasts Off! (Brett, 2006) from Chapter 5 is about the hedgehog astronaut who flies to the planet Mikkop to save the volcano Big Sparkler.

If You Decide to Go to the Moon (McNulty, 2005) from Chapters 5 and 11, tells about a boy who blasts off for the Moon, what it's like in space, what it's like on the Moon, and how different it is back on Earth.

On the Moon (Milbourne, 2006) shows a girl pretending to be an astronaut, and the real astronauts blasting off, landing on the Moon, and exploring the Moon. This is a book for your youngest children. Help children make astronauts helmets.

Child Development Checklist

Name _____ Sherry _____   Observer _____ Carolyn _____

Program _____ N. Ave. _____   Dates _____ 3/12 _____

Directions:
Put an **X** for items you see the child perform regularly. Put **N** for items where there is no opportunity to observe. Leave all other items blank.

Item	Evidence	Dates
11. Dramatic Play Skills		
_N_ Does pretend play by him/herself	Seldom plays by herself	3/12
_X_ Assigns roles or takes assigned roles	Took role as daughter but later tried to assign this role to Ann	3/12
_X_ Needs particular props to do pretend play	Uses props such as real boxes & bags in grocery play	3/12
_X_ Takes on characteristics & actions related to role	Got groceries off shelf; put them in bag; went to cashier; took them home	3/12
_X_ Can pretend with imaginary objects	I have seen her pretend she is holding a spoon	3/12
_X_ Uses language for creating & sustaining the plot	Talked constantly during grocery store plot	3/12
___ Enacts exciting, danger-packed themes	No	3/12
_X_ Uses elaborate themes, ideas, details	Carried out detailed actions in grocery store plot	3/12

Figure 13–2   Dramatic Play Observations for Sherry

OBSERVING, RECORDING, AND INTERPRETING DRAMATIC PLAY SKILLS

Information from the running record on 3-year-old Sherry can be transferred to the checklist in Figure 13–2. This information shows Sherry as a mature player in this imaginative role. The only blank on her checklist ("Uses exciting, danger-packed themes") is more typically observed in a 4-year-old, especially a boy. Table 13–1, which describes the ages and stages of pretend play, can help you interpret your findings.

Table 13–1 Development of dramatic play skills

Age	Child's Pretend Play Behavior
1–2	Goes through pretend routines of eating or other brief actions, in some cases
2–3	Replays fragments of everyday experience (e.g., putting baby to bed) Repeats routine over and over in ritualistic manner Uses realistic props (if uses props at all)
3–4	Insists often on particular props in order to play May have imaginary playmate at home Uses family, doll play, hospital, cars, trains, planes, and firefighting themes Assigns roles or takes assigned roles May switch roles without warning
4–5	Uses exciting, danger-packed themes (e.g., superheroes, shooting, and running) Is more flexible about taking assigned roles during play Uses more rigid gender roles (e.g., girls as mother, waitress, or teacher; boys as father, doctor, or police officer)
5–6	Plays more with dollhouse, block structure Includes many more details, much dialogue Carries play over from one day to next sometimes Plays more in groups of same gender

Because imaginative play is an area of strength and confidence for Sherry, her teacher should consider using a dramatic play activity to help Sherry in a checklist area that needs strengthening. For example, Sherry has shown little development in the area of written language. Perhaps she could make a sign for the grocery store or pretend to write out a grocery list of things to buy in mock writing. All children's development is interrelated. We should remember to use strengths from other areas of a child's development when we design an individual plan to strengthen a child's particular needs.

LEARNING ACTIVITIES

1. Use the dramatic play section of the Child Development Checklist as a screening tool to observe all the children in your classroom. Compare the checkmarks for children who score well in the sequences of dramatic play development with their checks in social play and language development. Can you draw any conclusions from this comparison?

2. Choose a child with high-level skills in imagination and make a running record of him or her on three different days. What new details did you learn about the child's pretending?

3. Look over the activities suggested, and choose one for use with one of the children who you have determined needs help in this area. Carry

out the activity you have prescribed for the child. Record the results.

4. Take a field trip with your children to a site of interest where they can see and meet people at work in a special field. Put out appropriate props in your dramatic play and/or block areas after you return and record the kinds of pre-

tend play that take place. Is the play any different from what went on previously? If so, how do you account for this?

5. Carry out one of the book activities from this chapter with one child or a small group and see if it stimulates any pretending. How could you extend this pretending?

SUGGESTED READINGS

Bromer, B. L. (1999). Who's in the house corner? Including young children with disabilities in pretend play. *Dimensions of Early Childhood, 27*(2), 17–33.

Burton, S. J., & Edwards, L. C. (2006). Creative play: Building connections with children who are learning English. *Dimensions of Early Childhood, 34*(2), 3–8.

Isbell, R. T., & Raines, S. C. (2007). *Creativity and the arts with young children* (2nd ed.). Clifton Park, NY: Cengage.

Isenberg, J. P., & Jalongo, M. R. (2006). *Creative thinking and arts-based learning: Preschool through fourth grade* (4th ed.). Upper Saddle River, NJ: Merrill/Prentice Hall.

Jones, E., & Reynolds, G. (1992). *The play's the thing: Teachers' roles in children's play*. New York: Teachers College Press.

Levin, D. E., & Carlsson-Paige, N. (1995). The Mighty Morphin Power Rangers: Teachers voice concern. *Young Children, 50*(6), 67–72.

Paley, V. G. (2004). *A child's work: The importance of fantasy play*. Chicago: University of Chicago Press.

Perry, J. P. (2003). Making sense of outdoor pretend play. *Young Children, 58*(3), 26–30.

CHILDREN'S BOOKS

Beaty, A. (2007). *Iggy Peck, architect*. New York: Abrams.

Bergman, M., & Maland, N. (2007). *Oliver who would not sleep*. New York: Arthur A. Levine.

Best, C. (2006). *Sally Jean, the bicycle queen*. New York: Melanie Kroupa Books.

Breen, S. (2008). *Violet the pilot*. New York: Dial.

Brett, J. (2006). *Hedgie blasts off!* New York: G. P. Putnam's Sons.

Gebhard, W. (2004). *What Eddie can do*. La Jolla, CA: Kane/Miller.

Golding, S., & Oliver, M. (2004). *Foley and Jem*. New York: Sterling Publishing.

Heap, S. (2002). *What shall we play?* Cambridge, MA: Candlewick Press.*

Hoffman, M. (1991). *Amazing Grace*. New York: Dial.*

James, B. (2004). *My chair*. New York: Arthur A. Levine Books.*

Kuklin, S. (2001). *Hoops with Swoopes*. New York: Hyperion.*

Maclean, C. K. (2002). *Even fire fighters hug their moms*. New York: Dutton.

McLeod, B. (2006). *Superhero ABC*. New York: HarperCollins.

McNulty, F. (2005). *If you decide to go to the Moon*. New York: Scholastic.

Milbourne, A. (2006). *On the Moon*. London: Usborne Publishing.

Moore, J. (2007) *Freckleface Strawberry*. New York: Bloomsbury.

Peck, J. (2006). *Way far away on a wild safari*. New York: Simon & Schuster.

Richmond, M. (2006). *My shoes take me where I want to go*. Minneapolis, MN: Marianne Richmond Studios.

Seeger, P. (1986). *Abiyoyo*. New York: Macmillan.*

Soman, D., & Davis, J. (2008). *Ladybug girl*. New York: Dial.

Soto, G. (1993). *Too many tamales*. New York: Putnam's.*

Ward, M. (2005). *Mike and the bike*. Salt Lake City, UT: Cookie Jar Publishing.

Weeks, S. (2004). *If I were a lion*. New York: Atheneum.

*Multicultural.

14

Sharing Observational Data with Families

INVOLVING FAMILIES IN THEIR CHILDREN'S PROGRAMS

Early childhood programs have recognized the importance of involving families in their children's education and development. Many preschools, Head Starts, nursery schools, child-care centers, prekindergartens, and kindergartens have done everything in their power to bring parents and other family members closer to their children's programs. They schedule parent visits, parent conferences, family newsletters, family volunteer opportunities, and parenting workshops. Such programs are aware of the overwhelming research that shows:

> One of the most accurate predictors of achievement in school is not family income or parents' education level, but the extent to which parents believe they can be key resources in their children's education and become involved at school and in the community. (DiNatale, 2002, p. 91)

There is no doubt about it. When parents (or primary caregivers) are closely involved with their children's preschool programs, children tend to bloom. Youngsters seem to understand that if Mom and Dad and Grandma know the teacher and the teacher knows Mom and Dad and Grandma, whatever happens in school is all right. All these significant people will be talking about the child, making sure she is on the right track, and helping her along whenever she needs help.

Nevertheless, it is not always easy or even possible to involve all parents in their children's education. Most parents work and thus find it difficult to participate or even visit their children's programs. Some parents find it uncomfortable to visit schools where they may feel out of their element. Others think it is the teaching staff's responsibility to care for their children during the school day, while they take responsibility for their children at home. Is there some way all parents can be convinced to become involved?

Focusing on the Child

A most effective approach that many preschools have adopted is to focus on the child, not on the program. Both family members and teachers want the child to succeed in school and develop to his greatest ability. Thus it is the child who should concern them first and foremost. What is he or she like? What are his interests at home and at school? What is his favorite activity? How does he get along with others? What would his parents like to see him accomplish this year?

411

As teachers begin to develop a closer rapport with family members, they can communicate their own strong interest in this child as an individual and their commitment to helping him grow and develop in preschool. They can describe to the parents how they start by determining where each child in their class stands in his development. Then they are able to plan activities to meet each child's needs.

They can talk about finding out how the child handles herself in a strange, new environment; how she deals with stressful situations; whether she plays with others; and whether she can share and take turns. They can discuss what they want to know about the child's physical development; whether she can climb, draw with crayons, cut with scissors, build with blocks, sort things that are alike, ask questions; whether she ever tries to write or if she likes to paint; and what kind of pretending she does. At the same time, they will be asking the parents what kinds of things they would like to know about their child in school.

Such discussions need to be completely informal and not overwhelming to the parents. There is no need to pursue a long list of questions or child developmental needs. Play it by ear. The idea is for the parents and family members to understand your personal concern for their child, as well as the specific activities the children will be involved with. Stipek, Rosenblatt, and DiRocco (1994) found that

> The more specific she was about what children gained from the activities, the more parents appreciated the activities' value; thus, for example, she pointed out that playing with Legos and pinching and pulling clay help children develop the coordination necessary to hold a pencil and form letters. (p. 8)

Such conversations with parents should also let them know that the teaching staff spends time looking at their child individually to determine where she stands developmentally, and that the staff has found that the best way to determine where the child stands is to observe her by using an observation checklist to guide them.

Using the Child Development Checklist

When the time is right, give the parents a blank copy of the Child Development Checklist, telling them that this is what you and the teaching staff use as a guide to look at where their child is developmentally. Have them flip through the checklist with you, looking at the main topics. Together you might go through the items under Self-Esteem. Because their child has already been in school for a week, you can tell them what you have been able to check off so far in this area.

Are they surprised? Did they realize how well their child was able to adjust? If this is not the case, you may have to ease their concern that their child isn't "seeking other children to play with" yet, but that he no longer clings to the parent as he did during the first week of school.

Make sure that the parents understand the purpose of the Child Development Checklist: that it is not a test, but an observational guide to child development, that helps you look for the areas of strength that each child possesses and note the areas that need strengthening. No two children develop the same, nor should we expect them to.

Tell parents what you have been able to check off under Self-Esteem so far.

Such a checklist helps you note where each child stands and how to help each one progress in specific areas of his development.

Then take the next important step in involving parents/primary caregivers in their child's program: Ask them if they would like to try observing their child at home in this same way. Tell them that you realize they have been observing their child for many years. Using the checklist, they will have a chance to record what they have seen. If they agree, tell them you would like to give them a blank copy of the checklist to put somewhere handy in their house—maybe on the refrigerator door—where they can check off items they see their children performing. Point out that this can be very helpful to them as they note the different items their children accomplish. It can also help you, if they care to share any of their observations. But make sure they understand that you are not asking them to do this observing for you, but rather for them to learn more about their child in the same way you do in the classroom.

This is a big step for parents to take, and a completely different type of activity than most are used to. Be sure you have established some sort of rapport with the parents before you present this idea. Make sure they understand that looking at their child by using a checklist should be interesting and fun for them, not a chore, that it is not a test, and that it can be "for their eyes only." They do not need to share it with you or anyone else unless they feel like it. Tell them that there is no "right" or "wrong" involved. Whatever they see, they can check off. If they feel like writing down what the child does under "evidence," so much the better. Keyser (2006) has found that "parents are most interested in child development information when it directly relates to what is happening with their child" (p. 44).

If parents agree with the idea and begin to observe and record their children's behavior at home, they will often want to share what they find with you because: (a) they will want to know what certain items mean, and (b) they will want you to know how their children are doing. Point out that they may not be able to check off some of the items because the checklist is designed to look at classroom activities rather than those in the home, and because children cannot be expected to accomplish every item all at once. Development occurs over time, with maturity and practice.

What you are doing by giving parents the Child Development Checklist is much more important than merely involving them in observing their child more closely. You are *making them a part of the teaching team.* You are helping to *make them partners in the education of their children.*

MAKING PARENTS PARTNERS

One of the reasons most parents often feel so ill at ease with teachers is because they occupy such a different role. Teachers are the professionals and they, the parents, are not. In fact, most parent involvement programs focus on "helping parents learn more effective ways of working with their children" (Kasting, 1994, p. 150). There is nothing wrong with this focus. It does, however, imply a superior position for the teacher, and therefore an inferior role for the parent. The teacher has information to impart that the parent needs to learn. As Kasting (1994) noted, "Rarely do parents and teachers collaborate on the basis of mutual respect and shared responsibilities" (p. 159).

Parents who accept the role of observing their child just like the teacher does can begin to change the balance of this relationship. They can, in fact, begin to become educational partners in their own right. After all, they know more about their child than anyone else. Their influence on their child is more powerful than anyone else's. But they need to be aware of the significance of child behavior. By observing their child using the Child Development Checklist just as the teacher does, they learn what is important to look for. As they discuss this information with the teacher, they learn what these findings mean.

Parents who have become child observers get really excited about what they are discovering. After all, their child is of great importance to them. Now they are beginning to unlock the "secrets" of child development that teachers seem to know, but they do not. As they share their findings with the teacher and the teacher responds by sharing her observations with the parent, their relationship changes dramatically. They become true partners in education and care.

Arlene Kasting, coordinator of the Child Study Centre of the University of British Columbia in Vancouver, Canada, reports on the model parent involvement program (1994) using shared observations that her center has developed: Addressing the Needs of Children Through Observation and Response (ANCHOR). In this project, parents and educators observe together children's activities in the preschool classroom either on closed-circuit television or in video-taped sequences. She noted.

The shared observation experience brings parents and educators together in a common educational task. Parent and educator relationships are defined as partnerships. This view of parenting and teaching as complementary processes is integral to the project. (p. 146)

Although this was a group observation of a classroom of children containing the parents' own children, and not a home observation of a single child as discussed here, the resulting relationships of parents and educators changed for the better. Parents were not treated as persons needing instruction by educators, but as full partners in the observation process. Their input about their child's behavior was valued as a key to understanding the child. Parents felt most respected when teachers listened attentively to their remarks and asked them to give even more details. Suddenly they, not the teachers, had become the source of information.

Kasting (1994) recorded the remarks of one parent:

I have better observation skills. When you look at kids, you tend to look more closely at their interaction; how they are doing it and also why they are doing it.... And there are differences in people. We all come out to the same end, but there are so many different ways of reaching it. And you somehow have more confidence in yourself as a parent. You're more secure about the decisions that you make. (pp. 147–148)

Although the parent does not mention it, there is another important outcome for parents who do shared observations. They develop a trust in the program because the program has entrusted them enough to give them a professional's checklist and believe they are capable of using it. And, of course, they are. They may need your help in explaining what some of the items mean and your suggestions for looking at one section of the checklist at a time, but you should be just as happy as they are about their new role.

As they look at the checklist items and realize that the teaching staff is also using these same items to observe their child, parents are brought much closer to the teaching team because they feel a part of it. They may feel shy at first about showing you their filled-out checklist (of course, this is not necessary), but most parents will at least tell you what they observed for specific items. This information should be extremely helpful to you when you discover how the child behaves in his home setting—which is often quite different from school behavior.

Conversing about checklist results makes family involvement a real joy for all parties concerned. You and the families will develop reciprocal trust, and you will look forward to hearing from families about their children. Still, you may wonder how you will have the time to keep up such a running commentary with the many families of your children.

SHARING OBSERVATION RESULTS

Communication Methods

Programs that have tried using the checklist as described report a wide number of program/family communication methods.

Figure 14—1   Communication
Methods between Early
Childhood Programs and Families

- Exchanging information when parents bring or pick up children
- Phone conversations
- Faxes or e-mail
- Planned parent conferences or home visits
- Informal breakfast meetings before work
- Information sent home and returned via the child

This last method seems the most popular. Teachers run off many copies of the checklist and send out one sheet at a time to share with parents what they have checked off on a particular day. Parents are free to write on the same sheet what they have observed and return it with the child the next day, if they choose to do this. Teachers are the ones who need to initiate the use of the checklist, but once parents become involved, they often reply without prompting.

All of the written communications are kept in a child's folder or portfolio (see section later in this chapter) along with a record of phone or e-mail messages and a summary of conference results. Once a checklist has been completed by a parent or teacher, the program can invite the parent to help interpret the results and discuss how they can be used in the program or at home.

Interpreting Checklist Results

When the teacher of one preschool class, Laura S., had finished observing 4-year-old Andy on three different days for about half an hour each time (see Figure 14–2), she had a much better idea of Andy's strengths as well as areas that needed strengthening. Her observation confirmed for her that Andy did not usually play with other children, but seemed to prefer doing things on his own. He seemed independent, making choices on his own, defending his rights, being enthusiastic about the things he chose to do, and smiling much of the time. She chuckled about his characteristic tuneless humming as he busily engaged himself in block building or racing little cars. She always could tell where Andy was by his humming.

Being happy and smiling were especially important clues to Laura about the overall status of any child in her class. Andy demonstrated few inappropriate behaviors, in fact, except for his quick temper when other children tried to interfere with his activities. Laura had tried to get him to express his feelings in words, but without success. Now she noted that he really did not speak all that much. Somehow she had missed that

CHILD DEVELOPMENT CHECKLIST

Name _____ Andy _____ Observer _____ Laura S. _____

Program _____ RHead Start _____ Dates _____ 10/5, 10/7, 10/8 _____

Directions:

Put an **X** for items you see the child perform regularly. Put **N** for items where there is no opportunity to observe. Leave all other items blank.

Item	Evidence	Dates
1. Self-Esteem		
_____ Separates from primary caregiver without difficulty	Upset when mother leaves	10/5
_X_ Develops a secure attachment with teacher	Too soon to tell Okay	10/5 10/7
_X_ Completes a task successfully	Built road for race car	10/5
_X_ Makes activity choices without teacher's help	Goes directly to activity area of his choice	10/5
_____ Seeks other children to play with	Plays by himself	10/5
_____ Plays roles confidently in dramatic play	Does not do this play	10/5
_X_ Stands up for own rights	Will not let others take his toys pushes, grabs, hits	10/7
_X_ Displays enthusiasm about doing things for self	Hums a tune while he plays	10/5
2. Emotional Development		
_X_ Releases stressful feelings in appropriate manner	Lets teacher hold him	10/7
_____ Expresses anger in words rather than negative actions	Sometimes hits or pushes when angry. No words	10/7
_N_ Can be calmed in difficult or dangerous situations		
_____ Overcomes sad feelings in appropriate manner	Shows sadness when mother leaves	10/5
_N_ Handles surprising situations with control		

Figure 14–2 Child Development Checklist for Andy

Item	Evidence	Dates
__X__ Shows fondness, affection, love toward others	Lets teacher hold him	10/7
__X__ Shows interest, attention in classroom activities	Goes around trying out things	10/7
__X__ Smiles, seems happy much of the time	Always smiles & hums	10/5
3. Social Play		
_____ Spends time watching others play	Is beyond this level	10/5
__X__ Plays by self with own toys/materials	Pretends with small cars, people	10/5
__X__ Plays parallel to others with similar toys/materials	Plays with cars next to others	10/5
_____ Plays with others in group play	Not often	10/8
_____ Makes friends with other children	Has no close friends	10/8
_____ Gains access to ongoing play in positive manner	Does not try to gain access	10/8
_____ Maintains role in ongoing play in positive manner	Does not play much with others	10/8
_____ Resolves play conflicts in positive manner	Sometimes hits or pushes	10/7
4. Prosocial Behavior		
__X__ Shows concern for someone in distress	Comes near to child who is crying	10/5
_____ Can tell how another feels during conflict	Does not respond when asked about this	10/7
_____ Shares something with another	Does not seem to know how to share, hits	10/7
_____ Gives something to another	Does not do this	10/7
__X__ Takes turns without a fuss	Has trouble with favorite toys	10/7
__X__ Complies with requests without a fuss	Does what teacher asks	10/5
__X__ Helps another do a task	Helps Nat with building	10/7
__N__ Helps (cares for) another in need		

Figure 14–2 *continued*

Item	Evidence	Dates
5. Large Motor Development		
_X_ Walks down steps alternating feet	Yes	10/5
_X_ Runs with control over speed & direction	Does a lot of running	10/5
_X_ Jumps with feet together	Jumps on playground	10/5
_N_ Hops on one foot		
_X_ Climbs up, down, across climbing equipment	On playground, good control	10/5
_X_ Throws, catches & kicks balls	On playground	10/5
_X_ Rides trikes, bikes, & scooters	On playground	10/7
_N_ Does creative movement		
6. Small Motor Development		
_X_ Turns knobs, lids, eggbeaters	Uses eggbeater easily in water play	10/7
_X_ Pours liquids without Spilling	Fills plastic bottles at water table	10/7
_____ Fastens/unfastens zippers, buttons, Velcro	Needs help taking off & putting on jacket	10/5
_X_ Picks up & inserts objects with dexterity	Puzzles	10/8
_N_ Molds play dough/clay with dexterity	Not available	
_____ Uses drawing/writing tools with control	Does not draw, write	10/5
_____ Uses scissors with control	Does not use scissors	10/5
_N_ Uses hammer with control	Not available	
7. Cognitive Development		
_X_ Sorts objects by shape, color	Yes	10/5
_X_ Classifies objects by size	Sorts little cars by size	10/5

Item	Evidence	Dates
__X__ Places objects in a sequence or series	Places cars in a sequence	10/5
__N__ Recognizes, creates patterns		
_____ Counts by rote to 20	Can only count to 10	10/8
_____ Displays 1-to-1 correspondence with numbers	No, doesn't understand	10/8
__X__ Problem-solves with concrete objects	Finds ways to make tunnels for cars	10/8
__N__ Problem solves with computer programs		
8. Spoken Language		
__N__ Listens but does not speak	Beyond this level	10/5
__X__ Gives single-word answers	Sometimes	10/5
__X__ Gives short phrase Responses	Sometimes, speaks softly	10/05
_____ Does chanting	Not usually	10/05
_____ Takes part in conversations	Not usually	10/5
__X__ Speaks in expanded Sentences	Sometimes	10/5
__X__ Asks questions	Asks "When Mama will come?"	10/5
__N__ Can tell a story		
9. Emergent Writing and Reading Skills		
_____ Pretends to write with pictures & scribbles	Does not use writing tools	10/5
_____ Makes horizontal lines of writing scribbles	No	10/5
_____ Includes letterlike forms in writing	No	10/5
_____ Makes some letters, prints name or initial	No	10/5
__X__ Holds book right-side up; turns pages right to left	Likes to look at books	10/8
__X__ Pretends to read using pictures to tell story	Likes hearing stories, sometimes tells parts of them	10/8

Figure 14—2 *continued*

Item	Evidence	Dates
_____ Retells stories from books with increasing accuracy	*His speaking is limited*	*10/8*
_____ Shows awareness that print in books tells story	*No*	*10/8*
10. Art and Music Skills		
_____ Makes basic scribble shapes	*Does not use art tools, likes finger painting*	*10/7*
_____ Combines circles/squares with crossed lines	*No*	*10/7*
_____ Draws person as sun-face with arms & legs	*No*	*10/7*
_____ Combines objects together in a picture	*No*	*10/7*
N Moves legs & feet in rhythm to a beat		
N Moves arms & hands in rhythm to a beat		
N Plays instruments		
_____ Sings with group or by him/herself	*No*	*10/7*
11. Dramatic Play Skills		
X Does pretend play by him/herself	*Pretends with little cars & people*	*10/5*
_____ Assigns roles or takes assigned roles	*Does not play much with others*	*10/5*
X Needs particular props to do pretend play	*Cars, people*	*10/5*
X Takes on characteristics & actions related to role	*Motorcycle driver makes sounds*	*10/05*
_____ Can pretend with imaginary objects	*No*	
X Uses language for creating & sustaining the plot	*Talks to himself while pretending*	*10/5*
X Enacts exciting, danger-packed themes	*In solitary play with cars, people*	*10/5*
X Uses elaborate themes, ideas, details	*In solitary play*	*10/5*

important aspect of his behavior because he seemed content, and possibly because he did vocalize—if only to hum.

Now she noted that although she could understand him if she listened closely, his speaking skills were not at the level of the other 4-year-olds. She began to wonder if this might be the reason he did not get involved in playing with the others. Because dialogue is so much a part of make-believe play, a child without verbal skills might feel out of place, she reasoned. She couldn't wait to hear from Andy's mother to see what she had observed on the same items.

Laura had a strong hunch that Andy was highly creative. Watching him build elaborate roads for his race car and talk to himself as he played alone or parallel to the others, he seemed to invent all kinds of situations for the miniature people he played with. She noted that creativity certainly did not show up in his arts skills, but she reasoned that his difficulty with small motor skills may have caused him to avoid painting, drawing, and cutting.

In looking for areas of strength, Laura picked out his enthusiasm and good self-concept, his large motor skills, his cognitive skills, and his imaginative play. His special interests seemed to be block building, water play, and all kinds of outdoor play. She thought he was a bright boy who used his cognitive ability in playing by himself, rather than joining others. Areas needing strengthening included language; small motor skills; using writing, drawing, and painting tools; controlling his temper; and especially playing with the other children.

Sharing Checklist Results with Staff

To confirm her interpretation of the Child Development Checklist observation, Laura shared the results with the two other classroom workers. They were also surprised about how little Andy verbalized, and that they too hadn't picked up this fact previously. What had they missed about the other children, they wondered? One of them decided to observe Andy on her own, using the checklist to see how her results compared with Laura's. The teacher assistants were fascinated by the details Laura had gleaned in a very short time and by the way she had interpreted Andy's inability to join in group play.

Sharing Checklist Results with Parents

Laura contacted Andy's mother and found that she, too, had completed her copy of the checklist. Because she worked all day, she wondered if Laura could meet her at a nearby restaurant for coffee after work in the late afternoon. Andy's grandmother would pick up Andy and take him home. When they met for this first conference, both teacher and parent were full of enthusiasm for what they had discovered. Laura confided to the mother that she always looked for a child's areas of strength first because that gave her the best picture of the youngster. Also she used the child's areas of strength to help him improve in areas where he might need strengthening. The two decided to exchange checklists to see what each had observed.

This was the first time that the teacher, Laura, had exchanged checklists with a parent. Usually she was the one who had done the observing and the parent was on the other side of the fence waiting for her pronouncement. This way was so much better, she decided. First of all, she did not have to explain the observation method to the mother. Also, she found herself waiting with anticipation to examine the mother's checklist to see how it compared with her own, and whether it would shed any more light on Andy's development.

The mother was a bit hesitant to exchange checklists at first because she didn't know if she had done it right. But Laura assured her that everyone felt that way at first, even the classroom staff. She said all the items on the list were positive, so you couldn't really go wrong. If you saw the behavior, you checked the item. If you didn't see the behavior, you left the item blank. If there was no opportunity to observe, then you wrote N.

Laura noted that Andy's mother put Ns for some of the items related to classroom activities. Sometimes she crossed off a word or two and changed the item to something similar from the home. For example, she changed "dramatic play" to "car and truck" play. She seemed to have written many Ns where toys and materials were concerned. But the main difference between the two checklists seemed to be Andy's play with others. At home he sometimes played with his brothers, shared and took turns, and did not express aggression. The mother had written in brief explanations under the evidence section, just as Laura had done.

Andy's mother was very interested in Laura's observations. She told Laura that Andy was the youngest of three brothers and did not seem to have the language skills at age 4 that his older brothers had shown. She also noted that Andy preferred to play alone, but she had never considered that his speaking skills might be the cause.

She told how all three boys invented their own games because they had few toys at home. As a single working parent, she had all she could do to provide for their food and clothing needs. When Laura suggested that Andy might like to continue water play at home in the sink with empty containers, his mother thought this was a fine idea and also a way that he might help her with the dishes! She was especially pleased that Laura thought Andy was bright on the basis of his water play games and block building in the center. She asked Laura for other ideas for making up games with household throwaway items. Laura offered to lend her a booklet full of ideas. When Laura also mentioned that the center liked to send home picture books for parents to read to their children, Andy's mother said she thought Andy would like this a lot.

Planning for the Child Based on Checklist Results

Laura was delighted with the outcome of the meeting. She had never had a parent conference go so well. Andy's mother wanted to continue observing, so Laura gave her another checklist to use. Then she took out a learning prescription form for Andy and showed the parent how she and the staff used it to plan for a child based on checklist results. This time she and the parent filled it in with areas of strength and confidence that they had detected from their two checklist observations (see Figure 14–3). Then they discussed three areas needing strengthening for Andy and recorded them on the form as well.

LEARNING PRESCRIPTION

Name _____ Andy _____ Age ____ 4 ____ Date ____ 10/12 ____

Areas of Strength and Confidence

1. Good self-concept, happy, helpful
2. Creative in block building, water play
3. Good large motor skills on outside playground

Areas Needing Strengthening

1. Learn to play with others
2. Develop better speaking skills
3. Improve small motor coordination, writing

Activities to Help

1. Ask Andy to help new boy learn to use climber

2. Read "Louie" and give him puppet to play with

3. Do medicine dropper, water & food colors in muffin tins

Figure 14-3 Learning Prescription for Andy

Next they considered ways to use Andy's strengths to help him improve in learning to play with others, develop better speaking skills, and improve his small motor coordination. Laura, of course, had a better idea of what activities were available in the classroom, but she listened closely to the mother's suggestions. She told Laura that Andy did know how to play with others just like he did with his brothers, so they both agreed to list as the first activity "Ask Andy to help new boy learn to use climber." This might help him make a friend he could play with. Laura said she thought he might like to help Russ learn to use the outside climber because Andy was so good at it. Talking with and helping one other child should not be so difficult for Andy in the beginning as playing with a larger group.

Laura told the mother about the book *Louie* (Keats, 1975), with its title character who was never heard to speak until he first saw puppets speaking. She thought he would enjoy the story, and that maybe she could make a paper cone puppet with him. Laura said they both could read the *Louie* book because children enjoy hearing the same story repeated. She would send home a paperback copy of the book. Meanwhile, she would read the classroom copy to Andy and a small group of children and have them each make a simple paper cone puppet like the ones in the book. Laura then would use her own puppet to engage the children in talking through their puppets. Once they got the idea, she would extract herself from the pretending and let them play on their own.

Laura said she planned to do this during the activity period every day with small groups of children, always trying to include Andy. She hoped Andy and the others would like the activity enough to make other puppets on their own. This would also involve Andy with small motor and art skills. She also decided to work on Andy's problem of learning to control his temper through the puppet play by having her own puppet get angry and hit her, and asking the others to help her puppet express anger differently.

In case Andy did not get involved in making his own puppet, she thought the medicine dropper activity with colored water in a muffin tin should interest him because of his fascination with water play. The staff decided to try these activities for a week and then discuss the results at their planning session the following week. They had already planned to do similar observations for each of the children as time permitted and to involve their parents in observing at home.

Ongoing Observations by Parents and Staff

Parents had been introduced to the idea of observing at home when they enrolled their children for preschool at the beginning of the year. They were told it was voluntary on their part, but that many parents found it to be an interesting way to learn more about their child. Not all the parents in Andy's class agreed to observe at first. But during the first parent meeting when they heard other parents talking about how much they liked the activity, several more agreed to try it. They were impressed with how the teachers were asking them to find out important things about their child by doing the same thing the teachers did. Only parents who had trouble speaking English were still unsure of what to do. Laura suggested maybe one of their neighbors with children in the program could help them, and maybe their older children could translate the checklist for them.

When home observing really caught on among most of the parents, Laura kept several copies of *Observing Development of the Young Child* on hand for the parents to borrow so they could read about the items they were observing. The classroom staff of three adults took turns observing each child at three different times during a week, and soon had completed a checklist for all 18 of the children.

Parent Observation in the Classroom

Keyser (2006) tells that "some teachers invite family members to observe with them in the classroom. A short observation of children building a spaceship out of blocks can offer families a chance to understand children's ability to learn many things simultaneously: teamwork, science, physics, and physical coordination. Short interactions like these can enable parents to learn important child development information" (p. 44).

Laura invited parents one by one to observe in the program using their own copy of the checklist.

Laura decided to try it with her parents. She invited parents one by one to observe in the classroom using their own copy of the checklist. Although those who worked all day felt they could not participate, Andy's mother got so caught up with observing her child that she arranged for time off to visit the classroom and observe once a month.

Laura decided that shared observations like this gave her the most successful family involvement program she had ever known. The parents were so pleased with what they learned about their children and the program that they wanted to continue it next year when their children attended a public school kindergarten. Laura agreed to meet with a group of the parents and school personnel to make the arrangements.

DEVELOPING COLLABORATIVE PORTFOLIOS

Teachers who have initiated shared observing with parents sometimes carry this sharing one step further. They ask parents to participate in helping create a portfolio for their children. Many early childhood educators have adopted the portfolio as one of the best methods for assessing ongoing development of each child. A portfolio is an individual systematic collection of documents that reflects what a child does in a classroom. It is usually assembled by both teachers and children, and emphasizes both process and product in the documents collected (Tierney, Carter, & Desai, 1991).

Teachers of preschool children have long participated in collecting youngsters' artwork and writing scribbles. So have parents. Bringing together such a collection allows all involved to provide a more in-depth assessment of children's development. The teacher must provide the framework for collecting items; otherwise, the results may become a meaningless hodgepodge.

Helm, Beneke, and Steinheimer (2007) tell us: "There are many different approaches to systematizing a portfolio collection process. They discuss a variety of portfolios that have been effectively used in early childhood programs. Some programs use a three-folio system with separate portfolios for ongoing work, current work, and permanently kept work" (p. 41).

The purpose for creating the portfolio may be the deciding factor in how to assemble it. Teachers who need to document a child's development will be assembling a *developmental portfolio.* Jones and Shelton (2006) explained that "portfolios in which the primary purpose is to facilitate and chart development emphasize work in progress. They foster the development of knowledge, skills, and dispositions that will be employed in subsequent learning and practice contexts. The builder is not alone in these endeavors" (p. 29).

Such portfolios can be used for assessment of a child's development by the teachers, the program, outside evaluators, and of course, the parents. This author suggests using the Child Development Checklist as an outline for collecting documentation materials. Observing and documenting can then go hand-in-glove in helping teachers, children, and parents to illustrate where the child stands in each of the development areas.

Appropriate Portfolio Items (Evidence of Development)

- Products representing each area of child development
- Products related to learning objectives of teachers and parents
- Products showing ongoing development over time
- A variety of products including teachers' records, parents' records, photos, artwork, writing scribbles, lists of favorite books, completed checklists, anecdotal records, communications from parents, tapes of child's speech, children's journals, children's narratives of science experiments, field trips, made-up stories
- Products that can be used for meaningful communication with parents and other professionals
- Products that can be used for making curricular decisions

Why Make Portfolios?

Before beginning to create a portfolio for each child, it should be clearly understood what the portfolios will be used for, thus what work samples will best illustrate this use. In the case of collaborative developmental portfolios assembled by teachers and parents who are doing checklist observations of each child, the portfolios will be used to support observational data throughout the year about the children's development in the areas of self-esteem, emotional development, social play, prosocial behavior, large motor development, small motor development, cognitive development, spoken language, emergent writing and reading skills, art and music skills, and dramatic play skills (all areas of the Child Skills Checklist).

Mindes (2003) tells us:

> Observational notes form the foundation of the portfolio. To enrich the observational record, add to the collection examples of each child's work. A collection of children's paintings, drawings, and stories show what children know. Besides the artifacts, include lists of books read, transcripts of discussions with children about their work, and other products collected throughout the year provide a good progress report. (pp. 74–75)

At first this may look like an overwhelming task, but once the observers realize the portfolio can be assembled over the entire school year, they may be more willing to take on the task of adding a piece of evidence to one of the 11 areas of development only when appropriate. For example, the teacher may add a sample of a child's writing at the beginning, middle, and end of the year. Or she may decide to include only a copy of a child's journal. Photos of children at work and play can be excellent illustrations of their development. Some examples of possible portfolio products for the 11 checklist areas might include

Self-esteem

- Photos of child showing classroom accomplishments
- Anecdotal records about child from classroom meetings
- Parents' communications about child at home

Emotional development

- Teacher's records of how child handles stress, anger, joy
- Photo of books child likes to hear when under stress
- Finger painting child made to relieve stress

One child chooses to include a photo of books he likes to hear.

Social play

- Photos of child playing with others
- List of dramatic play themes child participates in
- Parent communication about child playing in neighborhood

Prosocial behavior

- Teacher's records on how child shares, takes turns, helps
- Parent communication of child's helping at home
- Name of helping storybook child likes to hear

Large motor development

- Photo of child on outside climber
- Photo of large hollow block building child helped build
- Parent communication on child climbing stairs up and down

A teacher chose to include a photo of a child on an outside climber.

Small motor development
- Sample of cut-and-paste artwork
- Anecdotal record of child zipping jacket, tying shoes
- Photo of child pounding nails into wood

Cognitive development
- Pictures with colors child identified
- Photo of block enclosure child built
- Computer printout of child's number game

Spoken language
- Tape of story child tells
- List of songs child sings
- Funny words child likes to say

Emergent literacy
- Page of scribbles child makes
- List of books parent has read to child
- Sign-up sheet with name child prints

Art and music skills
- Sample of easel painting
- Tape of child singing
- Photo of playdough creation

Dramatic play skills
- Hand puppet child made for pretending
- Videotape of child in dramatic play role
- Running record of child pretending with small figures

Once the collecting has started, teachers must date each piece of evidence and include who chose it and what it represents. For example, a sheet of art scribbles may represent emergent drawing or it may be emergent writing, depending on how it is done and what the child has to say about it.

What Form Should a Portfolio Take?

Where will you keep these products for each child? Puckett and Black (2000) suggest:

> There is no one way to assemble, store, and retrieve portfolio contents. Methods will depend upon the types of portfolio products chosen.... File folders, expandable folders, hanging files,

pocket folders, oversized sheets of construction paper folded in half and stapled, stacking baskets, corrugated cubbyhole units, wall filing units, and uniform sized boxes are just a few of the possibilities. (p. 199)

How a portfolio will be used also helps determine its size and method of material storage. Portfolios should not be too large or heavy if you intend to carry them to meetings with staff, parents, or other professionals. A large three-ring binder with transparent sheets and pockets is the choice for some collectors. An accordion file folder is used by others. Labeled dividers or index cards are also necessary for handy data retrieval.

How Can Portfolios Be Used?

As the school year progresses, teachers need to add to each child's portfolio regularly. This can happen if portfolios are actually used in an appropriate fashion, and not just as storage containers for children's products. They should be the focus for classroom planning sessions and team meetings with parents. Whether or not parents contribute, they will want to view and discuss the contents of their child's portfolio from time to time.

Many educators, including Mindes, Ireton, and Mardell-Czudnowski (1996), are beginning to realize the value of a portfolio's use with parents:

One promising use of portfolio is a parent-education piece. That is, you review the portfolio with parents. Besides seeing child progress, parents learn about developmentally appropriate practice in a practical, specific way. Examples of organizational categories for portfolios include products from a theme on personal growth, favorite stories, special science projects, or other materials chosen by child and teacher to show to parent. (p. 234)

During team meetings and parent sessions, the focus should be on what you have observed the child accomplishing and what you have interpreted her present needs to

When you know the strengths of each child, you can design your program to meet his needs.

be. Activities for helping the child to accomplish these needs can be discussed and planned as the child's products and observational data are shared. Both parents and staff can contribute to such discussions in a meaningful way as they learn how children develop through the observations they have done.

Observing the development of young children is thus a teaching as well as a learning technique that should benefit all of its participants—teachers, college students, children, and families—because it outlines each aspect of child development carefully, objectively, and positively. Promoting development in young children works best when it focuses on assessing their strengths. When you know the strengths of each child in every aspect of development, you will be able to design your program to meet an individual's needs as the children in your classroom work and play together creating their own unique selves.

LEARNING ACTIVITIES

1. Discuss with members of the classroom team how parents have been involved in your program in past years and whether this method has been successful. Record in some detail what the role of the different team members has been and what they have to say about it.

2. Make a list of ideas of how team members can focus on the child when meeting with parents. Include what materials they will need to take to parent meetings and how they will discuss these materials with the parents. Also note how the team members will elicit information about the child from the parents. (Sit in on a parent meeting, if possible.)

3. Discuss with team members the possibility of using the Child Development Checklist with the parents for home observation of their child. Record their comments about this idea, both negative and positive. Make a list of what you believe parents could learn from such observations and the sharing of results with the teaching team.

4. Discuss with team members the idea of making parents partners. Why would they want to do it? How can they do it? What would be accomplished if this happened?

5. Put together a portfolio for one of the children. Involve other team members, the child, and parents if possible. What did you include? Why? How did you organize the portfolio? How will you use it?

SUGGESTED READINGS

Bennett, T. (2006). Future teachers forge family connections, *Young Children, 61*(1), 22–27.

Mass, Y., & Cohan, K. A. (2006). Home connections to learning: Supporting parents as teachers. *Young Children, 61*(1), 54–55.

Ray, J. A., & Shelton, D. (2004). E-pals: Connecting with families through technology. *Young Children, 59*(3), 30–32.

Weldin, D. J., & Tumarkin, S. R. (1998–99). Parent involvement: More power in the portfolio process. *Childhood Education, 75*(2), 90–95.

Wright, K., Stegelin, D. A., & Hartle, L. (2007). *Building family, school, and community partnerships* (3rd ed.). Upper Saddle River, NJ: Merrill/Prentice Hall.

References

Ahola, D., & Kovacik, A. (2007). *Observing and understanding child development: A child study manual.* Clifton Park, NY: Delmar/Cengage.

Ainsworth, M. D. S., Bell, S. M., & Stayton, D. J. (1974). Infant-mother attachment and social development: "Socialization" as a product of reciprocal responsiveness to signals. In M. M Richards (Ed.), *The integration of the child into the social world.* London: Cambridge University Press.

Alexander, N. P. (2005). "Tell her I'll pay with a credit card." *Dimensions of Early Childhood, 33*(1), 30–31.

Allen, K. E., & Marotz (2007). *Developmental profiles: Pre-birth through twelve.* Clifton Park, NY: Cengage.

Althouse, R., Johnson, M. H., & Mitchell, S. T. (2003). *The colors of learning: Integrating the visual arts into the early childhood curriculum.* New York: Teachers College.

Anderson, G. T., & Robinson, C. C. (2006). Rethinking the dynamics of young children's social play. *Dimensions of Early Childhood, 34*(1), 11–16.

Andrews, T. (1997). Wordworking: Winning from the beginning. *Texas Child Care, 21*(2), 28–33.

Ariza-Evans, M. (2004). Self-esteem and young children: Guiding principles. *Dimensions of Early Childhood, 32*(1), 21–27.

Baghban, M. (2007). Scribbles, labels, and stories: The role of drawing in the development of writing. *Young Children, 62*(1), 20–26.

Balaban, N. (2006). *Everyday goodbyes: Starting school and early care: A guide to the separation process.* New York: Teachers College Press.

Barron, M. (1999). Three- and four-year-olds completing 150-piece puzzles? Impossible? *Young Children, 54*(5), 10–11.

Baumeister, R. F., Bushman, B. J., Campbell, J. D., Krueger, J. L., & Vohs, K. D. (2004). Exploding the self-esteem myth. *Scientific American, 292*(1), 84–91.

Beaty, J. J., & Pratt, L. (2007). *Early literacy in preschool and kindergarten* (2nd ed.). Upper Saddle River, NJ: Merrill/Prentice Hall.

Beaty, J. J. (2004). *Safety in preschool programs.* Upper Saddle River, NJ: Merrill/Prentice Hall

Beaty, J. J. (2008). *Skills for preschool teachers* (8th ed.). Upper Saddle River, NJ: Merrill/Prentice Hall.

Benjamin, A. C. (1994). Observations in early childhood classrooms: Advice for the field. *Young Children, 49*(6), 14–20.

Bentzen, W. R. (2005). *Seeing young children: A guide to observing and recording behavior* (5th ed.). Clifton Park, NY: Cengage.

Bergen, D., & Coscia, J. (2001). *Brain research and childhood education.* Olney, MD: Association for Childhood Education International.

Berk, L. E. (1994). Vygotsky's theory: The importance of make-believe play. *Young Children, 50*(1), 30–39.

Bodrova, E., & Leong, D. J. (1996). *Tools of the mind: A Vygostskian approach to early childhood education.* Upper Saddle River, NJ: Merrill/Prentice Hall.

Bowlby, J. (1969). *Attachment and loss: Vol. 1. Attachment.* New York: Basic Books.

Bowling, H. J., & Rogers, S. (2001). The value of healing in education. *Young Children, 56*(2), 79–81.

434

Brazelton, T. B., & Sparrow, J. D. (2001). *Touchpoints 3 to 6. Your child's emotional and behavioral development.* Cambridge, MA: Perseus Publishing.

Bridge, C. A. (1986). Predictable books for beginning readers and writers. In M. R. Sampson (Ed.), *The pursuit of literacy: Early reading and writing* (pp. 81–96). Dubuque, IA: Kendall/Hunt.

Bronson, M. B. (1995). *The right stuff for children birth to 6.* Washington, DC: National Association for the Education of Young Children.

Brooks-Gunn, J., & Matthews, W. S. (1979). *He & she: How children develop their sex-role identity.* Upper Saddle River, NJ: Merrill/Prentice Hall.

Buchoff, R. (1994). Joyful voices: Facilitating language growth through the rhythmic response to chanting. *Young Children, 49*(4), 26–30

Burton, S. J., & Edwards, L. C. (2006). Creative play: Building connections with children who are learning English. *Dimensions of Early Childhood, 34*(2), 3–8.

Caplan, T., & Caplan, F. (1983). *The early childhood years: The 2 to 6 year old.* New York: Putnam.

Charlesworth, R. (1996). *Experiences in math for young children* (3rd ed.). Clifton Park, NY: Cengage.

Charlesworth, R., & Lind, K. K. (2007). *Math & science for young children* (5th ed.). Clifton Park, NY: Cengage.

Cherry, C. (1972). *Creative art for the developing child.* Belmont, CA: Fearon.

Cherry, C. (1976). *Creative play for the developing child.* Belmont, CA: Fearon.

Chiron, C., Jambaque, I., Nabbout, R., Lounes, R. Syrota, A., & Dulac, O. (1997). The right brain hemisphere is dominant in infants. *Brain, 120*(6), 1057–1065.

Clay, M. J. (1991). *Becoming literate.* Portsmouth, NH: Heinemann.

Clemens, S. G. (1991). Art in the classroom: Making every day special. *Young Children, 46*(2), 4–11.

Clements, R., & Schneider, S. L. (2006). *Movement-based learning.* Reston, VA: National Association for Sport & Physical Education.

Copley, J. B. (2000). *The young child and mathematics.* Washington, DC: National Association for the Education of Young Children.

Corsaro, W. A. (2003). *We're friends, right? Inside kids' culture.* Washington, DC: Joseph Henry Press.

Cosgrove, M. S. (1991). Cooking in the classroom: The doorway to nutrition. *Young Children, 46*(3), 43–46.

Cratty, B. J. (1982). Motor development in early childhood: Critical issues for researchers in the 1980's. In B. Spodek (Ed.), *Handbook of research in early childhood education.* New York: The Free Press.

Cratty, B. J. (1986). *Perceptual and motor development in infants and children* (3rd ed.). Englewood Cliffs, NJ: Prentice Hall.

Curenton, S. M. (2006). Oral storytelling: A cultural art that promotes school readiness. *Young Children, 61*(5), 78–87.

Curtis, D., & Carter, M. (2006). *The art of awareness: How observation can transform your teaching.* Upper Saddle River, NJ: Merrill/Prentice Hall.

Damon, W. (1983). *Social and personality development: Infancy through adolescence.* New York: Norton.

Damon, W. (1988). *The moral child: Nurturing children's natural moral growth.* New York: Macmillan.

Davidson, J. I. (1996). *Emergent literacy and dramatic play in early education.* Clifton Park, NY: Cengage.

De la Roche, E. (1996). Snowflakes are not all the same: Developing meaningful art experiences for young children. *Young Children, 51*(2), 82–83.

Deerwester, K. (2006). Hitting, biting, & pushing, oh my! *Children Our Concern, 29*(1), 9.

Deerwester, K. (2007). Teaching about feelings. *Children Our Concern, 30*(1), 7.

Denham, S. A. (1998). *Emotional development in young children.* New York: Guilford Press.

Dickinson, D. K., & Tabors, P. O. (2002). Fostering language and literacy in classrooms and homes. *Young Children, 57*(2), 10–18.

DiNatale, L. (2002). Developing high-quality family involvement programs in early childhood settings. *Young Children, 57*(5), 90–95.

Dodge, D. T., Heroman, C., Charles, J., & Maioca, J. (2004). Beyond outcomes: How ongoing assessment supports children's learning and leads to meaningful curriculum. *Young Children, 59*(1), 20–28.

Dunn, M. (2003). Getting along while getting ahead: Meeting children's social and emotional needs in a climate of academic accountability. *Dimensions of Early Childhood, 31*(3), 18–26.

Edwards, L. C. (2002). *The creative arts: A process approach for teachers and children* (3rd ed.). Upper Saddle River, NJ: Merrill/Prentice Hall.

Edwards, L. C. (2006). *The creative arts: A process approach for teachers and children* (4th ed.). Upper Saddle River, NJ: Merrill/Prentice Hall.

Egertson, H. A. (2006). In praise of butterflies: Linking self-esteem and learning. *Young Children, 61*(6), 58–60.

Eisenberg, N. Lennon, R., & Roth, K. (1983). Prosocial development: A longitudinal study. *Developmental Psychology, 19*(6), 846–855.

Eliot, L. (1999). *What's going on in there? How the brain and mind develop in the first five years of life.* New York: Bantam.

Ellis, S. M., Gallingane, C., & Kemple, K. M. (2006). Fiction, fables, & fairytales: Children's books support friendships. *Dimensions of Early Childhood, 34*(3), 28–35.

Engel, B. S. (1996). Learning to look: Appreciating child art. *Young Children, 51*(3), 74–79.

Entz, S., & Galarza, S. (2000). *Picture this: Digital and instant photography activities for early childhood learning.* Thousand Oaks, CA: Corwin Press.

Fabes, R. A., Eisenberg, N., Nyman, M., & Michealieu, Q. (1991). Young children's appraisal of others' spontaneous emotional reactions. *Developmental Psychology, 27*, 858–866.

Farish, J. M. (2001). Helping young children in frightening times. *Young Children, 59*(6), 6–7.

Feeney, S., & Moravcik, E. (2005). Children's literature: A window to understanding self and others. *Young Children, 60*(5), 20–27.

Ferreiro, E., & Teberosky, A. (1982). *Literacy before schooling.* Portsmouth, NH: Heinemann.

Fischer, M. A., & Gillespie, C. W. (2003). Computers and young children's development. *Young Children, 58*(4), 85–91.

Frey, W. H., & Langseth, M. (1985). *Crying: The mystery of tears.* Minneapolis, MN: Winston.

Fromberg, D. P. (1998). Play issues in early childhood education. In C. Seefeldt & A. Galper (Eds.), *Continuing issues in early childhood education.* Upper Saddle River, NJ: Merrill/ Prentice Hall.

Frost, J. L., Wortham, S. C., & Reifel, S.(2005). *Play and child development.* Upper Saddle River, NJ: Merrill/Prentice Hall.

Furman, R. A. (1995). Helping children cope with stress and deal with feelings. *Young Children, 50*(2), 33–41.

Gallagher, K. C. (2005). Brain research and early childhood development: A primer for developmentally appropriate practice. *Young Children, 60*(4), 12–20.

Gallahue, D. L. (1993). *Developmental physical education for today's children.* Dubuque, IA: Brown & Benchmark.

Gambrell, L. B., & Mazzoni, S. A. (1999). Emergent literacy: What research reveals about learning to read. In C. Seefeldt (Ed.), *The early childhood curriculum: Current findings in theory and practice.* New York: Teachers College Press.

Gellens, S. (1996). Children's art must be child produced. *Children Our Concern, 21*(1), 7–9.

Gellens, S. (2005). Integrate movement to enhance children's brain development. *Dimensions of Early Childhood, 53*(3), 14–21

Gelman, S. A. (1998). Categories in young children's thinking. *Young Children, 53*(1), 20–26.

Goleman, D. (1997). *Emotional intelligence.* New York: Bantam.

Gottschall, S. (1995). Hug-a-book: A program to nurture a young child's love of books and reading. *Young Children, 50*(4), 29–35.

Gottschall, S. (1989). Understand and accepting separation feelings. *Young Children, 44*(6), 11–16.

Gowen, J. W. (1995). The early development of symbolic play. *Young Children, 50*(3), 75–84.

Greenspan, S. I. (1997). *The growth of the mind and the endangered origins of intelligence.* Reading, MA: Addison-Wesley.

Gronlund, G., & James, M. (2005). *Focused observations: How to observe children for assessment and curriculum planning.* St. Paul, MN: Redleaf Press.

Hale, J., & Roy, J. (1996, 16 March). *How art activities can be used to enhance the education of young children.* Paper presented at the Southern Early Childhood Association Conference, Little Rock, AR. (ERIC Document No. ED 394937)

Harter, S. (1998). The development of self-separation. In W. Damon & N. Eisenberg (Eds.), *Handbook of child psychology: Social, emotional and personality development* (5th ed.). New York: Wiley

Hatcher, B., & Petty, K. (2004). Seeing is believing: Visible thought in dramatic play. *Young Children, 59*(6), 79–82.

Hayes, A. H. (1990). From scribbling to writing: Smoothing the way. *Young Children, 45*(3), 62–68.

Hearron, P. F., & Hildebrand, V. (2005). *Guiding young children* (7th ed.). Upper Saddle River, NJ: Merrill/Prentice Hall.

Helm, J. H., Beneke, S., & Steinheimer, K. (2007). *Windows on learning: Documenting young children's work.* New York: Teachers College Press.

Hoffman, E. (2004). *Magic capes, amazing powers: Transforming superhero play in the classroom.* St. Paul, MN: Redleaf Press.

Holzman, M. (1983). *The language of children.* Upper Saddle River, NJ: Merrill/Prentice Hall.

Honig, A. S., & Wittmer, S. A. (1996). Helping children become more prosocial: Ideas for classrooms, families, schools, and communities. *Young Children, 51*(2), 62–70.

Hopkins, A. R. (2002). Children and grief: The role of the early childhood educator. *Young Children, 57*(1), 40–47.

Howes, C., & Ritchie, (2002). *A matter of trust: Connecting teachers and learners in the early childhood classroom.* New York: Teachers College Press.

Howes, C. (1996). The earliest friendships. In W. M. Bukowski, A. F. Newcomb, & W. W. Hartup (Eds.), *The company they keep: Friendship in early childhood and adolescence.* New York: Cambridge University Press.

Huber, L. K. (1999). Woodworking with young children: You can do it! *Young Children, 54*(6), 32–34.

Hughes, F. P. (1991). *Children, play and development.* Boston: Allyn and Bacon.

Hunter, R. (2000). Some thoughts about sitting still. *Young Children, 55*(3), 50.

Hyson, M. C. (2004). *The emotional development of young children: Building an emotion-centered curriculum.* New York: Teachers College Press.

Isbell, R. T. (2002). Telling and retelling stories: Language learning and literacy. *Young Children, 57*(2), 26–30.

Izard, C. E. (1991). *The psychology of emotions.* New York: Plenum.

Izard, C. E. (1977). *Human emotions.* New York: Plenum.

Jablon, J. R., Dombro, A. L., & Dichtelmiller, M. L. (2007). *The power of observation for birth through eight* (2nd ed.). Washington, DC: Teaching Strategies/NAEYC.

Jalongo, M. R. (2008). *Learning to listen, listening to learn.* Washington, DC: National Association for the Education of Young Children.

Jensen, E. (1998). *Teaching with the brain in mind.* Alexandria, VA: Association for Supervision and Curriculum Development.

Johnston, C. B. (2003). Effects of television violence on young children: Viewed from Vtgotsky's sociocultural perspective. *Dimensions of Early Childhood, 31*(2), 22–30.

Jones, M., & Shelton, M. (2006). *Developing your portfolio: Enhancing your learning & showing your stuff.* New York: Routledge.

Kalmar, K. (2008). Let's give children something to talk about! Oral language and preschool literacy. *Young Children, 63*(1), 88–92.

Kaplan, L. J. (1978). *Oneness and separateness: From infant to individual.* New York: Simon & Schuster.

Kasting, A. (1994). Respect, responsibility and reciprocity: The 3 Rs of parent involvement. *Childhood Education, 70*(3), 146–150.

Keats, E. J. (1975). *Louie.* New York: Scholastic.

Kellogg, R. (1970). *Analyzing children's art.* Palo Alto, CA: National Press Books.

Kemple, K. M. (1991). Preschool children's peer acceptance and social interaction. *Young Children, 46*(5), 37–54.

Kemple, K. M. (1996). Teachers' beliefs and reported practices concerning sociodramatic play. *Journal of Early Childhood Teacher Education, 17*(2), 19–30.

Kemple, K. M. (2004). *Let's be friends: Peer competence and social inclusion in early childhood programs.* New York: Teachers College Press.

Keyser, J. (2006). *From parents to partners: Building a family-centered childhood program.* St. Paul, MN: Redleaf Press.

Kosnik, C. (1993). Everyone is a V.I.P. in this class. *Young Children, 49*(1), 32–37.

Koster, J. B. (1999). Clay for little fingers. *Young Children, 54*(2), 18–22.

Kyoung-Hye Seo. (2003). What children's play tells us about teaching mathematics. *Young Children, 58*(1), 28–34.

LeDoux, J. (1996). *The emotional brain: The mysterious underpinnings of emotional life.* New York: Simon & Schuster.

Leithead, M. (1996). Happy hammering: A hammering activity center with build-in success. *Young Children, 51*(3), 12.

Leppo, M. L., Davis, D., & Crim, B. (2000). The basics of exercising the mind and body. *Childhood Education, 76*(3), 142–148.

Levin, D. E. (2003). Beyond banning war and superhero play: Meeting children's needs in violent times. *Young Children, 58*(3), 60–63.

Linder, T., Holm, C. B., & Walsh, K. A. (1999). Transdisciplinary play-based assessment. In E. V. Nuttall, I. Romero, & J. Kalesnik (Eds.), *Assessing and screening preschoolers' psychological and educational dimensions.* Boston: Allyn & Bacon.

Lucos, L. (2007–08). The pain of attachment—"You have to put a little wedge in there." *Childhood Education, 84*(2), 85–90.

Machado, J. M. (1995). *Early childhood experiences in language arts: Emerging literacy.* Clifton Park, NY: Cengage.

Maldonado, N. S. (1996). Puzzles: A pathetically neglected, commonly available resource. *Young Children, 51*(4), 4–10.

Marion, M. (1997). Guiding young children's understanding and management of anger. *Young Children, 52*(7), 62–67.

Marion, M. (2003). *Guidance of young children* (6th ed.). Upper Saddle River, NJ: Merrill/Prentice Hall.

Markus, H. R., & Kitayama, S. (1991). Cultural and the self: Implications for cognition, emotion, and motivation. *Psychological Review, 98,* 224–253.

Marshall, H. (2001). Cultural influence on the development of self-concept: Updating our thinking. *Young Children, 56*(6), 19–25.

Martin, S. (1994). *Take a look: Observation and portfolio assessment in early childhood education.* Menlo Park, CA: Addison-Wesley.

Mayer, K. (2007). Emerging knowledge about emergent writing. *Young Children, 62*(1), 34–40.

McDevitt, T. M., & Ormrod, J. E. (2004), *Child development: Educating and working with children and adolescents.* Upper Saddle River, NJ: Merrill/Prentice Hall.

McFarland, L. (2008). Anecdotal records: Valuable tools for assessing young children's development. *Dimensions of Early Childhood, 36*(1), 31–36.

McGhee, P. E. (2005). The importance of nurturing children's sense of humor. *Children Our Concern, 28*(1), 16–17.

McNair, J. C. (2007). Say my name, say my name! Using children's names to enhance early literacy. *Young Children, 62*(5), 84–89.

McVicker, C. J. (2007). Young readers respond: The importance of child participation in emerging literacy. *Young Children, 62*(3), 18–22.

Micklo, S. J. (1995). Developing young children's classification and logical thinking skills. *Childhood Education, 72*(1), 24–28.

Mindes, G. (2003). *Assessing young children* (2nd ed.). Upper Saddle River, NJ: Merrill/Prentice Hall.

Mindes, G., Ireton, H., & Mardell-Czudnowski, C. (1996). *Assessing young children,* Clifton Park, NY: Cengage.

Mitchell-Copeland, J. Denham, S. A., & DeMulder, E. K. (1997). Q-sort assessment of child-teacher attachment relationships and social competence in the preschool. *Early Education and Development, 8*(1), 27–36.

Moomaw, S., & Hieronymus, B. (1995). *More than counting: Whole math activities for preschool and kindergarten.* St. Paul, MN: Redleaf Press.

Mooney, C. B. (2000). *Theories of childhood: An introduction to Dewey, Montessori, Erikson, Piaget, and Vygotsky.* St. Paul, MN: Redleaf Press.

Moore, S. G. (1982). Prosocial behavior in the early years: Parent and peer influences. In B. Spodek (Ed.), *Handbook of research in early childhood education.* New York: The Free Press.

Morrow, L. M., & Grambell, L. B. (2004). *Using children's literature in preschool: Comprehending and enjoying books.* Newark, DE: International Reading Association.

National Association for the Education of Young Children. (1991). Guidelines for appropriate curriculum content and assessment in programs serving children ages 3 through 8. *Young Children, 48*(5), 29–33.

National Association for the Education of Young Children. (1996). NAEYC position statement: Responding to linguistic and cultural diversity—recommendations for effective early childhood education. *Young Children, 51*(2), 4–12.

National Association for the Education of Young Children. (1998). Learning to read and write: Developmentally appropriate practices for young children. *Young Children, 53*(4), 30–46.

National Association for the Education of Young Children. (2004). Where we stand on curriculum, assessment, and program evaluation. *Young Children, 59*(1), 51–53.

Neuman, S. B., & Roskos, K. A. (1993). *Language and literacy learning in the early years.* Ft. Worth, TX: Harcourt Brace.

Newberger, J. J. (1997). New brain development research: A wonderful window of opportunity to build public support for early childhood education. *Young Children, 52*(4), 4–9.

Oken-Wright, P. (1998). Transition to writing: Drawing as a scaffold for emergent writers. *Young Children, 53*(2), 76–81.

Olds, A. R. (1994). From cartwheels to caterpillars: Children's need to move indoors and out. *Child Care Information Exchange,* No. 5, 32–36.

Opitz, M. F. (2000). *Rhymes and reasons: Literature and language play for phonological awareness.* Portsmouth, NH: Heinemann.

Otto, B. (2002). *Language development in early education.* Upper Saddle River, NJ: Merrill/Prentice Hall.

Palmer, H. (2001). The music, movement, and learning connection. *Young Children, 56*(5), 13–17.

Paneque, O. M. (2006). Good intentions, bad advice for bilingual families. *Childhood Education, 82*(3), 171–174.

Parker, J. G., & Asher, S. R. (1987). Peer relations and later personal adjustments: Are low accepted children at risk? *Psychological Bulletin, 102,* 357–389.

Parten, M. B. (1932). Social participation among preschool children. *Journal of Abnormal and Social Psychology, 27,* 243–369.

Piaget, J. (1976). *The child and reality.* New York; Penguin Books.

Pica, R. (1995). *Experiences in movement: With music, activities, and theory.* Clifton Park, NY: Cengage.

Pica, R. (1997). Beyond physical development: Why young children need to move. *Young Children, 52*(6), 4–11.

Puckett, M. B., & Black, J. K. (2000). *Authentic assessment of the young child.* Upper Saddle River, NJ: Merrill/Prentice Hall.

Puckett, M. B., & Black, J. K. (2005). *The young child: Development from prebirth through age eight* (4th ed.). Upper Saddler River, NJ: Merrill/Prentice Hall.

Raikes, H. (1996). A secure base for babies: Applying attachment concepts to the infant care setting. *Young Children, 51*(5), 59–67.

Ramsey, P. B. (1991). *Making friends in school: Promoting peer relationships in early childhood.* New York: Teachers College Press.

Ramsey, P. G. (1987). *Teaching and learning in a diverse world: Multicultural education for young children.* New York: Teachers College Press.

Resnick, L. B. (1989). Developing mathematical knowledge. *American Psychologist. 44*(2), 162–169.

Richardson, L. I. Goodman, K. L., Hartman, N. N., & LePique, H. C. (1980). *A mathematics activity curriculum for early childhood and special education.* New York: Macmillan.

Riley, D, San Juan, R. R., Klinker, J., & Ramminger, A. (2008). *Social and emotional development: Connecting science and practice in early childhood settings.* St. Paul, MN: Redleaf Press.

Robinson, E. H. M., & Curry, J. R. (2005–06). Promoting altruism in the classroom. *Childhood Education, 82*(2), 68–73.

Rodrigues, D., Smith-Carter, L., & Voytecki, K. (2007). Freedom from social isolation for young students with disabilities. *Childhood Education, 83*(5), 316–321.

Rojas-Cortez, M. (2001). It's all about talking: Oral language development in a bilingual classroom. *Dimensions of Early Childhood, 29*(1), 11–15.

Romero, I. (1999). Individual assessment procedures with preschool children. In E. V. Nuttall, I. Romero, & J. Kalesnik (Eds.), *Assessing and screening preschoolers' psychological and educational dimensions.* Boston: Allyn & Bacon.

Roskos, K., & Christie, J. (2001). On not pushing too hard: A few cautionary remarks about linking literacy and play. *Young Children, 56*(3), 64–66.

Roskos, K. A., Christie, J. F., & Richgels, D. J. (2003). The essentials of early literacy instruction. *Young Children, 58*(2), 52–60.

Rubin, K. H. (1983). Recent perspectives on social competence and peer status: Some introductory re-marks. *Child Development, 54,* 1383–1385.

Sanders, S. W. (1992). *Designing preschool movement programs.* Champaign, IL: Human Kinetics.

Sanders, S. W. (2002). *Active for life: Developmentally appropriate programs for young children.* Champaign, IL: Human Kinetics.

Sanders, S. W. (2006). Physically active for life: Eight essential motor skills for all children. *Dimensions of Early Childhood, 34*(1), 3–10.

Saunders, R., & Bingham-Newman, A. M. (1984). *Piagetian perspective for preschools: A thinking book for teachers.* Upper Saddler River, NJ: Merrill/Prentice Hall.

Schickedanz, J. A., & Casbergue, R. M. (2004). *Writing in preschool: Learning to orchestrate meaning and marks.* Newark, DE: International Reading Association.

Schickedanz, J. A. (1986). *More than the ABCs: The early stages of reading and writing.* Washington, DC: National Association for the Education of Young Children.

Schickedanz, J. A. (1999). *Much more than the ABCs: The early stages of reading and writing.* Washington, DC: NAEYC.

Schrader, C. T., & Hoffman, S. (1987). Encouraging children's early writing efforts. *Day Care and Early Education, 15*(2), 9–13.

Schwartz, J. I. (1981), Children's experiments with language. *Young Children, 36*(5), 16–26.

Seagull, E. A. W., & Kallen, D. J. (1978). Normal social and emotional development of the preschool-age child. In N. B. Enzer & K. W. Goin (Eds.), *Social and emotional development: The preschooler.* New York: Walker & Co.

Seefeldt, C., & Wasik, B. A. (2006). *Early education: Three-, four-, and five-year-olds go to school* (2nd ed.). Upper Saddle River, NJ: Merrill/Prentice Hall.

Seefeldt, C. (1995). Art—A serious work. *Young Children, 50*(3), 39–45.

Seefeldt, C. (1998). Assessing young children. In C. Seefeldt & A. Galper (Eds.), *Continuing issues in early childhood education* (pp. 314–338). Upper Saddle River, NJ: Merrill/ Prentice Hall.

Segati, L., Brown-DuPaul, J., & Keyes, T. L. (2003). Using everyday materials to promote problem-solving in toddlers. *Young Children, 58*(5), 12–18.

Shaw, J., & Blake, S. (1998). *Mathematics for young children.* Upper Saddle River, NJ: Merrill/Prentice Hall.

Shore, R., & Strasser, J. (2006). Music for their minds. *Young Children, 61*(2), 62–67.

Shore, R. (1997). *Rethinking the brain: New insights into early development.* New York: Families and Work Institute.

Shore, R. (2005). The magic of music. *Children Our Concern, 20*(2), 4–7.

Siegler, R. S. (1986). *Children's thinking.* Upper Saddle River, NJ: Merrill/Prentice Hall.

Singer, D. G., & Singer, J. L. (1977). *Partners in play: A step-by-step guide to imaginative play in children.* New York: HarperCollins.

Smilansky, S. (1968). *The effects of sociodramatic play on disadvantaged preschool children.* New York: John Wiley & Co.

Smith, C. A. (1982). *Promoting social development of young children: Strategies and activities.* Palo Alto, CA: Mayfield Publishing Company.

Smith, N. R. (1993). *Experience and art.* New York: Teachers College Press.

Snyder, S. (1997). Developing music intelligence: Why and how. *Early Childhood Education Journal, 24*(3), 165–171.

Solter, A. (1992). Understanding tears and tantrums. *Young Children, 47*(4), 64–68.

Soundy, C. S., & Genisio, M. H. (1994). Asking young children to tell the story. *Childhood Education, 71*(1), 20–23.

Soundy, C. S., & Stout, N. L. (2002). Pillow talk: Fostering the emotional and language needs of young learners. *Young Children, 57*(2), 20–24.

Staley, L., & Portman, R. A. (2000). Red Rover, Red Rover, it's time to move over! *Young Children, 55*(1), 67–72.

Stipek, D., Rosenblatt, L., & DeRocco, L. (1994). Making parents your allies. *Young Children, 49*(3), 4–9.

Stone, S. J. (1995). Wanted: Advocates for play in the primary grades. *Young Children, 50*(6), 45–54.

Strickland, D. C., & Schickedanz, J. A. (2004). *Learning about print in preschool: Working with letters, words, and beginning links with phonemic awareness.* Newark, DE: International Reading Association.

Swartz, M. I. (2005). Playdough: What's standard about it? *Young Children, 60*(2), 100–109.

Teale, W. H. (1986). The beginnings of reading and writing: Written language development during the preschool and kindergarten years. In M. R. Sampson (Ed.) *The pursuit of early reading and writing* (pp. 81–95). Dubuque, IA: Kendall/Hunt.

Temple, C. A., Nathan, R. G., & Burris, N A. (1993). *The beginnings of writing* (3rd ed.). Boston: Allyn & Bacon.

Tierney, R. J., Carter, M. A., & Desai, L. E. (1991). *Portfolio assessment in the reading-writing classroom.* Norwood, MA: Christopher-Gordon.

Unglaub, K. W. (1997). What counts in learning to count? *Young Children, 52*(4), 48–49.

Van Hoorn, J., Nourot, P., Scales, B. & Alward, K. (2003). *Play at the center of the curriculum* (3rd ed.). Upper Saddle River, NJ: Merrill/Prentice Hall.

Vukelich, C., & Golden, J. (1984). Early writing: Development and teaching strategies. *Young Children, 39*(2), 3–8.

Vygoksky, L. S. (1962). *Thought and language.* Cambridge, MA: Harvard University Press.

Vygotsky, L. S. (1976). Play and its role in the mental development of the child. In J. S. Bruner, A. Jolly, & K. Sylva (Eds.), *Play: Its role in development and evolution.* New York: Basic Books.

Wachtel, L. C. (2008). "Mommy, look what I made!" Open-ended art. *Children Our Concern, 31*(1), 18–21.

Wardle, F. (1995). How young children build images of themselves. *Child Care and Information Exchange, 7,* 44–47.

Watson, M. (2003). Attachment theory and challenging behavior: Reconstructing the nature of relationships. *Young Children, 58*(4), 12–20.

Weitzman, E., & Greenberg, J. (2002). *Learning language and loving it.* Toronto: The Hanen Centre.

Wenner, G. (1988). *Predictive validity of three preschool developmental assessment instruments for the academic performance of kindergarten students.* State University of New York at Buffalo. (ERIC Document #331 867, EDRS)

Werner, R., Timms, S., & Almond, L. (1996). Health stops: Practical ideas of health-related exercises in preschool and primary classrooms. *Young Children, 51*(6), 48–55.

Willis, J. (2007). Brain-based teaching strategies for improving students' memory, learning, and test-taking success. *Childhood Education, 83*(5), 310–315.

Wittmer, D. S., & Honig, A. S. (1994). Encouraging positive social development in young children. *Young Children, 49*(5), 4–19.

Worthham, S. C. (2008). *Assessment in early childhood education* (5th ed.). Upper Saddle River, NJ: Merrill/Prentice Hall.

Yarrow, M. R. Scott, P. M., & Waxler, C. Z. (1973). Learning concern for others. *Developmental Psychology, 8*(2), 21–23.

Zaichkowsky, L. D., Zaichkowsky, L. B., & Martineck, T. J. (1980). *Growth and development: The child and physical activity.* St. Louis: Mosby.

Zero to Three. (2005). *Terms frequently used in developmental assessment.* Retrieved from http://www.childrensnurturingproject.org/pdf/Brain%20Development%20List%20of%20Terms.pdf.

Web Sites

Action for Healthy Kids	www.actionforhealthykids.org
Association for Childhood Education International	www.acei.org
American Obesity Association	www.obesity.org
Assessing Young Children's Progress Appropriately	www.ncrel.org
Best Children's Music	www.bestchildrensmusic.org
Better Brains for Babies	www.fcs.uga.edu
The Association for the Study of Play	www.csuchico.edu
Center on the Social and Emotional Foundations for Early Learning	www.csefel.uiuc.edu
Center for the Study of Teaching, Evaluation & Educational Policy	www.csteep.bec.edu
Children's Music Web	www.childrensmusic.org
The Collaborative for Academic, Social, & Emotional Learning	www.casel.org
Early Childhood Education Assessment Consortium	www.ccsso.org
International Child Art Foundation	www.icaf.org
International Reading Association	www.reading.org
Math and Literature Idea Bank	www.mathcats.com
Mathematical Perspectives Teacher Center	www.mathperspectives.com
Mind in the Making	www.mindinthemaking.org
National Art Education Association	www.naea-reston.org
National Association for Bilingual Education	www.nabe.org
National Association for the Education of Young Children	www.naeyc.org
National Association for Sport and Physical Education	www.aahperd.org/NASPE
National Coalition for Parent Involvement in Education	www.ncpie.org
National Dance Education Organization	www.ndeo.org
Parents as Teachers	www.parentsasteachers.org
Read Write Think	www.readwritethink.org
Reading Is Fundamental	www.rif.org
Reading Rockets	www.readingrockets.org
Teaching Strategies	www.teachingstrategies.org

Index of Children's Books

Chapter 1
Observing and Assessing
Children's Development
Freckleface Strawberry (2007), 17
I Will Never Not Ever Eat a Tomato (2000), 17
Looking for a Moose (2006), 21
Tabitha's Terrifically Tough Tooth (2001), 17
Ten Terrible Dinosaurs (1997), 16–17
The Forest Has Eyes (1998)*, 21
Through Georgia's Eyes (2006), 21

Chapter 3
Self-Esteem
Click, Clack, Moo: Cows That Type (2000), 74
D. W.'s Guide to Preschool (2003), 66
Drum, Chavi, Drum (2003)*, 64
I Will Never Not Ever Eat a Tomato (2000), 74
Ella Sarah Gets Dressed (2003)*, 74
Jingle Dancer (2000)*, 64
Magic Thinks Big (2004), 64
Margaret and Margarita (1993)*, 68
Mouse's First Day at School (2003), 66
My First Day at Nursery School (2002), 59
See You Later, Mom (2006)*, 59
What Shall We Play? (2002)*, 71–72
Wow! School! (2007)*, 77

Chapter 4
Emotional Development
A Saw an Ant in a Parking Lot (2007)*,
Aliens Love Underpants (2007), 116
Aunt Minie and the Twister (2002), 103
Big Bug Surprise (2007), 108
Bootsie Barker Bites (1992), 99

Calor (1995)*, 110
Don't Forget to Come Back (2004), 103
Francis the Scaredy Cat (2002), 102
Full, Full, Full of Love (2003)*, 110–111
Goodbye Mousie (2001), 106
Ha, Ha, Baby! (2008), 116
How Do Dinosaurs Go to School? (2007)*, 113
Hurty Feelings (2004), 94
I Love It When You Smile (2005), 116
I Miss You Every Day (2007), 105
"I'm Not Scared" (2007), 102–103
K is for Kiss Goodnight, a Bedtime Alphabet (1994)*, 110
Llama Llama Mad a Mama (2007), 98–99
Love Is a Family (2001)*, 110
Mama, Do You Love Me? (1991)*, 110
Papa, Do You Love Me? (2005)*, 110
Patches Lost and Found (2001), 106
Saturday Night at the Dinosaur Stomp (1997), 113
Sometimes I'm Bombaloo (2002), 97
Stop Drop and Roll (2001), 103
Stuck in the Mud (2008), 108
The Owl Who Was Afraid of the Dark (2000), 102
The Story of My Feelings (2007), 93
The Way I Feel (2000), 93–94
Two Cool Coyotes (1999), 106
What Pet to Get (2008), 108
When Sophie Gets Angry—Really, Really Angry (1999), 97
Whopper Cake (2007), 108
Yesterday I Had the Blues (2003)*, 105

Chapter 5
Social Play
Bones, Bones, Dinosaur Bones (1990), 137
Building a Bridge (1993)*, 134–135

Chatterbox Jamie (1993), 132
Feast for 10 (1993)*, 136
Haircuts at Sleepy Sam's (1998)*, 146
Hedgie Blasts Off (2006), 150
Hunter's Best Friend at School (2002), 141
I Am Absolutely too Small for School (2004)*, 141
If You Decide to Go to the Moon (2005), 150
In the Diner (1993)*, 146
Jessica (1989), 141
Mel's Diner (1994)*, 146
My First Day a Nursery School (2002)*, 132
Saturday at the New You (1994)*, 146
Tar Beach (1991)*, 136
What Shall We Play? (2002)*, 149–150
Zoom! Zoom! Zoom! I'm Off to the Moon (1997), 150

Chapter 6
Prosocial Behavior
Alejandro's Gift (1994)*,
A Birthday Basket for Tia (1992)*, 168
Carlos and the Squash Plant (1993)*, 172
Clink Clank Clunk! (2006), 178
Coconut Mon (1995)*, 168
Dumpling Soup (1993)*, 175
Flower Garden (1994)*, 168
Grumpy Gloria (2006), 160
Ha Ha, Baby! (2008), 160
Haircuts at Sleepy Sam's (1998)*, 171
How Are You Peeling? Foods with Moods (1999), 162
Love Can Build a Bridge (1999)*, 178
Me First (1992), 171
Mine! Mine! Mine! (2006), 166

Pedritro's Day (1997)*, 172
Rabbit's Gift (2007), 168
Some Dog! (2007), 172–173
Stuck in the Mud (2008), 178
The Way I Feel (2000), 163
Too Many Tamales (1993)*, 174–175

Chapter 7
Large Motor Development
Arroz con Leche: Popular Songs and
    Rhymes from Latin America
    (1989)*, 207
Bounce (2007), 195
Chicken Chickens (2001), 197
Clip-Clop (2006), 191
Duck on a Bike (2002), 205
Five Little Monkeys Jumping on the
    Bed (1989), 194
From Head to Toe (1997), 198
Funny Walks (1994)*, 189
Harry and Willy and Carrothead
    (1991), 202
Hit the Ball Duck (2006)
Hoops with Swoopes (2001)*, 193
Just Like Josh Gibson (2004)*, 202
Luke Goes to Bat (2005)*, 202
Magic Moonberry Jump Ropes
    (1996)*, 194
Mammoths on the Move (2006), 188
Mike and the Bike (2005), 205
Mother Goose: Numbers on the Loose
    (2007)*, 207
Move (2006), 206
Oh, Look! (2004), 189
One, Two, Three, Jump! (1998), 194
Rap-a-Tap-Tap: Here's Bojangles,
    Think of That! (2002)*, 189
Ready, Set, Skip! (2007), 195
Sally Jean, the Bicycle Queen
    (2006), 205
Saturday Night at the Dinosaur
    Stomp (1997), 187–188
Twist with a Burger, Jitter with a Bug
    (1995)*, 207
We're Going on a Bear Hunt
    (1989), 189

Chapter 8
Small Motor Development
A String of Beads (1997)*, 226
Alphabet Under Construction
    (2002), 236–237

Busy Toes (1998)*, 228
Cleversticks (1991)*, 228
Cook-a-Doodle-Doo (1999), 220
Cool Kids Cook (2000), 221
Duck Soup (2008), 220
Dumpling Soup (1993)*, 220
Ella Sarah Gets Dressed
    (2003)*, 224
Famous Seaweed Soup (1993), 227
Grandmother's Dreamcatcher
    (1998)*, 227–228
I Can Do It Too! (2003)*, 224
I Love Tools! (2006), 237
Iggy Peck, Architect (2007),
    230–231
My Crayons Talk (1996), 233
Oliver's Milk Shake (2000), 221
Pablo's Tree (1994)*, 235
Patches Lost and Found (2001), 233
The Empanadas that Abuela Made
    (2003)*, 230
The Mud Family (1994)*, 231
Thump, Quack, Moo: A Whacky
    Adventure (2008), 237
Warthogs in the Kitchen: A Sloppy
    Counting Book (1998), 221

Chapter 9
Cognitive Development
Anna Banana: 101 Jump Rope
    Rhymes (1989),
Astronaut Piggy Wiggy (2002), 266
Butterfly Butterfly (2007), 256
Click, Clack, Splish, Splash
    (2006), 269
Construction Countdown (2004), 266
Hats Off to Hair! (1995)*, 263
Hit the Ball Duck (2005), 261–262
How Big Were the Dinosaurs?
    (1994), 259
If I Had a Dragon (2006), 273
If Mom Had Three Arms (2006), 273
If You Give a Pig a Pancake
    (1998), 273
Just Enough Carrots (1997), 259–260
Kente Colors (1996)*, 263
Kofi and his Magic (1996)*,
    263–264
Look! Look! Look! (2006), 254
Luka's Quilt (1994)*, 264
Magic Thinks Big (2004), 273
Maisy's Rainbow Dream (2003),
    256

Max Counts His Chickens (2007),
    269
Mother Goose: Numbers on the Loose
    (2007)*, 266
Mouse Shapes (2007), 254
New Shoes for Sylvia (1993)*,
Planting a Rainbow (1988), 256
The Runaway Tortilla (2000)*, 255
We All Went on Safari (2003)*, 269

Chapter 10
Spoken Language
Abuela (1991)*, 305, 310
Anna Banana, 101 Jump Rope
    Rhymes (1989), 295
Arroz con leche: Popular Songs and
    Rhymes from Latin America
    (1989)*, 304
Bear Snores On (2002), 293
Bebe Goes Shopping (2006)*, 305
Can You Say Peace? (2006)*, 291
Chatterbox Jamie (1993), 289
Do Donkeys Dance? (2000), 291
Does a Kangaroo Have a Mother,
    Too? (2000), 291
I Am Absolutely Too Small for School
    (2003)*, 301
I Am Not Sleepy and I Will Not Go
    to Bed (2001), 301
I Can Do It Too! (2003)*, 289
I Love Saturdays y domingos
    (2002)*, 305
I Will Never Not Ever Eat a Tomato
    (2000), 301
I'm Calling Molly (1990)*, 300
Is Your Mama a Llama? (1989), 293
Knots on a Counting Rope (1987)*,
    310
Little Raccoon's Big Question
    (2004), 307
Mama, Do You Love Me?
    (1991)*, 307, 310
Mice Squeak, We Speak (1997)*,
    293
Miss Mary Mack (1998)*, 296
Mother Goose: Numbers on the Loose
    (2007)*, 295
Oliver Has Something to Say!
    (2007), 288–289
Papa, Do You Love Me? (2005)*, 307
Snow Is My Favorite and My Best
    (2006)*,
The Lady with the Alligator Purse
    (1988), 295

The Seals on the Bus (2000), 296
The Three Billy Goats Gruff (2001), 309
There Was a Coyote Who Swallowed a Flea (2007), 296
There Was an Old Lady Who Swallowed Some Snow (2003), 296
We All Go Traveling By (2003), 305

Chapter 11
Emergent Writing and Reading Skills
A Letter to Amy (1968)*, 326
Abiyoyo (1994)*,
Abuela (1991)*, 333
Aliens Love Underpants (2006), 340
Alphabet Under Construction (2002), 331
B is for Bulldozer, a Construction ABC (2003), 331
Bunny Cakes (1997), 320
Carlo Likes Reading (2001), 321
Chicka Chicka Boom Boom (1989), 331
Clarabella's Teeth (2003), 116–337
Click, Clack, Moo: Cows that Type (2000), 326, 330
Click, Clack, Quackity-Quack (2005), 331–332
Diary of a Worm (2003), 332, 334
Drat That Fat Cat! (2003), 340
Duck for President (2004), 326, 333
Giggle, Giggle Quack (2002), 326
Grumpy Gloria (2006), 340
Homemade Love (2002)*, 344
How Do Dinosaurs Get Well Soon? (2003)*, 337
I Know a Rhino (2002), 344
I Love You! A Bushel and a Peck (2005), 342
I Will Never Not Ever Eat a Tomato (2000), 337

If You Decide to Go to the Moon (2005), 333
If You're Happy and You Know It (2007), 342
Llama Llama Red Pajama (2005), 340
My Crayons Talk (1996), 333
My Truck Is Stuck! (2002), 344
Nice Try, Tooth Fairy (2000), 326
On Top of Spaghetti (2006), 343
Patches Lost and Found (2001),
Please, Baby, Please (2002)*, 344
She'll Be Coming 'Round the Mountain (2006), 343
Silly Sally (1992), 334, 340
Snip Snap! What's That? (2005), 340
Stuck in the Mud (2007), 340
The Three Billy Goats Gruff (1973), 334, 341
Twist with a Burger, Jitter with a Bug (1995)*, 340

Chapter 12
Art and Music Skills
Ballerina Dreams (2007)*, 366–367
Dooby Dooby Moo (2006), 374
Drum, Chavi, Drum (2003)*, 371
Giraffes Can't Dance (1999), 367
Hilda Must Be Dancing (2004), 367
Jazz on a Saturay Night (2007)*, 371
Josephine Wants to Dance (2007), 367
My Crayons Talk (1996), 359
Peter's Picture (2000), 364
Planting a Rainbow (1988), 364
Red Red Red (2007), 359
Rock-a-Baby Band (2004)*, 371
Summer Beat (2007), 369
Take Me out of the Bathtub and Other Silly Dilly Songs (2001), 374

The Jelly Beans and the Big Dance (2007), 367
Twist with a Burger, Jitter with a Bug (1995)*, 367

Chapter 13
Dramatic Play Skills
Abiyoyo (1986)*, 402–403
Amazing Grace (1991)*, 391
Even Fire Fighters Hug their Moms (2002), 395–396
Foley and Jem (2004), 404
Freckleface Strawberry (2007), 393
Hedgie Blasts Off! (2006), 404
Hoops with Swoopes (2001)*, 393
If I Were a Lion (2004), 384
If You Decide to Go to the Moon (2005), 393, 404
Iggy Peck, Architect (2007), 393
Ladybug Girl (2008), 391, 401
Mike and the Bike (2005), 393
My Chair (2004)*, 396
My Shoes Take Me Where I Want to Go (2006), 391
Oliver Who Would Not Sleep (2007), 384
On the Moon (2006), 404
Sally Jean, the Bicycle Queen (2006), 393
Superhero ABC (2006), 402
Too Many Tamales (1993), 390
Violet the Pilot (2008), 391
Way Far Away on a Wild Safari (2006), 403
What Eddie Can Do (2004), 392
What Shall We Play? (2002)*, 387

*Multicultural characters.

Index

Access rituals, 126–127

Activity choices without teacher's help, 64–66

Ada, A. F., 305

Affection, handling, 109–111

Aggression, handling, 97–99

Ahola, D., 4, 9, 15, 17, 20, 29, 41

Ainsworth, M. D. S., 56

Alborough, J., 202, 261–262

Alexander, N. P., 397–398

Allen, J., 102–103

Allwright, D., 343

Almond, L., 185

Alphabet cards, 329

Alphabet hammering activity, 236–237

Alphabet letters, learning and printing, 327–332

Althouse, R., 232, 364

Alward, K., 125, 387

Anderson, G. T., 128–129, 133

Andreae, G., 367

Andrews, T., 236

Anecdotal records, 26–28, 40

Angelou, M., 263–264

Anger, handling, 94–97

Animal charades, 187

Archambault, J., 310, 331

Ariza-Evans, M., 59

Aroner, M., 178

Art skills
  checklist, 349
  combines circles/squares with crossed lines, 356–357
  combines objects together in a picture, 360–364
  developing, 349–352
  draws person with sun face with arms and legs, 357–360
  observing, recording, and interpreting, 364

scribble shapes, makes basic, 352–356
  stages of art development, 353
  talking with children about their art, 360

Asher, S. R., 138

Ashley, B., 228

Assessment(s)
  defined, 4, 6
  reasons for, 6

Assessment methods, 5
  child interviews, 15–17
  documentation panels, 20
  play-based, 15
  tests, 12–14
  visual documentation, 17–20

Attachment and separation, from primary caregiver
  helpful ideas, 57–59
  initial attachment, 55–56
  initial separation, 56–57
  separation from caregiver and attending school, 57

Attachment relationship with teacher, development of, 60–62

Audiotapes, 19–20

Autonomy, self-esteem and, 75–77

Baghban, M., 318

Baicker, K., 224, 289

Balaban, N., 57, 60

Bang, M., 97

Barber, B. E., 146

Barron, M., 218

Barton, B., 137

Baumeister, R. F., 53

Bead-stringing, 226

Beaty, A., 230–231, 393

Beaty, J. J., 101, 248, 274, 336, 390

Becker, S., 166

Begaye, L. S., 68, 134

Behavior modification interventions, 35

Beneke, S., 427

Benjamin, A. C., 10, 11, 50

Bentzen, W. R., 20, 22

Bergen, D., 247

Bergman, M., 340, 384

Berk, L. E., 395

Berkner, L., 93

Bertrand, D. G., 230

Best, C., 205, 393

Bingham-Newman, A. M., 260

Biting, 99

Black, J. K., 215, 430–431

Blake, S., 249, 262–263, 270, 271

Bodrova, E., 234

Bottner, B., 99

Bowie, C. W., 228

Bowlby, J., 56

Bowling, H. J., 92

Boxall, E., 102

Brain
  research, 246–248
  right versus left side, 352

Brazelton, T. B., 99

Breer, S., 391

Brett, J., 150, 404

Bridge, C. A., 340

Bronson, M. B., 394

Brooks-Gunn, J., 97

Brown, M., 66

Brown-DuPaul, J., 269

Buchoff, R., 295

Bunting, E., 168

Burris, N. A., 316

Burton, S. J., 304, 388

Bushman, B. J., 53

Buttons, fastening and unfastening, 222–224

Cain, J., 93–94, 163
Campbell, J. D., 53
Caplan, F., 186
Caplan, T., 186
Caregiving
  helping another in need,
      175–178
  helping to do tasks, 173–175
Carle, E., 198, 291
Carter, M., 21, 25
Carter, M. A., 426
Casbergue, R. M., 324
Caseley, J., 202
Catching, 200–201
Chanting, 293–296
Charles, J., 13
Charlesworth, R., 245, 251, 257,
      258, 265
Checklists, 37–39, 40
Cherry, C., 196, 232, 233
Child, L., 74, 141, 301, 337
Child development
  checklist, 7–8
  defined, 3
  stages, 3
  watching versus observing, 3–6
Child Development Checklist
  example of, 42–47
  how to use, 41–50
  interpreting data, 48–49
Child interviews, 15–17
Chiron, C., 247
Chocolate, D., 263
Chodos-Irvine, M., 74, 224
Christelow, E., 194
Christie, J. F., 315, 382
Clarke, J., 108, 178, 340
Classifying and sorting
  color, 255–256
  comparing objects, 257, 258
  how children do, 249–251
  patterns, 262–264
  sequence, 260–262
  shape, 251–255
  size, 257–260
Clay, M. J., 322, 342
Clay, molding with dexterity,
      228–231
Cleaning and picking up, 174

Clemens, S. G., 232
Clements, R., 191
Climbing equipment, 197
Climbing up and down, 195–198
Cognitive development
  assessing, 251
  brain research, 246–248
  checklist, 243
  classifying and sorting, 249–251
  collections, 258–259
  color classifying/sorting,
      255–256
  comparing objects, 257, 258
  counting, 1-to-1 correspondence
      with, 266–269
  counting, rote, 264–266
  counting, using picture and
      number symbols to
      record, 267–269
  exploratory play, 248–249
  observing, recording, and
      interpreting, 276–277
  opposites, using, 258
  patterns, recognition and
      creation of, 262–264
  Piaget's stages of, 243–246
  problem-solving using computer
      programs, 273–276
  problem-solving with concrete
      objects, 269–273
  reasoning, types of, 269–273
  sequence classification, 260–262
  shape classifying/sorting,
      251–255
  size classifying/sorting, 257–260
  Vygotsky's theories, 245–246
Colandro, L., 296
Cole, J., 295
Color classifying/sorting, 255–256
Communicating with parents,
      415–416
Comparing objects, 257, 258
Complying with requests,
      171–173
Computers
  alphabet games, 330
  comparing objects using, 259
  play and use of, 134
  problem-solving using, 273–276

what children need to know
      about operating, 274
Confidentiality issues, 9
Conflict resolution
  other-esteem conflict
      conversion, 160–163
  in play, 146–150
Conversations
  child-child, 299–300
  rules of, 297–298
  takes part in, 296–230
  teacher-child, 298–299
  telephone, 300
Cooke, T., 110–111
Cooking, 218–219
Cooney, N. E., 132, 289
Cooper, E., 64, 273
Cooperation
  complying with requests,
      171–173
  turn-taking, 169–171
Copley, J. B., 262
Corsaro, W. A., 141–142
Cort, B., 116, 340
Coscia, J., 247
Cosgrove, M. S., 218
Counting
  1-to-1 correspondence with,
      266–269
  rote, 264–266
  using picture and number
      symbols to record,
      267–269
Cousins, L., 256
Cratty, B. J., 200, 218, 231, 366
Creative movement activities,
      205–207
Crim, B., 184
Cronin, D., 74, 195, 237, 269,
      326, 330–333, 374
Crummel, S., 220
Crying, 92, 101
Curenton, S. M., 308
Curriculum planning, 4
Curry, J. R., 176
Curtis, D., 21, 25
Cutting with scissors, 233–235
Cutout characters, 393
Cuyler, M., 103

Damon, W., 56, 159
Dance, 366
Davidson, J. I., 70, 283, 322, 382, 387, 394
Davis, D., 184
Davis, J., 391
Dawe, H., 97
Death, 104, 106
Decontextualized talk, 308
Deductive reasoning, 270
Deerwester, K., 89, 99
Delacre, L., 207, 304
De la Roche, E., 350
DeMulder, E. K., 65, 156
Denham, S. A., 65, 104, 156
dePaola, T., 293
Desai, L. E., 426
Dewdney, A., 98–99, 160, 340
Dexterity, 215
Dichtelmiller, M. L., 10
Dickinson, D. K., 299
Dillon, D., 189, 207, 266, 295, 371
Dillon, L., 189, 207, 266, 295, 371
DiNatale, L., 411
DiRocco, L., 412
Distress, handling, 90–94
Documentation panels, 20
Dodd, E., 109
Dodge, D. T., 13
Dole, M. L., 64, 371
Dolls, dressing and undressing, 223
Dombro, A. L., 10
Doolittle, B., 21
Dorros, A., 305, 333
Downey, R., 110
Dramatic play skills
    age comparison, 406
    assign roles or takes on assigned roles, 384–387
    checklist, 379
    developing, 379–381
    dialogue, use of, 396–398
    group play, 401–402
    improvisation, encouraging, 398
    observing, recording, and interpreting, 405–406
    observing children in, 381–382
    pretend by themself, 382–384

pretending using imaginary objects, 393–396
props needed for pretend play, 384, 388–391
superhero and war play, 399–401
takes on characteristics and actions related to role, 391–393
themes, use of exciting/danger-packed, 398–403
themes and details, expanded use of, 403–404
Drawing/writing tools, using with control, 231–233
Dunn, M., 127

Edwards, B. 59, 132
Edwards, L. C., 304, 380, 388, 392, 398
Edwards, P., 288–289
Edwards, P. D., 221
Egertson, H. A., 54
Ehlert, L., 256, 364
Eisenberg, N., 97
Elffers, J., 162
Eliot, L., 56, 157, 214, 281–282, 352
Ellen, 63
Ellery, A., 273
Ellery, T., 273
Ellis, S. M., 137
Elya, S. M., 305
Emergent literacy, 316
Emmett, J., 343
Emotional development
    description of, 87–88
    observing, recording, and interpreting, 117–118
Emotions
    affection, 109–111
    aggression, 97–99
    anger, 94–97
    checklist, 87
    common causes and results, 117
    distress, 90–94
    fear, 99–103
    helping children manage inappropriate, 89–90
    interest, 111–113
    joy, 114–116

sadness, 103–106
surprise, 106–108
Empathy
    cultural differences, 158
    feeling what another child feels, 160–163
    modeling, 159
    for someone in distress, 157–160
Engel, B. S., 360
English as a second language learners, 291–292, 303–304
Entz, S., 19
Erikson, E., 56
Event sampling, 35–36, 40
Exercise, need for, 184–185
Exploratory play, 248–249

Fabes, R. A., 97, 103
Falwell, C., 136
Farish, J. M., 100
Fastening and unfastening zippers, buttons, and tabs, 222–224
Fear
    of being left alone, 103
    of fire, 103
    handling, 99–103
    of storms, 103
Feelie bag, 290–291
Feelings, talking about, 96
Feeney, S., 64
Ferreiro, E., 319
Field trips
    dramatic play and role of, 390–391
    drawing about, 363
    play and, 136, 145
    spoken language skills and role of, 304–305
Finch, M., 309
Finger painting, use of, 133
Fischer, M. A., 273
Flannel boards, 393
Fleming, D., 236–237, 331
Fox, C., 266
Fox, D., 266
Frame, J. A., 1005
Franco, B., 369

Frazier, N., 21
Freedman, C., 116, 340
French, J., 367
French, V., 221
Frey, W. H., 92
Freymann, S., 162
Friends, making, 137–141
Fromberg, D. P., 132
Frost, J. L., 125
Fuge, C., 344
Furman, R. A., 95

Galarza, S., 19
Galdone, P., 341
Gallagher, K. C., 88, 91
Gallahue, D. L., 201
Gallingane, C., 137
Gambrell, L. B., 316,
    340–341
Garay, L., 172
Gebhard, W., 392
Gellens, S., 187, 200, 218, 219,
    364, 366
Gelman, S. A., 250
Gender differences, manipulative
    activities and, 225–226
Generosity, sharing with another,
    163–168
Genisio, M. H., 308
Geoboard, 226
Gillespie, C. W., 273
Golden, J., 319
Golding, S., 404
Goleman, D., 109
Goodman, K. L., 255
Gorbachev, V., 197, 359, 364
Gottschall, S., 57, 334
Gowen, J. W., 390, 394–395
Gran, J., 108
Greenberg, J., 297
Greenspan, S. I., 109, 247
Gronlund, G., 4
Group/cooperative play, 135–137,
    401–402
Group role play, conflict
    resolution and, 149
Group storytelling, 309–310
Guarino, D., 293
Guback, G., 264

Hale, J., 350
Hammering, with control,
    235–237
Handedness, 215
Harris, R. H., 103, 106
Harter, S., 54
Hartman, N. N., 255
Hatcher, B., 382
Hawthorne effect, 9
Hay, D., 221
Hayes, A. H., 325
Heap, S., 71–72, 149–150, 387
Hearron, P. F., 164
Helm, J. H., 427
Henkes, K., 141
Heroman, C., 13
Hieronymus, B., 259
Hildebrand, V., 164
Hillenbrand, W., 108
Hindley, J., 189
Hoberman, M. A., 296
Hoffman, E., 400–401
Hoffman, M., 391
Hoffman, S., 316
Holm, C. B., 14
Holzman, M., 296, 302
Honig, A. S., 162, 164, 171
Hooks, B., 344
Hopkins, A. R., 104
Hopping on one foot, 194–195
Horacek, P., 256
Hort, L., 296
Howard, P., 110–111
Howes, C., 61, 62, 126
Hru, D., 194
Hubbard, P., 233, 333, 359
Huber, L. K., 236
Huggable toy, use of, 93
Hughes, F. P., 388
Humor, 115
Hunter, R., 184
Hyson, M. C., 88, 97, 100, 111,
    114, 161

Inductive reasoning, 270
Inserting objects, 224–228
Interest, encouraging, 111–113
International Reading Association
    (IRA), 317

Intuitive reasoning, 269
Ireton, H., 431
Isadora, R., 202
Isbell, R. T., 309
Izard, C. E., 88, 89, 95, 99, 100,
    107, 114

Jablon, J. R., 10
Jalongo, M. R., 288
James, B., 231, 396
James, M., 4
Jenkins, S., 206
Jensen, E., 269
Johnson, A., 202
Johnson, M. H., 232, 364
Johnson, P. B., 343
Johnston, C. B., 146
Jones, M., 427
Joosse, B. M., 110, 307
Journal writing, 332
Joy, 114–116
Judd, N., 178
Jumping with feet together,
    191–194

Kallen, D. J., 56
Kalmar, K., 282, 288
Kaplan, L. J., 56
Kasting, A., 414–415
Katz, A., 374
Katz, K., 291
Keats, E. J., 326, 424
Kellogg, R., 354, 357, 358, 361
Kemple, K. M., 69, 123, 137,
    138, 142
Kent, C., 21
Keyes, T. L., 269
Keyser, J., 413, 425
Kicking balls, 201
Kimmel, E. A., 255
Kitayama, S., 73
Klinker, J., 138, 156
Kosnik, C., 54
Koster, J. B., 230
Kovacik, A., 4, 9, 15, 17, 20,
    29, 41
Krebs, L., 269
Kroll, S., 106, 233, 321
Kroll, V., 263

Krueger, J. L., 53
Kuklin, S., 193, 393
Kurtz, J., 300
Kyoung-Hye Seo, 224

Langseth, M., 92
Language development. *See*
    Spoken language
Learning center logs, 33–34
Learning prescription, 82–84
LeDoux, J., 87
Lee, S., 344
Lee, T. L., 344
Leithead, M., 235
Leong, D. J., 234
LePique, H. C., 255
Leppo, M. L., 184
Lester, H., 94, 171
Levin, D. E., 399
Lewin, B., 237
Lewis, K., 344
Lind, K. K., 251, 257, 258, 265
Linder, T., 14
Linguistic scaffolding, 306
Listens but does not speak,
    285–289
Literacy skills
    See also Reading skills; Writing
        skills
    developing early, 315–317
Lively, P., 194
Loesser, F., 342
Logico-mathematical knowledge,
    245, 260
Loomis, C., 146
Lowery, L., 207, 340, 367
Lucos, L., 60–61
Lund, J., 106

Machado, J. M., 298
Maclay, E., 21
Maclean, C. K., 395–396
Maioca, J., 13
Maldonado, N. S., 217, 225
Manipulative materials, 224–225
Mardell-Czudnowski, C., 431
Marion, M., 96, 159, 161
Markus, H. R., 73
Marshall, H., 73

Martin, A., 227
Martin, B., 310, 331
Martin, S., 34, 35
Martineck, T. J., 199
Matthews, W. S., 97
Mayer, K., 318
Mazzoni, S. A., 316
McBratney, S., 116
McCain, B., 227–228
McDevitt, T. M., 100, 243–244, 283
McFarland, L., 26
McGhee, P. E., 115
McLeod, B., 402
McMullan, K., 371
McNair, J. C., 327
McNulty, F., 150, 333, 393
McVicker, C. J., 332
Meaning play, 294
Michealieu, Q., 97
Micklo, S. J., 249
Milbourne, A., 404
Milstein, L., 168
Mindes, G., 428, 431
Mitchell, S. T., 232, 364
Mitchell-Copeland, J., 65, 156
Mitton, T., 207
Molding clay/play dough, with
    dexterity, 228–231
Montessori, M., 220
Moomaw, S., 259
Mooney, C. B., 7, 56
Moore, J., 393
Moore, S. G., 173
Mora, P., 168, 235
Moratz, 63
Moravcik, E., 64
Morrow, L. M., 340–341
Moss, M., 146
Most, B., 259
Motor skills, large
    age comparison, 198
    catching, 200–201
    checklist, 183
    climbing up and down, 195–198
    creative movement activities,
        205–207
    development of, 183–186
    exercise, need for, 184–185
    hopping on one foot, 194–195

    jumping with feet together,
        191–194
    kicking balls, 201
    observing, recording, and
        interpreting, 207–209
    in preschool years, 185–186
    riding bikes, 204–205
    riding scooters, 204–205
    riding trikes, 203, 204–205
    running with control, 189–191
    throwing, 199–200, 201–203
    walking down steps alternating
        feet, 186–189
Motor skills, small
    checklist, 213
    cooking, 218–219
    development of, 213–215
    dexterity and handedness, 215
    drawing/writing tools, using
        with control, 231–233
    fastening and unfastening
        zippers, buttons, and tabs,
        222–224
    gender differences, 225–226
    hammer, using with control,
        235–237
    manipulative materials, 224–225
    molding clay/play dough, with
        dexterity, 228–231
    observing, recording, and
        interpreting, 237–240
    picking up and inserting objects,
        224–228
    pouring liquids without spilling,
        220–221
    puzzles, 217–218
    reflexes, 214
    scissors, using with control,
        233–235
    timing, 214–215
    turning/twisting objects,
        216–220
Murphy, S. J., 259–260
Music play center, 369
Music skills
    checklist, 349
    dance, 366
    developing, 365
    instruments, playing, 369–371

Music skills (continued)
    moves arms and hands in
        rhythm to a beat, 368–369
    moves legs and feet in rhythm to
        a beat, 365–367
    name clapping, 368–369
    sings in a group or by themself,
        371–374

Narratives, 25–29
Nathan, R. G., 316
National Association for the
    Education of Young Children
    (NAEYC), 6, 13–14, 303, 317
National Association of Early
    Childhood Specialists in State
    Departments of Education, 6,
    13–14
Neubecker, R., 77
Neuman, S. B., 341
Newberger, J. J., 101, 246, 247
Northway, J., 59
Nourot, P., 125, 387
Numeroff, L., 273, 367
Nyman, M., 97

Observation(s)
    confidentiality issues, 9
    guidelines for objective, 32
    how to start, 9–10
    planning for, 10–11
    practicing, 21–22
    recording, 9
    systematic, 11–12
    timing of, 10
Observation, purpose of
    assessments, 4–5
    curriculum planning, 4
Observational data, recording
    anecdotal records, 26–28, 40
    checklists, 37–39, 40
    choosing method, 39–41
    learning center logs, 33–34
    narratives, 25–29
    rating scales, 36–37, 40
    running records, 28–29, 40
    sampling, event, 35–36, 40
    sampling, time, 34–35, 40
    shorthand methods, 33

Observer, errors made by
    insufficient evidence, 30
    omitting or adding facts, 32
    rating scales and, 37
Observer, how to become an, 8–9
O'Connor, J., 195
O'Keeffe, G., 21
Oken-Wright, P., 323
Olds, A. R., 192, 193
Olson, K. C., 266
Olson, M. W., 326
Onlooker, play and, 128–130
Opitz, M. F., 294, 340
Orloff, K., 273
Ormrod, J. E., 100, 243–244, 283
Otto, B., 306
Oxenbury, H., 189

Palmer, H., 365
Paneque, O. M., 303
Parallel play, 130, 133–135
Parents, involving
    checklist, use of, 412–414
    checklist results, interpreting
        and sharing, 416–423
    checklist results, planning for
        child based on, 423–425
    communication methods,
        415–416
    focus on child, 411–412
    having parents as child
        observers, 414–415
    parent observation in classroom,
        425–426
    portfolios, developing
        collaborative, 426–432
Parker, J. G., 138
Parten, M. B., 125–126, 128,
    130, 133
Pattern play, 294
Patterns, recognition and creation
    of, 262–264
Peck, J., 403
Peer acceptance, helping children
    develop skills for, 127
Peer pressure, 127
Pegboards, use of, 226–227
Pena, A., 110
Pet, lost, 106

Petty, K., 116, 160, 382
Photographs, 18–19
Physical knowledge, 245
Piaget, J., 16, 125, 243–246,
    248, 294
Piaget's stages of cognitive
    development, 243–246
Pica, R., 199, 206
Picking up and inserting objects,
    224–228
Play
    See also Dramatic play skills
    access rituals, 126–127
    categories, 125
    checklist, 123
    conflicts, resolving, 146–150
    exploratory, 248–249
    gaining access to ongoing,
        141–143
    group/cooperative, 135–137
    importance of, 124–125
    involving children in,
        128–130
    maintaining a role in ongoing,
        144–146
    meaning, 294
    observing, recording, and
        interpreting, 150–152
    onlooker, 128–130
    parallel, 130, 133–135
    pattern, 294
    research on, 125–126
    self-esteem and, 66–68
    solitary, 130–132
    sound, 294
Play-based assessment, 15
Play dough
    commercial sources, 229
    molding with dexterity,
        228–231
    recipe for, 228–229
Playmates, 137–141
Play skills, development of,
    123–124, 126–127
    teacher's role, 127–128, 137
Polacco, P., 189
Portfolios, developing
    collaborative, 426
    contents of, 427

form for, 430–431
how to use, 431–432
reasons for making, 427–429
Portman, R. A., 184, 185
Posters, making, 233
Pottery clay, 230
Pouring liquids without spilling, 220–221
Pratt, L., 336, 390
Predictable books, 340–341
Pretend roles, self-esteem and playing, 68–72
Prigger, M. S., 103
Prince, J., 113
Problem-solving
  using computer programs, 273–276
  with concrete objects, 269–273
Prosocial behavior
  caregiving, 173–178
  checklist, 155
  cooperation, 169–173
  developing, 155–157
  empathy, 157–163
  generosity, 163–168
  observing, recording, and interpreting, 178–179
Puckett, M. B., 215, 430–431
Puppets, use of
  dramatic play and, 398
  emotion development and, 93, 102
  play skills and, 143, 149
  prosocial behavior and, 162
  spoken language skills and, 288
Puzzles, 217–218

Questions, asks, 305–307

Raikes, H., 92
Ramminger, A., 138, 156
Ramsey, P. B., 137, 138, 162
Ramsey, P. G., 303, 304
Rating scales, 36–37, 40
Rattigan, J. K., 175, 220
Reading skills
  awareness that print in books tells the story, 341–344

checklist, 315
holds book right-side up or turns pages right to left, 332–334
observing, recording, and interpreting, 345
pretends to read using pictures to tell story, 335–337
retelling stories with increasing accuracy, 337–341
stages of reading development, 338
Reasoning, types of, 269–273
Reflexes, 214
Reid, M. S., 226
Reifel, S., 125
Reiser, L., 68
Resnick, L. B., 266
Richardson, L. I., 255
Richgels, D. J., 315
Richmond, M., 391
Riding
  bikes, 204–205
  helmets for, 203
  safety issues, 205
  scooters, 204–205
  trikes, 203, 204–205
Rights
  choice of participation, 72
  completing independent projects, 72
  cultural differences, 73
  of possession, 72
  protecting property, 72
  self-esteem and standing up for own, 72–74
Riley, D., 138, 139, 156, 157
Ringgold, F., 136
Ritchie, S., 61, 62
Roberts, S., 305
Robinson, C. C., 128–129, 133
Robinson, E. H. M., 176
Rodrigues, D., 127, 140
Rodriguez, R., 21
Rogers, S., 92
Rojas-Cortez, M., 299
Romero, I., 13
Root, P., 21
Rosen, M., 189

Rosenblatt, L., 412
Roskos, K. A., 315, 341, 382
Roy, J., 350
Rubin, K. H., 131
Running
  directed, 190
  games, 190
  imaginative, 191
  to music, 190
  in place, 190–191
  with control, 189–191
Running records, assessment method, 28–29, 40

Sadness, handling, 103–106
Sampling
  event, 35–36, 40
  time, 34–35, 40
Sanders, S. W., 183–184, 188, 201, 202
Sand table, use of, 219, 227
San Juan, R. R., 138, 156
Sardegna, J., 110
Saunders, R., 260
Scaffolding, 183, 245–246
  linguistic, 306
Scales, B., 125, 387
Schickedanz, J. A., 324, 327, 328, 335, 338, 339
Schlein, M., 307
Schneider, S. L., 191
Schrader, C. T., 316
Schwartz, J. I., 294
Scissors, using with control, 233–235
Scott, P. M., 176
Scribbling
  art development and making basic shapes, 352–356
  horizontal lines from, 321–324
  pictures and, 318–321
Seagull, E. A. W., 56
Seefeldt, C., 5, 17, 105, 225, 254, 282
Seeger, P., 402–403
Segati, L., 269
Self-concept, 53

Self-esteem
  activity choices without teacher's help, 64–66
  attachment relationship with teacher, development of, 60–62
  autonomy, 75–77
  checklist, 53
  developing, 53–55
  learning prescription, 82–84
  observing, recording, and interpreting, 77–84
  playing with other children, 66–68
  pretend roles, playing, 68–72
  rights, stands up for own, 72–74
  separates from primary caregiver without difficulty, 55–59
  task completion, successful, 62–64
Self-image, 53
Separation. See Attachment and separation
Sequence classification, 260–262
Shannon, D., 205
Shannon, G., 168
Shape classifying/sorting, 251–255
Sharing, 163–168
Shaw, J., 249, 262–263, 270, 271
Shelton, M., 427
Shields, C. D., 113, 187–188
Shore, A., 365
Shore, R., 247, 365
Siegler, R. S., 257, 264
Singer, D. G., 380, 382
Singer, J. L., 380, 382
Singing, group or solo, 371–374
Size classifying/sorting, 257–260
Smee, N., 191
Smilansky, S., 131, 144, 382, 388, 396–397
Smith, C. L., 64
Smith, N. R., 361
Snyder, S., 365
Sobel, J., 331
Social knowledge, 245
Solitary play, 130–132
Solter, A., 92
Soman, D., 391

Song storybooks, 342–343, 373
Sorting. See Classifying and sorting
Soto, G., 174–175, 390
Sound play, 294
Soundy, C. S., 105, 308
Spanyol, J., 321
Sparrow, J. D., 99
Spoken language
  chanting, 293–296
  checklist, 281
  conversations, takes part in, 296–230
  decontextualized talk, 308
  developing, 281–282
  English as a second language learners, 291–292, 303–304
  language acquisition, stages of, 282–285
  listens but does not speak, 285–289
  observing, recording, and interpreting, 310–311
  preproduction, 284, 285–289
  production, early, 284, 285, 291–230
  production expansion, 284, 285, 301–310
  production transition, 284, 285, 289–291
  questions, asks, 305–307
  short-phrase responses, 291–293
  single-word answers, 289–291
  speaks in expanded sentences, 301–305
  story, can tell a, 307–310
Staley, L., 184, 185
Steinheimer, K., 427
Step climbing, 187
Stevens, J., 220
Stevens, J. R., 172
Stickland, P., 16
Stipek, D., 412
Stone, S. J., 124
Storytelling, 307–310
  decontextualized talk, 308
  predictable books and, 340–341

retelling stories from picture books, 309
Stout, N. L., 105
Strasser, J., 365
Stress, emotional, 90–94
Strickland, D. C., 339
Strickland, M. R., 146, 171
Sturges, P., 237
Surprise, handling, 106–108
Surprise bag, using a, 108
Swartz, M. I., 228
Systematic observation, 11–12

Taback, S., 105
Tabors, P. O., 299
Tape recording
  music and, 369
  play and, 134
  storytelling and, 310
Task completion, self-esteem and successful, 62–64
Tasks, helping to do, 173–175
Teacher, self-esteem and attachment relationship with, 60–62
Teale, W. H., 338
Teberosky, A., 319
Temple, C. A., 316, 321, 322, 324
Tests, as assessment tools, 12–14
Thompson, L., 66
Thomson, L., 366–367
Thomson, P., 340
Throwing, 199–200, 201–203
Tierney, R. J., 426
Time sampling, 34–35, 40
Timms, S., 185
Tomlinson, J., 102
Turning/twisting objects, 216–220
Turn-taking, 169–171

Unglaub, K. W., 267
Urbanovic, J., 220

Vail, R., 97
Van Hoorn, J., 125, 135, 387
Videotapes, 19
Visual documentation, 17–20
Vohs, K. D., 53
Vrombaut, A., 336–337

Vukelich, C., 319
Vygotsky, L. S., 7, 125, 183, 243, 245–246, 248, 294
Vygotsky's zone of proximal development, 124–125, 183, 245–246

Wachtel, L. C., 350–351
Walking down steps alternating feet, 186–189
Wallace, N. E., 254
Walsh, E. S., 254
Walsh, K. A., 14
Walsh, M., 291
Ward, J., 296
Ward, M., 205, 393
Wardle, F., 59
Warhola, J., 342
Wasik, B. A., 105, 225, 282
Watson, M., 60, 61
Waxler, C. Z., 176

Weeks, S., 384
Weitzman, E., 297
Wells, R., 269, 320, 332, 342
Wenner, G., 13
Werner, R., 185
Westcott, N. B., 295
Wheeler, L., 188
Willis, J., 251
Wilson, K., 108, 207, 293, 367
Wittmer, D. S., 162, 164, 171
Wood, A., 340
Wortham, S. C., 3, 15–16, 125
Writing center, 232–233, 320
Writing skills
    alphabet letters, learning, 327–332
    checklist, 315
    horizontal lines from scribbles, 321–324
    journals, keeping, 332
    letterlike forms, 324–326

    mock, 324–325
    observing, recording, and interpreting, 345
    principles and concepts of, 322
    prints some letters, name, or initial, 326–332
    scribbling and pictures, 318–321
Writing tools, using with control, 231–233

Yaccarino, D., 150
Yarrow, M. R., 176
Yolen, J., 113, 337

Zaichkowsky, L. B., 199
Zaichkowsky, L. D., 199
Zero to Three, 15
Zippers, fastening and unfastening, 222–224
Zone of proximal development, 124–125, 183, 245–246